:

d CATHERINE BASKIN

orn near Duncannon, Pa.
Died in Georgia in 1792

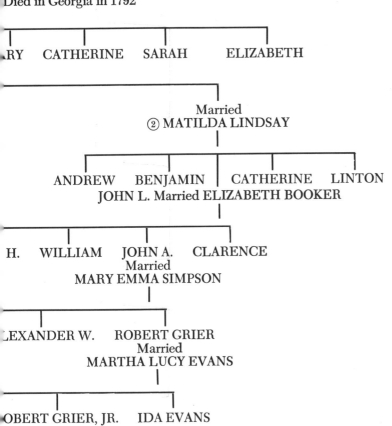

RY   CATHERINE   SARAH   ELIZABETH

Married
② MATILDA LINDSAY

ANDREW   BENJAMIN   CATHERINE   LINTON
JOHN L. Married ELIZABETH BOOKER

H.   WILLIAM   JOHN A.   CLARENCE
Married
MARY EMMA SIMPSON

LEXANDER W.   ROBERT GRIER
Married
MARTHA LUCY EVANS

OBERT GRIER, JR.   IDA EVANS

Intrepid Warrior

CLEMENT ANSELM EVANS

GEN. CLEMENT ANSELM EVANS, C.S.A.

Intrepid Warrior

CLEMENT ANSELM EVANS

Confederate General
from Georgia

Life, Letters, and Diaries
of the War Years

Compiled and Edited by
ROBERT GRIER STEPHENS, JR.

Morningside
1992

ISBN: 0-89029-540-9

This book was composed on the Intertype in
Morningside's own printing plant in eleven
and eight point Caledonia.

Morningside House, Inc.
260 Oak Street, Dayton, Ohio 45410

This Book is Dedicated
to My Wife,
Grace Winston,
with Appreciation of Her
Friendship, Companionship, and
Deep Love for Almost
Sixty Years

TABLE OF CONTENTS
Part I

Part II

Part III

Part IV

MAPS
(by John Heiser)

ACKNOWLEDGEMENTS

It would be remiss on my part if I did not make acknowledgement of the many persons who have had influence in the completion of this work.

My first acknowledgement must be of my family. When I grew up "history" was not an academic exercise. It was a synonym for "story." Our parents gave all of us the viewpoint that history was the way to enjoy the fascinating stories about people: what they did; what they said; where they went; how they acted; and what they looked like. It made the heroes of old come alive and made them again into human beings of flesh and blood with all their virtues and all their vices. Our parents wanted us to appreciate the good examples of great persons and they encouraged us to want to look up to and appreciate their ideals.

Among my first acknowledgements, too, is to give thanks to my public school teachers who steeped my early life in the love of our American heritage. One simple memory is an admonishment one teacher gave our class. She taught me that George Washington said never to commence a letter with the pronoun "I." It sounded conceited. That made President Washington more real to me than Parson Weems' tale about chopping down the cherry tree.

The school textbooks my uncle, Lawton B. Evans, wrote that told the story of Georgia were a delight. His young folks books published by Milton Bradley Co., such as *America First, With Pack and Saddle,* and *With Whip and Spurr,* were inspiring stories as well as instructive.

In my college years my studies were enriched by the history professors at the University of Georgia. Dr. John Hanson Thompson McPherson, head of the department for more than fifty years, had the best grasp of his chosen field of any teacher I ever had. Merritt B. Pound and W. O. Payne were fascinating in their presentations. I had, too, every course under the foremost scholar

ix

in antebellum and Civil War history in the first half of the twentieth century, E. Merton Coulter. These are general acknowledgements of persons who helped me to love history.

There are, in addition, a great number of people whom I must thank who are closer to this specific book than the foregoing persons. When I wrote my thesis for my M.A. in history, using just my grandfather's diaries, Frazier Moore, then in the Georgia English department, reviewed the thesis and gave me valuable suggestions. Later when he became professor of journalism at Georgia, I discussed off and on with him my hopes of combining the diaries and the letters of my grandparents into one volume. He gave me continued encouragement and was the first to recognize that besides the value of these papers to the military annals of the Civil War, that putting them together made a great love story.

Other persons who in recent years have given me encouragement to complete the job include Robert Krick, chief historian, Fredericksburg and Spotsylvania National Military Park; William S. McFeely, Richard B. Russell Foundation Professor of American History at the University of Georgia and his wife, Mary Drake McFeely; Emory Thomas, also of the Georgia history department; my nephew, Edward H. Reynolds, who teaches history in Griffin, Georgia, and whose interest has never flagged; and my cousins, the late Adelaide Henderson and her husband, William F. Eve Cabaniss who read the manuscripts some years ago and hoped for them to be published.

Among the other Civil War enthusiasts and scholars who have read various versions and parts of my manuscripts and given me encouragement, I would like to thank James Hudson, Athens attorney, Morgan "Bucky" Redwine, Athens businessman and banker, Owen "Sonny" Roberts also a businessman of Athens and Judge Joseph Gaines, Our Superior court judge. I especially want to thank Mrs. Anthony "Tommie" LaCavera of Athens, now historian general for the United Daughters of the Confederacy. She has been following the progress of this book for many years, as an historian in her own right and through her dedication to the perpetuation of the memory of those who lived and fought through the Confederate War. She has devoted many years in service in the various leadership offices of the U.D.C. in Georgia.

It would also not do for me to fail to recognize some who have done a great service in the "spade and shovel" work. Historian Roger Long of Port Clinton, Ohio, Joyce Claypool of Houston, Texas, and Thomas Elmer of Dayton, Ohio, were engaged by the publishers to review my manuscripts, correct and edit my mistakes, and remedy my shortcomings. They have been exceedingly helpful. And, finally, there are my secretaries over the years who have had the job of not only typing drafts, but also of deciphering my handwriting and interlinear scribblings. They include Jan (Mrs. Peter) Banks of Barnesville, Georgia, Martha Comolli from Elberton, Georgia, Anne Strickland and Mary Stowe Boyd, and most recently, the person who has ably assisted in whipping into shape the final manuscripts, Mrs. Tony (Diane) Russell. And, last I thank my daughter, Winston Stephens, for reading and editing many pages, straightening out my research files, typing many corrections, and making valuable suggestions.

THE EDITOR'S EXPLANATION

The story that unfolds hereafter tells the part my grandfather played in political events in Georgia just before the Civil War and of his role in the Army of Northern Virginia after June 1862, all as recorded in his heretofore unpublished diaries, several official reports, and some 245 letters exchanged with my grandmother, Allie Walton Evans.

My earliest recollection of any "ancestor" was of this grandfather. His picture in a gray uniform hung in our library in Atlanta. His Confederate belt buckle was on the bookshelf. His portrait hung in our state capitol. My first knowledge of Heaven was associated with him. I remember asking Mother where Grandfather was, and she told me he was in Heaven and that perhaps someday I would see him. He was born 158 years ago. That seems to be a long, long time. Then I realized that he died only 2 years before I was born and that does not seem so far away. On my very first birthday, August 14, 1914, the act passed by the Georgia Legislature to create Evans County in his honor was signed by the governor of Georgia. It was carved out of Bulloch and Tattnall counties.[1]

My original acquaintance with my grandfather's papers commenced when I was in my first year of teaching in the history department at the University of Georgia. I had a graduate fellowship to complete my Master of Arts in history. A thesis was required for that degree and, while I sought a subject, my parents told me about the diaries in their possession, diaries written during

1. *Georgia Official and Statistical Register, 1957-58.* Department of Archives and History. Office of Secretary of State, State of Georgia, Archives Building, Atlanta, Georgia, p. 1102. Several successive issues of *Georgia Official and Statistical Register,* compiled biannually by the Department of Archives and History, (Atlanta, Georgia) give a complete list of Georgia counties with the date of acts creating each and the land taken to form each. See pages 671-78 of the 1957-58 issue as a specific reference. Cited hereafter as *Georgia Official and Stat. Reg.* with date of volume.

the Civil War by my grandfather. I seized upon the opportunity to use them and the department approved my work in editing these diaries so as to complete, in 1937, the M.A. requirements.

In 1938 I discovered from my cousins in Augusta, Georgia, that they had a collection of letters my grandfather and grandmother had written each other during the Civil War. These had been kept by their mother, my aunt Ida, (Mrs. William F. Eve), the little girl so frequently mentioned in the correspondence. She was ten years old when the War was over. These cousins, Sarah Eve and Allie Eve Cabaniss, gave these letters to me, and my first job was to get them typed, as a step in preservation, as well as to make them easier to read. This job was well-done by a young undergraduate student, Ned Bond, assigned to the history department under the National Youth Administration, established as part of the war on the Depression launched in the first term of Franklin D. Roosevelt.

I did not do much with them for some time thereafter because I got married; I began the law school in 1939, teaching a full load in history and taking a full load at the law school; then I went into the army for nearly five years; and then got into politics. This latter step proved fortuitous. While serving in the Georgia legislature, I chaired a committee which worked eight years to build the Georgia Archives building. In working with the staff of the archives department I found their service of laminating historical papers very valuable, as they laminated and bound all of Evans' letters and papers. It was while on a trip to the National Archives with the Georgia Archives Committee that I got a chance to review and copy the Confederate records of my grandfather. Before I could work further on editing my grandfather's papers in serious fashion, I was elected to Congress in 1961. However, as time passed, I got back to the task while in Washington. For part of each year, my wife and children stayed home, and I occupied myself many nights drafting and editing my grandfather's papers with the hope of one day publishing them. In 1977 when I left Congress, I had more opportunity to work on this ambition which, after nearly fifty-five years, is becoming a reality.

The letters and diaries were obviously not written for publication, but in haste, many on battlefields and around campsites. Thus, a few editorial changes were necessary for the sake of clarity. My grandfather's and grandmother's spelling and punctuation are sometimes eclectic because of their haste, and occasionally it takes several readings to extract the exact meaning. The few corrections made should help the reader of the book over these rough spots, without taking away any of the spontaneity which makes letters and diaries so charming. General Evans was, after all, an editor himself. Had he chosen to publish these writings in his own lifetime, he would surely have amended the obscurities.

It has been a pleasure for me, over many years, to gather together the threads of his life. Capt. John Smith, Pocahontas' friend, was right when he wrote: "History is the memory of time, the life of the dead, and the happiness of the living."[2]

Robert Grier Stephens, Jr.
Athens, Georgia, 1991

2. Philip Barbour, *The Three Worlds of Captain John Smith* (Chicago: The Riverside Press, 1964), p. 355.

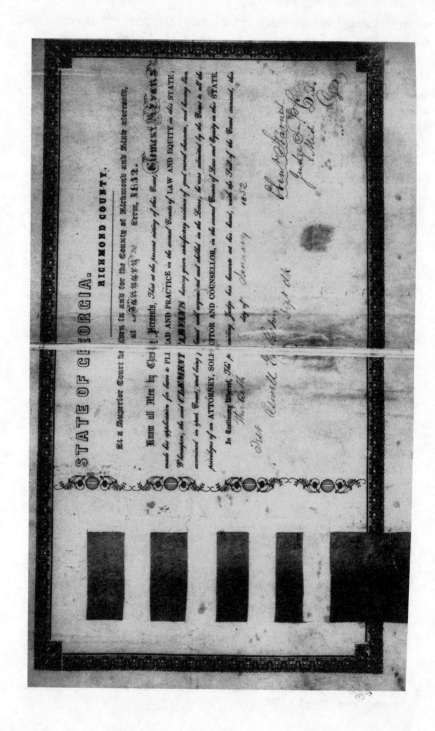

STATE OF GEORGIA.

RICHMOND COUNTY.

At a Superior Court held in and for the County of Richmond and State aforesaid, at _____ Term, 1852.

Know all Men by these Presents, That at the present sitting of this Court, Clement M. Evans made his application for license to PLEAD AND PRACTICE in the several Courts of LAW AND EQUITY in this STATE; Whereupon, the said CLEMENT M. EVANS having given satisfactory evidence of good moral character, and having been examined in open Court, and being found well organized and skilled in the Law, he was admitted by the Bench to all the privileges of an ATTORNEY, SOLICITOR AND COUNSELLOR, in the several Courts of Law and Equity in this STATE.

In Testimony Whereof, The presiding Judge has hereunto set his hand, with the Teste of the Court annexed, this twenty-ninth day of January 1852.

Thos. G. Holt

Wm. Starnes
Judge S. C. M. D.

Test: Averill G. Holt
      Dept. Clk.

INTRODUCTION

Clement Anselm Evans was born February 25, 1833, in Stewart County, Georgia, near the Alabama border. The year he was born, Georgia was 100 years old, the United States was 44. Andrew Jackson was inaugurated president for a second term that March. On November 13 the phenomenon of the "Shower of the Stars" occurred for the thirteenth time in 900 years. It was like St. John's revelation when "the stars of heaven fell unto the earth, even as a fig tree casteth her untimely figs, when she is shaken of a mighty wind."[1] The year of 1833 was also the year that Great Britain appropriated £20,000,000 to pay for the emancipation of slaves in all her colonial possessions.[2] It was the year the Charleston and Hamburg Railroad reached Hamburg, South Carolina, opposite Augusta. The rails spanned 136 miles and, when completed, it was the longest railway in the world.[3]

The year of Clement Evans' birth was when the nation was in the throws of the nullification movement after the Protective Tariff Act of 1832 had been passed by Congress. Southern states, led by South Carolina, most vigorously protested this act, alleging it consisted of gross discrimination against the agricultural South by favoring the manufacturers in New England. The protest foreshadowed the broader underlying cause of the secession movement in 1860-1861, *the principle of states rights*. In March 1833, when Clement Evans was a month old, a compromise on the issue was agreed to by Congress and the sectional confrontation on states rights that became the Civil War was postponed for twenty-five years.[4]

Clement Anselm Evans was named for his grandfather, Clement Bryan, and for his father, Anselm Lynch Evans. Both names

1. R. M. Devens, *Our First Century: Being Popular Descriptive Portraiture of the One Great and Memorable Events of Perpetual Interest in the History of our Country* (Atlanta: E. Nebhut & Co., 1876), p. 329. See also Rev. 6:13.
2. Arthur L. Cross, *A Shorter History of England* (New York: Macmillan Company, 1930), p. 656.
3. Ulrich Bonnell Phillips, *A History of Transportation in the Eastern Cotton Belt to 1860* (New York: Columbia University Press, 1908), p. 152-53.
4. E. Merton Coulter, *A Short History of Georgia* (Chapel Hill: University of North Carolina Press, 1933), p. 230; Alexander H. Stephens, *Pictorial History of the United States* (Philadelphia: The National Publishing Co., 1882), p. 451.

prophesied his major roles in life as a Methodist preacher and as a Confederate general. *Clement* means "peace and mercy," and *Anselm* means "the helmet of a warrior."

Professor Sylvanus Morris, in his *Strolls About Athens During the Early Seventies*, gives witness to these attributes, saying as he passed the Methodist church: "That gallant soldier and strong man, Gen. Clement A. Evans, was pastor. He was an inspiration to any man to hear him."[5] Both of these qualities became evident in Evans' final days, after he had suffered a stroke. The illness caused his mind to revert to his days in the war, and he issued orders and commands as if still on a Virginia battlefield. And yet, his last words on his deathbed were from the Christmas story of St. Luke in the Bible: "Glory to God in the highest, and on earth peace, good will toward man."

Clement married Mary Allen Walton in 1854. Allie, as she was called, was fifteen years old when they married and Clement was twenty. Although the greater part of this work consists of Clement Evans' diaries and letters during the Confederate War as a soldier, Allie's letters complement what he wrote to her and add considerably to the historical value of the exchange. It must also be remarked that if she had not had the good judgment to preserve his letters, an irreplaceable contribution to that era would have been lost.

A lawyer before the war, Evans joined the Confederate army as a private in 1861 and, when surrendered at Appomattox on April 9, 1865, he held permanent rank in the Army of Northern Virginia as a brigadier general, with temporary command as a major general. The only major battle he missed after June 1862 was Antietam (Sharpsburg).

During the war he was wounded five times, twice severely. His first wound was on June 27, 1862 in the Battle of Gaines' Mill (First Cold Harbor); the second at Chancellorsville, May 3, 1863; the next one on the first day at Gettysburg, July 1, 1863; the fourth, in the Wilderness in May 1864; and his most serious, when he was shot from his horse as he led a charge at the Battle of Monocacy, July 9, 1864.[6]

5. Sylvanus Morris, *Strolls About Athens During the Early Seventies*, (1912; Athens, Georgia: Athens Historical Society, 1969), p. 17.
6. Lillian Henderson, *Roster of the Confederate Soldiers of Georgia*, 1861-1865, 6 vols. (Hapeville, Georgia: Longino & Porter, 1960), vol. 3, pp. 576, 613.

He took part briefly, in the Valley Campaign of 1862 with Stonewall Jackson's "foot cavalry." In the 1863 Gettysburg Campaign, he marched with Maj. Gen. Jubal Early beyond York, Pennsylvania, the deepest penetration of Confederate infantry troops into the North. Evans fought through the three hard July days at Gettysburg and, on July 5, was in command of the last regiment to leave the battlefield as the rear guard of Gen. Robert E. Lee's army. On July 13 Evans and his Thirty-first Georgia regiment were the last Confederates to leave enemy soil at Williamsport.

In the first action of Lt. Gen. Richard S. Ewell's corps in the Wilderness in May 1864, Evans' Thirty-first Georgia advanced in Gordon's brigade down the Orange Turnpike. When the attack penetrated the Federal center, leaving both Confederate flanks exposed, Evans held the Confederate center stable so that Brig. Gen. John B. Gordon could align the right and left in flanking maneuvers to face the enemy and prevent encirclement of the brigade.

A week later Evans held the center of the Confederates at the "Bloody Angle" at Spotsylvania Court House, stemming the tide of the Federal breakthrough at the apex until General Gordon could organize a counterattack. Evans was with General Early in the last Valley Campaign, when, for the only time in the war, the city of Washington was seriously threatened. In October 1864, at Cedar Creek, he helped plan the surprise attack that routed Maj. Gen. Philip H. Sheridan's army and was in command of the last Confederates on that battlefield after Sheridan's famous ride rallied the Union troops to victory.

In April 1865 Evans led the Confederates who held the gap at Fort Stedman in front of Petersburg in Gen. Robert E. Lee's last attempt to launch an offensive against Lt. Gen. Ulysses S. Grant. And Evans again commanded the rear guard action of General Lee's army, as it evacuated Petersburg and commenced the con-

---

Volume 3 contains the record of Evans' Thirty-first Georgia Regiment. While on the Georgia Prison Commission, General Evans compiled a roster of men from Georgia who served in the Confederate army. His work on this is stated in his diaries of 1903 and 1904. These records were eventually housed in the state library, and in 1958 the state librarian, Miss Lillian Henderson, who had preserved, edited, and added to the lists, had Governor Marvin Griffin authorize publication of this collection of six volumes.

tinuous running battle from that city to Appomattox Court House. As a finale, Evans ordered and commanded the last charge of the war in Virginia at Appomattox on April 9.

General Evans and General Gordon became friends and comrades-in-arms from the time their paths came together in April 1863, when Gordon relieved Evans, who had become temporary commander of Alexander R. Lawton's brigade. They mutually recognized and admired the qualities of leadership possessed by each of them. In his *Reminiscences,*[7] Gordon calls Evans "that intrepid leader" and when he recommended Evans for promotion to brigadier general in March 1864, Gordon commented: "I have observed him closely in camp, on the march and in every battle in which this brigade has been engaged since my connection with it, and for deliberate courage, quick perception and ability in handling his men, I believe he has but few, if any, superior among officers of his rank in the service."[8] And Evans reciprocated his own confidence in General Gordon, which Evans expressed to his wife in his letter after the disaster at Cedar Creek, October 19, 1864: "But oh, if we had Gordon at the head with a harmonious, cooperating set of Major-Generals what a splendid army this would be."

Robert Grier Stephens, Jr.
Athens, Georgia, 1991

7. Gen. John B. Gordon, *Reminiscences of the Civil War* (New York: Charles Scribner's Sons, 1903), p. 312.
8. Evans left many papers, letters, and memoranda that are unbound, which will hereafter be indicated as EVANS PAPERS, and are in the possession of the writer. Other memoranda have been bound and entitled MANUSCRIPT COLLECTION and will be hereafter referred to as MC. This collection is also in the writer's possession.

FOREWORD

"Verily the works and words of those gone before us have become instances and examples to men of our modern day, that folk may view what admonishing chances befell other folk and may therefrom take warning; and that they may peruse the annals of antique peoples and all that hath betided them, and be thereby ruled and restrained. Praise, therefore, be to Him who hath made the histories of the past an admonition unto the present."

The Arabian Nights.

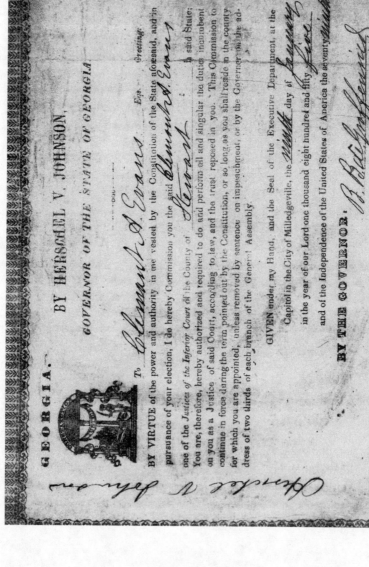

GEORGIA.

BY HERSCHEL V. JOHNSON,

GOVERNOR OF THE STATE OF GEORGIA

To _Elisenik A. Evans_ Esqr. ———— Greeting:

BY VIRTUE of the power and authority in me vested by the Constitution of the State aforesaid, and in pursuance of your election, I do hereby Commission you the said _Elisenik A. Evans_ ————— a said State:

one of the _Justices_ of the _Inferior Court_ of the County of _Stewart_ ————— You are, therefore, hereby authorized and required to do and perform all and singular the duties incumbent on you as a Justice of said Court, according to law, and the trust reposed in you. This Commission to continue in force during the term pointed out by the Constitution, or so long as you shall reside in the county for which you are appointed, unless removed by sentence on impeachment, or by the Governor on the address of two thirds of each branch of the General Assembly.

GIVEN under my Hand, and the Seal of the Executive Department, at the Capitol in the City of Milledgeville, the _ninth_ day of _January_ in the year of our Lord one thousand eight hundred and fifty _five_ and of the Independence of the United States of America the seventy _ninth_

BY THE GOVERNOR. _B. Ruthiffeurs_

Secretary Executive Department.

Herschel V. Johnson

Part I

Chapter 1

CLOUDS OF SECESSION, 1859

On November 2, 1859, the Georgia Senate convened in the picturesque capitol at Milledgeville. Twenty-six-year-old Clement Evans, a handsome young lawyer from Stewart County, rose with the others to be sworn into office. The former judge (at twenty-two) and rising politician took his seat as one of the youngest senators in Georgia history.

The clerk of the Georgia House at that time described him: "The first time I saw him was one day when I took a message to the upper chamber. He was speaking on some leading question of the day. I shall never forget how he looked. His hair was coal black, rather long, and his figure was as erect as an Indian. Character was written in every line of his face. Though quite a young man he was quick in debate. His language was lucid and clear."[1]

The Senate president, Theodore LeGrand Guerry, rapped the gavel for order and gave this advice: "You gentlemen are chosen depositories for the time being of the legislative power of this great state. You are in part the legitimate guardians of its rights, its interests, and its honor."[2]

The political campaign that had brought Clement to the Senate was a vigorously-contested one. He had aligned himself with a somewhat secret political group, the American Party, generally referred to as the "Know-Nothings" or "Opposition" party.[3] The

---

1. The *Atlanta Constitution* (July 4, 1911). Statement of Judge Hillyer at the time of Evans' funeral.
2. *Milledgeville* (Georgia) *Federal Union* (October 11 and November 11, 1859). Library of Congress, Washington, D.C. Speaker Guerry represented Quitman County, 1859-60.
3. The American Party members were often referred to as "Know-Nothings" because, when asked about the purposes of their party, they shrugged and said, "I know nothing." By the time that Evans was affiliated with the American

23

contest, first publicized in the *Columbus Daily Enquirer* of July 8, 1859, commenced with the report that the American Party of Stewart County had met at Lumpkin that week: "C. A. Evans, Esq., responded to a call by stating the objects of the meeting and moved that the chairman appoint a committee of five, to report the names of suitable persons to represent Stewart County in the approaching gubernatorial and congressional conventions."[4]

After the committee had met and reported, Col. Bedford S. Worrill, Evans' law partner, "addressed the meeting, in his usual happy style, in favor of nominating a candidate to oppose the election of Joseph E. Brown for Governor."[5] In July a "Know-Nothing" candidate, Marcellus Douglas, was put up from nearby Randolph County to run for Congress from the Second District. In the first weeks of August, the party's state convention met in Atlanta and endorsed Warren Akin for Governor. The so-called "Know-Nothings" had indeed entered the political arena with serious intent.

This show of strength encouraged many Stewart Countians, and the "Know-Nothings" gathered again in Lumpkin on August 22. They sent this account to the *Columbus Daily Enquirer*: "At an early hour our streets were crowded with delegates and members of the party generally from every part of the county. . . . The roll of delegates being called, fifty in number were found to be in attendance."[6] After a lunch recess, the delegates reconvened at 2:00 p.m. and adopted three resolutions. The first endorsed the candidacy of Warren Akin for governor; the next, that of Marcellus Douglass for Congress; and the third proposed "that we unanimously place in nomination for the Senate, our friend and fellow-citizen, Clement A. Evans, Esq., and for the House of Representatives, Messrs. Samuel B. Walton and Mark Holloman."

The convention reporter continued:

Party, there was little that was secret about the political tenets; members were xenophobic, anti-Catholic, anti-every-thing that was not white, Protestant and home-grown. At one time or another many American politicians had some connection with the "Know-Nothing" philosophy, including Presidents Millard Fillmore and James Buchanan. Even Abraham Lincoln, it was suggested, had a brief flirtation with the American Party, although he denied it.

4. *Columbus* (Georgia) *Daily Enquirer* (July 29 and August 12, 1859). University of Georgia Library, Athens, Georgia.
5. *Ibid.*, August 26, 1859.
6. *Ibid.*, August 22, 1859.

The nominations were hailed with enthusiastic applause, and the proceedings of the Convention unanimously ratified by the meeting. Clement A. Evans, the nominee for the [Georgia] Senate, being loudly called for, accepted the nomination in a short and eloquent speech, in which he displayed that ability and clearness of thought and expression which so eminently qualify him for the position assigned him.

It was a hot campaign in the Georgia tradition. Evans had been opposed by old-line politicians, who supported Dr. Jubilee Smith of Richland.[7] The *Lumpkin Palladium* printed an editorial on the race in the issue of August 25, using a pun on the name of his opponent:

> The opposition party of Stewart [County] have nominated C. A. Evans, Esq., for [state] Senator, and Messrs. S. B. Walton and Mark Holloman for Representative—all clever men. Mr. Evans is a new nag upon the political turf, and we can at this date form no definite opinion as regards his strength. We hope, however, to be able to convince him that, "The year of Jubilee has come". . . . Democrats to your posts. . . . Teach these loudmouth denunciators of Democracy that Democrats, and Democrats alone, are the only custodians of Southern Rights and honor![8]

The exhortation was not exactly prophetic. The election results of Monday, October 3, 1859, showed 573 votes for Evans and 542 for Dr. Smith. After the election, the *Daily Enquirer*, which had supported the "Opposition" ticket, editorialized on October 6: "We are glad to learn that old Stewart has been fully redeemed by the election of the entire opposition ticket."[9]

The *Milledgeville Federal Union*, though, was smug over Joe

7. *Georgia Official and Stat. Reg.*, 1957-58, p. 891; Helen E. Terrill and Sara R. Dixon, *History of Stewart County* (Columbus, Georgia: Columbus Office Supply Co., 1958), pp. 95, 167, on Dr. Smith as longtime pastor of providence Chapel Christain Church.
8. *Lumpkin Palladium* was the small weekly paper of Lumpkin, Georgia.
9. *Columbus* (Georgia) *Daily Enquirer* (October 6, 1859); *Milledgeville* (Georgia) *Federal Union* (October 11, 1859).

Brown's election as governor in an October 11 editorial column: "We might crow a little over the result, but our opponents are sore enough. . . . We are satisfied if they are."[10]

Clement Evans began his Senate term under rather unpropitious circumstances. He was very young and inexperienced; he belonged to the minority party; he had not supported the winning candidate for governor; and he was alone, having left his young, twenty-one-year-old wife, Allie, in Lumpkin with three babies: Ida, Clement, Jr., and Charles Crawford, all under four-years old.

During his first week as a Senator, the youthful legislator attended the Inaugural Ball on November 5 at Newell's Hall in the capital city and heard Governor Joseph E. Brown's inaugural message, which was climaxed with these resounding sentiments:

> In the present condition of affairs, I would advise the citizens of Georgia to stand united with the National Democracy, so long as they continue to stand by her rights and to protect them in the Union. But should this organization be broken down, and her constitutional rights be denied, and her equality in the Union destroyed, I would then advise her citizens to strike for independence of the Union and to pledge to each other "their lives, their fortunes, and their most sacred honor," never to forsake each other till triumphant success shall have crowned their efforts. My fervent prayer to Almighty God is, that this necessity may be averted—that wisdom, moderation and justice may control all our National and State councils—and that the rights of the States, and the Union of the United States, may be thus perpetuated.[11]

It was while Evans was in this session of the legislature that he began to write to his wife, Allie. From this session, only one letter survived, but it began a series that covered the next six

---

10. *Milledgeville* (Georgia) *Federal Union* (November 8, 1859) gives election results as Akin, 680 votes and Brown, 568 votes in Stewart county.
11. This issue prints Governor Brown's whole speech. In the quoted part included in the text, he cites the words of the Declaration of Independence and the motto of Georgia.

momentous years of the nation's history. In this first letter, he commented on his initiation into state politics, then moved on to a topic which was obviously more interesting to him:

Milledgeville, Nov. 26, 1859

My dear little wife

It is half past nine o'clock and I have returned from that abomination of abominations the Governor's Levee. I would not have had you there to be crushed, jostled, and suffocated in that motley throng for a half interest in the Governor's honors and emoluments of office. The whole mansion thrown open to the public and thronged by a sweltering mass of humanity, afforded in no single spot a desirable position for this individual. The Governor has made quite an improvement on the *tallow* candles of his last Levee as he had in use tonight genuine (not Sperm as you might suppose) adamantine. I observed quite a number of his poor "brethren and sistern" sitting about looking oddly enough, but still I cannot remark this as censurable because doubtless the invitation to them was prompted by the best of all motives, and why a distinction of classes in this free government? Miss Taylor I left at the piano, singing to the best of her ability and resting her reputation on a dying effort. Whether she yet continues that laudable occupation or not the telegraph has not informed me. The "patent leather" smile was on hand you may be sure.

But apart from Levees and such stuff—I had rather think of you, my jewel—I thought I would sometime or other reveal to you a great secret of my life, and when we have been talking together, I desired then to make it known, but I shrank from the revelation because I knew how much you prized the idea that you were the first, the last and the only woman that I had ever loved, or even dreamed of loving. Now Darling shall I tell the history of my first great love—That love of Loves, so much purer, so much higher, better, nobler, more absorbing than all love that ordinary human affection becomes an indifference compared to it, and other love a tame sentiment! And a love that still haunts my dreams,

27

and makes sleep a heaven, and ministers like an angel of light to me in my waking hours.

Though years have passed away since that Love first assailed my heart and storming every post demanded and obtained a surrender without terms, yet still it holds the key of the fortress and refuses to admit any other Love!

What do you think now, my Love, of this intimation of my first great affection?

Nearly ten years—ten years ago—What a long time when we think of it as ten years ahead!

But nearly ten years have passed since the first gentle, almost imperceptible beginnings of this love! For a while its soft approaches wooed my thoughts to *One*—my thoughts were taught to wander to a little school-girl, who day after day met and passed me, perhaps herself little dreaming that every faint foot-fall was treasured, every expression of her face was garnered up, every movement of her lithe and graceful form so many jewels—And so from day to day the bonds increased, the silken fetters tightened—the flood of love increased until the bonds yielded not, the fetters imprisoned, and the flood overwhelmed—

Such my first love for woman—no not for woman then, for she was but a little girl, and I not yet arrived to manhood, and the Love was pure, and holy,—unmixed with selfishness, no sensual grossness was its accompaniment, but it was a love that passeth all understanding, such as we might suppose a mortal in an hour of innocence could feel for an angel.

And so I have revealed to you my first love—and what does your own good heart teach you! Does a solitary stray doubt linger there, my Love, causing you to distrust who was the object of that first—last, only, great love! Or does not your own affections and the experience of the past point out as the little angel of my first adoration the mother of my own three little angels?

Your Husband

Chapter 2

LIFE IN EARLY FRONTIER GEORGIA

When the 1859 session of the General Assembly recessed on December 16, Clement Evans returned home to Lumpkin. For his daughter, Lucy, born twenty years later, Clement left this vignette of that frontier community:

> Tradition tells of the glory of Lumpkin in the decade between 1850 and 1860. The lovely little town was among the youngest and was by far the prettiest of all the towns of Southern Georgia. The people belonged to the very best class of Georgians and were intent on educating their children. The social life was refined, cordial, and intimate. In these conditions young people were thrown together in a truly cordial and beautiful social life almost from childhood.

In another memorandum, he wrote that the first settlers of Stewart County "are not to be thought of as being like the first settlers of the wild regions of the Western states. They were families that had moved in upon the fertile lands bringing with them education and . . . refinement. Generally the land was owned by purchase. It was not 'squatted on' as much of the western lands were. . . ."

The Evans home, where Clement was born, lay between the villages of Richland and Lumpkin on the Jackson Trail,[1] the first known trace made by white men through this wilderness. It was hewn in 1818 by Tennessee riflemen from the command of Maj. Gen. Andrew Jackson, who had it cut to facilitate the control of Florida Indians after an 1817 uprising. The trail ran through Dis-

1. Terrill and Dixon, *Stewart County*, pp. 2-6, 34-37, 316. Also Deed Book D, 468, Superior Court Clerk's Office, Stewart County, Georgia, conveying land in Ninteenth District to Anselm Evans.

trict 19 of the state survey of land ceded by Creek Indians in 1826. A land lottery was decreed by Georgia in 1827 and, under the category of head of a family, Anselm Evans (Clement's father) drew the sttandard plot of 202½ acres.[2] About 1828 the Evans family moved to the ceded Indian land near the Alabama line. This was shortly before Stewart County was created by a legislative act passed just before Christmas in December 1830. The county was named in honor of Brig. Gen. Daniel Stewart, a Revolutionary soldier of Liberty County, renowned Indian fighter, and one who was destined to be the great-grandfather of President Theodore Roosevelt.[3]

Very few facts are known about the Evans family in these frontier days. The name is Welsh. The first recorded ancestor was George Evans, who came from North Carolina to Georgia before 1800 and died there in Clarke County in 1818.[4] His son, John Evans, the grandfather of Clement, served in the Revolutionary War in the company of Capt. John Clark under the command of Elijah Clarke.[5] Anselm Lynch Evans, Clement's father, was born in 1792 in North Carolina.

On October 30, 1824, Anselm married Sarah Hinton Bryan in Jones County, Georgia. The Bryan family also came from North Carolina. Sarah Hinton Bryan had been born in Johnston County on August 8, 1793, and when her parents, Clement and Edith Smith Bryan, came to Georgia in 1805, Sarah was twelve years old, the oldest of eleven children. According to family tradition, the Bryans were of Irish stock and kin to the O'Briens of Thomond, descendants of early Irish kings. The first ancestor to come to America was William Bryan, who migrated to Virginia in 1689 after marrying Lady Alice Needham. Clement Bryan's mother, Sarah Hinton, was the daughter of Col. John Hinton, a North Carolina hero of the American Revolution.[6]

2. Coulter, *Short History*, pp. 204-05, 215.
3. George White, *Historical Collections of Georgia* (New York: Pudney & Russell Publishers, 1854), p. 523, tells about General Stewart. Also Terrill and Dixon, *Stewart County*, pp. 2-6.
4. Will Book A (1802-1822), Office of Probate Court, Clarke County Court House, Athens, Georgia, pp. 105-07.
5. Written statement of W. C. Gill, state senator from Lee County, Georgia, in 1890, in Evans' papers.
6. The 1790 United States census lists Clement Bryan in the New Bern District of Johnston County as owner of thirteen slaves. Letter in Evans' papers of 1882 by Loverd Bryan, uncle of Clement Evans.

Not too long after the creation of Stewart County, the last Indian battle in Georgia took place near Lumpkin. The United States began the movement of Cherokees out of North Carolina, Tennessee, and Georgia in 1836. A group of young firebrand Indians, filled with resentment, made forays down and across the Chattahoochee River, intending to proceed into Florida to join the Seminoles. On Sunday morning, May 13, this band attacked and burned the little village of Roanoke, about twenty miles from Lumpkin.[7] To escape this turmoil, Sarah Bryan Evans and her children, Clement, Martha, and Jane, went to visit her sister, Edith Bryan Brown,[8] in a safer spot, Macon, Georgia. Anselm Evans wrote, with many misspelled words and no punctuation, to Sarah on May 29, 1836, from Stewart County:

> The Indians burnt the house of Samual Quals some few miles above fort Twiggs kill'd the overseerer and wounded another man in the arm, the troups from the fort persued them immediately and gave them a brush they fled to the swamp we do not know that any of the Indians was killed non on our side hurt save one man was shot in the arm nother further particular.

Things were unsettled for several weeks. The *Milledgeville Southern Recorder* of August 30 published an article called "Full Report of the Final Cornering" of the Indians.[9] It was written by Capt. H. W. Jernigan of the Stewart Rangers. He said the Indians had crossed Pataula Creek and gained the west side of the Cuthbert Road, where they made their way to the Ichowanotchaway Swamp.

On July 15, the first day of pursuit, a brisk but undecisive skirmish ensued with losses on both sides:

> My loss was three killed and seven wounded. The names of the wounded are Clement Bryan, of Randolph, in the shoulder, severly; Robert Wellbron, through the chest: ———— Felder, arm broke: ———— Martin in the leg; N. R. Bryan, in the throat, by a spent ball; William

7. *Columbus Daily Enquirer* (May 20, 1836).
8. For relatives see Appendix A.
9. *Milledgeville* (Georgia) *Southern Recorder* (August 30, 1836).

ANSELM EVANS

32

Shield in the foot; one other slightly wounded. . . . The battle continued about fifty minutes.

Two days after Clement Bryan was shot, the Indians were encountered again in the Ichowanotchaway Swamp and, in an engagement that lasted forty-five minutes, were defeated. Jernigan said his forces "returned to the camp bearing on twelve pack horses and two ponies, captured from the Indians, near $1000 worth of Roanoke goods. . . . " In conclusion, Jernigan said that he owed it to his brave men to state that they "moved forward with the fearless courage which moved our forefathers in '76."

Thus, almost as a climax to his life, Clement Bryan (at age sixty-six) volunteered to fight in this last Indian raid. In a family letter of 1882, his son, Loverd Bryan, wrote: "My father was shot by the Indians in the Battle of the Ichowanotchaway. He survived two years and died in 1839. Needham, David and I were all in this little war."

Clement Evans said that one of his earliest recollections, at the age of three, was to see these uncles bringing his grandfather home on a litter with an Indian arrow sticking out of his back. The boy watched in fascination while his grandmother extracted the shaft and dressed the wound.

A few years later, tragedy struck. Late one night in the 1840s, when Clement was a young man, he was rudely awakened by his excited father, who pulled him out of bed and told him to go for the doctor because his mother had suddenly been taken ill. The boy hurriedly dressed, saddled a horse, and rode at breakneck pace for the doctor. By the time they returned, Clement's mother was dead. This sad occurrence was a major turning point in his life. After his mother's death, he lived a good part of the time in Lumpkin with his uncle, Loverd Bryan.

About 1851 Clement Evans began his studies at the law office of Col. Bedford Worrill, who tutored him and allowed him to use the Worrill library. Clement contemplated attending the Yale law school and wrote for information. Among Evans' papers is an interesting reply from James Hamilton, an official from Yale:

I received your letter this morn—making inquiries with reference to the advantages of Yale. . . . I know of no institution in the country whose diploma I would rather have. Like all American Colleges the student is subject to quite a school room discipline, and the tutorial system—which I consider the greatest curse to any college—is here in full blast. This also is a necessary evil—but still the advantages of Yale are such that I would prefer leading the mill house life which the student here is found to do, than resort to another institution, where discipline may be more lax, but course of study not half so thorough. There is little doubt but that Yale turns out the finest scholars in the country. . . . The expenses vary according to the habits of the student. . . . The Treasurer bill in the catalogue—which you have I believe—is no criterion of the necessary expenses. You can get board from two to three dollars per week. A good many room out of college, where there is an additional charge of from $1.50 to $2.00 per week. . . . One can go through college comfortably for $500.00 a year.

Clement gave up such ambitious plans and, in late October, enrolled in a well-known Georgia law school conducted by the Honorable William Tracy Gould at Augusta. Clement took with him several impressive letters of introduction. One was from his pastor, who recommended Evans to the Methodist minister as "an acceptable gentleman, & a thorough Christian." A second letter was from Legislator John A. Tucker of Lumpkin to Charles J. Jenkins of Augusta, a future governor, recommending Evans as a "young man of gentlemanly deportment and of sterling moral worth." In December 1851, Clement took the bar examinations before Judge Ebenezer Starnes, judge of the Superior Court of the Middle District of Georgia, in Augusta, and was licensed to practice law on January 30, 1852, less than a month before his nineteenth birthday.

Also in his papers is a letter of March 1852, from Clement's teacher, Judge Gould, which gave him a high recommendation. Gould said that Evans had studied under him since October 22, 1851, and had been admitted to the bar after a "very creditable examination. His deportment, while under my instruction, & the improvement he had made of it, authorize me in recommending him—as I do, with pleasure—to the confidence of the public."

It was at this time, too, that Evans became serious about mar-

34

rying Allie. About 1850, James and Lucy Harrison Walton came to Stewart County, Georgia, from Person County, North Carolina. Allie had been born there on April 13, 1838. The homeplace was about nine miles from the Virginia border at Halifax County and some twenty miles from South Boston, Virginia. There were two other Walton girls, Clementine M. and Anne E., and one brother, Robert.[10]

James Walton settled a plantation in Stewart County, but occupied a residence in Lumpkin for the more convenient education of his children. The 1853 catalogue of the Lumpkin Female Academy lists the Walton girls among its ninety-five pupils. This institution had been sponsored in 1852 by trustees from the Cross Lodge No. 12 of the Free and Associated Masons, to which Clement Evans belonged.

One of Allie's classmates, Lucy Ellen Harris, wrote that on graduation day in June 1855, nine young girls "marched between two rows of Masons formed in line in front of the building into the Auditorium." She added that "Allie Walton began with this class but early in her Junior year the wedding bells began ringing in her head and she asked Dr. Branham to let her do two years in one. To this he gave his consent and she was graduated in 1854. . . ."[11]

As Clement confessed in his letter from the legislature, he first fell in love with Allie when he saw her as she passed in attendance at the academy. After a period of courtship, he married her on February 8, 1854. She was fifteen, he was twenty.

From the Evans papers we find one school event of the next term involving Allie's sister, Clementine, known as "Clem." She delivered a debate paper as part of the graduation exercises for the 1855 class. Her subject was entitled "Is the Mind of Man Superior to That of Woman?"

At the head of this order of creation stands man to whom has been given dominion over every earthly creature. He rules, controls and governs all.

When he stood in his unsullied strength and dignity in the Garden of Eden he was "monarch of all he sur-

10. See Appendix A for relatives.
11. Terrill and Dixon, *Stewart County*, pp. 215-17, 233, 339.

veyed," but this extent of domain did not make him happy. Here indeed his physical strength could be exerted and his intellect fully employed, but there was another element in this composition that wandered like Noah's dove without a place to rest. This was his affections.

The world was sad, the garden was wild, and man the hermit sighed "til woman smiled."

When woman was given to man it was for the purpose of companionship, not in the strife of intellectual nor physical power to be his competitor but a real helpmate for him, the solace of his home, the sunlight of his heart, a pillow for his forehead. . . .

Her field is a limited one, bounded within the circle of home and friends.

The negative side of the question was presented by Mary Pope, but has been lost. By family tradition, both sides of the "debate" were written by the young lawyer, Clement Evans.

Evans worked hard at the practice of law, and his efforts were rewarded by his appointment on January 9, 1855, as Justice of the Inferior Court of the County. Governor Herschel V. Johnson signed the commission of young Clement, who was just twenty-one. Two of his uncles had both previously held this job: Needham Rupert Bryan and Loverd Bryan.[12]

In the last year of his judgeship, Evans signed a partnership agreement with his first law teacher, Colonel Worrill.[13] The younger partner was to "receive one-third of the whole of the net profits." Shortly thereafter, the newspaper carried the advertisement of Worrill & Evans, Attorneys. A promising and lucrative career beckoned, but state and national politics would change everything—forever.

---

12. *Ibid.*, pp. 81-83.
13. *Georgia Official and Stat. Reg.*, 1955-56, p. 432. Bedford S. Worrill was the grandfather of Judge Charles William Worrill, justice, Supreme Court of Georgia from 1949-57.

LOVERD BRYAN

37

STEWART GREYS.

First Company

OFFICERS.

JANUARY 26, 1861.

JARED I. BALL,..................................CAPTAIN
CLEMENT A. EVANS,........FIRST LIEUTENANT
WM. C. RICHARDSON,...SECOND LIEUTENANT
JOSEPH B. NEWELL......THIRD LIEUTENANT

SOUTH-WEST GEORGIAN PRINT, CUTHBERT, GA.

Chapter 3
"A STEW OF EXCITEMENT"

The year 1860 found State Senator Evans still in the midst of fateful events—a cataclysmic national election year that tore asunder old allegiances and coalitions. The emerging parties were the Constitutional Union Party, which nominated John Bell of Tennessee and Edward Everett[1] of Massachusetts; the old line Democratic Party, which nominated Stephen A. Douglas of Illinois and Herschel V. Johnson of Georgia; the Southern Democratic Party, which sponsored John C. Breckinridge of Kentucky, the incumbent United States vice-president, and Joseph Lane of Oregon; and the Republican Party, which chose Abraham Lincoln of Illinois and Hannibal Hamlin of Maine.

The national schisms had their local counterparts on the Georgia scene, as well as in other Southern states. Tempestuous U. S. Senator Robert Toombs supported Breckinridge and Lane. His law partner and retiring Congressman, Alexander Stephens, headed the Douglas Democratic ticket and was an elector on the ballot. Clement Evans took a "strong" stand with Toombs for the Southern Democratic candidates, Breckinridge and Lane. Evans stumped his section of the state for his candidates and was chosen as an alternate elector to the national Electoral College.[2] On general election day (November 6, 1860) the split of the Democrats, plus the Bell ticket, threw a majority of electoral college votes for president to Lincoln. The day after Lincoln's elec-

1. *Biographical Directory of Members of Congress, 1775 to 1971.* U.S. Printing Office: Washington, D.C., 1971. At Lincoln's Gettysburg Address, Everett was the main orator of the day.
2. Letter of August 13, 1860, in Evans' papers from W. M. Kirby, chairman, executive committee, Democratic Party, from Milledgeville: "By resolution of the Democratic Convention of 8th inst., of the State of Georgia . . . you were unanimously chosen to be one of the candidates for Alternate Elector of President and Vice-President of the U.S. . . ."

tion, Evans went again to Milledgeville for the legislature, which convened on November 7.

Clement to Allie:

> Milledgeville, Saturday, Nov. 10 [1860]
>
> My dear Darling,
>
> I received your letter written on Tuesday, this morning, and I was glad that you promised to be cheerful and pass the "days of absence" as pleasantly as possible. I have not yet located myself permanently. I can find no place that suits me exactly, but I shall perhaps change my quarters to day.
>
> I have not enjoyed myself as I did last year when you were with me. I feel like I ought to be at home. There are plenty of men here to ruin the State without my help.
>
> Everybody here is in a stew of excitement about the election of Lincoln, and various counsels are given. A disposition to write all parties and individuals is *professed* by leaders, but I solemnly believe that it is only *professed*, not intended to be accomplished. I have done my best to bring Toombs and Ben Hill to an agreement but I believe I shall utterly fail on account of Hill's distrust of Toombs' sincerity and unbiased patriotism, and of Toombs' indifference about Hill's cooperation. I believe Toombs is in the wrong about Hill. I am the only man in the Breckinridge Party with whom Mr. Hill has freely consulted and after my conversation with him I talked to Toombs for the purpose of bringing them together. But I was sorry to see that Toombs appeared careless about the alliance. I know precisely what is the matter and I am ashamed for Toombs that he has not the unselfish patriotism in this hour of trouble to look more to his country and less to himself: This is the difficulty. If Hill and Toombs agree upon a course of action looking to a Southern republic and the movement is endorsed by Georgia, Hill will be *Governor* next year and that is the place desired by Toombs. Therefore he desires to keep Hill in the back ground, notwithstanding

the whole movement is imperiled by that course. The truth is Mr. Toombs is dealing ruin to the cause of Southern rights while to all appearance he is the most ultra Southern rights man here out of Georgia for twelve months from this date. Two parties will doubtless be formed by the action of this legislature. One for Separate State Secession and the other for Submission. I shall speak on the question some day next week perhaps toward the last of the week, and I fear I shall please nobody by my plan.

I have received compliment after compliment for my efforts this year in behalf of Breckinridge & Lane. My review of Ben Hill's speech had a tremendous circulation all over the state. A great anxiety to hear from Stewart County was manifested. I suppose I was asked over a hundred times about my County, & you may know I felt really good when your letter brought me the news.

I am going to consult Gov. Brown this morning concerning an endowment of our College. He has proposed to the legislature to appropriate $100,000 dollars for a Female College to educate young Ladies who are paupers, to become teachers. I intend to offer him our College for nothing, and get him to assist me in obtaining an endowment of $50,000, the interest to be employed in educating & half-boarding about 50 girls per annum. I am afraid I will fail and I do not want a word said about it unless I succeed.

Well I have written this whole letter about myself. Tell our daughter[3] that Pa loves her mighty good, and wants her to be a good little lady. He wants her to study her book and learn to read a little before Pa comes home next Christmas and he will bring her a nice little present. Ask her what is it she wants the most. Tell Master Charlie Crawford to behave himself—

I have had some enquiring made of us about Mrs. Thornton since I have been here. John Price has written to Dr. Green about her.

3. See Appendix A for relatives. This is Ida.

41

I shall write to Bob[4] to day about matters in general. You can show this to *home folks*.

Mrs. Seward sends her kindest regards to you.

The principal keeper of the Penitentiary sends his polite respects to one Mr. Collier—[5]

Good by my Love—Be a good child and don't fret about my absence.

Good bye. I will write to morrow. I send you some papers etc.

Your Husband

Milledgeville, Sunday, November 11, 1860

My Dear Darling

I have been very lonesome yesterday and to day. To day I went to Church morning and night, for I thought it was better for me to do that than to sleep off the time. I think I am improving some. I have been told that I look better than I did last session, but I feel bad tonight because I gorged myself with too much dinner. I want to come home bad enough and see my little wife. I think about you all day and wonder what you are doing. I am afraid you are not taking good care of yourself. You are so precious to me, Darling, that I want you to live always—

Newsom and Humber are here. They seemed to be low spirited about Stewart County voting for Breckinridge, but I told them that if they had done right, they would now be rejoicing with me.

The Douglas leading politicians are courting the Bell men with a perfect inflamatory love. I never saw men so loving in all my days. It is astonishing to me what India-rubber consciences some men have. The ambition of political leaders is the ruin of this country.

Herschel Johnson [vice presidential candidate on the Douglas ticket] is here looking like a Comic Almanac picture. He is disgusting to me. He cares nothing for the good of his State, but looks only for his own promotion to official station. The truth is that Toombs on one side,

4. See Appendix A for relatives.
5. See Appendix A for relatives.

and Johnson on the other are pulling the government to pieces.

The resistance feeling here is strong but is assuming a more moderate and a safer aspect. The only difficulty in the way is that certain men are trying to organize a party on the question of Union and disunion. The safest advisers are seeking to prevent party lines being drawn on that question, but I fear that their desires cannot be fulfilled. We shall make an effort to harmonize all parties as much as possible. A convention of the people will probably be called. I believe it is a very unwise step, but still I do not see how it is to be avoided. There seems to be a general demand for it, in various parts of the country. It is to be hoped that we shall be able to pilot the State into a clear sea, by some decisive, honest, and patriotic measure.

You can say to Bob, and any others that it is the safest policy now to assail the action of South Carolina and Alabama. I believe South Carolina will Secede. In that event doubtless Georgia will follow, either in Secession or in some steps to lend South Carolina material aid. At present the formation of a Secession party in Georgia is simply and purely bringing down inevitable defeat & with it abject submission. My idea is to prevent there being any *Union* party at all. That is any party pledged to unconditional Submission, but to have one united vote in Georgia upon resistance, after formal demand.

I know you are interested in politics because I am and have therefore written the above.

Tell Bob, to tell Jim Wimberly to send me the *Bill* that McRee desires to be passed, at once. Tell Redding & Carter that an act has to be passed to relieve them from their bond. Tell Kedd to advertise my Lucinda Burke fifa for January sales.[6]

I will come home Friday next, if nothing happens.

6. *"Fi.Fa."* is an abbreviation for a legal writ that begins in Latin "Fieri facias." These first two words translated as "you cause to make." *Black's* Law Dictionary defines it further: "In practice, a writ of execution commanding the sheriff to levy and make the amount of a judgment from the goods and chattels of the judgment debtor."

Will be on the stage Friday from Cuthbert. You must be patient. I am entirely well.

Why did you not put your picture in my trunk. Must I have mine taken! Give Miss Ida a sweet smack for Pa. Tell her she must write to her Pa all about her Ma's doings at home. Tell old Goody Two shoes[7] not to eat all the apples you buy. Make her work for you all you can.

I suppose Probe[8] has gone to Baker. I told Fleuellen all about him. He appears to like Probe very much.

Good bye. I hope to get a letter from you soon. I have not received but one from you so far.

Goodbye Darling———
Your Husband

Milledgeville, Ga. Nov. 12, 1860.

My dear Darling

I do not know what to write to you about. I have done nothing here yet. I have not once opened my mouth in the Senate. The time has not come for me yet. Others here are rampant, I am cool. This is not the time for me to be hasty in anything I do. There are indications ahead which show me that the coolest and the most prudent are the ones who must direct the Storms— In a few days I shall make a speech and will send you papers that contain a notice of it.

I am busy all the time. I scarcely find time to do what I desire. But it is best for me to be busy so I can keep out of mischief. I have been nowhere. I keep to my room all the time except when in the Senate. I wish you were here with me.

Tell everybody to keep perfectly cool about politics— That the final day has come when judgment must begin.

Nothing is going on here to write to you about. And you must excuse the short letter, for I have a whole evenings work before me. Mr. Alex. Stephens[9] is to speak to night & Ben. Hill tomorrow night.

---

7. "Goody Two Shoes" is an unidentified person. This may have been a nickname for a slave.
8. See Appendix A for relatives.
9. Stephens, *Pictorial History*, pp. 570-82. Displays text of this speech.

Tell Bob to write me at once how the people stand on the question of *immediate separation by the State of Georgia alone.* Tell him to write fully & give me the names of those who are in favor of immediate Secession or for secession at all. I know he knows them—I am very anxious to hear from home. If they call a meeting I hope there will be no dissenting to some feasible plan of resistance: either by Gov. Brown's plan—or some other:

Write to me often Darling I have received only two letters from you.

Good bye. *I am getting fat.* You need not be uneasy about my health. Take care of your dear self. Kiss Ida & Charlie for Pa. Goodbye.

Your Husband

Shortly before the Senate adjourned in Milledgeville, Clement delivered that speech which he had felt coming on. It is preserved in a notebook among his papers:

It may be, but it may not be too late for the North to prevent the disunity of the two sections. They know our grounds of complaint and apprehension. The thief on the cross saved his soul even in the last agony of his death, by repentance & a prayer of faith for forgiveness. Perhaps the north may yet save itself even in the last hour by a concession of all we ask, but I confess to you frankly that such a hope has left my heart. Ever since they imposed Lincoln on us as the President-elect of these states, no official demonstration has been made by them toward preserving the union on our basis. The sands are rapidly running and time never pausing is pointing its long finger to the 4th of March 1861. We look vainly for that long deferred returning sense of justice.

We are dealing with no question of policy transient in its nature & which will admit of delay, but with a question of human rights & states' rights involving all the great principles that underlie our system of government. States have offended us, and states must redress—It is a government that has wronged us, and the government must act. When you ask me then, what I would do if before the separation was actually done every grievance was redressed, and threatened wrong was securely provided against, I have no hesitancy in replying that it would be the duty of the south to continue her connection with the north. But I confess frankly that I cannot see how the threatened wrongs that we anticipate under Lincoln's rule can be so securely provided against as to furnish peace and content at the south. What is that government worth, whatever be its name or form, or however great, powerful & extensive unless the citizen is at peace with his government.

Milledgeville, GA
Nov. 16, 1860

My dear Darling

I am so sorry you have been sick. I know you have not taken good care of yourself. Did you not want your Darling home to love you some while you were sick? Tell Charlie, Pa will bring him something if he will be a good boy & Ida too.

I will come home some day next week—Look for me Wednesday—& from then on until I come. I will write every day.

Nothing is doing in the legislature that I feel any great interest in. I would come home and stay, if that would be right. I have improved in my health every day.

You must not be alarmed at *insurrections.* We are securer now from them than we have been for years, because the people are so excited, that the Yankees are afraid to come among us, and every man is watching. You may sleep in perfect peace—

I suppose the people at home are excited about Lincoln's election. Well tell them to be perfectly cool. The Union is just as sure to be dissolved as the world *stands until January the first 1862.* Men may try to save it but they had as well have tried to save the world from the deluge! Abraham tried to save Sodom from fire & brimstone by begging for Lot & his household—but all he accomplished was the *secession of Lot from Sodom* before the fire from heaven came. That is the duty of us all now. Some here still hope our grievances may be redressed in time to save the Government—well I tell those to come with us, and we will march forward to preparation for the early separation, and if before the final appointed day comes, these grievances are redressed, we will take the Union on further probation, asking guarantees for future safety. You must continue [to be a] politician and tell everybody to quit praising the Union until the war on slavery ceases at the North, and to praise the South, and the great state of Georgia. Tell them to hold on to Georgia—the Union will save itself if it is worth saving. It is a question of strength now between the love of slavery and the love of Union—So long as the Northern mind stands unchanged from its present state slavery will have no friend in the administration of the Government. It is my deliberate opinion that the North designed to continue its oppressions and based on that my opinion is my solemn conviction that if the Union stands slavery will fall.

There is no need of alarm when the Union dissolves. It will be the peaceful death of a decrepit old man, and the North shall take the body, and we will be the disenthralled Soul.

When Jeroboam was appointed King over Israel the Southern states of that nation examined his platform & they said to him do you intend to rule us on that platform? He said to them "Your burdens were heavy under King David but my little finger shall be as weighty as Davids' loins." Then they raised the standards of secession & said "There is no inheritance for us—To your tents Oh Israel!" All that we desire now is for the "Sons of Liberty" to have patience. Samuel Adams said to the excited patriots of 1774, just prior to actual disunion between us & Britain, "Violence of submission is now equally fatal." Let true men take the movement in hand and the Fourth day of July next will be re-baptised and re-christened as the second birth of Liberty and the mother-day of the Republic of Washington.

Goodbye—We will raise Charlie for the Presidency in

47

the New Republic—Goodbye—show this to who you please.

Your Husband
C. A. Evans

Milledgeville, GA. Nov. 17, 1860

My dear Darling

Look for me home soon. The nature of business here is such that I find it to be difficult to select the precise time for starting home. But commence looking on Wednesdays Stage. I can't stay with you though but two or three days. The legislature will not sit very much longer. Perhaps two weeks only.

The bill calling the [Secession] convention to resume passed *without a dissenting voice.* The election takes place on 1st Wednesday in January 1861. The feeling here now is not to have any contest for delegates, but for a general convention of each county to be called and select good men without any party lines. Our county will be entitled to three delegates.

The legislature have appropriated *One Million* of dollars to defend the State if invaded. South Carolina, Alabama, Florida, Mississippi and Texas are pledged with us. North Carolina, Virginia, Tennessee, Louisiana and Arkansas are consulting but will follow. If we separate, all will go together on the same day.

Am getting very tired of staying here. I hope our people will not want me to return again next legislature. Why has Bob not written to me about the state of affairs at home! I have been *no where* since I have been here, not even to the Asylum. I have kept myself close for fear I would get into mischief—I hope I will get a letter from you tomorrow or anyhow next day. I am still improving perfectly. I am getting almost *red* in the face. But it is not *whiskey.* It is the advantage of place and habits; We shall provide our removal when I come.

I had rather be talking to you than writing to you, for I want to say many things that I do not know how to write. The humor for writing has not been on me this winter. But I have done some terrible hard thinking.

Good bye. I will write to morrow again. You need not write after receiving this until I come. Kiss the children.

Your Husband

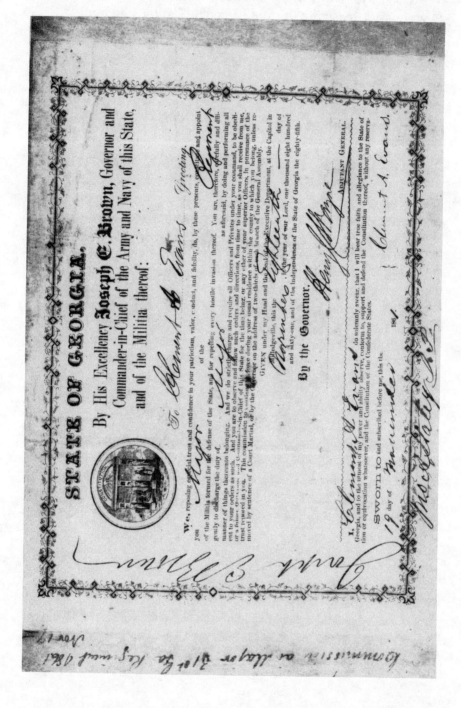

STATE OF GEORGIA.

By His Excellency Joseph E. Brown, Governor and Commander-in-Chief of the Army and Navy of this State, and of the Militia thereof:

To *Clement A. Evans* *Greeting.*

We, reposing especial trust and confidence in your patriotism, valor, conduct, and fidelity, do, by these presents, constitute and appoint you *Major* of the

of the Militia formed for the defense of the State, and for repelling every hostile invasion thereof. You are, therefore, carefully and diligently to discharge the duty of *Major*

in that manner of things thereunto belonging. And we do strictly charge and require all Officers and Privates under your command, to be obedient to your orders as such. And you are to observe and follow such orders and directions, from time to time, as you shall receive from me, or a future Governor, or your Commander-in-Chief of this State for the time being, or any other of your superior Officers, in pursuance of the trust reposed in you. This commission to continue in force during your usual residence within the county to which you belong, unless removed by sentence of a Court Martial, or by the Governor on the address of two-thirds of each branch of the General Assembly.

GIVEN under my Hand and the Seal of the Executive Department, at the Capitol in Milledgeville, this the *eighteenth* day of *November*, in the year of our Lord, one thousand eight hundred and sixty-one, and of the Independence of the State of Georgia the eighty-fifth.

By the Governor.

Joseph E. Brown

Henry C. Wayne
ADJUTANT GENERAL.

I, *Clement A. Evans* do solemnly swear, that I will bear true faith and allegiance to the State of Georgia, and to the utmost of my power and ability observe, conform to, support and defend the Constitution thereof, without any reservation or equivocation whatsoever, and the Constitution of the Confederate States.

SWORN TO and subscribed before me, this the

19 day of *November* 186 1. } *Clement A. Evans*

Thos. Colley J.P.

Commission as Major 31st Ga. Regiment 1861
Nov 19

Chapter 4
WAR FEVER

Events had moved rapidly after realization in the South that the Republicans had won a victory in 1860. On December 20, South Carolina promulgated her Secession Ordinance and urged her sister states of the South to follow her example. Many years hence, Evans conducted the funeral service of his friend, Ben Hill, who had become United States Senator. At the graveside, he spoke of those restless times:

> We walked together one day, while in the old state capital at Milledgeville, and sat on the bank of the Oconee River. It was in 1860, when the fearful question of the Union's disruption was tossing all minds in a tempest of trouble. He was dreadfully afraid of secession, and I, many years his junior, could not share his alarm. We were both members of the State senate, members of the church, and responsible for the part we were taking. The die, however, was cast, and nothing could stay the calamity. As we sat and talked, he suddenly said to me: "Is it not strange that we, who are both Christians, should trust so much, in this matter, to human wisdom? We are praying men, and yet now we differ! I am afraid," said he, "as much of the moral as of the political dangers of secession."[1]

In anticipation of war, the young bloods of Stewart County organized a company about which Evans wrote: "My first com-

1. Benjamin Harvey Hill, Jr., *Senator Benjamin H. Hill of Georgia, His Life, Speeches and Writings* (Atlanta: H. C. Hudgin and Company, Publisher, 1891), pp. 17-41.

mission in the Confederate War was First Lieutenant. The Company was formed in December 1860 while I was away from home in the Senate, and before the secession of the State, and I was elected 1st Lieut. without having known anything about it until after the election." Upon notice of his election, Evans did not accept, but retained his seat in the legislature.

Georgia's Secession Convention met in Milledgeville a month later and passed the state's Secession Ordinance on January 19, 1861. Action to form the new union of Southern states did not lag after the secession of Georgia. In February, Southern states' representatives journeyed to Montgomery, Alabama, to form a temporary *Confederate States of America*. They chose Senator Jefferson Davis of Mississippi and Congressman Alexander H. Stephens of Georgia as president and vice-president, respectively, of the provisional government, the capital of which was in May to be moved to Richmond, Virginia.

Clement Evans wanted to be in the mainstream of events, but hesitated to jump in because of his family responsibilities. However, as a civilian observer, he set out with the Stewart Grays in late July 1861 for Richmond, the vortex of action still swirling from the first Battle of Manassas in July. As this local company formed ranks to depart from Lumpkin, Miss Sallie Tucker of that village presented the Grays with a flag made by the hands of local women. She climaxed her farewell speech with these brave words: "Take this flag, and may it be the first to float in the field and the last to leave it."[2]

Although not yet in the army, Clement wrote this first "war letter":

> Macon, Tuesday Night 10½ p.m.
> July 30th, 1861
>
> Dear Allie
>
> You must excuse the shortness of this letter, and I will write you a long one in Atlanta. We have had an excellent trip so far, for our comfort has been well provided for all along the route. I suppose you have been told about the good dinner at Ward's, and the entertainment for the night at "Camp Douglass" as well as the

2. Terrill and Dixon, *Stewart County*, pp. 266-70.

generosity of the clever people at Cuthbert. Everything has gone well so far. "The Grays" have done themselves great credit by their orderly behavior and general good appearance. I have heard frequent praises bestowed upon them in different places where we have stopped. Their faces look cheerful but I can once in a while catch an occasional serious expression, that tells me they are thinking of home. Tonight no doubt, while travelling along to Atlanta, many a suppressed sigh will be given by the poor fellows.

You want to hear about me—don't you? Well, I have spent the time since I left as well as could be expected. I am not much fatigued, and feel in body perfectly well, but of course I had much rather be home with you than anywhere in the wide world. It was my duty to go, and between a desire to stay, and duty to go I was left no choice. I have often today felt that I have been deprived of a great privilege, when I was deprived of the opportunity to serve permanently during the war as a soldier. We must all bear our part in this great struggle, and you can bear yours in giving me up for a time. You have I know your share of patriotism and you must not let your great love for me stand between you and your country.

I will take good care of myself & you need not be uneasy about me. I want you to enjoy yourself in every possible way. You must visit your neighbors every day— Interest yourself in something—Keep a diary of every thing you do, see, & think—and love me all the time: Go to Riddles [local photographer] & have you & the children taken in a group. I will pay him on my return, as there is a settlement between us; Have Father's ambrotype taken also; Probe is doing finely; He sends his love to "Annie & Walt." *Probe feels bad about leaving home*: Give my love to Mat. & Minerva & sister & all; Kiss the babies.[3] Goodbye—

Your Husband

3. See Appendix A for relatives.

Atlanta, GA—9 o'clock a.m.
Wednesday, July 31, 1861

Dear Allie—

We arrived here this morning all safe and sound. I thought I would have time to write you a long letter today but in an hour I shall leave for "Camp McDonald" which is 27 miles beyond this place on the state road to witness a review of the troops stationed there. I am getting along finely & so are all the boys. You know I feel lonesome without you anywhere, but except [for] that I am getting along splendidly. You must not be downhearted about my absence, and be certain not to be crying all day about your being unhappy, at a time when I need your encouragement: Write me a cheerful letter, all about yourself; Tell Mr. Richardson that Bill Tom is well—in good spirits &c.

Probe gets on well enough: He is bad off now to "take a wash"—Goodbye—Kiss the babies

Your Husband

Dalton, Ga. Thursday
August 1st, 1861 2 o'clock p.m.

Dear Allie

We are detained here nearly 24 hours, on account of a failure to make connection. The boys are grievously disappointed, but they bear it with a great deal of fortitude. The Governor furnished them with all necessary camp equipage including tents: We got 22 good tents with knapsacks — Haversacks, canteens — cups — coffeepots — water buckets &c.

The provision furnished us is a *hogshead* of dry bread: It eats like fodder, but by soaking it a minute in a mud puddle it eats finely. All are contented & cheerful. No sickness among us. I spent yesterday at Camp McDonald & witnessed the review of the Governor, of the 2500 troops there. All these troops are to be sent at once to Va. The first 500 start next Saturday. We will reach Richmond about Saturday night. I hope you are not uneasy about me, or at least that you have become resigned to my absence. Whatever I do you must be satis-

54

fied, because I shall do what is my duty. I cannot, of course, tell now, how long I shall be absent, but perhaps a month is the longest time.

You must take good care of yourself, and be well & fine looking when I come. Don't let your love for me make you unhappy. Talk to the children about their Pa every day, and tell Charlie to eat a heap & grow fast so he can go to the war, & fight the "Yankees." And make Ida read every day & write some also: You have written by this time to Richmond to me. You must write two or three times a week. So far I have written every day, but my next letter will be from Richmond & then I will write as often as I have opportunity. Goodbye, take good care of your precious dear self & love me all the time, but don't grieve about me. Kiss all the babies for me.

Probe is well—give my love to all—
Goodbye—Goodbye—

Your Husband

Allie wrote, from Lumpkin, the only letter of hers which has survived from this period:

Lumpkin, Stewart County, Ga.
Sunday night August 4, 1861

My own dear Darling

I have just put my last little one away for the night, and am all alone for Sister is in bed sometime ago. I am really glad too to see night come after having worried through this long lonesome Sunday. It has been raining off and on all day which made the day seem longer than otherwise. I have missed you more than ever today. I did not go to church this morning and tonight there is none. How I wonder where you are tonight and what you are doing. I have been wishing all day for a magic mirror. If there was such a thing I would be tempted to pay a big price for one.

I have received two letters from you since I wrote last. You did not tell me where to write. I shall keep sending my letters to Richmond though until I hear from you again, which I hope will be very soon. You say I must write you a cheerful letter all about myself. I don't know what to write that would at all interest you about myself for I travel the same road every day one after another. I have subscribed for the *Daily Sun*. Received two last mail. The Columbus mail comes now on Saturday instead of Sunday. They will rest here one day.

We had quite a thunder storm Friday evening. Lightning struck Cooper's house and set the pantry on fire, nobody was hurt, but it produced a good deal of excitement. I was spending the day at Mother's and saw it all.

I hear Amos Way has made up another company in this county. I don't know how true it is. I hope it is so for if he gets a company there will not be men enough for another left in the county.

A terrible storm passed down the river on Friday ruined Uncle Loverd's [Bryan] crop blowed off the house tops killed the cattle and ruined everything generally.

It is reported here that Tom [Crocker] and Sinclair were discharged and left in Atlanta for getting drunk. If it is so they were served right.

Sister [Annie Collier] says tell Probe that she will look for one of his long and very interesting letters in about a month. She is not well at all. She stays in bed most of the time. Walt is well. The old lady Richardson [a neighbor] begs me to mention her in all my letters. Let William [unidentifiable] know they are all well. I hear of nobodies being sick except Dr. Barnum he is quite sick with bilious fever. You must write me in your first letter after getting this when you expect to come home, how long you will stay. Take good care of yourself and keep well, write often. I am doing as well as I could do without you.

The children speak of you very often. Bud[4] said tonight he reckoned there was a heap of good things there where Pa was. God bless you. I want to see you so bad.

Allie

4. *Ibid.*

The next series of letters are from Clement to Allie:

Richmond [Virginia]
Tuesday Morning
August 6, 1861

My Dear Darling—

We reached this place yesterday evening after the most fatiguing ride I ever endured. We rode all night in an *open* car, made to transport cattle in, and as there was considerable danger to those who slept Dr. Moon & myself staid awake to watch or on our feet all night. So you may judge that I was too tired to write or do anything else yesterday. But I am actually fattening under this kind of life. I believe I have a better condition than three-fourths of the company. We have several sick—Tom Crocker (sore-feet)—Josh Wimberly—Folks-Westerman—(diarrhea) Folks (fever)—none sick much except Folks.

I have a very poor chance to write. I am stopping at the Exchange Hotel for the present but will move my quarters today. There is some expectation that our company will go to Manassas & farther in a few days. I am going to see Genl. Toombs[5] this morning to make arrangements to go myself. We are in his Brigade—But don't be uneasy. Mansfield goes also. I have not had time to see anything to write you about.

Nobody here knows anything about the movement of Genl. [P. G. T.] Beauregard. It is stated that he still advances, but everything is under profound secrecy. Nobody can get off from here without a passport, and it is very difficult to get permission to travel in the state.

5. Douglas S. Freeman, *Lee's Lieutenants*, 3 vols. (New York: Charles Scribner's Sons, 1942), vol. 1, pp. 621-29, for an evaluation of Robert Toombs' military career. "When the Confederate government was organized, Toombs was disappointed in not being elected to the Presidency, and he was not placated by the tender of the first position in the Cabinet. He accepted and labored, furiously if sullenly for about five months. Then he resigned to accept command of a Georgia brigade of infantry. He did not believe that the war would be long, and he did not intend that it should stop his political career, but for the time, he felt that more of service was to be rendered and more of honor won in the field than in the forum" (Freeman, *Lieutenants*, vol. 1, p. 622).

CLEMENT ANSELM EVANS (1870s)

MARY ALLEN "ALLIE" WALTON EVANS (1870s)

I saw Col. Semmes'[6] Regt. [Second Georgia Infantry] parade yesterday. Seven of his Cos. are well drilled. Our company will be mustered into service today. Most of the boys are cheerful, but I could name several who would give anything in the world to be at home. I will write more fully this evening. I go this evening to see Bob. He is about a mile from here.

Goodbye Honey—Take care of yourself. I am Home sick all ready.

Love to all.

Your Husband
C. A. Evans

Richmond, Virginia
Tuesday 8 o'clock p.m. Aug. 6th, 1861

My dear Darling

This morning I mailed a short letter to you, and also four morning papers. This evening I received your first letter, and I felt like I was almost home again. I have had no good opportunities of writing to you as I desired, and you must not think that I don't love you good because I have only written four letters to you during the week since I left. I hardly remember what I have written to you, and now that I have a good chance to write a long letter I hardly know where to begin. You were disappointed because I did not send you a message from Cuthbert. Well, Judge Barry gave me a very fine large peach, and I wrapped it up nicely in a piece of paper, and told Redding that I wanted him to carry it to you, but in the bustle & confusion of getting off, I lost sight of Redding and thus the message & the peach both failed of being sent. I did not forget you. I think of you a hundred times every day.

We are here in Richmond at last after suffering greater hardships than you have any idea of. We got along very well as far as Atlanta. Then as you know we were detained about eight or ten hours. Up to that time the

6. Henderson, *Roster*, vol. 1, p. 373. Paul Jones Semmes; also Ezra J. Warner, *Generals in Gray* (1959; Baton Rouge: Louisiana State University Press, 1991), p. 272.

trip was a frolic. Everyone was in good humor and no one had become fatigued with travel. Jokes were passed, the laugh went around and fun was the order of the day. Some little uneasiness was manifested when it became known that Wethersby had the mumps, but we left him at Fort Valley to come on when he got well.

I believe I wrote to you about attending the Review by the Governor of the troops, at Camp McDonald. The war fever came on me terribly bad, and if you had been there I expect you would have been contented to see me a soldier. After leaving Atlanta our hard time commenced. The principal trouble was want of sleep and water. After leaving Bristol [Virginia] we were sixty hours getting to Richmond and I had the good fortune to sleep four hours out of sixty. But you would be surprised at the incredible amount of fatigue which I can bear and at the same time thrive & fatten. I was intended for a soldier. I have never been satisfied with any other life so well as a soldier's life. If you and the children could be with me I would like to adopt the military profession and enter the regular army. I am in perfect health and have not seen a sick hour since I left home, except a slight headache one evening. Tonight I am comfortable, situated in an elegant private home at 75 cents per day, about half way between the camp of the Stewart Grays, and the Stewart Infantry. Hotel board is two & ½ dollars per diem. If I had known we could board at 75 cts. I think I would have brought you anyhow. I went to Lynch's Camp[7] today. Bob is perfectly well & I believe all of the company are up. Some few complain of colds. Bob is anxious to get a letter from home. All of you must write to him. I think that the regiment which Lynch is in, will probably remain here several weeks, but our Regiment is expected to be ordered off in a very few days. The Major's place is vacant in the Regiment Lynch is in & possibly it will be offered to your humble servant, if so I will either return home & bring you on,

7. Henderson, *Roster*, vol. 2, p. 918. Capt. Michael Lynch, Company I, Twenty-first Regiment Georgia Volunteer Infantry.

or you must fix up & come. I shall do no juggling for the Majorship, but I have good reason for supposing that an unsolicited effort will be made to place me there. You must not interpose any objections because I feel that my services must be given at an early date. I have qualified myself for a command, and if offered to me I could not decline. I am ashamed at the office seekers here. They fill every corner in the city. I told my Georgia acquaintances here not to be uneasy. I did not want any office. That I came on my own hook & was not going to trouble them at all. It is time I was closing this epistle. You must not be uneasy if you do not receive letters regularly. I do not expect one half my letters will reach you. The mails are deranged, & it is not certain that every letter will get to you:—

Bill Tom [unidentifiable] is getting along capitally. He makes a good officer & stands hardships well. The boys are all writing cheerful letters home. They don't want the old folks to be uneasy. They grumble terribly when they happen to think of some of the boys who stayed in Lumpkin enjoying themselves. Tell all my kinfolks I am well. Tell father to be certain to have his Ambrotype taken good large size—Give my love to all. I will write again to you and father. Good bye—Good bye.

Your Husband

August 8, 1861
Richmond-Friday 9 o'clock a.m.

My dear wife—

I wish you was with me this morning, or I was with you, for I am getting so anxious to see you that I will have to get a furlough soon, unless I get over my homesickness. I walk & ride all day long and often in the night about the city, so that when bed time comes I am tired enough to sleep like a log. There are many things worth seeing here, but you cannot turn around without having to pay money. I never saw such a set of swindlers in my life as now are in the blessed city. I will except from censure the citizens who are out of trade, for many excellent families have & continue to take sick &

wounded soldiers & nurse them without charge. Two of
[the] "Grays" (Tom Bridges & Tip Gregory) are now
quartered with private families and will soon be well:—
I have been to see the Yankee prisoners, and the Guns
lately captured [in First Battle of Manassas]. Some of
the prisoners are old men, many quite young & a few
Negroes. One likely Black young Negro boy I saw worth
1400 dollars in our market, who was taken prisoner. It
is believed that the Government will hold all the captured Negroes until our fugitive slaves are restored: The
prisoners are well treated when they conduct themselves properly. Some of them say they have been deceived and will not fight any more, but others curse
Southern men through their windows & declare they will
yet have revenge. One rascal was shot through the head
a few days ago by a sentinel. The orders are, that they
shall not put their heads out of the windows, nor insult
persons passing. This fellow saw a genteel lady passing
by and exposed himself to her in the most devilish &
brutish manner. A sentinel off about 50 or 100 yards
happened to see him, and in a moment his rifle was to
his shoulder, and his eye ran along the barrel, his fingers
pulled the trigger and a minnie [minié] ball went
through the rascal's head. The punishment was summary, but it will stop all such Yankee brutalities: A
congressman named Ely[8] is a prisoner. He is tremen-
dously frightened, and sent for Col. [Louis T.] Wigfall
(of Texas) with whom he was acquainted, to help him
get his liberty. He said—"Wigfall, is there no chance to
get me out of this horrible place."

"None sir" said Wigfall—

"My god" says the Yankee, "what will they do with
me?"

8. *Biographical Directory of the American Congress, 1774-1961* (Washington:
United States Government Printing Office, 1961, p. 860. Alfred Ely, a rep-
resentative from New York, was taken prisoner while witnessing the Battle
of Manassas and was held in Richmond for nearly six months; also Margaret
Leach, *Reveille in Washington* (New York: Harper and Brothers, 1941), pp.
100, 103. At this point, the summer of 1861, the best known Richmond
prisons, Libby and Belle Isle, were not yet in operation. Federal prisoners,
mostly from Manassas, were held at several buildings in Richmond and in
Charleston harbor.

"Hang you by G-D sir" said Wigfall "Hang you like a dog if your d--nd President hurts a hair of any of our boys' heads."[9]

The muskets which we took from the Yankees are all of superior kind. A great many of them are precisely like the "Stewart Grays" muskets, and what is strange thousands of them were found *loaded*. A Southern man would have *fired* his loaded Gun, at the enemy before throwing it away. I have a musket ball & three buckshot & some powder taken from one of the Guns. A gentleman told me that some of the Guns were partly filled with *peas* & *corn*, but I hardly believe they were fools enough to load their guns in that way.

Many of the Guns are bent, broken, & otherwise damaged—Clots of blood stick about on many of them showing that those who used them were wounded. The number of small arms taken is a little over 22,000, and I was told that the whole of them, have been engaged by Southern Volunteers. We will have to get up another fight soon, so as to get more guns:—Hundreds of troops are coming into Virginia every day. All do not come by Richmond. They turn off at Lynchburg, Bristol, & other points: There are now 210,000 troops *in the field* belonging to the Confederate army. This includes all the army raised in the South: Congress has authorized the raising of 400,000 troops.

It is just as hard to get news in Richmond as in Lumpkin. Genl. Beauregard is certainly advancing & strengthening as he advances, but this is all we can know. No citizens are allowed to leave Richmond without a pass-

9. W. A. Swanberg, *First Blood, The Story of Fort Sumter* (New York: Charles Scribner's Sons, 1957), p. 110, describes Wigfall as "Washington's most violent and uninhibited character . . . a former South Carolinian noted for his willingness to shoot people who disagreed with him." Congressman Ely's version of this encounter with Senator Wigfall is quite different. According to Ely's diary, the incident took place on July 26, 1861. Ely did not send for Wigfall: the senator was at the prison to visit another prisoner. Ely had frequently seen Wigfall in the pre-war Congress, but never met him before this day. The senator did assure Ely that the Confederate government intended to hang him if the Federal government carried through with its threat to hang privateers from the schooner *Savanna*. See *Journal of Alfred Ely, A Prisoner of War in Richmond*, Charles Lanman, ed. (New York: D. Appleton and Company, 1862), p. 35.

port to go anywhere, and not at all toward Manassas unless to visit a wounded sick relative. (Mr. McNab passed through here yesterday to see John. He is sick at Fairfax C. H. [Court House] James McNab, is at Meriwether Spring for his health) I shall have to turn soldier or come home. I think that it will be impossible for me to go farther with the company as a traveling citizen. I am anxious to go & may buy me a uniform & borrow a gun for a few weeks. I am quietly waiting to see what will turn up as to my *Majorship*. I would press it with vigor if you was not so much opposed to it.

There is yet no certainty about the time when either the "Grays" or "Stewart infantry" will be ordered forward. I think however that the "Grays" will go soon perhaps in a week, but the Stewart infantry will be here a month. However no one knows anything on the subject—not even the Colonels themselves.

Unless I can be allowed to go farther I shall return home soon. Perhaps in ten days from now. I should like very much however to engage in one battle just to know something about it. But the probability is that two months will elapse before another general engagement.

You will see by the paper that the Yankees are becoming frightened down about Newport News and Hampton. Hampton it appears has been entirely destroyed by fire. The general impression here is, that the North is allready whipped, but don't know how to propose peace & yet pretend to be able to conquer us if they wanted to.

Well I must close now. I will write again tomorrow. I have not written every day because I have really a bad chance to write. I am perfectly well—so is Bob & Probe & Charley Davis. Bill Tom, I think will make the most active officer in the Grays. He keeps well, takes a pride in his position—does his duty & will become a favorite in the Regiment. This is all true. Many of the Boys are very homesick, I tell you they feel good about getting enlisted for 8 months. Their time is up eight months today.

Goodbye. Give my love to Father—Mat, Sis Jane & all the balance of the family. Bob & Probe send their love.[10] Kiss the little darlings for Pa. Tell Ida to study her book and learn to write so she can write to Pa. Goodbye—Goodbye.

Your Husband

Saturday, Aug. 10th, 1861
Richmond, Virginia
10 o'clock p.m.

My dear Darling

I am getting allready very tired of Richmond, and unless our Regiment is ordered forward soon I shall make my way home. I wish I was with you tonight instead of taking my night's sleep on a sofa. I have slept only two nights in a bed since I left home, but when I do sleep all the drums in the army can't wake me up. This evening I lay down on two big rocks under a shade on the river bank and slept about an hour as sound as if I had been on a feather bed. I expect to walk ten to twelve miles every day going about from place to place restless as the [James] river itself. There is still no certainty as to the time when the Regiments will leave here, although last evening the men were ordered to dispose of surplus baggage. This created the impression that the stay at this place would be a day or two longer, and many have written home to that effect. You need not believe they are certainly gone until letters are received from the place to which they are ordered. Toombs himself, Commanding the Brigade does not know how soon the Regiment can move. Much depends upon the advance movements of General Beauregard, and his own requisitions on the department here, for more troops to cover his rear. Opinion here as to the probability of an early fight is considerably divided, but after all, it is mere opinion, mere conjecture. The greatest strictness prevails as to the movements of Beauregard. Nothing whatever is permitted to be published and all persons who are so fortunate as to be able to get passports, are put upon honor to communicate no fact that may come to their knowledge.

10. See Appendix A for relatives.

Mr. Mansfield has after much difficulty obtained leave to go to Manassas as Chaplain to the Stewart Grays. My only chance to go is to go as a soldier during my stay, and I am not sure that I can get to go in that capacity without being regularly mustered into service. I shall see however in a few days, when I will be allowed to serve two weeks on my own hook and if so I will at once write to you. If I cannot I will be at home by the 20th of this month. The chance for the Majorship still stands as it was, and I believe I might get it by a little juggling, but I do not feel like doing that. I wish you was here to give me the benefit of your advice.

I am very anxious to get another letter from you. I have received but one, and that was written a day or two after we left. I think this is the 7th or 8th letter I have written to you. I am now writing late at night and you must look over my short & dull letters. I send you papers every day, and have subscribed for the "Daily Dispatch" for you. I wish I had some news to write, but positively there is none, except that soldiers are coming every day by companies & Regiments, and thousands offering their services and all accepted. It is the calculation to continue the increase of the army just as rapidly as they can provide transportation and arms. Georgia stands high here. She has sent more troops to Virginia than any other State. The iron works here are turning out guns & heavy ordnance rapidly but not enough to supply one half the demand. The Yankee muskets are distributed daily. There were 27 Captains at one time to day in the building where they are kept Selecting for their Companies; and this happens every day. Lynch has received his muskets. They are the same as the "Stewart Grays" musket. Lynch is the best Captain in his regiment. This is strictly true & not buncombe in my judgment the Grays are doing finely receiving many well deserved praises. All their sick are getting well.

It is a hard matter here to pick up any information on which to base a reliable opinion as to the future. None believe the war will be of long duration, but all differ as to the probabilities of any heavy battles soon.

Some say that Genl Beauregard is planning a forward movement on Philadelphia, others that he only designs expelling the Yankees from Virginia, & still others say he will soon attack Washington. All these things you will see in the papers, but believe none of them as the truth, for some are published to blind the enemy, others merely for sensation.

Nelson[11] of Tennessee elected a few days ago in Tennessee by the Union party of Tennessee to Congress, was brought in here today under a guard of forty soldiers. He was captured in the North West of Va. trying to get to the *Washington Congress.*

Well—Good bye I will go to sleep & write to you again tomorrow. I wish I was with you or you with me. If I can have one *pull* at the Yankees I will come home & not leave you any more but if I don't get the chance this time you must fix me up to go next winter. My love to all *and all my love to you.* Kiss the babies for Pa. Bob & Probe all well—Good bye—Good bye—

Your Husband

Richmond, VA.
Sunday, Aug. 11th, 1861
8 o'clock p.m.

My dear Love.

Today nothing of particular interest has occured for me to write to you about. I went to the Methodist Church on Broad street to hear Mr. Duncan preach. The church is a very fine building indeed. Everything was conducted in the city style very different from our own mode of worship. I can never get accustomed to fashionable worship. Mr. Mansfield also preached yes-

---

11. Thomas A. R. Nelson of Tennessee, "long-time friend and associate of Andrew Johnson, Chairman of the Greenville convention which had tried to keep Tennessee from secession, and one of the representatives which East Tennessee had sent to the national House of Representatives during the first year of the war" (Robert Selph Henry, *The Story of Reconstruction, 1865-1877* [New York: Grossett & Dunlap, 1938], p. 305). Nelson was also one of Andrew Johnson's defense counsels in the Senate trial of impeachment during Reconstruction.

terday in one of the Baptist Churches. I passed a Catholic Church & saw two *Nuns*, sisters of Mercy—dressed in singular style. A loose brown colored gown. I will be home perhaps a day or two after this letter reaches you. If I can go on I will write immediately—The Stewart Grays will get off Wednesday. They would have left on tomorrow but a heavy rain fell last night & has damaged the track so much as to cause this delay. Good bye—Love to all & all my love to you again.—

Your Husband

Richmond, Va.
Monday, Aug. 12th, 1861

My dear darling

I expect from present indications that I shall soon be at home, for the Military authorities here are very particular about granting passports. Even persons who have sons in the army at Manassas come here and cannot go any farther. I can get a passport to Norfolk and I shall probably go down there in a day or two.

I have allready written all the news in the city, and I hope you are getting the "Daily Dispatch" which will give you all that is current here.

Several of the "Stewart Grays" have been unfortunate in the money matters. Over $160.00 have been stolen from them: Randolph Hines lost $70. Mat Brown about $20. Frank Wats $15. John Mansfield $15. Joe Singer $32. This money has actually been stolen, but who by no one now knows. Suspicion points out no particular person. Some think it is Negros in the company, others suspect loafers about the camp. I expect the company will certainly leave on Wednesday although that rail road accident to which I referred in my last [letter] may delay them still farther.

Perhaps the next immediate fights will occur in North West Va. or somewhere down at Fortress Monroe. I hope if a fight does take place I will be back in Norfolk in time to witness it. But don't be uneasy. I bear a Charmed life. Bullets can't hurt me as long as you love me like you do.

69

Our Congress will adjourn in a week. I went to the Capitol again to day and saw some of our *great men.* Several looked about as common as myself.

I have up to this date received but one letter from you and I think this is about the eleventh I have written to you. Either you do not write or the mails fail to bring your letters. I am afraid many of my letters do not reach you. I write nearly every day. I think about you all the time. Everytime I see anything worth looking at I wish you were with me to enjoy yourself also. I have been sorry a hundred times you did not come with me, and yet the passage from Lumpkin to this place would have been very unpleasant to you. Never mind, when I get home we will manage to find some enjoyment even in Lumpkin. But when I come home you must not object to my making up a company to go to the war. I feel like the war is passing off and I have not contributed anything to my country's independence.

I shall not be satisfied unless I am permitted to participate in some way in the fight. I expect that Georgia will have to be defended next winter. That is, I think unless a heavy force is placed near our sea coast, Lincoln will be tempted to invade us from that quarter. But we will talk all this over at home. Don't be uneasy. I am safe while you love me—Goodbye—Think about me all the time—Good bye—My love to Mother, Clem, Mat & all & all.

I have written to Father—Tell him I will be home soon. Good bye my dear.

Your Husband

Tuesday, Aug 13th.

No letter from you yet! What is the matter? Surely you have written since the 30th [of] last month. Probe is anxious to get a letter before he goes off. Not yet certain that the "Grays" leave tomorrow—Goodbye—Maybe I will be home soon—

Richmond, Va. Thursday
11 o'clock a.m. August 15th, 1861

My dear Darling

Yesterday orders were sent to Col. Semmes to move his regiment [Second Georgia] Friday morning to Manassas, and many have written home to that effect. Last night about nine o'clock these orders were countermanded, and the regiment ordered forthwith to move to *Aquia Creek*. Accordingly this morning at 8 o'clock the trains carried them off, our company among the rest. I had been begging a passport to Manassas about ten days & failed, but this morning I obtained a passport to go to Aquia Creek & Norfolk, and this evening at 5 o'clock I shall be off to remain there however but a day or two unless [obliterated]. But don't you be at all uneasy. If it was not right I would not keep you informed of my movements, but I know you are entitled to be acquainted with all I do. I promised to bring myself home safe, and no Yankee bullets are yet moulded to hurt me. Before this reaches you, the telegraph will bear the news from Aquia Creek, and I shall not be surprised if the work is warm:—I think I smell *gunpowder in that direction*. Why the advance on Richmond has not been made from that point is a mystery to me. Perhaps if our batteries there can be stormed, Beauregard will have his hands full again—

I am in perfect good health, but feel low spirited because I cannot hear from home—Bob & Probe are well—

Tom Crocker & Rufus Thornton were left here sick. I believe both of them will have to return home. The balance are well or but very little sick.

I shall be home a few days after this reaches you, so don't be uneasy. I think you may commence looking for me on the 23rd.

Give my love to all—I wish you were here or I was there.

MAJ. GEN. ALEXANDER ROBERT LAWTON

72

Chapter 5
SOLDIER

Upon returning to Lumpkin, Senator Evans wrote to Governor Brown of Georgia on August 23 to inquire as to prospects for service for other Stewart volunteers besides the Grays:

> To his Excellency Joseph E. Brown
> Sir,
> At the instance of a number of citizens I write to ask information concerning the organization of either infantry or mounted Rifle Companies, and their acceptance for the defence of the Coast of the State; — This County has in the field about 400 men, and three other companies can be organized, one for Virginia (or elsewhere) and two for Georgia. A number of citizens are so situated as to be unable to leave their homes for Virginia but who desire to engage in the service in this State, being anxious to contribute to their utmost, in the present war; One company of light Cavalry, and one of infantry for the latter purpose can be readily raised, and drilled at home until such time as you may direct, without expense to the Government; Can you furnish the Cavalry with breech loading guns, sabres & pistols, and will the infantry armed with double barrell shotguns be accepted? Your early reply will confer a considerable favor on a number of citizens. . . .[1]

Evans had, no doubt, voiced his own status in the foregoing letter to Governor Brown. This assumption is borne out by his correspondence with his former senate colleague, Brig. Gen.

1. Original letter in Department of Archives and History, Office of Secretary, State of Georgia, Atlanta, Georgia.

Alexander R. Lawton, who had formed a volunteer brigade of Georgia militia in Savannah. General Lawton was a West Pointer by education, a lawyer by profession, and the renowned captor of Fort Pulaski, Savannah's chief Federal stronghold in early January 1861.[2] General Lawton replied:

> Sept. 2, 1861
> Savannah, Ga.
>
> My Dear Sir
>
> I am truly glad to hear from your note of the 30th inst. that you people are feeling such a deep interest in our coast defence. The great pressure on the War Department from the Northern frontiers of the Confederacy has turned all eyes (and unfortunately arms) in that direction and caused us to be sadly neglected here. But we are doing everything that energy and industry can accomplish with small means—and will hope to be prepared for the advent of our Northern friends.
>
> The Confederacy has no *arms* at its disposal and the Governor informs me that the State supply is exhausted. I am powerless therefore in that respect. But would receive with pleasure any companies from your section of the State (with such arms as they can furnish themselves) and attach them to Regiments here, or would receive a battalion properly organized and officiered.
>
> Permit me to add that I would be pleased to have you transferred with me from the Senate to the camp, and amid other scenes renew the pleasant association of the past years.
>
> A. R. Lawton

By that fall, Evans could not stand the "war fever" any longer and enlisted as a private in another one of the volunteer companies from Stewart County—the Bartow Guards.[3] This company was named for one of the heroes of the hour, Francis S. Bartow, who sacrificed his life in the first big engagement of the war at Manas-

2. Warner, *Generals in Gray*, p. 175. Brig. Gen. Alexander Robert Lawton.
3. Henderson, *Roster*, vol. 3, pp. 576, 609, 613. The Bartow Guards became Company E of the Thirty-first Georgia Regiment of Lawton's brigade.

sas.[4] The Bartow Guards were sent to Savannah in November to join Col. Pleasant J. Phillips'[5] regiment and became part of the aforementioned volunteer brigade of General Lawton.

Leaving home had been no light and frivolous escapade for Evans as his letters from the Savannah camp indicate:

Savannah. Nov. 13, 1861

My dear Allie

Last night I commenced to write you a letter and before I had to finish it I was hurried off to the [railroad] Cars. This will explain why you received no letter from Macon, but I have been troubled all day thinking that you would be uneasy. Let me beg you not to think I am sick or in danger or anything else wrong because you happen to miss one or two or even three mails once in a while, because a thousand things can happen to prevent me from writing every mail.

We got along finely. No accident happened. We had plenty to eat, good cars to ride in and everything pleasant. We reached here this morning about sun-rise, and the company was marched to the Parade Ground, while I remained to have the baggage cared for and transported. I remained at the Parade ground until 2½ o'clock when the company was marched down to the barracks and mustered into service by *Major Wm. S. Rockwell*. He is the ugliest man I ever saw. Take a *bag pudding*, dip it in a quart of Poke-berry juice, and then mash it against a gridiron, and you have a very good likeness of the man's face. I have met him occasionally before. He is Grand Master of the Grand Lodge of Masons in this state. All the boys submitted cheerfully to the yoke

4. Francis S. Bartow was an 1835 graduate of the University of Georgia. A. L. Hull, *A Historical Sketch of the University of Georgia* (Atlanta: Foote & Davies Co., 1894), 74. Bartow was killed at Manassas in July 1861, at the same time as Brig. Gen. Barnard Bee, who has been credited for naming "Stonewall" Jackson at that battle. The names of Bee and Bartow, especially in Georgia, are nearly synonymous; Freeman, *Lieutenants*, vol. 1, pp. 55-73. In December 1861, Georgia changed the name of Cass County to Bartow, having become disenchanted with Lewis Cass for whom it was originally named. *Georgia Official and Stat. Reg.*, 1957-58, p. 671.
5. Henderson, *Roster*, vol. 3, p. 576. Col. Pleasant J. Phillips.

he put on them, but I could not help from feeling sorry for them although I have to incur the same danger, and equal hardships of different character. Our Regiment has been ordered to encamp about two miles from Savannah for the present, and perhaps for several weeks. We will organize next Saturday with either nine or ten companies. Genl Lawton has ordered me to go down to the junction of the Gulf-road and bring forward some companies there. I will leave for that purpose early tomorrow and may not be back for two days and therefore if you should not get a letter soon after receiving this do not be uneasy. I have met a large number of acquaintances here from all parts of the state in various positions from private to General. I have just seen old Commodore [Josiah] Tatnall. He appears to be about sixty or sixty five years of age, and weighs about one hundred and seventy five pounds. He is in all excitement this morning and so indeed is the whole city by the reported arrival of a steel-clad steamer [*Fingal*] purchased in Europe bringing between seven and eight thousand Enfield rifles. The steamer is said to be almost if not quite cannon-proof. I judge the report to be true as General Lawton was telegraphed to that effect, and the Commodore has sent down troops & boats to guard and unload her. Gov. Brown is here but I have not yet seen him. We intend to get the use of the Enfield rifles for our Regiment if we can possibly influence the Governor to let us have them.

There are said to be between twelve & fifteen thousand troops encamped here, and I observe a good supply of light artillery. The Savannah people have been greatly frightened. Numbers have left here, not only of women and children but men. I have seen to day several houses where their owners were taking out and packing up furniture, although at present not much danger of an attack is apprehended.

The Bartow Guards have been highly complimented on the route and since their arrival they have 70 men besides 4 commanding officers. Col. [Pleasant J.] Phillips is here busy as a bee. He is very popular with his regiment.

Capt Redding[6] draws tents, knapsacks &c &c this evening and will go regularly to duty at once. I tell you old Stewart [County] may well be proud of the companies she has sent off. As soon as I return I will write you in full. I find I left many little things which I shall need and will give you a list of them. Make your arrangements to come down in three weeks, and be cheerful— There is not the least danger in my opinion of any fight here in that time, and therefore I know we shall meet again—I shall take good care of my health—Don't be uneasy on that score. I have commenced to fatten allready—and before long my jaws will be hanging in great rolls of fat like a Berkshire hog—Goodbye—Give my love to all of the folks at home. Tell them I will write often, and they must write to me. Good bye—Good bye—Kiss the "*little darlings.*"

Your Husband

Toombs' Brigade & Semmes' Regiment are not ordered here, as you have been told.

Sav[annah] Nov. 13/[18]61

Dear Darling

Sure enough the "Steel Clad Steamer" has come in and a glorious looking vessel she is. Completely mailed with steel so as to be cannon proof—She brought over 12000 Enfield rifles—Several rifles cannon-ammunition in abundance millions of percussion caps—*4000 kegs* of powder—cartridge boxes—leather &c &c.

She did not expect to land here but was nosing her way along, saw no fleet, nothing to obstruct her entrance and in she came. Her arrival is a victory in Itself. She is such a splendid vessel that I am tempted to quit the land and take water. I believe I would if I had another little steel vessel with you & the babies in it tugging along with me.

It is reported that the fleet has gone. If so look out for

6. *Ibid.*, p. 609. Leonidas R. Redding.

another Port Royal affair somewhere else. They intended to sneak round the coast & when we are not prepared to meet them & they can put 20 war vessels on one poor little fort they will pitch in.—Cowardly scamps!

They are doing a regular Negro stealing business on the coast. This morning one planter on an island ordered his 300 Negros to go with him to a place he had provided for them in the interior & they rebeled & refused to go. Some troops were sent from here to force them off but I have not heard the result.

Savannah has disappointed me—Streets narrow—Houses common—Women ugly (I wouldn't give you for all of them).[7]

Good bye—in haste—I wrote once before today & will leave for the Junction & perhaps Brunswick tomorrow to return Friday—

> Good bye
> Your Husband

Savannah Nov. 18th 1861

My dear Allie,

I will first write to you again & then I would take time to write to several others.

The Regiment was organized to day by holding an election resulting in the unanimous selection of Col. Phillips —Hill[8]—& myself for field officers. [Evans was elected major.] We held this election in order to get commissions from the State, as well as from the Confederate States. Everything passed off agreeably although at one time yesterday and this morning we feared that Hill would have opposition. With this exception nothing of any interest has transpired. Our remaining three companies will all be in this week when our Regiment will be full. Some of the companies are very small indeed, but recruiting officers will be sent out to fill their ranks. Capt. Redding's company is the third or fourth largest company, and I think his commission will rank him about

7. In deference to the women of Savannah, one would not expect Clement to write his wife anything other than this opinion.
8. Henderson, *Roster*, vol. 3, p. 576. Daniel Pike Hill.

letter D. That however cannot be ascertained until all the companies come in. So far I am pleased with the Commissioned officers of the companies. A strong moral & religious influence shall be brought to bear on the regiment with the hope that we shall be distinguished as much for moral & religious conduct as some regiments are for the contrary. Nearly all the companies are un-drilled, but we expect to commence a systematic course of drilling at once which will put the Regiment in proper training for service. We do not know how soon we may be needed, although there are no immediate prospects of fighting so far as I can judge. I try to keep down the blues, and endeavor to be as cheerful as possible, but I would give a twelve months Major's pay freely to be at home and my duty all discharged. This morning I com-menced a practice which I intend to keep up as far as possible, of taking a long walk to think of home and you, until you come. I am afraid when you come that you & the children will soon become tired. If we were rich & could keep a carriage & horses here it would be far more comfortable but if you stay in the City, you can come to the camps only occasionally & I will have 2½ miles to ride or walk to visit you. I don't mind my part of the trouble if you can be made comfortable. I want you with me by all means, for I cannot get through the war without you. I am waiting to get a letter from you & get fixed before hunting a boarding house. Don't read any more of this letter to anybody.

I am very much cramped on account of my slender purse. A thousand unexpected things have reduced me down to only Sixteen dollars, and many things yet to buy. My uniform must be purchased at once at a cost of 50 dollars. I have been almost slavishly economical. And to tell you the truth I had as soon be a private as to be a Major without money. I write this to you because I have no secrets from you. Don't think of sending me any money. But keep it all yourself. You can press Frank Pierce—J. T. Thornton—George Bull &c so as to get up any how $150 for your self. You will be obliged to have that much. I will manage to get along.

Don't sell our "Sausage grinder" I want it bad to grind up beef.

Goodbye my darling. I shall devote my whole future to your happiness. Kiss the little darling children for Pa—Goodbye—My love to all.

Your Husband

Savannah, Nov. 20 1861
Camp Phillips

Dear Allie

I have just a moment to write to you my daily letter and it will be a short one, but you had rather get a short letter than none at all. I am in excellent health and I believe all the Bartow Guards are well except Durham & he is getting well.

I received my commission yesterday, drew two tents, which gives me three to myself including the one I brought from home. I bought me a cot costing six dollars & worth about three, but it was the best I could do. My funds are melting like snow.

Don't be alarmed about Dr. Park's letter. It is true that the place may be attacked, but you can get here and get away too whenever I say so. Dr. Parks is looking out for a good boarding house in the city for you. He thinks that you & all can get good board for 50 dollars per month. The only difficulty about getting here & staying here is money enough. If that article can be had you can come on when you please.

Lieutenant Orr[9] will be at home by the first of December to return by the 4th or 5th. You can come with him. He can bring Mose[10] without expense.

I expect you had better put me up a matress out of cotton in the pantry, but I will write again this evening. I have but time to say good bye. Kiss the babies.—Love to all.

Your Husband

9. *Ibid.*, p. 609. Isaac W. Orr.
10. Moses Evans was a slave of Clement Evans and accompanied him to Virginia. See Moses' letter of December 26, 1862, hereafter.

Savannah Nov. 20, 1861
Headquarters Col. Phillips' Reg.

My dear darling

It is very hard to keep from having the blues when night comes, and supper is over. My mind will run back at home, for where my treasure is my heart is there also. If I did not dream about home I would get along better; but to have these dreams about being with you and the children, enjoying myself so well; then to wake and here I am surrounded by military camps amid thousands of strangers,—these are the things that give me the blues.

Today I had two of my tents put up and as I am to occupy all three alone of course I have room abundant. They are good roomy tents with flies to them and afford a good protection against the weather. I have caught no cold, and really today I felt physically better than any day since leaving home. For the first time today the Field officers dined together alone. We three mess together alone, not from any aristocracy or anything of that sort, but because the Staff officers and all others have friends in the companies with whom they chose to mess. *My everlasting Trunk* supplied a most bountiful dinner, and it was three o'clock before we had time to eat. You may be assured that I filled nature's haversack to its full capacity. I did not go down to the City today, and have no news for you. In fact you get by the papers the same news that I get, but you need not believe half the tales you hear about Savannah. The simple truth is this, that the Yankee fleet may take a notion to attack the city. When that notion will be taken no body knows, but we are prepared here to make a good defence which if well managed will be successful. From the beginning of the attack time will be plentiful in which to move every woman & child into the country far enough off to be safe. All that we will have to do is to make a contract before hand with some man who keeps horses & carriages to hire to give him twenty five dollars to carry you twenty five miles, which can be done. Then select the twenty five miles to some point on either the Central or the Gulf Rail Road and you are safe: If you want to go, that will be our plan, if not you can go with me through the fight. I would as soon trust you by my side as any soldier here. If I can keep you with me I shall see this war through, and if it lasts until Charlie gets fourteen he shall have his gun shouldered with the rest. I shall love to be a soldier, if you can be happy while I am a soldier.

I stated that we had a moral Regiment and truly we have. I have not heard an *obscene* word since I have been in the Camps, while in other regiments I have been shocked by open-mouthed vulgarity. Col. Phillips is a good man. Lieut. Col. Hill, although in no Church has an excellent appreciation of religion.

Many Captains & Lieuts are professors of religion, and every night prayer is held in several companies in the regiment. If we can keep up this state of things you will soon see a good fighting regiment, for when a man is prepared to die, he can face danger in the discharge of duty without fear.

No sickness in the Bartow Guards. They are drilled just enough to give them needful exercise, and every attention is paid to their health. Tell everybody to have no apprehensions on this score. The boys shall be provided for. I drilled them to day and find them progressing rapidly.

I do hope you will get money enough to come with and not feel cramped. My situation is somewhat unpleasant by reason of the scantiness of my funds. I shall soon be entirely out unless I get the fifty dollars due me here which is doubtful. I will find that out to morrow. I have my measure and an order to I. E. Daniel & Co. for my uniform which will cost me another fifty. I must blunder along somehow until I get some from the Government. I shall write to W. A. Rawson to day about paying for my uniform at Columbus. I want you to buy me a good pocket knife not an expensive one—not too heavy—but strong; Make Mose bring a saw—¾ auger & chisel—Hammer—Small mallet—(I have an axe & a hatchet)—bring some nails—either *6s, 8s, or 10s*—Small smoothing plane—draw knife—Send Charlie Warren word to make me a good pair of boots at once, so as to have them ready when you or Orr comes. Tell him not to make them too heavy, nor too course, but with good thick soles.

Well good bye darling—I write all about myself—you must excuse that—Kiss the children. Tell Mrs. Collier[11] with all her faults I love her still.

Your Husband

Headquarters Phillips' Regt.
Sav[annah,] Ga. Nov. 21, 1861

Dear Darling

My every day letters to you amount to nothing more than a mere diary of what I do every day and can hardly be interesting to any one except yourself. I know they interest you more on that account, and for that reason I fill all of my letters about myself. You may take it for granted that I am in perfect health until I mention the contrary for I will tell you when I get the least sick.

Your second letter written Tuesday came this morning and has given me the blues. I wish I was with you to help you while the children are sick; Don't fail to send an express at once to Columbus & telegraph to me here if any of you get very sick. Tell Buddy Pa is so sorry he has been sick, but is glad he is a good boy. Tell Ida, she must love her Buddy.[12] Pa has been waiting to get a letter from her ever since he has been here. Bless the dear little children.

To day I went to the City and made a requisition for plank to floor both my tents, and got two hundred feet of splendid seasoned lumber, which has been delivered here ready for me to have it fixed tomorrow. I will then be almost as comfortable as if I was in a house. We intend as soon as possible to procure plank floors for the entire Regiment. Some companies have plank for their tents now.

11. This is a little pleasantry to Allie's sister Anne, Mrs. Probert Collier. See Appendix A for relatives.
12. "Buddy" is the baby, Charles Crawford, who died the next summer. "Ida" is the oldest daughter who will be referred to in many letters through the war. See Appendix A.

A great deal of attention is paid here to the comfort of soldiers, both well and sick. I see the greatest difference in those things here, and in Virginia. It is true that there are many inconveniences and hardships which must be endured and which demand the exercise of patriotic patience. Still the weather so far is soft, the ground is level, and porous so as to be easy to travel over and yet soon becomes dry after a rain, the tents are good and new, and many companies have provided themselves with large wall tents, and generally the officers who have charge of the various departments here such as quartermaster general, comissary General &c are as accommodating as could be expected. Therefore we can say to all at home, 'Here is the place where the State is threatened with invasion at any hour;—you are needed badly to assist in repelling the invasion—you can spare twelve months from your business, your homes & families—Come, give that much to the State which protects you—Come! and you shall have good quarters, good provisions—good surgeons—and when the war is over and independence won you can sit by your fireside in peace with the conscious pride in your hearts that liberty was won by your help, and not without you, nor in spite of you—Ah me! would that the boys who refused to come could hear our brave boys talk around the camp fires about them.

We bought a bellows & anvil to day and to morrow our gun-smith will go to work to repair all the guns in the Regiment which are out of order. (General Lawton has promised to arm three companies with musket and bayonet, but do not say anything about this, for we have to promise the muskets to two companies in order to get them).

Our Regiment will be complete this week. Another company came in tonight making eight on the ground— This company is from Pulaski county has 70 men and commanded by Captain Wood.[13] Capt. Forrester[14] is

13. Henderson, *Roster*, vol. 3, p. 620. Warren D. Wood.
14. *Ibid.* Apollus Forrester.

yet on St Simons Island but we expect his company here Saturday. Another company is on Green Island which we send for to morrow. Our commissary has been appointed and is now acting. I wish Bob[15] was here but there is no place vacant which he would have.

Tom Hines, son of Uncle Jeff, came in to day and enlisted in Captain Lowe's company. He says he went out *possum hunting* and came off without Uncle Jeff's knowledge. I look for the old man Jeff down here in a day or two.

Nothing of any interest has happened to day in the City or camp. Some Yankee Vessels are reported off the bar & two inside, but don't be alarmed at these demonstrations. They mean nothing. No such notice will likely be given of an attack. As soon as Generals Lawton & [Robert E.] Lee[16] return from Brunswick I look for a more active system of preparation for defence.

With reference to Frank Bush's pistol tell Graham[17] not to buy it, without trying it good and not to pay over twenty dollars for it on a credit. If he could borrow a good repeater for two months I would have the opportunity & the cash in that time to make a good purchase. I think I can do without one anyhow. If a battle comes off I can easily get a pistol from some soldier & until that time I have no need for one. Please ask him to see Jesse Latimer & if Latimer will do it, borrow his sword for two months. I cannot get one here, nor can I have mine fixed up at present to my notion. I will have to send it to Columbus. I am putting you all to a heap of trouble, but you must bear with me. I am sorry you are getting along slow in collecting money for I want you here bad, but don't come without getting one hundred & fifty dollars. I want you to have a plenty and I hate to commence drawing on the government as soon as I receive

15. See Appendix A for relatives.
16. In November 1861, Robert E. Lee, who was acting as advisor to President Jefferson Davis in Richmond, was ordered to South Carolina and Georgia to direct and supervise construction of defenses on the coast. R. E. Lee, Jr., *Recollections of Letters of General Lee* (New York: Doubleday, Page, and Co., 1904), p. 54.
17. James Graham, husband of Clement's sister, Mat. See Appendix A.

85

my commission. I wish I was rich for your sake. You should have your carriage and horses here. Lieut. Orr will be home soon, and it is a good chance for you to come with him. I will meet you in Macon I reckon, if I can find out when you are coming. Buy me a *Lantern* from Chamberlin. Good bye. The paper is filled. Kiss me & good bye again.

Your Husband

Headquarters Phillips' Regt
Savannah, Ga.
Nov. 23, 1861

My dear Darling

You must again be satisfied with a short letter for I am not only much fatigued, but I do not feel well. Do not be uneasy; I shall take a big blue pill tonight and Ep. Salts tomorrow which will put me straight. I have been eating too much and my stomach and bowels have got out of order.

To day I tramped all over the City to find McMillen, the man who owes me the fifty dollars, but I could not get up with him. I found *his wife*, but failed to see him. I visited the extensive rice mills down near the wharf. Everything is on the grand scale for cleaning the rice. There is too much noise, and dust & steam & bustle to enjoy a visit to such places. The foundrys here are turning out iron in abundance ready for the Yankees. I wish I could hear from [Fort] Pickens.[18] I do hope our boys are standing their place well down there.

I received your third letter this morning. You must not be uneasy about my taking care of myself. I am comfortably fixed, with a good cot, plenty of bed clothes, a good tight tent & plank floor, and will after a while get me a stove. I need Mose almost every day, to do many little things for me. I get along very well however.

To day I looked round for a saddle &c, and find that it will cost me nearly fifty dollars to buy a saddle & briddle & blanket. What shall I do? Would it not be best to

18. This refers to troops at Pensacola, Florida, that had been bombarded by Union warships on November 22-23.

buy a saddle at home? John Rockwell has a large deep saddle which I think will do. It is a fine one & priced I think $25.00 but perhaps he will take less. Tell Graham or go yourself and examine the saddles in town, & get it if you can a *deep seated black saddle with a horn on it*, but if there are none such buy the one at John Rockwell's [store]. Tell John I will write to him soon. I have been too busy to write during the day time & too sleepy to write at night.

Darling, I want you here so bad, until I do not know how to advise you about coming at once. My last letter will show you that the city may be attacked at any time, but I am satisfied that you can get out of danger. Much will depend on the fight at Fort Pickens. If the Yankees take Pensacola, they will be greatly emboldened. But, [if] money is the article you want, send Mose down to Jim T. Thornton with a letter begging him to get you a hundred dollars. Tell him I am here out of money & must have some. He lives near Mansfield's Mill where Mose is at work. Get the money due from Frank Pierce and George Bull &c. Raise $150 & come early in December if you can. I expect I can get a short furlough commencing the 8th of December & ending the 15th. Had you better wait until then and let me come & fix up my business & sister Collier's & all come down together?

> Good bye—Good bye.
> Your Husband

> Phillips' Reg.
> Savannah, Ga.
> Nov. 24, 1861

My dear Allie

A second Sunday has passed since we were together, and to look back at it seems years instead of weeks. The time passed rapidly with reference to everything else except as to the time when I shall see your dear self again. The nights are terribly long from Sundown to bedtime because you are not here to make the hours pass away. The truth is we must get together again and stay together. Life is short at the best and why should our best years be spent away from each other when absence makes us mutually unhappy? Men who do not want their wives here have not the love for them which I bear for you, or else they love the money which must be spent in supporting their wives here, more than the society of their families. Of course I allude to those who have the means, and whose wives desire to come.

I write you so many letters that I forget what I have written and therefore if I write anything twice you must overlook it. I expect my friends grumble at my negligence in not writing to them but really I have no convenient time to write except at night and am not yet fixed so as to write conveniently even then.

We had preaching twice to day. This evening Rev. H. Caldwell formerly of Cuthbert preached an excellent sermon, to a very attentive congregation of our soldiers. We have erected a Gun Smith shop and are putting our guns in order. Genl. Lawton tells us to get ready for an hours call. Tomorrow we shall make a requisition for ammunition for the Regiment & also for knapsacks &c &c for the men yet unprovided. I think we shall be stationed here some time, perhaps the whole winter, for the necessity to guard this point is very urgent. Any day may commence the fight here. This morning part of the fleet fired off Tybee Island just below here. Doubtless taking ranges &c. There are supposed to be spies lurking in the city giving information to the enemy and a strong vigilance committee has been organized by the mayor to ferret them out. Last night a horse was stolen from a Cavalry company here by some one and ridden rapidly toward the sea coast. It is supposed that one of these fellows have escaped to the enemy. There are considerable cases of measles among the troops. We have a few cases in our Regiment but I hope our hospital arrangements are sufficient to soon cure them up. No case in the Bartow Guards yet. We need another company badly. If Dick Cherry will get up a company in 8 or ten days of sixty men & come down without uniform, we will receive him & give him time

88

to uniform his men & recruit afterwards. I think we can also provide him sixty muskets with bayonets, but I will write more fully on this tomorrow.

[The balance of this letter is lost.]

Headquarters Phillips' Reg.
Savannah, Ga. Nov. 26, 1861

My dear darling,

It is very late at night and I ought to have been in bed long since, but I must write you one letter every day at least. If the mail could reach you twice per day you should hear from me that often. I hear no news of interest to day. The enemy have withdrawn from Tybee island & now occupy another little island below. The blockading fleet is (of course) still on hand. Commodore Tatnall went down this morning to give them a few shots from his little fleet without damage. Savannah is dull, very different from the Savannah in times of peace. Our Regiment still getting on well. The Bartow Guards were furnished Blankets & Bed-sacks to day. Only one case of sickness among them I believe; that is Jimmy Goode[19] who has the measles just started. The measles is in our camp in very mild form, generally running its course in a week. I think there is but little danger in taking it.

I shall look for a letter from you tomorrow morning. Write as often as possible and let me know all the news about town.

Does anybody ever enquire about me?

I hope soon to get time to write in the day so that I can be more interesting to you.

I do want to see you so bad, can't you get a pair of wings and fly to me? You are so nearly an angel that you ought to be entitled to a pair of wings. If all the women in the world were like you this world would be a happy world, for the men would be better.

Good bye my darling—we will soon meet—goodbye.

Your husband

19. Henderson, *Roster*, vol. 3, p. 614. James Thomas Goode.

Allie, give the enclosed letters to Mr. Graham & ask him to see to them at once. They explain themselves.

Headquarters Phillips' Reg
Sav., Ga. Nov 29/[18]61

Dear Allie

Lieut. Orr will hand you this letter. I expect I shall get a furlough to come home in a week from now. I want to get to Columbus Saturday morning & come down on the stage Sunday. I have to come by Columbus to pay for my uniform. Look over my notes in the package and you will find one for about $500 on F. M. Pressly. Enclose it securely in a letter to me at *Columbus* Ga. "Care of *Wm. A. Rawson.*

"Thus—C. A. Evans
"care of Wm. A. Rawson
"Columbus,
"Ga."

I shall have to deposit this note with Rawson to accept for me. The note is on F. M. Pressly, endorsed on the back by *"Gideon Massey."* If you know of any one going to Columbus *Friday* or *Saturday*, tell them to look for me at the Hotels & at T. H. Daniel & Co. Don't write anything particular in the letter, because if I cannot go, I will have to write to Rawson to break open the letter & take out the note. Remember this.

Write to me at once what the prospect is to get Worrill & Lyle to attend to that business. The fifty dollars is waiting for me, and I will get it as soon as their letters come.

Send the letter enclosing the Pressly note by the *Wednesday's* mail from Lumpkin to Columbus. This will cause me to get it in time.

I do hope everything will work for me to get home to you. Good bye my dear.

Your Husband

Have the *Carter* pistols sent to me by Orr & everything else you get ready. Put all in a box & mark my name on it. He will bring it safe and we will not be troubled with it, in coming down, & perhaps I may not come. I think it best for you not to tell that I am coming home. It may prevent you from collecting.

Head Quarters, Phillips' Reg.
Savannah, Nov. 29th [1861]

My dear darling

I sent you a letter to day by Lieutenant Orr, which perhaps you will not receive before Tuesday. I mentioned in that letter that I expected to be in Columbus Saturday morning and wanted you to send me a note of F. M. Pressley endorsed by Gideon Massey for about $500, which you will find in the package. Make out an exact copy of the note to keep, before you send it, & enclose it in a letter directed to me at Columbus Ga. to the Care of Wm. A. Rawson.

Rawson will accept for me for $150, and do not write anything special in the letter because if I do not get a chance to go home, I will have to write to him to break open the letter.

I am very lonesome and homesick tonight. I do want to see you more than anything else on the earth. What shall we do, if the situation of affairs here shall render the place totally unsafe for you? The prospect is very threatening. No person can enter or leave Savannah now without a permit. From the observatory over the exchange the enemy's great fleet is plainly visible with a glass. All soldiers here are required to be kept in constant readiness, & any morning may begin [lines obliterated] Regiment will have nothing to do except resist and advance by land, and the victory over the enemy may be achieved without our firing a gun. On account of our being without bayonets & having guns of short range, we will not have the privileges and posts of honor & danger accorded to Regiments better armed.

Now my dear you are a soldier's wife, and I write all these plain things to get you accustomed to the contemplation of danger. I know you are brave as a lion, but your love for me makes you unhappy. When you come down, let me see a cheerful face, not assumed, but real. I do not expect you to be as happy as you would be if

91

our situation was different, for that would be requiring you not to love me, but I want you to make the best of circumstances, and render yourself as happy as possible, because that will add to my happiness. I am far from being happy here. I envy the position of the humblest private here, who has no dear wife and little ones at home to think of, and who has nothing to do, but serve his eight hours of duty out of twenty four, and then sleep, eat & drink at his leisure. But I intend when this war ends to live for you. You shall have the sole direction of my life so long as you control it for your own happiness—

Don't I write to you too often? Every day after dark comes on, the first duty is to write to you. Until the letter is written I feel like some duty remains undischarged. I am afraid my letters are very dull for it seems like I write nothing at all. In fact there is no news here except what you get through the *Columbus Sun*. Some things it is not prudent to write for fear that by possibility they should become known to the enemy.

This war has assumed a fearful magnitude. I am not disheartened as to the speedy results, but the most gigantic effort will be made by the enemy this winter to crush us at every point. Memphis—New Orleans—Mobile—Apalachicola—Savannah—Charleston—and so on all round to the island border again will be centers of attack. Recent partial success [by the Federal navy] has encouraged Lincoln, & the greatest confidence is felt in the result of their naval expeditions. But we will fight even unto death & let every soul find its exit from a battle field. If they will have war—war—war, we must answer their continued appeal to arms without fear—If you were happy, how defiantly could I tell them to come on.

I am still well. I believe all the Bartow Guards are well. Dr. Baldwin (our Chaplain)[20] has come. I saw a brother of Ed Davis to day. He is an Assistant Surgeon in Wilson's Regiment [Twenty-fifth Georgia Infantry].

20. *Ibid.*, p. 576. Benjamin J. Baldwin.

We have got our cartridges—powder & lead & have distributed several rounds to each man. I wonder how many Yankees will be killed by them?

What is the news at home? I am very sorry for you my darling. I know you live hard, and that you are unhappy. You sometimes feel like all your friends have left you, don't you? Be cheerful my love.

Do not stint yourself on anything you want. I am willing to work like a Negro to make you happy.

Write to me at once and tell me how everything is at home. How are you getting on winding up, selling off & hiring out? You will get to be quite business woman before this war ends.

Do take good care of that dear self. I want you to come fresh & blooming to me.

Kiss my little innocents. Good bye

Give my love to all.

Your Husband

Head quarter Phillips' Reg.
Sunday December 1st 1861
Sav[annah], Ga.

My dear darling

Another letter from you written last Thursday, and one also from Father reached me to day. I am sorry you distress yourself so much about the prospect of an early battle at this place. If you were here, your anxiety would not be so great about me, because you would know the truth, and not be frightened by exaggerated rumors. I try to tell you the truth in my letters, which you cannot get from any newspaper or telegraphic dispatch.

Looking at probabilities we readily conclude that the enemy will attack Savannah, but not immediately. The force of the enemy borne by the fleet is by very correct information nearly twenty thousand strong. The city will be attacked by different approaches, but to make the attack successful Fort Pulaski must be reduced—that is taken by them or evacuated by us. To do all these things the enemy are not yet strong enough. It is therefore

93

probable for the present they will content themselves with taking & occupying certain islands along the coast, and also establishing & fortifying themselves at Port Royal & Tybee and in the meantime await reinforcements which will be sent forward from the New England States. Their best fighting plan is to compose the fleet of New England Yankees, and let the North western men do their land fighting. Still, Savannah, or rather Fort Pulaski may be attacked any day, but we will have no opportunity to participate in that fight—

In Savannah we have many secret enemys. There is a class of Yankee population (chiefly merchants, fattening off the war), whom we believe will run up the Yankee flag and take Federal protection as soon as the city is taken. Many of them have made themselves rich out of us, and although making great outward pretense of devotion to our cause are yet at heart the meanest of tories. I talked to day with a member of the Vigilance Committee of the City, who gave me these facts and said that their eyes were on this class. That all their patriotic pretenses did not save them from a close watching. We have many a *wolf in sheep's clothing* all over the South—

We had an inspection of the Regiment to day, by order of Col. Wilson commanding the post. I was very proud of the Bartow Guards. Capt. Redding was absent, & Lieut. Harrison[21] was in command. The excellent appearance of the company, their prompt execution of the commands, and the military bearing of Lieut. Harrison, attracted Col. [Claudius C.] Wilson's attention & he paid them the highest compliment. I think that without partiality it is the best company old Stewart [County] has sent—I do hope Lieut. Orr will be able to get twenty or thirty recruits.

Dr. Baldwin preached for us this evening a most excellent sermon. He will be popular in the Regiment, as Chaplain, because he knows his duty and will attend to it. The Chief of the Medical Department for this district says we have the best surgeon (Dr. Forbes) of

21. *Ibid.*, p. 609. William Henry "Tip" Harrison.

any regiment here. We commence tomorrow to erect a large Hospital for our own Regiment, near by here where our sick will be well provided for—We have Dr. Forbes, Dr. Kimbrough, Dr. Jones, Dr. Busch, and the volunteered services of Dr. Park, with several excellent nurses, for our sick boys.[22] At present we have no sickness except a mild type of Measles. The weather is glorious & as our tents are new & all floored with plank, and our doctors all active, we soon cure them up. Besides this we put no duty on any man who reports himself sick until he gets sound. Therefore we have had not a single relapse. We enforce *cleanliness* rigidly & give the well men exercise enough to keep them healthy.

I expect no regiment has less immorality practised in it than ours. As I told you before our commissioned officers are all moral men and many of them Christians. We have *four* preachers besides the Chaplain, and many of the Lieutenants and privates were prominent church members at home.

The three field officers are Masons, and also several Captains & Lieutenants. From as near as I can judge I think there are nearly a hundred Masons in the Regiment.

We have one company whose four commissioned officers (Captain & 3 Lieuts.) weigh *800 lbs*, and they have 80 whose average weight is *156 lbs*.

We look for the men we sent off several days since, after our tenth company to be here in two or three days. We then shall be full as to companies, but one of our companies is yet small.

After all, our situation is as pleasant as can well be made, and we have every prospect of doing fighting enough to *distinguish* or *extinguish* ourselves. If the balance of the war men about Lumpkin will just come along and help us a little, by joining the Bartow Guards everything will move off smoothly. But the boys here do talk some terrible hard things of the boys left behind. I want the Bartow Guards to sum up to a hundred men

22. *Ibid.*, pp. 576, 615. Only Forbes and Jones are listed here.

by Christmas. I take a great deal of interest in their drilling & in their general comfort. And I must not forget to tell you about our other company from Stewart & Chattahoochee, for they are also one of my companies—"The County-line Guards" [under] Capt. Lowe.[23] Gus Redding is 1st Lieutenant.[24] It is a splendid company & splendidly officered. All the best set of fellows in the world. Little *Tom Hines* ran away from Uncle Jeff & came here a few days ago & joined Capt. Lowe.

Well I have spun this letter out a long ways, and almost about nothing. I feel ashamed about not writing to several fellows in Lumpkin, but I have so much to see to & bother about, that I really do not find time to write but one letter a day.

Do you get all my letters?

Give my love to all.

Your Husband

Head quarter Phillips' Reg.
Sav[annah], Ga. Dec. 3, 1861
(Tuesday)

My dear darling,

Shall I write you an old fashioned love letter? How well could I play the lover to you if you were here tonight in my great roomy tent! I am getting almost unfit for service on account of my anxiety to see home & you once more. This would be home if you were here and no place can be home without you.—

I am almost afraid to say that I am coming soon, so fearful am I that I shall be disappointed. My greatest hope is founded on the probable necessity of my going to Columbus soon, to look after our rifles. If I get to Columbus Friday morning I shall come home by stage Saturday, but if I reach Columbus Saturday morning I will have to come home Sunday, or wait for a chance. Have everything ready to come back with me, for my stay will be very limited.

23. *Ibid.*, p. 628. John H. Lowe. On the promotion of Colonel Evans to brigadier general, Lowe succeeded him as colonel of the Thirty-first Georgia.
24. *Ibid.* Augustus B. Redding.

I had such unpleasant dreams about home and the children last night, that I have been gloomy all day. I want you all here. I am willing to serve my country in her day of trouble to the sacrifice of all my property, all my time, and all my life, but you and the children must be with me.

Why did you send me your money? Didn't you know that I would have been better pleased for you to have kept it, or did you think I wrote about my own scarcity as a hint to you to send me some? Now darling, don't you do that any more. I shall have plenty if I get the Millen papers in time.

Dr. Park will get you a good boarding house at a reasonable price. He thinks you all can get board at the Gibbon Hotel, with two good rooms for sixty dollars a month. It is the best hotel in the place, and several wealthy ladies from the Islands are boarding there so that you will have excellent society.

It is also near the heart of the city, so that you will not have far to walk for pleasure or shopping. I will make arrangements before I leave.

I received a letter from Hurly to day about the sale of a land lot at a sacrifice & all the furniture on a credit. We cannot afford to do that. I think I can make a much better arrangement with Graham & E. T. Beall. Graham can sell the furniture for cash or on credit to good men. We have but little to sell, it is true, but we need not throw it away. Many things you can pack away rather than sell for nothing. I wrote to Hurly to day telling him, that if he desires to buy my house on a credit he must give me a credit price for it.

He wrote me that Jim Wimberly had sued the Vernor note. I am not surprised that my absence should be taken advantage of by some men. Tell Clem that she must not put herself in the power of another Yankee scamp. The conduct of Chamberlin shows the contemptible cowardly meanness of such scamps.

I am glad that Graham has bought the Selig Saddle—I have never seen it, but I have no doubt it will suit me. I received a letter from Mat to day. She tells me that

97

you are looking well—bless your heart I want you to look your prettiest when I come home. I expect to eat you up.

I have done all the Battalion drilling since I have been here. I could soon get the Regiment in good training, if I did not go home. Don't be afraid about my health. I believe I am the soundest man in the Regiment. I take good care of myself, and the constant exercise keeps me well & strong.

I am glad that Sister [Annie Collier] has a chance to rent her Baker [County] property. How does it happen that neither her, nor Mother nor Clem, ever send any word to me? Well I suppose as I am out of sight & liable to get killed out of their way, they do not care anything about me. Never mind when this war is over I shall take you clean off out of hearing.

I was very glad to get the messages from Mr. Richardson & Mrs. Holloman. I believe they do care something for me. I used to think I was tolerably popular at home, especially among the good women, but since I came off to the war, it looks like all have forgotten me. Well darling, if you stand by me, I shall have abundant happiness.

Good bye now. The rain & wind is testing my tent thoroughly. So far it proves good. You need not write any more after getting this letter. I shall expect a letter for me at Columbus when I reach there.

Good bye—Good bye until we meet.

Your Husband

Head quarters Phillips' Reg.
Savannah, Ga. Dec 3/[18]61

My dear darling,

Tomorrow will decide whether I am to come home or not. From present indications I think I will get a furlough, because just at this time there is less apprehension of an attack on Savannah than existed a few days ago. Not that the project is abandoned by the enemy, but postponed. How I will jump for joy when the General approves my leave of absence.

I received no letter from you today. Surely I will get one from you tomorrow.

I am tired to night from drilling the Regiment in the *double quick*. The boys perform most admirably for so short practice. I am delighted with them.

The measles is spreading among us very much and the present damp cold weather is very unfavorable but our system is rigid and our doctors attentive & skilled. I have no fear so far of losing any. I think there is not yet a single case of measles among either of our companies here. Captains Redding & Lowe are both excellent disciplinarians, and keep their tents clean & their men well provided. A great deal depends upon the Captain about the health of his men. In our regiment those captains who properly attend to their men have but little sickness while others who are inattentive have much sickness.

If I fail to get leave to come home I shall be half crazy, for I have thought about and dreamed over it until *going home* has become part of my life. You must remember that I will have not over three days to stay at home when I come, and you must have everything ready if possible. Can Sis come up to see me? If not we must pay her a flying visit. If any of the "home folks" want to send anything to the soldiers they must have it ready, but I expect Lieut. Orr will bring all that is to send.

I am in first rate health, but not fat yet. I am afraid that my ambition to be a fat man will never be gratified. You will have to do all the *fattening* that is done in the family. You must get Mose cured up & fixed to come. I need him very much.

And the little precious darlings must be fixed up to *shine* down here. Pike Hill has a son about eleven years old. I expect him & Miss Ida will take on together. Bless her heart I expect she will take on powerfully down here.

I must leave room to say whether I am coming before I put this letter in the office tomorrow. [In the margin of the letter.]

I am coming—Be in Columbus Friday if nothing
happens.

Your Husband

Allie to Clement:

Lumpkin [Georgia] Dec. 5, 1861
(Thursday)

My dear Darling.

Last night I got Worrill's letter to Millen, which
Graham says will enable you to get your money without
Lyle's letter but I doubt it. I have done everything I can
to hurry it up. I am so afraid you won't get it and will
miss coming home on that account. Three more days
before Sunday. I know you won't get this letter. I shall
be so disappointed. Yesterday I got no letter from you.
I very seldom ever get one by the Cuthbert mail. I have
made no further progress toward selling and hiring out.
Worthington says he don't want Charles and Nance next
year. I tried to hire Beck to Grimes till Christmas [These
are slaves] to pick out cotton, but he wouldn't have her
on account of her baby. He is well of the Whooping
cough. Has your cough got well I am afraid not.

Carter has sold his dueling pistols, but says he has
another splendid pair of horsemans pistols that you can
have if they will do you. I will send them by Orr. I sent
your note to Frank Pierce. He sent me word that he
would be here to see me yesterday, but of course failed
to come. Twenty dollars is all the money I have got yet.
I make slow progress toward getting a hundred and
fifty. I won't give up though I will keep trying.

I went yesterday and bought your shirts, got a very
pretty piece of cassimere from Selig. Went to work on
them right away. Rose don't get any work at all to do.
Dan gets a little but not enough to keep him constantly.
Times get worse and worse instead of better. When I get
money I can't find anything to eat to buy with it.

Palmer is gone to Virginia as assistant Surgeon in the
hospital for three years. Tom Kidd came home a few

days ago. He got an honorable discharge, on account of his health.

You must not feel bad about my living hard. I do very well, as well as half the people around me. John Rockwell told me yesterday morning that he didn't have a bit of meat, lard nor butter in his house, said he had some spare ribs for breakfast but a neighbor sent these in. I was no worse off than he was. If I could see you, that is all I want. I don't want anything to eat, never think of it. Old Gripes [unidentifiable] says the reason she don't write is she can't get no five cents. Matt and Father have both written. Darling I do hope you will come home. I do want to see you so bad. I hope today that I will get a letter that you are coming then I will be so happy.

Take good care of your precious self for me. Good bye darling. The children want to see Pa so bad. Good bye my love.

Your wife
Allie Evans

Here the letters stop for almost six months because Clement and Allie were together in Savannah. Only one letter is dated in this interim. Very little was happening during most of this period in the Eastern theater of operations. Both armies were in camp except for occasional skirmishes. The status quo was also preserved on the Georgia coast.

Skidaway Island
Mar. 8, 1862

My dear Allie

I believe this is Ida's birth day and I would like to be home to give her a little party, but she must wait until the first of May and I will give her a May party and she shall be queen of May.

We had a little excitement this morning. About half past eleven o'clock a small boat with between 15 & 20 Yankees left the shipping in the sound and was rowed towards the landing where Wright's legion is camped, near the *lookout* on the bay tree which I showed you. From the lookout the pickets saw them approaching and permitted them to come within 800 yards. The boat commenced to turn back & the pickets commenced to fire with their Enfield Rifles and scattered their balls all about the boat. As soon as the first shot was fired the Yankees all lay flat in the boat except one fellow who had a glass looking toward the shore. Deliberate aim was taken at him, and at the crack of the rifle he fell forward on his face, quite likely he was killed.

It is a false report about the *Ida* being captured, Capt. Crowder[25] saw her today. And was told that she had succeeded in getting to Ft. Pulaski & back.

Old Man Jimmy Hilliard & Williamson Perkins have just arrived from Stewart. They report that there is considerable uneasiness about our position on Skidaway island. You must set them all right about it—They are going to stay about a week—Capt. Redding lost one of his men to day from brain fever. His name was Slocum[26] from Webster County—One also died at Benly belonging to Capt. Lowe's company.

The map I promised you is not ready yet, but I will send it soon.

I am in first rate health and taking good care of myself. I hope you are on "good behavior." There is still a possibility that Skidaway island will be abandoned, but I cannot yet say whether it will become necessary or prudent. But you are not restless about my being here—

Write soon—Give my love to everybody. Maj. Mose sends his polite compliments to Miss Elizabeth.[27]

Dont let Charlie forget his fencing exercises.

> goodbye (my love)
> Your Husband

Fort Pulaski was surrendered to Federal besiegers on April 11, 1862, after Evans had departed for another arena. Savannah remained in Confederate control until December 1864, when it was taken by Maj. Gen. William T. Sherman's forces, not from the sea but at the end of their march from Atlanta to the sea.

25. *Ibid.*, p. 600. John T. Crowder.
26. *Ibid.*, p. 619. Stephen W. Slocumb.
27. "Major Mose" is Clement's joking reference to his previously mentioned slave. "Miss Elizabeth" is evidently a girlfriend of Mose.

Chapter 6
"BAPTISM OF FIRE"

Evans had enlisted in September 1861 for twelve months. However, in April 1862 the Confederate Congress enacted a conscription law which, among its features, extended enlistments to three years. This was the first law of its kind in American history. Thereafter, the brigade of General Lawton was reorganized. Six regiments were formally assigned and reorganized for a three-year tour of duty, being given the numerical designations they retained for the duration of hostilities.[1] The Bartow Guard became the Thirty-first Georgia Regiment, and Evans was elected colonel to command it. His commission ranked him from May 13, 1862. The next letter was from Clement while at Camp "Beulah,"[2] near Savannah, written on May 31:

> My dearest little wife
> Your precious letter came to me just now and told me you had been sick. How I wish I could have been with you. Before this reaches you, my other letters will have told you not to expect me home soon. My health keeps too good for me to get home, since none but the sick can go. Don't look for me at all—I will take advantage of the first opportunity to come to you. I do feel so sorry for the poor men here who want to go home that my heart bleeds for them, but I can't help them. One poor fellow has just left here. He received tonight a letter from his

1. George W. Nichols, *A Soldier's Story of His Regiment (61st Ga.)* (Jessup, Georgia: Privately Printed, 1898), pp. 18-19.
2. Clement gave it the Biblical spelling. "Beaulieu . . . is located twelve miles south of Savannah. . . . General Robert E. Lee . . . in planning the defense around Savannah . . . visited Beaulieu and established a battery on Beaulieu Point as a defense against the approach to the mainland from Greene Island Sound" (Robert Walker Groves, "Beaulieu Plantation," *Georgia Historical Quarterly* 37 [September 1953]: pp. 200-09).

wife. One of his children had died, his other was expected to die, and his wife was about to be confined, and yet I cannot grant his furlough. I am going to send him to [General] Lawton, but I know it is useless. Nearly every day some such application comes to me. I thought of my own little babies at home while I read the poor fellow's letter, and under such circumstances I would almost if not quite resign and go to you.

I am getting along very well with the Regiment. We have quite a different state of things here now. I don't think I am too strict, but the discipline is so much stricter than it was before that it goes harder with the trifling ones who have been shirking from duty.

No certainty of any fight here. Everything stands just as when you were here.

I will soon have a fine Regimental band of Music. What about my flag? Has John Rockwell that fine red Merino on hand yet? It will make a splendid flag. I sold my boots for ten dollars. I expect Warren charged me 15 for them. They were too large & coarse. All my underclothes are lost. I believe I have three pair socks and one & a half pair of drawers. But don't trouble yourself.

Why don't you write to me what you get to eat? Can you buy any chickens, turkeys, mutton, beef & eggs? Do you have [letter torn] good flour, meal, ham, lard, butter, milk and vegetables? Have you enjoyed Mrs. Gregory's butter? Don't deny yourself nothing that your heart covets. Send me a list of everything you would like to have and I will get them and send to you.

I do believe I have the strangest kin folks in the world.

Are you living by yourself, and do you see nobody at all that ever was related to me in any way?

Write to me again [as] soon as you get this. Tell me all the news. Archer Harrison[3] though very sick is better. He can get a discharge if he wants it, but I wish he could stay as one of my Regimental Drummers!

I had a thorough inspection today of everything. I

3. Henderson, *Roster*, vol. 3, p. 610. Archer Burwell Harrison. See appendix for relatives.

have the nicest camp about Savannah. Everything perfectly clean and neat. I wish you were here to see it.

I am still eating *cake* every day. Your present is on hand yet.

Tell Mr. Simpson that Charley[4] is one of my *aides* and does splendidly. He will buy his uniform next Tuesday.—Is Waddy Palmer coming down? Lucius Richardson[5] is my skirmish Bugler. He has learned the call and I will commence the practice next Monday.

Good bye now "be of good cheer." "Let not your heart be troubled." All things are ordered aright, and the day is not far ahead when the strife will be over and the poor soldier will be closed in the arms of his wife and little ones at home. Good bye my dear.

Your husband

In May Maj. Gen. George B. McClellan's Federal troops moved up the Peninsula between the York and James rivers, in an advance on Richmond. The Confederate capital was in imminent danger. In the last few days of May 1862, Governor Joe Brown of Georgia was requested to send Lawton's brigade to Virginia to strengthen the army there. Rations for several days were cooked and equipment was packed; then tents were struck and the troops mounted open train cars, and lay exposed to cold rains. Undue exposure on the trip to Virginia caused much suffering among the soldiers from Georgia. Several luckless fellows succumbed without ever striking a blow for their native state.[6]

Lawton's brigade, including Evans and his Thirty-first Georgians arrived in Richmond, Virginia, on or about the 4th or 5th of June 1862, just a few days after the Battle of Seven Pines (May 31, June 1, 1862), where Gen. Joseph E. Johnston was severely wounded. This caused the vacancy that was to be filled by the appointment of Gen. Robert E. Lee as commander of the forces which would gain fame as the Army of Northern Virginia.

On June 11 Maj. Gen. Thomas "Stonewall" Jackson, who was still in the Shenandoah Valley concluding his famous campaign,[7] had re-

---

4. *Ibid.* Charles N. Simpson, Jr.
5. *Ibid.* Lucius J. Richardson.
6. Nichols, *Soldier's Story*, pp. 18-19.
7. Freeman, *Lieutenants*, vol. 3, p. 274; *The War of the Rebellion: A Compila-*

quested reinforcements if available. General Lee, when writing Jackson a letter of praise for Jackson's "skill and boldness," added that he [Lee] was dispatching General Lawton with six regiments from Georgia as reinforcements. The brigade went by train to Staunton, beyond the Blue Ridge, and to their astonishment, the troop train went straight through the mountains by a tunnel.[8] At Staunton the reinforcements disembarked and began their firts long march on Virginia soil. A halt was called on June 16, near Port Republic, where the troops of Jackson had made history in a battle the week before.[9]

Port Republic had been the climax of Jackson's Valley Campaign. He had rendered ineffective the numerically superior Federal forces and had so aroused the fears that Washington might be attacked that Federal troops were recalled from the Valley to defend that city. After a rest at Port Republic, Jackson was ordered to join Lee, who was being pressed by McClellan at Richmond. Jackson's strategic "retreat" to meet Lee was begun on June 17. It was one of his typical driving marches, and the troops went so fast that wagon trains could not keep up with them. Many of the raw soldiers of Lawton's brigade were hampered by excessive baggage, and heavy rains discomforted them. Pvt. George W. Nichols relates a detail of this "shake down" march of Lawton's brigade: "Ive Summerin, of Company D, wrapped in his blankets, was lying down with the water ponding around him. He raised up a little and said, 'Boys, it rains very well tonight.' It created a big laugh."[10]

Jackson so cleverly screened his activities that he had his troops within 16 miles of Richmond before the enemy knew of their presence. The troops, including Lawton's brigade, had made a grueling march of more than 120 miles in eight days. They encamped at Ashland north of Richmond, on June 25, being preceded by Jackson, who on June 23 had ridden out to the Dabbs House, on the Nine-Mile Road, six miles east of Richmond to consult with Lee. At this conference it was planned that Jackson

tion of the Official Records of the Union and Confederate Armies, 70 vols. in 128 parts (Washington, D.C.: Government Printing Office, 1880-1901), series 1, vol. 11, part 3, pp. 585, 589. Cited hereafter as O.R.

8. Nichols, Soldier's Story, pp. 38-39.

9. Col. William Allan, "Stonewall Jackson's Valley Campaign" in The Annals of the War (Philadelphia: The Times Publishing Company, 1878), pp. 724-49.

10. Nichols, Soldier's Story, pp. 39-40.

would open the attack at Beaverdam Creek on June 26 as th
signal for a general offensive. Although Jackson started his me
on the morning of June 26, they had had such trying march
that they fell exhausted. So did Jackson. Douglas Southall Fre
man, in *Lee's Lieutenants*, wrote, "physical exhaustion and th
resulting benumbent of mind that depended on much sleep" wa
the cause of Jackson's failure to attack.[11]

Therefore, it was not until the second day of the Seven Day
Battle around Richmond that Evans and his fellow Georgian
got, as General Lawton called it, their "baptism of fire."[12]

Shortly after midday on June 2, the Confederates passed to th
east of Gaines' Mill and began to attack. Jackson was sent aroun
to the enemy's right in a flanking maneuver at Old Cold Harbor
and Lawton's brigade came up in the rear of Jackson's veterans
One participant described the action of Evans and his command
in the battle:

> After marching at double-quick time about four miles,
> we went into the fight about 4 o'clock in the evening.
> We went into the action under a very heavy fire from
> the enemy, which they kept up until after dark, during
> which time we charged them and took a battery. . . .
>
> Just before the charge [ordered by] the field officers
> of the 38th regiment, Lieut. Col. J. D. Mathews, fell
> wounded and L. J. Parr had his arm shot off. Col. Clem-
> ent A. Evans, of the 31st Georgia, came over to order
> the charge and went to our Color Bearer Sergeant, James
> W. Wright, and asked him for the battle flag. Wright
> refused to give him the flag; told Col. Evans that he
> would carry the flag as long as he was able, and all he
> wanted Col. Evans to do was to tell him where to carry
> it and it should go to the cannon's mouth. The Colonel
> ordered him to carry it to the enemy's battery, which he
> did. The command to charge was given, the "Rebel yell"

11. Freeman, *Lieutenants*, vol. 1, pp. 655-69.
12. Letter to General Evans from General Lawton in Evans' papers dated November 9, 1871, from Savannah: "I have no papers whatever touching the history
of the Brigade. Such as I had were consumed by fire with my Law Office,
Library, etc. nearly three years since. . . . Official Reports, no doubt accessible
to you, give an outline of our services in the 'Seven Days' around Richmond,
where we received our first 'Baptism of Fire'—."

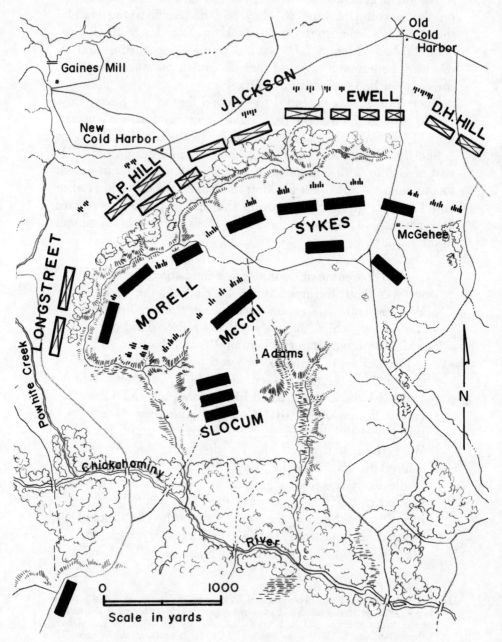

Gaines Mill

Old
Cold
Harbor

JACKSON

EWELL

D.H. HILL

New
Cold Harbor

A.P. HILL

SYKES

McGehee

LONGSTREET

MORELL

McCall

Adams

Powhite Creek

SLOCUM

N

Chickahominy

River

0   1000

Scale in yards

Battle of Gaines' Mill—(First Cold Harbor)—June 28, 1862

108

was raised, the battery was taken and the enemy routed. Three men were captured on the guns. Col. Evans complimented Wright for his bravery and daring; told him that he wanted to carry him home and show him to his wife.[13]

Lawton's men were complimented by Jackson for their part in the action.[14] This charge was the first major action in which Evans participated, and was also the engagement in which he received his first wound. He wrote: "I was wounded (shot in the leg) at Cold Harbor [Gaines' Mill], June 27, 1862, while leading my regiment in Jackson's famous flank attack which turned the Federal right. There I lost in killed and wounded 200 men in the space of one hour. Lawton's Brigade did fine service in that charge." The series of battles which raged at Cold Harbor, had begun on June 26 at Beaverdam Creek, and finally ceased at Malvern Hill on July 2, during which time a semi-circle of death had been drawn around Richmond. Many bloody engagements marked the progress of the Seven Days: Beaverdam Creek, Gaines' Mill, Savage's Station, Frayser's Farm (Glendale), White Oak Swamp, and Malvern Hill.

13. George H. Lester, *This They Remember* (Washington, Georgia: Washington Publishing Co., 1985), p. 103. This book is a collection of memoirs of various contributors.
14. Nichols, *Soldier's Story*, pp. 39-45.

LT. GEN. THOMAS JONATHAN "STONEWALL" JACKSON

110

Chapter 7
SICK LEAVE AND INVASION

After the Seven Days' Battles around Richmond, Stonewall Jackson, with Lawton's brigade and other units, was sent to Gordonsville, Virginia. They were to oppose the operation of a consolidated army of the Union forces which had previously been disjointed by Jackson's campaigns in the Valley during May and June. This new Federal army, designated the Army of Virginia, was placed under the command of a veteran of the West, Maj. Gen. John Pope.

In the latter part of July 1862, Lawton's brigade of Georgians was assigned to the division of Maj. Gen. Richard S. Ewell, one of three divisions that by early August reported to Jackson. This change occurred about the time Evans went home to Lumpkin, Georgia, on sick leave. He had been struck by a chill soon after reaching Gordonsville and had fallen seriously ill with typhoid fever.

Shortly after Evans left the army at Gordonsville, Jackson's men, including Ewell's division, helped to win the Second Battle of Manassas. At Brawner's Farm (Grovetown) on the day before that battle, General Ewell had been badly wounded. He had gone forward to direct a charge by the Twenty-first Georgia, and "Ole Bald Head himself was found on the field . . . unconscious from loss of blood, one knee badly shattered by a minié [ball]." Surgeons assessed the damage and amputated his leg, and Ewell was incapacitated for some time. General Lawton, who had held the rank of brigadier general for sixteen months, was put in temporary command of the division.[1]

After being defeated at Manassas and Chantilly (Ox Hill), General Pope retreated until he entered Washington, leaving Virginia

1. Shelby Foote, *The Civil War, A Narrative*, 3 vols. (New York: Random House, 1958), vol. 1, p. 627.

practically free of invaders. Lee, realizing that the Southern army was in the best of condition and flushed with victory, decided to invade the North. The Battle of Antietam (Sharpsburg), September 17, 1862, culminated this first invasion. It was the single bloodiest day up to that time of the war, with many of Lawton's brigade falling in the carnage. While leading a division, General Lawton himself received a serious wound and was never again a field commander. Temporary brigade commander Col. Marcellus Douglass, recent candidate for Congress from Evans' home district, was killed, and Col. E. N. Atkinson of the Twenty-Sixth Georgia then took command of the brigade. The night of the 18th, under cover of darkness, Lee quietly withdrew his army back across the Potomac into Virginia. Lawton's brigade guarded the rear.

Subsequent to the Battle of Antietam, the two corps system which had been introduced to the Army of Northern Virginia in July, one under Stonewall Jackson and the other under Lt. Gen. James Longstreet of Georgia, was formally constituted.

There are no Evans letters from August up to the first week of September 1862, because Colonel Evans was on leave. He was on his way back to Virginia when the letters started again.

Clement to Allie:

> Macon, [Georgia] Tuesday Evening
> Sept. 10th, 1862
>
> My dear darling
> This morning I sent a letter to Columbus by Bryan Watts and I hope you received it Thursday night, for I do not feel right about not getting you one on Wednesday.
> Bryan is just from Savannah on a short furlough. He says there is a great deal of sickness among the troops and that a good many are dying. Ben Watts[2] he says is in Richmond wounded. I met Dr. Parks also just from Sav. and going back to night. He tells me the same thing about the sickness of the soldiers. He is employed by the Government to collect botanic medicines & is located

2. See Appendix A for relatives.

112

at this place. He tells me that the Negroes at Sav. are employed in part in obstructing [the] Savannah river & strengthening the old fortifications. Bryan Watts says that surveys are made to extend the line of works all around the city from the river above [to] the river below and also to construct a railway around the city and mount siege guns movable by steam engines. This you know is an idea I advocated to you eight months ago.

I have heard nothing from our Regiment except that Lawton's Brigade was in the fight[3] and that was hardly news for I was certain of that before. I have seen no accounts for the 2nd or 31st Ga. Reg. The report of the killed and wounded come in very slowly. When I get to Richmond I will telegraph back anything that will be of general interest, and if I can get any list of killed & wounded from Stewart [County] I will send it on. I have seen no one at all who was in those late fights. I am afraid I will have a tedious time in getting to the Regiment even after reaching Gordonsville. I do not know whether any train runs farther than that place and if it does not we will have several days marching to do to get to them. I think however that we will find wagons or something else to ride in. Don't think from this that I am going to break myself down. I am anxious enough to reach the army, but I want to be of some service when I get there. I will keep my promises to you about taking care of myself. I hope many years of pleasure in each others society are still ahead, and I look forward to those good days believing they are going to be our happiest. We have many sorrows[4] but our life has not been all sorrow. We have both enjoyed each other as a blessing. No married pair have lived more uninterruptedly happy with each other than ourselves. I recognize plainly written as the letters of a book the hand of Providence controlling many events of my life, and I am satisfied that my marriage with you was one of them.

Let us therefore, my dear darling, take this blessing of Heaven with gratitude and trusting in God lead with

3. Second Battle of Manassas on August 29 and 30, 1862.
4. This refers to the three little boys who died. See Appendix A.

113

each other an humble Christian life, looking forward hopefully and cheerfully to the coming day when we shall be transported to a home of eternal happiness.

You must give my kindest regards to all my good lady friends at home. Tell them that I will be faithful to my promises about their boys as far as I am able. They shall share with me all the comfort that I can command and when sick or wounded I will see that they have attention. Give my respects also to Bro. Davies.[5] Tell him I I am sorry I could not be with him more while I was at home, but I hope he will stay with us another year, when perhaps the war may be over and I will be at home.

My kinfolks have my love of course. I will write to them when I get the opportunity; send Uncle Loverd word about Ben Watts being wounded.

Good bye now, my love. I must put this in the [post] office in time. I envy the piece of paper which can go to you while I cannot. Be cheerful as possible. Don't grieve about my absence. The next four months will roll away soon and we will be together again. Kiss my little lady for her Pa. She is the sweetest thing in the world except her Ma. Pa wants her to learn to read and write good this term.

Good bye—Good bye my dear darling. I do wish I could stay with you always. I would almost be willing to be a helpless invalid to be with you all the time. Good bye a thousand times.

Your Husband

Clement Evans rejoined his regiment in the Shenandoah Valley of Virginia on either September 19 or 20, 1862. On the 20th, because of the absence of Colonel Atkinson, Evans became senior colonel in command of the brigade of the wounded Lawton, a post Evans held for three months until Atkinson returned shortly before the Battle of Fredericksburg in mid-December.

In Allie's doleful letter of October 26—her third letter of 1862

5. Terrill and Dixon, *Stewart County*, p. 150. "Brother Davies" was Daniel C. Davies, Methodist minister in Lumpkin.

—she longs for delivery of an anticipated baby so she can go to Virginia.

Lumpkin Oct. 26, 1862

My dear darling husband,

This is a cold, windy, cloudy, Sunday morning. I wish my dear darling was here to spend the day with me. How pleasantly it would pass. As it is how long the day will be. I know it is so cold there where you are. I wonder if you are comfortable. I know you are not. How can you be, with no house to stay in, no good warm bed to sleep in and no wife to talk with you? I have got so much to tell you, so much to talk to you about. I don't think I would get through in six months. My tongue would never grow tired. I don't love to talk to anybody else but you. I am afraid I love you too good darling. You ask me in your letters if my heart aches at the thought of our long separation. Don't you know it does. I would give anything on earth to shorten our separation. I would make any sacrifice to be with you. I am afraid our parting will be longer than we calculated on. It is now the last of October and I am not sick yet. It may be the middle of November yet before I am sick. If it is my baby won't be old enough to start to see you the first of January as we expected. It would be running too much risk to go when it was only six weeks old both to me and the baby. I hope it won't be that long before I get sick. I am so tired of waiting for it. I try not to have the blues and to be as cheerful as possible. But if my darling was only here all would be right. What will I do for you darling. How can I get along without you. I know you cannot be here so what is the use of wishing it.

Mark Holloman's wife died yesterday. She was confined about a week ago. She took the mumps and imprudence killed her. I am sorry for poor old Freeman Walker.[6] I shall be very careful and take good care of

6. *Ibid.*, pp. 97, 134, 316. Amanda Walker married Mark Holloman on October 18, 1860, and died within two years. Mark was elected to the House of the General Assembly for the 1859-60 session, when Evans was the senator. Amanda's father, Freeman Walker, was an Evans family neighbor in the old Nineteenth District of Stewart County.

myself. You need not be uneasy about my acting impru-
dently. I love life too good to do anything to kill myself.

Tip Harrison got home night before last about midnight. He stole in and went to bed without waking anybody up. They didn't know that he was there until next
morning. I haven't seen him. He has a thirty days furlough. Joe Clifton[7] started home with him but somebody
stole his furlough and transportation. He went back to
try to get another.

Archer gave Tip Lucious Richardson's[8] pants the old
lady sent by him. She is mighty distressed about it. She
says she knows he will get what you carried him. Mrs.
Harrison hated it as bad as Mrs. Richardson she says
she had rather anybody else had taken them than Tip
because Arch carried them.

I see in last night's papers that they have had a little
fight down here on the coast near Charleston. Everybody is dreadfully frightened about the Yankees coming this winter but as for my part I had as soon they
would be here as in Virginia. You have got them to fight
wherever they are and of course I would rather you fight
them near home. The Virginians have suffered long
enough. Let some of these extortioners and speculators
have it awhile. I don't care how soon the Yankees come
if you come when they do. They can't hurt me any worse
than they have already. They have separated me from
you and what worse could happen to me?

Ida has been to Sunday school, just got back. She
sends a great deal of love to Pa. Says she wants him to
come home and that she hopes to have a nice present for
him when she sees him. She wore a new hat to church
or at least an old one made new. She said old Mrs. Everett admired it very much. She is so proud of that letter
she sent you she don't know what to do with herself. She
carried it to the post office and told Seymore to be sure
to send it for she had written one and put it there.

I have got the letter you sent by Forsyth Sapp.[9] The

7. Henderson, *Roster*, vol. 2, p. 12. Joseph H. Clifton.
8. *Ibid.*, p. 610. Lucius T. Richardson.
9. *Ibid.*, p. 634. Forsyth H. Sapp.

money was all right. You must not stint yourself to send me money. I had a plenty before you sent this. I shall save this last fifty to pay a debt with Christmas. I wish I knew you were faring as well as I am. I have a plenty good to eat and every other comfort that is necessary. All I want and haven't got is you to be at home.

Brother Davies is gone to Green Hill today. There is no preaching at our church. Everybody has gone to the Presbyterian church. They will all have a right cold time of it. Brother Davies leaves in a few weeks for conference. I hope he will be sent back to preach for us next year.

Father has been staying at Mr. Hill's ever since you went off. He hasn't been to town but once. I haven't seen Sis Jane either. P. I. comes up occasionally.[10] I think their wine speculation proved a failure. They are troubled about salt. Mr. Hill was to have started down on the coast yesterday to buy salt but he didn't go. Bacon will be scarce and high next year. The farmers can't get salt to salt meat for their own use and of course there will be none to sell.

Sister Richardson says I must write to you to detail one or two men and send them back here for clothing for the soldiers. If you could do it I do not think it would be a bad idea. It makes me heart sick to read of the suffering of our soldiers. If you need anything let me know. I can find a chance to send you bundles right often. Have you got bed clothes enough. What have you done about pants. I know if you have not bought any you are needing them. I wish I could get some flannel for you. I am afraid what you have got is not thick enough. Ida is sitting here by me singing so I cannot hear a thing for her. She sings more than she ever did. She is a good little girl at least we think so.

I wish you were here darling to spend this lonesome evening with me. Good bye. Good bye.

Your Wife

10. See Appendix A for relatives.

Allie's anticipated "sickness" arrived sooner than she predicted in this letter to her husband. The very next day a baby boy was born to her. Months would pass before he would receive the name of his father's departed friend, Lawton.[11]

Clement to Allie:

Camp of Brigade
Sunday November 9 [1862]

My dear darling

If you had been here this morning you would have been furnished with a good illustration of Soldier-life. About ten o'clock last night we received orders to move this morning at sunrise toward Middletown. We were up at dawn, the wagons all sent on and the Brigade drawn in line across the field where the cold winds blew through us, and there we received orders to go back into camp again and cook two days rations—Now we are under orders to move in quite a different direction and perhaps will not move at all—We have become so much accustomed to this that it is received as a matter of course and goes in, as a part of our Services for "three years or during the war." Soldiers generally are cheerful fellows. They crack many a joke on each other, and on passing citizens, as they march along, and play many a wicked prank on the good farmers while we lay in camp. We generally send a small guard to each farm house near the camp to prevent depredations. On one occasion a small party of Louisiana soldiers [of Hay's brigade], about a dozen, went to a house about sundown and reported themselves as being sent there as a guard. The owner of the house was glad to see them sent them out a good supper and went back in the house feeling quite secure. Poor fellow, as soon as darkness came on, his bee gums, and sundry fat turkeys, went the way of all the earth along with his curlytailed pet pig, and the self appointed

11. Lawton Bryan Evans was named for Clement's friend, Capt. Edward Lawton, mortally wounded at the Battle of Fredericksburg. Captain Lawton was the brother of Gen. A. R. Lawton. See Appendix A on relatives. See Clement's letter of January 3, 1863 and his official report hereafter.

guard. At another time Three of the 6th Louisiana Reg. reported themselves about dark to a farmer to guard his house and after being there about an hour, sent in to ask him to lend them his watch during the night, so that they might know when to relieve each other. He sent it out and in a short while he found that his guard had departed, and so had his watch. Sometimes I hear or witness some very amusing things done by them. This same Regt. about two weeks ago, was marched near by my Hdquarters, and Lieut. Jackson's overcoat, which he had laid down a moment to saddle his horse, was quietly picked up, from near his feet and carried off. As soon as he discovered his loss he galloped forward & finding the fellow with the coat carried him to his Col. By this means he got his coat, but every time he has to pass this Regt. they will ask him for mischief how "he likes his coat."

The troops usually cheer Genl. Jackson whenever he passes by them, and he invariably takes off his hat and holds it in his hand as long as they cheer him. A few days ago a woodenleg Negro came riding along, while they were all standing still in the road, and the boys commenced to cheer him—The old fellow pulled off his hat and trying to look like Jackson as much as possible trotted his horse the whole length of the line. You might have heard the whoop they gave him for a mile.

Notwithstanding the many hardships they have to endure and privations they have to suffer, yet they are remarkably cheerful and spirited. And although it may be reasonably expected that when so large a body of soldiers were camping in a country, the inhabitants would be badly treated yet, with exceptional instances, they are respectful and polite, observing like gentlemen the rights of the farmers. They go to the farm houses by hundreds to buy provisions, but the price is politely asked and paid, and every respect paid to the man and his family. The Yankee soldiers on the contrary are cross and insulting in their language toward the citizens both male and female and show by their conduct either a want of, or a neglect of the principles which should

119

guide the conduct of gentlemen—Well I have actually written you a letter about the soldiers. Poor fellows if they had [word obliterated] and blankets how good I would feel. I hope Lieut. Cox & Harrison will bring on some clothes for their company. I must send my boy [the new baby] his commission as Aid-de-camp soon, and order him to report here forthwith for duty. He must have a fine horse, saddle, & bridle, with a new uniform right away. Give my love to my daughter. Tell her to write to me soon. Good bye.

Your Husband

Chapter 8

FREDERICKSBURG AND A PROMISE TO GOD

For some unexplained reason there are no letters after Allie's letter of October 26 until December 26, 1863. However, Clement was busy with the war. General McClellan had crossed the Potomac River to keep a watch on General Lee. However, the government in Washington replaced McClellan with Maj. Gen. Ambrose E. Burnside. Burnside's intentions to advance directly on Richmond through Fredericksburg were divined by General Lee in the latter part of November. In order to meet this advance, Lee sent Longstreet to Fredericksburg where his corps arrived on November 21. Shortly thereafter, Lee called Jackson and his corps from the Valley to come on to Fredericksburg. Lee then drew together his forces behind the town of Fredericksburg and fortified the heights.

The Confederate lines on the south side of the Rappahannock River faced toward Washington, the troops stretched from northwest to southeast along a ridge overlooking Fredericksburg. Gen. R. H. Anderson held the Southern left nearest the river. Longstreet held the Confederate center. Stonewall Jackson and his corps of some thirty thousand at Hamilton's Crossing, defended the right where Ewell's division (now led by Maj. Gen. Jubal A. Early), including Lawton's brigade and Evans' regiment, was placed in reserve the right of the Confederate infantry. They were buttressed by "the gallant" Maj. John Pelham's horse artillery under the command of Maj. Gen. "Jeb" Stuart on the extreme right.[1]

Before the battle began, the Federal commander gave a stern warning to the townspeople that he would give them sixteen

---

1. Robert Underwood Johnson and Clarence Clough Buel, eds., *Battles and Leaders of the Civil War*, 4 vols. (New York: The Century Co., 1884), vol. 3, pp. 70-147. The Fredericksburg battle accounts herein are from these pages.

hours to leave, after which the town would be bombarded by artillery.

On the 11th and 12th of December, a portion of Burnside's army crossed the Rappahannock, and on the 13th began the ground force attack. The fight started by a charge against the Confederate right flank where Evans was with Stonewall Jackson's command. Federal Maj. Gen. William Franklin launched the assault with his force of thirty thousand men.

The attack was beaten off after great loss of life in the lines of the exposed troops of the Union. Lawton's brigade (led by Colonel Atkinson) swept in a countercharge but was savaged by strategically disposed batteries on the road to the Federal rear. The rest of the Federal efforts were then directed to the center of the Confederates, and for the remainder of the battle, Lawton's brigade was not actively engaged.

After Franklin's attack was beaten off, General Burnside, mistaking the Confederate center as its most vulnerable spot, hurled attack after attack at what was, in fact, the most invulnerable point of the Confederate defense at Marye's Heights. A sunken road, revetted by a stone fence, was the juncture of death.

The Federals made at least six charges which were driven back before night came, leaving the battlefield heaped with dead and wounded bodies. General Longstreet wrote that "the Federals had fallen like the steady dripping of rain from the eaves of a house. . . . The dead were piled sometimes three deep, and when morning broke, the spectacle that we saw upon the battlefield was one of the most depressing I ever witnessed."

Burnside was repulsed all along the line with heavy losses and did not renew the attack on the 14th. On the night of the 15th of December he retreated across the Rappahannock and hostilities for 1862 were completed.

General Lawton, still suffering from wounds, was not in command of the brigade during the battle and his brigade had been under its senior colonel, E. N. Atkinson of the Twenty-sixth Georgia. Division commander Early's official report said:

To Brigadier-General Hays and Colonels Walker, [E.N.] Atkinson, and Hoke credit is due for having promptly obeyed my orders and managed their respective commands with coolness, courage and intelligence, and the same need of praise is due Colonel [C.A.] Evans who succeeded to the command of Lawton's brigade after Colonel Atkinson was wounded.[2]

The Battle of Fredericksburg marked a milestone in Evans' life. It was here at Fredericksburg that the call to the ministry was so vividly impressed upon him. He revealed this after the war, in a letter to his old Methodist pastor at Lumpkin, Reverend Mr. Daniel C. Davies:

> Enough of wealth, of money making and money spending has been mine to satisfy me how empty are the joys they give; enough of popular favor, and popular distinction; of struggle for place, and position; enough of the inner chamber of the Temple of Fame has been revealed to me, to show me how bitter are its sweets, and how restless, how unhappy are its votaries. In looking back to the past I feel like a pupil who has been led by the hand and shown, the world and the kingdoms thereof, to learn the vanity, the wickedness and the wretchedness which abound, and to love and cherish the unnoticed virtues, the unsought truth, and the simple piety of the few who keep themselves unspotted from the world. After the hard battle at Fredericksburg, and while still on the battlefield my mind was engaged in reflection upon the misery which the armies were inflicting upon each other, and in general upon the disposition of man to be cruel to his fellow man, when again the ever recurring subject intruded itself, in the form of the enquiry "Will you not devote your life in teaching your fellow creatures lessons of humility, brotherly love, and Christian forbearance." And then I said to the good prompting Spirit, "if God will show me that it is His will, for me to do this as soon as my duty to my country is done, then I will gladly engage in the work."[3]

After the Fredericksburg battle, both forces went into winter

2. O.R., series 1, vol. 21, p. 667.
3. Clement wrote this letter to Mr. Davies on June 7, 1865. The balance of that letter is contained in the Epilogue.

GEN. ROBERT E. LEE

124

quarters. The majority of Lee's army stayed in around Fredericksburg, but Lawton's brigade was posted at Port Royal. General Jubal A. Early now commanded the division, which remained in Jackson's Second Corps. The weather was excessively cold at Port Royal. A great deal of snow fell and was used by the soldiers for great snow battles, there being no threats from the Yankees.

Two letters close the year of 1862. Moses Evans (Mose), slave and childhood playmate of Colonel Evans, had someone write for him a dutiful letter to Mrs. Evans. The other letter was from Allie to Clement.

Moses' letter was prefaced by a picture of an officer standing by his horse and a Confederate flag flying in front of a tent. This picture was drawn in pencil on a sheet of lined writing paper and the letter was penned below:

> Head quarters
> Camp near Port Royal,
> Va. Dec. 26th, 1862

To my Dear Mistress

I have taken great pleasure my good mistress to have these few lines riten to you hoping that they may find you enjoying the blessing of good health as it have me and the Colonel. Remember me to my little boy and the rest of my children and remember me to my old Mistress and may God Bless you through this troublesome war is my Prayers. I hope this war will soon be ended that the Colonel and me may be spared to see our dear old home once more. Give my respects to Brother George Bull and all the Brothers and Sisters of the Baptist Church. I remain your ever faithful servant.

> Moses Evans

The following letter from Allie acknowledges the "secret" of Clement's resolve to be a minister.

> Lumpkin Dec. 29, 1862

My dear darling

This is the last day of the old year. How earnestly do

125

I hope that the coming year may bring peace and happiness to us all. How many poor souls that were alive and full of hope one year ago to day have now gone to their long rest. Thank God darling that while so many have been taken that you have been spared. I received your letter with the secret in it. I have thought a good deal about it darling and made it a subject of prayer ever since I got your letter. If darling you feel that you are called to preach and that it is your duty then by all means decide right away that just as soon as your duty to your country is done that you will join the ministry and it will be the happiest day of your wife's life when she heard the gospel out of the pulpit from your lips. Have you never heard me express the wish that you were a preacher. The first thing I did darling after reading your letter was to go to myself and get on my knees and thank God if you were to be a minister of the gospel and beg him to direct you and help you to decide to do your duty. I have often thought and felt that you ought to be a preacher and darling if our heavy applications have been sent to this end then ought we not and won't we receive them as blessings. I had rather see you in the pulpit my dear husband than in the presidential chair. I am honest darling in what I say. I could say much more to you on the subject but I will see you soon I hope and then we will talk it all over fully and freely.

I am still working to get ready to leave by the tenth. You must come to see me just as soon as you can. Newman and Nelson hired for the same that they did last year. A Mr. Fitzgerald hired them. He will be a good master to them. He says he knows you and told me to give his love to you. Fillis is hired to Mrs. Odam at five dollars a month to be paid monthly. It is a good home. The other Negroes are not hired yet. I got a letter from Sister yesterday. She has the rheumatism bad again. They rented a house to live in. Probe's leg gives him a good deal of pain yet. She says and he is trying to get out of the service. [He had been wounded.] Ida sends her love and says she is coming to see you the tenth of January. Matt has just sent for me to come and spend

126

the day with her. It won't be long before we will meet darling and won't it be a happy meeting. I love you now better than I ever did.

Your Wife

H'D-QUAR'S, ARMY NOR'N VA.,
OCTOBER 2, 1862.

GENERAL ORDERS,
NO. 116.

In reviewing the achievements of the Army during the present campaign, the Commanding General cannot withhold the expression of his admiration of the indomitable courage it has displayed in battle, and its cheerful endurance of privation and hardship, on the march.

Since your great victories around Richmond, you have defeated the enemy at Cedar Mountain, expelled him from the Rappahannock, and after a conflict of three days, utterly repulsed him on the plains of Manassas, and forced him to take shelter within the fortifications around his capital.

Without halting for repose, you crossed the Potomac, stormed the heights of Harper's Ferry, made prisoners of more than eleven thousand men, and captured upwards of seventy pieces of artillery, all their small arms, and other munitions of war.

While one corps of the Army was thus engaged, the other insured its success by arresting at Boonsboro', the combined armies of the enemy, advancing under their favorite General, to the relief of their beleaguered comrades.

On the field of Sharpsburg, with less than one-third his numbers, you resisted from daylight until dark, the whole army of the enemy, and repulsed every attack along his entire front of more than four miles in extent.

The whole of the following day you stood prepared to resume the conflict on the same ground, and retired next morning without molestation, across the Potomac.

Two attempts subsequently made by the enemy to follow you across the river, have resulted in his complete discomfiture, and being driven back with loss.

Achievements such as these, demanded much valor and patriotism. History records few examples of greater fortitude and endurance than this army has exhibited, and I am commissioned by the President, to thank you in the name of the Confederate States, for the undying fame you have won for their arms.

Much as you have done, much more remains to be accomplished. The enemy again threatens us with invasion, and to your tried valor and patriotism, the country looks with confidence for deliverance and safety. Your past exploits give assurance that this confidence is not misplaced.

R. E. LEE,
Gen'l Comd'g.

Chapter 9

"HAPPY NEW YEAR TO YOU, MY DARLING"

Winter quarters of 1863 at Port Royal on the Rappahannock River, some fifteen miles below Fredericksburg, proved to be an ideal location for Colonel Evans. It was near rail connections, and, moreover, Allie had kin in Person County, North Carolina, and in South Boston, Virginia, in Halifax County. This made it easy to justify her trip to Virginia. Nevertheless, she was brave to face the strenuous journey which commenced about January 10 from Lumpkin, with little Ida, the eight-week-old baby, and all their baggage. The first miles were by wagon to the Cuthbert railway station to catch the "cars."

Allie took the same route Lawton's brigade had traveled in June 1862, but as the war progressed, railroad service had grown worse. Tracks, crossties, locomotives, and wheels were wearing out, with little hope for repair or replacement. The average train speed was down to about ten miles per hour by 1863. Passenger cars had little (if any) drinking water and were crowded in every corner with sick, wounded, and well soldiers, along with a motley assortment of civilians.[1]

In his second letter of 1863, Evans wrote of General Early's reluctance to let him meet Allie. Early (who never married) in a letter to General Jackson protested "against the interruptions visiting wives, mothers and sisters created in the work of the army." Jackson refused to support Early and remarked to his staff: "I wish my wife could come to see me!"[2]

---

1. E. Merton Coulter, *The Confederate States of America,* 1861-1865, of the series *A History of the South,* Wendell H. Stephenson and E. Merton Coulter, eds., 7 vols. (Baton Rouge: Louisiana State University Press, 1950), vol. 7, p. 276.
2. Freeman, *Lieutenants,* vol. 1, p. 729.

LT. GEN. JUBAL ANDERSON EARLY

130

Camp near Port Royal, Va.
New Year's day, Wednesday, 1863

My dear Allie

A happy new year to you my darling! The old year went out last night in a dark cloud, cold comfortless, and with a drizzling rain—Fit enough that a year so bloody—so miserable should have been wept out of existence by the pitying skies. But the new year was ushered in by a bright sun, smiling skies & pleasant atmosphere—May it prove a happy omen of returning Peace on earth & good will *among* men." Two years of bitterness have passed away recording events that will be long—long remembered—not forgotten in centuries— Two years of strife between two powerful nations whose boundaries are continuous for over a thousand miles, have caused the expenditure of six billions of dollars, the destruction of a larger sum in property, and the death of five hundred thousand men—not estimating the untold sufferings of the millions whose hearts have been wrung with agony over the fate of the loved ones in the Armies—is not war a device of the Devil? Certainly no Spirit less than Satan's himself could make men so full of evil as to be willing to shed so much blood & produce so much suffering.

Although everything is quiet here, yet while I write the deadly work is going on in the west, or else tremendous preparations are making for it. The "one great Battle which is to end the war," so often foretold may now be going on. If we are successful the calculations may be well made upon a speedy peace, but if Vicksburg falls, & Tennessee slips our grasp—If our western army is beaten the Lincolnites with new hope will enter upon another year's campaign. In thinking about it I cannot but wish that our Corps of forty thousand men could be ordered there to help in the great struggle. Perhaps it would turn the scales, give us victory, and produce peace—But we can only await in patience the result, hoping that our western compatriots may rival the Veteran Soldiers of the Army of the East.

Some Northern papers are extremely bold in their

131

attacks upon the administration of Lincoln. Their new liberty of free speech given them by recent elections seems to be enjoyed by them amazingly—But they do not yet say "let the South go"—They all seem to entertain a hope that the Southern States will return to the embrace of the old Union; I think that New York thinks that if New England was kicked out of the Union, that we would unite with the remaining Northern States— But it will be better for all parties to have four Governments—One New England States & others nearly identical with each other in interest—another of Western states—another of Pacific States & the fourth the present Confederate States—These would all be powerful enough, & would be a check on each other.

I have almost written you a political letter. I know you had rather hear about myself than about Governments—What do you think then is my anxiety about you, since I have received no letter from you later than the one dated Dec. 14th. Eighteen days have passed. I cannot imagine the cause. If you had started here upon receiving news of the battle of Fredericksburg you would have been here before this. If anything has happened certainly someone would write! I know you have written and the blame belongs to the mails. I could not help looking for your coming during the last two weeks. You may be sure that no frowns would have met you. Your letters when they do come will probably tell me when I can begin to count the weeks and then the days. I shall be busy enough making arrangements for your reception. My daughter will have a great many things to tell me when she comes. All about home,—about her Grand Pa—Grand Ma—Uncle Jesse, Aunt Clem & Mat, & her cousins—and all about her *travels*—She will eclipse all the Virginia little girls I know—

And that Great boy—Pa wants to see how he looks— Never saw his Pappa in all his long life!—You must not let the little hands and feet get cold, Ma and you must not let him run about in cars—and when you get to Richmond he will run a way and join the soldiers if you do not watch him—you know Ma, he was *born a soldier*.

132

I want you to leave twenty or twenty-five dollars with Geo. Singer to have me a pair of No. 1 boots made—with legs to come up to the knees—but without the flap above the knee. The top of the boots to be shaped so as to be as high as the knee in front & cut so as not to interfere with the bend of the leg—The leg to be of the same material *throughout* as the foot—intended to be worn outside of the pants altogether—He will understand "regular military boot."

Give my love to all. I sent Father by Capt. Orr a pipe made from laurel root from [the] battle field of Fredericksburg—Good bye and [obliterated] my love.

                                        Your Husband

Clement to Allie:

                        Camp near Port Royal, Va.
                        Jan. 3rd, 1863

My dearest darling

I am truly glad to see by your letter of the 24 Dec. that your anxiety for me is satisfied by hearing that I am safe. I know you must have suffered during those long days from the time you heard of the battle until you heard of myself. You write desponding and cheerless, my darling—I hope you will banish gloominess from your thoughts, and look to the bright side of the present and future—We must cease to mourn for our little jewels who have been taken from us. God bless the dear little Angels—how happy they are! Let us be cheerful and enjoy as happily as possible the life before us. I promise you my darling that no thought for myself shall ever interfere with your future happiness. Everything shall contribute to your pleasure,—your enjoyment so long as we both live—I know you are in trouble about coming out here and bringing the "little one," for fear the exposure may not be well for him—I am not there to comfort you, in your loneliness and many things cause you to be sad, which you would not notice if I was there—But my dear, ought you not to be grateful that I am spared to you? How many poor wives are sorrowing now

133

for their husbands slain in battle! Think of Mrs. [Edward] Lawton whose husband was wounded taken by the Yankees, carried away, and she had no tidings of him, whether dead or alive, until the 31st of Dec.—and even then only knew that he was in hospital at Alexandria wounded—Mrs. Captain Miles is here at a farm house nursing her husband who is shot through the body—Let us not give over to the spirit of murmuring and discontent, but thank our Maker that we are spared for each other, and count not the taking of our little darlings from earth as unendurable grief, but as the preparation for our own entrance to a happier Home—you shall be happy, my own love,—Time will soften our natural grief—another home, other scenes will give to us a new spirit of existence—perhaps other duties, different from any we have ever performed yet, will contribute to our real happiness—At least, darling, all my selfishness is gone—Ambition and self love has all died within me—I desire to live for you—to make you the happiest woman on earth—Can I do it? Will you tell me all your wants—tell me how I can fill you with joy? Will you help me make yourself happy? Will you school yourself against discontent—will you search your own mind and find what kind of life you prefer to lead? Where you had rather live, what you had rather do—how you would love to be employed what pleasures, what enjoyments you desire? And let me know all, so I can prepare them all for you! It does not require money to make you happy—if it did I might be in despair—but all else (except the gifts that come alone from Above) I know is within my power.

Of course while the war exists my duty to my country keeps me where I am—but even pending the war you may find many sources to divert your mind—You are coming here to stay with me—During the winter I can be with you a great deal, and you will be near enough to get instant news of me at any time. You will be subjected to many inconveniences out here, and in a great measure will have to depend upon yourself, but with a plentiful supply of money, you have already learned how to get along. Still in future days our talks in old

134

Virginia will fill many a pleasant hour—I think I can contrive to make your visit to Virginia pleasant, and should you desire, after visiting your relatives, to return for a time again home, there will be nothing in the way—Make up your mind to be happy—Take the events of life as they come—Praise God for his mercies, accept his chastenings with an humble heart & prepare in this brief life for the great unending existence after death—Do not suffer yourself to be dispirited by others—go to your sister's in Baker [County], or anywhere else—Do not stay where your mind has been accustomed so much to be occupied with sadness. [the loss of three little boys] [This letter ended here]

Camp near Port Royal, Va.
Jan. 3rd, 1863

My dearest darling

Another letter written the 22nd Dec. from you has just come only partially relieving my anxiety for it appears that you had not still heard of my safety. I wrote to you on the 13th (day of the battle) the 14th & 15th and besides told Lieut. Carey Cox who was going to Richmond on the 14th to telegraph to Graham for me. I am sorry that he has failed to do this because my duties were so urgent all this time that I scarcely had time even to write, and besides being in order of battle all the time & expecting at any moment to be called upon to go into action, I had no opportunities to see to the sending of any despatch— hope you do not feel that I neglected to think of you all this time. My letter of the 14th ought to have reached you on the 22nd. Surely it did on the next day—So you are coming sure enough—Well my brave little wife is more welcome than I can express. It will be impossible for me to meet you at your relatives—From the way Genl. Early talks he will not trust the Brigade into other hands than mine until Genl. Lawton returns—I have become a sort of favorite with the old fellow who *rarely has a favorite*—I think I can get a home for you near by. I am going out tomorrow to look up a place, there are several houses not far off and I do not think I can fail to get you a comfortable place—I sent you four hundred dollars by Everett Harris who has probably reached home about this time. This will make you perfectly easy in the money line— I have over five hundred more on hand so you need not stint yourself in your preparation to come. I wish Bob was coming back with you. It would be so much more pleasant for you to travel with him—But Everett Harris will give you every necessary attention—

I will write again tomorrow more fully about your coming if I succeed in getting a house—

Goodbye darling.

Your Husband

Camp near Port Royal, Va.
Sunday, Jan. 4th, 1863

My dearest Wife

I can write you only a few more letters before you are to start to see me. This will get to you about the 14th, and I suppose by the 20th you will be on your way. I am almost like a crazy man in thinking of the day when I shall see you again. I dread for you the hardships and inconveniences of the trip—The crowded cars & omnibuses—the unaccomodating Hotels—the troublesome baggage—the long weary days and nights of the journey—the disappointments in making connections, and all the other train of inconveniences that attend the traveler in these days of general confusion. When you get to Richmond if you can get a carriage or omnibus to take you to the *Edgemont House* you will find it more retired & better than the "American Hotel" or Spottswood house. It is not so pretentious as to style but those latter hotels are crowded with visitors, officers and soldiers: Here you will find an agreeable Lady who will perhaps find you company to stroll around Richmond a day or two while you send me word that you are coming so I can meet you at Hanover [Junction]. I am pretty well satisfied that I can get you a place to stay where you will be comfortable & where I can stay with you every night—I shall get a carriage & take two horses

136

to drive you about over the country—All my dread is about your getting here—If someone was with you who felt enough interest to take time in bringing you on I would not be uneasy—But you must write every day for several days before you start and also *on the day*, and fix one or two envelopes *stamped* with paper inside so you can drop them in the mail at Augusta, Petersburg or anywhere along the route. When you reach Petersburg you will be in a few hours of Richmond & if delayed can write from there. I think it would be well for you to stop two or three days in Richmond if you get in a good house—If you get in the Edgemont House or a private house, you will find someone who will show you the city. Congress will be in session—You must by all means go once or twice there—Congress I suppose will sit in the Exchange Hotel—You will be very apt to find someone in Richmond whom you know—I hardly feel like writing to you. It almost seem like "ending the war" for *you* to be coming here—

Lieut. Snider who resigned some months since has been sent back as a *Conscript*—

The great victories east and west I hope will bring about peace—but it is only a hope—

> Goodbye my
> darling, Goodbye
> Your husband

It was about the first of the year that Evans received the sad communique that Capt. Edward P. Lawton, brother of General Lawton, had died of wounds received at Fredericksburg. Evans' official report of December 19 had said:

I cannot forbear to mention in terms of unqualified praise the heroism of Capt. E. P. Lawton, assistant adjutant general of the brigade, from the beginning of the advance until near the close of the fight, when he received a dangerous wound and was unavoidably left in the open plain where he fell. Cheering on the men, leading this regiment, or restoring the line of another, encouraging officers, he was everywhere along the whole line

137

the bravest among the brave. Just as the four regiments emerged from the neck of the woods referred to, his horse was shot under him, and in falling so far disabled him that thousands less ardent or determined would have felt justified in leaving the field, but, limping on, he rejoined the line again in their advance toward the battery, but soon received the wound with which he fell.[3]

It was a loss deeply felt by all the officers because of the popularity of this young man. Their esteem was attested to by a letter and resolution dated January 11, which the officers addressed to the editors of both the *Savannah Republican* and the *Savannah Morning News*.

The memory of Lawton's death lasted many years, for in a diary of 1903, Evans entered for Sunday, December 13: "Anniversary of the bloody battle of Fredericksburg 1862 in which I was engaged. My friend . . . E. P. Lawton adjt. Genl. of brigade was mortally wounded in my presence. I was commanding the brigade in a charge. In honor of this noble officer, I gave his name Lawton to my boy. . . ."[4]

Allie had great concern about travel hazards, yet reunion prospects were most fervently betrayed in the couple's letters of the 16th to the 22d of January.

Camp near Port Royal, Va.
Jan. 16, 1863

My dear Allie

I do not know whether you have reached South Boston, but I will send a letter there to you, in care of your relatives—I expected to get permission to go to Richmond on the 20th (Monday) but the rascally Yankees have again appeared opposite to us, and make some pretensions as if they desired again to cross. I wish they had postponed their demonstration until I could have got to see you. Whether they are really in earnest about crossing or are only making a feint will be determined in a few days, and then perhaps I can get a short leave of

3. *O.R.*, series 1, vol. 21, p. 671.
4. Lawton B. Evans. See Appendix A.

absence. For the present I think you had better stay with your relatives and write to me. It is delightful to feel that you are so near, and as soon as possible I will be to see you, or meet you in Richmond—I have a thousand—thousand things to say to you. It is too bad, is it not? But I know you will enjoy yourself better where you are than you could in Lumpkin.

I fear now that you received my last letters telling you to come to Richmond. I hope, however, that you have carried out your original intention of going first to Halifax [North Carolina]. I do not know what I shall do if I find out you are in Richmond among strangers.

My little daughter I know is in fine spirits and the little Emperor, how did he stand the trip? Good bye, it is late & I have ridden 16 miles to day and four to night —Good bye we will soon meet God bless & preserve you & my little ones.

Your Husband

A letter from Allie of January 8 is lost but Clement's next letter described its contents:

Camp near Port Royal, VA.
Jan. 17, 1863

A letter from you written on the 8th instant reached me to day. It stated that you would start Saturday and I do hope indeed that you are now safely in South Boston. The tone of your letter shows you to have been no little excited at the prospect of soon meeting me in Virginia. I have myself been so restless for some weeks that I have hardly been of any use to the Brigade. The little Emperor showed his blood [that is, courage] by not flinching when the doctor cut his little arm [for smallpox vaccination]. I do feel so proud of this early evidence of his nerve. He is Pa's own little lion-hearted boy and Ma must not claim him any more. Every night I see you and the children in my dreams. But the sweetest dream I have had in a long time, but which has kept me sad ever since, happened to me two nights ago. I dreamed I was at home and in the yard frolicking with Charlie. It was so natural, so much like my old enjoy-

139

ments with the dear little fellow. His form, features actions everything about him, was just as he appeared just a few short months ago. I am afraid I have not yet schooled myself to patient resignation. Bless his dear noble heart! How bright the home he now enjoys, and how he will fly to welcome his Pa and Ma, when they go to him!

I expect our daughter was the queen of the Lumpkin society. She is good and will not be vain I know when everybody praises her. She must write to her cousins and her Aunts at home, and to her grand Ma, too.

I have no further news to write to you concerning the threatened attack of the enemy except what I gathered from the two officers whom I sent out to day to reconnoitre. They state that the enemy do not appear to be in any unusual force across the river. It is possible that the whole may be a false alarm, but the whole army is made ready to receive them.

I hope still to have the opportunity to come to see you at South Boston or at least to meet you in Richmond. If I get a furlough I will telegraph to you provided there is an office where you are, and if not I will write, so that you can meet me in Richmond. However, should you come to Richmond at any time without my meeting you, do not stop at the "American Hotel." It is in bad repute. I think, however, you had better remain where you are for the present. I am anxious enough to see you but do not come until I write. I think I shall be able to procure board near here for you. If you think your relatives would not object I suggest that you propose to them, to permit you to board there occasionally during the year. I shall not be able all the time, you know, to provide for you a safe and comfortable home, and you will be within two or three days travel from me instead of eight to ten. Besides you will be so much more contented staying with them.

I am still earnestly debating the important question of my future life. I hesitate to decide for fear the decision may be wrong. Your noble letter on the subject has endeared you to me ten thousand fold more than ever. I have in addition to the question of simple duty, looked into the bright and the dark features of such a calling. I do not believe I could be influenced by any considerations of ease, enjoyment, or love of applause, for surely I can find all these in other pursuits. I think few men, as young as myself, have tasted more of public favor than I have, and I can say to you that few enjoy greater prospective advantages, then surely a love for fame or notoriety cannot be the cause of this question obtruding itself upon my attention. I have suffered myself to think with pleasure, upon the opportunities I shall thus have of being almost constantly with you, without being useless to everybody else, and I feel no compunction of conscience in dwelling upon our future happiness, because it does not in the least interfere with the duties of so great an office, but on the contrary your opportunities for doing good will equal mine.

I remember when a long time ago, being only about fifteen years of age I was on a visit to old Mother Gary & Lucy Gary when this subject was introduced, and I told them that I then had a presentiment that when I reached thirty years of age I would receive certain evidence of my duty in this regard and at that age I should become a minister. This is singular is it not, since just as the time approaches when I am to arrive at this age the impressions of my duty should be so strongly brought before my mind.

I know that you have often said to me that it would make you happy to see me in this position, but I did not know how strongly you felt about it until I read your letter.

Strange is it not, that on the battle field, the day after one hard fought battle, and hourly expecting another, my mind should be drawn irresistibly to this great subject?

I feel that the decision must soon be made, and I trust in an all wise Providence that I do make no mistake.

I hope soon to see you. Give my best regards to your relatives and friends and say to them I hope to have the pleasure soon of making their acquaintance.

I am sorry to hear that Probe is not getting well of

his wound. I would write to your sister but I do not know where to direct the letter. I suppose, however, to Newton. I shall write to your Mother to night—

Goodbye—The Angels be around you my precious one—

Good bye
Your Husband

Camp of Brigade, near Port Royal, Va.
January 20th, 1863

My dear Allie

I was no little disappointed to night when the postmaster came and brought me no letter from you. I hoped to hear that you were safe and snug in South Boston, anxious to hear from me and to come where I am. I know you must be there by this time, since your letter written on the 7th which I received some few days ago, told me that you would start on the 10th. You do not know how anxious I am to know how you and the little cherubs fared during your long tedious trip. When the wind was blowing hard here on the 14th to 17th I know that you were exposed to it, and the past three days although without wind has been bitter cold, but I hope you have been warmly housed during this time.

You have seen by the Richmond papers that some expectation of another advance still exists, but I really believe that the design of the enemy is to keep this army here and prevent any part of it from being sent to North Carolina. Still the Yankees may be crazy enough to try us again. We are all well prepared and in the finest possible spirit. If a good warm spell should come I believe the Army would be glad to have another fight.

I have procured a nice place for you to board about a mile from my camp. Several ladies are there and I am sure you will be entertained well. I tried again to day to get a furlough for six days, but Genl. Early would not listen to it. He seemed determined not to give me any chance to get away from the Brigade. His only encouragement was "to wait a few days." As I have made arrangements for you, you can come as soon as you please.

I suppose this will reach you on the 22nd inst, and you could be in Richmond on the 24th and come to Guiney's Station on the 25th or you can stop in Richmond a few days and write to me, so that I may know exactly when to meet you at Guiney's Station.

You will write to me from South Boston as soon as you get this telling me what day you will go to Richmond and how many days you expect to stay there. Richmond is very much crowded, and I am really afraid you will be put to a good deal of inconvenience. If you cannot get with a good private Hotel, would you be willing to stop at [the] McMurry's? I want you to visit all that is worth seeing in the city, including the capitol grounds, the Congress, The cemetery &c, but the state of society is so bad there that you must not go without protection—If possible I will meet you there about the 26th or 28th, but I hardly think I can get the opportunity. I feel almost like a new man in thinking about seeing you so soon. I shall not easily consent to your return to Georgia, if your relatives will be kind enough to afford me a "house of refuge" occasionally. Perhaps in a few months we shall be tramping all over Virginia again, and it will be hard for you to follow, but you can be near me a great deal. You must promise not to give way to anxiety and alarms on my account. Here you will be in the very midst of the terrible war, and you may often bid me good bye in the morning knowing that before night I shall have to participate in a fierce battle but instead of yielding yourself up to fear and grief you must rejoice that you are so near me, to nurse me should I be wounded. You have been with me a good deal since the war opened, but your future experience will differ from the former. I hope, however, that with it all, your life in Virginia will have many, many pleasant days.—If my two letters addressed to you at South Boston have not failed to reach you, you will know from them everything else.

Kiss my daughter and "the boys" for me—

Good bye.
Your Husband

143

Allie to Clement:

At Mr. Fourquesen's, Halifax Co.
Thursday night Jan. 22, 1863

My dear darling.

A letter from you [came] to night telling me to come on to you. It made me so happy to think I would so soon see you. I wish you could have come to have gone with me. I am almost afraid to go alone through Richmond. Nevertheless I shall try it. I have been begging cousin William to go with me. Perhaps he may. I shall do my best to get him to go. I shall write to Mr. Riddle to night asking him to meet me at the depot. I would go direct to Mr. McMurry's if I know where he lived. I might not meet up with anybody in some time that knows where he lived. You must be sure to meet me at Guiney's Station on the twenty ninth. If I am not there on that day I will be sure to be there on the thirtieth. Be sure to meet me darling. If you can't come try to send some of the boys for I won't know what to do when I get there if you are not there. If I was alone I wouldn't care a cent. But travelling with children is not so little trouble. Suppose he gets the small pox, papa, what will we do for he is the dearest little thing you ever saw. Vaccination won't take on him. As soon as we get there you will get some physician to vaccinate us all again. I don't think we have ever had any real good matter. I am afraid of the small pox only on account of the baby. I would start tomorrow morning if you knew I was coming. The reason why I put it off so long is for you to get my letter and know I am coming. I leave South Boston at eight o'clock in the morning and get to Richmond at four in the evening. I know you will meet me there if it is possible. Do your best darling to come. Mr. Riddle may not be there and not get my letter. I mentioned to Cousin William to night about boarding me off and on through the year. He was very willing to it. So this will be my headquarters for this year for I have no desire to go home till you can go with me.

All the trouble I have got on hand now is the small

144

pox and scarlet fever. One good look at you my darling will doubly repay me for all the trouble I have had in coming here. The children are both very well. Cousin Eliza is opposed to my coming there. She wants you to come here. She is anxious to see you. In less than one week I will see my darling. A blessed privilege is it not.

Goodbye. Goodbye. Your Wife

[P.S.] I don't want to stop in Richmond an hour if it could be prevented. I hear such dreadful tales from there I am afraid.

Allie did finally arrive and spent several months close by. This explains, of course, why there were no letters from January 22 to May 5, 1863. During most of this period, the Army of Northern Virginia remained in camp around Fredericksburg. The winter hiatus of fighting ended spectacularly with the Battle of Chancellorsville.

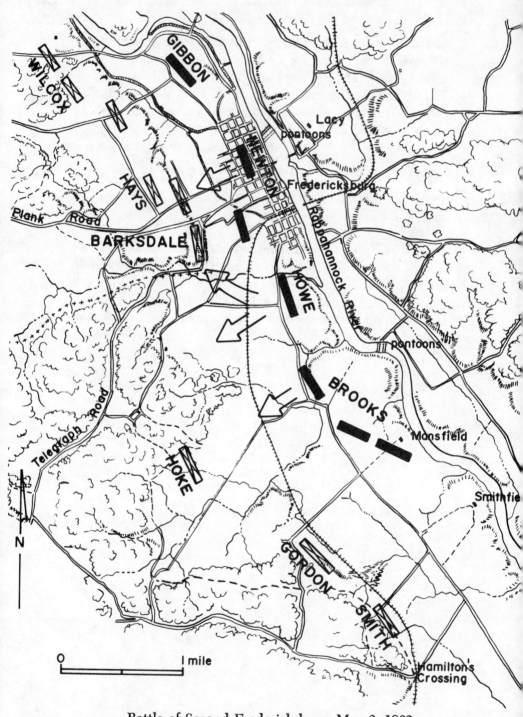

Battle of Second Fredericksburg, May 3, 1863

146

Part II

Chapter 10

"REST UNDER THE SHADE
OF THE TREES"

Since the Battle of Second Manassas, on August 28, 1862, Lawton's brigade had been without an officer of the proper rank to command a brigade. As previously noted, when General Ewell had been wounded in that battle, General Lawton was put in temporary command of the division. A month later Lawton was wounded at Antietam. It finally became certain that General Lawton would not return. Colonel Evans had proved to be an efficient officer, popular with his subordinates, and, in addition, he was a Georgian. Fifty-two officers signed the following letter asking that Evans be promoted and sent the request to Gen. Samuel Cooper, adjutant and inspector general of the Confederate army:

Camp of Lawton's Brigade
Near Port Royal, Va. Feb. 12, 1863

Genl. S. Cooper A & I Genl.
Richmond, Va.
    General,
    The undersigned officers of Lawton's Brigade, Early's Division would respectfully ask to be permitted to state to his Excellency the President that it is their desire if the same can be done consistently with the public interest, that Colonel C. A. Evans of the 31st Ga. Regiment may be made a Brigadier General. Col. Evans with one short interval has been in command of Lawton's Brigade since the 20th day of September last, and by his gallantry in action and his uniform good conduct in the manage-

ment of the brigade has in our opinion, demonstrated his fitness for the position to which we have suggested his promotion.

> We have the honor to be General,
> Very respectfully
> Your obt. Servants[1]

The petition to promote Evans was unsuccessful. In April 1863, John B. Gordon of Georgia was assigned to command Lawton's brigade. Gordon had distinguished himself at Antietam, where he had been forced from the field only after a fifth wound had rendered him unconscious. He was thirty-one—just a year older than Evans.[2] Colonel Evans resumed command of his Thirty-first Georgian. General Lawton was made quartermaster general of the Confederacy in the fall, much against his will, as confirmed in his appealing letter[3] from Richmond.

Col. C. A. Evans
31st Ga. Regiment
My dear Colonel:
You have doubtless heard that I reported here for duty about four weeks since—During all that time, I have been expecting orders daily; but have not yet been assigned to duty—Whether this results from embarrassment felt at the war office in assigning me again to the command of a Brigade, after the promotion over my head of so many of its favorites, or from a disposition to force me to accept a position for which they want me, and for which I have no relish (about which you may learn more soon), I am not yet able fully to decide—Certain it is, however, that General Lee's army is in motion, and that I have no command in it; though I have asked *unconditionally* for orders almost every day for four weeks—One pretext is that I have not sufficiently recovered from my wound (lameness) to enter upon an active campaign in the field.
The uniform kindness and consideration which you

1. Evans' Papers.
2. Gordon, *Reminiscences*, p. 90, 95.
3. Evans' Papers.

have always shown me, Colonel, induces me to call your attention (privately) to a petition recently sent by the officers of the Brigade to General Lee, to retain Genl. Gordon in the command—I feel very sure that this petition was signed under the confident belief that I would not be again reduced to the command of a Brigade, after the events of the last campaign; but I fear it has been misunderstood in certain quarters—If this petition was signed under the impression (as I have indicated), it would be grateful to my feelings to have the officers say so; now that my official connection with the Brigade is probably dissolved for the war—Should you deem it advisable, and the officers of the Brigade be inclined to say this much to me, I beg that nothing may be said which could possibly be objectionable to Genl. Gordon, who I am happy to learn, is a worthy gentleman and gallant officer—I do not wish to publish, or make present use of, such a paper; but it may be necessary to correct errors in the future.

God bless and preserve the good ole Brigade

Very sincerely,

your friend,

A. R. Lawton

The remainder of April 1863 was spent by Early's Confederates in drills and maneuvers about the camp at Port Royal in preparation for the spring campaign. Reorganization in the Army of the Potomac found Maj. Gen. "Fighting Joe" Hooker in command, after the Burnside debacle at Fredericksburg. Hooker sent Maj. Gen. George Stoneman with the cavalry toward Richmond and ordered Maj. Gen. John Sedgwick to demonstrate near Fredericksburg. Then, with the main portion of the army, Hooker crossed the Rappahannock and moved in the direction of Chancellorsville. On April 29 Evans' camp at Port Royal was thrown into a tumult because of a sharp skirmish on the Rappahannock River. By April 30, however, Lee decided that the main attack would not be made at Fredericksburg, but would instead be made to the west on the Rappahannock. Evans remained with General Early's division to guard against a Federal attack on Fredericksburg.

Lee ordered the rest of the army (except Longstreet's command near Suffolk) toward the area around Chancellorsville. There, late in the afternoon of May 2, Stonewall Jackson, with a well-conceived flank march, attacked Hooker's right flank and rear and drove the Yankees back in confusion. After dark, Jackson went forward to reconnoiter somewhat beyond the Confederate lines. As he returned, he was mortally wounded by his own pickets, a tragic mistake that was to affect the Confederate cause to the end.

On the morning of May 3, Jeb Stuart led Jackson's men to the attack, and by midday, the Confederates had decisively defeated Hooker at Chancellorsville. A great victory was won, but at the irreplaceable loss of General Jackson, who died from complications of his wound a few days later.

While the battle was transpiring at Chancellorsville on the 2d and 3d of May, Gordon's brigade was still posted below Fredericksburg between Deep Run and Hamilton's Crossing. The brigade was not in the main battle at Chancellorsville on the 2d, but worked to strengthen the fortifications below Fredericksburg. Early in the morning of Sunday, May 3, General Sedgwick moved the Union forces against the heights of Fredericksburg and, in a determined attack, captured the Confederate position on Marye's Heights where Brig. Gen. T. R. R. Cobb of Georgia had bled to death on December 13, 1862. Gordon's brigade, however, had not been called into action, even though it was just three miles away. After taking the high ground at Fredericksburg, Sedgwick left a a part of his army to hold them and pushed toward Chancellorsville to join Hooker.

In the early morning of May 4, Gordon's brigade, being nearest the Rappahannock River, advanced two miles through woods and bushes, drove in the Yankee skirmish line at Marye's Heights,[4] and retook it with very little loss. Having secured the position, the brigade remained inactive up to nightfall.

General Lee, having overawed Hooker at Chancellorsville, dispatched a large force under Maj. Gen. Lafayette McLaw, back toward General Sedgwick, near Fredericksburg. There, about 6 p.m. on the 4th, the Federals were caught between two Confederate forces. General Early launched his men in a fierce attack near Taylor's Hill and the Yankees were driven back. The next day, May 5, all of Sedgwick's forces were back across the Rappahan-

4. The significance of this taking of Marye's Heights is more fully developed in Evans' letter of May 30, 1863, and the footnote there.

nock and the Army of Northern Virginia had won a great victory, but had suffered an even greater blow: the loss of Stonewall Jackson.

Between these actions, and before Allie's departure for southern Virginia, Clement wrote several short letters. Of these, one was about the battle.

May 5th, 1863
9 o'clock a.m.

Dear Allie

On my very first opportunity I hasten to send you word to join me in thanks to the Great Preserver that I am still unhurt. I have had many miraculous escapes, but surely yesterday I was most signally shielded by a merciful Providence. My Regiment, deployed as skirmishers, advanced over two miles, captured about 30 prisoners, several wagons full of stores, about 30 or 40 horses & mules, & drove everything before them. This was from about sunrise yesterday morning. My brave boys covered themselves with glory. All yesterday we fought the enemy until near sunset [when] our line of battle was changed. My regiment was placed in the regular line and we made a charge of the line over hills, ravines, woods, & fields, under a storm of shell & Grape, completely routing the enemy. On our line, the victory was most glorious. I have not heard from the left. It is said that we have that part of the enemy still on this side, at our mercy. Firing of artillery is heard in the distance, proceeding from our side.

I am in good health, although almost worn out. This is the 6th day that we have been in the presence of the enemy under full range of his guns. My loss is not heavy. Capt. Shorter slightly wounded, Lieut. Haws seriously wounded, Lt. Acree killed. So far as I can learn, I have had only about 5 or six killed in all—This is a strange result to me—to be accounted for only by attributing it to the interposition of Providence. I have a fine captured Horse and Bridle. My boys have helped themselves to Yankee fixins.

I am nearly dead to see you, but of course, cannot be

spared now. Write to me. Do not be uneasy—That is restrain yourself as much as possible.

Give my love to Ida & the boy.   Your Husband

> Near Hamilton Crossing
> May 6, 1863

Dear Allie

Lieut. Henry has just returned & told me he sent on my letter to you. I was very much provoked because he did not see you and bring a letter to me from you. He says you are all well & I am satisfied. We took the heavy rain yesterday, last night, & this morning. I had but little protection & fared badly. I am not sick at all, but very much fatigued. I think I shall go through safely, but if I get at all sick I will retire at once & recruit my health. I will try & come to see you in a day or two, or as soon as we know certainly what we are going to do. I am so anxious to see you that I can hardly keep from asking permission to go to day. The Yankees are still in small squads opposite Fredericksburg. I have not heard from the victory yet, but I expect it is very complete. Send me a letter by someone. If you will send it to Lieut. McGinty, acting quartermaster, he can send to me.

I send a few Yankee trifles—I was too busy to get anything for myself.

Give my love to Ida. Write home to our folks at once. Good-bye & God bless you my darling.

                    Your Husband

The next letter from Allie was from the rail junction at Guiney's Station. It is not dated but must have been written after May 6 and before May 10. She acknowledged the items Clement called "Yankee trifles" in his letter of the 6th, but refers to Stonewall Jackson as nearby "and doing very well," which was surely before Sunday May 10, the day he died.

> At Mr. Mottley's near Guiney's
> Wednesday morning, May [6] 1863

Dear Darling.

I received your letter this morning with the Yankees' portfolio and letters. I gave the portfolio to Ida. She is

Head Quarters, Military District
Savannah Sept 2nd 1861

My Dear Sir

I am truly glad to hear
from your note of the 30th inst, that your
people are feeling such a deep interest in
our Coast defences. The great pressure on
the War Department from the Northern
frontiers of the Confederacy has turned all
eyes (and unfortunately arms) in that direction, and caused us to be sadly neglected here. But we are doing everything
that energy and industry can accomplish with small means. And still hope to
be prepared for the advent of our Northern
friends.

The Confederacy has no arms
at its disposal and the Governor informs
me that the State supply is exhausted. I am
powerless therefore in that regard. But tried

receive with pleasure any companies from your section of the State, (with such arms as they can furnish themselves) and attach them to Regiments here, or would receive a battalion properly organized and officered—

Permit me to add, that I would be pleased to have you transferred with me from the Senate to the Camp, and amid other scenes renew the pleasant associations of the two past years.

I remain very truly
Yours—
A R Lawton
Brig: General

Camp of Lawtons Brigade.
Near Port Royal Va Feby 12th 1863.

Genl S Cooper. A & I Genl
    Richmond Va
                General

                    The undersigned
Officers of Lawtons Brigade Earlys Division
Would respectfully ask to be permitted to
state to His Excellency the President that
it is their desire if the same can be done
consistently with the public interest. that
Colonel C A Evans of the 31st Ga Regiment
may be made a Brigadier General
Col Evans with one short interval has
been in command of Lawtons Brigade
since the 20th day of September last, and
by his gallantry in action and his uniform
good conduct in the management
of the Brigade has in our opinion
demonstrated his fitness for the position

ch we have suggested his promotion

We have the honor to be General

Very Respectfully

Your Obt Servants

James M Smith, Col 13th Ga Regt

J N Baker Lt Col 13th Ga Regt

C W McArthur Maj Comdg 61st Ga Regt

J S Blain Maj Comdg 26th Ga Regt

R P Eberhart Capt Comdg 38th Ga Regt

J H Lowd Maj Comdg 31st Ga Regt

Tho J Barrett 1st Lt Comdg Co "A" 13th Ga Regt

J T Horsley 1st Lt " Co "B" 13th " "

John Orean 2nd Lt " Co "C" 13th " "

W W Hartsfield Capt Co "D" 13th " "

W Kaigler 2nd Lt Comdg Co "E" 13th " "

S W Jones Capt Co "F" 13th " "

W M Patten 2nd Lt Comdg Co "G" 13th " "

T G Middoy 1st Lt Comdg Co "H" 13th " "

S C Mitchell 1st Lt " Co "J" 13th " "

B F Cartwright 2nd Lt " Co "K" 13th " "

David Rayal	Lt Comdg Co "C"	61st Ga Reg
Peter Brenan	Capt Co F.	61st " "
S R A Johnson	Capt Co C	61st " "
E F Sharp	Capt Co K	61st " "
S H Kennedy	Comdg Co K	61st " " "
John F Erwin	Capt Co G	61st " "
John S Henderson	1st Lt Comdg Co Fi	61st " "
Thomas M McRae	Capt Co E	61st " "
Eugene Jeffers	2 Lt Comdg Co I	61st " "
James E Deloatch	Capt Co H	61st " "
Joseph Hilton	1st Lt Comdg Co B	26th Ga Regt
J E McDonald	1st Lt Comdg Co I	26th " "
Henry A Smith	Capt Co K	26th " "
Urbanus Darl	1st Lt Comdg Co "A"	26th " "
H J Lowther	1st Lt Comdg Co G	26th " "
J P Cason	1st Lt Comdg Co K	26th " "
N J Rogers	1st Lt Comdg Co C	26th " "

John Oglesby — Lt Comdg Co E 38th Ga Regt
L W Farmer — Capt Co G 38th " "
J J Maddox — 1st Lt Comdg Co B 38th " "
Chas A Hawkins — Capt Co E 38th " " & Brig Insptr
R T Dorough — Lt Comdg Co E 38th " "
J G Rankin — Capt Co D 38th " "
G W Stubbs — Lt Comdg Co K 38th " "
John Gorwick — Lt Comdg Co H 38th " "
Johns J Maralle — Lt Comdg Co A 38th " "
Thos D Thornton — Lt Comdg Co F 38th " "
J D Grantham — 2d Lt Comdg Co J 38th " "

A S Shorter — Capt Co A 31st Ga Regt
G W Lewis — Capt Co D 31st " "
Thos J Vaughn — Capt Co L 31st " "
H J W Bozeman — 1st Lt Comdg Co F 31st Ga Regt
W H Harrison — Capt Co E 31st Ga Regt
R S Fletcher — Capt Co K 31st " "
J G Sanders — Capt Co C 31st " "
John W Murphy — Capt Co H 31st " "
John T Jordan — Lt Comdg Co G 31st " "
R T Pride — Capt Co B 31st " "

Richmond Va
8th June 1863

Col. H A Evans
31st Geo: Regt

Dear Colonel

You have doubtless heard
that I reported here for duty about four
weeks since — During all that time, I have
been expecting orders daily; but have not
yet been assigned to duty — Whether this
results from embarassment felt at the
War office, in assigning me again to the
command of a Brigade, after the promotion
over my head of so many of its favorites; or
from a disposition to force me to accept
a position, for which they want me, &
for which I have no relish (about which
you may learn more soon) I am not yet
able fully to decide — Certain it is, however,
that General Lee's army is in motion, &
that I have no command in it; though
I have asked unconditionally for orders, al=
most every day for four weeks — One pre=
text is, that I have not sufficiently recovered
from my wound (lameness) to enter upon
an active campaign in the field

Very sincerely
your friend
A R Lawton
Geo: and receive this not
only as not ——

The uniform kindness and consideration which you have always shown me, Colonel, induces me to call your attention (privately) to a Petition recently sent by the officers of the Brigade to General Lee, to retain Genl Gordon in the command — I feel very ~~confident~~ sure that this Petition was signed under the confident belief that I would not be again reduced to the command of a Brigade, after the events of the last campaign; but I fear it has been misunderstood in certain quarters — If this Petition was signed, under the impression, (as I have indicated), it would be grateful to my feelings to have the officers say so; now that my official connection with the Brigade is probably dissolved for the war — Should you deem it adviseable, and the officers of the Brigade be inclined to say this much to me, I beg that nothing may be said which could possibly be objectionable to Genl Gordon who I am happy to learn is a worthy gentleman and gallant officer — I do not wish to publish, or make present use of, such a paper; but it may be necessary to correct errors in the future —

As this letter might fall into the hands of some person less discreet than yourself, I beg that you will destroy it

Gettysburg

This was a Splendid battle — 3 days battle —
occurs July 1. 2. & 3 — 1863 —

[Antecedent events]

You know about the Campaign into Pennsylvania &
~~When~~ After we invaded Pa, Gordon was sent to penetrate
to the Susquehannah: I was ~~in Command of his~~
~~brigade~~ with him. We marched through the
beautiful, fresh looking Country — We passed
on Sunday through the lovely City of York
and many of the people dressed in their
Sunday Clothes turned out to see our Division
march through. The rebs behaved beautifully
— not one depredation was Committed
& very little demonstration of any sort —
The troops were jolly, & joked each other &
the Citizens as they passed —

Confederate buttons were in demand
especially from the Coats of Officers in
Command & I do not know how Gordon
managed to keep his Coat on him — But
he was fond of Good Clothes & must have fought
~~wants to keep~~ his buttons.

We reached the river in time to see
~~find the~~ a retreating force set the long
bridge on fire at the little City of <u>Wrightsville</u>
on the Susquannah! The flames rushed
through the bridge like they were fed
by oil — It was a useless destruction
because fifty men at the other end
could have kept the bridge against
a hundred thousand —

The flames rushed through & caught the houses
at the abutment on our shore & seemed
to threaten the little town with destruction.

And what do you suppose the rebs did? —
Why they stacked arms at once, & although
worn with a days march, went to work with
a will to <u>put out the fire</u>, <u>North & South</u>
met together there to save a town. The Citizens
& the Confed. soldiers mixed like they had
no fear +

— We were recalled to join the main body
rapidly + & reached Gettysburg July 1
just in time to form & go into action

Early held the left & made the attack
with all his Command. It was a brilliant
advance + (Give Early Credit for this first
Success of the Gettysburg battle) Also Gordon
— Doles brigade of Georgians did
Splendid work.

— In this battle the Federal line in our
front held their line until we were
nearly on them. The Command to fix bayonets
ran along their line and just as they
Changed from the act of firing to the act of
fixing bayonets the line broke in our front
& fell back in Confusion scarcely firing
    Upon the Second line
at all after breaking & the Second line soon also
broke in retreat toward Gettysburg
We pursued the retreating troops &
occupied Gettysburg —

I was wounded just at the moment
when the Federal line gave way — but did
not leave my Command —

Gettysburg (4)

~~I was in favor of~~ with rest of Early's Corps

My Command ^ occupied Gettysburg the
first day + ~~the~~ enemy were beaten back
to ~~the~~ hills which they fortified —

~~Early's Corps~~ ~~occupied the~~ was placed
~~the made~~ on the left of Lee's army in
that fight.

~~My command faced over to side~~

We made a night-attack on the left
but only carried a part of the ground +

I was in the action at Gettysburg the
2nd & 3r days also, although my wound
was painful + kept me half bent on my
saddle +

(The wound was not dangerous at all. It
was caused by a Minnie ball tearing across my
left side cutting & bruising skin, muscle &c
+ producing a sore irritating wound,
Ordinarily I would have taken a week odd
of rest ~~for~~ but the ~~time~~ circumstances forbade
my being absent a moment from my brigade. I
eat, slept, fought &c right in their ranks during all
that Gettysburg fight —)

3

The 4ᵗʰ day which was July 4ᵗʰ we
waited in our lines + On night of the
4ᵗʰ we began the retreat —
+ I was placed in Command of the rear
of that part of Lees retreating Columns
which belonged to our Corps + And
I had a dreadful time of it — as I was
harrassed all day long with ~~some~~
pursuing light artillery + Cavalry which
I could not furnish. ~~I constantly~~
~~kept them off by~~

~~Alone~~ in Enemy County on retreat
responsible for ~~protection~~ of an army
is one of the most trying positions in
Military life. I have advanced into
a hostile County + I have retreated
~~from it~~ — The ~~former~~ latter is ~~far more~~
~~this~~ much more perilous than the former +

=

Hd:Qrs. 2ᵈ Corps. Army. No. Va.
9ᵗ Feby, 1864

Col. C. A. Evans,
          Comg Gordon's Brigade,
                    Colonel;

          I have received with great
pleasure, your letter of the fifth instant,
announcing the re-enlistment of your gallant Brigade & showing that the move commenced by Gen.
Rodes' Division is still continued. This spontaneous proof of devotion is hardly less gratifying than the spirited conduct of the Brigade
on Saturday, near Morton's Ford.

          The deeds of "Gordon's Brigade" are already suffi-
cient to ennoble all who have shared its
dangers & its glories.

                    I remain, Colonel,
                              With great respect,
                                        Yrs. very truly,
                                        R. S. Ewell
                                        Lt Genl.

Hd. Qrs. Army of Northern Va.
14th May 1864.

General Orders }
No 41 }

I The Commanding General takes great pleasure in announcing to the army the series of successes that, by the favor of God, have been recently achieved by our arms.

II A part of the enemy's force threatening the Valley of Virginia has been routed by Genl. Imboden, and driven back to the Potomac, with the loss of their train and a number of prisoners.

III Another body of the enemy under Genl Averell penetrated to the Virginia & Tennessee Rail Road at Dublin Depot. A portion of this force has been dispersed by Genls Morgan and W. E. Jones, who are in pursuit of the remainder.

IV The army of Genl. Banks sustained a severe defeat in Western Louisiana by the forces of Genl Kirby Smith, and retreated to Alexandria, losing several thousand prisoners, thirty five pieces of artillery, and a large number of wagons. Some of the most formidable gunboats that accompanied the expedition were destroyed to save them from capture.

V The expedition of Genl Steele into Western Arkansas has ended in a complete disaster. Northern journals of the 10th inst. announce his surrender with an army of nine thousand men to General Price.

VI The Cavalry force sent by General Grant to attack Richmond has been repulsed and retired towards the Peninsula. Every demonstration of the enemy south of James River has up to this time been successfully repelled.

VII The heroic valor of this army with the blessing of Almighty God has thus far checked the advance of the principal army of the enemy and inflicted upon it heavy loss.

The eyes and hearts of your countrymen are turned to you with confidence, and their prayers attend you in your gallant struggle. Encouraged by the success that has been vouchsafed to us, and stimulated by the great interests that depend upon the issue let every man resolve to endure all and brave all until by the assistance of a just and merciful God, the enemy shall be driven back and peace secured to our country.

Continue to emulate the valor of your comrades who have fallen, and remember that it depends upon us whether they shall have died in vain.

It is in your power, under God, to defeat the last great effort of the enemy, establish the independence of your native land and earn the lasting love and gratitude of your countrymen and the admiration of mankind.

R E Lee
Genl.

Brig. Genl. Jno B. Gordon
Com'd'g Division

The situation at this time, (about 2½ o'Clock P.M.,) taken in connection with the facts just mentioned, was as follows; viz — My Brigade constituted as stated the left of Gordon's division; on the left of my brigade on the prolongation of its line was first a small open field three hundred yards wide; next a neck of woods one hundred and fifty yards wide; next a large open field twelve hundred yards wide; next a body of woods (width not known,) from which the two regiments of our Cavalry referred to has been driven. Beyond these woods, still farther to the left, Rosser's Cavalry were reported to be in position, and apparently from those woods or some field immediately beyond them the enemy was firing about two pieces of artillery in the direction where Rosser's Command was reported to be. Across this large open field a skirmish line of the enemy appeared in view, deployed on the elevated grounds lying near the North Eastern edge of the field; and his Vedettes were discerned on the skirt of the woods from which our Cavalry had retired. Behind this skirmish line it was correctly conjectured that Cavalry was concealed in the woods, for as soon as the latter against once they Succeeded this Cavalry advanced dismounting to one or two brigades advanced into the open field. I will state here also that at the left of the skirmish line was deployed opposite to fill in rear of the left of the enemy line of infantry concealed in a ravine — line from these elevated grounds on which the enemy's skirmish was posted, the view extended as far as Bell's Grove, unobstructed; and this large open field presented to his Cavalry an excellent opportunity to operate against our flank or even penetrate to our rear unopposed.

This was the position about at the time here mentioned when my brigade was ordered to this large open space and placed in position to support several pieces of artillery, which were momentarily expected to arrive, and with orders to oppose in any direction from which the

(See paper marked ⅔)

my been now, to call your attention to a careful
study of the map accompanying this report, which was
executed by Capt C. S. Shack Engr from a skeleton
made and carefully explained to him by myself, and
which has been pronounced correct in its topographical features
as well as in the given positions of troops, by several officers
who were present at the time and had good opportunity
for observing the places and positions represented by it.

From this map can be understood the position of my
brigade and the like at the time the enemy
moved forward to attack. The position of his line
of infantry, overlapping our left. His skirmishers on
the elevated ground, his Cavalry behind this skirmish
line, the artillery firing on Rosser, and also the
position of Gordon's Division & Kershaw's left. It
represents also the enemy having advanced his line
of infantry; the "small open field" is penetrated, and
his attack begins. The gap in Gordon's division
although that portion which advanced immediately
in front is checked for a time; It represents also
my brigade having advanced and attacked the enemy and
he was driving back the part of the line in its immediate
front, and in that position where I received
orders to retire. My skirmish line is represented
advanced on my left flank in the open field —
I offer that map as a better explanation of the reasons
why the attack of the enemy was successful than any
I can write, and beg you to give it a careful
scrutiny.

2

About 3³⁰' or 4 O'Clock P.M. the enemy advanced his infantry and attacked the left of our main line of infantry. At the instant that this attack commenced my brigade advanced at double quick, attacked the enemy near the right of his advancing line, driving ~~the right back a short distance~~ that portion in its front back a short distance, but in the meantime "the small open field" had been penetrated by the enemy, who then filled the gap between ~~the~~ ~~remainder~~ my brigade and the remainder of the Division and were directing an enfilading fire upon the latter, causing it to commence breaking from the left, At this juncture orders were received from the Maj Genl Comdg for my brigade to withdraw ~~this~~ attack was sufficiently wanting in determination and force, as to have been repelled if the large gap in the Center of Gordon's division had been filled. That is the attack as made, might have been repelled if there had been one continuous line of infantry across "the small open field" and "narrow neck of woods" aided by a few pieces of artillery. ^

Here introduce the statements concerning the map — which appears on the reverse side of paper marked 1

Control ready for any order it might receive. ~~I conjecture now, that the enemy did not continue immediately to advance forward that portion of his line which attacked Gordons Division, but employed his force in gradually turning the left of each brigade of the Army in succession.~~

My Command being organized was ~~directed by Maj Gen Gordon to advance to the support of~~ Ramseurs Division, which was still in line on the right, but although moving rapidly we could not reach this Division before it also gave way in retreat, and my command faced ~~by the rear rank and~~ in line of battle marched to Belle Grove hill, (Sheridans Ho Qrs) where it again halted in support of two pieces of Artillery which were here placed in position to fire upon the enemy. These ~~pieces~~ being withdrawn and the retreat still turning on the right the brigade faced ~~by the rear rank~~ about in line of battle marched to the enemys works near Cedar Creek on the West side of the pike where another stand was made, Checking the enemy until it was supposed that all Artillery and trains were safely in the rear. This position was held so long that an organized retreat across Cedar Creek by its difficult crossing above the regular Ford became impracticable. ~~The enemy chiefly~~ in our immediate front had moved Cavalry around our left flank; Cedar Creek was only about two hundred yards distant with no crossing except a bridge of loose poles and fence rails, and to attempt to cross there in order by the flank, would have subjected half the Command to Capture at the Creek, or else the enemy reaching his works which perfectly commanded the Crossing in easy rifle range, could have killed and wounded large numbers of the troops. Orders were therefore given for a precipitate retreat to reform as soon as the creek was passed. After the creek was crossed an imperfect organization was made, but it soon became night coming on, various commands became mixed indiscriminately in the dark. I was not present when the Enemys Cavalry attacked our trains our Artillery, having waited to see my whole Command pass, and the Cavalry having come in on the pike from its West side beyond the head of the Column of my brigade, not encountering the Brigade at all, but moving up the pike in the direction of Strasburg. In the darkness of the night amid the Confusion arising from commands being mixed together, all available organization was lost and the retreat was continued in this manner to Fishers Hill.—

I desire to remark that the Division behaved with Commendable Courage in the mornings attacks there being remarkably few skulkers or plunderers while the pursuit was vigorous. I desire also to say in behalf of my immediate Command which made the gravest and fought in retreat. With exceptional cases of grace. I have caused charges to be preferred against men in flagrant cases of Cowardice during the recent battle have caused plunderers to be punished — guns & accoutrements to be paid for have suitable rewarded a few cases of merit and distinguished gallantry and only ask for the brave soldiers in my command a careful study of the Circumstances and situation under which they fought an impartial judgment upon this evidence.

I have the honor to be Major

Very Respectfully Your Obt Servt

Major R. W. Hunter
Asst Gen

Camp of Evans Brigade
Gordon's Division
Octo. 30, 1864.

Brig. Gen. C. A. Evans
Commdg &c

Official report
of the Battle of the
19th October 1864

Battle of Cedar Creek
Oct 19, 1864

Hd qrs Evans Brigade
Oct 30th 1864

Major,

In accordance with a previously arranged plan, Gordon's division followed by Ramseurs and Pegrams Divis, (my brigade with the other 3 brigades of) all under the Command of Maj Genl Gordon, his division being temporarily under my command, moved from their Camps near Fisher Hill, about 9 O'clock P.m. Oct 18 1864, followed the Valley Pike across the Stone bridge over Fishers Creek, near Strasburg, then filed to the right, and were marched along the base of three top mountain, over a dim & difficult path, leading down the North Fork Shenandoah river to the Front Royal & Strasburg roads, which was reached at Midnight and where the head of the Column was halted to allow time for the divisions to Close. From this point the march was continued along the Front Royal road, until the Command arrived opposite Bowmans Ford an obscure Crossing above Buck Fords on the North Fork Shenandoah, where at 4 O'Clock A.m the 19th inst, the pickets of the enemy were driven away by a detachment of Cavalry which here preceded the infantry, and the Command hurried across with great rapidity, moved by the flank right in front, directly to the Buck-ford & Middletown road and on that road to a distance of one & 1/4 miles from the ford over which the troops had Crossed. Five O'Clock A.m, the time designated for attack, having arrived Gordons Division was halted, faced to the front, placed in line of battle nearly parallel to the Valley Pike, and about one 1/4 miles east of the River and immediately advanced. The ground over which the advance was made found to be very rough, broken into ravines & hills, & covered with woods,

in consequence of which the unity of the line was not well preserved, but after an advance of something over three fourths of a mile, the enemy were discovered in line about four hundred yards distant, posted nearly parallel with the pike across a range of wooded hills, a temporary halt was ordered, to reconstruct the line, which was very quickly done, the halt not lasting three or four minutes, when the Division moved forward rapidly with spirit, encountered the enemy, who made a brief but somewhat stubborn resistance (part of the lines actually engaging hand to hand) and then fled, leaving four pieces of artillery, over which the left of the command passed, after a detachment from the 12th Ga batt. had taken possession & turned these guns against the retreating columns of the enemy; the pursuit was continued across the pike through the camps of the enemy, beyond Bell Grove the H.Q. of Maj Gen. Sheridan U.S.A. — and until about 8 o'clock a.m. — capturing in addition to the artillery mentioned & colors, a large among of camp equipage, besides a number of small arms

Special Orders,
No.
} Extract:

At this time I returned to the immediate command
of my brigade Maj. Gen. Gordon having
assumed immediate command of his Division;
the pursuit of the enemy being discontinued
In the last line of battle taken up by the army
near Middletown my brigade was at first placed
on the left of Gordons Division, that Division
Constituting the left of the line. About one
O'Clock P.M. it was observed that the enemy
were moving Cavalry to the left of our line of battle
about 3/4 of a mile from our front passing behind
a thick piece of woods out of sight, and soon
afterwards Couriers from Brig. Gen. Rosser
came to me & were by myself directed to go
to Maj. Gen. Gordon, or directly to Lt. Gen. early
with their verbal despatches which were to the
effect, that the enemy had massed Cavalry in
his front, had driven back two of his regiments
other couriers came afterwards at short intervals with similar information
and they had been compelled to fall back
About the same time it was discovered that the enemy
was extending their line of infantry to the left
which fact was made known to the major general
commanding. At the same time to develop the
enemys position the skirmish line, deployed to
cover not only the brigade, but extending over three
hundred yards to the left more than the line
of the brigade advanced through the woods in
front of the line of battle, attached & drove in
the enemys skirmishers, receiving a volley from
the enemys main line the full length of our
skirmish line. fell back to their original position,
the fact being thus ascertained that the enemy had
extended his more line at least three
hundred yards beyond our left.

1864.

Special Orders, }
No. }   *Extract:*

Leave of absence is hereby granted the following named Officers

At this time the ~~position of off~~ situation was as follows—
To the left of my brigade on the prolongation of its line
was first, an open ~~with~~ out a ~~picket~~ field 200 yards, open ~~woods~~ 150 yards, open field 1200
yards wide, next woods width not known ~~four~~ which the
two regiments of Cavalry referred to above had been
~~posted but~~ driven away; beyond these woods, I understood
Rosser's Cavalry to in posted; about ½ mile distant; this open field presented
to the enemy Cavalry an excellent opportunity to operate
against our flank & even to penetrate to our rear
unopposed, and my brigade except one regiment & part of
another was ordered to this open space concealing the
right of the line to prevent the enemy from discovering
its extent, in order to be ready to move in any direction from which an attack might be made; —
Immediately threw out an extended line of Skirmishers
to present as much front as possible without further
weakening my main line already ~~reduced~~ by over
over one hundred killed & wounded and on the skirmish
line of one hundred men; the over Skirmish line; —
About 3½ or 4 o'Clock P.M. the enemy advanced his
infantry to the attack. It was a real attack as all
who were present know, but one which might have been
repelled if there had been troops enough in position to the left of
the line occupying By Command of Major General Sheridan:
ground four hundred 150 yards in length on the prolongation
of that line; As soon as this attack was made my brigade
advanced at double quick from the field where they
~~still~~ posted, attacked the enemy, near the right of their line Assistant Adjutant General.
driving it back a short distance, but in the mean time the

Small open field on the left of the Division, had
been penetrated by the enemy, who there filled the
gap between the remainder of the division and
my brigade and were enfilading the line of the
former; — This caused a retreat of the line, which
and of my brigade at first in confusion, but
the brigade was again organized on the open
field about 800 yards in rear of the line
from which the retreat was made, and was held
by itself under good control, ready for any orders
it might receive. I conjecture now, that the enemy
did not continue immediately to advance forward that portion
of his line which attacked Gordon's Division, but employed
his force in gradually turning the left of each brigade
in succession: —

With My organized command was directed
by Maj Genl Gordon to advance to the support
of Ramseurs Divn which was still in line on
the right, but although the enemy was
moving rapidly I could not reach
this division before it also gave way in retreat, and
my assistance being useless, the command retreated
in line of battle to Belle
Grove Hill — Sheridan's Head Qrs, when it again
halted in support of two pieces of artillery which
were here placed in position to fire upon the
enemy. These pieces being withdrawn, and
organized line appearing
and the retreat still continuing
on the right, the brigade faced by the rear rank
marched to the enemys works near Cedar Creek
on the west side of the Valley Pike, when another stand
was made the command by rapid firing
checking the enemy, until
it was supposed all artillery & trains were safely in the rear

Hd Qr Evans Divn
Appomattox C. H. Va
Apr. 11. 1865

Col Lowe
        Please ask the officers
of my Brigade to gratify
me with their autograph
Signatures, and Post Office
address, in this book
            Resptly
            C. A. Evans
            Brig. Genl

very proud of it. I am so thankful that you are safe my darling that I hardly know how to behave myself. My anxiety has been very great as you know, but yesterday I felt contented, having no idea that you were in any fight. I am glad now that I did not know it. The opinion here is that the fighting is over. God grant it may be, I say from the bottom of my heart. There are about four or five thousand of our wounded down here at the depot. A great many of them lying out in the mud. The shrieks and groans; they sure are heart-rending. I wouldn't see them if I could. I know I could do them no good. The field in front of the house is covered with prisoners. Gen. Jackson is about a quarter of a mile from here. He is doing very well. If the fighting is over you can come down in a day or so, can't you. I shall be obliged to stay here till the train can go through to Richmond. It is mighty bad to be paying ten dollars a day, though—I don't care for anything now my darling is safe. Last night was a terrible night and I am afraid you were out all night. I hope it will not make you sick. We were looking for the Yankees here all day Yesterday—But they didn't come. Maj. Speer comes to see how I am getting on every day. He has promised to send you this letter by the first one [courier] that goes up. I hear so many rumors here I don't know what to believe. They say all the enemy have recrossed the river. I hope it is so.

We are all well but the baby. He is a little sick this morning, but I think it is from his teeth. Write to me by the first opportunnity. I want to see you so bad. I believe I would almost shout if I were to see you safe and alive again.

Goodbye darling. God bless you and take care of you—Goodbye—Your Wife

Clement to Allie:

Hamilton's Crossing
[near Fredericksburg, Va.]
May 10, [18]63

My dear Allie
I would not come down yesterday because we have

said good-bye once, and that is a *luxury* not to be indulged in. I do not love to say "good-bye" especially to you, and I know how it makes you feel. It is best for us not to allow ourselves to give way to our feelings.

I send you my trunk. It is full of a little of everything. You will find a "silk signal flag" which belonged to Lieut. Marston, captured by us on Marye's Heights. I send it to the "emperor." Keep it for him.

Green Clifton will go with you, and Capt. Orr, will also be down on the train, if he can get on. You must take good care of yourself.

If you do not get off to day, send me word by Mose & I will come down to night.

God bless you. Good-bye.

Your Husband

After Jackson was shot on May 2, a team of Confederate doctors examined the wounds. A ball in his right hand was readily extracted. The general's left arm was shattered beyond repair and was amputated by the most skilled army surgeons on May 3. For several days it looked as if Jackson would be all right. He had been carried out of danger from the enemy, to the plantation office near the home of Mr. Thomas Chandler of Guiney's Station, to convalesce. By May 7 Jackson had taken a turn for the worse, developing pneumonia, and on May 10, whispered his last words to his wife: "Let us cross over the river, and rest under the shade of the trees."[5]

Jackson's body was placed on a special railroad car that would carry the remains from Guiney's Station to Richmond to lie in state at the capitol, where a warrior's funeral was to be held. As the train left the station, bedecked in mourning crepe, a crowd had gathered. Among them were Allie Evans and her little eight-year-old daughter, Ida, who was held high by her nurse so she could better see the departing cortege.[6]

---

5. Henry Kyd Douglas, *I Rode with Stonewall* (Chapel Hill: University of North Carolina Press, 1940), p. 228.
6. A story from family tradition.

Chapter 11
"SURPLUS BAGGAGE"

After Chancellorsville the Confederates returned to their old camps around Fredericksburg. They spent the rest of May regrouping and recruiting the army up to its full fighting strength. The news of the great victory at Chancellorsville gave a new impetus to the Southern cause, and the ranks were more readily filled.

When Jackson died, Lee reorganized the Army of Northern Virginia. Where he had previously established two corps, he now divided the army into three. He placed the First Corps under experienced General Longstreet, just returned from near Suffolk; the Second Corps under "Ole Bald Head," General Ewell, now back at the front with an ill-fitting peg leg; and the Third Corps Lee placed under the bold, red-haired fighter, Lt. Gen. A. P. Hill. Gordon's brigade, as part of Early's division, was in the Second Corps.[1]

Clement to Allie:

In camp near Fredericksburg, Va.
May 14, 1863

My dear Darling.

This commences another series of letters to you, and the interval which has occurred between this and my last shows that we have been together. I could not help a little melancholy and a feeling of loneliness when I rode back to camp, after parting with you, knowing that several long, long months must pass by before I could see you again. But I will not indulge in melancholy. You know my theory is that we must be content with everything we cannot avoid. It is not right

1. Douglas S. Freeman, *R.E. Lee*, 4 vols. (New York: Charles Scribner's Sons, 1946), vol. 3, p. 11; *O.R.*, series 1, vol. 25, part 2, p. 810.

LT. GEN. RICHARD STODDERT EWELL

156

to indulge in useless sorrow at any event, nor in sorrow at all except such as shall make our hearts better. Mose told me you got on the train all safely & comfortably and that other ladies besides yourself were in the cars. I was afraid you would have to travel with the sick & wounded, and I knew that would be so unpleasant.

I have no news of the enemy to write to you. So far as can be judged, everything is as you left it, but I believe that Hooker will not remain inactive long. We had to day a very heavy fall of rain and the atmosphere is now quite cool. I hope you had a rain also to add to your comfort in travelling.

I am getting all straight again, and although I do not expect to be fat again until next winter, yet I believe my prudence will keep me from becoming sick, but you may be sure that so soon as I feel at all incapacitated for duty by any sickness that I shall come to you immediately. You may rest perfectly assured of that.

I have received a letter from Clem which I enclose. I wrote to Father last night and shall write to Mother tomorrow. Our first letters have reached home by this time and their uneasiness quieted.

I have had milk yesterday and to day. I shall get it everyday from Mrs. Alsop.[2] I sent Eugene Granbery after it, and he said they asked many questions about you. Genl. Gordon's wife is staying there. Col. [D. B.] Penn is looking for his wife back. How I wish mine was here too. I am sorry I let you go.

You must send up & buy a Richmond paper every day. Either the Examiner or Sentinel.

Tell all your kinfolks that I shall not leave Virginia without going to see all of them.

Take good care of your precious self. Kiss Ida & the Emperor for Pa. My love to all our cousins.

Good bye,
Your Husband

May 15, 8 o'clock a.m. Heavy fall of rain last evening.

---

2. Mrs. Alsop ran a boardinghouse near Fredericksburg and Allie stayed there on part of her visit to Virginia in the early days of 1863.

Cool & pleasant this morning. No news. I am well. Good bye.

In camp near Fredericksburg, Va.
May 17, 1863

My dear Darling

Your welcomed first letter written the 15th reached me this morning. It is so pleasant to know that in two days I can hear from you. I am very glad you found your relatives well, for I was afraid that the whooping cough would drive you to wandering about for a month or two. I feel much more contented now, because I know you have a fixed home where you can stay as long as you please. My first letter to you will tell you how much I miss you. I feel again like I was in the war sure enough, for the hardest part of the campaign is my absence from you. I never see old Alsop's house without thinking of you and the happy hours we passed there together, but I look forward to the ending of this struggle when we shall pass our lives together usefully,—making up for the many years we have idled away. I feel like I have done nothing worthy of having lived for. Surely I might have accomplished much more for our own good and that of our fellows than I have done since I came to "man's estate." I have no news from the enemy; up to this time. So far as I can observe no demonstration has been made by Hooker. In fact the daily Richmond papers will inform you much quicker than I can of everything that occurs and you must be sure to get one or two every day or so as to keep posted. If cousin William[3] takes any particular paper, you can take a different one.

I received a nice present of a pair of India Rubber leggins from my friend Maj. Reid yesterday, so I have an India Rubber Cap, overcoat, and leggins complete and can defy the rain. I am in all respects better fixed up now than I have been since the war began and at very little expense. My wounded sorrel horse is getting well & will be the finest horse of all. He is a noble

---

3. See Appendix A for relatives.

fellow. *The Canadian* made a polite bow and sent his love to his Miss Ida & young Master, "the Emperor." My Yankee brethren supplied my necessities very liberally in the late fight in exchange for my complement of bullets & bayonetts.

Your letter written at Richmond has not reached me. I expect Clifton did not go after it. You must write home at least once every week so as not to keep our folks in suspense. I will write also that often or oftener.

I am still on Court martial duty & probably shall be for a month. I regret it because it keeps me away from my regiment so much. Capt. Murphy has sent in his resignation. He is laboring under a disease which prevents him from doing much duty. The health of the regiment is improving. We will soon be in as good [a] fighting trim as ever. My own health is number one. I have fully recovered from all fatigue.

I shall write to you often, say about three times per week and you must write to me *every day*.

Give my love to all, & tell them that I hope not to be wounded or get sick, but if I do I shall trespass on their hospitality. Anyhow, I shall see them all before the war closes. I am sorry to hear of Uncle Sidney's loss. You must go to see him by all means if possible. Good bye. Good bye.

Your Husband

Tell Ida she must study hard; Pa will learn her to read French as soon as the war is over.

In camp near Fredericksburg
May 19, 1863

My dearest Darling

Your letter written at Richmond reached me to day, so you may rest easy about your correspondence being read by any person for whom it was not intended. My boots also came yesterday and such a disappointment I did have. They not only do not suit me at all—at all, even if they fitted; but the worst is, that I cannot get them on. They are entirely too small. I wrote very particularly how I wanted them made and my instructions were not complied with in scarcely anything. I am very much provoked about it, and have written back that I shall return them to Singer by the first opportunity.

I have, as usual, no news to write to you. Everything is just like it was before the battle. We shall probably change our camp in a few days and perhaps occupy old Alsop's woods. The men are to be furnished with tent flies for the summer campaign, and there is a general fixing up going on now, betokening some considerable degree of activity for the summer, but of course nothing is known now.

I want to see you almost as much as I ever did, but I have made up my mind to endure a three months separation, and surely I ought to be grateful that I can see you so often when so many do not see their wives for 12 months at a time. I cannot convince you to become a philosopher, because you think that the misery of others does not by comparison, make yours more endurable.

I suppose the little Gentleman [Lawton] attracts attention during his travels. He is certainly a remarkable boy, and his mother is so easily flattered about him. Well, it is very natural and excusable.

You must pardon my short letters. I have commenced writing just before drill & the drum is beating. My love to my sweet little daughter & to all our kinfolks. Goodbye & God bless my darling.

Your Husband

Clement from Allie:

Halifax Co., Va.
May 20, 1863

Dear Darling

I had one letter from you since I have been down here. That was written Friday after I left Wednesday. I looked for another last night, but was disappointed. It will come this evening, I know it will. I was so glad to get your letter. I miss you so much when night comes on, the time when you usually come. It is more lonesome then than at any other time. They generally get back from the post office about that time and when I get a letter it will relieve that feeling of loneliness some. I am so selfish that I don't want any other woman to be with her husband if I can [not] be with you. I know it is mean, but I can't help the feeling. I felt right mad at the ladies at Mrs. Alsop's when I read your letter. I wished mighty hard I was there with my husband.

Well, darling I was very much surprised on looking over your trunk after I got down here to find my picture sent off with your surplus baggage. Now darling that shows what is what. I always told you I loved you the best. Now I wouldn't take anything on earth for your picture while I am away from you. I love to look at them and wish I had a dozen more of them. I was thinking of me having mine taken to send to you [at] the first opportunity. It is not worth while though. Is it? It would be throwing away money wouldn't it? I expect Mose put it in there and you didn't know it. You remember you said he had it to take care of for you.

Ida has gone to school this morning. I make her go regularly. She likes it very well. Must I make He go too, papa? Mama thinks he is smart enough to learn. Don't you, papa? You wouldn't say so if you thought so. He is a man, pa. He can call the dogs. I am going to learn him to say papa before he comes to see you. Cousin William left yesterday morning. He didn't know whether he would go any further than Richmond or not. I told him where he could find you and hope he will look you up. Nancy has got well. I believe I am straight again. I don't want to get sick so far from you. I am so glad you will get milk. You must buy it as long as you stay there. If you can get any syrup, send Miss Sarah a bottle full for old Mrs. Philips. I told her you would before I left there. I have been shoe making and think I will have as nice a pair of shoes as old George Singer[4] could

4. Terrill and Dixon, *Stewart County*, p. 590. Johan George Singer was born in Stuttgart, Germany, and settled in Lumpkin in 1838, where his uncle had previously located: "Mr. Singer was a shoemaker and had a prosperous shoemaking establishment, furnishing fine boots and shoes to this section. During the Civil War he rendered valuable service in making shoes for the Confederate Government."

turn out when I get them done, but I don't like the trade much.

We have had peas once. No other vegetables yet. Cousin Lewis's garden looks fine. I wish you could get vegetables. I remember how fond you are of them. Ida told me to give her love to pa and tell him she was studying very hard. She kissed me for you, of course, before she left. My Yankee letters have been almost worn out by reading. I sent one picture home. Good bye darling. One week ago this morning I parted with you. Good bye.

Your Wife

Clement to Allie:

In camp near Fredericksburg, Va.
Thursday morning, May 21, 1863

My dear Darling

I have nothing to say to you worth writing about, unless I write you a letter about yourself. However, I have sold my boots (which did not fit me) for cost, and although I'm in almost bootless condition I am not out of the money I paid for them. New troops are arriving here constantly, and one Brigade (Colquitt's) is going off to North Carolina. The movements look a good deal like something was meditated by General Lee in the way of a demonstration against the enemy. We have been provided with new tent flies, our transportation is all fixed, the men are closely confined to camp, and all else needed to meet an emergency has been provided. *Uncle Richard*[5] was here yesterday. He says that Miss Mary is just recovering from a severe attack of Pneumonia. The rest are all well. I sent my *love* to them.

The camp is terribly dull now, but I can get along in the day time because I have enough to do to pass away the hours, but I do so much miss my walk to Alsop's and my evenings enjoyed with you. Three more months sounds like a long time yet to roll off—June—July—

5. See Appendix A for relatives.

August—These are to pass away before I can see you again. However, when they are gone it will appear like a short time, for the days are slipping by. It is almost a month now since we commenced the late fighting & it scarcely seems like a week. When we commence marching the time will go away much more rapidly. It may be wrong to count another day as gone. Nearly five months of the year is gone. The remaining seven will soon pass and I hope they will develop some plans of settlement of the war.

Tell Ida she must not waste any more of her time. She must now go to studying in earnest or she will grow up to be an ignorant young lady and all her Pa's hopes in her be disappointed. Tell the "man" he must study too and quit all his meanness.

Good bye. My love to all. God bless you.

Your Husband

In camp near Fredericksburg, Va.
May 27/[18]63

My dear Darling

I have been sick two days with the prevailing scourge of the camp—dysentery—, but by careful dieting & medicine I am again on sound footing. I almost wished to get sick enough to go to see you, but I would not wish it.

I wish I had that precious piece of "surplus baggage" which I sent off—not in my trunk—but from old Motleys' —I cannot help thinking about how you imagined you had such a good thing on me about your picture. I expect to hear of that "surplus baggage" for the next twenty-five years. That will be added to the long list of delinquencies which you have maliciously cherished against me—How different I am! I forget all your little faults, and remember only your goodness. If I had a *record* like yourself, I could tell some things too, that would close your lips on the "surplus baggage."—But I will have to endure all my sufferings patiently—for love is ever forgiving, forbearing—bears no malice &c. &c.

I have no news at all to write. We are all impatient to

hear from Vicksburg. We hope that today's papers will furnish some news. The Yankees opposite us are just as you left them. We may have a fight any day or may not fight in a month.—It is reported that all our cavalary is being concentrated near Culpeper—this may mean an extensive raid into Pennsylvania or some movement against Hooker's Base.

I have received no other letter from home. I am surprised that Bob did not answer my letter. I suppose he has gone to Jackson, Miss. to follow the 46th Ga. ([Peyton] Colquitt's).

I hoped to have rec'd a letter from you today, but none came. Do I write too often? I wonder if you want to see me really bad, like I want to see you, or are you content with beholding my *painted image*, which you said so much about. You must try to keep from forgetting how I look.

I hope Ida is trying to learn. Pa is very much afraid that his daughter will not become the intelligent young lady that he hoped she would be—Pa wants her to be good, modest, and smart—She must study hard while she has the opportunity. The little gentleman can do just as he pleases. Pa don't count much on him no how— His Ma brags [a] heap about him, but Pa has never seen much to brag about—

Tell Nance that President Davis sends his special thanks to her for the two swords she sent to his cavalry.

My love to all—

Good bye my darling.

Your Husband

Allie to Clement:

Halifax Co., Vir.
May 27, 1863

Dear Darling

Since I wrote to you last I have received two letters from you written one on the seventeenth and one on the nineteenth. I ought to have got them both last week, I have been terribly bothered about my letters. You say you will write to me three times a week and I must write every day. Just reverse it and you will have it right. You write to me every day and I will write three times a week. It has been just two weeks this morning since I parted from you. It looks like a long—long time to look back to that morning. How will it be before three or four months are gone. I wonder where you will be and what will turn up in that time. I hope all will be well for us. I do wish I could know when this war would end. It is terrible to think that it may last for years yet. I have almost despaired of its ever ending. I have heard it said that the darkest hour is just before dawn. I think it is dark enough now for day to break. Cousin William has got back home and didn't see you. I was so disappointed. He said he tried his best to find you, but could not find a man that could tell him where Gordon's Brigade was. He says men are going about through the country here making speeches and saying that Gen. Lee says if the farmers don't send the army provisions he will be obliged to fall back. That his position is worth fifty thousand men, but that he can't hold it unless they send him more to eat. He don't believe it and wants to know what you think about it.

I dreamed about you again last night. Indeed I dream about you almost every time I go to sleep day or night. It is mighty lonesome down here in the country. I miss your coming so much at night. Everybody here goes to bed at dark and I have nobody to talk with me. Then is when I want to see you worse.

Ida is going to write to you this morning. I don't think she is learning anything at school and have concluded to make her study at home. I think they have a very poor teacher.

Cousin Eliza is getting well of her fall. Her eye looks very badly yet.

Mama has got him [Lawton] sitting on a pallet, pa, while Nancy has gone to eat her breakfast. He don't like it a bit and is growling mightily. You say his mother is very easily flattered about him. His papa likes to hear him praised as well as his mama. He is seven months old today. Everybody says he looks like he was a year old. I

165

stay in a little office out in the yard. I like it a great deal better than staying in the house. It is off to myself and feels like a little home. I am away from the children and they certainly are the worst children that ever lived. I would soon wear them out if they belonged to me. I try to keep Ida straight, but you know evil communications corrupt good manners. Cousin William has had a good many applications to take families to board from Richmond, but he has not the house room. It is well I engaged board before I left here or I would have been cut out. Are you going to write to me often darling? You must for all the pleasure and company I have is your letters. Ida and the little man send love to pa.

Good bye. Good bye.

Your Wife

I am so sorry your boots didn't fit. What will you do for another pair? It is very provoking.

Clement to Allie:

In camp near Fredericksburg, Va.
May 28, 1863

My dear Darling

The events of camp life are so much alike day after day, that I hardly see how you can place any value on my letters. Certainly you do not prize them according to their contents of news, for then the paper on which they are written had as well be unsoiled—

But I do have something to write about this time. Yesterday we had a review of our Division—4 brigades— by the old hero General Lee himself. I was so sorry you were not there to see the old gentleman; But you have seen "Uncle Richard" and at a distance of fifty yards they look very much alike about the face & head. But General Lee has a much better figure, is not so large, and on horseback looks splendidly. He is an old cavalry officer and his riding is superb. After our Division, came Jackson's old division now commanded by General Ed Johnson—General A. P. Hill now Lieutenant General was present. After the review was over three cheers were given for General Lee, Hill, & Johnson,—but poor old

166

Early was left out. He looked deeply cut. I went out at the head of the regiment & Brigade, although sick, because General Gordon wanted me to do so. I am not fully well, but I have not given up duty. I shall be well in one more day.

The Sec. of War has decided my rank and placed me Senior Colonel as it was at first. I feel mortified to think that after I had rightfully commanded the Brigade so many months that the attempted trick on my rank succeeded even for a month, but now it is all settled, and without my writing a line or moving a single step in my own favour. General Early's letter to the Sec. of War, on the subject written two months ago, was more against me than otherwise, and has just been replied to fully & finally settling the question. So far as I can hear, it has given very general satisfaction. So far as the question affected my future promotion I do not honestly care a particle about it, for I am fully content to serve just as I am. I hope I have fully cured myself of ambition for place, merely for self-gratification.

Have you quit writing to me, or are you mad about that "surplus baggage" yet? I write every other day, so that you ought to get three letters per week, and if anything "turns up" I will write to you every day until quiet is restored. Could you afford to love me enough just to write that often? Give me a full description of everything you see. Tell me about everybody you meet, & every place you go to. You must see all your old friends & kinfolks. I wish you had Mose along with you. You could hire some kind of a carriage & travel generally.

Give my love to the little darlings. They are very precious to their Pa.

Take good care of your own priceless self.

Good bye. God bless you.
Your Husband

Allie to Clement:

Halifax Co., Va.
May 29, 1863

My dear darling.

It has been a week yesterday since my last letter from

you was written. I do wonder what is the matter. I can't help but think it is the mail, for I know you wrote. I never was so put out in my life by anything. I thought yesterday evening I certainly would get a letter, but when I enquired I got the same old answer that I dread so much to hear. No letter from you. Cousin Liza tells me you were so tired of me and so glad I am gone, you have forgotten me—but I know better than that, I tell her. I know there are letters somewhere if you are alive and able to write. Suppose you were to get sick darling and write to me to come to see you and the letter should be delayed. What would I do? If you get sick don't trust to writing but send somebody after me. I am afraid you are sick now, but I hope not. I could hear from you as soon at home as I can here. Your letter written on the twenty-first I received on the twenty-third, but have had none since except two that were written before that one. I don't expect you get any of my letters either and you are thinking I don't write. It is very provoking. We are having a good rain this morning and it is very much needed. Everything was needing rain. I wish you could be here to spend this rainy day with me. I could enjoy it so much. Would you believe I was foolish enough to look for you sometimes, thinking something might turn up or happen for you to get a short furlough and run down here to see me a little while. But vain is the hope I know. I have written to Matt this week. Have you had any letters from home? I am anxious to hear from Hannah. It is time for her to be sick. You must write to Sister. I have written to her once since I have been down here. I wish you could hear the baby call the dogs. He is calling them now. I think he will talk soon. You must take care of that little pony for him to ride papa. He will soon be man enough to ride him. Ida is well and getting right fat. She wrote to you day before yesterday. Good bye. Bless your heart.

Your Wife.

Clement to Allie:

Camp near Fredericksburg
May 29, [18]63

My dear Darling

Your letter written six days ago came to day. I cannot imagine why this delay in the mails. I learn from it with surprise that but two of my letters had reached you to that date. I know they were written, and I feel hurt that you should intimate in your letters that it was my neglect. I have written usually every two days, and sometimes daily.

I am very glad you find some enjoyment where you are, but you do not tell me all about yourself. I want to know everything you do, and all about everything you see. You must not get *blue* to see me, nor to go home. As long as you can enjoy yourself I want you to stay & not think of going home until November, and then only to stay until January. If it was not our duty to look after our Negroes I would not let you go home until the war closed.

As you have not said anything about visiting, I suppose you will stay at Cousin William's for the present. Is there a telegraph office at South Boston so I could send a dispatch if necessary? Enquire and let me know.

I am not entirely well, but you need not be uneasy about me at all, for I am not really *sick*, but only on the *puny* list. My *full cheeks* and fat is all gone, and I am your same *old coon-jawed, hollow-eyed husband*. The summer does not suit me like the winter. For your sake I take splendid good care of myself—because I want to enjoy many years of happiness with my dearest darling when the war is over.

I believe that we shall be very happy and our life will be that smooth undisturbed current which we have so often dreamed of and hoped for. Certainly the life we have chosen is one eminently qualified to produce happiness. I confess to some anxiety to enter upon it, but perhaps that grows out of my weariness of the continuance of this war.

I wrote to Mother yesterday a long letter. I hope you have done your duty in that regard also.

No news from the enemy. Everything is held in suspense to see how "Vicksburg" is going to turn out. I am afraid the Yankees now have the advantage & will take the place. Do you see the daily papers? You must by all means get them every day.

If the Yankee cavalry get around towards South Boston you must put a gun in the "man's" hands and make him stand up to his post. Tell him he must fight for his Ma while Pa is gone. Has he quit all his meanness and bad doings Ma?

I am glad Ida is studying. Tell her I am looking for a letter from her next week.

Give my love to all. Write soon & often. Tell Nance when the war is over, I intend to turn her and Mose out to graze & kick up their heels in clover pastures.

Good bye. God bless my darlings.

Good bye.

Your Husband

Allie to Clement:

Halifax Co., Va.
May 30, 1863
(Saturday)

Dear darling

Two letters from you at last. I am so proud of them.

You say you want to make me happy and want me to be contented. I can't be either without you write to me oftener and long letters. You promised me to write every day. Didn't you ask me in one of your letters if you write too often? No indeed you don't. Please darling write every day. I will make a bargain with you. If you will promise to write to me every day I will promise not to say anything more about that surplus baggage you sent off. You know that is a good deal for me to give up. I have got you good and you are trying your best to get out of it. But you can't do it. Ida is very much insulted with President Davis because he didn't send one of his respects to her. She says she sent him [also] one of them swords. He says he went strawberry hunting this evening, papa, and eat his full. He started home with some for Mama, but eat them up before he got here. He does love them so good. You give him privilege to do as he pleases [but] you know he will do it anyhow and you can't

170

help yourself. You would like mighty well to master him, papa, but you can't. He is free himself. He sends all his sausy talk to you papa.

It is almost dark and I am straining my eyes out to see. I do want to see you so bad, and you have been sick. Were you sick much? Worse than you told me you were I expect. Did you want your darling there to wait on you. I wish she could have been. The folks here laugh at me about writing to you so often. They say I am determined you shall not forget me if writing you will do any good.

This is Saturday night. I will spend a lonely day tomorrow. It is the fifth Sunday and there is no preaching in the neighborhood. I don't know what I shall do with myself for it don't matter how many are around me I am lonely if my darling is not there. I am very sorry to hear of Sister's bad health. I have written to her twice since I have been down here. You must write to her too. She would be so glad to get a letter from you. Ida burnt her hand a little while ago and such another fuss as she is having over it. She has got her hand in a sling and seems to be almost dead. I have just called her old Mr. Motly. She says tell Pa "I study as hard as I can but I can't learn anything here with such a teacher as I have got. She hasn't got much of an opinion of him.

Do you sit in the moonlight and think about me any these nights or do you go to bed and go to sleep? I sit up and think about you till late every night. I wish we were together in our dear old home tonight. How I could enjoy a good quiet talk on the front porch. I love the old house and everything connected with it. I have spent many happy hours there as well as many very, very sad ones. I do wonder how long it will be before we will be in a home of our own again together. When we can gather our little family again and live in peace and happiness. God grant it may not be long. I am getting so tired of roaming about from place to place. But home is not home without you. I wonder if you long for us to be together as I do. I ask no greater happiness on this earth than to be allowed to spend the balance of my days with you and our dear little ones. That we may never be parted again.

Good bye. Good bye.

Your Wife

[Written in the margin and unsigned.]

Be sure you write to me every day. Please do. It is so good to get a letter every day. I can't live without them. I was almost crazy all last week because I didn't get any letter.

Clement to Allie:

In camp near Fredericksburg, Va.
May 30th, 1863—

My dear Darling

Another letter came from you to day making my heart glad, and the burden of absence lighter, enclosing also one from my little daughter which contains a very amusing account of the way her Ma is conducting herself about Pa's absence, and *Nancy* is grumbling about going back to Georgia. I am afraid you are not contented. You do not write like you enjoyed yourself and I suspect the truth is, you coop yourself up in that little office there to brood over the war and make yourslf miserable. If such is the case, Darling, you had better make a visit to Georgia—Don't you think so?

I hoped to have received accounts of your pleasant times and instead of that, your letters seem to avoid mentioning whether you are pleased or not. Do tell me fully all about yourself, your situation, your enjoyments, present & prospective, so I can form some idea of your condition.

I am sorry I did not see Cos William during his visit. With reference to the provisions for the army I have no idea that Genl. Lee said what he is reported to have said about falling back from want of provisions. An army that has been on half rations for six months, will remain on half rations still rather than fall back on that account. But ought not the people to feed such a noble, self-sacrificing, all-enduring army well? Think of six months living on a pound and three fourths of Bacon *per week* to the man. Our Negroes get twice as much. The Government is strained to its utmost to feed the army, and if the men at home do not come like patriots to the rescue, by opening their meat houses and granaries, this suffering, half-rationed army will have to fight on, suffering still, half-rationed still until the power of the Government through the late acts of congress can be exercised. The prices now allowed will make any farmer rich who will raise subsistence, sell it to the Government and invest his money in the bonds of the Government.

Everybody is regretting the controversy in the Richmond papers between General [William] Barksdale and Genl. Early about the loss and recapture of Marye's Heights.[6] Particularly among ourselves, because Barksdale has lugged Gordon's Brigade into the war of words. Barksdale has very strangely written that we retook Marye's Heights after it was evacuated.—Very strange indeed, that my Regiment should be under a hot fire, capture prisoners, wagons, horses, mules, and drive Yankees off an evacuated hill. Barksdale & his brigade was a mile and a half behind when I reached the crest of the heights, and came in to his old position behind the stonewall after I had placed two companies in it. No one censures his Brigade for being forced back when flanked or overpowered by numbers so much greater than his own. But he seems to be filled with envy because the same position was taken by a bold rapid assault next morning. Old Early is the same as ever—neither loving, lovely, or loved. I rarely hear him spoken well of.

How much I miss you while I am sick. I want some nice little eating, cooked by you, brought in by you, and

6. Barksdale became excited when he heard "a report" that Early had said Gordon's brigade had recaptured Marye's Hill on the 4th that Barksdale lost on the 3d. Barksdale's official report, dated May 15, says "It was soon discovered that Lee's and Marye's Hills had been abandoned by the enemy. General Gordon took possession of Marye's Hill without opposition" (*O.R.*, series 1, vol. 25, part 1, p. 839-41). Barksdale was in error. One of his scouts had gone to Willis Hill before Gordon reached it and found no Federal troops. Evans' account in this letter bears out the fact that Marye's Hill was occupied.

173

you sitting down by me scolding and fretting because I eat so much. It is a luxury to *have been sick*, and while convalescing to have my dear like angel wife hovering around me.

I am not yet fully well. But be quiet. I am not sick much. Only puny for the past week. I discharge all my duties except drilling. I keep quiet, diet myself, and think of you.

Give my love to all. Kiss the Emperor for his Pa. You say everybody says there is something *uncommon* about him. Pa didn't see it.

Good bye.

Your Husband

In camp near Fredericksburg, Va.
June 1st, 1863

My dear Darling

I do hope my letters have been reaching you more regularly for I have been so sorry for you, knowing what little fortitude you possess. It is strange that a woman who could brave all the perils you have in order to see & be with me, should allow herself to be distressed because three or four days pass away without bringing a letter. The mails are terribly irregular, or rather the distributing office at Richmond is wretchedly managed. Yesterday I rec'd a letter from you written on the 29th day, only two days ago—in fact not quite two days for I rec'd it about two o'clock of the 31st, and it may have been written later on the 29th. But never mind. If you hear from me twice per week be satisfied— All seem to agree that [General] Hooker is on the move, but no one appears to know his purposes. In fact he may not have any purpose more than to hunt a healthier camp. But a few more days will tell—I am almost well.— But my hearty looks are all gone and I am poor old Mr. *Cadaverous* again. I am afraid another winter will have to come before I will be presentable to your kinfolks. Will you be ashamed to own me, Darling?—I do not know what to fill this letter up with. Captain Redding has returned, but brings no news. They have plenty of wheat at home, and it is all saved. "Biscuit" is once more seen on the tables of the Georgians. The peach crop and all the fruit except apples will be abundant. Corn very small, but the rains which fell the day he left if continued will make that all right. He went to Lumpkin, but saw none of our folks. He says the 31st [Georgia] stand No. 1 in Georgia.—I have not rec'd a letter from home in over a week. I expect someone is coming, who is bringing the mail, instead of its being sent through the P. O. [post office].

It is getting so dark, Darling that I am writing at random, guessing where the lines are. My letters I know must be miserably dull to you.—How good I would feel if I could talk to you instead of writing. Every day I pass Alsop's to attend Court Martial and look at the room where we spent a happy time together. I wish you was there again. But I must stop this sort of writing, or we will be planning another trip for you to come to see me. Three months—June—July—August—the longest, dullest, hottest of the year and then we will meet.

Good bye.—Give my love to my daughter. *Bump his head for Pa.*

Good bye.
Your Husband

Allie to Clement:

Halifax Co., Va.
June 2, 1863

Dear Darling.

Another month is gone. I am glad of it. How swiftly the time would fly if I were with you. How slowly it goes when away from you. This evening I start on my visiting tour. I did not expect to go until Saturday. But Cousin William told me this morning it would be more convenient to send me to day. I wanted to write to you several days before I left so you could direct your letters to Black Walnut. You must direct your letters to Black Walnut to the care of Thomas E. Owen. Remember they have a daily mail there as well as they do here. But I don't think you ever intend to write to me often again. Yesterday I got no letter nor day before either. If you could know how anxious I felt to get a letter when the mail comes you certainly would write oftener. Write often darling so I may not be troubled about my letters while I am gone. I can't enjoy myself nor be cheerful or agreeable if I don't get letters from you. And I want to enjoy my trip. It is with you whether or not I shall. I am almost out of writing paper and it sells for twenty five cts. a sheet here. Can't you put a sheet in your letter occasionally when you write. Your paper does not cost anything, does it? If you have it to buy, I had as well buy it here, if it is no cheaper there. If you get sick, remember your promises. I shall be almost as near South Boston as I am here. Only a mile or two further. I am afraid you have not got well yet. If you get sick come here and Cousin William will send for me.

I have had no letter from home since I have been down here. If you get any, be sure to mention it. I wonder what you are doing to day. I imagine you are Gen. officer of the day and will have to ride all day. If you are I wish I could go with you. I reckon you think I am always wondering what you are doing and about you. Well I am. How can I help it when I love you so good and want to see you so bad. Papa, he can whistle. You ought to hear the little sweet mouth every time he does sweet and smart. Mama tells [him] how much papa would give to see him. Ida says give my love to Pa and tell him why don't he write to me? If he has got my letter he must write to me. We are all well. Ida is getting fat. Good bye darling. Write—write. Please sir write. Good bye good bye.

Your Wife

I don't believe you love me as good as you used to, because you don't love to write to me as well as you did. Good bye.

Clement to Allie:

Camp near Fredericksburg, Va.
June 2, 1863—"night"

My dear Darling
   I have just finished an abominable novel which made

me mad. It was *The Mother in Law* by Mrs. Southworth—rather a poor affair—but I got mad over it anyhow. A young fellow 18 years old married the girl he loves (16 years old) both immensely rich & of lofty families. A family falling out takes place between his father, a widower, and her mother—a widow. The mother steals the young chap's wife, shuts her up &c, &c, and he takes on about it like a sentimental fool instead of taking his gun in one hand and a torch in the other, and demanding a surrender of his wife under penalty of fire and sword to her captors—She, poor simpleton, submits to be humbugged by her mother & pines away, instead of cutting her way out, and rejoining her husband—what would you do under such circumstances? These novelists do not write true to nature—Gamblers, rum drinkers, and novel writers ought all to be classed together, for all three are the bane of society.

Do you believe that any person, or a dozen of them could weave up a tissue of circumstances ever so artfully as to make you discredit my love? Would anything that others say or do induce you to distrust me a moment? Yet you are the most jealously-tempered woman by nature I ever saw—But you love me—and you loved me naturally—You couldn't help it—you didn't know it, you did not cultivate it, nor discourage it—You never loved before and you have never since then doubted that I loved you, nor have I ever since our first meeting doubted that you loved me. Perfect trust, unlimited confidence, we have reposed on each other. But a novelist would take up our cases, and have us in a world of agony over each other with me in the war, and you roving about generally—Somebody would tell you something about me & somebody would whisper to me about you, & we could both turn fools & be pining away, avoiding each other &c &c instead of cowhiding the slanderers and clearing up the matter at the start. I call that nature—the novelist would have to give up his trade if he dealt in that article—Well this is a funny letter, but I am mad with the ninny which that book described.

The war news is that [General] Hooker is moving about, some say up, others down, & that the enemy are fortifying at Centreville for fear we have an idea of taking breakfast in Washington. Our army is now divided into three corps commanded by Lieut. Generals Longstreet, Ewell, and A. P. Hill;—General Lee commanding the whole. I suppose we will know more in a few days.

I want to see you bad enough—but June, July, August—and then—

No letter in two days—one tomorrow I hope. Could you send me that "surplus baggage?" [i.e., her photograph]

Tell my daughter she must try to be just like her dear Ma in everything if she wants to take her Pa's eye. Tell the "old man" to be just what he pleases. Pa don't count on him much no how.

My love to all. Good bye.

God bless you darling.

Your Husband

Camp near Fredericksburg, Va.
June 3rd, 1863

My dear Darling

Certainly it is a pleasure to me to write to you every day, and your request in the letter of June 1st just rec'd is not hard to comply with. It is the next pleasure that is. I do not ask you to offer me the bid that you will not say anything about the "surplus baggage" if I will write every day, because that is no bid at all. Remember that you need my picture always with you to keep you from forgetting me, but that is not the case with me.

When the war ends and we find our home again in peace I am resolved to remunerate myself for all this suffering—all this absence. To be with you always—to have you for my bosom friends,—my co-worker in good —my monitress to keep me from evil; to console me in sorrow—to cheer me up when desponding, to rejoice with me, to weep with me—to be my second self—all this comprehended in the one word—my dear, dear wife.— We are under orders to be ready to march at a moment's notice. I understand that the army is to move toward

Culpeper, but how true the rumor is I cannot tell. Possibly other great trials of your fortitude, your faith & your resignation are before you. A month has passed since the last battle. I supposed that we would have been engaged again before this, and we can hardly look for another month to pass without another battle. Certainly if Hooker moves up to Manassas we will engage him there very speedily. This move will interrupt the regularity of our correspondence somewhat—That is it will prevent my hearing from you, but I can continue to write to you every day by some means. My health is about restored. I am lean and gaunt, but not sick. I do not forget my promise not to risk my health—You have been my brave worthy little wife so far—Do not despond now. Be cheerful, trust in the Good Being and all will be well. We had a little rain last night, and it still looks like more will soon come. This has settled the dust, cooled off the air, and made us all feel so much better. The march will not be disagreeable. If we go near enough I shall call to see Mrs. Amos, and if we stay any length of time, with prospect of operating from Gordonsville this summer you can after a little while visit her. That would be so delightful wouldn't it?

My brass band is doing finely. I had them out on dress parade yesterday and excited a sensation. The regiment is in excellent spirits. A good state of feeling exists among men and officers, and harmony is one of the best characteristics of the command.

My new Chaplain is doing much good having entered upon his work in the right manner. The court martial still sits and I pass by Alsop's every day and look up to our room, wishing you were there again. I have been sorry ever since I left you off. If you had stayed until now our separation would have been a month shorter.

Did I write to you that Capt. J. W. Murphy[7] was going to send me a splendid pair of boots as a present? He went home a few days since. My present boots will

7. Henderson, *Roster*, vol. 3, p. 636.

last very well a month longer. I must begin to look around now for my next winter's uniform. I wonder if you could hire some one to weave me a good piece of gray. It costs two hundred dollars now to get a coat & pants in Richmond of even ordinary material, and three hundred dollars if got up in style.

I have no news to write. Do you get the Richmond news papers? We are all anxious about Vicksburg. I am afraid yet that the place will be taken—

Write soon. Give my love to my daughter. Smash that saucy mouth for talking to Pa so.

Good bye. God bless you.
Your Husband

Allie to Clement:

Black Walnut, Va.
June 4, 1863

My dear Darling.

Yesterday I received three letters from you. I don't know what can be the matter with the mail. I have not had a letter before since Saturday and this is Thursday. I am very uneasy about you darling. I know you are sick when you tell me you are. Why don't you get a furlough and come to me? I do wish you would. If you are not well yet go and try right away to get off and come to see me and let me nurse you. I can cure you. I do wish I could fix you something nice to eat. Poor darling. Do try and get off darling and come down here. If you don't and are sick you must send for me right away. Don't trust to writing. There is a telegraph office at [South] Boston. You could send me a dispatch. Perhaps it would come safe. You must live on rice altogether. Don't eat anything else while you are sick. I would give anything on earth to be with you this morning. I feel so very, very uneasy about you. Write to me just how you are darling. I am afraid you may have another spell of the typhoid fever. I look for you a little all the time. I would be so glad if you were to come. You are afraid I am not contented and don't enjoy myself. I am just as well satisfied here as I could be anywhere from you. I can't help from having the blues sometimes when it is almost a week between my letters and you sick too.

It was right lonesome at cousin Eliza's. Every day was just alike. I went nowhere nor saw anybody. But it is very different up here. The house is full of lively company all the time. They all want to know when you are coming. They are anxious to see you. I don't know how long I shall stay here about two weeks I suppose. Anyhow I shan't leave till I know you are perfectly well. The measles is here. Cousin Mary's little girl is broken out thick this morning. I hope the baby won't take it now. I keep him away from it as much as possible. I have had no letter from home yet. I think they treat me badly. I hope I will get another letter from you this evening that will relieve my mind. Now don't be fretted with me for saying I am uneasy about you. How can I help it?

He has another tooth, papa. It did not make him sick like the first one he cut. He is dressing to go up to the store to weigh. Nance is grunting again. She was up vomiting in the night last night. Don't you feel uneasy about my enjoying myself. Take care of yourself and get well. That is the best way to promote happiness now—Do you have any fruit? We have plenty of strawberries and cherries. You must not eat anything of the kind. Oh darling, I feel so much better after taking a cry. Take good care of yourself darling for my sake and let me know just exactly how you are. God bless you my love.

Your Wife.

Confederate States of America,

WAR DEPARTMENT,

Richmond, *March 13th* 186*3*

To:

You are hereby informed that the President has appointed you

Colonel

Thirty-First Georgia Regiment

In the Provisional Army in the service of the Confederate States: *to rank as such from the Thirteenth day of May one thousand eight hundred and sixty two. Should the Senate, at their next session, advice and consent thereto, you will be commissioned accordingly.*

Immediately on receipt hereof, please to communicate to this Department, through the Adjutant and Inspector General's Office, your acceptance or non-acceptance of said appointment; and with your letter of acceptance, return to the Adjutant and Inspector General the OATH, *herewith enclosed, properly filled up,* SUBSCRIBED *and* ATTESTED, *reporting at the same time your* AGE, RESIDENCE *when appointed, and the* STATE *in which you were* BORN.

Should you accept, you will report for duty to

Jas. A. Seddon

Secretary of War.

Col. C. A. Evans
31st Georgia Regt.

Through Hon. Mr. Trippe of Geo.

Chapter 12

DIARY AND LETTERS OF THE GETTYSBURG CAMPAIGN

As Colonel Evans and his wife exchanged the preceding letters, daring plans for the Army of Northern Virginia were being made. Lee decided that the best defense for the capital at Richmond would be a thrust into Pennsylvania, perhaps to Harrisburg and beyond. The first invasion of the North had been partly to encourage Maryland to join with the rest of the South. This time, Lee wanted to carry the fight to the soil of the foe so that their states could taste of the ravages of war. This move would also divert Union forces from the West, where Southern arms were suffering reverses, especially in and around Vicksburg. Thus, in early June 1863 Lee began his second invasion of the North.

Prior to this campaign, Evans seems to have jotted down nothing except his letters. But, starting June 4, 1863, he began to keep a diary of sorts. In a pocket-sized, leather-bound ledger, soiled from constant use and with scant punctuation, Evans wrote the events of this 1863 campaign which took him and his brigade farther North than any other Confederate infantry. At the same time, he augmented the details of the campaign in letters to his wife. The Thirty-first Georgia, led by Colonel Evans, was in General Gordon's brigade of Early's division of Ewell's corps, in the van of the second invasion. The first entry in the little book was made about twilight:

In camp near Hamilton's [Crossing, south of Fredericksburg] June 4th 1863—6 o'clock p.m. Tents are all down & packed. Baggage in the wagons, arms stacked & all ready to move.

June 5th. At one o'clock a.m. the march commenced

and with it the beginning to us of the summer's campaign against the enemy. Marched nearly twenty miles passing through Spotsylvania Court House.

[No entries were made for the next two days, but letters for these days give some details.]

Clement to Allie:

Camp near Fredericksburg
June 4, 1863

My dear Darling
    We certainly move to night or to morrow morning up the river. The main body of the army is already gone in that direction and I suppose we will consolidate again somewhere about Culpeper. [General] Hooker appears to fear an invasion from us, for his army has also moved to get between us and Washington. The rascals are afraid we are going to overrun Pennsylvania. That would indeed be glorious, if we could ravage that state making her desolate like Virginia. It would be a just punishment. I do not know what we are to do, but I look for nothing else but a fight before June is out. Do not be down hearted. It is not my plan to deceive you about what is going on, but to let you know all the truth trusting to your fortitude faith & resignation to the Divine will. I was riding along a few days ago thinking of the probability of another exposure of my life in battle, and was saddened to think of your anxiety about me and your grief should I be taken from you, when the assurance came upon me suddenly irresistably "your enemies have no power over you except by the will of God"—This was enough, and I know that I am invulnerable until the will of God is otherwise. No Yankee sharpshooter, however well practiced his aim, can reach my life unless my Great Preserver is willing. Therefore I trust in Him and can do my duty to my country.
    The weather is delightful and the march will not be unpleasant. My health & spirits will be improved and the "lingering hours of absence" will pass more swiftly

than they do in camp. I can ride along and think of my darling and when night comes I will raise my fly-tent, and sitting under it will dream of "wife, children, & home."

I am so sorry I did not get another letter to day as probably it will be a week now before I will hear from you again, but I will manage somehow to write to you every day. Should you fail to get a letter do not think I have neglected to write. Do not forget that "Frederick's Hall" is on the route to Gordonville and that "Nat Harris" will board you. My health is about as good as usual—my looks still *lean* and *scrawny*.

Tell my daughter to write to her Grand Ma.

Tell that great saucy boy, Pa intends to lam him on sight.

> My love to all.
> Good bye.
> God bless you my dear
> Your Husband

You had better address your letters, simply "31 Ga. Reg. Gordon's Brigade, Early's Division Ewell's Corps, *via* Richmond, Va."

> Camp on March
> June 5th, 1863
> 7 o'clock p.m.

My dearest wife

I rec'd yours of June 2nd to day and I am distressed that my letters do not reach you, because you unjustly accuse me of neglect. You never did that before. I have recently written every day & previous to that I wrote three times each week. I feel so mortified that you should believe I did not write as I promised to do. I hope my daily letters are now reaching you, and you are ready to beg me to forgive you for writing that letter of June 2nd.

This morning at one o'clock we moved from our camp near Hamilton's Crossing and have come about sixteen miles in the direction of Gordonsville, passing through Spotsylvania Court House in the route. The march was most disagreeably dusty and fatiguing. Our camp is near a branch and as soon as we halted I ordered a rest of one hour and then sent the regiment down to bathe their feet and legs—Poor fellows, we have done very little marching in six months and their feet were badly blistered. Tomorrow it will be worse. A portion of A. P. Hill's Corps still remains at Fredericksburg. What the programme is I do not know, but I will keep you posted as far as possible. I rec'd a letter from Mat—nothing new—The catalogue of prices still kept up. Says our Negroes are well & that Dan is getting work at $2.50 pr. day.

For some days my letters will be in pencil & short. Don't think now that this too is because I do not love you. You wish for the time to roll away. How can the wish be helped? There is no pleasure in being separated from you, and I think now I will never voluntarily part from you. Bless your dear heart I do love you even when you write me such an unloving letter as the one just received.

Tell Ida I have written to her.

So He can whistle. Pa will make him whistle if he gets hold of him.

Good bye. God bless & keep you for me.

Your Husband

Camp on March. June 6th, 1863
12 o'clock

My dear darling

Contrary to my expectations we have not marched today. Yesterday evening I wrote to you about our march from Fredericksburg in the direction of Gordonsville. Today the report is that the enemy crossed the Rappahannock at Fredericksburg and we are halted to await the turn of affairs. I have heard occasional cannon firing in the direction of Fredericksburg. We have sufficient force there for all our present purposes. I am really glad of this halt because the troops were excessively fatigued & sore from the march yesterday.

186

To day my camp has been honored by two visits of separate bevys of Ladies. Don't be jealous—they did not come to see me—Indeed I was not any part of the attraction—but my *brass band* was the cause of the honor. I looked at them and wished—wished that you were one of the party—that is all. I cannot tell whether we go back, go on, or stay here. We are convenient to help either Longstreet or A. P. Hill. You must not be unhappy about the present prospects of another battle. All will be well. If I send a dispatch to you or Mr. Fourquesen, it will get to you without delay. I hope my daily letters will reach you, since you no longer attribute your failure to receive them to the mails, but to my neglect. I did not think you would ever write me such a letter as the one I rec'd yesterday—I shall not forgive you easily for it.

My health, appetite &c is improving. I feel a hundred per cent better to day than I did the day before we started. The prospect of a fight always cures me. You had rather I would select such occasions to be sick would you not?

I want the fighting to begin, to keep on, until it is ended. I hope that all of the fighting of the war will come off this summer, and let the war end. Our success in the end is so absolutely certain that we can afford to crowd a dozen campaigns in one year.

The old confidence in Jackson, has found a new birth in our faith in Ewell. Always a favorite with his division, he is now the idol of his corps. Our army is now splendidly organized—Better than ever before & though fewer in real numbers than Hooker's army still the spirit of the men and the skill of our officers, with the justice of our cause sanctioned by the approval of the Great Being will render us invincible. We shall march to victory when we march toward the enemy: Good bye. God bless you.

Your Husband

[written in margin] June 7—On way to Orange Court House.

Raccoon Ford
12 o'clock M-
June 7, 1863

My dear Allie

Instead of continuing the direct route to Orange Court House we turned aside this morning and have just crossed the Rapidan River at Raccoon Ford. The morning has been delightful. Yesterday evening a heavy rain fell, laying the dust and cooling the air very much to our comfort. The troops waded the river after the Confederate style, pontoons being a Yankee contrivance. I suppose we will go toward Culpeper Court House which is ten miles distant. The country we are now passing through is much better than that part of Virginia seen by you between Richmond & Fredericksburg. The farms are in better condition also, because the army has not encamped upon them. Our horses find good pasturage, very needful too, as we only get five pounds of corn **per** day for them. My own health improves every day. Perhaps I shall fatten again.

8 o'clock p.m. We were camped near Culpeper Court House, & have orders to move at sunrise to morrow. The Stewart Grays are about a mile & a half off but I haven't gone to see them. I have seen no newspaper in two days and am in the dark as to what is going on. I do not even know our own movements. I understand that we have possession of Warrenton and that the enemy are concentrating about Centreville. They are moving up one side of the river as we move up the other.

I do hope my recent letters will reach you. I am afraid however that some of them will fail and you will be scolding me unjustly again. I have not got over that *June 2nd* letter yet. Do you remember what you did write? You will be so sorry when I show you the letter some day.

We are camped in sight of Cedar Mountain where the fight was made last . . . [August]. The country is beautiful about here.

I am improving every day.
Good bye and God bless you.

188

My love to my children.
Your Husband

[Evans entered in the diary for the enusuing days:]

June 8. Passed through Culpeper Court House & camped two miles beyond the town.

June 9th. Battle [Brandy Station] between the Cavalry of Genl. Pleasonton of the Yankee army, and Genl. Stuart.

About three o'clock p.m. we were moved in quick time to . . . [Brandy] Station to support Genl. Stuart. The enemy had retired however before we reached there—camped in the fields.

June 10th. Marched to the Front Royal Road & then to the same camp we had left the evening before.

About three o'clock p.m. marched again toward Sperryville. Marched five miles.

June 11. Marched through Sperryville & [Little] Washington camping about three miles beyond Washington.

June 12. Passed the cross roads & turned to the left to cross the mountains toward Front Royal.

About 8 o'clock p.m. marched through Front Royal & on the Shenandoah.

June 13. At sunrise forded the Shenandoah, although our pontoon train lay on the banks. Pontoons are Yankee ideas—Confederates wade rivers—

About one o'clock p.m. formed first line of Battle four or five miles from Winchester.

3 o'clock p.m. moved by the left flank to a new position nearer the enemy and in an hour were charging them through woods & fields.

Yankees acted cowardly.

—Receiving orders from Genl. Gordon to exercise my discretion in protecting the flank of the Brigade I moved the regiment about two hundred yards to the right of the Brigade to resist a threatened attack of cavalry & infantry from that direction.

As soon as I placed the regiment in position the enemy retired from our right & massed their forces against the left flank of the division—My loss only one killed & 8 wounded—

Night coming on with a very hard & continued rain ended the struggle for the day. During the night I necessarily did heavy picket duty since I had my own front & flank to protect.

[The Union troops encountered were under Maj. Gen. Robert H. Milroy and were strongly ensconced at a well-fortified position called Main Fort. On the day following the above action, little took place.]

June 14. Morning opened with a stray picket shot or two. I advanced my skirmishers and took possession of the positions before me, and soon afterwards advanced my line about two hundred yards—

Remained in line today—Principal fighting between artillery.

At Winchester June 15, 1863. At daylight moved with two other regiments to the Romney road & took position to join in the assault upon [Main Fort], the orders being to storm all the positions of the enemy.

But just at this time we observed the flag no longer *waved* over the fort & moving rapidly forward we pressed by the Fort on to the Martinsburg road in pursuit of the enemy.

The victory was completed. Everything belonging to the enemy fell into our hands except portions of his Cavalry & Infantry. 3000 prisoners—with artillery, small arms, ordnances, quartermaster & commissary stores abundant.

—My regiment deployed as skirmishers covering the Brigade—The enemy however had too much the start and we halted in camp about five miles from Winchester.

[So hasty had been the retreat of General Milroy's forces that a beautiful, solid-black horse, that reputedly belonged to him, was captured and turned over to General Gordon. The beast was promptly named "Milroy," but proved to be such a coward in battle that he was of no use to the general.]

[Letters for these days implemented the brief diary entries.]

Clement to Allie:

Near Culpeper Court House
Culpeper county, Virginia
Monday, June 8th, 1863
4 o'clock p.m.

My dear Darling—

We have rested here to day after a pleasant march of five miles, and I learn we are to move to morrow at sunrise, in the direction of Rappahannock county. If you will take a map of Virginia, you can trace our route up the Rappahannock river to the Rapidan river, passing through Spotsylvania Court House and Verdiersville and up the Rapidan to Raccoon Ford where we forded the stream and from thence through Culpeper. From this place the railroad which runs from Gordonsville passes on to Alexandria, but on our side I think the cars run no farther than this place. And the public road runs on to Warrenton where Lieut. Wm. Richardson died, and another runs through Rappahannock county crossing the Blue Ridge mountains at Front Royal. This latter road is the one I am informed, we shall travel to morrow. But we may continue that route only for ten or fifteen miles, and then turn to the right toward Warrenton. A portion of Ewell's corps have already passed on. Longstreet's Corps is encamped around us here and perhaps will not move immediately. If we have been completely successful at Vicksburg our present aggressive attitude will be very alarming to the Yankees, and will unsettle Joe Hooker's nerves.

We shall probably pass very near the residence of Dr. Amiss. Don't you wish now you had gone there instead of going below Richmond? I could have seen you as we passed and you would have been comparatively close to me. Well we may hold this country all the summer; and if so your promised visit can be paid yet. Dr. Amiss has gone to see his family. I understand that the mail facilities are very bad beyond this point and I fear my letters cannot be regular, but I will do my best

191

to get you a letter off somehow every day. You must direct your letters to Culpeper Court House for the present. Do not despond. All will be well. Kiss Pa's little darlins for him. Tell he to grow fast and be a big boy by the time Pa sees him again. Tell my Daughter to make herself a perfect little lady. I write on one sheet, so you can answer on the other.

You must think about me Darling, and love me like I love you. You do not know how much I do love you nor how anxious I am to see you. I am afraid to write about my anxiety to see you because it makes me still more anxious and I know it creates a greater anxiety in you. But never mind we will see each other again under happier circumstances and a whole life time of love will be ours.

Good bye. God bless you my darling.

Your Husband

Addressed to:

Mrs. Allie Evans
c/o Mr. Thos. E. Owens
Black Walnut
Halifax Co.
Virginia

Camp near Culpeper C. H.
June 8th, 1863

My dear Darling

We passed through Culpeper Court House this morning about 8 o'clock a.m. Like all the Virginia towns in this section it is built on Rocky uneven ground and can make no claim to beauty. Many of the houses appear old, and the town wears a desolate appearance. Much of this of course is attributable to the war. I met up with the Stewart Grays on the route, and had a general shake hands all round. Capt. Newell is with them and looks rather used up. Lieut. Rockwell also. They have had a hard winter, marching with but little rest. I have no news from the enemy. I suppose they move on the other side of the Rappahannock so as to confront us. I do not know whether we are to fight or not, the probability is however that a battle will take place at no distant day. You must not take on, and be uneasy. All will go well.

I am writing hurriedly so as to send this off to day. I will write again to night. We move again to morrow. Write to me to Culpeper C.H. Good bye. My love to the darlings.　　　Good bye.

Your Husband

Culpeper C. H., Va.
Friday morning, June 9 [18]63

My dear darling

Orders to move at sunrise are not always followed by an actual march. Therefore we are still here making ourselves comfortable. Heavy artillery firing is heard south east of us on the Rappahannock and my surmise is that the enemy are shelling the woods opposite Kelly's ford to see what we are up to. They have quite a number of pieces of artillery planted at that ford, and in fact at every passable point along the Rappahannock where they have possession. Evidently they fear that we are about to get after them on the old ground of our victories. If we do, then "farewell to all your greatness, Joe Hooker." The "Finest army on the planet" will turn comet with its tail this way—I am going over to visit the Stewart Grays—I promised them to do so. I saw Dr. Palmer also yesterday.

You must get hold of a map of Virginia and familiarize yourself with the country. You will see that you can get here by way of Lynchburg to Charlottesville & Gordonsville as well as by way of Richmond. And if we go up to the valley you can get to Staunton by way of Lynchburg. I suppose you would prefer avoiding Richmond in your route. I am anxious for you to travel from Lynchburg to Staunton and I hope we will stay up in this region during the summer so you can have the opportunity. If you can get a history & geography of Virginia I would like for you to read it pretty closely so as to acquaint yourself with the location of places & their history. Tell Ida all she wants to know about Virginia. She will come with you also, but you can leave that big man behind for his meanness. Pa thinks it is time to wean him anyhow. I am writing every day to you, and I do hope my letters will reach you.

Good bye. God bless my sweet wife & dear little babies. Good bye.

Your Husband

7 o'clock P.M. There has been considerable cavalry fighting on the Rappahannock to day. The infantry was also crossed over by the Yankees, and we have moved up the line of the railroad and are now not far from Brandy Station. If there is a battle you will hear of it in the papers before this reaches you. I cannot give now any certain opinion what to morrow may bring forth, but my trust is in the Good Being who orders all things aright. My health is very good & the fatigue is not hurting me at all. But how much would I not give to snatch a hasty kiss before going into battle as I did before the last battle. But God bless my sweet little wife, it is a great consolation to me that she is not now suffering on my account as she did at the last battle.

Good bye. I will write at every opportunity. Good bye. Kiss in imagination—Good bye.

Your Husband

[In margin of letter]

There is writing paper in the trunk which I sent you.

Near [Little] Washington, Rappahannock Co., Va.
6 o'clock P.M. June 11, 1863

My dearest darling

I can well imagine your uneasiness at the rumors of our movements, and my own letters reach you. I wrote to you hastily a few lines from Sperryville to day just to let you know where I was at a certain date and I write for the same purpose now. For in truth the intentions of Genl. Lee are known to but few. From this point we can turn to the left, cross the mountains at Chester Gap by Front Royal on to Winchester and down the Valley; or we can turn to the right and march toward Manassas, to drive Hooker back toward Washington. The probabilities of either course being taken are so nearly equal that I cannot prophesy which will be the route taken. I said in a letter written a day or two since that I seriously doubted whether we would invade the North, but I begin to be somewhat shaken in that opinion. Our army is so well organized, disciplined, armed, and enthusiastic, enjoys such remarkable health & is encumbered with so little baggage, that it is a splendid instrument in the hands of such skillful generals as we have to punish the invasion of our country by a counter invasion.

Remember that Mrs. Dr. Amiss lives at Sperryville & that a regular stage coach runs that far from Culpeper Court House. I am so sorry now that you did not come to Sperryville. It is a beautiful little—very little—village right in the midst of the mountains and the people seem to have plenty of everything. You would enjoy a month or two there so much. After a little I will make arrangements for you to come, if we continue up here which is very probable. From Sperryville the only chance to get farther would be by the great uncertainty of private vehicles. I see that an accommodation train runs on the *Central Rail Road* from Richmond by Gordonsville to Charlottesville. You can see the time of running in the advertisement in the papers. This would probably be a better route than by way of Lynchburg. If anything occurs or I get sick I will send Cpt. Orr, or Mose immediately after you. Keep in good heart my Darling. These trials will soon end, and we shall love each other all the better for our separation & sufferings.

Punch out them teeth, Ma. He has no business with them. Tell Ida Pa wants to see her very much.

Good bye. God bless you.

Your husband

I read a letter from you today written the 4th from Black Walnut. Give my respects to our kinfolks & tell them I shall come to see all of them.

Camp five miles north of
Winchester, Va.
Monday June 15, 1863

My dear Darling
I have been trying all day to get a dispatch to you by

telegraph but so far have failed completely. I shall still continue to try, for I know the Richmond papers have contained the news of our attack upon Winchester and you are very uneasy I know. This letter will record another victory in which I have participated, and another occasion of great Thankfulness to the Good Being who has so wonderfully preserved me. You will read the whole account in the newspapers. The battle or attack was not a severe one, our loss being small. The enemy attempted a retreat this morning before daylight having found our weakest point and succeeded in effecting a partial escape. But our capture of prisoners and stores, Horses, wagons, Artillery &c &c was very complete. We pursued after them and found the streets of Winchester and the road leading toward Martinsburg & Charles Town crowded with every considerable species of plunder. We were advanced so rapidly that we had but little opportunity to obtain any Yankee Goods. However the men would dash into the wagons & Knapsacks as they went along and grab the first thing they saw—As usual our troops are feasting over the Yankee eatibles, wearing Yankee shoes, boots, hats, and pants, and underclothing. I have but few Yankee trophies and they were given to me by the men. I have a *Yankee woman's ambrotype* to look at. Do you feel jealous—some more Yankee pictures and I would have saved you some letters, but the few which I have read are very uninteresting. Several Yankee Ladies who were staying with their husbands were captured. Genl. Milroy & his family escaped.

Four men of the Stewart Guards were wounded but you do not know any of them.

I have supplied myself with a new pair of good boots and am therefore all right again. The men brought me about four dozen cigars, paper, envelopes, dried fruit, jam, preserves &c. I wish you could have followed us on and been there to witness the effects of our rout of the enemy. I do hope I will get a chance to send you this letter. Good bye. Good bye. God bless you.

Your Husband

June 15, 9 o'clock a.m.
We move this morning but I do not know where.

[The events at Winchester had one bit of relief from the serious side. Among Evans' papers is this anecdote about the confirmed bachelor, General Early.]

Winchester had been heavily garrisoned by the Federals and General Milroy was in charge of the forces there. Early spread out his regiments and they advanced in line of battle with cheers and enthusiasm expecting every minute to meet the enemy in force. Soon couriers and scouts came announcing that Milroy had entirely withdrawn his forces and was not preparing to offer any resistance to the advancing Confederates.

General Early discontinued the advance of his infantry and artillery and sent only his cavalry in pursuit of the flying Yankees. He then rode back into the town of Winchester accompanied by his staff and other officers of his command.

Winchester was an old-fashioned town with a square in the centre, but, contrary to most towns of that time, it had no building or structure in the centre of this square; it was an open plaza. Into this the Confederate party rode. The women, young and old, of the little city had come out from their homes to greet and welcome the boys in gray and to rejoice in their occupancy of the town instead of the much dreaded, much hated Yankees.

With handkerchiefs waving and with a buzz and a chatter, as only women can make, they crowded the streets and gathered around the Confederate party in the square. Two of the fairest of the young ladies were appointed as a committee by the hundreds of others to wait upon General Early and they approached him with handkerchiefs waving and calling as they drew near.

"Address us, General. General Early, address us."

It was too much for the bluff old veteran of many battles. Drawing himself up in the stirrups he replied in his brisk, brusk manner:

197

"I have never had the courage to address one lady and and I cannot now face hundreds of them!"

[By the time Winchester was taken, some of Allie's letters of the same days had reached Clement.]

Halifax Co., Virginia
June 6, 1863

Dear Darling

My letters are coming right at last and I feel like another being. In your last letter you said nothing at all about being sick and of course I infer from that you are well. I hope you are anyway. I have been very uneasy about you. If you are not well you must try to get a furlough and come to see me. I am having quite a lively time of it now! Enjoying myself finely all but you not here. But your dear letters come every day and that is next to seeing you. The papers report both armies moving. I wonder where you are going. I hope you will move back this way. I don't want you to get any farther than you are—It has been raining for two days and nights but this morning it is clear and pleasant. I went to see a cousin of mine yesterday evening Mrs. Owen—Cornelia Williams she was. She was very glad to see me and gave me a very pressing invitation to come and stay with her some.

He has got another tooth, papa. Mama weighed him yesterday. He weighs twenty-five pounds. Don't you know he was a man, papa? He is. Everybody notices and loves him so much. It is almost impossible to make Ida study while I am visiting around.

What do you think I have to pay for Nance a common homespun dress? Three dollars a yard. It hurts mighty hard but there is no help for it. She is obliged to have some dresses. She is not decent now. I have at last had a letter from home. I send it for you to read. I wish Sister would write. I have written to her twice. I hope her health is better. I have made me a new fashion headdress and I think it quite becoming. Wish you could see me with it on as you know you are the only person I care to look well before. You must continue to

198

write often, darling. I feel so much better since my letters come every day and only two or three days after they are written.

I shall answer Clem's letter to day. Good bye. Bless your dear heart I wish you were here. Good bye. Good bye.

Your Wife

Black Walnut, Halifax Co., Va.
June 11, 1863

My dear darling

Yesterday evening I rec'd a letter from you and sure enough you are moving. I had hoped to the last that you would stay where you were and not move. I feel just like you were leaving me again, and that you are a great deal further off than you were when you were at Fredericksburg. I hope you will not try to invade the enemy's country. Then you will be far off. You say I wrote you a very unloving letter last week and that you never expected to get such a one from me. Now darling I don't have any recollection of writing any such letter as that. All I remember saying is that you didn't love me as well as you used to because you did not write to me as often. Well darling you know yourself that you used to write to me every day and that you had not been writing but three times a week then. If I said anything wrong in the letter of course I am ready to make amends, ask pardon or do anything else. I hope your health has continued to improve while you are marching. If you get sick come back right away. I dreamed about you last night and you were sick. I hope my dream will not come to pass. We are all well except Ida and she is not so very sick but ailing a little. She has a dreadful bad cough and threatened with croup. I gave her hive syrup all last night but she is very tight in her chest and hoarse this morning. I think she will be better soon. If she is not I will give her a good emetic and that I know will relieve her. He is well, papa, and says he whistled louder than ever when mama read he what you said in your letter about him. He said he ain't fraid of you one bit papa.

199

You need not try to scare he for you can't do it—You want to know what county Black Walnut is in. It is in Halifax only a few miles from South Boston. I don't know how much longer I will stay here. About a week I expect. I shall go from here to Joe Painter's in [North] Carolina. I don't know his post office but will write to you about it in my next letter. It is about eight miles from here. I am still having a good time and enjoying myself as much as I could anywhere away from you. It is almost the middle of June and soon the three months of our absence will be gone and we will meet again. Already one month has passed but it has been a very long month.

Good bye darling. Good bye.

Your Wife

Black Walnut, Halifax Co., Va.
Monday, June 14, 1863

My dear darling—

What shall I write to you about this morning? I live over the same thing every day with very little change. I don't see nor hear anything to write about. I have written home this morning. A good long letter to Clem. Don't you wish we were in our dear old home together this morning? I would give all of my earthly possessions to be with you and to know we did not have to part again. I do not live away from you. It is my greatest happiness to be with you. When will that happy, happy day come I do wonder. Your little man is sick, papa. Not much though. He is cutting two upper teeth. I think that is making him sick. Ida is well except a very bad cough. I bought her a nice little reading book this morning which she is very proud of. I reckon she won't be quite so proud of it when I get her down by me reading it. She will wish it back at the store before she is done with it. I am so anxious for you to stop near Mrs. Amiss' so I can come up to see you. I have built up a good many hopes on that but fear I am doomed to be disappointed.

I wrote to you a day or so ago to direct your letter to Cunningham store, Person Co., N. C. to the care of

Joe Painter. I thought I had better write it again for fear you would not get the other letter. Yesterday was Sunday and there was no church to go to so I spent the day in sleeping. It was a long day although I was asleep half the day. Are you having any cherries? We are having any quantity of the nicest kind. I wish you had some of the nice raspberries we are having now, too. I wonder if you ever have any vegetables. We are having Irish potatoes, beets, and peas. I believe these are the only vegetables we have had yet.

He has lost his appetite, papa. He don't eat anything like he is the largest baby you ever saw and the finest looking. I hope to get a letter this evening from you. Your letters are coming very regularly now everyday. It takes them about three days to reach me.

Good bye.   Good bye.

Your Wife

Clement to Allie:

Near Winchester, Va.
Tuesday, June 16, [18]63
10 o'clock A.M.

My dear Darling

I received a precious letter from you to day. The first for several days. I am so sorry you do not get my letters regularly when I write, and now the opportunities for writing are so few that all your patience will be required. I wrote you yesterday about the battle of Winchester. The full account you will get in the newspapers. My loss was small. None killed in Harrison's company.

I am surprised that you have been told that your money is not good. It is as good as any, and is still fundable at 7 per cent in bonds until August. After that time it is not fundable. I calculated that you would spend it before that time. I will send you more money as soon as possible. I paid out $300 for my horse, but I can send you two hundred dollars by someone. Let me know fully how much you have. How long it will last you &c.

Your board need not be paid until I send you more funds. I suppose you have two or three hundred dollars still.

We move at twelve o'clock to day toward Charles Town, I understand. Mrs. Amiss sent word to send after you and bring you to her house. She lives you know at Sperryville & a stage runs from Culpeper there.

You must not be uneasy about me. Trusting in the Good Being we will abide His will whatever it may be.

We must begin the education of our daughter in earnest. I am not sorry that she is now traveling about so as to lay the foundation for good health but we must not neglect her mind. I want that cultivated as highly as possible but not at the expense of either her heart or her health.

So my little man has joined the cavalry and is learning to ride. He must have a sabre & pistols, Ma.

I wish you were in Winchester to see the sight. The Yankees as usual had everything to make them comfortable. Our captures were very considerable although they burned as much as they could.

I will still write & keep a letter always ready. I shall send this to Black Walnut & with another to South Boston for fear you have returned.

I know you are so uneasy & yet I cannot get the chance to send you a dispatch.

Good bye & God bless my dear darling.

Your Husband

Tell Ida to name her little waiting maid whatever she pleases. It shall be hers.

Near Winchester, Va.
Tuesday, June 16, [18]63
10 o'clock a.m.

My dear Wife

We leave here at 12 o'clock in the direction of Charles Town. I have written one letter to Black Walnut, but learning you have gone back to South Boston I will write there also.

You have read about the battle of Winchester. Poor

202

darling you are so uneasy to day, and I am safe and well and you do not know it. I have no chance to send you a dispatch & do not even know whether this letter will go. But darling you must have a trusting patience. Resign your self fully to the will of God as to myself. Whatever may happen you must feel that it is right because it is the Divine will.

I am not a fatalist or predestinarian by any means, but I have so fully & unreservedly committed myself to my Maker that I fear no harm until it is His Will, and then it will be for the best.

At the last fire I received so many shots & so close that my regimental officers once all begged me to dismount from my horse, yet not one touched me even in my clothing. All this my darling was from God.

I am enjoying excellent health and spirits. The only drawback to my pleasure is absence from Home & you. But when the war is over I still promise myself full enjoyment of both.

I write short letters because I write often and hurriedly. On the march or in camp my time is fully taken up, my mind is engrossed and I cannot write.

Good bye my darling, kiss my little babies.

Good bye.

Your Husband

[The next several days of events are in the diary.]

June 16th—Marched toward Martinsburg.

June 17th—Wednesday—Marched ten miles—passed through Martinsburg & camped at splendid spring near a little village.

June 18—Remained in same camp all day—Preaching at 4 o'clock p.m. by Rev. Wm. Lacy—formerly Gen'l Jackson's chaplain.

June 19th at 6½ o'clock a.m. marched toward Shepherdstown. Passed through about 6 o'clock & marched along the Potomac to the ford where we remained until sunset. Went into camp near the ford to remain for the night—

June 20th Saturday—Very heavy rain last night. Potomac swollen very much.

Yesterday it was easily fordable not reaching to the hips. This morning it will reach the waists of the men. The air is much cooler.

An issue of captured sugar, coffee, dried apples, soap, cigars, tobacco &c was made this morning.

Heavy rain at 2 o'clock p.m. Potomac rising—clouds still heaving indicating more rain.

June 21st Sunday—Still in camp at Shepherdstown ford on Banks of Potomac. Clouds lowering—Potomac considerably swollen.

June 22. With two days rations in Haversacks & five days in wagons, we crossed the Potomac just after sunrise by wading.

The cutting of the canal & recent rains had deepened the waters, so that up to the waist & sometimes to the armpits the soldiers struggled through. As soon as the regiments were re-formed on the Maryland shore the line of March was resumed in the direction of Sharpsburg. We soon came in sight of the great battle ground along the Antietam river or creek, fought nine months ago.

The citizens of this county (Washington) are thoroughly Union & we met with not a single sign of encouragement until we reached Boonsboro. Here the feeling is better and many expressed their hearty wishes for our success against the detested tyranny of the Yankees. Marching through Boonsboro on the Hagerstown road, about two miles, we are encamped.

June 23rd—Tuesday—Entered Pennsylvania—marching from Boonsboro to Waynesboro. Find the citizens uneasy at our approach, looking as if they scarcely knew how to conduct themselves.

Clement to Allie:

> Darkesville, Va.
> Wednesday, June 17, [18]63
> 6 o'clock.

Dear Darling

The postmaster for the Brigade has just informed me

that he is going back with a mail in a few minutes, & I write hurriedly to tell you I am well. Before this reaches you we will probably be in Maryland or Pennsylvania provided Genl. Lee has been as successful in managing [General] Hooker as we have in taking care of Milroy.

We left our camp yesterday about twelve o'clock, and marched through Bunker Hill & Darkesville toward Martinsburg which is about six miles from here. We move in half an hour & will probably encamp near Martinsburg or a few miles beyond there. I want to urge you not to be uneasy about me, for if a fight comes off & I am hurt either Capt. Orr, or Mose or someone will start for you at once on a fleet horse toward Culpeper & from there will telegraph to you to meet them in Richmond. It will take only two days ride to Culpeper, so in two days if I am hurt you shall hear from me. Now when you read of a fight and *three* days have passed since the battle don't be at all uneasy because that will assure you I am safe. I shall be sure to attend to this.

Your money is perfectly good. You can exchange it in Richmond for the new issue if you desire. I will send you more as soon as I can. How much do you need?

I believe the spirit of adventure is rising in our troops. In fact I feel its influence very considerable and *but for you* I should enjoy an invasion very much.

It takes me by surprise but I am prepared for it. My health is good. I put on a *clean white Yankee shirt & clean collar* yesterday and caught quite a cold in consequence of my *daring*.

My letters now are so hurriedly written that I can give you no account of what we do. The country is all delightful. We get butter & milk abundant and are living like princes. I do wish so much that you could travel along with me. If we take Baltimore I shall send for you at once.

How is my little "cavalry officer?" Pa must send him a commission. I do so much wish you and Ida were with me this morning. What a delightful trip with a good carriage and horses.

The people about here are nearly all Unionist. We

received however many cheers in Darkesville, but saw scores of sour Tory faces.

Good bye. Write to me at least once or twice a week. The mail will be very irregular or I would want you to write every day.

Remember I shall send at once if I get hurt & if I can I will meet you at Sperryville.

Good bye. May the blessing of Heaven be given to my precious wife and babies. Good bye.

Your Husband

In camp five miles north of Martinsburg, Va.
Wednesday eveng., June 17, [18]63

My dearest Darling

You will see we are still moving toward the Potomac. Tonight we are camped in a nice grove near a large spring which is two feet deep, ten feet wide, and twenty feet long. The water is excellent and after a hot & dusty march of ten miles such water is a luxury. We move again at 6 o'clock tomorrow morning but I do not know the course. I suppose however we will go either toward Williamsport or Shepherdstown. I expect a regular mail line will now be established to Winchester & I hope to be able to send you a letter often. I write nearly every day & sometimes two a day to send different ways. I am enjoying myself just as well as it is possible for me to do, absent from you. This kind of life suits my health very well. Please do not be uneasy about me. If you hear of a battle and three days have passed do not be uneasy, for if anything happens to me someone will go at once at good speed to the nearest telegraph office to notify you. If wounded I will meet you at Sperryville or Staunton. Please do not be uneasy. I do so much wish you were with me. How much you would enjoy this trip, especially if we go over to Maryland.

The people generally about here look sour at us, but many seem overjoyed at our possession of the Valley again.

It is very dry and dusty. The wheat, clover & grasses

do not look so well as in the country just beyond the mountains.

I am glad my daughter is looking so well and that *He* is such a man. I know I shall be proud of my daughter when she grows to be a young lady.

I look forward to an early meeting yet. I do trust that we are now closing up the war. This campaign I hope will be the last. Good bye. God bless you my dearest darling. Kiss the babies.

Your Husband

In camp five miles north of Martinsburg [Va.]
Thursday, June 18, 1863

My dear Darling

We did not move this morning as I expected, and as I wrote in yesterday's letter. We are waiting I suppose for other portions of the army, or indeed an actual invasion may not be on foot. It is said that our cavalry is in Maryland now. It is only about seven miles to Williamsport from here and we can easily move there to night & cross at daylight to morrow. After all if the invasion is properly conducted it will lead to very important results. We have no news here from Vicksburg later than that contained in the Richmond papers of the 13th. Nor do we know what disposition Gen. Lee is making or Hooker. The troops appear to be in excellent spirits and I believe are anxious to cross into the enemy's country. The spirit of adventure runs very high among Southern soldiers.

We get plenty of good milk & butter sometimes for nothing & generally very cheap. One of the greatest inconveniences to me is the absence of your letters. I have received three since June 4th, but may not get another letter in some time.

June 19th. 6 o'clock a.m. We move to day. I have had no chance for two days to send you a letter & now I am hurried. Good bye—Good bye.

Your Husband

Allie to Clement:

Black Walnut, Halifax Co., Va.
Saturday, June 18, 1863

My dear darling

Yesterday evening I got another letter from you telling me about your march. I should like so much to know which way you went, where you are. The papers give no information whatever about it. Every time the mail comes in I expect news of a battle. I hope it will be a long time though before the next battle is fought. I always want to put off the evil day as long as possible. I wish they would put it off until I come to pay Mrs. Amiss that promised visit. If you stay up there long I am coming sure enough, darling. It would be so pleasant wouldn't it to spend the summer up in the mountains and to be near you too? But I am afraid it will be like it was last summer. You won't stay in one place long enough for me to get to you if I were to start. Last night I thought of my poor darling when I went to bed. I knew that he was so tired and had to lie down on the hard ground to sleep—and I don't expect you had anything for supper but old bacon and hard crackers. Poor darling I am so sorry for you.

Mr. Owens says you must come and make them a visit. That he would be very glad to see you. Indeed they all have a great curiosity to see you. I reckon it is because I talk about you so much, for you know that out of the abundance of the heart the mouth speaketh and surely my heart is filled with you. Ida has been threatened with pneumonia but the danger is all past now. Her cough is very loose and she expectorates freely. There is some very good sulphur springs about a mile from here. We walk there right often in the evening and drink the water. If it was not quite so far I would go every evening. I think it would be very beneficial to us all. Yesterday evening I brought home a bottle full of the water for Ida.

He says he is growing just as fast as he can papa—eats all he can and he will be a grown man when you see him. You must direct your next letter to Cunningham's store Person Co., North C[arolina]—To the care of Joe Painter. I shall go up there next week. I will write to him to send for

208

me. He sent me word to do it. If you get sick or anything happens send a dispatch to [South] Boston, [Va.] to Cousin William he will send it to me.

Good bye.—Good bye.

Your Wife

Clement to Allie:

Shepherdstown Ford, Va.
Saturday, June 20, 1863

My dearest Darling

Almost hopeless of a chance to send this off yet I will write just for the pleasure it affords myself, and to be ready for any opportunity to communicate with you.

Yesterday we marched to this ford which is a mile below Shepherdstown, passing through that little town where we were received with many demonstrations of joy by the citizens. The girls are pretty and dressed in their best raiment, with smiling faces greeted us, waving Confederate flags, and throwing bouquets to our awkward & dusty soldiers. The Unionists had nearly all left before our approach for fear that we would treat them as Milroy's brutal soldiers had treated the true Virginians. But they could have remained in safety, for our troops are as gentlemanly as they are brave. Not one Unionist has been insulted nor a particle of their property destroyed by our men. We expected to ford the Potomac yesterday & for that purpose were drawn up along the shore, but [the opportunity] to cross did not come and we are still encamped on the Virginia side. A part of our troops have crossed and the cavalry is all ready making a pretty extensive circuit. Other portions of the army are coming on. Everything is favorable to the success of our enterprise. The rain fell in torrents last night & the Potomac is much swollen, but it can still be forded. The clouds are still black & we shall have more rain today.

Sunday morning June 21st—I still write a little every day, but how slight is the possibility of sending this off. It rained again last evening and the clouds still lower and threaten. The Potomac is swollen & could be forded only with great difficulty. We are still lying in camp near Shepherdstown on the river shore. Perhaps the rains have caused this delay or perhaps Longstreet & A. P. Hill have not reached their position. I hear no news. From the papers you will get information much sooner than from my letters. Just as I write, a volley of musketry is heard in the direction of Harpers Ferry which is only seven miles distant, but as there is no artillery firing, nor any continuance of the musketry, I think that it is only a discharge of loaded arms for the purpose of cleaning up.

Yesterday the troops received coffee, sugar, soap, dried apples &c which had been captured at Winchester. I forgot to mention *cigars* and tobacco also. Milroy proves to be a good commissary & quartermaster & ordnance officer for Ewell. Think of our Confederate soldiers smoking cigars, drinking pure coffee with sugar in it too.

The *Band* serenaded Shepherdstown last night & had a fine time. I did not go with them.

I do wish so much that you was with me to day.

Good bye.

Your Husband

Near Waynesboro, Pennsylvania
Tuesday, June 23rd, 1863

My dearest Darling.

It will seem to you that I am gone for good when you receive this letter, perhaps ten days after it is written & find it dated & sent from Pennsylvania. I did not know when we commenced marching that Genl. Lee intended to send us back in the Union, but here we are all in the Union again.

I wrote to you from Shepherdstown on the 21st. On the morning of the 22nd at sunrise we waded the Potomac. The water was deep coming up to the waist & breasts of the men, but they passed over cheerfully, even joyously. This placed us in "Maryland My Maryland" and we marched through to Sharpsburg passing the famous battle ground. We met scarcely any but Unionists at the beginning of the march but after a while the way brightened and since then even until now in Pennsylvania we meet with warm sympathizers. Our army has done no wanton damage. The discipline is strict and order is preserved.

You will be glad to learn that I do not think the Maryland & Pennsylvania women at all pretty. The specimens seen by me on the route are rather coarse in appearance & manners. A certain free & easy air rather surprises those of us accustomed to the gentle modesty of Southern girls. One of them told us to give "the devil to the Yankees." All of them stood along the road side or sat in groups on logs or fences and either cheered us on, or made sport of us in a bold & coarse way.

Maryland is full of stout men *fit for war*. They have a happy time. Lincoln does not draft them, and they do not feel the war. All have been lately enrolled & about the time a draft is ordered you may look out for emigration to the South.

I do not know what we are to do, but there is nothing to oppose us yet except Yankee Militia. Before this gets to you, you will know everything through the papers. My health is good. I suffered a little to day, because I ate too much yesterday. But not much. I wish you could see this country. War has not touched it, & everything looks blooming.

You must not be uneasy about me. My chance to send off letters are bad indeed. But if I get sick I have my arrangements well made to get back. It is not over a day's hard drive to Winchester from here & I can be sent there easy enough. Trust me for making arrangements. Above all however trust in the Good Being for my safety. You must still write twice each week. After awhile I want you to come on to Sperryville. I would not have you miss that visit for a great deal. But the last of July or first of August will be time enough. Give my love to my Daughter. Pa dreamed about He, ma. I thought he was walking good. I rec'd your letter of June 15th & 16th yesterday.

Good bye and God bless you.

Your Husband

211

My dear darling

I have just sent you a letter to North Carolina, but I am afraid you will go back to South Boston before it reaches you, and therefore will write also to that place. I cannot help feeling sorry for you my Darling, because I know how restless and uneasy you are now that you know we have crossed into Maryland & invaded Pennsylvania. I do hope my letters about the Winchester fight reached you safely. I could not get any chance to send a dispatch. If I get sick up here I have my arrangements made so I can reach Winchester in one day & from there I can telegraph you to meet me at Sperryville. Do not be uneasy as long as you hear nothing. For I will not keep you in suspense when I can help it. I wrote to you on the 21st from Shepherdstown. . . .

[Evans repeats almost verbatim his earlier letter of the same day, so it will not be repeated here.]

The Pennsylvanians seem to be taken by surprise and do not know how to act. Some say they are "Secesh"—many oppose Lincoln & *all* oppose the draft of *themselves.*

I do not know where we are going. Ewell's corps can sweep like a hurricane over Pennsylvania, if he will just say the word. I hope we will go to Harrisburg, the capital. It can be taken easily, for there is but little defence except Militia & a very few volunteer regiments.

I am in good health & excellent spirits. I have eaten too much yesterday—that is all. I have so much appetite for milk, butter &c.

I do hope you are enjoying yourself. You had better send your money down to Richmond & exchange it for the new issue. I hope to have a chance to send you some next month. I do not suppose, however, you are suffering any inconveniences. But you had as well be a little saving until I can send you two hundred dollars more.

You must address your letters very plainly especially

the "*31st Ga.*" Your letter of June 6th went to another regiment & travelled around until it got to me. It had been broken open. Make the "31st Ga." very plain.

Well my dearest Dear I do hope this campaign shall end the war. Oh how much I long for our good little home again. Certainly the Yankees will be satisfied when this campaign is over & a treaty of separation & peace can be made. Pray for it earnestly.

Do not be uneasy about me. Trust in the Good Being who will order all things aright. Pa dreamed about his babies last night & about ma too. Give my love to my Daughter. Good bye.

Your Husband

[Clement's diary continues the next day.]

June 24. Wednesday—Marched from Waynesboro toward Chambersburg passing through Quincy, Funkstown & other small villages. Encamped near Greenwood, on the Baltimore and Chambersburg turnpike.

The class of Pennsylvanian met with on this route do not impress one favorably. We find them generally living in pretty good style, but coarse, uneducated and apparently having little knowledge of the outside world. Some of them had never seen a cannon and expressed great anxiety to see the big guns.

The Southern troops were considerably surprised at the rough & profane language of the Pennsylvania belles. To us who never hear a rough word from the lips of a Southern *Lady*, it sounds very strange to hear these Northern women curse—

Considerable alarm is manifested among some at our approach. In some instances the citizens leave their houses to our mercy, but I am glad to write that generally the orders have been observed.

At a halt to rest today my regiment rested near a house from which the people had fled. Some soldiers were passing into the yard to get cherries & fearing they might be tempted in some mischief I went where they were. I found them in the rear of the house, near the

milk & butter House or cellar & although it was unlocked & they knew it was well stocked, not a particle
had been touched—

The citizens supply our troops *too* liberally with the
article of *whiskey*. Certainly they can ruin our army by
a liberality of that sort unless the orders are enforced.

In Quincy the merchants were selling their goods to
our soldiers, taking Confederate money freely.

The country we passed through resembles the Valley
of Virginia. But we have reached a much poorer region,
settled by poorer people.

June 25. Thursday—It was intended that we should
have marched to Gettysburg today for the purpose of
capturing the place & force there but for some cause
the expedition was abandoned & we have remained in
camp. I sent four companies in command of Captain
Pride on picket about 3 miles in direction of Shippen-
burg. Went with the picket to their posts & took dinner
with a Pennsylvania Dutch Lady. Talked to some of the
peace Democrats. They appear to be very hostile to the
Abolitionists & in favor of Peace. They hope for a res-
toration of the Union by a peace policy. The inhabitants
have run off or concealed all their horses & cattle & have
taken one or more wheels from each of their wagons.
This is to keep them from being impressed for their use.

Allie to Clement:

Person Co., N.C.
June 25, 1863

My dear darling

You see I am at Mr. Painter's. I came up last Friday
morning. The baby has been quite sick ever since I have
been here. He is better now but not well. I sent for a
doctor. Dr. Terrell a cousin of mother's. He cut his
gums. He has six teeth coming through all at once and
the worst of all is [that] I am very much afraid he has the
whooping cough. He has a very bad cough and occasionally whoops. Almost everybody who sees him thinks it is
but I still hope it is nothing but a bad cold and that he

214

will soon be over with it. If he has been exposed to the whooping cough I don't know when nor where it was. It was an impossibility for him to take it from cousin Eliza's children as they were what you might call well when I first got there. He is terrible cross. Worries me almost to death and to complete the matter I have caught cold in my breast and am very much afraid it will rise. I am doing my best doctoring it. Got it all covered in collard leaves now. Nance and Ida for a wonder are both well.

Yesterday I heard the army had crossed into Maryland. It is nothing more than I expected. I have been looking for it sometime. We have a mail here only twice a week. It is ten miles from the railroad—that is the great objection to staying up here and visiting around. If I could hear from you as I want to I could spend several months visiting among my relatives very pleasantly. Several of them have been over here to see me since I have been up here and all seem glad to see me and all want me to visit them. If I could just hear from you often and the baby was just well and would stay so I could enjoy myself very much. All are anxious for you to come and make them a visit. I do wish you could come. It would be so delightful. Wouldn't it?

I am looking constantly to hear of another fight but I take it all, darling, the best I can hoping always for the best. My belief is, darling, that you will be spared to go through this war safe and live to do a great deal of good in the future. With how much pleasure I look forward to the close of the war. When we shall be together again never to be parted again on this earth. I have the blues while the baby was sick. You know I couldn't help it, darling. For what would I do if he were to die so far from home and you so far away too? It would be terrible. I do hope he will soon be well. I think he is better and I am not anything like as uneasy about him as I was a day or so ago. But I want him to be well, for how could I give up my darling little baby? It would be more than I could bear. I try not to think of it any more than I can help.

There must be a great deal of desertion going on in the army. This whole country is full of deserters. They form themselves into companies. Have camps and resist all attempts to take them. It is too bad and our army will soon be ruined if there is not a stop put to it soon. I don't think there is anything like as much patriotism in Virginia and North Carolina as there is in Georgia or any of the other more Southern states. I see a great many people here who are opposed to the war. Cousin Joe has three grown sons, all healthy hearty young men, and all three have substitutes. It looks bad to me. Ida got after one of them yesterday telling him he was a coward to have a substitute. That her Pa wouldn't have one. That Ma had begged and done everything to get him to have one and he wouldn't have it. Don't you think she is coming out?

I haven't heard any further news from home since I wrote you last. My mind was soon relieved about you after the fight at Winchester. I saw in the papers that no officers were hurt. But I don't know but that before now you have been in another fight worse than that. Oh that these troubles would end. Suspense is awful. Tomorrow we have a mail and I will get letters from you. I wish it would come faster than it does. Time passes so slowly. If the baby has the whooping cough sure enough I will go back to Mr. Fourquesen's. It would not do for me to visit around with the baby. He would spread it all over the country. I don't know how long I shall stay here. Continue to direct your letters here a while longer. I will write by Saturday's mail what I intend doing. Good bye darling. God bless, protect and preserve you my darling husband. Good bye, good bye.

Your Wife

Person Co., N. C.
June 25, 1863

My dear darling

It has been a week day before yesterday since I have had a letter from you. I know you did not get my letter telling you to direct my letters here and they have been coming to Black Walnut since I left. I know you have written every opportunity and that it is not your fault that I get no letters. They promised me to send my letters from Black Walnut up here. I am worried about their not doing it. I am afraid you won't get any of mine while you are in Maryland. I do hope that when tomorrow's mail comes I will hear that the army has recrossed the Potomac. I feel like you were so far away. Almost out of my reach. If you were to get sick where you are, how could I ever get to you? I do hope and trust you will not be sick and that nothing will happen to you.

When I wrote to you last I had a pack of troubles on hand but we are about well now. The baby didn't have the whooping cough. It was three days before I got the cold out of him. The baby is a great deal better. Almost well but he coughs right bad yet. I am delighted to think he hasn't got the whooping cough. If I could just hear from you I would feel right good but there is always something to trouble.

I have not been anywhere but here at cousin Joe's yet. The baby has been too sick to visit about. A good many of my old friends and relatives have been to see me. I didn't know I had so many kinfolks. Do you dream about me any darling? I see you almost every night in my dreams. I dreamed last night about you. Thought I was sitting in your lap talking to you. Enjoying myself finely. I feel mighty bad when I wake in the morning and find it is but a dream and that you are not here. I sometimes wish I could sleep till the war ends if I could wake and find it ended to my notion. I feel so uneasy about you. Perhaps while I am writing you are engaged in a battle and exposed to thousands of Yankee bullets. You never can imagine my feelings, darling. How awful the suspense is. When I hear of a fight I do not know what I shall do. If I could only be near you always as I was at the last fight it would be so much better. But maybe it is better as it is. Good bye darling. Would that I could see you this morning.

[Written crosswise on the paper at the heading: Your Wife]

He sends his specks [respects] to you papa and say

217

he will have a mouth full of teeth when you see him again and then you had better not fool with he; if you do somebody will get bit. Ida sends her love to Pa and of course wants to see him bad enough, for ma don't.

Clement to Allie:

Greenwood Franklin County, Pennsylvania
June 25, 1863

My dear Darling

I have an opportunity to send this letter off and I do hope it may reach you. We have advanced very considerably into Pennsylvania without opposition so far. As far as I can learn the enemy are not yet prepared to oppose us. This place is seventy miles from Baltimore & about sixty from Harrisburg, the capital of the state. It is situated among the mountains and settled by a poor class of people. The women have been to visit us to hear my regimental band. They are pretty coarse I tell you. Their hands are large & rough, fingers blunt at the ends. They have evidently been accustomed to labor. The Negroes have nearly all run off from fear of us. There is a Negro settlement close by called *Africa* but they have nearly all gone. The *Bushwhackers* occasionally fire on our stragglers, but this helps us to keep them in camp and in ranks. The people say that volunteering for Lincoln's army is over with and that the men will hide from the draft. It seems that they have some difficulty in getting their Militia together.

I do not know what we are to do. We are in camp today, but may move at any moment. Our troops are faring finely. Whatever is needed for the army is impressed & paid for just like we do in Virginia. This does not seem right after they have plundered Virginia so much. But we can be gentlemen as well as soldiers, and that mixture seems to be an impossibility with the Yankees. I have no question now of the wisdom of the invasion & believe that it will accomplish much good.

The soldiers generally are behaving well. These people who have been unaccustomed to any army think that the loss of a beehive or a dozen poultry quite a hardship. But they ought to see the Virginia farms despoiled, houses burned, Negroes run off, women & children turned out of doors.—then they would not complain.

I know you are very uneasy about me, but do not distress yourself. My health is very, very good. I will certainly return if I get sick. I expect to see you again in six weeks from today.

I have bought you twenty-four yards of small red-check Gingham for 25 cts. per yard. If I could have been allowed to leave my regiment I would have been able to supply you with all you needed for yourself & children. Perhaps I can yet.

Pa will buy something for the little pets in the next town. Pa thinks about his little darlings a great deal.

Good bye now, my dear Love. Do not trouble yourself on my account. In a month after this reaches you we will meet again somewhere. Keep in good heart after this many are the happy days before us still.

Good bye. My love to all our kinfolks.

Your Husband

[At this point, the letters from Colonel Evans ceased for a few days. Nevertheless, his diary covers the events of this period.]

June 26th. Friday. Marched on the road to Gettysburg. Destroyed the Furnace & rolling mills of the arch abolitionist, Thaddeus Stevens.[1]

The militia abolitionists at Gettysburg made scarcely any show of resistance— Our cavalry defeat & run them off—

My regiment was left in the town as Guard. We occu-

1. Thaddeus Stevens, after the war, emerged as the most radical Republican reconstructionist in Congress. For more details on the destruction of his Caledonia Iron Works, near Greenwood, Pennsylvania, see Edwin B. Coddington, *The Gettysburg Campaign* (New York: Charles Scribner's Sons, 1968), p. 166. Loss of a $65,000 investment, $10,000 of goods from the company store, bar iron at $4,000, all fence rails, eighty tons of grass and other minor damages, to one of Stevens' vindictive temperament could not but have left a deep resentment. Also, see Claude G. Bowers, *The Tragic Era* (Cambridge, Massachusetts: Houghton Mifflin, 1929), pp. 65-84. The Confederate attack was the second loss of Stevens' ironworks.

pied the Court House as quarters. The town was kept very orderly & quiet. The citizens expected us to revel & riot all night, burning & destroying property. They were therefore very much surprised at the quiet of the town.

I paroled 46 Yankee prisoners & left them at Gettysburg.

June 27—Saturday. Marched out of Gettysburg in direction of York. Encamped at a little town of two stores.

June 28th. Sunday. Triumphal entry into York. I was sent ahead to establish a Guard & preserve order in the town. The troops passed through in admirable order. Before marching through I took down the U.S. colors which were flying over the town at the Market place—A very large stand of colors—Citizens in the streets dressed in their best, all full of curiosity to see the Rebels—

Marched through toward Wrightsville—Reached the enemy's position. In attempting to get his position we frightened them off.

—All militia, who ran as fast as possible & burned the Bridge. Town on fire.—Rebel Regiments which had marched 25 miles that day work to stop the fire. Tear down houses & at last the fire stops, after burning six or eight houses.

Wrightsville was a scene of confusion & excitement. But the splendid behavior of Rebel troops soon restored quiet—

I again guarded the town.

June 29—Monday Marched back to York & camped.

June 30—Marched in direction of Chambersburg. Encamp near Heidlersburg—Long weary march—

[On July 4 Evans wrote more of the York-Wrightsville episode in a letter to Allie]

> Gettysburg battlefield
> July 4th, 1863

My dear darling:

For many long days I have had no opportunity to write you a letter, nor do I know when or how this will ever reach you. I have written to you but twice since we crossed the Potomac. The last time I wrote from Greenwood in Pennsylvania about two weeks ago. Since then I have been in action three times—twice very lightly engaged, but one time in as severe a battle as ever. Thank God my dear for us both that I am still alive. Do not be uneasy when I tell you that I was again slightly wounded in the side, for it did not stop me but a few minutes. I have not left the regiment for it at all, and will in a few days be entirely well.

When we left Greenwood we marched to Gettysburg & took possession of the town with very little opposition. I was placed in charge of the town to preserve order and quartered the Regiment in the Court House. Very little disturbance occurred and the citizens were very agreeably surprised to find that after ten o'clock at night their town was as quiet as usual and they could sleep in peace with the *terrible* Rebels all around them. We found very few boots, shoes or hats for the men, but in provisions or rations so far there has been no stint.

We left Gettysburg & marched upon York, which is a very beautiful town indeed. I was sent there ahead to take possession and to establish guards for the security of the place. I found the Yankee flag flying over the city, and as our troops had to pass directly under it, I hauled it down and sent it to the General. It is a very large flag being nearly thirty feet in length. Passing through York, our Brigade alone, marched rapidly to Wrightsville on the Susquehanna. About one mile from the town some Militia had formed in line protected by rudely constructed trenches. Not knowing their strength we cautiously advanced upon them from two directions, dividing the Brigade. I was sent along the railroad in command of a portion of the Brigade to attack their flank, but the timid Militia, who equalled us in numbers fled at the bursting of the first shell. They had not been in action before, and believed that the shelling was terrible, although only two pieces were fired. They fled so rapidly that we captured only about thirty. At this place the Susquehanna is, or rather was, spanned by a splendid bridge, over a mile in length. This Bridge the frightened

Militia set on fire as soon as they crossed, although two or three pieces of artillery judiciously placed on the opposite side could have saved it. We rushed forward to stop the burning but were too late. Seeing that the town of Wrightsville on this side would probably be burned also our noble hearted men, who had marched twenty five miles that day & chased the Yankees a mile or more stacked their arms and worked until nearly midnight to arrest the fire. By tearing down a few houses the burning was arrested. It was a singular sight to see those *marching* Rebels work so eagerly to save a Yankee town which the scamps had themselves set on fire, and this too after reading in Northern papers of the entire destruction of Darien in our own state by some Massachusetts & two other Negro regiments on the 16th of this month.[2]

Next day we returned to York and on the first day of this month marched again upon Gettysburg to meet the Yankee army.

[This letter will be continued after his journal entries in order to keep the sequence of events in order.]

All this time, the Union forces had not been idle. General Hooker had been relieved on June 28 as commander of the Army of the Potomac and was succeeded by Maj. Gen. George G. Meade, who moved his forces into Pennsylvania, keeping them between Lee and Washington and Baltimore. When Lee understood that Union forces were approaching his invading army, he began to assemble his scattered corps.

2. In 1893 General Evans wrote to Lt. Col. James Lachlin of Darien, Georgia, an interesting addition to this incident at Wrightsville, Pennsylvania.

"When my brigade had driven the enemy across the Susquehannah River, the fleeing enemy set fire to the bridge and the flames caught the little town. But instead of letting it burn down we stacked arms and by bringing water in buckets we succeeded in arresting the flames. While the town was burning I chanced to kick up a stray piece of newspaper that the wind blew to my feet and then by the light of a fire which we were putting out I read a northern account of the invasion and fire at Darien in Ga. McIntosh and Darien boys like gallant Southerners were putting out fires kindled in a Northern town while invaders of Ga. were burning our towns. Such incidents show the noble spirit of Confederate men."

This letter is from James Hilton papers in the Georgia Historical Society archives in Savannah, Georgia, and was furnished to me by Lt. Col. Pharris Johnson of Evans County, Georgia.

Confederates under A. P. Hill approached Gettysburg on the morning of July 1, and the greatest battle of the war commenced. Ewell's command came up with Rodes' division in the early afternoon, and shortly thereafter Early's division, including Evans' regiment, came on the field. The date at the top of Evans' diary page was written in heavily shaded characters and much larger than usual.

July 1st. Wednesday. Marched toward Gettysburg from camp. Heavy firing heard in our front, occasional skirmishing with cavalry by our advance.

About 3 o'clock p.m. formed in line of battle about two and a half miles from Gettysburg. The 11th and 1st U.S. army corps were formed in the front of our Corps.

About 4 o'clock an advance was ordered. The charge was handsomely made from all points driving the enemy through the town and into his entrenched position among the hills & mountains—The slaughter of the enemy was very heavy. About 6000 prisoners & a few pieces of artillery captured—I received a slight wound on my side, near the ribs, but not sufficient to force me from the field. The Brigade slept on the field of Battle that night. I went to the hospital at dark—

July 2nd. Thursday. Had my wound examined & dressed. Dr. Butts gave me a certificate that I was unfit for duty on account of my wound. Put it in my pocket & rejoined my regiment.

Brigade moved frequently during the day to various points.

About 5 o'clock p.m. a very heavy artillery fight between ours and the enemy's batteries—

They were strongly & skillfully fortified—During the day our infantry charged the enemy in his entrenchments repeatedly, often taking them but unable to hold them.

At dark we were ordered to support Hays' Brigade[3]

3. Louisiana Brigade in Early's division commanded by Brig. Gen. Harry Hays of New Orleans.

in a charge upon the enemy entrenchments near town—
The assault failed of success. We held however an advanced position all night within 800 yards of the Yankee redoubts.

July 3rd. Friday. Heavy fighting all along the line—Repeated attacks upon our part. The enemy driven a little farther but their strong position still held.

The heaviest artillery fighting of the war—[4]

Weather exceedingly hot—

July 4th. Saturday—Moved back the lines to afford the enemy an opportunity to attack. All day long battle was offered which he declined.

Rain falling in torrents.

Our Brigade held in reserve.

Battle field becomes very offensive on account of the unburied dead—

For miles the dead Yankees lay scattered along.

Yankee prisoners have been ordered to bury their dead but they work very slowly.

All of our dead have been buried—

[In order to keep the proper sequence of events, Clement's letter of July 4 is continued here. As Ewell's corps came to Gettysburg on July 1, after a thirty-five mile march, Evans wrote:]

When we reached our position about two miles from the town we formed in line, advanced & soon met the enemy. He had the advantage of position & one time they gave us a few minutes of stubborn resistance; but our boys were impetuous & drove them back through the woods, fields & town with most terrible slaughter. It was in this charge that I received my wound. The Yankees retreating through the town got a strong position

---

4. Coddington, *Gettysburg,* p. 469, says there were three Union rifled batteries and two light twelve-pounder batteries, twenty-six guns in all as the engagement commenced about 4:30 a.m. "One hundred and forty-five cannon were massed to cover the advance of the attacking column. After one of the most terrific and prolonged cannonades ever witnessed, the assaulting column . . . appeared from behind the ridge. . . ." (Joseph T. Derry, *Story of the Confederacy* [Richmond, Virginia: Johnson Publishing Co., 1895], p. 252). See letter to Allie hereafter.

on a commanding hill. Next day [July 2] the heaviest artillery fighting I ever witnessed took place but did not avail us in getting possession. A charge of infantry on their intrenchments was ordered. It was made over open fields & made gallantly, but failed—the assault was renewed by other troops yesterday [July 3] but failed again as to any material advantage.

We have over six thousand prisoners, killed the Yankees in hordes, & their wounded fill the houses of the town. Our loss is tolerably heavy, but nothing like the Yankee loss.

Thus the matter still stands, and the question of strength, skill & courage is still to be tested. In Him who rules all things well we put our trust for victory.

I am quite well—although very *very* much fatigued. Hope for the best my Darling. If I get sick or wounded I will start for Winchester immediately & send someone to telegraph to you to meet me in Sperryville.

Kiss my precious babies for their Pa. I hope we will meet soon. All seem to think that the great struggle of the war is on us & that Peace will follow.

Do not forget my Darling to place all your trust in the Good One & be resigned to His will whatever may happen.

Tell that Little Lady of mine that Pa will bring her something nice from Yankee Land if he lives.

Pa will bring something for the Boy, too & bring himself for Ma.

Good bye and God bless my Darling.
Your Husband
Hagerstown, [Maryland] July 7th, 1863

My dear dear Darling

I have so much to write to you about that I do not know how to begin, but I know how grateful to the Good Being you will be to see my handwriting again after so long a silence during the last week of danger. I have felt so sorry for you my darling, but if my letters while on the other side of the Potomac reached you I do hope that you were resigned to whatever may be the will of God, and that after you heard of the battle you were satisfied that I was not hurt or you would have been notified.

[He repeats here the same information given in the diary about capturing York and saving it from fire so that is omitted.]

I had command of all the principal towns we passed through as well as Wrightsville & almost perfect order was preserved. Generally the stores were closed, but our quartermasters & Commissaries were ordered to search them to find army supplies. All private property & private rights were scrupulously respected. The people had been told that we would destroy their houses, barns & stores, insult their women and commit all sorts of ravages, but they were most agreeably deceived.

They soon learned that we were gentlemen—so different from the Yankee army—and the women and children turned out to see us. Not one woman was rudely spoken to by a single soldier. We have friends among the Pennsylvanians who are willing to let us go in peace. 1st of July, we reached the battlefield of Gettysburg about 3 o'clock p.m. We were soon in line advancing against the enemy, completely routing him at all points with horrid slaughter. We ran them through the town, & drove them back into their entrenched hills and mountains. The victory on the first day was of the most complete character. Do not be alarmed when I tell you I was again wounded. Just before the charge ended I was struck by a passing fragment of shell on the side. At first I was impressed with the idea that I was very seriously hurt as the blow was upon the points of my ribs, near where they join the backbone. I stopped & sat down, made an examination & finding I could still travel I got up & went on. Unluckily I had just left my horse, the ground being cut up with fences, & ravines & therefore I had to walk. However the fighting soon ceased and at night I went to the hospital. We had so many wounded seriously that I had Mose stretch me a tent in the field & I slept there until next morning. Dr. Butts examined my wound &

advised me to remain at the hospital, but I did not think I ought to, & therefore went to the regiment again. I suffered a great deal for two or three days, but I stayed on duty although I could hardly get on my horse & had to walk doubled up like an old man.

On the 2nd of July we were ordered in again to support a charge made just at night, but Providentially only a few men of our Brigade were wounded. The battle on the 2nd & 3rd was not successful. On the 4th we offered the enemy battle but he declined & on the 5th the army moved away. I lost fifty men—nine killed & forty-one wounded—many very seriously. Dave Adams is badly wounded in the leg. Lieut. Patterson killed, Capt. Cody slightly [wounded]— Our Brigade was the last to move off, & I had charge of two regiments in rear of the whole army—The enemy followed and we had to fight them a little on the way—We are now about six miles from the Potomac near Williamsport but I do not know what we are going to do. I can only again entreat you to rely upon our Maker for my safety. How much better could I do my duty if I did not have you & my sweet little babies to think about.

I hear that part of our wagon train has been captured & I fear my baggage is gone. But I have enough with me.

I must close, I hope this will go safely. I have tried so often to send you a letter during the last two weeks. I know how uneasy you are.

Tell my little daughter her Pa thinks of her everyday & wants to see her & the little man so bad. Pa does hope they fare well. Keep in good heart, we shall meet soon. Give my love to all.

Good bye and God bless you. I send this to South Boston for I expect you are there by the time this gets to you. My love to all. Good bye. Good bye and God bless my darling.

Your Husband

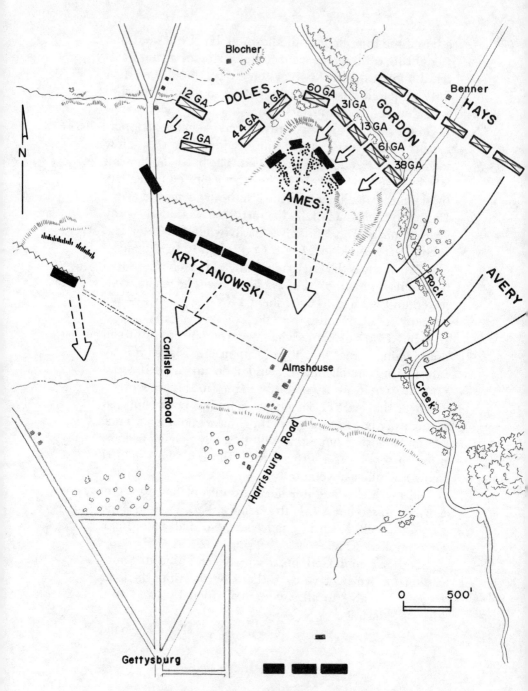

Battle of Gettysburg, July 1, 1863—
Ewell breaks the Eleventh Corps

228

Chapter 13
AFTER GETTYSBURG

Diary recordings fit in at this time to bridge some of the gaps not covered by Evans in the letters. As noted, the Confederates began to leave the field on July 4, but the rear of the army did not leave until the morning of July 5.

July 5th. Sunday. Moved in direction of the mountain Gap at Fairfield toward Chambersburg—Our Brigade was placed in rear of army & mine & Col. Atkinson's reg. in rear of Brigade.

A small force of Infantry, cavalry & artillery follow to harass us—

Near Fairfield Co., Atkinson deploys and charging back drives them back.

They then shell our division from a good position but not a man is wounded.

We encamp near Fairfield. I took charge of the picket line of Hays' & Gordon's Brigades with about 40 cavalry—Push my line nearly to Fairfield until about daylight when I returned.

July 6th. Monday—We cross the mountains & encamp with Ewell's & Hill's corp[s] de'armee.

July 7th. Tuesday—Marched to Hagerstown where we found most of the army.

July 8th. Wednesday in camp at Hagerstown. Hagerstown begins to show the effects of war. Pennsylvania & Maryland can now sympathize somewhat with Southern states which have [been] invaded.

Fencing is being destroyed by both armies a great deal, but it is unavoidable. Our wagon trains are parked at Williamsport on the Potomac. The river is very much swollen & cannot be crossed by our troops even if that was an object.

Clement to Allie:

Hagerstown, Pa. [Maryland]
July 8, 1863

My dearest Darling

I wrote you again this morning at a venture hoping that some means will offer to send to you what I write. I have had two nights rest & am getting over my fatigue. I have been almost exhausted—so tired, tired that I could scarcely move. My wound does not hurt me now. The pain is all gone and the sore is healing rapidly. I have done a great deal of hard duty. For four nights in succession during the battle & while we were retiring I was on duty without sleep. The fourth night I volunteered to take charge of a line to cover our forces at the foot of the mountain. At eleven o'clock at night, with a part of our Brigade, Hays' brigade & forty cavalry, I advanced toward the enemy's lines approaching them as nearly as possible. Of course this was hazardous duty & kept me awake. However about three o'clock I sat down by a fence holding my horse & I suppose I scarcely touched the ground before I was fast asleep without intending it. I could have slept not half an hour when I awoke with the strangest feelings I ever experienced. I did not know where I was nor what I was doing, but felt like I was losing my senses. In a few minutes however I aroused myself. It was nearly day and as my object was accomplished I slowly withdrew my line until I was within six hundred yards of the camp. Soon after day we had a little skirmishing & then marched across the mountains. This was the night of the 5th & morning of the 6th. I believe that one can lose their mind from want of sleep and every sentinel who sleeps on his post ought not to be *shot*. My regiment is very much reduced. I have about seventy-five in killed & wounded since I left Hamilton Crossing & about a hundred from sickness sent to hospital. The weather is very gloomy. Raining a great deal. But I think it is better than hot sunshine & dust.

We are all standing still here. I expect Genl. Lee intends to give the Yankees another turn somewhere. I have bought you some few things, but the chance for carrying anything is so bad that I bought very little. You must write home for me & let them know I am safe so far.

I want to see you so bad. When this war is over I shall live for you, my Darling.

Give my love to my Daughter & to the little Man for Pa.

Good bye. God bless you.
Your Husband

Hagerstown, Pa. [Maryland]
July 8, 1863

My dear Darling

I wish I could telegraph you a letter this evening & receive an answer in the same manner. But I must write and send by some uncertain hand. Perhaps it will be two weeks before you read this. I know you are now calling it all to your aid. I have had no chance until yesterday for two weeks to send you a single line. Do not think I have been indifferent.

The last fight at Gettysburg was a very fearful affair. At some points the Yankees fought pretty stubborn but where ever we had a fair field we whipped & slaughtered them in great numbers. Both armies are now maneuvering & preparing for another battle. It will soon come. I do hope that these fights may be decisive. If I knew that this was indeed the last year of the war how much better I would feel. Then I could be assured that next year if I lived would be spent with you.

We must begin to make arrangements for another meeting soon. It will soon be August and you know we are to see each other then or by the first of September. Will not the meeting be delightful? I look forward to it with so much pleasure.

The Yankees captured nearly all my band. I had sixteen instruments & they got twelve. The band was with the wagon train & the Yankee cavalry dashed in and got them. I think they have Ben Hames prisoner.

231

I have seen no paper from Richmond in two weeks and know nothing of what is going on. We have the news that [General] Pemberton whipped Grant at Vicksburg again. [Of course, Vicksburg had already fallen on July 4, but the news had not yet reached Evans.]

8 o'clock p.m.

It is now nightfall and we are still in camp. I have no further news to write. I can only repeat what I have urged so often. Put your trust in the Good One. We will meet again & I trust we have many happy years before us. If I get wounded I shall send some one to you without delay. Try to be satisfied. I want you to come to Sperryville whenever it becomes safe. I will let you know. Give my love to my sweet little daughter & kiss my little man.

Good bye.

Your Husband

[Evans' diary and letters of the next six days complete the Gettysburg Campaign.]

July 9th. In camp near Hagerstown: Rumors that the enemy is approaching in two or three directions. We hear pretty constant cannonading in the direction of Boonsboro Gap. The enemy seems to be exceedingly slow and cautious in their approach, and several days may pass before another general engagement.

Our army is strengthening and the losses of the Battle of Gettysburg will soon be supplied. The greatest difficulty we have is in supplying regular rations. But for this the Campaign in Maryland and Pennsylvania could be prolonged indefinitely but this difficulty will force us back to Virginia sooner than all the Yankee army ever could. The Yankee Cavalry hovers around us to pick up every straggler & stray wagons.

Hagerstown appears to contain about 2000 inhabitants —the effects of war are visible in its closed doors & gloomy look. But little damage has been done so far to houses or fencing, but in the event of a battle the usual destruction will of course follow—

Moved today through Hagerstown on the National Pike—turned left and encamped about two miles from town.

Hagerstown, Md.
July 9, 1863

Dear Darling

We are still at the camp and no orders to move. But I am looking for something to turn up every minute. The morning is very foggy and the weather unsettled. The Potomac is *booming* and our ambulances with the wounded have to cross over on flats two at a time every fifteen minutes. This is slow work. I suppose however in a day or two the river can be forded if it does not rain again.

I wonder what you are doing this morning. I know you have so anxiously looked for a letter from me since the battle of Gettysburg, and how you have trembled from fear of hearing bad news. I know you cannot help this anxiety and your suffering is much greater than mine. I shall recompense you for it all as soon as this bloody war shall end by being always with you.

I am getting over my fatigue and will soon be all well.

I have written several letters in the last two days & placed them in various hands hoping that some chance would offer or that some of them would reach you. I write this in the same way & the man is waiting.

Good bye. God bless you my darling. My love to my dear daughter & noble boy.

Good bye.
Your Husband

Hagerstown, Md.
July 10, 1863

My dear Darling

Before this letter reaches you another terrible battle will in all probability be fought near this place. The enemy are reported to be approaching from two directions —Boonsboro & Waynesboro, and we will give them battle near here. I trust in Providence for victory. For your sake

& that of my little ones I pray for my own safety. I shall make arrangements to send you news as speedily as possible & if possible will, whether safe or not, have a dispatch sent to you from Winchester. I am well. Keep in good heart my darling. I commit you and my little dears to the Great Father & Protector. He will bring no trial on you to crush you, but His all-providing arm will sustain you.

I am in good health. Kiss my babies for their Pa. Good bye. God be with you my darling.

Good bye.

Your Husband

Hagerstown, Md.

July 10, [18]63

Dear Darling I am getting short of paper & you must be satisfied with short letters. I have been sending my letters to South Boston but today I will send three off, to Black Walnut, Cunningham's Store & South Boston, one each, in hope one will reach you. Your letter of June 25th was brought to me today & you had received no letter in three weeks. Poor darling. I am afraid many weeks passed in suspense without any letter to you. After we left the Potomac I found no chance at all to write to you. My darling must be as patient as possible. Pa was so sorry to hear that his little man had been sick. His pa loves he so good, mama. But Pa has given him to the Good Being to do as to Him seems best. I wish I could be with you to talk to you about the events of the last thirty days. I can imagine your troubles when the reports of the battle of Gettysburg began to come in. Even yet you do not feel certain of my safety, but I hope you remember I have made arrangements for you to hear of my safety almost as soon as you hear of the battle. It is now seven days since the last fight & my message would have reached you in some shape by this time. I am well. Several times I have been almost broken down, but I would hang on & come out straight with a little rest. If I get sick I will put my horse in a little wagon and come to Winchester where you can join me, as I will send you a dispatch from there & send my horse after you to Staunton or Sperryville.

I expect it is Genl. Lee's intention to fight them again on this side of the Potomac. Perhaps he designs maintaining his ground during the whole summer. Our army is in fine condition considering all that has been endured so far. I have no fear of final results. The enemy are uneasy—not confident of their ability to whip us. The first day's fight at Gettysburg demonstrated how easily we can whip them on fair ground.

I am looking forward to an early meeting. Six months of the year are gone and the days roll away rapidly. It will soon be fall, and then you shall be with me. I am almost entirely well of my wound.

We are ordered to move.

Good bye and God bless you my darling.

Your Husband

Hagerstown, Md.
July 10, 1863

My dearest Darling

I have no additional news to send to you, nor any certainty that I shall have an opportunity to send this off. It sickens me to think how seldom you get a letter from me & how uneasy you are. I dream of you but my dreams are always pleasant. Last night we were young again, unmarried, and in love—I passed over some of the happy scenes of the sweet days or "Auld Lang Syne." We shall soon meet & I trust not many months will go by before we can go home in peace—I am expecting another heavy battle. Cannonading is going on toward Boonsboro Gap, but I do not know who is engaged.—I am told that the Yankee papers claim a great victory at Gettysburg, but do not believe a word of it. We whipped them utterly on the first day & slaughtered them on the 2nd & 3rd; on the 4th we offered them battle on fair ground which they declined & on the 5th both armies moved back. We certainly sustained much less loss by half than they did.

Your Husband

[In the diary, he wrote more:]

July 11th. Saturday. Early in the morning we were placed in line of battle about a mile from Hagerstown with the remainder of Early's division, Johnson's division on our right & Rodes' on the left; In the centre of the line is A. P. Hill's Corps, and Longstreet on the right. Our position naturally strong is made more so by entrenchments. The enemy have fortified at Waynesboro & Boonsboro, & their columns are slowly moving upon us. Light skirmishing takes place along the line. We still hold possession of the main portion of the town with cavalry & our infantry pickets are nearly a mile in advance of the line.

July 12th. The enemy have massed their forces principally against our centre—Our cavalry retire from the town and move to the left of our entire line. The infantry skirmishers in front of Ewell's corps hold their position.

Opposite A. P. Hill's corps the enemy attack our skirmishers very vigorously. They are repulsed for some hours but coming in force our skirmishers are driven back. At night our division is moved to the centre & support [Henry] Heth's & Pender's [Pettigrew's] Divisions.

Clement to Allie:

> Hagerstown Battle ground
> Monday, July 13th, 1863

My dear Darling

When will the time come that I can date my letters from some other place besides battlefields? Will you not rejoice, my dear, when wars shall cease, and we learn to live in charity with each other?

This is the third day that we have been in line of battle but nothing more than skirmishing has yet occurred. The enemy is fortifying his position & probably will not attack us until his own lines are secure. We are sure of victory if he does attack, because our position is a good one & the troops will fight with great heroism. Our line

236

extends from the Potomac to beyond Hagerstown. A pretty long line but it is well defended.

I am well—that is, today I am not sick. I feel very much fatigued—worn out. I am so anxious to see you & the little ones again. Six more weeks & I hope to see you my darling again. I write this in much uncertainty of sending it off. Give my love to my dear little daughter & "my boy." Good bye & God bless you.

Your Husband

July 13th. Monday. Brisk skirmish firing in A. P. Hill's front. The Yankee skirmishers have protected themselves during the night within about a thousand yards of our main line. Our skirmishers are about equidistant between our main line & their skirmish line. The weather is very gloomy. At 7½ o'clock p.m. our division ready to move immediately.

At 8 o'clock we commenced the march to recross the Potomac with our Corps D'armee at Williamsport. Our Division [Ewell's] was placed in the rear, our brigade [Gordon's] in rear of the Division & my regiment [Thirty-first Georgia] in rear of the Brigade. It was only a march of five miles to reach the Potomac, but that occupied the entire night. The rain came down in torrers. The road was full of mud, the night was dark & in all it was the most miserable night of my whole life. Moving at a snail's pace when we did move, halting every fifty yards, & frequently halted for an hour, overpowered with want of sleep & excessive fatigue I could scarcely endure through the night. I fell asleep frequently on my horse— I sat down in the mud & slept—Most of all attacked with dysentery I suffered from acute pains all night.

July 14. Tuesday. But soon after daylight we reach the Potomac once again. Longstreet & Ewell were crossing on pontoons lower down, but our corps was from necessity to wade the river. The rain had swollen the Potomac, so as almost to swim a horse & the water reaches above the waists & nearly to the arm-pits of the men. But at last the passage was effected and we marched on the road toward Martinsburg.

237

At one o'clock p.m. we stopped in a grove to rest—
The enemy made no pursuit upon our corps, but followed Longstreet & Hill very cautiously with artillery.

[General Lee was not sure exactly what Gettysburg had meant,
nor did General Meade assess the battle's full significance. Both
President Lincoln and President Davis were disappointed. In
fact, nobody fully evaluated the events at the time of the Battle
of Gettysburg. Only years later did historians, in retrospect, dub
it the "high tide of the Confederacy." However, Colonel Evans'
contemporary view of what the battle meant is scarcely to be
improved upon as he closed the diary]:

Thus ended for the time being the Pennsylvania Campaign. The success of the movement was not as great as
was to be desired—Had *our wishes* been gratified the
Yankee Army would have been demolished & Washington captured, but I doubt if either was expected—We
remained on the enemy's territory as long as it was
possible to subsist the army there. Short rations will always compel *short* campaigns of invasion, unless we
could invade where railroad & water communications
could be kept up. The general results of the last 40 days
however are not at all unsatisfactory. The Federal army
of the Potomac has been forced out of Virginia—The
enemy have learned to their cost what invasion is, and
have one great battlefield with all its horrors on their
own soil to contemplate. We have given the Federal
army a shock at Gettysburg in the loss of over 40,000
killed, wounded & prisoners from which it will not
recover. We have drawn from the enemy subsistence
stores for the whole army for two months. We have
furnished our trains, cavalry & artillery with new & good
horses—We have supplied ourselves with quite a thousand new wagons. The capture of ordnance & ordnance
stores have been abundant.
We have possession of the Valley of Virginia with its
abundant crop of grain & hay—

238

Our loss during the 40 days will reach 20,000. That
of the enemy will not fall short of 60,000.[1]

With the exception of the gallant souls who have. . . .

[Unfortunately at this point a page, the last entry in this diary,
is torn out.]

1. The official Confederate casualties were 20,451 and the official Federal casualties were 23,049. See *O.R.*, series 1, vol. 27, part 2, p. 187.

Confederate States of America,

WAR DEPARTMENT,

Richmond, _May 20th_ 186_4_,

Sir:

(by and with the advice and consent of the Senate)

You are hereby informed that the President has appointed you

Brigadier General,

In the Provisional Army in the service of the Confederate States: _to rank as such from_ the _Nineteenth_ day of _May_ one thousand eight hundred and sixty _four._ _Should the Senate, at their next session, advise and consent thereto, you will be commissioned accordingly._

Immediately on receipt hereof, please to communicate to this Department, through the Adjutant and Inspector General's Office, your acceptance or non-acceptance of said appointment; and with your letter of acceptance, return to the Adjutant and Inspector General the OATH, herewith enclosed, properly filled up, SUBSCRIBED and ATTESTED, reporting at the same time your AGE, RESIDENCE when appointed, and the STATE in which you were BORN.

Should you accept, you will report for duty to _General R. E. Lee for assignment to the command of Atkinson's Brigade, vice Brig. Gen. J. B. Gordon promoted_

James A. Seddon
Secretary of War.

Brig Gen C. A. Evans,

Commanding &c
_P. A. C. S._

Chapter 14

AND WHAT OF ALLIE
AFTER GETTYSBURG?

Allie's everyday life went on, in spite of the carnage of war. Her line, "Oh darling I feel you are clean out of my reach," is very appropriate.

Allie to Clement:

At Mr. Painter's Person Co., N.C.
Friday, July 3, 1863

My darling Husband

This morning I received three letters from you, one from Clem and one from Sister. I took them and run off down in the garden so I could have a good time reading all to myself. Your last letter was written ten days ago from Pennsylvania. Oh darling, I feel like you are clean out of my reach. So far from me. I bear it all the very best I can darling, control my feelings and am just as cheerful as I can possibly be. I do pray so earnestly for your safety, darling. I know you will be spared. For what would I do without my darling? We hear little or nothing of the movements of the army from the papers. All is kept dark.

I know if anything had happened to you, you would send for me. I am so glad to know you are living so well. That is some consolation. Clem writes me Hannah's [a slave] baby is dead. She thinks she smothered it. I didn't calculate on its living anyway and was not surprised at all to hear of its death. Nellie she said was right sick with the measles. They were preparing for a grand concert

241

for the benefit of the wounded soldiers in which she is to take a very active part. You will have to write to her what you heard about it while you were in Yankee land. Sister says her health is wretched. She never sees a well day. She says Probe is still going on one crutch and has no idea of going back in the service.[1] She says he expects to sell his land soon for fifteen or eighteen dollars per acre and that we shall have a full benefit when they close. Joe Campfield was killed in the last fight. Probe, she says, has almost killed himself fishing. She says you must write to her. She was so uneasy about you in the last fight. She wonders if you ever think of her. Ida is very busy this evening writing to her grandma. She says tell Pa how bad I want to see him and how good I love him— and don't you want to see he, papa? He has got right well again. He can most talk, papa.

You seem to be afraid I will get out of money. I have two hundred dollars and that is as much as I want if it is good. I shall send it down to Richmond and exchange it for new issue before the first of August. I didn't write to you about it because I wanted you to send me more. I wanted to know if it was good. You need not trouble about sending me more.

Uncle Sydney's wife's funeral is to be preached near here next Sunday. I am going and will see him I reckon. You must continue to send your letters here for a while. I shall be at Mr. Fourquesen's in about three weeks. You will know when to send your letters there. I am still at Mr. Painter's but will go to Mr. Williams' next week. If anything happens to you send to [South] Boston. I will hear it right away. I am writing but I do not feel like you will ever get my letters. I hope you will. I hope you have not had as much rain where you are as we have here. If you have I know you have suffered. Poor darling, I know you are having a hard time of it. If this war ever ends and it is in your wife's power to make you happy you shall be a happy man the rest of your life. I do want to see you so much. Must I come to Sperry-

1. See appendix A on kinfolks.

ville? Write me what to do about it. Good bye, darling. God bless you my own dear, dear husband.

Your Wife

At Mr. Williams'—Person Co. N. C.
July 13, 1863

My dear Darling—

How I wonder how and where my dear darling is this morning. More than a week has passed since the big fight and I have heard nothing from you as yet. Therefore I take it for granted that you are safe. God grant that you are my darling. I never believed that I would be able to control my feelings as I have done. To feel as calm and contented about your safety as I have done since the fight. I have such faith in your being protected by the Good Being. Although I have seen no account of the battle—No list of casualties—Yet darling I feel sure of your safety. I feel that I have entirely given you up into the hands of our Heavenly Father and that all will be well. I have never felt so before. I believe darling that you will pass safely through the war and live to do a great deal of good in the world yet. I wrote you no letter at all last week. We had no mail. The river was up so high that no one could cross at all. The railroad is on the other side of the river. I seldom ever get a letter from you now. I know it is not your fault. You have no opportunity to mail letters. I don't fret about it as I use to. I almost know you are safe. I may be deceived but I don't believe it.

Yesterday I came up here to Mr. Williams. I am right in my old neighborhood. About a mile from our old place. I have not been up to see it yet but will in a few days. I passed the old school house yesterday as I came up here. I was astonished to see things so little changed. Every little path was familiar to me. It made me almost a child again in my feelings. It is a very great pleasure to me to visit my old home and friends. You have no idea how much I am enjoying my visit. If you could only be with me. That is the only thing that is a drawback to my happiness. I know it is an impossibility for you to be with me and I am just learning to take things as I should. My relations are all glad to see me and everyone anxious for me to spend some time with them. When I get to a place it is hard for me to get away. I went to Mr. Painter's to stay a week and stayed over three and they let me off then only with a promise to go back and stay with them again. I shall have to stay here at least two or three weeks before I can get off I know. I went to church last Sunday—saw uncle Sydney and his children. He was very glad to see me and insisted on my coming down and staying with them some. Almost everybody I meet knows me. They all say I have changed very little. Even the old Negroes I used to know are glad to see me.

I wonder if you have had as much rain where you are as we have had here. The farmers' crops are all ruined. You never saw such long looking faces in your life. Vicksburg has at last fallen. Everybody predicts the war prolonged by it. The papers say the darkest hour of the Confederacy has come. I hope so. Our last account from Gen. Lee was that he was moving back this way. I do so hope he will recross the Potomac. Then I will come on up to Sperryville right away and see my darling. It has been two months today darling since I parted from you. I wasn't to stay but three months. I wrote to you some time ago how well Ida was looking. But she has fallen off in the last two weeks to nothing in the world but skin and bones. She has no appetite to eat. I don't know what can be the matter with her. She plays about as usual but she is not well. Nance is most always sick too. She is looking very badly.

She has chronic diarrhea. This country agrees with me better than any of us. I am as fat as you ever saw me. He is fat too, papa, and just as smart and as sweet as ever. I do wish you could see him now. You wouldn't want to sell he, pa. You would be too proud of him. I have had no letter from home since I wrote to you last. I know they are all very uneasy about you. We have a mail here tomorrow. I hope I will hear from you. I have written to [South] Boston for my letters to be sent on here. The mail goes direct from here to [South] Boston. My last letter from you was written on the twenty-third.

You can continue to send your letters to [South] Boston. I get them just as soon from there as if you were to direct them here. I shall go from here to Uncle Sydney's and stay there a week or two and then go to Mr. Fourquesen's and then on up to Sperryville. I wish I could see you this morning. I want to see you so bad. Bless your dear heart I love you better than any other woman ever did love a husband. Ida says give my love to Pa. But she sends more love than all.

Good bye. God bless you my darling. Good bye.

Your Wife

Person Co., N. C.
Friday, July 16, 1863

My dear Darling—

No letter yet written since the fight—I do wish I could get one—I have had one since I wrote to you last on the Twenty-fifth of last month. That was a long time ago. Don't think I am complaining of you. I know it is not your fault. I don't think you are hurt. But I do want a letter so bad I am almost crazy. I keep writing to you but when I write a letter I don't feel like you will ever see it. I wish the army had never crossed the Potomac. Everybody is low spirited and discouraged about the war. Nobody seems to see any end to it and I am like everybody else. I begin to think it will never end. If I could just take you and go home I would be the happiest mortal on earth. We are all well except Ida. She is puny yet but better than she was last week I think. Papa, if you could just hear this little man here say My Papa you would mash his mouth sure enough. He can say it as good as anybody. You never saw a little thing try as hard to talk as he does. He calls Nance—Nannie very plain. Mama thinks it is the smartest thing she ever saw. He has two more teeth and can stand up by a chair and walk around it. Mama is trying to have him very smart by the time you see him again, papa. You will be proud of your little man.

I went to see a shoe maker yesterday and engaged a pair of leather shoes for myself at the enormous price of twenty dollars. I am almost without shoes and had begun to think

I should have to go barefooted. I shall be so proud of my gingham dresses. Tell Mose not to let them get lost. To hold on to them but I shall be prouder if my darling gets back safe than I would be of all the goods in the whole of Yankeedom. I wonder when we will have another happy meeting. Write to me when I must come to Sperryville.

I have been to my old home. It looks quite natural. I went all through the old house. I was a child again in my feelings. It made me sad to think of the changes since I left it. It seems but just the other day I left here a mere child and now I am back again with children almost as old as I was when I left. We are growing old fast darling and it hurts me to think our best days are spent apart from each other. We could be so happy but for this war. But never mind. It is obliged to have an end sometime and then we will be so happy.

Good bye my darling. Good bye.

Your Wife

At Mr. Williams', Person Co., N. C
Wednesday, July 23, 1863

My dear darling

How I wish I could exchange pen, ink, and paper for a seat by your side with your head in my lap for a good long talk such as we used to have in bygone days. It would be happiness enough for me. To day has been the happiest day I have spent in some time. Three weeks ago the big fight commenced and I have just today got your letter written since the battle. Got six all at once. I was getting very uneasy and had concluded to go to [South] Boston and telegraph to Riddle to know if there was any of the Thirty-first Georgia in Richmond. I thought in that way I might hear something from you. I felt like you were safe but I wanted to know it. I feel a little restless and uneasy about the wound you received in your side. I do hope it is well. Couldn't you have gotten a furlough on account of it? You ought to have tried. I would have given you a warm welcome. I do want to see you so bad I don't know what to do. Always after a battle I want to see you worse than ever. I reckon it is because you have been in such danger. My heart has been overflowing with gratitude all day to the good being Who has been so wonderful as to spare you to me. I do so sincerely hope you may never be in another battle. That the last battle of the war has been fought. I am afraid it is in vain to hope for peace in a long time yet. What do you think of the prospect? Everybody here looks on the dark side. I am so sorry the Yankees got your band. Did they get my dresses? If they did I shall hate it mortally. I was afraid maybe they had Uncle Moses too as they captured a good many Negroes. I am very anxious to make my visit up to Sperryville but will hold off as long as possible I look forward to our next meeting with a great deal of pleasure. If I could only be with you always I would ask no greater earthly blessing —no greater happiness. If the war would only end.

I had a letter from Clem a few days since and I know you will be sorry to hear of Charles Carter's death. He was killed by lightning while out on his plantation. Willie Palmer I am afraid is dead too. His mother got a letter to come on to Atlanta immediately if she wanted to see him alive. She and Pink started right away. Oh I am so thankful while so many have died and been killed that I still have my darling. Ida's health seems to have improved some. She goes to school part of the time. There is a very good school here in the yard. She has been all day writing a letter to old Aunt Rachel for Nance [slaves]. It is a very interesting epistle. Well papa I reckon you want to hear something from your little man.

He is just as saucy as he can be—got two more teeth and tries to see how hard he can bite me every time he goes to suck. He is not as fat as he has been but is perfectly well. I had rather he was not so fat. He suffered so much with heat. He has got a little hat. A young lad cousin of mine plaited it of straw and gave it to him. It is very nice. I have made him say my papa so much and worried him so about it that now when I ask him to say it he won't open his lips. A contrary little rascal. He is a dear little fellow, papa I expect it will be a month yet before I get back to [South] Boston unless you write for me to come to Sperryville sooner. I find it very pleasant visiting much more so than staying down there. You may continue to direct your letters there as I get them just as soon. They get to [South] Boston one evening and are sent up here the next day. It has been so long since I got a letter until to day. I am right foolish about them. I can't tell the number of times I have read them over. I got my new twenty dollar shoes today. They are right rough but it was the best I could do. Do you know what Green Clifton done with the bundle they sent me from home by him? Please ask him. Ida had a pair of shoes in it. This is a beautiful moonlight night. How I wish we were in our dear old home together out on the front porch. How I would talk to you. I think of the old home often. How lonely and desolate it must look all shut up. I have spent many happy hours there as well as many sorrowful ones. I wish I knew tonight that you were perfectly well I am uneasy about your [wounded] side. Good bye darling. God bless you.

Your Wife

Clement to Allie:

Near Martinsburg, [West] Va.
July 15, 1863

My dearest Darling

I have just received your letters of the 27th of June & 3rd of July. They make me so anxious to see you again. I have been sending all my late letters to South Boston & I am afraid you have, on that account, failed to hear from me. I wrote three one day sending one each to South Boston, Black Walnut & Cunningham's store. From this time I think you can hear from me more regularly—Well, darling the Pennsylvania campaign is over & we are back again on our own soil. We have accomplished a good deal but still the army & the Public are both disappointed. We expected to do too much. To capture Washington, destroy the Federal army & end the war in six weeks was a physical impossibility—but we have done a great deal. We have brought off over a thousand wagons—Perhaps two thousand horses—Pro-

248

visions for the army during its stay & for a month more. We have taught the Pennsylvanians what war is & left in their state a great battle field to contemplate, with a large town full of their thousands of wounded.

I hope that no necessity will occur for another invasion. We can make the Yankee army behave very respectfully in Virginia for the balance of the Summer.

Our army is moving toward Winchester. Probably we will cross the mountains again in part, our Corps remaining in the Valley. As soon as I can find out enough of our probable movements & whether it will do for you to come to Sperryville, I will write & send for you. I am very anxious for you to come down & see Mrs. Amiss. I know you will enjoy yourself and I will see you again.

July 16. 6 o'clock a.m. We are still marching toward Winchester but I think we will soon come to a halt & rest of some duration. I have no news additional to write to you. Take care of yourself. Pa is so glad that his little man is well. Pa wants to hear him talk some. My little daughter will enjoy the trip to Sperryville very much I think. Much of the road runs in sight of and along the mountains & the views are delightful.

Good bye—God preserve my treasures—
Good bye.
Your Husband

[During the twenty days Allie was writing those letters and waiting for word from Clement, the Army of Northern Virginia had retreated in orderly fashion and was cautiously waiting, for the Potomac, then at flood stage to crest and subside, when it re-crossed the river on the night of July 13-14, and marched slowly up the Shenandoah Valley. By the middle of July, Clement's letters began to say less about the Gettysburg Campaign and to pick up the current situation.

Subsequent to July 13-14, when the Confederates crossed the Potomac, the Union army gingerly pursued, making feints and maneuvers. In all these marches and countermarches on Virginia soil, there occurred only two noteworthy expeditions involving the infantry. The first was at Bristoe Station in October. The second was an abortive confrontation at Mine Run and Rappahannock Station in November and the early days of December.

Very little of the army's actions in these next five months is covered in the Evans' correspondence. This is not only because of the fact that nothing of consequence took place in his sector, but is also because Allie had joined Clement just after August 27 and remained near the army until almost November.

Because of Evans' relatively uneventful days and Allie's relatively quiet domestic life, their letters are longer and more personal throughout July and August.]

Clement to Allie:

> In camp near Darkesville, [West] Va.
> July 18, 1863
> 5 o'clock p.m.

My dear Darling

I have just packed you a little black greasy box about two feet long, one broad & one foot deep to send to you from Staunton by express to South Boston. You may look for it I think about the first of August. Perhaps a little earlier or later, as I expect Orr to carry it to Staunton & send it from there. It contains a few things which I purchased in Pennsylvania for you. You will be disappointed, I know, but I had no transportation at all at the very time when I could have bought such things as you needed; several of the articles were given to me, among them several yards of black cotton velvet which I send although I do not know what you will do with it. The merchants had run off all their fine goods and therefore I could buy nothing of the kind. The one piece of calico which I send was the best I saw. The 20 yards of check Gingham will do for you & the little Lady I suppose— Perhaps "He" may come in for a showing. The other two muslin dresses are quite common, for I bought them in the night & could not tell their quality. The needles & thread you will appreciate most I know—There is such a jumbled mess of everything in such a *dirty box* that I advise you not to open your *treasure* until you have it in your room.

Green Clifton brought me another pair of excellent

boots which fit me well enough—He says he left a bundle for you in Richmond with "*Martha*," Mrs. Matheien's Negro woman. I shall write to *McGarie* to have it sent to you by express.

You will find also in the box nearly two yards of woolen gray tweed or flannel, which will make me a sack or shirt for next winter, unless "He" wants it, Mama, for something. I shall have to begin to look out for a winter uniform coat soon. I was foolish enough to trouble you about getting some cloth in the country where you are, but I recall the request. I know you cannot do it.

Mose is on the sick list and I am living according to circumstances. Happily an occasional starving benefits my health. In all my troubles I think of the happy, happy future, darling. You promise in your letters to devote yourself to my happiness to repay me for all these sufferings & privations. The *mere promise* darling, pays me for all. The actual performance will be all clear profit.

Some are desponding about our country now because of our recent heavy reverses. They have been heavy certainly—But I do not see how the ability of the Confederacy to maintain itself has been impaired. We have not for a whole year been able to help Louisiana, Texas, Arkansas, Missouri, or Kentucky. We can help either as much now as ever, or rather each can take care of itself as well as before. I do not believe that these events will prolong the war. On the contrary, the European nations are not waiting to see if we can maintain ourselves, but are waiting to interfere whenever we are about to be subdued. You see if the country is not full of rumors, of mediation, intervention & recognition immediately. I should not be surprised to hear within sixty days that our independence was recognized by the leading nations of Europe, upon a basis that forced a peace before Christmas. Am I too hopeful?

Mrs. General Gordon is here. She has no little children to trouble with. I could so easily arrange for you to be with me all the time, if the *little man* would stay—

But he has to travel wherever Ma does. But have you not enjoyed yourself this year much more than you would have done in Lumpkin? Tell me has not your sojourn among your relations and old friends been *very* pleasant? I do hope you have enjoyed yourself to your heart's content.

I wrote to Mother that she might look for you next winter, perhaps in November—but of course I must have you with me two or three months first—say August, September & October—Here I am telling of your coming to me in August and it is the 18th of July—Time slips away so fast! Two months since we parted! I *must* see you in one more month. I want Ida to travel some through the mountains & see as much of Virginia as possible. She is old enough to be benefitted physically & mentally by the trip.

I have no news of army movements. We are all lying still & Genl. Lee is planning. I hope he won't plan any more "Gettysburg mountains" for us to storm.

Good bye now & the Good Being bless you, my darling. Kiss my little dears.

Good bye.   Your Husband

In camp near Darkesville, [West] Va.
July 19, 1863
Sunday 7 o'clock p.m.

My dearest Darling

I still write from the camp. Our rest has been a long one and we have all recovered from the fatigue of the Pennsylvania campaign. I suppose Genl. Lee will hardly remain inactive many more days, but will soon have us on the tramp somewhere, either across the mountains or across the Potomac. The impression seems to be growing that we are to have another invasion, but I do not know upon what foundation it rests. At present I can see no indications of a move in any particular direction. It is reported that we have another pontoon train on the way, but this like a thousand such reports may be utterly without foundation. I hear also that portions of our cavalry have recrossed the Potomac again—but of this

I also know nothing positive. The only objection I have to going again into Maryland is personal, being because it interrupts our regular correspondence, and places me so far from you. Since their recent successes the Yankees may get it into their heads to try the capture of Richmond again, by moving their main force directly forward. In that event we may move with them, or indeed, Genl. Lee may leave Richmond to its present defences and march boldly into Maryland. But these are all *speculations* and only waste the paper they are written on.

Orr is still here and therefore your box is not on its way to Staunton, but he will leave about the 21st and get to Staunton about the 25th. You ought therefore to get your box at least by the 30th, or even sooner. Don't be at all excited about what it contains for I assure you I am almost ashamed to send it to you. The dresses are so coarse that I advise you to trade them off. Pa promised to send "He" something, but, Ma, there was nothing to be had for him.

One [man] of my regiment came from Lumpkin lately & says we have a splendid garden of vegetables of all sorts. Don't you wish we were there! What a nice shade in the yard & how comfortable and cozy the house looks. Think of the Porch in the cool of the evening & our walks to the college—Ah this makes me tired of war!

I wrote to Bro. Davies today and sent him a *Yankee sermon*. It was full of bitterness & blasphemy. Did I write to you that Charlie Carter was killed by lightning? He was found dead in the field. I understand that Jared Ball has been conscripted. His substitute has reached 21 years of age, & he is trying to be exempted on the ground of being a miller, but Curt Lowe put him through. I understand that Curtis is putting everyone in that he can get his hands on.

Lieut. Miller from the Harris Co. Company has just come in from Richmond. He has been on the way about two weeks and says large numbers of convalescent soldiers are returning. In a short time the losses across the Potomac will be made up and the army will be as strong as ever.

253

Apples are beginning to ripen where you are, now, are they not? I hope your good appetite for them will be satisfied this year. You must not go home until you have received complete satisfaction. Enjoy yourself my dear. Commit my safety to Providence, bear our separation with cheerfulness, and amuse yourself in every way that you can.

One more month and I hope to see you by some means. I can arrange very easily for you to meet Orr in Richmond & he will see you safely through. But a month from now may find us somewhere else besides the Valley of Virginia. Perhaps nearer to you than we are now, perhaps farther off. Any how we must meet by the first of September. Can't you live on this hope? I do. I have been counting by months, and now I can begin to count the weeks. They will soon pass. I was so much disappointed last night when the mail came and there was no letter for me. Certainly I will get one to night, or tomorrow, as your last was written on the 6th two weeks ago. Your letters are of the right sort. They are long, cheerful and about yourself and the little darlings. Pa could read a bushel of them daily if he could get them. Did you receive all the short pencil letters I wrote to you, about the time we were at Winchester?

Tell me if you are afraid to venture so far with the little ones as Winchester—& could you endure a stage passage of a *hundred miles*? Poor darling—perhaps next winter if Major [John H.] Lowe & Captain [Rudolphus T.] Pride (who will soon be Lieut. Col. Lowe & Major Pride) both keep well so as to be on duty with the regiment, I can get a leave of absence to go home. Now, how shall we manage so as to make the most of it? Don't you think you had better stay with me until November—Then go home and let me come in January & you return with me in February? I think this would be "so nice," as our old friend says.

Kiss my little dears as usual. Pa is so anxious to see them—& Ma too.

Good bye.
Your Husband

254

Camp near Darkesville, [West] Va.
July 20, 1863
Monday 8 o'clock a.m.

My dear Allie

I wrote to you last night and I hope the letter went off this morning, but I am not certain, and as I have another opportunity, I will write again. I know I cannot send you more letters than you want to read.

The weather has cleared up again and the last few days have been quite warm—that is, warm in the middle of the day, but the evening & morning are very delightful. All this is quite in contrast to the almost constant rain or cloudy weather we have had for weeks.

I have just sent out to have a pretty girl make me a Gingham shirt. Don't you wish it was you? Well darling I suppose she may be pretty, I have never seen her. Don't be jealous—all my thoughts are for you. The shirt will not please me half so well as it would if you were the manufacturer.

I told you in one of my letters that the Yankees had captured my band. Since then I have managed around & got it up again by getting other instruments, but not so many. The Yankees got 14 splendid instruments from me. The band was getting along splendidly, before this misfortune.

Among the various camp rumors I now hear it surmised that our Division is to be kept in the Valley for its protection, while the rest of the army crosses the mountains. I shall be satisfied with this arrangement provided they will make it permanent enough for me to send for you.

I have lain almost still for the five days we have been in camp here. I have hardly felt like moving my bones for any purpose, but now I am rested & restless again. Again would I like to be on the march—not the hard, toilsome night march—but the short easy tramps of fifteen miles per day. The change of place with its exercise & excitement keeps my spirits up, keeps off the Dyspepsia & blues & gallops off the wearisome days.

How heartily I can sing

Roll on, Roll on, sweet moments roll on,
When I shall go home, go home, go home.

I shall keep off my homesickness as much as possible.
The hope of seeing you soon buoys me up beyond measure. Where you are, home & heart are, my dear. If I had
to count months, instead of weeks, before I could see
you again I should be blue indeed. But my calculation
is for me to be with you in September & October, & then
for me to be with you in January again.

We have just received orders to cook two days' rations
preparatory for a move. Longstreet's Corps has gone toward Smithfield, which is between Winchester & Harpers
Ferry. We may travel in the same direction. 12 o'clock
M. No news yet. But we will certainly go in a day or two
somewhere. Good bye. Kiss my little darlings. Good bye.

Your Husband

Camp near Darkesville
6 o'clock a.m. July 20, 1863

My dear Darling
I think I might commence or end this letter with
these two sublime lines.

My hand is bad my ink is pale
My love for you will never fail.

Any how I will abandon the ink & take up a pencil, although a pencil letter may be suggestive to you of battles & marches, for generally I write in pencil under such
circumstances. I have just awaked out of a long sleep. I
try to sleep off the long, long days. I love to see the sun
set because I can say one more day is gone, one day
less of war, of toil, of suffering, of separation from you.
One day nearer our meeting, one day nearer that time
we have promised ourselves to be together with none
but God to put us asunder. There is no variety in our
life now—one day is the twin of the day preceding—
cook & eat beef & flour—sleep, drink—make morning reports—send off the sick—all alike the dull monotony of
life in camp. It is hard to be satisfied, while toiling on

the march, weary, worn, without sleep & sick how I long for a few days of rest, now I want to march again. Sometimes I even catch myself sighing for the hot excitement of battle—but the recurring thought of blood—wounds—death—widows, orphans & bereaved Mothers chill every such heartless aspiration. Oh if there could always be peace in the earth! What a glorious home for man prepared for him was this planet before his first disobedience brought sin into this world with all its woe. How glorious still it might be if *love* reigned in the hearts of men instead of *hate*.

I want to see my little family so much. Having cut myself loose from a permanent home I have ceased to think of the particular spot of ground where our house stands as home. But to whatever place you go there I think of home. We will meet soon either by my coming to you or you coming to me.

I understand we are only to move for a change of camp & perhaps a few miles will cover the march. I hear no news from any quarter. Since the terrible commotion about the 1st of July at Gettysburg & Vicksburg all seems to have become quiet & inactive. The leaders on each side have to take time to look about them & determine what mischief to do next. I can't guess even at what may be the next great move on the chess board. We are ordered to move at once.

Good bye
Your Husband

[The following was added as a postscript to the preceding letter of July 20.]

July 22nd 4 o'clock p.m. Sure enough the pencil does indicate hard marching & fighting. I was scarcely done writing my sighs for another march & another fight before both were on hand. We marched until eleven o'clock at night. Up again at day break & marched 20 miles rapidly in the hot sun, for the purpose in conjunction with Johnson & Rodes, of surrounding & capturing Genls. [Benjamin F.] Kelley & [Col. James] Mulligan who with about 7 or 8000 men had crossed at Williamsport & stationed themselves at Hodgesville, about six miles from Martinsburg. But we found the nest warm & the birds flown. The Yankees had run off before we could get around them. We had nothing to do but encamp. This morning at sunrise we marched back again to Bunker Hill on the road to Winchester. I am so tired that I would write a letter to but *one* person in the world. Longstreet's corps has crossed the mountains & A. P. Hill is following him. We will come next & I suppose the march will continue to morrow. This will bring me nearer to you and we will soon meet again.

I received two letters from you to day. One dated *June* 13th, the day the battle of Winchester was fought. Perhaps at the very hour you were writing so confidently in the protection of the Good Being over me, I was indeed shielded by Him from the thousand dangers of that fierce little battle. The other letter was dated July 13th and you had heard of the terrible battle of Gettysburg, but not one word of me, yet you say you know I am safe. You feel confident that Providence has spared me. How I love you darling for such faith as that. You say you have committed me into His keeping. God bless you for it my dear wife. Whatever He does now will all be right.

I am so sorry to hear that my poor little daughter has fallen off. What can be the reason that she falls away so suddenly sometimes, & when she commences to get well she fattens about as fast? I am so much afraid that we cannot give her a healthy robust constitution. We have tried a variety of climates & none seem to favor her peculiarly.

Would it not be well to leave Nancy & hire a nurse when you come to see me?

Orr has not started yet, but will in a day or two. I think your box ought to be at South Boston, by the first week in August. Do not make sport of my purchases. I did the best I could under the circumstances.

In three more days we will in all likelihood be across the mountains. I expect my chances to write to you will be bad, for several days, but I will do my best. I look for another great battle in August somewhere on the Rappahannock again. I tell you this to prepare your mind.

July 23rd—Sunrise.

We march toward Winchester & across the mountains.

Good bye.

Your Husband

Winchester, [Va.] July 23, 1863
Marching—9 o'clock a.m.

My dear Darling

I almost feel like I was going to you, as we march again toward Richmond. Now if you were at Sperryville I would see you to morrow. What a pity we did not arrange for you to go to Sperryville from Hamilton's Crossing. Then I could have seen you as we marched toward Maryland and again as we march back. But we foreknow nothing and it is well that we do not. Even now I do not know whether to send you "orders" to cook rations & move. I am sorry however that you will likely miss your visit to Sperryville altogether. For we shall move beyond there doubtless. We certainly will be nearer Culpeper or Gordonsville in a few days unless the Yankees change their programme.

Well you have been enjoying yourself better where you are a great deal than you would have done, generally, at Sperryville, for you have been among old friends and old scenes. But I must find out enough soon to let you know where to come.

Good bye.

I only write just to let you know where we are from time to time. Give my loving to my little darlings.

Good bye.

Your Husband

6 miles from Winchester [Va.]
July 23rd, 1863
8 o'clock P.M.

My dear Darling

We are on the route to cross the mountains. We move

259

to morrow at dawn toward Front Royal. I write by fire-
light just because the mail leaves to morrow, & I want to
send you a letter by every opportunity. I have heard
some cannonading in the direction of Snicker's Gap. I
suppose we go to place ourselves between the enemy &
Richmond. How many noble lives have been offered up
to save Richmond! And still they must be offered.

I rec'd a letter from Mat today. She sends no news at
all. I have written to her to have a supply of wheat &
corn bought for you, and also to have your smoke house
provided. I fear you will have to board out even when
you go home.

What do you think of our letting your sister have
Hannah? She does not suit us now at all & will be only
a constant source of trouble. I do not want any one to
have her but your sister.

I may send you a dispatch to meet Capt. Orr in Richmond sometime soon. But do not hurry back to [South]
Boston on that account for it may be several weeks yet. If
I find out that you can come earlier I will send you a
dispatch.

Tell your kinfolks that if the war continues I shall
quarter you on them next year again and they must bear
it with the best grace possible. I want to visit all of
them & tell them how much I am obliged to them for
their kindness to you.

I must close—Goodbye my dearest. How much I do
love you. You are in all my thoughts. Tell Ida she must
get well & look rosy again. Smash that old boy for Pa.
Good bye.

Your Husband

Allie to Clement:

At Mr. Williams', Person Co., N.C.
July 26, 1863
(Monday)

My dear darling

I want to see you so bad this morning. I have got so
much to talk to you about. So much to tell you. I can't

write like I want to. If I could be with you my tongue would never tire. July is almost gone and I am glad of it. One more month and then it will be September and you know I was to come to you then. How glad I will be to see you. Nobody but me knows. I think of you all the time. All day long my thoughts are of my darling and all night I dream of him. It never was intended for us to be separated darling and I don't believe it is right. If I had it in my power I would injure the Confederacy one soldier. I do wish you could get out but I know there is no chance now less than there ever was before. I wish you had got a substitute last year for now it is past all hope. I wonder if this war will ever end. I don't believe it will. I am enjoying myself just as well as I could anywhere away from you. I have been here two weeks and will probably be here two weeks longer. They seem very anxious for me to stay and it is very pleasant here and don't cost anything—The longer I stay here the longer I can stay with you when I come to see you. Everybody predicts that Charleston [South Carolina] will soon fall and that then all communication will be cut off with the other Southern states. If that is the case I won't be able to get home. If it is to be so, I am very glad it caught me on this side for I couldn't stay away at home and not hear from you. It is bad enough here. I think every postmaster ought to be turned out of office. My last letter from you was written on the other side of the Potomac on the tenth—two weeks ago. I know you have written often enough but it is the fault of the mails. It takes all the patience and fortitude I have to bear with it. Everybody else's letters come in the same way—two weeks after they are written. It is too bad but I console myself thinking if there was anything the matter with you, you would send for me. You promised me to and I know you will do it and therefore I am conttented. I went to church yesterday. Saw a good many of my old acquaintances. As a matter of course they were all glad to see me and all anxious for me to visit them. I am afraid you are almost drowned by the rain. I never saw as much rain fall in my life.

I don't expect your clothes have been dry now in a week. Poor darling how do you sleep at night? I am so sorry for you. I wish I could come and take your place and let you rest. I would willingly do it. I know you are worn out. I wonder if there will ever be an end to all this. Everybody I see has given up the Confederacy. Say that we will be subjugated. That we are whipped. If it is to be I hope it will come quick and let you come home. That is the only thing on earth that I ask for. You ought to see He chew sweet gum, papa. Mama is afraid that he will get to chewing tobacco. The little rascal will chew a piece of sweet gum an hour at the time. He can talk right good but is mighty mean about it. It won't be long before you can put He in as a substitute papa. He can take your place. You never heard such a fuss as he makes when he sees a horse. I think he will have to join the cavalry.

Ida is well and as frisky as ever. Always talking about pa and how bad she wants to see him. She has picked up another little sweetheart down here. A little better looking choice than Joe Massy. Did I write you about her getting scalded? She scalded her left hand very badly last week and of all the capering you ever saw done she did it. She has a right bad sore on her leg that she is taking on about now. I hope I will get some letters from you today. Do you get my letters? I wish I could see you. Good bye. Good bye.

Your Wife.

Clement to Allie:

En route for Madison C.H., Va.
July 29th, 1863

My dear Allie.

I write hastily just to let you know that we have crossed the Blue Ridge again and are "marching on." Some surmise that we will turn up again at Hamilton's Crossing. I would not be surprised at all to see old Alsop's house again at the end of a week.

We crossed at the same high crooked gap where we marched through last year. We had a time of it. I assure you. Yesterday it rained a young flood & the clouds are heavy & threatening this morning. I have had no letter from you in nearly two weeks. I know I shall get several if they are not lost in our miserable mail arrangements.

Good bye. I shall write again tomorrow—Good bye—Kiss my precious little treasures—

Your Husband

Allie to Clement:

Person Co., N.C.
July 30, 1863

My dear darling

Last night I dreamed I got nine letters from you and before I got through reading them you came yourself. I was so glad to see you, so happy in my dream that I wished it could have lasted a month. This morning soon after breakfast I got two letters from you and I could not help from looking up to see if you were not coming sure enough before I got through reading them. But darling didn't come—my dream did not come to pass. Poor darling what you have suffered since I saw you. I am uneasy for you darling. My heart aches to think of it. I can't enjoy myself for thinking of you. How tired you are. How sleepy and often so hungry while I am living at my ease. A plenty of the best of everything in the country. What would you give for one good night's rest in a good bed such as I have every night. Never mind darling if this war ever does end and we get home together again I will do my part in making your life comfortable and happy and try to repay you and make up for all this suffering and hardship you are going through with now. You shall have the softest bed and the best of eatables that it will be in my power to provide for you. Bless your dear heart. I could cry my eyes out for you if it would do any good. But time will put an end to it all sooner or later.

Yesterday I spent the day with a cousin of mine. Left the

baby and Ida here. They are very anxious to have me stay with them sometime but their children have the whooping cough the very worst sort. I am afraid to go for fear the baby will take it. He told me if you should get sick or wounded at any time and I should need a friend to go with me to see you or to go after you, he would go willingly and bring you to his house for all of which I was very much obliged to him. Ida is sitting down here by me playing with her rag doll. She says give my love to pa and tell him I want to see him mighty bad. That she was mighty sorry he got wounded but she was mighty glad it was slight. You just ought to see he, papa, with his new hat on. He is a man sure enough now. He has most got two more teeth. Nance works day and night on him trying to learn him so many little smart tricks before he comes to see him papa, but he is the contrariest little rascal that ever lived. Mama wants to whip him right good sometimes. I do hope you are in camp now and rested. I am afraid you are sick. I have but one more half sheet of paper and don't know where I shall get any more. I will try though and make out a letter to you two or three times a week even if I have to beg it. Good bye darling. I wonder when I will see you. Good bye God bless you and take care of you my darling.

Your Wife.

Clement to Allie:

In camp near Madison C. H., Va.
July 30th, 1863

My dear Allie

We are encamped at the same spot we were last winter when we halted here for a few days rest on our march from the Valley to Fredericksburg. We will in all probability still rest here for a few days and then perhaps the same march to Fredericksburg will be repeated.

I received today your letter of the 23rd telling me that you had just received my letters written after the Gettysburg battle. I knew there would be a long delay, for I think the battle had been over a week or more before I had any opportunity at all to send you a letter, and then it required another week or more to get the letter far enough into Virginia to be mailed. I expect some of my letters did not reach you at all.

Ma tries to make out he can say "My papa" but Pa don't believe one word of it. It is like some of his other smart doings which Pa never saw. I am so glad to hear that Ida's health improves. Do not confine her to school if it affects her health.

Your Sperryville trip is all knocked in the head now. The Yankees are in that region and probably our army will not again soon occupy such a line as will enable you to visit Mrs. Amiss. In fact if you had gone while we invaded Pennsylvania I should have been uneasy about you all the time for fear the Yankee cavalry should march into the place. But instead of that we may soon be back at the old stand point near Hamilton's Crossing where you can get to me easily.

I have just come in from a good vegetable dinner at a citizen's house. I ate today my first vegetable *this summer*. Over four months of the vegetable season with us at home is gone, and I have had my first dinner. I shall continue my dinner there so long as we stay here.

I almost envy Capt. Cody's wound, which is slight enough to do him no harm and severe enough to enable him to stay at home two or three months. He has gone home on a sixty days furlough just in the season when everything is flourishing & plenty at home, and when the service is the hardest here. Was it not today a year ago when I reached home? I wonder when I can go again? Perhaps if nothing happens I can spend January there. How glad I would be to know I did not have to endure another year of this kind of life. I want quiet and rest once more. A home and my family with me at home again. I know I can appreciate these enjoyments when they become mine again. I want to see you so much, but our movements are so uncertain that I am afraid if I should write for you to come to any point, we might be a long ways off before you would reach us. Anyhow it will not be long before the plans of the enemy will be so far developed that I can make a reasonable calculation about when and where we shall meet. In the meantime go on and enjoy yourself. Stay where you are among your relatives and be contented. You are better off there than you would be at home in Georgia so far from me, or if you were with the army exposed to all the uncertainties of a campaign. Do not be uneasy about my wound. It is entirely well. In fact after I recovered from the effects of the blow I suffered no pain, and the slight cut soon healed. Scarcely a trace of it now remains. It was so slight that I did not have it reported at all.

I wrote to you that Green Clifton had left your bundle in Richmond & that I would have it sent to you by express. I am afraid it may be lost yet. Has the little greasy Pennsylvania box came to you? Didn't you laugh when you opened it and found such a mixed mess of everything? I hope it has gone safely through for although it is a small affair, yet there are many useful things to be found in it.

If we go to Fredericksburg my first care will be to find a boarding place for you to come. This I hope will all happen in August so I can soon cease to count by weeks and commence to count the days that are to pass before we meet again. I shall find some other place than Alsop for I cannot endure the idea of your staying there. I know I can do better for us both than to go to that place again. But after all the enemy may so dispose his armies as to force us immediately around Richmond. This will be very much to be regretted because of the unhealthiness & want of comfort in our position there.

You must make your arrangements to either wait until the first of September or to come by the middle of August according to circumstances. The time will be soon past. Before this letter reaches you it will be August and then only a few more weeks of separation. We can bear it my darling with the hope of reunion before us.

Kiss my little darlings for their Pa. Write a heap about them in your letters. Tell me all their "smart doings."

Pa knows he can't talk. You needn't try to fool Pa in that way. But in a few more months the little tongue will be rattling & the little feet pattering on the floor.

Good bye: My best wishes to all our kin-folks.

Good bye.

Your Husband

Near Madison C. H. [Va.]
July 31st, [18]63
9 o'clock a.m.

My dear Darling

We move this morning I suppose toward Culpeper C. H. The balance of the army is in that region & we are to join them. I have no news of any interest to you. The Yankees I suppose are feeling about for a weak spot, or only dallying until they can concentrate larger armies for an advance upon Richmond.

August 2nd

We have two short marches and are now about three miles from Orange Court House and within two days march of Fredericksburg. I think in all likelihood that we will be near that place by the 5th of this month. What say you to an early visit in that event? By the time all arrangements can be made it will be toward the middle of August, or last of August before you can come I suppose.

I have nothing of interest to write. The army is strengthening every day, & is invincible in its defensive policy.

Your letters give a glowing account of the progress of the little gentleman in all accomplishments. I can't believe all but I will do my best, and let you play on my credulity to a considerable extent. I don't believe one word about all his talking & walking—next time he will be whistling &c. Smart boy, Ma, but Pa don't believe it. Pa thinks his little lady is the smartest thing on earth now.

Write to me a good long letter about yourself & everything.

Good bye.   Your Husband

In camp six miles from Orange C. H. [Va.]
5 o'clock p.m.
Aug 2nd, 1863

My dear Darling

I have just received another letter from you dated the
26th. I don't think I get all your letters, and they come
very irregularly, but I try to be satisfied. You complain
also of the long delay which attend my letters to you.
I hope those which I have written since we recrossed
the Potomac have gone to you more promptly. Lately I
have written at every possible opportunity; sometimes
every day.

It is not yet certain that we are going to Fredericksburg as all this depends on the enemy. Yesterday part
of the army commenced crossing at that place, but the
enemy commenced crossing at Kelly's Ford, which caused
a general halt. It may be that Meade intends to try this
route to Richmond.

If Charleston [South Carolina] is taken it will be sometime before Augusta will fall and that route home will
still be open. But any how we will be governed by circumstances & you can remain in Virginia where you are.
I regard Virginia as home until the war end, for I make
no calculations on your staying in Georgia for any length
of time.

You don't know how much I want to see you, & my
little lady and the *talking prodigy* too. Pa don't believe
all those great tales Ma writes about him. It won't be
long now before we see each other. Only a few weeks
at most. I shall make arrangements for you as soon as
we get to our stand point. This month will not pass off
without something definite.

Aug 3rd Morning:

No move yet, but we are still under orders to move at
daylight. The enemy crossed in some force at Kelly's
Ford and we have been under orders to keep every man
in camp & be ready to move at a moment's notice.

The weather is intensely hot. I think the days & nights
are both sultry. This makes marching very oppressive
and I hope we shall have but little of it to do.

I send you this letter leaving you in uncertainty as to whether we will soon go to Fredericksburg or not, but as no mail has been sent off for three or four days you will be impatient for a letter. This I send by a private opportunity. Good bye.

Who is the little gentleman that has stolen my daughter's heart?

Tell him he will have to make himself a man before he can have my little darling.

Good bye.
Your Husband

Allie to Clement:

Person Co., N.C.
August 3, 1863

My dear darling—

I am glad that I can count another month with the past. July is gone and soon August will be gone and then it will be September and then I am to go to see my darling. Time passes rapidly. Am I wrong in wishing it to go still faster? I don't care how swift it goes while the war lasts and I am separated from you but when it ends and we can be together again I want it to stop right still. I have just been amusing myself looking at the baby stripped naked playing in a bowl of water. He does love to play in it. He is so fat and it is so warm I have to keep him almost naked. . . . [Torn off here]

I am going visiting this evening to spend two or three days at Mrs. Trotter's. You have heard me speak of the family. I will see brother's [Robert Walton] old flame, Pat. She has been to see me. Yesterday and today are the first real summer days we have had this summer. This is equal to Georgia weather. Yesterday morning I received four long and very interesting letters from you. You have no idea how much good they have done me. I felt happy all day long after I got them. What would I do if it was not for my letters. I shall write to Mr. Fourquesen to take care of my box until I come. I will be so proud of it—for anything in the shape of dry goods now is appreciated by me. I am almost crazy to get hold of it. I am needing my shoes very much. Papa, He said it don't make any difference if you didn't get he anything in Pennsylvania. He has got a new hat and that will do him. He is the proudest little rascal of it you ever saw. Will sit all day with it on his head. Don't want anybody to touch it. Mama thinks he is just the greatest boy in the Confederacy. He is so much company for me. Our little lady is as frisky as ever. She is a great gal too. I have been reading *Shady Side of Life in a Country Parsonage* to day. I have read it before but it is more interesting to me now than it was the first time I read it. You want to know if I am enjoying the apples down here. I can assure you I am taking full benefit. Take three or four bites everyday. I eat so many apples that I haven't. . . . [Torn out here.]

I had to tell Ida today that if I caught her eating any more I would have to whip her. She eats so much fruit and nothing else that she is as poor as a snake. She don't eat one meal a day. You ought to see him eat peaches and apples too, Papa. He can hide them in a hurry. He cries after every blackberry bush he sees. I have made me a new head dress and laid it away to wear when I come to see you. I think it is powerful pretty. All I think about is going to see my darling and it is the most I talk about too. I want to see you so bad, darling, how can I help it? I feel like I had not seen you in a year. I got the Yankee letter you sent me. I can sympathize with the poor woman and hope he will be able to get back home safe. I am so warm I am about to melt. I wish you were here with me. I have enjoyed my visit up here very much. . . . [The rest of this letter from Allie is missing.]

Clement to Allie:

Camp near Orange C.H. [Va.]
August 5, 1863

Dear darling

I think I will keep a guessing book for my own amusement, in which I will put down my guesses of what will be done by the army just to show myself how often & easily I am deceived. I verily believed that to day we would have been at Hamilton's Crossing, but instead of that it seems now that we will be here a week or more or longer. I think Gen. Lee was fooled too for he started part of the army toward Fredericksburg four days ago and then ordered it back. At present Meade seems to be at a halt, and whether he intends to fight or not is yet uncertain. Your letter of the 29th ult. came to me to day. You write desponding. Just because that woman had her husband with her and yours is not! My darling would you swap husbands with her to day? Or do you think a husband is worthy of a good wife and two nice little children who would not take up arms to defend them? That woman ought to envy you, or any other wife who has a husband doing his duty in the field. You shall come to me just as soon as I can ascertain where we are to stay for any length of time. I will make enquiries and write to you tomorrow. I am so sorry my letters do not reach you. I wrote several to you from the fifteenth to the 25th of July. I wrote about the box I sent by Orr to have expressed to you at [South] Boston. I had it marked to the care of Wm. Fourquesen at South Boston & I expected it to reach you by this time, as Orr reached Staunton with it about the 25th. Orr has not returned yet & I do not know for a certainty that he has yet sent it off.

I received a letter from Mat. She says that Mother & Clem have gone down to Baker to Sister's. She tells me that everybody is going off to the war under the new call, but makes no mention of Jessie. She is anxious for you to come home and speaks of coming where you are if you do not conclude to go back.

Keep in good heart. We will meet soon. Do not despond. The war will close after awhile and then we can go home with good consciences. All will be well with us. "Let not your heart be troubled," all things will work together for our good for do we not love and adore our great Preserver? This is "the valley & shadow" but we will "walk through it & fear no evil for he will guide & comfort us."

If that little man comes about me talking his chat, Pa will just smash that mouth. Pa won't take any impudence from him, Ma, not one bit. You had better not bring him along for Pa will just take him & throw him in the river just as soon as he sees him.

I want to see my new "son in law." Do you think he will do? He will have to be something extra to get my little lady. Love to all. Good bye.

Your husband

Allie to Clement:

Person Co., N.C.
August 6, 1863

My dear darling—

I have just today returned from my visit. Stayed longer than I expected to and you will miss one letter by my visit being prolonged. Yesterday was my day to write as the mail went out today. I had a very pleasant visit—enjoyed it very much and will start on another in the morning to Black Walnut to be gone two days. I am having a fine time but all that don't keep me from wanting to see my darling for I am never so happy as when I am with you. Oh I do want to see you so bad. When I think about it I can't set still. I just want to jump up and run to you. Ida says tell pa if I could just see him I would try to eat him up. She is tolerable well but looks badly yet. I do wish she would get well. I don't send her to school at all now. She don't want to go and I won't compel her. You say you don't believe he can talk, Papa. Do you know what you are talking about? He can talk. He can say Aunt Dina, the name of Cousin Ann's servant that waits on the table. Nance says tell papa he has got six teeth and he makes good use of them for when he gets mad with her he bites her equal to a little squirrel. She says he can make a mouth at any body and points his finger at you. When he sees anybody he asks her who is that. He can say buttermilk and apple. Calls his sister "tis" and her Nannie. Says eat. If you give him an apple he sticks it to her mouth and tells her to bite. He can't eat until she bites a place to start on. He will go under the bed and hide and call you to come and find him. He can pull up by a chair and she tells papa that

272

ain't half he could do but she can't think of it all tonight. He is certainly a great baby. So mama thinks any how. Nance says tell pa him tips about with his hat set on one side of his head and his mouth full of sweetgum as big as any man. Ida insists on my telling pa that she wishes that the war was ended so we could have our old days back again, like we have had and so we could enjoy ourselves again. She says she is so sleepy she can't think of any more to tell but Good night, she says she is ashamed to send him such a message.

I got two letters from Clem today. Would you believe it she and Mother were both at Sister's flying around and having a good time generally. They went through Albany. Took the cars in Cuthbert—carried Hannah with them. They say they are just as miserable as they can be about you. Clem writes me that sister has joined the Methodist church. I am so glad to hear it and I know you will be too. She says that Walt has improved considerably. That he is a right good boy. I haven't got my box yet. I expect it is at [South] Boston. I am going down next week to get it. I am very anxious to get hold of it. You say I must not laugh at it. If I do laugh it will be because I am so glad to get it. I am so glad you are getting down here close to me again. It is so much nearer for me to come. I expect to see you soon and, oh the joy of that meeting. Good bye. God bless you.

Your Wife

Clement to Allie:

Camp near Orange C.H. [Va.]
August 10, 1863

My dear Darling

Will you become alarmed if I tell you about my everyday headaches, or will you not remember that I am so subject to such attacks every summer? Well I know you will understand it to be nothing serious when I tell you I have suffered more or less every day for a week. The weather is so intensely hot that I can hardly expect anything else but headaches. Luckily we are resting in camp and I can take good care of myself. How easily it

273

could all be cured if you were here where I could rest my head in your lap. I am getting so much the more anxious for you to come that I must prepare you for an early summons to come. Perhaps by the 20th and I think anyhow by the 25th I shall send you the dispatch. You will reach Orange Court House by Eleven O'clock a.m. When I send you word I will arrange for someone to meet you at Powhatan Hotel. You will probably get this letter on or about the 15th. I think you had better go at once to South Boston and make your preparations for it will not be long before I shall send you the dispatch. I thought I would put it off until September, but I have been gradually coming down until I would not surprise myself at all if my dispatch to you to come reached you as soon as this letter.

Orr will go to Richmond in a day or two and if he stays any length of time I will arrange for him to see you safely on the cars, and I am thinking of having "Old Moses" to go to Richmond to help about your baggage. I could go on and write a dozen pages if I should write all I thought about you coming, and the ways and means—Only two more weeks and you will be with me. In all likelihood from present appearances our principal fighting will be in September & October and had you not rather be with me or near me during that time? Or would you feel better in case of any casualty befalling me, if the news could be shortened by distance & lapse of time? You hardly know how to reply, but my good little wife, will under any circumstances do right.

You have been reading again "Life in a Country Parsonage" with peculiar interest. Did your heart sink, my darling, at the picture presented there of the trials which may be in store for you? Are there no misgivings on your part that these trials will be beyond endurance and that such a life will prove too hard for you? The wife of an obscure minister is a different character from the wife of what might, in wordly position, become that of your husband. For my part I confess to an occasional shrinking as I try to work into the future, but generally I experience a growing anxiety to be what I trust is my true calling. I do not know what stronger evidences others may have felt but if mine are not strong enough I am satisfied they will be strengthened, or my eyes will be fully opened before I take the final steps in this important matter. These things are known only to you, myself and to God—and our reliance being in the direction he shall give, there is no possibility of being mistaken.

I want to see the two little darlings and the one "dearest darling" so much. Come—come.

Good bye.

Your Husband

Allie to Clement:

Person Co., N.C.

August 10, 1863

My dear husband

Did you ever feel such hot weather in all your life? I don't think I ever felt any hotter weather in Georgia than we have had for the last week. It is thundering in the distance and I am very much in hopes it will rain and cool the air. I have been very unwell for the last two days. It is such an unusual thing for me to be sick that I don't know how to take it. I have had better health this year than I have had in six or eight years. I hope I shall be all right in a day or so. The baby is almost well again but he has fallen off so much. Mama don't want him to be a little delicate looking baby. Yesterday I got a letter from you and after I got through reading it I handed it to him to read. If you just could have heard him trying to read it, papa. It was a mixture of all the languages. I have made my new gingham dress and it is so pretty. I shall save it to wear when I come to see you. I have been trying all day to make my new homespun but felt so sick I couldn't do much towards it. Mama gave him a new dress of the gingham, papa. Nance is making it. He thinks he is somebody, papa. Ida is having a time of it with her risings—got boils over her. He [Lawton] has had about fifty in his head papa. None anywhere else but in his head. I have had another letter from Clem. They are still at Sister's and having a jolly time. Clem says they expect to stay until the first of next month, if all keep well. Hannah she says is in bad health. Hasn't been well since her baby was born. She can't account for it in any way for she says no white woman ever had better care taken of them than she did. I know she was well taken care of. Sister will be confined in November. That is the secret of her bad health. Don't you think that Probe had better come back to the army? Willie Palmer did not die as I wrote you he did. He is at home but looking like a ghost Clem says. I will leave here tomorrow if I am well enough.

I should like to stay here until you write for me to come but the little Negroes have the whooping cough and I am afraid to stay. I shall go back to Mr. Painter's, stay there about a week; from there I will go to Uncle Sydney's and stay a week and then back to [South] Boston to stay till I go to you. You continue to send your letters to Boston. I get them regularly now. I want to see you so badly. Wish I was with you this evening. I don't think of anything else but coming to see you. I live on it. Ida says tell pa I want to see him so bad I don't know what to do and that I have had a mighty sore foot this week. A cloud has come up since I have been writing and we are having a delightful rain. The air is cooler and I feel better already. Good bye darling. I hope I will be well in a day or so and then I will write again. Good bye. God bless you.

Your Wife

Clement to Allie:

Orange C.H. [Va.]
Aug. 12, 1863

Dear Darling

I write hastily just to say the word "Come"—come at once. I have secured a place to board about one mile from camp, where I think you will be comfortable. I shall make my calculations for you to leave on the 20th to be at Powhatan Hotel on the 20th and at Orange C.H. on the 21st, but if you come earlier you will find a hotel at Orange C.H. to stop at until you can get me word. This letter will certainly reach you by the 18th

276

and I shall be at Orange on the 21st ready for you. I will try to have some one at Powhatan Hotel to help you on, and if any one goes from here on the 19th or 20th I will send Mose also. I am considerably excited about your coming and may send a dispatch yet, so great is my anxiety to see you. I will write to McGary to leave that bundle for you at the Hotel which Clifton brought. Bring a dress or two with you to make. I can get Orr to swap your shoes for you. Good bye until we meet— Good bye.

Your Husband

Allie to Clement:

Person Co. N.C.
August 18, 1863

My dear darling

Yesterday I received a letter from you written on the eighth telling me to be ready to move at a moment's notice, that I might receive orders any hour to come to you. I am almost crazy, so afraid you will send for me before I can get back to [South] Boston. I am getting back as fast as I can. This is a very busy time with the farmers and I have to wait until it is convenient to send me from one place to another. I am so impatient about it that I can't enjoy myself one bit now. Cousin Joe will send me to Uncle Sydney's in a few days. As soon as he gets through threshing out his wheat. Uncle Sydney lives about eight miles from here and nine from [South] Boston. I will stay there a few days and then get him to send me to [South] Boston and then I shall be ready to go to my darling. Must I bring all my baggage? I think it will be best to bring it all as I shall go home from up there and that will save a trip to Boston when I start home. Write to me what to do about it. You say you are anxious to hear my criticisms on my box. You have got my letters about it before now. Everybody envies me the contents of that box—but I am as stingy as you please with it. It is appreciated highly and you need not doubt it. I have worked myself almost to death since I have had it. Is not this the most changeable climate you ever saw? Yesterday it was so warm we could scarcely live and this morning it is really cold—cold enough for winter clothes. I am so anxious to see you darling. I expect, as you say, I shall deliberately pancake when I do see you. Your little man is better this week than he was last. Nance is some better too. Ida is about the same—and all anxious to start to see you. I am going to spend the day about a half mile away. Will have to walk. Wish you were here to go with me. It is time for me to be going. Good bye darling. I will see you soon.

Good bye. Good bye.

Your Wife

Halifax Co., Va.
August 22, 1863

My dear darling

I am back in Halifax again at Uncle Sydney's but so impatient and restless I can hardly contain myself. My last letter from you was written on the eighth. I have been moving about so that your letters have failed to reach me. I shall be so glad when I get with you and letters will be no longer necessary. I am looking for letters this morning. I wrote to [South] Boston for them to be sent down here. I hope they will contain the order for me to move. I shall go to Mr. Fourquesen's in three or four days at the farthest and then I shall be ready to come. I have been sewing so hard all day that I am broke down. Working for Uncle Sydney's children. Poor little things, I am so sorry for them. They need a mother's care so much. I am sorry I didn't come down here two or three weeks sooner, so I could have fixed their clothes for them. I am so sorry for the old man. I expect though that he will soon have another wife. He has marrying in his head I think. His oldest daughter is almost grown— in her fifteenth year. He has four children, three girls and one boy. He is very well fixed and [I] think next summer, if the war lasts, I will come and stay sometime with him. He lives only three miles from the depot.

The baby is still very unwell. He has a very bad cough and I am again frightened about its being the whooping cough. It is in nearly every family in the country. I wouldn't have him to have it for all the money in the Confederacy. He is as cross as he well can be. I will be so glad when I get to you. I feel like if I only can get there my troubles will all vanish then. An old lady has just come in to see me—one of Uncle Sydney's neighbors. They have sent up for me and I shall have to go down. I hope this is the last letter I shall have to write to you in some time. I am almost dead to come darling. Good bye till I come. Good bye. God bless you.

Your Wife

South Boston, Va.
August 23, 1863
(Sunday)

My dear darling

Last night I got your letter to come to you two days after I was to have been there. I was so troubled about it last night that I couldn't sleep. I wouldn't have disappointed you for anything in the world. I am afraid you are sick. If I had got your letter as I ought to in time I might have been with you this lonesome Sunday evening. I shall start Thursday morning if the baby is well enough and will be there Friday. You must meet me at the depot. I would start sooner but a cousin of mine is going up to Fredericksburg Thursday and I can go with him to Hanover Junction. If you knew I was coming I would start in the morning for I don't know how I can stay here until Thursday morning—three days. If I had just have gotten your letter what a happy day I should have spent. It is too bad and I am afraid you are uneasy about my not coming. The baby is still very unwell. He is so sleepy and drowsy today I can scarcely keep his eyes open a moment. Been asleep all day. I can scarcely live for thinking of coming so soon. Good bye darling. Meet me Friday morning.

Your Wife

Clement to Allie:

Orange C. H., [Va.]
Aug. 27, 1863

My dear Darling

Your long looked for letter has come telling me you will be at Orange [Court House] on the 28th, Friday. I will be there waiting for you. I have been into Orange every day since the 20th hoping to meet you, but [was] disappointed every time. But I am sure of you now. Good bye until we meet.

Your Husband

Part III

Chapter 15

SKIRMISHES AT BRISTOE STATION AND MINE RUN

During the couple's happy reunion of two months, there were naturally no letters because Allie was close by during the Bristoe Station Campaign of some thirty days' duration. In that foray the corps of Generals Ewell and Hill were advanced across the Rapidan River on October 9 to make a flanking movement on General Meade's Army of the Potomac. Evans' command, as part of Gordon's brigade, moved with Ewell. Meade's countermoves kept the Federal forces between Lee's army and Washington. General Stuart and his cavalry scouted ahead and skirmished with the enemy. From near Warrenton on October 13, Stuart sent word that he was in danger of being cut off. Ewell's men were advanced the next morning and created a diversion that allowed Stuart to escape. Lee ordered General Ewell to march on to engage the enemy at Bristoe Station by one route and sent Hill by another. Before Evans' Thirty-first Georgia arrived with Ewell's forces on October 14, Hill had launched an unfortunate attack and had been badly mauled by the Federals. The fight had lasted only forty minutes but Confederate losses totalled 1,361. The conflict at Bristoe Station has been called as "badly managed a battle as had ever been fought under the flag of the Army of Northern Virginia."[1] Meade withdrew soon afterward, and the Confederates also fell back slowly, reaching the Rappahannock by October 18.

Before the close of this episode, Allie and the children had

1. Freeman, *R. E. Lee*, vol. 3, p. 181. *O.R.*, series 1, vol. 29, part 1, p. 426-35.

started on the tedious journey to Georgia by train. She had been away from Lumpkin since January 1863. Her letters to her husband soon resumed.

Allie to Clement:

Thursday Oct. 26, 1863
Augusta, Ga.

My dear darling

We arrived here this morning safe after a long tiresome travel. We failed to make the connection here for the first time. Got here this morning at seven o'clock and will have to stay over till five this evening. They travel so very slow. I expected to have been in Macon this morning but I have another day and night before me. I am not very sorry of the delay as it gives me an opportunity of writing to let you know how we are all getting on. We have got on finely till we got here this morning and I found that Mose[2] had lost my bag of wool. I never was so vexed in my life about anything. I had as soon he had lost one of my trunks. I don't know how he managed to lose it. I won't let him talk to me about it. It is enough for me to know it is gone. I sent him back to the depot to look for it, although I knew it was no use. I am sorry. I can't enjoy going home without my bag of wool. I had my heart set on making you a nice suit of clothes and now to think it is gone. It is too provoking is it not? Darling I am so mad about it I don't know what to do.

Ida got acquainted with a very nice gentleman at Wilmington and he volunteered to take charge of us this far for which I was very grateful for I don't know what we should have done last night if it had not been for him. The worse part of our trip has been from Kingsville here. We were so crowded. The gentleman put us through safe. He is a good traveler—very attentive and seems to be a perfect gentleman. I don't know his name

2. "Mose" is a familiar name for Moses Evans, the slave belonging to Clement. Allie uses this more than Clement. See Chapter 17 for more about Moses in the Diary of Winter Quarters of 1864.

—he lives in Richmond. He will see me safe off from here and will try to find me an escort to Macon.

Old man Cox [unidentifiable] left us this morning— Went on to Atlanta—he didn't even take leave of me. I think he was very ungrateful after I had taken such good care of him and brought him through safe. It was a very happy deliverance to get rid of him. I assure you it was. He didn't of course pay any attention to me or my baggage when the conductor came along and wanted to know what he was doing in the ladies' car, he would point to me out as the lady he had under his charge. He secured a seat in the ladies' car and that was all he was after—

He [Lawton] has been a perfect little man every bit of the way papa—he has not cried any at all. Do you remember a little fidgety fussy woman we met in Milledgeville Mrs. Judge Thomas. I met her here this morning at the breakfast table. She was still talking about Judge Thomas. She did not recognize me nor I her— Mose has just come back and as I expected did not find my bag. It is hard but I shall have to give it up. I am so out of sorts about it—feel like pitching into everybody I see. The red blanket was in the bag too besides a good many other things but nothing hurts like the wool. Mose tries hard to explain and to clear himself. Seems very much hurt—An old rascal. It is almost impossible to keep your baggage now while traveling. Everybody you see has lost something. I reckon I ought to consider myself fortunate in not losing any more— but it seems to me I could have borne anything else better than the loss of my wool. I shan't go out to look around at all today. I am so tried—tired and want to see my darling so bad. I hope your cold is well before now. I wish I could get a letter from you today. It would be such a consolation. Ida and Nance are out on the street looking around and seeing what is to be seen. They are at home anywhere.

It has taken one hundred and thirty dollars to bring us this far and I have not paid but seven dollars fare for Ida —We have eat only one meal since we left Richmond.

283

Moses's twenty dollars gave out at Kingsville. It will take twenty more to carry him home. They charge almost as much for servants as they do for white people. I will write again as soon as I get to Cuthbert and just as soon as we get home. I have not seen any person that I knew yet. Good bye my darling—my heart aches as the distance widens between us. I can see you now standing when I left you at Orange [Court House, Virginia]. I do love you so good. Good bye my own dear husband—Good bye. God bless you.

Your Wife

Lumpkin, Ga.
Nov. 31, 1863

My dear darling—

I am at last at home and as I had to come I am not sorry the trip is over. I sent Mose on home Friday evening to tell the news and to hire [a] horse sent for me. It was two o'clock Sunday morning before they started for me and didn't get here before three. They got Joe Cox and his horse and the livery stable hack. Charlie Burk wouldn't let them have it without the promise to come back that night and what do you reckon the trip cost me—only *twenty eight dollars*. We started from Cuthbert [Georgia] at four o'clock and got here at half past eight. Matt,[3] Mr. Graham, the children and Clem were looking for us but we slipped up to the gate without their hearing us and I jumped out and ran in as easy as I could opened the door and said "how do you do" before they knew we had come. You never heard such a racket in your life. You could not hear a word that was said. They grabbed the baby and that like to have frightened him to death. You never saw people gladder to see anybody in your life. You never heard such talking everybody at once. Matt went home about four o'clock. It has been so very cold today that nobody scarcely has been to see me besides nobody knows that I am here. Mrs. Holloman was over before

---

3. This is Clement's sister, Martha. In his letters he writes her nickname as "Mat." Allie always adds the extra "t" in her letters: "Matt." See Appendix A.

we ate breakfast. She and Matt and Mr. Graham dined with us today and had a big old gobbler that Sister sent up for me the next day after I got here. Mrs. McCullah [who] came up this evening is all the company I have had. Clem says I need not be uneasy about everybody coming to see me for she knows that they will all come as soon as they find out and it turns warmer. I have got so much to tell you darling I don't know how to begin. I can only write you a short letter tonight for I am writing by firelight and have the headache so bad I can scarcely see. I had such a cold ride last night that it has given me a dreadful cold and I don't feel well at all. I never suffered more from cold in my life. I promise you a real feast by the next mail. A real long interesting letter. I wrote to you Mother [Lucy Walton] was at Sister's. Sister is buying up our pork down there at forty five cents. It is a dollar here and in less than a week it will be two dollars. Clem is writing to her tonight to buy me five hundred lbs. and ten gallons of syrup. It is five dollars a gallon. Sugar down there is only one dollar a pound and I have written to her to buy me fifty pounds. She has plenty of money to buy with and we will manage some way to get it home. Don't you think it is a good arrangement?

I think I shall be able to sell the lot for three or four thousand dollars and soon pay every debt we owe. Confederate money is received by everybody in payment for old debts. I am in high spirits about our getting out of debt. I will write you all about everything in my next. I think I could fill a book [and] you shall have a full benefit. Beck has a fine boy aunt Rachel saved our doctor's bill which is fifty dollars. Brother has given you eight pounds of the nicest of wool to make you clothes and says if it is necessary you shall have more. Matt will give you the balance and they will not cost you anything. That consoles me for the loss of my wool. I think your coat will be very nice. Father came in from P.D.[4]

4. "Father" is Anselm L. Evans who was seventy-one in 1863. "P.D." is Peyton D. Hill. See Appendix A for relatives.

Today. The old man was glad to see us. He don't look as well as he did when I saw him last but he says his health is perfectly good. I have got so much to tell you. Goodbye. God bless you

Your Wife

In two days after this gets there look out for one of them letters.

By the time Allie reached Lumpkin, Georgia, there occurred in Virginia the last noteworthy event of the fall of 1863. This was the Mine Run encounter. On November 10, Lee had returned to the Rapidan from Bristoe Station and on November 26, General Meade crossed the Rapidan and passed to the right of Lee's main force, hoping to isolate and defeat General Ewell's corps, with Gordon's brigade and Evans' regiment, twenty miles west of Fredericksburg.

Colonel Evans made a report of the Mine Run expedition in his papers in which he stated that on November 26 the brigade was disposed for action:

On the morning of the next day [the 27th] the brigade was advanced across Mine Run and came in contact with the enemy at Locust Grove. The 16th Georgia was deployed as skirmishers advanced, engaged the skirmishers of the enemy, drove them nearly upon the main line, took up a position in their front and held it during the day against repeated assaults. During the night our line was drawn to the right side of Mine Run about two and a half miles distant, where position was again taken and fortified. The enemy followed, crossed a heavy line of skirmishes in front of Early's division, drove in our skirmishers but the lost ground was soon recovered, the enemy again retiring their skirmish line across the Run. On the 29th and 30th no operations of importance occurred. On the 2nd of December the discovery having been made that the enemy had retreated, the brigade, as a part of the Division, pursued, but without results, as the enemy had recrossed the Rapidan. On the same day the brigade returned to its former camp near Somerville Ford.

[As a conclusion to this matter, Clement wrote Allie a succinct summary of the fighting in his letter of December 3]:

In camp near Rapidan, Va.
Dec. 3rd, 1863

My dear Allie

The fighting is all over. Meade has ingloriously retreated across the river after boldly presenting himself with the vaunt that he was to fight Lee wherever he could find him. We have been gone just a week. At first we formed a line of battle in a position unsatisfactory to us from which we fell back about a mile, Again our position was not good & we withdrew another mile to a very strong position which we fortified and awaited an attack. The prisoners say that Meade ordered an attack Sunday morning [the 29th] but the soldiers refused although the officers made speeches to them & did all they could to get them to attack. On Monday night we arranged to attack them Tuesday morning. A. P. Hill was to commence the attack on their left flank & we then would attack in front. The result would inevitably have been a most thorough and decided victory. My regiment was in the front as skirmishers and I discovered that they were withdrawing. At daylight it was perfectly clear that the enemy had gone & we commenced pursuit, but he crossed in safety. We have captured in all about one thousand prisoners. Their killed & wounded will amount to as many more. Our loss in the whole army is very-trifling indeed.[5]

I think that the campaign now closes, but I will not be too sure for there are yet fifteen or twenty days in which we may have an engagement. The weather has been very cold, but has moderated a little. No snow and but little rain.

Now I shall begin to miss you so much. For we shall doubtless go into winter quarters and I shall have nothing scarcely to do. But I will find some employment so

5. *O.R.*, series 1, vol. 29, part 1, p. 838, lists 601 Confederates killed and wounded at Mine Run, and on p. 686 shows Federal losses at 1,653.

as to make the months fly away on swift wing. I shall not begin to count the months yet.

I hope you are now safely lodged at home with the home folks. Do write me about all the taking on over you. Give me a full history of the excitement on your arrival and tell me all your troubles in getting home. I have received Clem's letter written on the 23rd. That Gobbler from your sister I suppose has gone to his last resting place by this time. He has fallen a sacrifice, or rather he has died in honor of your return.

"Joe Hooker" [Clement's horse] has met with a sad accident. His flowing tail has been curtailed—shorn of its fair and full proportions and now goes "Bobbing around." Some mules got loose and ate about half of it off.

Goodbye. I must cut my letter off short to get it off. I will write tomorrow. Good bye. God bless you. My love to Ida.

Your Husband

[Shortly thereafter weather conditions prompted both armies to go into winter quarters on opposite sides of the Rapidan.]

Chapter 16
THE CURTAIN FALLS ON 1863

The letters in the closing months of 1863 and in early 1864 begin to have a marked difference from the communications in 1861 and 1862 when the war was young. The élan of the days when the local citizenry wined and dined the Stewart Grays as they marched out of Lumpkin was gone. The fervor of Sallie Tucker's farewell address to those "heroes" as they left home had waned under the realities of war. The "warfever" of Clement's reports as a civilian observer, when he accompanied the Grays to Richmond, had abated. The enthusiasm while training in Lawton's brigade in Savannah was now missing. Death and destruction, disillusion and disappointment, and the revelation of the frailties of human beings in wartime had taken their toll on the sensibilities of Allie and Clement.

Allie to Clement:

Lumpkin Dec. 6, 1863

My dear darling.

Day before yesterday I wrote you a real small pox letter. I was frightened but as I might have known then it all turned out to be nothing at all. I mean in town. They certainly have got it at Green Mill and out at Hurley's only one mile and a quarter from town. You can hear as many reports about the small pox now as you could soon after the big fight at Richmond. You can just step out and hear that anybody has it. It is well enough to frighten the people about it I reckon it will be best. Everybody will be vaccinated and that is the only preventative of small pox. Is it anywhere near you? Old man Hurley had to bury his son himself without any help.

289

Meb is dead and I miss her just as much as if it was somebody. I think she must have been poisoned. I don't know who done it, without it was some of Hannah's beaux. She would always bark when anything came about at night. I couldn't help but cry when I saw her dead. Ida and Sis buried her. Ida said she was buried very neatly. They tied black lace on her feet. Put her in a nice grave down in the orchard. They sang "Hark, from the Tomb" over her grave when they buried her.

Dr. Palmer has written to Mrs. Palmer that he will take Christmas dinner with her. Can't you come and take dinner with us Christmas day? I will give you such a good dinner. If I thought you could come I would commence to make preparations now. Ida is rocking the baby and he is squalling. He says: "Papa when you gwine to send me a name?" He grows very fast and is just as pretty as he can be. Let's give him your name. He is just like you and ought to be named for you. I think I will have him vaccinated before I start with him to Virginia. Dr. Battle says he don't think it will hurt him. Better do that even if [it] makes him sick than for him to catch the small pox.

Florella [unidentifiable] is staying with me a few days. She still says she will go with me but I have no idea [if] she will. Johnny McNabb is here. He has been wounded in the leg and is home on a furlough. I haven't seen him. Matt says she is going over to Eufaula [Alabama] soon. Joe Singer is home. I expect old George got him out of service as a shoemaker. There seems to be more coming from the war than there is going. Gregory is here too. He says he came home to buy salt for his family. I didn't think they would grant furloughs for such an excuse as that. I don't expect he has joined the army at all. Florella says if you see her man up there anywhere, put him in a letter and send him to her.

I wish I could see you this morning. I have written this letter before breakfast. You don't know how smart I am since I have been fixing to come to see you. Good bye. Good bye darling.

Your Wife.

Clement to Allie:

In camp near Rapidan, Va.
Dec. 11, 1863

My dear Allie

Your two long and very interesting letters came to-night and put me in a good humor with everybody. You are safe at home, no matter at what cost and find most of our affairs in a condition to please you. I know you were met with open arms, and it does one so much good to know you are enjoying yourself.

You speak so hopefully too of settling up all of our affairs and placing us free of the world. I feel perfectly confident in your ability & energy in these matters because we have talked so much about it until we think precisely alike and you would do precisely in all things as I would if I were present. In fact I am expecting the best of results from your management. I wrote to you to get all my papers, notes & receipts. Look over all and do what you can or please concerning them. I think that those who owe us ought not to charge high prices for anything that we want to buy from them. If they do, I think you had better buy from somebody else. There is a vast deal of selfishness and meanness engendered by this war, but we will do well neither to encourage it, nor entangle ourselves with it.

You will perhaps have some trouble with the Negroes during Christmas, but if you provide homes for them beforehand I would send them off as soon as possible. You have received my letter containing Ward's proposition to buy Charly[1] & hire the rest. Consult Bob[2] about it. He is posted about this business of making sales and can give you good advice. If you hire to Ward he will pay in advance. But if you hire to others, require security and either keep the notes until I come or apply them to debts or—just as you see best.

Sell the House & lot and Cole place together if you can, but if not sell them separately—Be sure to sell—but

1. Charles is another slave. He is mentioned in later letters.
2. See Appendix A for relatives.

get the highest possible price for both. You might in selling the Cole place reserve one years wood privilege for yourself, but do not stickle on that point.

I have forgotten now what our Negroes hired for this year, but as I suppose Dan has done a good years work all together. He ought to be worth a very respectable sum. It was rather mean in that fellow to charge ten dollars per bushel for wheat when he had hired Charles at the old price. All our expenses at home have doubtless absorbed a great deal of what the Negroes hired for.

Mr. Kirksey can give you any information you may need about my business in court. You have done exactly right in buying sugar and bacon in Baker & Millen [Counties]. Some opportunity will occur for bringing it up. I am sorry to learn our premises are so much out of repair. That will affect the sale no doubt, but do the best you can.

I feel very happy about my new uniform which Mat is making at home. It will save me many a dollar—& besides being made at home is a recommendation beyond mere money value. If you think Mose can be trusted you can send me my black overcoat—& pack my cap & other things in the bonnet box. But if he is going to lose them don't send them by him, for I might chop off his head when he gets here. As I expected you have pardoned him and the old rascal is running at large just as if he had not lost a hundred dollars worth of things for me. Everett Harris is not here nor can I get him another pair of shoes, but I will pay him the cost of them. You need not fix my jacket until I come. I suppose Mose lost the blue cloth you expected to use in trimming.

Well I have written you a good long letter all about business and very much a repetition of what I have told you what I have written. You know I want you to become accustomed to managing my business and I had rather lose a little while you are gaining experience than not to have you for my agent. Therefore I write business letters to you.

I am feasting pretty high now off of other folks. Capt. Cody has just got a box from Home full of good things and so has Col. Lowe. We are making an egg nog now and will have cake to go with it.

Tell Dr. Battle I expect to come home next March in good health, but I want to get sick just a little while I am here, so I can stay at least a month. I did not have a fair chance last year, as I left home before I got well.

Tell Mat & Sis Jane, or rather send them this letter to read, that they must save me some fat turkeys & other nice fixins for my coming. If John & Jim have to go in the army under the last [conscription] act perhaps the best place for them is Capt. Frank George's company of cavalry in Columbus.

Well good bye—My love to all—Write often—Give me all the news—Kiss my little darlings for me—all of them— the little Curly head and the little name sake too.

There are rumors of another fight. Hooker is said to be in command here with reinforcements, but I hope we shall not have to tramp again. It is very cold—sleeting. Good bye.

Your Husband

Graham won't need any further order from me to give you all my papers. I have no receipt for them and these letters he can retain if he desires.

C. A. Evans

Camp near Rapidan, Va.
Dec. 12, 1863

Dear Darling

Tomorrow will be the anniversary of the Great battle of Fredericksburg, at which fell my good friend Captain Lawton. How sadly will his poor wife feel all day long tomorrow. Twelve months have gone. Three hard fights, many skirmishes, many exposures, many unseen dangers, have been in my history of these twelve months and yet I live. Let us join in thanks to the Good Being who has so wonderfully preserved me through it all. Still for some good purpose the Divine hand has turned the bullets aside, only allowing them to wound just enough to keep me mindful of His protection. I have to considerable extent become inured to hardship and hardened to dangers;—but I never fail to invoke the protection of the Good Being and to thank Him for saving me from death and wounds. I am glad to live, darling, for your sake and the sake of our little ones, with the hope too that the future is full of promises for me to be useful. Occasionally the old dream of ambition sweeps over me and from my present standpoint exhibits to me the probability of almost certainty of distinction at the hands of the world—but I feel ashamed of myself for ever being amused in an idle hour with anything so empty of real happiness.

No, indeed, darling—if I know my heart it has no pulsation but for you—no ambition but to make you happy, no hope save that of the joyous Heaven where we shall both be reunited forever. It is not wrong I trust to find so much present joy in anticipation of the serene and happy life which we have marked out in the future. Many are the hours delightfully spent in anticipating the real joys that await us, and in the foretaste of those delights which our future employment will surely bring. These reveries which I love so much to indulge in lighten the cares of my present life, and put new feathers in the wings of the hours of our separation. But for them these hardships & privations attendant on camp life would be almost intolerable, but with them they are scarcely felt. Let us therefore make every preparation both of hearts and fortunes to obey fully the Divine will concerning us. We will free ourselves from the travails of worldly obligations, we must have no annoyances of that kind otherwise we shall not be happy. We must commence by being able to say "We owe no man anything." Then with the blessing of God on what is left, and with our hearts sanctified, we will be ready for any and all the duties of life. I am disposed to be full of hope—perhaps too sanguine, but my very heart leaps to think of the days when, the war being over, I may be with you all the time, and when we together are employed in making ourselves & all around us happy.
[This letter from Clement stops here.]

[This letter to Allie has no salutation.]

You know how dull everything is here when no movements are on foot, and how little there is to write about. I do not know hardly what to tell you, unless it is interesting to you to know that I am entirely well, and doing as well as could be expected under the circumstances. I had almost forgotten that I had been sick until I received your last letter written after receiving my first. I was very sick coming back from Orange C. H. [Court House] I could scarcely ride because of pain in my back, chest & all over. I fully believed that I was going to have an attack of Pneumonia and I bitterly repented having sent you off. I had a very hard chill that evening, followed by a high fever all night. For two more days I was quite sick & during the time the enemy crossed the Rapidan and advanced against us. I got out of bed [and] took command of my regiment. The Brigade was divided leaving me two regiments I rode nearly all night—next morning we were in line of battle. I had two more regiments in a very advanced position. Had another hard shaking ague was so sick I could hardly ride. General Gordon requested me to go to the rear. I would not have done it just at that time for a kingdom. Rain and cold came. I had but one blanket. Slept without a tent—was up a greater part of every night—worked hard every day—and yet contrary to all the rules of health it did not kill me but I got well—absolutely was cured by exposure. If you had been here and no fight occurred I should have taken a bed at Graves and been sick two or more weeks. All this is strange is it not?

I dreamed of you again last night. Such a delightful dream of home & you. I awoke in the act of kissing my darling and was so mad. Night before last our dear little Charlie came to me in my dreams—just like he was—my bright noble little boy. All night I enjoyed his company—but the morning came and he was gone. Bless the dear angel boy.

The war cannot last always. The end is coming. I work

hard, keep myself employed so the days may appear to be short. After awhile the proclamation of peace will be made and then home, happiness. A new life, with new employment, new enjoyments. Your society all the time will be mine. You will ever be a joint laborer with me. A partner of joys, sorrows, and labors. Will we not be happy? How much better we will live—how much more useful. Certainly it is a comfort to look around to such a future as ours will be.

You know I told you I saw Henry Thomas at the review. I don't see what possessed me to make such a mistake. It was John Whit Thomas, and not Henry. I do not know what I could have been thinking of for I knew both of them well enough. I expect you told his wife that I saw him in Virginia. Henry is still in the west.

Joe Clifton is certainly a prisoner. We haven't heard from him since he arrived in Yankeeland. Tell Mrs. Clifton not to be uneasy about him. When you left we did not know where he was and therefore I did not tell you. It was thought then that he was perhaps a prisoner but there was no certainty of it until lately. He had plenty of good new clothes, and two good blankets when he was taken.

I am very glad to hear that Bro. Davies is our presiding Elder. You must get to see him when he comes.

I told you I have no news to write. You must write me good long letters. All about everything. Tell me how you are getting on paying off old scores. I wrote you a long letter the last time, all about our business. Do not let Confederate money get cold in your hands. Exchange it for our notes as fast as possible. The wind is blowing terribly hard. But not very cold. Good bye. My love to everybody. Kiss Ida and the Boy. Which name do you like best "Troup" or "Lawton." Good bye.

Your Husband

Camp near Rapidan, Va.
Dec. 19, 1863

My dear Allie

I wrote you yesterday evening a hasty note which

Scott Baldwin will carry with him and deposit in the mail somewhere on the route. He has gone home on a twenty-four day furlough and will go to Lumpkin about the first of January to see you. He may reach there earlier. I want you to have his measure taken by John Singer, to make my coat by. His measure taken exactly will fit me loosely and comfortable. I do not expect the cloth will be ready, nor have you any buttons, but if you have, and the cloth is ready the coat can be made and sent to me by him. He will also have me a good pair of boots made at Ward's; therefore it will not be necessary to have me another pair made for the winter. You can send by Baldwin anything which Mose does not bring. It is not necessary to send my blue pants, but I would like to have my cap & black overcoat. Capt. Redding is going to Richmond to see if he can buy me some grey cloth there also. He will return in five or six days when I will write to you immediately as to his success. I do not place much confidence, however, in this.

Tell Sis Jane that P. D. and Graham treated me very mean about those shirts & pants. I am sure they were good enough and would have been very acceptable. Two or three heavy shirts added now to my scanty wardrobe would add very materially to my comfort. Hereafter whenever I need a clean shirt this winter I will remember these two gentlemen.

I need Moses now very much and I do hope he is on his way with Ben Hawes. I shall be very comfortable as soon as I get Moses to look after my horses. I expect though to have my usual winter's hard labor for the Brigade.

I received another letter from you yesterday evening. I am so very sorry you have been sick. You must not allow that to happen anymore. I shall be sure to try to get home the first of next March & stay with you nearly a month. Can't you keep in good spirits until then?

Tell Bob to say to Charles Warren that when he pays the notes on my bond for title & has both recorded in the office of the Clerk of the Superior Court that he will have a good title, and when I come home I will make him a deed, or will send some one, say Bob, a power of attorney to execute the title to him. I was under the impression that Wimberly had Charles Warren's notes on the Fernor debt. I have really forgotten what notes Kimberly has.

I am afraid you are too sanguine about the sale of the lot. I do not now calculate on its sale at all. Our great chance was lost when Mrs. Dorsey bought elsewhere. But do the best you can according to my previous letters. You say nothing about the sale of Charles and the hire of the others to Ward. I expect you had not received my letter containing the one Ward wrote to me. I have no new suggestions to make to you with reference to Confederate currency. I still believe that the present issue will all be called in and placed out of circulation. Also that property of all kinds will depreciate in value fully one half.

Darling, you do not know how anxious I am to be free from debt. I fear that in letting the fall pass by with our affairs entrusted to agents who did not feel the same interest that we do, that we have committed a fatal mistake. It is the old story of our letting our love for each other's society run away with our reason. If I could only relieve myself of every pecuniary obligation I should at the close of the war be a happy man, but, as it is, when this war with the Yankees ends I shall be in as almost as great trouble about my affairs as I am now. Can we do nothing to avoid this bitterness?

I do hope you are passing a pleasant time at home, but somehow your letters breathe a different tale. Has Lumpkin and its people changed even since you were there before? Are the people less kind & sociable, more selfish & exacting? Have they not received you with open arms? If not come back to me. Wind up our affairs speedily—shake the dust of Lumpkin from your feet and we will enter it no more. I am counting largely on your being with me during the summer months. If you come alone, the difficulties of transportation will be but little. But can you leave the boy for three or four months? I expect not.

You will receive this letter during the Christmas holidays—in full enjoyment I hope of many good things. I shall have Christmas on a small scale too I reckon, but I have yet made no preparations.

What a glorious Christmas we could spend together if I could take the telegraph line and drop in Lumpkin suddenly on Christmas eve. Would there not be "joy in the land." Never mind, all will come around well yet.

For your comfort I can state that very heavy rains have fallen for two days & the prospects for snow is good, making fighting just here impossible.

Goodbye. Tell Ida to write. Kiss the boy.

Good bye.

Your Husband

Tell Aunt Katy Rooks that Davy is not yet exchanged. I will write as soon as he is.

Allie, in settling claims do not pay any accounts unless you know all about them. Pay only notes. Write to me about the election.

Allie to Clement:

Lumpkin, Stewart Co., Ga.
Sunday Morning Dec. 20, 1863

My dear darling

I know you are most frozed up this morning for it is so cold here that I can't stir an inch from the fire. It is Sunday morning but too cold to go to church. I have not been to church since I have been home. It has been either raining or too cold every Sunday and I haven't got my trunk home yet. I had to leave my largest trunk in Cuthbert. Couldn't bring it on the hack when I came up and have not been able to get anybody to bring it for me. I have begged everybody in town to hire me a wagon or something to send for it but it was no use. Charlie Burke says he will have it brought on the mail buggy tomorrow but I don't look for it. I am needing it very much. Ida is almost barefooted and I can't get her any shoes anywhere. She has a good pair in my trunk if I ever get it. I always thought that Lumpkin was the

299

most selfish place I ever saw but it is worse now than ever. The last place in creation I think. I have been trying to get my two trunks home from Columbus too but haven't heard a word from them yet. Wiley Pope was to have gone up there this week and promised to bring them for me but I haven't heard anything more from them. I do want the war to end so bad so I can have you home with me. I do get so tired of taking care of myself. Oh darling if anything should happen to you I do hope God in his mercy will take me and the children too, for I do not want to live a day without you. All the happiness I have now is in dreaming of the future when the war will end and we will be together again. I don't think of anything else. Oh if I only knew it was close at hand.

Do you remember we had a good many cows to stray off from our plantation? There is a man out here in the country I have forgotten his name says you told him he might have half of all he might find of them. He has found one and says that he will swear to it, that he knows all of the old Gauly stock of cows. Brother went with him to the man's house that had her and he says she has been there four or five years that he don't know whose cow she is. So we will take her but I have to pay the man fifty dollars for finding her. Is that right? She will be home in the morning. They say she is an excellent cow but very poor now. I think I can take her and feed her up and make her give milk enough for my family if I should go to housekeeping. She will give enough for the baby anyhow and he is obliged to have milk. Just such cows are selling for one hundred and fifty dollars. I am very glad indeed to get her. I am afraid darling I shan't be able to sell the lot. The chances were passed before I got home. I have had only one applicant since I have been here. That was a Baptist preacher. I asked him three thousand dollars but he was not willing to give it, said it was too much out of repair to pay so much for it. I don't intend to take a cent less than that. It may be best for us not to sell. We don't know what may happen that we may want a home before the

war ends and if we sell this one we won't be able to buy
another until peace is made, but still I should be glad if
I could sell and pay our debts. I had rather sell the lot
than Charles. I haven't got my money from Sister yet.
I don't know whether she has collected it yet. Mother
has not come home yet. I will know all about it when
she comes. I shall try to collect all our Negro hire the
first of Jan. and pay that out. Brother is speaking of
going back to Mississippi after Christmas—he is not satisfied yet—wants to make more money. That is the way.
We never know when we have enough. Always want to
make a little more.

Ben Gaines says now that he will start back to Va.
tomorrow week. I shall be sure to send Mose by him
when he goes. It is a shame for him to stay here so—he
is as well as he ever was and has been for the last four
or five months. You need not trouble about getting me
any more wool. It will be so much trouble to get it home.
I think I will have enough [of that which] brother gave
you to make three coats. I am afraid it won't be ready for
you when you get home and intend to hurry Matt up a
little. There was many a poor hog died around here yesterday. There is any quantity of pork in the country, but
everybody wants to hold it thinking they will get more
after awhile. Negroes I think will hire much better than
they did this year. I have heard of some hiring men for
two hundred and women for two hundred and fifty dollars. I don't think it would be best to hire ours to go on
the coast to make salt. They die off so down there. A great
many Negroes have died down there this year. It seems
to be very unhealthy. I think it would be best not to let
them go even if we had to take less for them. You just
ought to hear Lawton stand and call Pa just as loud as
he can bawl and then call Joe. I don't think he has forgotten you yet. I talk to him a great deal about you.
Ida has gone down to spend the day with Aunt Matt.
She would live there with Emma [Graham] if I would
let her. I am going down to spend the evening with
them. We have had such disagreeable weather that I
have not been out any since I have been home. I have

301

just gotten well, have been sick all the time. Goodbye my love. God bless you.

Your Wife

Clement to Allie:

Camp near Rapidan, Va.
Dec. 22, 1863

My Love

I am now occupying Brigade Hd. Qrs. and as soon as our permanent winter camp is established will fix myself off comfortably—that is as comfortably as the nature of the case will admit. With something to do all the time I shall pass the time pleasantly, but no matter how pleasantly, yet your presence would add a thousand fold to the enjoyment.

I have written to you very frequently every day, & at least an average of three letters each week since you left, yet yours dated the 12th inst speaks of your receiving only three letters up to that time. Surely there must be great delay in the mails. Write to me how long does it take a letter to reach you so I may know when mine are read by you. It is a pleasure while writing to think that your dear hands will hold the same paper and your dear eyes will read the lines which I write.

From your last description of Lumpkin I fear your stay there will be anything but pleasant. It almost dissuades me from paying the place a visit. But for seeing you and a few others I should feel no disposition to make the long trip.

You write me a great tale about the "boy's walking"—Pa don't believe one word of it. It is just like all that talking and other smart things which he always did when Pa was gone.

You despaired about the sale of the lot and said nothing about the sale or hire of the Negroes, nor of any other business matter—I know you are discouraged. So indeed am I, but I will be as stoical as possible about it. I do feel keenly the disappointment denied from the forever lost opportunities presented this fall to secure pecuniary independence. It will soon take five times as much property to pay us out as it would have done one month since. The lot in a few months will bring if sold about five or six hundred dollars and all else in proportion. We seem to be born to such peculiar misfortunes. I do not suppose you will get the money from Sister before January and then I fear the money will not be taken by the people. But, darling, we must be free from debt by some means.

I have endured its bitter slavery as long as I can bear it. But do not let my doleful writing make you gloomy. I had rather sacrifice all than give you unnecessary pain. I can toil for you with the utmost cheerfulness. I was only deeply regretting that we did not avail ourselves of the golden opportunity to pay off everything and yet have plenty left. It will make it necessary for me and you to save every possible dollar.

I must close immediately—the mail man has just arrived in a hurry.

I do so much wish you were with me this fine morning.

Goodbye my darling.
Your Husband

Allie to Clement:

Lumpkin, Stewart Co., Ga.
Dec. 24, 1863

My dear darling—

This evening I received a letter from you which had been written only six days [ago]. That is the shortest time I have ever had one to come in. It makes me feel good to hear from you in so short a time. Darling I would give anything in the world for you to be here tonight. I am on a trade with a Presbyterian preacher Mr. Carter for our lot. He wants me to give him possession now and wait about two weeks for the money. He says that he will certainly pay in that time. Graham is bitterly opposed to the trade. He advises me not to take it any way in the world. Brother is out of town and don't know anything about it. I can't get his advice.

I shall trade—what harm can there be done? I shan't give him any deed or anything of the kind until the money is paid and if he fails to pay in the two weeks he will have to get out of the house. If he don't I will make Brother put him out. Graham has done everything he can to keep me from trading but I shall trade contrary to all his advice and I do hope it will turn out well. I certainly think I am doing for the best. I would give anything in the world for a word of advice from you. I feel like if you were here you would say trade and I shall do it. We had a letter from Sister yesterday. She has six thousand dollars on hand and I have written her to send me two thousand by Mother and I will deliver the notes to Mother when I get the money. Mother will be here the first of next week. If I can make all the arrangements I am trying [to make] I can pay all of our debts without selling Charles. I have offered Graham the Cole place for a thousand dollars. If he don't take it I can get it I think. I think I shall have a little sale of my household plunder that I calculate will bring me at least five hundred dollars. I am doing my very best darling and do hope I will soon have the pleasure of writing you the good news that we are out of debt. This is a mighty sorry letter but I promise you a good one day after tomorrow. I am so anxious for my trade to turn out well. Tomorrow is Christmas. I shall spend a dull time. You must enjoy yourself, and try to have a good time too. Goodbye, write often and long letters. The children and all send love. I have got my trunks from Columbus all right.

> Goodbye. God bless you.
> Your Wife.

Clement to Allie:

> Camp near Rapidan, Va.
> Dec. 24 [1863]
> *Christmas eve—*

My love

    I wish you may enjoy a very happy Christmas. I know

you would if I was at home to join you. Will the little ones hang up their stockings for Santa Claus to fill? If I had the old fellow's faculties for locomotion I would mount my chariot and swifter than the wind would fly to Lumpkin to present myself as your Christmas present tomorrow morning. I shall perhaps eat a Christmas turkey tomorrow and thus end my share of the festivities. Our Brigade will change camp on Saturday and go into permanent winter quarters about a mile & a half from our present position. I shall then fix as comfortably as possible to spend the next four dreadful months. We have had comparatively mild & unusually dry weather so far, but I look forward to a few months now upon the other extreme. Thus matters here will be at a standstill until about the first of May next.

My last letter was rather petulant was it not? Well I am not in good spirits yet. I am so disappointed about everything in general and many things in particular that I have been even lowspirited, although nobody could have observed it. I believe I get along better while you are here. Your absence causes me to think so much of home that I begin sometimes to have homesickness. What will I do if you have to stay from me the whole of next year? I can scarcely endure the idea of such a long separation. But I must not depress your spirits. I want you to be lively, cheerful, even happy. Do not distress yourself about anything. You will find enough employment & amusement to occupy your time I hope.

You do not know how uneasy I am for fear you may not be comfortably fixed for the coming year. You must provide yourself with a good supply of everything. Be sure to get all that you need in sufficient plenty not to be at all cramped during the year. You have not written to me even where you are staying—whether with Mother or at home. I shall have to ask questions & get your answers in order to find out what I wish to know. I am afraid you don't read my letters carefully because you never refer to anything which I have written about. I have written several letters of a business nature which I was anxious for you to receive, but I cannot tell from your answers if they have reached you.

Can you take a little scolding? Has Graham given you my papers? Have you taken all of my papers away from Matt? I could ask a thousand questions, but they are all embraced in my previous letters and I still hope that your letters written after the 18th instant will contain all that I desire to know.

I am afraid now that you will think that I am getting to be cross and illnatured. This is my second or third cross letter. But you must not imagine that you are the cause of my present state of mind. What could you do that would make me love you less? Nothing. But anything you do is eminently right, making me love you more dearly every day—

I need old Mose very much. I do hope he is on his way by this time and that I shall have him before next year begins. You do not seem to have received any of the letters I wrote concerning him.

I have nothing more to write about. We shall hardly have any more fighting until next spring, so be easy on that point. Mrs. Speer is still here but I have not seen her yet. My time is all occupied.

Send my love to Sister when you write. Tell her I cannot remember her post office or I would write. You must go to stay with her some after Christmas & then I can find out where the post office is.

I hope to get another letter tonight or at least tomorrow. Send your letters to me now as "Comdg. Gordon's Brigade—Early's Division &c" and I will get them one night sooner.—Kiss the little dears for Pa. Tell them Pa wants to see them so bad. Tell Ida to write. Ask Nellie[3] if she can't write to her Pa too.

Jim Graham wrote to me that John was very proud to get a gun &c. Tell Johnny that he cant get the gun until he joins the army. Goodbye—God bless you darling.

Your Husband

3. See Appendix A for kinfolk.

Allie to Clement:

Lumpkin, Stewart Co., Ga.
Dec. 25, 1863

My dear darling—

A merry Christmas darling. I would like so much to know just how you have spent the day. I have been busy sewing all day. I see nothing to remind me that it is Christmas. The day looks a little like Sunday. None of the Negroes but Fillis has come in. I suppose they will all be in after awhile. How I wish we could have spent this Christmas together. It would have been so pleasant. Well darling the lot is sold if I ever get the money. The man has moved in and promises to have three thousand dollars for me in two weeks—he says he has a Negro to sell to raise the money and just as soon as he can affect the sale of the Negro I shall have my money. I talked right up to him about it—told him if he didn't bring the money at the appointed time he would have to hustle out of the house—that I should claim it and if he dont pay up to time I shall make brother put him out. I don't think though there will be any difficulty as he is a preacher; he will certainly keep his word; he is to take charge of the church here. I don't think he is much of a preacher. Graham wags his head mightily about it thinks I have acted very wrong but I can't see for my life it is. I have given him no deed or writing of any kind. He has no claim on the lot at all. If he fails to pay for it I may miss any other opportunity that may offer in the time to sell but I will still have my lot. I am very anxious for my trade to turn out well because I acted on my own hook. I have not seen brother—he has not been to town in several days. I believe I wrote to you I had offered the Cole place to Graham for a thousand dollars—he won't say whether he will give it or not—he shall not have it for any less. I think I can get that or more for it.

Wood has got to be quite an item here—a good load is five dollars. John Richardson wants the place and Graham will have to say soon what he will do. I have not made any disposition of our Negroes for another year yet. I think Negroes will hire very well—better than they ever did before. I want to hire all I can for the cash. Some are proposing to pay in advance. I don't think I shall let Ward have any of them. You have heard before now about the Yankees destroying the salt works—ruined everybody about here. They carried off about one hundred and fifty Negroes.

I think there is too much risk and the Negroes are very much opposed to going. I think you had better take Scott Baldwin's proposition about the boots. I can't have you a pair made here for less than seventy five or a hundred dollars and furnish the upper leather. They make very little difference in the charge when you furnish anything. I shan't have you any made until I hear from you again. They wouldn't make them anyhow until after Christmas. I tried to get them to send by Mose. Ben Hames leaves Monday. Mose will go with him. I wish I could go in the bonnet box to you too. Wouldn't you be glad to unlock it and find me in it? Sis Jane has been up again—came to show Matt how to draw in a piece of cloth in the loom.

You want to know how my factory is progressing. Slowly. I haven't got my wheel yet. I didn't calculate on getting it in operation until after Christmas. Matt hasn't made any farther progress in your suit she be making. I told her yesterday if she didn't hurry up you would be home before she got it done. Allen Lowry is to be married Sunday morning to a Miss Statum from the Richland neighborhood. There was a large party at Nutting's last night given by the young men. Randolph Hines is here and I understand is running against Mr. Kirksey. Since I have been writing the mail has come in and brought me a letter from you sent by Scott Baldwin. I wish my darling could have come home too this Christmas. I am invited to Dr. Battles to spend the day tomorrow. I know I will have a good dinner and wish you could enjoy it with me. I called in there a few minutes yesterday eve and was treated to eggnog and cake. I do want to see you so bad darling and the children want to see you too. Lawton brings Ma chips in his apron and when he gets to the door he stops to clean his feet—he runs the ducks and chickens all day long. He is getting to walk right good. Ida is very anxious for school to commence. She wants to go. She was very much shocked when she got home to find it reported all over town that she had put on long dresses and that I had written that I thought she would marry before she got here. She don't do much else but nurse the china doll. Santa Claus didn't come last night—the children didn't hang up their stockings. We told them it was no use he wasn't coming.

How shall I do about making a deed to the lot? Write to me about it. I am worried about it. So afraid the old man won't come up to the mark. I do wish you could have been here to tell me what to do. It is so cold and I know it is still colder where you are but I would like very much to be there. Did I write you that Sister would send us our pork and other things soon and it will not cost us anything to get it here? Goodbye my love. All send love. God bless you—

Your Wife

Clement to Allie:

Camp near Rapidan, Va.
8 o'clock P.M.
Dec. 26, 1863

Dear Allie

I have just returned from a dining given by Major Speer winding up with an abundance of egg nog. I tried to enjoy myself, but the dining was at Graves' where I had spent so many happy weeks with you. Everything looked so familiar, so homelike. Graves was there with his round red beaming face, but Ursula was gone. Mrs. Speer wished so much that you were here and I joined her very, very heartily. She said you had given our boy to her and insists that you shall bring him with you to deliver to her. The dinner was excellent and abundant— all did full justice, none more so than myself. This is my third Christmas away from home. I wonder if my next will be passed again in the army or at home in peace with you. Your cheering letter of the 16th was received on yesterday. It cheered my spirits, for it breathed cheerfulness and told that you could make yourself comfortable. You tell me you will *patiently* wait for the time when I can come to see you. This is right. You will remember that my time and services belong to the Government and therefore I can ask for leave of absence, I cannot demand it as a right. You ask me to forgive Mose. Well I do so because you ask it, and you may tell Mose that he owes his life to your intercession. I shall receive him with usual affection installed again in favor. I need him very much and hope he will be here in a few days more.

I have tendered your sympathies to General Joe, for the mournful loss of his tail. He has become resigned to his loss, even makes the most of it, lifting the remainder high in the air with the most graceful switch imaginable. The loss has made him feel light behind, which has caused him to form the playful habit of kicking up with me now & then. In short Joe has grown very fat and sleek. He feels his keeping and indulges himself in many sportive antics. He takes a great fancy to my leg or arm when I go about him & gives me many an affectionate bite. Poor Joe, he thinks now that the Yankee bullets will whistle near him no more, and bursting shells shall not again alarm him. But even now, we are under orders again to meet the enemy. A division of the enemy have advanced to Mitchell station, which is just opposite Clark's Mountain.[4] This may not mean anything serious, but a few days more will disclose it all. The telegraph will tell you the news before this reaches you.

I am afraid that those turkeys & chickens which are being saved for my coming will grow old before the time. Tell Clem not to save them. I am not afraid that she will be unable to entertain me. I shall enjoy that gallon of syrup and those dried apples will come in just at the right time. I am living very well, in good quarters with plenty to eat. I have duties enough to occupy my hours of labor, and my leisure moments

4. Clark's Mountain was a Confederate observation station. Freeman, *R. E. Lee*, vol. 3, p. 269.

I manage to pass pleasantly. You congratulated yourself that I still remained at the same camp but my last letter will tell you that we are about to change. However it will be but a little way. Clark's Mountain is still in view; Graves' house, the little white church, the fields & woods which you looked upon while you were here, are all still in view. You can still imagine me galloping across the field or up the lane. In "your mind's eye" you may still ride with me over these familiar places. Perhaps after a few months reality can take the place of imagination. I went so far as to promise Mrs. Speer that you should return with me next March. It is not certain that Speer leaves us. If he does not you will have his little wife for a traveling companion.

Capt. Redding has returned from Richmond without securing me any cloth, but I shall soon obtain a uniform coat anyhow. He brought me six small stars which I wear on my jacket. They are the same as the one you have only smaller, and are very pretty. I shall save them to put on the jacket you are trimming, or rather which you will trim when I come home & bring you some blue cloth for the purpose.

Capt. Redding has or will apply for a sick furlough soon to be at home in January. I suppose he will return about the first of February. He looks very badly. His homesickness has almost prostrated him. I do hope he may be elected. If he is, you will write to me at once to tell me whether Bob will come in the service as Quartermaster. He will have to give bond for twenty or thirty thousand dollars, but I suppose he can do that without trouble. Just as soon as the election returns come in get a copy and enclose it to me.

I am expecting some letters from Ida. Has she forgotten how to write or does she care so little for her Pa that she does not wish to write to him? Will Mrs. Harley be her teacher next year? If she is you must say to her that I am extremely anxious now for Ida's rapid improvement. I desire her to be very particular about her handwriting. I hope she will exert herself in this respect.

You see now I have written a long letter on my spare

311

half sheet by doubling the lines. Paper is so scarce that I have to economize. Write often, my love, write good long letters. It is all I can do to keep my spirits up, but your letters are great helpers. I think of you, dream of you all the time. How much I do miss you. How I do long for the day when I can enjoy your dear presence all the time. It will surely come and then I will give myself up to love and happiness.

Give my love to all. Ask Father if I have entirely passed out of his mind. Take good care of yourself. Dont get sick any more. It makes me so unhappy. Good bye.

Your Husband

Allie to Clement:

Lumpkin, Stewart Co., Ga.
Sunday Dec. 27, 1863

My dear darling

Mose leaves in the morning and I had promised myself to write a long letter to my darling this morning but I feel so bad I don't know whether I can or not. I have taken cold in my breast and it is making me right sick today. I haven't felt well enough to sit up scarcely today—something has been the matter with me ever since I have been home. I have fallen off about ten pounds. I don't know whether it is because I am away from you or what. I do wish I had something good to send you by Mose but there is nothing in the world to be had here. Matt charges me to tell you Graham sends the dried apples. Be sure to bear it in mind. Don't forget it. Mother sends the syrup. Matt sends the bottle of wine. It was made of our grapes. I am ashamed to send you so little. The cake Sister sent us by Mother but I would not suffer it out here. Mother got home yesterday—the old lady was glad to see us. Says she wants to see you very much. We have got all our meat home from down there without its costing us anything. Sister sent me eighteen hundred dollars by Mother. I have got on hand now two thousand to pay out. The next time brother comes in shall dispose of it.

Well darling my trade has fallen through the old man flew the track after moving into the lot. I went up yesterday and told him to get out in double quick time. I was just mad enough to say anything to him and gave him to understand that I thought he had acted in a very bad faith for a minister of the gospel. Graham came down this morning to laugh at me about it. Well I don't care. I have had fun enough about it to pay me for the disappointment. Our Methodist preacher Mr. Norris is to look at the place in the morning. He says if he likes he will buy. I think I will be able to sell anyhow. I will keep you advised of all my arrangements. The Negroes have all come in but Charles and Norman. I am afraid Matt won't have your coat ready to send back by Baldwin. She hasn't commenced spinning it yet. I told her that you wrote. She told me to tell you that various things had prevented her from getting it done. I dined with Mrs. Battle yesterday—told Battle I wanted to have a settlement with him —he says we don't owe him anything that we will just have to exchange accounts. I will write again soon darling—I feel so badly this evening that I can't write much. Goodbye—All send love—Goodbye darling—I wish I was going too—Good bye. God bless you.

Your Wife

Lumpkin, Stewart Co., Ga.
Dec. 30, 1863

My dear darling

Mose started two days ago and I reckon is half way to Virginia by now and will be there long before this letter gets there I hope. I know you are needing him very much and were anxious for him to start sometime before he did. He made twenty-nine dollars while he was here. I gave him thirty five when he started. He borrowed five dollars from me while he was here make him pay you for he gave it to Hannah Graham—Darling I am thinking about money so much that I am afraid I don't write to you about anything else. I am expecting all the energy I can to get up money to pay our debts. I have now on hand twenty seven hundred dollars and

313

as soon as I can get three hundred more I want to get Brother to go up to Columbus and settle the Hogan debt—that is the largest debt and I want it settled first. I have collected all our Negro hire for the year but two hundred and fifty dollars and I expect to get that in a few days. Graham takes the Cole place at a thousand dollars. I will get that next week and will pay Worrill for Uncle Sydney and I can get Charlie Warren to pay that note to go with it. If I could hire our Negroes for cash I could almost pay our debts without selling either Charles or the lot. Wimberly has collected right smart on the notes he has for the lot and has the others in judgment. I could just let that stay as it is—he will soon get it all. I am asking four hundred dollars for Charles. If I don't sell him, [I will get] three hundred a piece for all the rest except Beck. Everybody else that has Negroes to hire are asking at the same rates. I will have to take a little less if I get the cash. I had much rather have the money now. Graham is attending to it for me.

I found out that I could not get along without a great deal of trouble. I can't go up in town and see the men and they won't come to see me—it is no use sending for them and he is very kind, does everything I ask him cheerfully—you know he is slow and I have back bit him right smart to you but he is the best friend that I have got after all. Brother is good enough but he is most always gone and is so much engrossed in making money for himself that he don't think of anybody else. The lot is still on hand. Everybody else can sell but poor me. Every man I find to sell to somebody will step in between me and a trade. I wrote you I thought I would sell to the Methodist preacher. Bill Mansfield and Ed Davis have both sold to him for the same that I ask. He had money he wanted to invest. Mr. Kirksey has bought Mr. Turner's lot for five thousand and now wants to sell his. He is asking three thousand for it. Mrs. Tom Peter Simpson was here this evening to see me about mine. She says Mr. Kirksey wants her to buy his lot but she won't have it. She is trying to sell a Negro to buy her a home and says if she can sell her she will take my lot.

314

She is to let me know in a few days. If I don't sell in a week I shall sell Charles. I hate to sell him too and expect I will have some trouble in parting him and Nance. He makes us more than any of our Negroes. If I could hire all the Negroes for cash I don't think I would sell him but borrow a thousand dollars from Sister which I think would pay us out and we could pay her any time. One thousand dollars compared to our present indebtedness would be a very small sum. You may make yourself easy I don't intend that you shall owe anything two months from now. I have concluded to ask twenty-five hundred for my lot and see if that won't induce somebody to buy. I know if you were here I know it would have sold long ago but what is a poor woman worth without a man.

Scott Baldwin was to see me day before yesterday. I was really glad to see him. He went to have your measure taken but I expect Singer was too drunk to take it correctly. I am so sorry the coat couldn't be made to send by him Matt does work so slow on it. Everybody in the house is asleep but me. I have been trying all the evening to get an opportunity to write but failed and now it is about eleven o'clock. Sallie Campfield is staying with us a few days. Hollis is Lieutenant Col. of a cavalry Reg. and Arthur Hood is the Col. [Second Georgia Cavalry]. They are in camp down below Bainbridge. I will put up for tonight and add a little more in the morning but I must tell you while I think of it to send me the power of attorney to make deeds or do anything. I received a letter from you this evening dated the twenty third. Your letters come much quicker and more regular than they did when I first got home. I reckon you think I wrote you funny letters. Some times in high hopes about paying our debts and next time desponding—but darling I always write just as I feel at the time. You know I am right easily discouraged and I am so anxious to do what I want to do right away. I haven't got patience to wait. I want good news to write to you all the time. I am doing my very best darling and if I fail it won't be my fault. I would have given anything if you had been home this Christmas. It is pouring down rain now and I am afraid we will have a long rainy spell and I can do nothing in the time. Goodbye. God bless you my love. Goodbye.

Your wife

Clement to Allie:

New Camp—Orange Co., Va.
Dec. 30/[18]63

My dear Wife—

I have been engaged for two days in moving, building a new camp designated for our winter quarters. The weather for these two days had been very delightful, though the ground is still soft from the heavy rain of Sunday night. I received yesterday your letter written on the 20th. It was not so cheering as that which preceded it, but I laid its tone and tenor somewhat to your vexation at not receiving your trunks either from Columbus or Cuthbert, and at having to pay fifty dollars for the recovery of your own cow. I hope the first causes of your grief are by this time removed by the safe arrival of your trunks, and that you will not suffer any longer from the second, because the cow is worth the money in beef. Your report of being unable to sell the lot did surprise me as you will judge from my former letters if you receive them, but I am a little sorry that you did not trade with the Baptist Preacher on something less than three thousand dollars. However it may be all for the best. You have a home of your own and I suppose you will go to housekeeping without delay though you do not mention a word of your future plans. You talk despairingly of your ability to take care of yourself placing all your reliance on myself. This will not do. I can no more take care of you now than I could if I was dead. Therefore you must be self reliant. You find the world to be devoted to its own interests, & entertaining but little sympathy for the sufferings, and caring nothing about supplying [torn away] indeed different from the tender solicitation [torn away] with the very wind that blows upon you roughly, who only anticipate and joyfully supplies your smallest desires. The world has ever

316

been so, and while I am unhappy because my darling must endure all this, yet I accept the situation as preparation for the duties, responsibilities & trials yet before us both. I hardly know how I ought to write to you. If I tell you how much I miss your company, how lonely among the thousands around me I am, how much depression of spirits I suffer in thinking of you so far away, I only make you unhappy and create in you a feverish anxiety to be with me again, which cannot be gratified for some time to come. But a letter having no lines of love in it, such a one indeed as might pass between friends, would be unworthy [torn away] and do violence to that affection which for thirteen years has known no abatement. How dearly I do love you, my own [torn] wife, must be proven by the record of these thirteen years of devotion to you alone, and be confirmed by that future love which my heart tells me will be always yours, and yours undivided, unshared [torn away] earth. Ten years of marriage cures romance, but [torn away] strengthens true affection such as ours. You have ever been my ideal of womanhood, and my heart's brightest picture of a wife. How far short I have fallen of the true ideal of manhood and my own picture of a husband is only known and most deplored by myself.

Write very often. I am so glad that you are well again. Dont get sick any more. Kiss Ida & Lawton for Pa, & Nellie too. Bless their hearts. Good bye—God bless you—
Your Husband

Camp Rapidan, Va.
Jan. 8th/[18]64

Dear Allie

It has been an entire week since I received a letter from you, leaving me ignorant of all that has occurred at home for fourteen days. You may imagine how impatient I am, and how disappointed I feel as each day passes and no letter comes.

Moses has arrived, but the trunk (with a letter in it) is left in Orange C. H., so I may not get it for two more days. I do not know what to thank you for until the trunk does come, because Mose is unable to tell me what it contains.

You know I wrote you in my last letter that Joe [Hooker] was sick. Well the poor fellow [Evans' horse] is dead. You do not know how much I felt about it. He was sick all day, but I thought he was over the worst part, and would get well. About eleven o'clock at night I went to see him before going to sleep. He appeared a little more lively. I went close up to him and put my arms around his neck. He laid his head caressingly against my breast. I told him goodbye for the night, but did not think it was my last farewell to my horse. At daylight next morning they told me that Joe was dead. I know you will feel so sorry. I shall not soon get so good a horse again. Mose tells me that you and the Presbyterian did not trade at last. Well it is all right. If you have not sold the lot I suppose you are preparing to move it and can entertain me very hospitably when I come to see you next March. So much is being said in the newspapers now against the payment of debt in Confederate currency that I fear you are going to have trouble. Two months ago we could have arranged all our difficulties, but I fear now that we cannot. I believe it is the conscientious duty of all citizens to receive the currency in payment of debts. I have acted on that opinion all the time. The Government insists in paying me my pay monthly in its currency, although I cannot sell it for more than ten dollars per month in gold. Is it not just as fair for me to demand my pay in gold & silver from the Government & refuse to take its bills, as for the people to refuse to take from me the very money which the Government pays me?

I wrote to you that I was keeping a journal for your sake. I am working hard at it every night, strictly for your sake, for otherwise it would be a very great bore. It will not be interesting to anyone besides yourself, and to you, only because I wrote it. I am still on court martial. Have to go every morning stay six hours and return just before sunset. It is bitterly cold these mornings. The ground is frozen thick ice covers all the branches. We had quite a snow three or four days since. I am quite comfortably situated. Have a very large wall tent, making a room as large as our parlor. A good large fire place, piled up high with large logs; a good bed made of logs like a pen, 4½ feet wide, 7 feet long & a foot high. Some pine split boards placed crosswise make the slats, my mattress on that, & then my blankets &c, make me sufficiently comfortable for a soldier—still I sleep cold. You know I never complain of sleeping cold when you are here. Why does not Ida write to me? Scold her for me and say I shall not kiss her when I come home if she does not write. You must write very often. Paper is very scarce. We draw none scarcely from the Government, & office work takes all of that. The price at the Sutler's is from 25 to 50 cts. per sheet. Do not think hard of me then when I write only twice per week. As soon as I get paper I will write every day.

Good bye. God bless you. My love to all.

Your Husband

Allie to Clement:

Lumpkin, Stewart Co., Ga.
Jan. 11, 1864

My dear darling—

I have moved and am at home again and Oh how I wish my darling was here tonight. My happiness would then be complete. I moved up today and am about as well fixed up tonight as I was when I broke up—have worked myself down. I am so tired I can scarcely move. Clem has just left. She takes my leaving down there very hard—took a good cry just before she left. I am worried for her. Mother told me to be sure and write to you that she wanted me to stay and I would not. She is afraid you would think she didn't want me. The Bealls have had a real feast looking on today. All the neighbors say they are glad I am back but I think from the actions of the Bealls they are gladder than any—there has been a head to every pane of glass all day. Mrs. Harrison told me to tell you she was so glad I had come back she couldn't wait for it to hold up raining and for me to get

319

fixed up but she had to come down and spend the evening. Mrs. Richardson is sick in bed but she sent me word she was mighty glad. Matt is delighted but poor Clem is terribly distressed. Mother's house is so small that it is inconvenient and disagreeable staying down there. I have not hired Beck yet. It will be hard to get her a home and I am afraid I will have to keep her. Nobody wants her with her children. I sent the note you wrote to Brother Davies—he called to see me and told me to tell you that [the Methodist] conference did not appoint a minister to every brigade but appointed ten to be controlled by a committee in Macon to be sent where they were mostly needed and where there were no chaplains—he said he would write to you soon and explain it to you. My factory comes on slowly. It will be on a small scale though. I can't get a [spinning] wheel. Mr. Bass says he will have me one this month certain. If I can hire Beck I shall have no one but Hannah and Fillis. I think it would cost more to feed another one than they would make in cloth. I feel lonely tonight. What if you were to walk in now? Wouldn't there be joy in the land. The baby is asleep. Ida is sitting in your old rocking chair talking to Coon. Hannah is nodding and I am in the other corner sitting on the floor writing to you. We are in the room next to the parsonage. The bed is sitting up in the corner next to the door. Mother's old bureau in between the two windows. The wardrobe behind the door. Can't you see us all in your mind's eye?—how I wish you could see us with your sure enough eye. You must not grumble at the short letter tonight darling I am so tired. Goodbye. God bless you. Your wife.

Ida says give her love to pa and tell him to look for a letter soon.

Clement to Allie:

General Court Martial,
Early's Division Jan. 15, 1864

My dear Allie

While these dull proceedings of the court martial are

going on, I will try to keep one ear open to the testimony given by the witnesses, and at the same time cause the time to pass more pleasantly by writing to you. You have no idea how wearisome the monotony of my duties are. Every day without regard to the weather I have to ride or walk a mile & a half to this place, sit for six hours in trial of military offenders, back again in the evening to my tent, then papers &c to examine—then doze over the hours that pass until about Eleven o'clock p.m. when I go to bed to awake again for the same unvarying round.

Still somehow the time runs along. You have been gone nearly two months, and I could look with pleasant feelings to the end of the next two when I hope either to be with you, or on my way to see you. Looking back to the shortness of the last two I can anticipate the rapid passing of those to come, but they will not compare at all in speed with the one short fleeting month in which I am to be with you. But we will make the most of it, by abandoning all else to be with each other. I hope I can transact all my business affairs there in so short a time, that I can give myself wholly to your society. I received a letter a few days ago from Sid Cheatham. He is the Adjutant of the 5th Ga. Reg. and is stationed at Dalton, in Bragg's army. If I can get him any promotion I shall get him transferred here. He says that George Cheatham is also there. I also received a letter from Dr. Carter written in December about the elections. I wrote to him to come into the service as surgeon or asst surgeon. What has become of Dr. Gregory? If you see his wife tell her I would like to know where the Dr. is, so I can write to him. What has become of Whit Bryan & John Randall? All the men who furnished substitutes being now subject to conscription, they will have to enter the army. Write to me about Sam Beall and all the others who have substitutes. What do people say about Curt Lowe as an enrolling officer? Is he showing any favoritism? I know there are several absentees without leave in Stewart, and that he fails to arrest them. I shall wait a short time & then report him for neglect of duty.

Tell Mrs. Harrison that I am going to send Tip home in the course of a month. Tell her not to be uneasy. If nothing happens she shall see him this spring. Sam Everett will start in a few days. Furloughs to the soldiers are being granted now very liberally—Did I write to you to inquire about John Singer (son of old George)? I understand that he has grown very much and is now stout & able to do duty. You must be particular in making your inquiries so as not to excite any feeling against yourself.

Have you met Bro. Davies since you reached home? Describe the present pastor to me.

General Gordon is now at Columbus and writes that he has not improved much. I am pretty certain however that he will return about the first of March. Major Pride and Gus Redding are both at home.

I have seen Olinthus Turner. He has grown very much and I think he will make a good soldier. Your particular friend Gen. Early is still in the Valley.

There now haven't I written you all the news about everybody and everything? Do likewise.

Our camp looks like a little city. It is "laid off" in regular streets, and at night really looks splendidly. We are all fixed very well—both man and beast. So far the winter has not been near so unpleasant as the one you spent, but I must not forget that the hardest part of the winter is still ahead.

I am making ink by boiling Maple bark in water &c. Can you send me a good recipe? The Government fails to supply even that & *fluid*.

I am going to have me a military sack made out of my grey overcoat to wear home. It will look very well and will be the very coat I shall want for summer. Buying a uniform is now out of the question because I shall need more money than I can raise to buy me a horse. I am very sorry now that I sold the sorrel. But I will make out somehow. I now ride Captain Redding's horse.

Jan. 16th. A thousand kisses to you before I seal this letter. How much warmer they would be if the long thousand miles did not separate us. Kisses in imagination, though, will have to answer for the reality until we meet.

My love to Ida. You did not mention her in your last letter, nor the boy either. Nor have you said a word about Nellie for a long time. Goodbye I hope to get a letter from you tomorrow. It takes about 15 days for your letters to come.

Goodbye. God bless you my darling.

Your Husband

Allie to Clement:

Lumpkin, Stewart Co., Ga.
Jan. 27, 1863 [1864]

My dear darling

I received a long, loving letter from you today written on the eighteenth two days before the one Sam Everett brought. I am delighted to know you are living so well but you don't tell me who are the kind friends that sent you so many nice things. Are they lady friends? Do you prize your tobacco bag very high? You had better not bring it home with you for I might burn it. I bet I can guess who it was sent it. It was Miss Newman wasn't it? I told you not to go there any more after I left. How many times [have] you been? You had better not go any more or there might be a fuss when you get home. I know you were disappointed when Scott Baldwin got there and had nothing for you—but you have got your boots—I am glad of that.

I am at a loss to know what to write you about tonight. Shall I tell you what I have been doing all day? I got up this morning a little after sun up, ate my breakfast, which consisted of fried ham and eggs, biscuit. I then went to carding and spinning with all my might. I have succeeded in borrowing another wheel. After I had spun about an hour I took Lawton and washed him all over from his head to his heels, put clean clothes on him then got him to sleep, laid him down and went to work again. Hannah was scouring the house and Fillis gone to the mill for bran to feed the cow on, but she didn't get any so the old cow is eating meal at three dollars and a half a bushel. Mother sent for me to go and spend the day with her but I sent word I couldn't leave the wheel. After awhile Ida came from school. We had bread, milk and butter for dinner. I took Lawton, Coon and Fillis and went to mothers to spend the evening with her and to make Fillis wash cotton to spin. I found Mrs. Hollowman there and a little more talkative than usual. About three o'clock I sent to the [post] office, got a letter from you. Mother as usual insisted on hearing it read. I read only a part of it to her. I entertained them the balance of the evening talking about you. I left about sundown, came on by Mrs. Boynton and found Florella sitting in the front porch waiting for me—said she had been waiting an hour to walk with me. I had the fire filled with potatoes for supper as soon as I got here but the bell rang for prayer meeting before they got done. I sat down on the front steps to wait for somebody that I could go with when the Bells passed—they didn't see me and was talking how lonely they thought I must be and how much company I had. After awhile Mrs. Stubs, Mrs. Harrison came on. I went with them. We had a right good congregation but there was nobody to raise the tunes. Our preacher can't sing at all. He asked some of the brothers and sisters to raise the tunes but nobody done it.

As we came on home Sister Dennard and Mrs. Daniel came in and sit awhile and we ate my potatoes that I left by the fire. I talked to them about you about an hour. When they left, I sat down to write to you. Ida is staying with her grandma tonight. Clem is at Mollie Bells [not identifiable]. Ida told me to give her love to you and to tell you she would write to you again soon, that she is studying reading, writing, spelling and arithmetic. I can't buy any books for her, she just has to study the same ones she had last year. I will send you a list and let you get them for her when you come home.

Well darling I have read over all the letters I have rec'd from you since I have been home and I don't think there is anything in any of them but what I have answered. I hear some of the conscripts are saying they intend to resist the enrolling officer—that they never intend to go to the war. They had as soon die one way as another—they say it comes nearer killing Nutting than anybody else. There is a cavalry company camped out at the camp ground. The company that Lt. Bryan belongs to—they are picking up conscripts. I am looking every day for Uncle Loverd to send in for me. I don't think I can stay more than three or four days. I want to go and I don't want to go but of course I will go. The preacher came to make me a pastoral visit yesterday— I was at home but if I had known he was coming I don't expect I would have been. I haven't been to see them yet but intend going soon. Lawton is the fattest baby you ever saw. Florella was telling me this evening that one of the Miss Bealls said she thought he was the prettiest thing she ever saw in her life. This is not flattery for she didn't say it to me. He and Coon got on finely—he don't talk much. Makes signs for what he wants. Every time he wants to nurse I make him call Pa before I give it to him. I am trying to learn him to sleep in the cradle before you come home. Everything I do is with an eye to your coming home. It seems to me the time never will come. Another long month to drag through yet before you come. You must write to me as soon as you send up your application so I can be looking for you. I do want to see you so bad darling. You don't know how bad. The rogues have stolen one of my dinner pots. I have to lock all of my cooking utensils up in the smoke house every night by dark to keep them from being stolen. Good bye my darling. Good bye.

God bless you.

Your Wife

FORM OF OATH.

I _____ aged _____ years _____ months, born in

_____, appointed from _____

do solemnly swear or affirm that while I continue in the service I will bear
true faith, and yield obedience to the CONFEDERATE STATES OF AMERICA,
and that I will serve them honestly and faithfully against their enemies, and that
I will observe and obey the orders of the President of the Confederate States,
and the orders of the Officers appointed over me, according to the Rules and
Articles of War.

_____

Sworn and subscribed before me this _____ ⎫
   day of _____ 1862, ⎬
   at _____ ⎭

Chapter 17
WINTER QUARTERS DIARY, 1864

In winter quarters Colonel Evans began his second diary, a red leather ledger once used to keep accounts of regimental supplies. As he explained in his letter of January 8, this journal was for his wife. Evans thought his writing "a very great bore."

1864, January 1, Friday.

The beginning of the new year finds me encamped on the south side of mountain run, about eleven miles from Orange C. H. three or four miles from Verdiersville, and about five miles from the River Rapidan. The camp is traversed by several little streams emptying into Mountain Run some miles below, and as it has been located and occupied only since Wednesday last, the huts for winter quarters are still unfinished, and the fallen timber lies tangled on the ground.

Commanding the Brigade my mess consists of Captain James Mitchel, Assistant Adjutant-General, and Lieut. Eugene Gordon, acting aide-de-camp. Captain Mitchel, who is the son of John Mitchel, the Irish exile, is about twenty-three years of age, florid complexion, light curling hair, blue eyes, delicate features, and possesses a slight and trimly built figure. He first entered the war as a private, was afterwards made lieutenant, and about the first of January 1863, being appointed A. A. Genl., was assigned to duty with this Brigade to supply the vacancy occasioned by the death of the lamented Capt. E. P. Lawton, who was mortally wounded at the battle of Fredricksburg, Dec. 13, 1862. He has been wounded in three separate actions, on one occasion losing the fingers of his right hand and a portion of another; at another time in the leg and the third time in the side. Possessing courage, good judgment, affability, and industrious business habits, he has proven to be most valuable in his official position. Twelve months ago, being then in command of this brigade, he came with his orders of assignment and reported to me for duty.

This year, with its sad as well as its pleasant events, has gone—changes, momentous to many, have taken place, but we are thrown together again in the same relative position.

Lieutenant Eugene Gordon, brother of Brig. Genl. Gordon, (the commander proper of this brigade), stout and well built in frame, hair dark and eyes blue, about nineteen years old, unexceptionable in morals, courteous in demeanor, brave in action, ambitious withal—suits the position which he temporarily holds, and discharges its duties admirably.

Brigade headquarters is composed of various other parties, but those described are the chief.

After these come in order, first Emery Mattox, the lean, lank, sober looking, but not always sober *acting,* clerk in the office of the Assistant Adjutant-General. Uncle Hardy Slow, in the *Georgia Scenes* was doubtless in his early manhood the personification of this clerk of ours, although I doubt whether Uncle Hardy could ever fully have rivalled those quizzical, comical looks which spread over the countenance of this clerk in his less sober mood. But justice must be done by ascribing full clerkly qualifications to Mattox and recording his departure from perfect sobriety as occurring but twice or thrice per annum, and then upon such extraordinary occasions as a trip to Orange C. H. at Christmas or the reception of a box—and bottle—from home.

The couriers and teamsters, mess-mates with Mattox, must wind up these characters without further description and this headquarters is complete.

As the days shall roll on and this journal is extended, the passing events, and occupations if all recorded would be so much alike, that the description of one day would nearly suffice for all. For instance we rise with the sun, breakfast soon after, then I have a two miles ride to the General Court Martial for Early's division of which I am a member. This sits until three o'clock, after which I return and *vise* office papers, "forward," "return," or refer. The usual orders for the day, the usual routine of duties—this is every day work. The weather too must come in for its share of comment, but why keep a mere weather record? Yesterday the old year departed in heavy tears. The rain pattered down all day long and the miserable year went out in gloom. A fit ending for a wretched twelve months. But the new year came in with smiles subdued at first by thin clouds through which the sun rays struggled, at last conquering and covering the earth with brightness. Let this too be accepted as emblematical of the events of the year just born.

A letter today from my wife dated Dec. 23, 1863, and another promised soon. With this let this memorial of the New Year's day close, and let me listen to Gordon read a sketch from *Georgia Scenes*.

1864 Jan. 2nd Saturday

An unclouded sun shines upon the frozen earth; shivers as it touches the icy ground; but still woos, and still fails to thaw. Unrequited love; the keen, intermeddling, boisterous winds persuade the earth to still present its hard unlocked heart to the beseeching beams;—succeeds;—and at last the sun goes down beneath a cloudy veil hiding its disappointment, and chagrin.

A ride of fifteen minutes finds me at Mountain Run, and Mountain Run I find coated with treacherous ice—Attempting to ride across proves dangerous. I labor to break a path through the ice and labor vainly. I mount again warmed by the exercise, and impatient at the delay which would cause me to be late at the sitting of the Court Martial. But down the stream about a half mile the water ran swifter and the ice was unformed. At

1. *Georgia Scenes*, published in 1835, was a popular and humorous book by Augustus Baldwin Longstreet, a former president of Emory College at Oxford, Georgia, and Methodist minister. He was the father-in-law of Senator L. Q. C. Lamar of Mississippi. See J. D. Wade, *Augustus Baldwin Longstreet* (New York: McMillan Company, 1924), pp. 241-88.

this point a crossing was effected, the house where the Court is held soon gained—in time—all right. This duty will be daily & therefore need not be repeated—The Court meets at a house built of hewn logs, weatherboarded, and the interstices inside between the timbers well filled with clay. It contains two storys; two rooms above, two below, with stair case leading from a small entry built between the lower rooms, to the upper floor. One room is occupied by the Court, and the remaining rooms contain the wives of soldiers on visit to their husbands. This house now stands in an open field, its former fencing all destroyed, and having for company only a few dilapidated outhouses and a bucket-less well.

Brigadier General John Pegram is president of the court. He is small in stature, erect and carries himself well. Thick, coarse dark hair is brushed back from his forehead and his face lit up with good eyes exhibit to you a quick, nervous & industrious man. He was an officer in the United States regulars at the time of the Secession of Virginia, resigned, raised a Regiment of volunteers and subsequently was promoted to Brig. Genl. of Volunteers in our army. By a recent order these Courts Martial are required to sit six hours each day with [a] comforting addendum that this order need not be construed so as to prohibit sittings of greater length. This "comforting" assurance however is received as only a little joke from General Lee, not expected to become practical these short cold days. Our Court is sometimes dull, at others enlivened by merry trials, often saddened by exhibitions of human depravity. The trials of course vary in length. Sometimes four cases are despatched in one day, but occasionally four days can despatch one case. The principal offences are desertion & absence without leave, and as these are usually attended by few circumstances, provable by [a] few witnesses they are rapidly tried. There are about twelve such courts now sitting daily in this army alone, averaging two trials per day resulting in convictions. This makes six hundred convicts for one month from this army.

During this morning while the proceedings of a trial

which I had not attended were being read, I entered the adjoining room to sit by the soldier's fire. I found him there, a plain unlettered Virginian, surrounded with rude comforts, but having a comfort less rude in the person of his wife. She, poor woman, wore the humble habiliments of poverty, the manners disclosed the training rude and rough of early years, and her language revealed her illiterate;—but she had braved the winter's cold left the home she had, to find no home at all, unless indeed her humble heart found home alone where its affections rested.

The husband explained. He had served faithfully for the year past; furloughs they had told him would be sparingly granted, he had saved a little from his monthly pay, he could not go home himself and he wanted to see his "Nancy." She came to him; his Colonel allowed him to occupy this room near the camp, and as he told me this I saw contentment dwelling in his face—Happy even in the humility which surrounded them, content with the hard lot which was theirs in life, made harder by the deprivations, sufferings & separation caused by the war, content for a few short months of winter to rest upon a rude sort of boards, eating the coarse fare of the army. When the spring comes, bringing again the conflict of the two opposing armies the "twain whom God had joined together" will be put asunder, he to take again his place in the wearying tramp, the night's bivouac, the morning battle,—perhaps to die;—perhaps to be returned to her maimed, crippled, helpless, But no matter, he is but a poor unknown nonentity; bullet material counting but one in the great strife. Perhaps his name appears in the list of "killed or wounded," perhaps a narrow trench receives his stark, stiff, breathless frame, perhaps a board is placed at his head telling his name company and regiment, to the heedless passer by in the old field where the battle was fought. But the poor wife will mourn; for he is all the world to her.

1864 Jan. 3rd Sunday
    Sunday comes in the army like any other day scarcely

to be distinguished by anything you can observe from the less sacred days of the week. War which has wasted property, maimed scores of thousands, slain scores of thousands more, has in its train of evils, swept ruthlessly over the Sabbath also. This day of peace, holiness, & repose, has looked upon battling armies hurled against each other and reveling in a carnival of death. Its serene evenings have looked pityingly upon the trim & ghastly dead; its setting suns have hastened from the moanings of the wounded; its recorded angel has wept over the tale of blood.

The impossibility of a due observance of the Sabbath by opposing armies is a strong evidence of the sin of war. That cannot be right in itself which creates a state of circumstances that prevent obedience constantly to a plain command from Heaven. It is on this day that the mind, in the army, misses most its accustomed period of repose, the body its season of rest and the soul its devotions in the sanctuary. Instead of calmness there is clamor; instead of quiet, there is bustle; instead of the holy sanctuary there is the camp. We miss the music of the church-bell inviting the soul to adore the Supreme, and in its place the hubbub of the drum, beaten to the shrieks of the fife, salute our ear. On this day too is missed most of the dear delights of home;—This day enjoyed in sweet converse with those we love, in innocent relations from worldly care, in the heart's devotion to its affections, in the soul's adoration of its God. It belongs not to the mind, or the body, nor to brain or muscle, but to the heart and soul, the spirit and the affections.

1864 Jan. 4th Monday

The only peculiarity of this day to distinguish it from others is that it has furnished us the first snow of the season worthy of mention—There is something enlivening to the spirits in the light graceful falling of the feathery flakes, tingling your cheeks & drawing the rich blood nearer the surface. Then on the other hand there is something peculiarly disagreeable in the slush that envelopes your feet, & the damp that chills your frame. This is of light snows—Something there must be still more disagreeable where an ocean of snow descends from the skies & covers up the earth. Poetry and song may render snows enchanting, when read or sung on sultry summer days, but in the army we learn to dispense with sentiment, eschew romance, and particularly on the subject of snow storms, when rations are short, teams jaded, and roads impassable. Then we would gladly barter all our poetry for bread and the romance for bacon. Yet the snow is not suffered to disappear without contributing something to the enjoyments even of the camp. For what are the circumstances from which the soldier does not extract some fun? Snow fights, of course, occur. I have myself fought—often and hard. Sometimes singled off in pairs, often in groups and companies sometimes by regiment, occasionally even by opposing brigades with all the preludes, maneuverings & excitements of real battle. Happily the accidents are few and the fun is great.

I have intimated that a soldier finds something to be merry over under all circumstances. One would think that deprived of the society of his family, without opportunities to attend to his business, deprived of all luxury, of many comforts, sometimes even of necessaries, exposed to cold & heat, to storms of rain and snow, having no liberty of disposing his own time, labor, rest, place of habitation, or any habits of life but subject in nearly all things to a superior will; this reward in a mercenary point of view being his daily issued variety, his clothing often lacking, and his pay eleven dollars per month; these circumstances one may think would render the soldier morose, unhappy, spiritless, even mutinous. But fortunately for him for his country, fortunately for human liberty men endure all these things, and still find occasions of pleasure. Grumble they do indeed as a "constitutional privilege, and inalienable right, unresigned blessing," but they grumble and endure; they complain yet obey. They make a mock of their misery and utter witticisms over the sufferings. I have seen a whole column when worn and wearied from a long days march and still marching on as the sun was settling low, dust covered, foot-sore, and hungry, tramping in silence, broken by an occasional grumble—I have seen this apparently spiritless column suddenly and surprisingly enlivened through its whole tortuous length by the simple and innocent appearance of some poor citizen wight who, luckless, rides by with so simple a thing as a peculiarly shaped or uncommonly tall hat upon his unhappy head. At once the march is forgotten, the dusty faces gleam with merriment, and a thousand supremely ridiculous questions, remarks and witticisms assail the poor citizen's bewildered brain. Happy he who can command himself in apathy, and be phlegmatic, insensible during the fierce ordeal. I have seen hundreds of men chase a frightened rabbit, encouraged by such cheers as are never given except to that startled animal or General Jackson. They have become "children of a larger growth" many of them very bad children too as these pages may show hereafter.

1864 Jan. 5th to Jan. 9th Tuesday

Yesterday snow was the topic; it could scarcely have been otherwise for snow covered everything around us. Today, therefore, it should not be the topic because the snow no longer exists. Although the sky of the morning was of dull, unvarying leaden hue yet before midday the clear bright sun showered its beams upon the earth changing the white crisp carpet into universal *slush*. But ere this was done, the early morning found scores of soldiers traversing the fields, deployed like skirmishers, carefully exploring each copse, beating at each bush, stirring every tuft of sedge enjoying the profitable amusement of rabbit hunting. Many of the luckless animals died for the Confederate cause, contributing their all to increase the rations of the Confederate soldier. It is surprising to see how any of these animals are caught. I remember on one occasion about six weeks ago, when I marched my regiment to the Rapidan opposite Robertson's Ford to support Col. [Edmund N.] Atkinson in case he should be attacked, I caused arms to be stacked in a small piece of woods near an old sedge field, and in fifteen minutes after the command "rest" was given nine large rabbits were caught by being surrounded and run down by the troops. This may seem surprising but in truth the rabbit has but little chance of escape, even if he is not frightened to death by the shouts and clamor which surround him. At Brandy Station last fall I knew a soldier to run down and catch a fine wild turkey gobbler. Another in hot pursuit, when he supposed himself near enough, threw forward his hand and seized the turkey by the tail at the same time falling prostrate on the ground. Unhappily the feathers came out in his grasp, the bird going off tail-less and the soldier coming back turkey-less.

Appropos to "rabbits and rations" must be recorded the less praiseworthy deed of butchery committed upon the swine of a neighboring citizen. One of the numerous guards stationed at every house in the vicinity of the army brought under arrest today two soldiers of Hays' brigade, taken with the unlawfully acquired pork. They were sent to the commander of their brigade for disposal. These depradations upon the property of citizens is very difficult to be restrained, impossible to be entirely suppressed. Patrols traverse the country in all directions, guards remain at every house, yet the hogs, the sheep and even the cows disappear. It must not be understood from this that this army is composed of rogues and highway robbers. Among so many thousands there will be scores of evil men capable of any act of meanness. In comparison with the Yankee army in this particular our men are angels of light.

It is true however that the laws of *meum* and *teum* are not so conscientiously regarded in the army as would be desirable, and it is greatly to be hoped that this laxity of morals will cease with the war if not before. Thefts of anything to eat is not regarded in the light of crime, and even when discovered will scarcely produce shame. Tom Brown, who drives the cooking utensil wagon of my regiment, once lost his little sack of flour,

335

and in searching found that Cook, the soap man, was the thief. When discovered Cook had just mixed a portion of the flour with water and was kneading the dough. Tom, with wonderful good nature, not only withheld the well deserved punishment, but actually allowed him to keep the dough which he had allready wet, taking back only the flour. Now, would it be supposed that the fellow actually came within five minutes to borrow of Tom "just another cupfull of that flour, because he had wet up what he had too soft?" The day's history would be incomplete without the mention of the advent of Moses to his accustomed place of cook, hostler & servitor-general. He has just returned after a month's absence from the army at home entering upon his duties here at once. Moses, an old family servant, is utterly spoiled. He regards himself as my guardian, thinking doubtless that but for him I would have been lost long ago. I appreciate his fidelity and shall reward his services by affording him after the war a serene old age. Black as the ace of spades in color, and my bondsman and slave for life, yet he is happier than Greeley, Beecher, or Lincoln. It would be cruelty to give him his freedom and in fighting to retain my right of property over him, his children and fellow bondsmen. I contend but for their happiness. He went with me through the Pennsylvania Campaign last year, being well apprised that he had but to remain in order to be free. I offered him there the choice of remaining or returning and he scouted the idea of living among Yankees. While Moses thinks he is not so good as a Southern white man, yet he feels immeasurable superiority over the Yankee whites.

He rode his horse with serene dignity through the streets of Gettysburg and York dressed in full Yankee blue[2] often giving to the gaping Pennsylvanians a stiff military salute. Once he stopped at a house by the wayside to get some butter and was overpowered by the attentions of some Dutch damsels of the place. He came away offended at the familiarity they had presumed to

2. "Yankee blue" means Yankee uniform.

treat him with. I cannot boast much of his courage. Bursting shells demoralize him, and the singing Minie ball quickens the first law of his nature to wit, self-preservation. But I will say for him that he fears no danger if he is told I am wounded. Once he came to me on the false rumor of my being wounded, and at Gettysburg he came also to the very line where I was. He manifests great apprehensions for my safety. Said he once "They have shot you twice & shot all about you many times; some of these times, if you don't take care, they will shoot you bad, & then what will become of me?"

I have been thus minute in speaking of Mose, because he came into the service with me, and prefers enduring these campaigns rather than the more comfortable labor at home. Possibly his name may occasionally occur in these pages to be hereafter written. But, should it not, let him ever be remembered for his fidelity.

1864 Jan. 9th to Jan. 18th Saturday

The monotony of camp life when in winter quarters is so great that the soldier almost unwittingly sighs for the season to change, excitement and danger again. From day to day the round of duties is almost unvarying. The severity of the winter prevents those outdoor exercises which enliven the camp of summer time somewhat. *Nostalgia*, or homesickness, then begins its attacks, and although it seems incredible, yet numbers become seriously sick from a longing desire to be at home. The mind having no other occupation broods over the "dear family scenes of home" until the reveries of the imagination develop a real disease. Many a poor fellow has thus fed upon his anxieties to visit his family and friends until his diseased brain prompts him to commit the crime of desertion. While upon this subject, it may be noticed as part of the history of the times, that much of the soldier's happiness or contentment depends upon the character of the letters he receives from home. Some of those letters are hopeful, & encouraging, others gloomy and desponding. Some say to their husbands or sons, "do your duty faithfully to your country. We must make sacrifices, we must suffer, but we will endure & be cheerful." Others write complainingly, say that they are "getting along badly at home," speak of the war as endless; not only hint at desertion, but even advise or request it. Some poor fellows have lost their lives by sentence of Court Martial for desertion who abandonned the service to go back to their complaining, fretting, unhappy wives. Happily the encouraging letters exceed those of the other kind. The want of employment, however, has not yet been seriously felt. After nearly two weeks of constant and hard labour the huts are scarcely completed; well sheltered stables for the horses are yet to be built, to protect them from the snows, the cold winter rains and the bleak piercing winds; much clearing of camp, building of bridges, cross-laying, or corduroying of roads, are yet to be done, so that January will probably pass before we can really feel snugly in quarters for the winter.

In this portion of Virginia the public roads themselves become almost impassable, while the common dirt road as it is called, passing through woods or fields becomes entirely so. The earth appears to become rotten, and the mud without any bottom in a very short time after a rain or snow. Hence, in order to haul supplies to the army these roads must be *corduroyed*. This is done by having a sufficient number of stout poles cut about twelve or fifteen feet long and laying them close together across the road. A few inches of dirt is thrown on the poles thus completing the work. The labor is very great but is so absolutely necessary that it cannot be omitted. Even after this is done it is difficult, with our very limited transportation, to keep the army supplied with rations for men and forage for horses.

The regular ration now is a fourth of a pound of bacon, a fourth pound of lard, a pound and eighth of flour, besides salt, and occasionally some dried apples, rice, and sugar in small quantities. This is really a small allowance for a healthy man, but last winter for three months the same amount was issued and the troops kept healthy and really fattened. It is certainly true that a smaller allowance is necessary in winter than when we are active. I am building a house as a depository of the Bacon collected by the company as tax in kind from the neighboring citizens with a view of providing against the contingency of any occasional failure on the part of the Division company to supply the regular ration—With a view also to more easily forage the public animals I have sent a quartermaster to establish about fifty miles from here a depot to receive forage, where all animals not absolutely needed can be sent for the winter.

These arrangements, or extremities, have to be adopted in order to prevent starvation of men and horses in this region where King Mud reigns almost without dispute.

1864 Jan. 18th to Jan. 28th Monday
A week passes away in the army almost with the fleetness of a dream, notwithstanding the monotonous character of duties performed day after day. I was surprised upon reference to the last date in this journal that an entire week has passed without the usual record. But if the week gives birth to no event worthy of being named it can scarcely be accounted my fault that it is not celebrated in this journal.

But last week shall be celebrated for its beautiful days. Almost a week of pleasant Georgia winter. And it was well improved too; for now the huts are completed, the stables for horses built, the encampment cleared of brush and trash, and all now snugly in winter quarters.

Our Court Martial also having exhausted its docket has adjourned for a week thus allowing a pleasant rest.

A letter from "Sid Cheatham,"[3] his first to me since the war began, recalls vividly to my remembrance the days of "Auld Lang Syne." Sid is my first cousin, the son of my mother's sister, and the companion of my boyhood, youth, and earlier manhood. Having no brother, I attached myself naturally to this cousin who was nearly my own age, very similar in disposition in many

3. Sidney Cheatham. See Appendix A for relatives.

respects, and who was my constant associate. Sid is remarkable for a dashing reckless courage, which would have distinguished him, added to his other fine traits, had he entered the service in command of cavalry. I regard that branch of service as his forte particularly if allowed elbow room. He is now adjutant of the 5th Ga. Reg., served the first thirteen months of the war as a private, was four times elected captain of district infantry companies, each of which he declined. His fine penmanship, industrious & methodical habits fit him eminently for his position.

I have mentioned camp life several times in this Journal as monotonous, but it must not be understood as being an existence without pleasure. On the contrary, as a general rule soldiers are now the happiest inhabitants of the country. There are many sources of pleasure, among which the social conversational visits of friends are not esteemed the lightest. Suppose, for instance, the day has closed, dinner ended, a bright warm fire burning on the hearth of the stick and mud chimney, and the slightest perceptible yawn begins to exhibit its symptoms of ennui, when just in time steps in Lieut. Lyon, ordnance officer of the brigade;—Lyon the jovial, the "queer case," the man of good yarns well spun. The yawn disappears, then changes to a good round smile: Expectation is exhibited from the eye; If Lyon is in humor the evening will pass rapidly—He is not exactly "the spoiled child of fortune" for I think he is chiefly guilty of his own spoiling, but he has evidently been turned loose from a very early age. His college life had its ups and downs, particularly on those several occasions when his pugilistic skill was tested. Lyon has travelled too—That is, he has seen the *inside* of much, that to the outsiders is never known. He has enjoyed a brickbat row in New Haven, killed deer in the Canada lakes, holding them by the tail to prevent their sinking, has shot alligators in the south, and rode a tournament, with a red ribbon in the third button hole of the left side of his vest. He says that he is the model boy in his family and was regarded in *Mobile* as the pattern of propriety

340

which the mothers of younger boys pointed to for the emulation of their sons. He enjoys the pleasing faculty of giving wings to the dull hours, for according to his theory "we do not know what we are coming to, and should make most of the present hour"—The liberal system of furloughs instituted by Genl. Lee, under which a very large number of officers and men are going home, is producing a most happy effect on the army. Great despondency sometimes existed in the minds of many on account of their families at home, whom they had not seen for two or more years. I have frequently heard the excuse for desertion offered that their families were in distressed circumstances and no furloughs being given the consequences of desertion were braved. Even wounds were courted because "wounded furloughs" were liberally granted. At the first Battle of Fredericksburg a soldier in the brigade received a wound in the arm, rather slight, which he joyously displayed exclaiming "heres my thirty days furlough" when just at that moment another minie ball entered his leg which caused him to drop on the ground and cry out "furlough extended to sixty days but that'll do I don't want any more."

General Lee has offered a furlough of thirty days to every soldier who procures an able bodied recruit & has him mustered into service in this army. In consequence of this, numerous are the letters written home, numerous the arrangements attempted to be made, and heavy are the private bounties offered. I have heard it said that in one or two instances even a thousand dollars have been offered for the necessary recruit. These furloughs have a double beneficial effect. The soldier becomes satisfied and returns cheerfully to duty, and the people at home catch somewhat of the soldier's spirit of cheerfulness while he is at home. The principal gloom is among citizens, for the soldier is full of hope, cheerfulness, and confidence. Some on returning declare that the army is by far the most to be preferred as the place of enjoyment. That at home, long faces, dolorous groans, and fearful apprehensions meet them at every turn. They are

341

glad to get back to their commands to laugh over the distresses of the comfortable citizen.

The following admirable general order, from General Lee, becomes history and will be transmitted to posterity as illustration of his own peculiar style of writing, of his goodness of heart, his care for his army, and also as proof of the patient self-denial of the brave troops under his command.

Head'qrs Army of Northern Va.
January 22d, 1864

General Orders No. 7:

The commanding General considers it due to the army to state that the temporary reduction of rations has been caused by circumstances beyond the control of those charged with its support. Its welfare and comfort are the object of his constant and earnest solicitude and no effort has been spared to provide for its wants. It is hoped that the exertions now being made will render the necessity of but short duration, but the history of the army has shown that the country can require no sacrifice too great for its patriotic devotion.

Soldiers! You tread, with no unequal steps, the road by which your fathers marched through suffering, privation and blood to independence!

Continue to emulate in the future, as you have in the past, their valor in arms, their patient endurance of hardships, their high resolve to be free, which no trial could shake, no bribe seduce, no danger appall and be assured that the just God who crowned their efforts with success, will in His own good time, send down His blessings upon you.

(Signed) R. E. Lee, Genl

General Robt. E. Lee is regarded by his army as nearest approaching the character of the great & good Washington than any man living. He is the only man living in whom they would unreservedly trust all power for the preservation of their independence. They had enthusiasm for Jackson, but their love and reverence for

Lee is a far deeper and more general feeling. General Jackson had many enemies, (while living) among officers of high grade, and his peculiarities were sometimes a subject matter of jest, but General Lee has no enemies, and all his actions are so exalted that mirth at his expense is never known.

1864 Jan. 31st Sunday

The first month has well nigh gone. Reflections upon the rapid flight of time are now even comforting and soothing because *the end* of all these national & individual distresses growing out of existing war is thus brought nearer. An end there must be, and each day's departure, may be deemed one day of waiting—of long-deferred hope, less. It is singular how often we have deceived ourselves since the war commenced, with the belief of its speedy termination. At first many thought there would be no war at all. When Fort Sumter surrendered after a bloodless bombardment, it was accepted as an omen that the further negotiation for separation would be bloodless. When hostilities actually began, ambitious young men hastened to the field for fear that the war would end without their having participated in the strife. Many thousand more were tendered than the Government could arm and supply. It was supposed that European Governments would not permit any blockade of ports, and that the Yankee Government itself could not endure the loss of our trade and production by prolonging the war, but would soon be willing to adopt terms of peace and mutual comity. The brilliant victory of Bull Run & first Manassas graced our arms, and the unfavorable opinion always entertained at the South of Yankee courage in battle, increased. At the most the country believed that one year would close hostilities.

On the other hand, the Yankees appeared equally confident. First an army of seventy five thousand men enrolled for three months were commissioned to subdue the Rebellion. These three months having passed an extension of ninety days was added, and again and again, the world was officially promised that the "insurgents"

343

would be put down and the authority of the U. S. Government maintained over all the old Union—

Even now it is again stated that the three months which follow the opening of the Spring Campaign will "crush the rebellion & end the war"—But the South while still indulging a strong hope that 1864 is the last year of the war, has fortified herself to endure even to the end, let it be ever so distant. But hope of yearly peace will take possession of the mind. Every indication of exhaustion or yielding on the part of the enemy, every manifestation of increasing strength on our part, every appearance of weariness among European Governments at the prolonging of the struggle form so many inducements to hope. Even reason steps in to assist the soldier to believe that a war of this magnitude must soon expend its fury, like a fierce storm. Can the country which groaned under an expenditure of Eighty millions per annum, five years ago in time of peace and prosperity, continue to spend much longer twice that sum every month? Can the heavy increase in price of all cotton fabrics, so necessary to the comfort of the poorer classes at the North be borne for years to come? Will the trade in cotton find some other channel, and the world submit to the non-production of that staple to let the war go on? Will the people of the North not become tired of the effusion of blood with so little prospect of success to their schemes?

Thus does reason with a thousand other questions come to the support of Hope, and both together buoy up the spirit, and point the imagination to a delightful home, the joyous greeting, the blissful days, weeks—years of peace, comfort and independence. How many who thus dream, must yet yield up their precious lives, that others may realize the dream!

1864 Feby 1st to 9th Monday

The attention of the army has been engrossed for some weeks by the subject of re-enlistment for the war. At the opening of the struggle a large number of regiments were mustered into service for twelve months and

344

on the 16th of April 1862 an act of Congress was passed which continued these troops in service two additional years. This term expires in a few months and Congress is devising some plan for further continuation of their service. Fortunately the troops are taking the matter in their own hands and are voluntarily re-enlisting for the war. I felt quite a desire that this Brigade should also renew their services, and therefore addressed the following circular:

Hdqrs. Gordon's Brigade
Feby. 1st 1864

The spirit of the Confederate troops exhibited at the opening stages of this war with our country's enemies, is again being displayed in her armies by the voluntary re-enlistment of these brave and dauntless men for the war. The mercenary hirelings of the Yankee army continue their inglorious, but merciless and barbarous warfare against ourselves, our homes, and our families, only for the pay of hundreds of dollars in bounties and the sordid hope of future plunder. Such a degrading price of blood is scorned by men whose present reward is the delightful consciousness of doing right, and whose hopes rest unwearedly upon the independence of their country. Soldiers of Gordon's brigade—You who have never failed to win solid triumphs wherever you have fought—your attention is called to this noble conduct of your comrades in arms. Will you not emulate their patriotic devotion? Will you not say to Georgia, to hope on, though the foe despoils her borders, for her sons are undaunted? And to the Confederate Government, that it shall *ever* have your services, cheerfully, hopefully, without stint, and without draft, conscription or bribe?

Faithfully relying on the Good Being who, while permitting through His infinite Wisdom, many reverses to befall us, has still, wonderfully shielded our young Republic, we will meet the foe again, with renewed energies, conquer a lasting peace and preserve our liberties and Honor.

C. A. Evans
Col. comdg.

The immediate response to this address was exceedingly gratifying and showed that the troops appreciated fully the necessity of continuing in the army, and looked forward to the blessings of peace, and liberty as a result to follow their services as soldiers. Four Regiments with almost entire unanimity renewed their enlistment and the other two are rapidly approaching the same state of unanimity. The only question raised by any troops is as to their reorganization and reselection of officers. Many desire that this privilege should be conceded to them, and I believe it would be, if the spring campaign were not so near at hand. But there is a strong probability that this would disorganize the army just when perfect organization is most needed. The situation now is such that I believe it will be better to retain the old organization through the campaigns of 1864, and about December next, consolidate the small regiments & companies & allow re-elections in the commands which are consolidated.

* * * * *

[The last major diary account Evans entitled "The Affair at Morton's Ford" on February 6. Since a letter to Allie, which he started on February 2 and finished on February 9, introduced the subject of the "Affair," it seems appropriate to read the letter first:]

In Camp, Feby. 6th, 1864
Saturday

My dear Allie

I am so glad to write February at the head of my letters. It seemed as if January never would pass away. About one month from today I hope General Gordon will be back, and my application can go up, so I can leave here about the fifteenth, and get home about the twentieth of March. These are my calculations, and I do not believe that they are likely to fail. Your letter of the 27th Jan. was received today, notifying me to be particular as to who I received presents from, & how many visits I pay to certain young ladies about here. Well, you know that everything is so dull, and I want to pass the

346

time off swiftly so I can get to see you sooner, and therefore if I visit agreeable young misses, especially if they are very pretty, just so as to pass off the time, because I want to see you so bad and would do anything in the world, since I love you so much, just for your sake, to keep me thinking of you, and wishing it was you instead of them, you don't care do you?

That silk tobacco bag is very pretty, but it did not come from Miss N. I would prize it so much more if it had been the work of your hands, but you know if some real handsome Georgia girl will, anyhow, in spite of myself, send me such things, why of course I must take on a little mustn't I? I wear it dangling from my coat button, but if you insist on it, I will put it in my pocket— the left side coat pocket, and only take it out when necessary. All these things however amount to nothing in comparison with my thoughts of my darling. My dreams of you are delightful, and not an hour passes during the day that does not contain some moments filled with thoughts about you. I shall be so impatient when I start home, railroad time will be snail-pace. I will want to fly with the wind. Do not commence looking for me until I write to you definitely about the day. There is no prospect of my leaving here before the fifteenth. Unless Genl. Gordon should recover earlier than I think.

Somebody handed me a copy of the "Columbus Times" dated the 21st of Jany. containing a most complimentary article on my regiment written by the editor.[4] Have you seen it? If not get Graham to obtain the paper for you. I did not keep the one which I read, or I would send it to you.

I will get Ida all the books she will need if you will send me a list. She must have them at any cost. I feel a deep interest in her education, and of course you feel equally solicitous about her. I know she is capable of high improvement.

The only rumors afloat here concerning our army are that both Genl. Ewell and Genl. A. P. Hill are to be re-

4. *Columbus* (Georgia) (January 21, 1864).

moved, and new Lieut. Generals made or assigned in their places. These are mere rumors. The Army has re-inlisted for the war.

There is . . . [Letter ends here.]

Monday Feby. 9th. The sentence unfinished above must remain so, as a memorial of the uncertainty of all human calculations concerning the war. Just as the words were written a most hurried order came for me to bring the brigade without delay to Morton's Ford. Of course I went at it with a vim and was soon on the march. An-other courier met me to say I was in command of the Division. I at once turned over the command to Col. [Edmund N.] Atkinson, & went in great hurry to the Front, where I found Genl. Ewell. The enemy had crossed their infantry & were in line of battle. We reached our trenches in time & confronted them. I shall not trouble you with details, for I reserve all these to talk about. It is sufficient to say that Sunday morning before day the enemy retired & Genl. Ewell has compli-mented my management of the Division very highly. Told Genl. Lee that a bold move which I made Saturday evening by which after a half hours hard fighting I drove the enemy from a strong position at some houses, was in his opinion the cause of the enemys leaving us. They doubtless intended a reconnaissance in force & have gone away disappointed. I captured 32 prisoners, killed and wounded a good number. Our loss very tri-fling. I have a memento of the fight in the picture of two very pretty Yankee babies. . . .

[The remainder of the letter is missing. We return now to Evans' diary.]

"The Affair at Morton's Ford"

On Saturday morning the 6th of Febry. we were quietly enjoying our winter quarters when a sharp cannonading in the direction of Morton's Ford on the Rapidan lead us to expect that the enemy were making some demonstrations against that point. About nine o'clock a.m. a courier from Genl. Ewell came in great haste bringing me an order to march the brigade as rapidly as possible toward the Ford. We were very soon on the march, when another courier came for me personally with the statement that I was in command of the division. I at once turned the command of the brigade over to Col. E. N. Atkinson and galloped to the front. On reaching our line of entrenchments which cover this ford, I found that the enemy confronted us in line of battle about three fourths of a mile distant, while a small portion of our forces occupied the trenches. I sent Col. [Henry] Forno, commanding Hays' brigade to Raccoon Ford and placed Gordon's brigade in the trenches just opposite Dr. Morton's house, their left resting on the river, and their right on Pegram's brigade which I found already in position. A few pieces of artillery were scattered along the line.

Just as soon as the brigades occupied the trenches, a line of skirmishers was deployed and marched forward six hundred yards to the crest of a hill and halted. Early in the day the enemy, by a bold assault upon a particular point of the skirmish line, which covered the front of the Division on the right of Early's division, carried the position at a fence, which these skirmishers held, and thus were able to advance their sharpshooters near enough to annoy our main line. About the same time they advanced the right of their skirmish line (which up to that time rested at Dr. Morton's house) about one hundred and fifty yards, and filled the barns & outhouses with sharpshooters. It became apparent at once that they had gained an important advantage, and the necessity to dislodge them became urgent because their sharpshooters commanded our main line while they were . . . themselves under perfect protection. I observed by reconnoitering the ground, that three companies of infantry could be conducted down a valley under cover of two hills, one protecting them from observation & artillery fire from across the river, and the other from the observation of the enemy on this side, until they could approach within seventy-five or one hundred yards of the barn & other outhouses in which

349

these sharpshooters were concealed. I accordingly detached three companies from Gordon's Brigade under the command of Lt. Col. [Charles W.] McArthur and entrusted to him the execution of the plan of assault, which was to straighten & organize the division skirmish line, give them instructions to advance rapidly as soon as the attack was made and then march the three companies to their position & commence the attack.

At the same time I directed Col. Atkinson, commdg. Gordon's Brigade, & Col. [John S.] Hoffman, commdg. Pegram's brigade to advance one good company from each regiment of their respective brigade as soon as the skirmish line advanced, to act as reserves & support to the skirmish line. These arrangements were admirably executed, and immediately after sunset Col. McArthur commenced the attack with the three companies, having taken the enemy by surprise. The entire skirmish line advanced at the same moment, driving the enemy back, and gaining the particular position at which they were directed to halt, which was a fence that ran from Morton's house and parallel with our main line down the river. A very close and severe skirmish fight occurred around the Morton Buildings but the enemy were driven entirely beyond the houses, but receiving a heavy re-inforcement from their main-line came up again to the main dwelling house, & occupied that, our pickets falling back about seventy five yards . . . from the Morton dwelling, still holding the other buildings and extending the main skirmish line to the river on the left. This was the position in which I left them about eight o'clock at night and rode with Major [Samuel] Hale, A.A.G. of Early's division to the Hdqrs. of Brig. [Gen.] [George] Doles where I met Genl. Ewell, Genl. Doles & Genl. [Stephen D.] Ramseur in consultation. The result of this conference was that the enemy was to be watched. If he was discovered retiring, we were to attack, but if he remained, we were to meet again at 4 o'clock a.m. to arrange a plan of attack.

I sent out officers & scouts to watch their movements & about nine o'clock lay down in the rain without any blanket & a very light overcoat, by a bush fire to rest. It was too cold to sleep and too wet to be comfortable in any position. Therefore I mounted again at midnight and went out to the skirmish line. I became convinced that the enemy had gone as soon as I arrived. I therefore sent out scouts who found no one. I hastened then with three companies to the Ford hoping to overtake their scattering pickets, but they were all across.

I rode with Major Hale down to the Ford. It was pitch dark, but the tramp of our horses attracted the attention of a Yankee sentinel who was sitting by a fire on the opposite bank and he sent a minie ball whistling above our heads. I thought so great a fool did not deserve his life. I sent six good marksmen with instructions to slip to the river bank, and discharge a volley at him. My orders were obeyed, and next morning the sun rose on his corpse.

It is probable that this demonstration was intended only as a reconnaissance, and to divert our attention from other quarters. The enemy gained no information, but have retired with an impression that our strength is more than it really is. They sent over one Division in Command of Brig. Genl. [Alexander] Hay[s]. They left seventeen dead, thirty two prisoners, and carried off their wounded, which probably amounted to fifty or sixty. Our loss is about five killed & fifteen wounded in All.[5]

This affair is in miniature the same as the affair of Mine Run during the latter days of November 1863, when General Meade crossed his whole force, confronted us for a few days, and then retired under cover of night and the thick woods.

The following highly complimentary note from General Ewell is entitled to a place in this journal.

Hdqrs. 2nd Corps, Army N. Va.
9th Feby 1864

5. *O.R.* series 1, vol. 36, part 1, p. 114, gives the report of Maj. Gen. G. K. Warren, U.S. Army Second Corps, which is accompanied by a sketch of troop positions. The Federal casualties on p. 118 are higher than Evans' estimate: 11 killed, 204 wounded, and 40 captured or missing—total of 255.

Col. C. A. Evans,
Comdg. Gordon's Brigade
Colonel

I have received with great pleasure your letter of the fifth instant announcing the reenlistment of your gallant brigade, & showing that the movement commenced by Genl. Rodes' division is still continued. This spontaneous proof of devotion is hardly less gratifying than the spirited conduct of the brigade on Saturday near Morton's Ford.

The deeds of "Gordon's Brigade" are already sufficient to ennoble all who have shared its dangers and its Glories.

> I remain, Colonel
> with great respect
> Yrs. very truly
> R. S. Ewell
> Lt. Gen'l

"Gordon Minstrels"

It would scarcely be thought that out of the meager accommodations of a winter's camp in the woods that anything like an interesting exhibition of any sort could be produced. But in an army like ours scarcely a brigade exists which' does not contain some men of each profession & occupation known to the country. For instance you will find the Lawyer, Physician, Preacher, Teacher, Dentist, Silversmith, Blacksmith, Carpenter, Painter, and so to the conclusion of the list. Therefore you need not look in vain for Musicians, quondam actors and amateurs.

After a great deal of hard labor a huge log building capable of containing about five hundred persons is erected. It is certainly rough enough, covered with old tent flys to keep out the rain, and the openings between the logs chinked with grass and mud to keep out prying eyes. This building has been christened the "theatre" where three or four nights during the week an amateur troupe amuses the thronging crowd. Happily they have discovered that every piece must be comic in order to be appreciated, for the soldier pays his dollar for something to laugh at. This discovery was easily made for a more candid audience of critics never viewed a play. What fails to please is at once & publicly condemned, and the close of each piece is either uproariously applauded or else significantly condemned.

This troupe style themselves "the Gordon Minstrels" and employ their faculties in various delineations of Negro character.

[Evans' diary stopped on February 9, 1864, but his life in winter quarters was still described in several letters that extend to the leap year day of February, the 29th.]

In Camp. Feby. 10, 1864

My dear Allie

You have been very good lately about writing to me. I have received three letters in the last six days from you.—All good loving letters—such as make me feel cheerful. I write about three times every week and I hope you get them all. I wrote to you Monday about the fight at Morton's ford. I did not think it to be necessary for me to send you any dispatch, because the same paper which will tell you of the fight, will also tell the end of it & that our loss was very little.

I am almost afraid to write again that everything is quiet, and no anticipation of another fight this spring, for the weather is delightful and the roads in pretty fair order. It is possible therefore that we may be annoyed again, although I do not believe that we will.

I am thinking of nothing now except of my going home. I am getting so restless that I hardly can control myself. I think Genl. Gordon will certainly return by the first of March. Possibly a little earlier. *Possibly* therefore I may embrace you by the fifteenth of March. But I must prepare you for a disappointment. I will send a dispatch to you a day before I start. I don't intend to cut my hair until they give me a leave of absence. It is now long, jagged *& bearish.* I look fierce. Would you like to see me in that shape? The twenty days which I

353

am to stay with you will fly away like the wind. Only twenty short days! How will we best employ them! Can we spare even a minute from each other? I fear the good people will not give me any credit for sociability if I carry out my inclination to stay only with you, all the time.

I suppose Mrs. Harrison & Mrs. Richardson are enjoying the company of their boys now. Tell them your time comes next. I intended to arrange it so that we all should go home together, but I was afraid if I made them wait they would lose their opportunity.

You are uneasy about my getting another horse. Well you ought to see "Bullet." I rode Bullet in the last fight. He has no objection to cannon balls or shell. He behaved magnificently—even when right at the battery. But minie balls demoralized him. Poor "Joe," he used to squat low to the ground and stand still & kick when the balls came thick, but Bullet is disposed to cavort. Still he is a good horse and can stand much hard riding. On Saturday I was in the saddle riding hard much of the time from nine o'clock in the morning until nine at night. Then took three hours' rest, and was again riding from twelve midnight until after daybreak. But he stood it all well. I still have "Betsy." She is improving and next spring when she fattens I will be able to exchange her for a good saddle horse.

I am unable to buy me any uniform. My pay will not enable me to buy a horse & uniform also—& leave me any to go home. My trip home and back will cost me at least three hundred dollars, which will be all I can save up to the first of March, after paying my commissary bills. I expect I shall have to borrow some to go home. But I am making a shift to appear as decent as possible, but all who look for a fine dressed Colonel will be disappointed. I wish for your sake I had the means to go home in full uniform, but I must put up with what I can get— You will not receive me any less joyfully will you?

Your letter brings me the agreeable news that you have paid out five thousand dollars. All is right now. We cannot possibly be hurt in the future.

354

God bless you. You are very precious to me. Good bye.

Your Husband
Camp. Feby. 15, 1864

My dear Allie

We have a good snow this morning and the skies look like they could still furnish any additional supply of the same article that may be needed. Of course this makes us feel more comfortable and snug, because it is a token of the suspension of active hostilities. It is such a day as I would delight to spend with you at home in our own room, having a good fire, and "the curtains drawn" as Miss Ann A.——— used to say. Instead of that I am cooped up in the goodly sized tent, located in the woods, while I hope you have the warm fire & the cozy room, but I know it is less cheerful than it would be if I was by your side. However I will be by your side before many more weeks shall roll round. Furloughs are still being granted very liberally. We attribute our good fortune in this particular to the absence of old Genl. Early. It is probable that if he had not been sent to the valley very few officers would have seen home this winter. Cody has sent up his application and will go home about the twenty-second or twenty-third of this month. Nearly all will have had their furloughs before me, but I can get a longer in order of that account, because then, no one will be waiting for my return in order to go home. Are you not tired of my writing nothing except about going home? I cannot make my letters interesting because I have nothing here to write about, and as nearly all my thoughts are of home & you, it must be expected that my letters will be full of the same subject. I have, in my imagination, been over the journey, spent my twenty three days with you, parted, & returned. Even farther than that have I gone, to your visit to Virginia next summer, staying with me three months & then returning to our happy home when the war ends, to our children growing up around us—to our final reunion to part no more.

Have you forgiven me, for the apparent crossness of some of my previous letters. I have been feeling bad enough about them or rather because you construed them differently from my intention. I will make it all up when I see you—Will I not?

Everyone who returns from Georgia especially South west Georgia gives glowing accounts of the plenty which abounds everywhere and also of the increasing confidence & cheerfulness of the people. This is a good omen. The crisis in the history of our struggle was passed in December & January. There was about that time a spirit of gloom and disaffection spreading which would have ruined us had it not been checked in time. But the danger is safely passed. Everything is improving. Blockade running is checked, the currency will improve, the troops have reenlisted with great spirit. The army is strengthened; public confidence is better. The Yankee currency is depreciating slowly. In short I never was more hopeful.

Try to enjoy yourself for a few more weeks. In twenty days after you get this letter I shall be with you.

Kiss the babies for Pa. From your account "the boy" is a prodigy which I am very anxious to see. The little "rip" will not know me.

Good bye. God bless you.

Your Husband

Feby. 17. The mail man neglected to come for my letter yesterday & I reopen it to tell you the good news of General Gordon being expected here by the 25th. You may in that event begin to look for me on the 10th of March. Goodbye again until we meet.

In Camp Feby. 20—1864

Dear Darling

I received one letter from you and one from Sis Jane last night. I must exhaust my last sheet of paper in writing to you and trust to some chance to provide me the means to reply to Sis Jane. The first item of interest of course is the all absorbing theme of my going home. Genl. Gordon has not returned but is expected in a few days. I shall send up my application in time to leave here about the fourth of March, & will reach Cuthbert about the tenth of the same month. The recent currency bill & tax bill has played the wild with the present issue of Confederate money. I am afraid the railroads will raise their rates of travel so high that it will take more money than I can raise to get home, and after I get home how will I manage to pay my way back? I am not jesting at all. I have no doubt that it will cost me two hundred dollars to get home. You see by these bills all of our Confederate money will after April 1st be worth only 50 cents on the dollar & everybody is preparing for it, by raising the price of everything. The Richmond Merchants and traders have raised their prices 50 pr cent & will continue to raise until after April 1st. We will need all of ours to pay taxes. Our tax will be about six hundred dollars, to be paid about next June. I will have to try & save enough of our wages and pay that. Which is almost impossible, unless I do without the necessities of life. My mess bill is sixty dollars per month, my horse not yet bought, and at the end of this month after drawing my pay & settling up all my outstandings I will have just ninety dollars, & therefore will have to borrow to go home. But for seeing you I should not go. I do believe it is going to run me hard to keep even. I hope however that prices of everything will go down rapidly after April 1st. I understand also that the bill has passed Congress allowing rations to officers. This will also reduce my expenses. I have yet strong hopes of buying me some Government cloth for [a] uniform. I have just heard that a lot will be received in Richmond in a few days and have written to Major Gilbert on the subject. If I get any I think I will not have it made until next summer & then will have me a coat made in good style. I could not afford to have it made now at a cost of three or four hundred dollars, besides the cost of the cloth.

Well, I have laid bare all of my little troubles. My great trouble is about you. There will be for two or three months after April a great tightness in money.

Nobody will have any and you will not be able to hire Dan as you do now.

But you have a supply of provisions on hand & I trust will not suffer. And what money you get will buy five times as much as at present. I hope Clem did not spend her Confederate money in Calico. She will need it all to pay her taxes. Write to Sister about this tax bill & tell her to save her Confederate money by paying her taxes before the 1st of April or if she cannot do that to buy a 4% bond to about the amount of her taxes and ours also, & we will pay her back in the new currency. Her tax will be eight hundred or a thousand dollars, & she cannot pay it after the 1st of April in the present currency without losing 33 cents on every dollar unless before the 1st of April she buys a 4 percent bond under the new law to the amount of her tax, or pays her tax in money before April 1st. The same advice you must give to Clem & Mother.

There is going to spring up soon in Georgia a new party on some sort of a peace basis. Cold blooded treason is at the bottom of it, though it will make its appearance in a fair form, with delusive promises, supported by a few prominent names. Unless frowned down at the commencement the state will be deluged with blood, for I tell you now I shall be as ready to march my regiment against those men as against the Yankees. The Richmond Whig has published an editorial inaugurating the movement & you will observe soon that the scheme will be developed.

I am so sorry to learn that the little man has burned his little hand. Pa must come home and cure it for him. He will not know his Pa will he?

I am very proud to hear that Mrs. Hailey has complimented Ida so highly & know she merits all the praise.

Just as I expected you have worked yourself half to death. I expect to burn up the factory when I get home. I am in fine health. Do hope you will not be sick at all. Good bye. God bless you.

Your Husband

In Camp, Feby. 29th, 1864

My dear Allie

I am impatient to write to you that Genl. Gordon has arrived & that my application for leave of absence for 30 days has gone forward.[6] I shall leave here next Monday and will reach Cuthbert on next Saturday afternoon. That is, I will be in Cuthbert at 3 o'clock P.M. on Saturday the 12th of March. If Sister has not gone home by that time I shall expect to meet you there if you can come without inconvenience. The time shall pass so slowly and I shall be so impatient & restless that I will hardly be able to contain myself. I know the cars will travel at a snail's pace. But notwithstanding all this the time will assuredly go by and our re-union will take place. I will not harass myself with the speculation of any probable movement of our army this week, although the weather is delightful and the roads in most excellent order.

I received another letter from you last night. I hope you have continued to write since the 19th so I may get two or three more letters before I leave. I will not send you any telegram unless I fail from any cause to go at this time appointed; but I do not expect any such great disappointment as that would be.

Pa is most dead to see his great boy who has become so smart lately. He wont know his Pa at first, but we will get acquainted before we have been together long.

If you have room you must bring Ida to Cuthbert with you. She would enjoy the ride so much, I know.

I shall have money enough to come home with. I will explain the late currency & tax acts to you when I come. I cannot get any wool for Graham anywhere.

I anticipate so much enjoyment. Really I did not believe I could become so much excited about going home, but you must remember I have been absent 18 months & have not seen you in nearly 4 long weary months.

Good bye. My love to Sister and all the rest. Good bye. I will write one more letter.   Your Husband

6. Special Order No. 66, Hdqs., Dept. of Northern Virginia, dated 8 March 1864, granted Evans a thirty-day leave. Original in his Manuscript Collection, p. 169.

LT. GEN. JOHN BROWN GORDON

360

Chapter 18
WAR IS RESUMED

When Colonel Evans returned to Virginia from leave on April 12, the Confederate army was still in winter quarters at Clark's Mountain near Mountain Run. The Federal army was also within sight of the Confederates. General Lee had used the mountain top to observe the Union army spread out on the plain below.[1]

Evans now begins to mention some new names and some old names in new places. Ever since General Grant's successes in the West, he had been hailed as the most outstanding Federal general. It was, therefore, no surprise that President Lincoln called for Grant to open the spring offensive in Virginia.

On March 4 Lincoln sent orders to Grant at Nashville to report immediately to Washington. It took several days for the general to travel by train, so it was not until March 9 that Lincoln personally, at a small ceremony, delivered to Grant the commission of the newly established rank of lieutenant general and informed him of his assignment as supreme commander of all the armies of the United States.[2] By these steps Lincoln, ever the politician, avoided removing General Meade as commander of the Army of the Potomac; Lincoln simply gave Meade a superior commander.

Clement's first letter, after returning to duty, however, dwells little with the army.

In Camp, Orange Co., Va.
April 13, 1864

My dear Darling
I arrived here last night and as Everett Harris has just received a furlough and is going home to-morrow I must

1. Freeman, *R. E. Lee*, vol. 3, p. 269.
2. Only once before had this rank been created by Congress as a post of real authority. It was given to George Washington and was abolished when he retired. Winfield Scott held the rank but only as an honorary title.
William S. McFeely, *Grant* (New York: W. W. Norton & Col, 1981), p. 151.

write you a letter. But I hardly feel in the humor to write, because I feel so lonely and so far away from my dear wife and babies. But I will keep in good spirits and try to be as cheerful as possible. I have thought of you all the way, dreamed of you several times. Could imagine your kisses so warm on my lips. Never mind, we will soon meet again. Six months will not be long in rolling away. I am almost disposed to day that it shall only be five months, but I cannot yet promise myself such a great joy as meeting you so soon. I passed Graves' place this morning and thought of our happy time there. Everything looked so natural that I could almost imagine you to be standing on the porch looking for me. But my darling was many hundred miles away. —I have nothing particularly new to write to you. The application which I told you about has been sent up by Genl Gordon & he thinks it has been approved by Generals Early, Ewell & Lee. I am afraid of old Early endorsing. I am going to write to General Lawton about it tomorrow. And when I get all the news I will write to you again. Do not tell anybody about it, for it might all result in a disappointment after all. I care nothing about it except for your sake. I am afraid to be ambitious. You know what a snare my ambition has been to me and how much unhappiness it has caused me. I do really feel now that I have subdued it, but still very little encouragement would send me dancing after popular applause again.

You must remember all I have told you about taking care of yourself. Do keep in good health. Be lively, keep yourself young. We have so many years of happiness before us because we love each other so much. We can be so happy with each other even in the humblest circumstances, and if we do our duty, we shall be truly happy.

The band is serenading me in honor of my return. All seem glad to see me. You will excuse this short letter. I will write again tomorrow.

Love to Ida. Good bye my sweet wife. Good bye.

Your Husband

The "application" Clement mentions in such a secretive fashion was a recommendation for his promotion to brigadier general.[3] In captured Confederate war records preserved in the National Archives in Washington, D.C., the dossier on Clement A. Evans contains General Gordon's original recommendation and the endorsements through channels to the Secretary of War. The successive endorsements, as the recommendation was forwarded, are most interesting and appropriately placed here in Evans' story, as the spring campaign and army reorganization were beginning to ferment.

General Gordon started the process in an official letter of March 22, 1864, to Samuel Cooper, adjutant general at the War Department, in which Gordon urged the promotion of:

> Colonel C. A. Evans, 31st Georgia Regiment of my brigade for promotion to the rank of Brigadier General. Col. Evans in my opinion combines all the qualities necessary to make an excellent brigade commander. I have observed him closely in camp, on the march and in every battle in which this brigade has been engaged since my connection with it, and for deliberate courage, quick perception and [ability] in handling his men I believe he has but few, if any, superior among officers of his rank in the service. He is the only colonel of my acquaintance whom I would recommend for as important a position.

On the back of General Gordon's letter are endorsements in the handwriting of each successive superior commander, commencing with the terse: "Reply forwarded. Approved." by Gen. Jubal A. Early from Headquarters, Early's division, dated April 3. The next is from "Hd. Quar. 2nd Army Corps, 5 April 1864. Respy. forded. Col. Evans commanded the brigade to my satisfaction two months in the winter. He was in Command of three brigades of Early's Division on the occasion of the demonstration at Mor-

---

3. The comment that he had written to General Lawton also refers to the recommendation. After General Lawton's wounding at Antietam, he was, upon recovery, relieved of command of the brigade and assigned to Richmond as quartermaster general of the Confederate army. Evans knew that this was a "friend in court" at the capital city who could obtain information on the fate of his promotion.

ton's Ford in Feby. and by his promptness & decision in seizing the right moment contributed largely to turning back the enemy & capturing a number. I was very much gratified by his conduct & approve the recommendation. R. S. Ewell, Lt. Genl."

On April 6, from "Head. Qu. Army of No. Va." General Lee penned in longhand his endorsement: "Res. fwd. as evidence of the merit of Col. Evans. My attention has been previously directed to him. My observation is confirmed by the recommendations of Gordon & Ewell. I should dislike very much to lose his services from this army, & at present there is no command to which he could be assigned if promoted. R. E. Lee, Genl."

Adjutant General Cooper received these recommendations and forwarded all to Secretary of War James A. Seddon on April 15th: "Resply. sub. to the Secretary of War. I do not see how Col. Evans could be apptd at this time, as Genl. Lee has no brigade for him & I know of no vacant Ga. Brigade elsewhere. S. Cooper."

The final note was by Seddon: "File for future reference. JAS."

Clement to Allie:

Camp on Mountain Run.
Orange Co., Va. April 15, 1864

My dear Wife

I have been trying to recall my dream about you last night but I cannot. It was pleasant and in consequence I have been in good spirits all day. I am going to be very active every day because in employment the time passes so much more rapidly and pleasantly. It will not be long before the excitement of active hostilities will furnish me exercise and duties enough. It rained last night pretty heavily and is still cloudy. The great uncertainty about the weather will perhaps prevent any move before the 25th of this month, but a postponement will scarcely be later. I will telegraph to you after any important movement.

I believe that I wrote to you that Capt. Redding had sent up his resignation and started home. It will be accepted in a few days, and I want Bob to be sure to write to me immediately about his appointment I did not know that Redding intended resigning so soon. Bob must come *fixed up* in a good jeans uniform at least, and prepared to buy him a horse here. He will have to make his bond at home & he had better see right away about getting his securities. Each security has to be worth the amount of the bond which will be twenty or twenty-five thousand dollars. If Bob is sure of exemption it will be personally to his interest to remain at home, since the pay of Captain will barely support him, but if he is not sure he had better take this appointment. Anyhow he must write to me as this has to be done immediately & he will have to come without any delay, as soon as I notify him of his appointment which may be in a few weeks. If he cannot on account of the suddeness of the appointment take it, he must telegraph to me, directing his dispatch to "Col. C. A. Evans, 31st Ga. Reg. Early's Division, Army N. Va. to be mailed at Richmond" and must write also a letter at the same time. I shall write all of this to him also today, but for fear it would not reach him I have written to you also.

Dan Boone has sent you his great thanks for the ham you sent him. All the balance of the boys looked like they thought you ought to have sent them one too. Eugene especially looked very much slighted. You will have to get up some little present for him. By the way if we can get the material anywhere (say in Pennsylvania) I want you to get up a nice battle flag, with the names of the battles worked on it, to present to the Reg. Can we devise any plan this summer to have it fixed up so you can bring it on with you? You will have to make a big speech on the occasion which you know you can do in your happiest vein. We will make a grand affair of it. What do you say? Perhaps you had better commence at once to write the speech. Send me a few specimen pages. I am pretty hard run for rations for Mose. Unless Congress repeals the ration law, or allows officers to buy one ration, I hardly know how I can keep him. I shall have to hire some soldier to help me I have had a great appetite since I returned. It seems like I can hardly eat enough. Many were surprised on my return that I had fallen off so much. It does seem absolutely necessary to my health that I should live out doors and be active all the time.

Tell Mat I get prouder of my coat every day. Tell her I have made arrangements since I came to make a marker of Jim, if he comes to the Regt. so he will be relieved of carrying his knapsack, & relieved of guard duty & fatigue duty. But suppose he joins the Reg. and I am promoted away from it? All this will be knocked in the head. I rather think that after all, she had better keep Jim in the state this year and wait to see what turn things may take. You can say that much to her without telling her of my prospects of promotion. Unless Genl. Early has suffered his prejudices to rule him I think I will certainly get promotion. As soon as I hear from Genl. Lawton I will enclose you a copy of his letter. It will not be many days before I will hear from Lawton. I am anxious about it because I know then you can spend next winter with me. There are still rumors of large accessions to our strength here. Some think that we will number at least one hundred thousand men. But at present all is a mystery. All are full of confidence that we will be victorious.

I have written to Ida today and gave her a long string of Geography questions about Virginia. Help her to answer them. Write to me all about her improvement and ask Clem to take her in hand when you go away. I expect to hear in a few days that you are off for Miller. Had I not better write to you there after the 25th. Any how I will write to Sister about that time, and a few days afterwards to you. I suppose you will be in Miller by the 10th of May.

Take good care of your precious self. For your sake I will not be reckless of either health or life. Love to all. Goodbye.   Your Husband

[The next letter from Evans to his nine-year-old daughter, Ida, is worth a comment. He was rightfully worried about her education, for she had been shuttled about from Georgia to Virginia, from Virginia to North Carolina, and then, whether in Georgia, Virginia, or North Carolina, Ida was jumped from the home of

366

one relative to another. It is marvelous to see that a colonel in the army, responsible for the well-being and the problems of hundreds of soldiers, risking his life—at times almost daily—and exposed to the horrors of war at every turn, could put those pressures out of his mind and sit down to write a challenging letter to stimulate the mind of his little girl.]

In Camp, Mountain Run.
Orange Co., Va. April 15 [1864]

My dear daughter

I am going to write you a letter every week, and you must appoint some particular morning or evening of each week in which you will answer my letter. I cannot be with you so long as the war lasts, to attend to your education and general training, but if I write to you regularly and you will love me enough to remember that I write, and do what I say I shall not be so uneasy about the wasting of the present time, which is so important to you.

I am going to ask you a great many questions in all my letters and you must answer each of them. You know you spent nearly a year in Virginia and traveled through several portions of the state. Have you ever thought to take your map of Virginia and see where the state lies, and where the towns & cities are which you stayed in, and the railroad you traveled on, the rivers you crossed, and the mountains which you saw? Besides this, would you not like to know a great deal about the Geography of a State where your Pa has been so long & where so many bloody battles have been fought? Then you turn to the map of Virginia and I will turn to mine, and we will study Geography together just like we did at home last March. I will ask you the questions and you must write the answers to me in your letter. First we will take the Rivers. What River runs by Richmond? In what direction does it run and where does it empty? What River runs by Fredericksburg where the battles of Fredericksburg & Chancellorsville were fought? Don't you remember where we boarded at Mrs. Holloway's near Port Royal and at Capt. Alsop's near Fredericksburg? Well, you know that we were close to this river then. Be sure to spell it right. What river did we cross when we went from Mr. Graves' over to Culpeper Co. & boarded at Mrs. Geo. Fitzhugh's where you nearly went crazy over that large doll? Into what river does this river empty? What river did General Lee have to cross when he carried the army over into Maryland? Now, tell me the name of any other river in Virginia which you can find on the map

We will next take the towns. Tell me what city is the capital of Virginia & the seat of government of the Confederate States? Describe its position so I can find it. In what part of Virginia is it? What city is nearly south of Richmond?

[The rest of this letter is missing.]

Clement to Allie:

Camp, Orange Co., Va.
April 18, 1864

My dear darling

I have kept myself so constantly engaged since I arrived that the time is going off at a refreshing speed. I am afraid I have not written often enough to you. I missed yesterday's mail by riding to the river and not returning early enough for the closing of the mail. I will do better in the future. I love to write to you. We are so far apart that we can't talk to each other, but we can write some of our thoughts, and some of the things we would say to each other if we were together. I met Genl. Ewell today. The old gentleman appeared to be very glad to see me. He was in company with Genl. Johnson & Stewart[4] with whom I am acquainted, and also General M. L. Smith to whom he introduced me. General Smith was one of the Vicksburg generals and is now on the Staff of General Lee. Everything looks hopeful here.

---

4. Maj. Gen. Edward Johnson, nicknamed "Old Allegheny." He, like Evans, was in the Second Corps and had been at Gettysburg. Brig. Gen. George H. "Maryland" Steuart (Evans misspelled it). He, too, was in the Second Corps and led a brigade in General Johnson's division. Warner, *Generals in Gray*, pp. 158, 290.

We are still fortifying. [General] Longstreet is in helping distance. The Yankee camps look as usual from Clark's Mountain. They are very busy drilling. A Yankee deserter who came in yesterday says that Grant intends to cross the river in the night and attack us. "Guess" he will be badly sold when he tries.

I believe that I wrote to you that after all I was one day behind time getting here but it is all right. Even old Jubal [Early] said my explanation was satisfactory. My Regiment is on picket, but I do not have to go, because I am on the roster of "General Officers of the day." I go however and spend the day down there where they are. It is more pleasant than staying in camp.

Mrs. Gordon is going away in a few days. I believe that all officers are sending their wives away until the campaign is over. It is well that you did not return with me, as we would dislike to be exceptional cases, when it was so general for Ladies to go back.

It is useless almost for me to write to you mere speculations about the future movements of the army. I was told however by pretty good authority that unless we are attacked by Grant at an early day, we would advance on him with invasion again in view. All seem to regard the next battles as the turning point of the war. That is, whether it is to be long or short. Decisive victories on our part will cause an early peace. I cannot but hope that our present separation, is a short one, and that I shall soon again be blessed with your dear self.

You must begin to cast about in your mind where you will have that permanent homestead. On what river and near what railroad shall it be? Think well & satisfy yourself, for when we buy it is to be permanent & we are to go at once to fixing up for our life & for one of our Children after us. Don't you wish we were there now! How we would plan our orchards, our vineyard, our Garden, our Grove of trees, & our flower Garden. Wouldn't we build pantrys, dairys, spring houses, and every other sort of houses? Think of our pigs, turkeys, geese, ducks, & chickens, of our sheep, cows & horses. And then we are to have our fishpond with a little snug boat to row in & fish in. Ah me, we could make for ourselves a little paradise—With all this we could be happy because we love each other. Without them we could be happy for the same reason. *You* are enough for me. I could work my ten hours daily for you & be happy, because you love me so much & would meet me with so many sweet smiles every evening. Bless your dear good heart, how fortunate I was in securing you for my own dear wife.

Did Ida enjoy her letter which made her *study* as much as those which did not? She is very much disposed to procrastination, to put off duties from time to time. We must try to rid her of that disposition and teach her to be prompt.

I have no news yet from General Lawton. Hardly time enough yet. I think in two or three days more I shall hear from him.

I still keep in excellent health. I have a headache today in consequence of a cold which I have had since I left Richmond. You must take care of your health too. Nothing has more to do with health than the frame of mind in which one keeps himself. Nobody can be healthy long who indulges in gloomy desponding spirits. Do not be unhappy about me. Accept our present separation as from the Good Being, and trust in Him to make even this the cause of blessings to us both. For my sake, therefore, amuse yourself in every possible way. Think about me pleasantly. Think of our future reunion & its great happiness. My sufferings & hardships are nothing compared to the painfulness of our being separated.

I have received no letter from you yet, but one will come soon.

Kiss my babies. My love to all.

Goodbye my dear
Your Husband

Allie to Clement:

Lumpkin, Stewart Co., Ga.
April 18, 1864

My dear darling

I expected a letter today and could not help feeling disappointed when I sent to the office and got no letter. You must have gone straight on through without any delay. I hope you reached camp before your furlough was out. I am so anxious to get a letter. It looks like an age to look back to the day you started from home. When will the war end? I am low down darling—got the blues the worst sort. Ida came home yesterday evening with the hardest kind of a chill on her and she has been very sick ever since. I never saw any little thing suffer as she did last night with her head. She was a little delirious all night—had very high fever. She is something better this evening but still has fever. I think it is [a] cold. Dr. Battle doesn't think it anything serious. She is anxious for Pa to know how sick she is. I do wish you were here so much. Mother and Clem have been with me all day. Matt and Mr. Graham have just left. Sister Richardson has been over twice today, but if every body in town was to come, it would be a poor compensation for my darling's company. I do hope Ida will be better in the morning.

Saturday morning. I commenced this letter yesterday evening. Mrs. Daniel came in and stayed till bedtime with me and after supper Mrs. Richardson and father came in and sit with us. I had to put off writing until this morning. Ida is a great deal better and of course my spirits are raised a hundred percent. She slept very well after midnight and is almost clear of fever this morning. I am so glad she is better for I have been very uneasy about her. I think she will be well in a few days. Mrs. Hurley sent her word she was coming to see her today. She is very much excited about it. Liz has just come up to bring us some light rolls for our breakfast and she is sending her grandma word about it. She sends her love to pa. Every time she woke up last night she would talk about pa and ask me if I had sent her love to you. It is real winter weather yet. The middle of April and I have to keep large fires. I expect Sister will send for me next week. I dread to leave Ida so much. What

371

if I should carry her and teach her down there? I am afraid you wouldn't approve of it.

Lawton has just come in and told me good morning. He has been talking a good deal for the last few days. He is a bad boy, papa, and you say mama must not whip him. What is to be done with him? Ma slapped him yesterday for spitting on her. He is a worse boy now than he was when you went off. The small pox is all over Eufaula, Matt tells me. Next door to Mrs. McNab's. I expect the whole family will be over here soon if it is so. Graham is the bluest looking man you ever saw—he is going to Columbus next week to report. I am sorry for him and hope he won't have to go. He gives the Militia officers and young men at home fits. It is so lonesome here at home by myself darling. I miss you so much. I would give all but my life for the war to end and let you come home. I try to amuse myself and keep my spirits up thinking and planning to go to Virginia next winter. When I think of it now I am astonished at myself that I bore your leaving so well. I feel sometimes like if I had you back here nothing on earth could take you from me. I will write again next week.

Goodbye. God bless you.
Your Wife

Clement to Allie:

Orange Co., Va., April 20/[18]64
In camp on Mountain Run,

Dear Darling

It is cold and cloudy today, and the prospect of bad weather continues. This I expect is good news to you, as it postpones the inevitable conflict between the two armies. But if it is to come, why not early as well as late? The suspense you feel on my account I know is great, and in spite of yourself and in spite of all I write to you about being gay and happy you cannot help having occasional hours of gloom. But shake off these bad feelings, darling, and think of me, as being well provided for, think of my safety as being the will of God, and of

372

the hopeful future full of happiness for us both. I have pictured off a little Arcadia as our future home, where there will be toil enough to make rest sweet, but where love will be the inspirer of all our enjoyments. I wrote to you something about it in my last, and wait anxiously to hear your own opinion. This long separation, all these dangers, all our past griefs will better enable us to enjoy the future, fully appreciating the blessings which are left us. We are sadder but wiser, and happier, though sadder because wiser. We can even extract from ourselves a sweet, sad pleasure in contemplating our sore trial, having faith that all these things have worked together for our good.

My Regiment came off picket today. They brought no news. So far as can be observed, the Yankees occupy the same positions. I suppose they now number about sixty five thousand men, and will probably increase ten or fifteen thousand more. We will be fully able to cope with them. I think we ought to advance soon, unless Grant attacks us. Of course Gen. Lee knows what to do, but I am so anxious to whip these fellows and end the war. Portions of Longstreet's command are at Charlottesville, but I have not heard about Benning's Brigade. I shall try to see Probe if his regiment comes near enough. He will certainly be transferred when the two corps get together.

I have lost all my gloves except my fine buckskin. I left my old buckskin at home. Please send them by Everett Harris, & also a pair of woolen gloves if I left them also. That is, if you can get to see Everett. I expect, however, that you will go to Miller before he returns.

I hope to get a letter from you this evening & will suspend writing in hope.

April 21st. No letter last night. Thirteen days since I saw you have gone by and I naturally feel anxious to hear from you. But I suppose you did not write until the 11th or 12th and a few days more must elapse before I can get your letter.

April appears to be trying herself. A dozen changes of weather take place daily. A little rain, a little sunshine, a few clouds, then windy, & next moment calm; this is the history of each day.

I have kept my tobacco pledge so far, and see no reason why I should not continue my self denial. I will save about twelve dollars a month by not buying chewing tobacco, and in eight months I can present you a calico dress out of my saving. That stimulates me to hold out.

We drill a good deal now. The weather is very suitable except when it rains. My time is pretty well occupied with my various duties and therefore camp life is not entirely monotonous. I am sorry that I did not bring my fishing tackle. The soldiers are catching a good many fish in the river & if I had lines & hooks I could send out a little party every day on shares. Our rations are pretty short. Corn bread five days out of seven. But I don't care for that. The meal would be better if it could be sifted, but still independence is worth all these little privations.

I have every one of my company officers present. Two have sent up resignations on surgeons' certificate of disability—Lieut. Haynes, and Lieut. Ginn. I have not heard from Capt. Reddings resignation, but it may come back at any moment for his cousin, Captain Gordon, to fill the vacancy. I feel myself under obligations to the General, but could not accede to his wishes. I am quite sorry that he mentioned the subject to me.

As the grass has commenced springing up pretty freely I thought I would give my moustache another chance, and have therefore turned it out. Perhaps it may profit by last year's experience and do better. It seems to be making a heavy effort & is quite a drain upon my system. I hope however that I shall be able to stand it.

I have no more to write today. Your coming letter will furnish me subject matter.

Give my love to Ida—& the boy.

Good bye. God bless you.

Your Husband

In camp, Mountain Run, Orange Co., Va.
April 22, 1863 [1864]

Dear Allie

This is a beautiful day and if any dependence could be placed in April weather, we might prophesy now of a continued favorable season. Grant will, therefore, be without excuse provided he has really been waiting for the rainy spring to pass, before hazarding an advance.

We have another order reducing transportation. Only one wagon for all the officers, Field, staff, & company officers. I have reduced mine to the portable standard & shall send my trunk & band box & mattress to Richmond to care of *"Georgia relief association"* with my name distinctly marked on them. Remember this. I shall carry along in a knapsack all that I will need. Gen. Lee evidently intends not to be needlessly encumbered with baggage trains. If we go into Pennsylvania I shall at once seize some Yankee's wagon for Hdqrs.

I don't believe I wrote to you about the difficulty Joe Clayton is in. I wrote to Wm. Mansfield about it by Everett Harris, and I am surprised that I forgot to write to you about it. After Joe was paroled he stayed about Richmond awhile, appearing not to be disposed to go home. I suppose he must have sold his transportation & perhaps his furlough to somebody. Lieut. Cox was in Richmond and persuaded him at last to conclude to go home. He came after that to where Cox was staying & showed him a blank furlough, and sitting down he filled up the blank places and showed it to Lieut. Cox, remarking how easy it was to forge a furlough. Cox told him not to use it or he would get into Castle Thunder. He laughed, went out, & the next thing sure enough was his arrest & confinement at that place. This was told me by Lt. Cox. Before getting this I wrote to Wm. Mansfield that I believed that Joe had been victimized by some artful scamps in Richmond and I think now that some one did induce him to sell his regular furlough & transportation & buy the blank which he filled up—It is best for you not to tell what I have written except in the family. I am afraid Joe will not prove to be a reliable man.

375

9 o'clock P.M.

I finished this letter by a dim firelight. Lt. Haynes leaves tomorrow & will mail this on the route.

I received tonight your first letter written on the 13th. I was so glad to hear from you. I know you are so lonesome, but I hope you are at sister's and all right.

I have concluded to send the trunk I brought here back. It is full of old things which will be useful to you. Some leather, my old jacket to make you some shoes, my overcoat, a bundle belonging to Charley Simpson &c. &c. I have sent it to Mr. Otho P. Beall at Cuthbert Geo. & have written to him to take care of it for me, and deliver it either to your order or to Dr. Baldwin. I have also written to Dr. Baldwin to get it to his house & from there to Mr. Jackson's & ask Mr. Jackson to send it to Lumpkin when he sends to mill. So if the trunk gets to Cuthbert, it will get home. My band box I will send to Richmond, & I think of leaving my mattress with Mr. Graves;—

I have no more to write. Tell Ida I am *very* proud of your good account of her & she must write.

Good bye.   Haynes is waiting.

Good bye.
God bless you.
Your Husband

Camp on Mountain Run
Orange Co., Va. Apr. 24

My dear Darling;

I have just received orders to move tomorrow morning at 9 o'clock to the Rapidan not far below Clark's mountain. The entire brigade changes camp to that point and the object is to be near our line of fortifications, to prevent surprise by the enemy. As we are now situated the enemy might in the night dash across the river and get possession of our works before we could march there to defend them. The weather is very moderate, and the change will be very beneficial in point of health. Here we discard all surplus baggage, and all our tents, until next winter. We are in light marching order, well clothed, well shod, tolerably fed, splendidly armed, and in the finest spirits. Full of hopes that the war will be closed by the present campaign. Many poor fellows must of course lose their lives—precious lives too, to their families, but this is the price of liberty. A few must suffer for the general good of all.

I bought three quarts of milk today from "Ursula" and thereby made out a splendid dinner of milk & corn-bread. She has promised to let me have it as often as possible. I still guard Graves' place with the small party that stayed there when you did. You remember how the troops grazed at Hamilton Crossing last year? The same thing is being repeated now. The fields are full of them now gathering wild onions & wild cress. I have not experimented with either yet, but the men seem to enjoy them very much. We have not received any fish from the Rappahannock as was expected, but the rivers & creeks are diligently explored with hook & line. Not many are caught, however. I suppose it is too cold yet.

This letter will not probably reach you at Lumpkin as I suppose you will be gone from there before the 4th of May, but Clem will send it to you. I wrote to you yesterday, directing my letter to Pryor, Miller [County]. I am so glad you are with your sister in Miller. I know you will enjoy yourself so much, although it is in the back woods.

You must get acquainted with every body about the neighborhood, and do a great deal of visiting. I do want you to enjoy yourself so much. Try to accept our separation as something which ought not to be avoided if we could, and something not to be unhappy about. Why should you be unhappy, when grief will not restore us to each other? Be very cheerful and rejoice in thinking what a happy time we will have when we meet again. I shall keep my promise to you, not to engage in any more experimental expeditions against the Yankees, where my life will be exposed, without the general result being influenced. I love the excitement very much, but for your sake I will deprive myself of it. The Yanks do look so tempting just across the river, that I feel like pitching into them every time I go down there. There is

377

no news more than you see in the newspapers. I do not believe that Grant has an army larger than ours, nor is any better prepared to attack us, than other Yankee generals who have failed. I am not at all uneasy about the result of an engagement.

I am looking for a letter from Ida every day. I will write to her again on Tuesday.

Give my love to sister and her brats. Tell Walt I am going to pull his Pa's long red nose for him, if he comes poking it about me.

Good bye. God bless you.
Your Husband

[A period of inactivity ensued because of heavy spring rains between April 15 and May 4, 1864. This time was used by General Lee to gather, collate, and assess every bit of information that would lead to the intentions of General Grant. Lee accurately divined those plans. He saw three attacks forming: the major one across the Rapidan, a diversionary expedition in the Valley of Virginia, and an attack on the flank against Drewry's Bluff on the James River.]

Camp on Rapidan, Va.
May 1st, 1864

Dear Allie

I will write you another hurried & dull letter. LaFayette Hawes arrived here today & to my great disappointment could not tell me whether you were at home or had gone to Miller. He left Lumpkin last Sunday, just a week ago. I should have thought he would certainly have known that much. I take it for granted that you are gone, or at least will be in Miller after the first of this month and that my letters written now will not reach you until after the tenth.

I have no news. A thousand rumors are afloat and everything appears unsettled, but we can expect nothing except an early battle between these two great armies. The Good Being will give us the victory.

Last night was quite cold & dripping rain, but the sun is out now very bright. The winter is fully gone. Vegetation

378

is springing very rapidly clothing earth & trees in green. It is just warm enough to be decidedly pleasant, but I do dread so much the long hot days of July and August.

Cody played quite a trick on me today. He came up & confessed that two of his Company had killed a hog. I was considerably incensed about it, because I had been very lenient in punishing some others who had killed a hog about a week ago, & therefore said a good deal about what should be done to put a stop to it. Cody let me go on blowing him up for not being more watchful over his Company but after awhile he told me it was a ground hog. I acknowledged myself "sold!" But I got my revenge by selling Maj. Pride on sight.

Cody, poor fellow, overstayed his leave of absence two or three days was tried by Court Martial, convicted, & sentenced to lose one month's pay. He takes the matter rather hard. I don't think he ought to have been found guilty.

My Chaplain has sent in his tender of resignation in order to go to Mississippi. I have written to Dr. E. H. Myers at Augusta to select me a good Chaplain and send him on. I hope I shall get a real stirring fellow, for our Baptist brethren have it nearly their way here. It is quite natural for Gen. Gordon to give some preference to his own denomination.

I have not yet heard from Bob. I will have to make application for his appointment anyhow, although I fear he is not ready to come into service so early.

Did I tell you that I sent my string band down to serenade the Newmans, expecting, of course, to get an invitation to dinner the next day and no invitation yet! Serious disappointment! I shan't go any more, would you? I don't care "no how." We get genuine coffee three times a day with sugar in it & that is ahead of most people.

How are you living? What do you do every day. Do you have any fun out of Hilda?

Write fully all about yourself especially about that question. My love to all.

Good bye.

God bless you.   Your Husband

379

Camp on Rapidan,
May 2, 1864

My dearest Dearest

I received yours of the 22nd ultimo and you were still at Lumpkin. I have been writing lately all my letters to you at Pryor, Miller Co. I see I have been making a mistake in the county, but the post office being correct & both counties being near each other, the letters will go correctly. So you did not hear Ben Hill speak. I am sorry for it as you doubtless would have been well pleased, but Ben Hill scarcely has the right to speak too harshly of those out of the war, since he has never been in himself. It is true his position as Senator exempts him from military duty, but it is questionable whether even otherwise would he have any inclination to try the tented field. There is an abundance of cheap patriotism in the country, and no class of persons are more abusive of those who grieve over the separation caused by the war, than those who have never had such occasion for grief. But we will not be uncharitable to anyone. Our joys and our griefs are our own. Let them be private. They concern only ourselves.

I am so glad to hear that Ida is getting entirely well. I knew she would like the study of geography, because it introduces her to a knowledge of places & countries. I have not written another Geography letter to her, because I do not want to tire her, but I will send her another in a few days.

We have the news now that [Maj. Gen. Ambrose E.] Burnside['s Ninth Corps] is coming with his horde of Negroes, Dutchmen & substitutes, that the long expected fight will soon take place. I hope that Grant may take it into his head to attack us here, but I fear that he is not fool enough for that. A deserter who came to us a few days ago, says that Grant rode along our whole front examining our fortifications and said he was "not going to butt his brains out there." These deserters also report the usual sensation news that the army is demoralized & deserting in large droves, etc.

The weather is still delightful. I have just come off

380

picket. Last night I sent Lieut. Green & five men over the river to scout the Yankee lines & find out whether they were strengthened much at night. He went into about fifty yards of their lines examining them closely. They are very vigilant and a surprise would be difficult. The night was very dark & favorable to the little reconnaissance.

Dr. Butts has returned from a short leave of absence in the country to recruit his health. I expect he is well known in Bainbridge & you may meet some of his friends.

I am anxious to get a Miller county letter from you. Suppose you do not go to Miller—then you will not get a letter from me for sometime at Lumpkin. I must write to Ida so that you may at least hear from me in any event. So Mat is head over ears in McNabs' now. Ida is penetrating enough to observe that we are "cut" for the time.

Give love to Sister. No news from Probe or Bob yet. Give "old man" [a] big spank for Pa.

Goodbye.

God bless you.

Your Husband

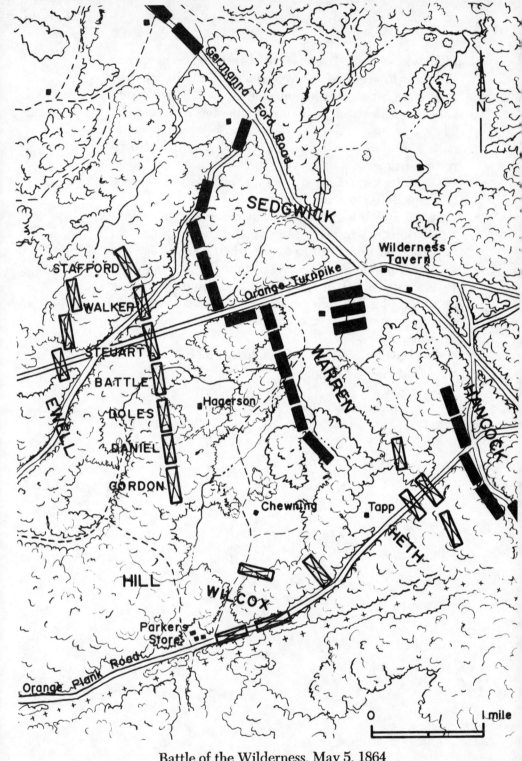

Battle of the Wilderness, May 5, 1864

Chapter 19
THE SPRING CAMPAIGN OF 1864

The spring campaign of 1864 began with the Federal advance across the fords of the Rapidan River. As pointed out previously, General Grant had delayed reopening hostilities because of wet weather and bad conditions of the roads. He gave orders finally for a general movement of all the armies by May 4. Confederate signal stations on Clark's Mountain[1] wig-wagged the news and Lee's Army of Northern Virginia prepared its counter-move.

As hostilities resumed, Grant revealed by his movements a major objective, the capture of the Confederate capital. Lee's objective, of necessity, was to keep Grant from taking Richmond. The ensuing history of the Army of Northern Virginia is in this struggle to protect the Confederate government.

Lee, having deduced what Grant was up to, had begun to gather his forces. He called upon Longstreet to move more rapidly from East Tennessee to Gordonsville and the War Department ordered Gen. P. G. T. Beauregard from North Carolina to Southside Virginia to face a Federal thrust up the James River by Gen. Benjamin F. Butler.

Evans wrote to Allie about some of the bitter strife in May. But his account to her of the next eventful weeks of the war is sparse.[2] It is evident that some of his letters were lost, perhaps in transit, for in his letter of May 15 he told Allie that he has not failed to write her.

Camp on Rapidan
May 4, 1864

Dear Allie

We awakened this morning and found that the extensive Yankee camps had all disappeared from our

1. *O.R.*, series 1, vol. 36, part 1, pp. 1, 8.
2. Lack of reports was not peculiar to Evans. The *O.R.'s* also lack many reports of the campaign, especially of the major day, at the "Bloody Angle" of Spotsylvania.

front, and soon the rumor was that they were moving down the river, perhaps to try over again the Fredericksburg battle grounds. I think this is very likely, and believe we are on the eve of another great battle.

I write to you hastily, hoping to get a chance to send this off, before we move, for in a few hours, we shall doubtless be on the tramp. I will seek every opportunity to communicate with you by letter, & will trust in our Heavenly Father for His blessing on us both. I commit you & my little darlings to Him believing that "He doeth all things well."

You will excuse short letters now, as I shall write every day if possible & by every one that passes from the army.

Goodbye,

God bless you my darling.

Your Husband

Bivouac near Mine Run, Va.
May 5, 1864

Dear Allie

Last night was the first regular bivouac of the year for our Regiment. Yesterday at about three o'clock p.m. we received orders to march at once in the direction of Fredericksburg, on the old turnpike road, and were immediately on the tramp. We marched ten miles, by nine o'clock p.m., and pitched our camp, on the turnpike not far from Mine Run, & Locust Grove. I cannot say that we pitched our tents, because tents we do not have on such occasions. An issue of two day's rations of the old familiar *hardtack*, & bacon was a token of the work before us. The news is that the enemy have crossed the river in force & occupy the country between this point and Fredericksburg. We have sufficient force to meet them successfully on fair ground.

I write just after sunrise, while under orders to continue to move, but we may not move today. The newspapers have doubtless put you under alarm. I feel so sorry for you, but your last letter encourages me to believe that you will bear the suspense with proper fortitude.

384

I have been directing all my letters to Pryor since the 20th, but your letter of the 24th, written from Lumpkin, still speaks of your continuing there for a week or so more. My letters will reach you at Lumpkin until about the 4th of May; and after that they will be going to Mitchell. I have written very often lately.

I have received a letter from Genl. Lawton at last. He says the endorsements of Genls. Early, Ewell & Lee are considered sufficient by the Sec. of War, & if there was a vacancy I would be appointed at once [to brigadier general]. He states that as soon as there is a vacancy he will give me a lift. Now, if your fears about yourself are groundless we may spend a happy winter together.

The wagons are just ordered back to Verdiersville & the rumor is that we will not move any further towards Fredericksburg, so uncertain are all army movements that one cannot even guess.

Now Darling I hope you will be enduring all this suspense in the manner I have so often recommended. We certainly have committed our all in the keeping of one who cannot err. I have fully committed myself to Him & let what will happen, I know it will all be right.

I close this letter now. Perhaps an early chance will offer to send it off. Good bye and God bless you.

Your Husband

Colonel Evans, in command of his regiment, advanced into the foreboding tangle of the Wilderness with the Second Corps. These troops brought up the rear of the extreme left of the Confederates as Gordon's brigade marched along the Orange Turnpike in an easterly direction toward Wilderness Tavern. This route was basically parallel to, but north of, the route of the Third Corps of A. P. Hill, which had taken the same easterly direction on the Orange Plank Road. Ewell's command ran into the enemy ahead of Hill's corps and became heavily involved on the left.

About noon Federal forces of Gen. Gouverneur K. Warren's corps were engaged by Ewell's advance units about two miles from Wilderness Tavern, and a situation developed that threatened to drive an enemy wedge between the two advancing Confederate corps.[3] The forward echelons of Ewell's men, struck by the enemy assault on their left flank, were driven back in some disarray. General Gordon received orders to attack, and this was done with such spirit it broke through Warren's left.

The success of this onslaught on such a narrow front put the Confederates of Gordon's brigade in the same precarious condition that had threatened to split the two Confederate corps earlier in the day, when the Union attack was first launched. Gordon's charge drove back the enemy left but left the enemy on both flanks of the Confederate brigade.[4]

Before the Federals could take advantage of this situation, Gordon ordered Evans' Thirty-first Georgia to hold a straight line in front of the enemy in the center position. The other regiments in Gordon's command, some on Evans' left and others on his right, Gordon deployed as follows: The units on the left were ordered to face left, form a front on the enemy flank and advance to the left, perpendicular to Evans' line; the units on the right were ordered to face right, form a front on the enemy flank on that side and advance to the right, also perpendicular to Evans' line. By these alignments, Colonel Evans not only held the exposed front and center line but also protected the rear of the other Confederate regiments as they struck the exposed Federal flanks on his left and right. That maneuver saved the day. By this time, supporting Confederate commands had joined in Gordon's assault, and by nightfall the Union advance had not only been halted but had been thrown back, with heavy casualties, to the positions held when the attack was begun.[5]

During the night there was little rest for Colonel Evans, because Gordon's brigade was ordered to march to the far left of the Confederate lines. There, Evans' Thirty-first Georgia regiment remained with the brigade in a combat-ready posture almost of the day on May 6.

A lack of action can be understood from General Gordon's accounts. He had made a reconnaissance to verify personally reports he had received that the Federal right was overlapped by his command. Convinced that the front lines of the enemy were the only adversary and that there were neither units on the Union right nor Union reserves backing up the front line, Gordon re-

3. *O.R.*, series 1, vol. 36, part 1, p. 1076.
4. Gordon, *Reminiscences*, p. 250.
5. *Ibid.*, p. 249.

ported this to Generals Ewell and Early before 9 a.m. on May 6, and asked for permission to attack. Those two could not believe that the Federal right was so completely vulnerable and withheld acquiescence to Gordon's morning request. About 5 p.m., General Lee rode into Ewell's battle station to seek support for troops of Longstreet's and Hill's corp had had been repulsed by Maj. Gen. Winfield S. Hancock's Yanks in a savage fight for the intersection of the Orange Plank and Brock roads. Gordon seized this opportune moment, in the presence of Ewell and Early, to inform Lee of the exposed Federal flank. Agreeing with Gordon, Lee instructed Ewell to let Gordon launch the attack forthwith. It was a signal success. Gordon wrote: "The Georgians, commanded by that intrepid leader, Clement A. Evans, were on the flank, and the North Carolinians, led by a brilliant young officer, Robert Johnston, were sweeping around to the rear, without a shot in their front."[6]

Perhaps the most gruesome rendering of the terrible Battle of the Wilderness is from the book of Union Bvt. Brig. Gen. Horace Porter: "Forest fires raged; ammunition-trains exploded; the dead were roasted in the conflagration; the wounded, roused by its hot breath, dragged themselves along, with their torn and mangled limbs, in the mad energy of despair, to escape the ravages of the flames and every bush seemed hung with shreds of blood-stained clothing."[7]

On May 7 Grant pulled away and began again shifting his armies to Lee's right in another approach to Richmond. As Private Nichols of Evans' command laconically put it, "Next day the enemy had left our front and I feel sure that General Grant decided that he had struck a 'snag,' and that if he ever got to Richmond he would have to try a different road."[8]

May 7, 8, and 9 were days spent by both the Federals and the Confederates maneuvering in The Wilderness near the town of

6. Gordon expresses himself more explicitly in his *Reminiscences* as to the obtuseness of Early and Ewell on page 255. In the official reports, neither Ewell nor Early mentioned the facts as reported by Gordon, that Lee had made a visit to Ewell. Lee did not criticize Ewell and Early, but singled out Gordon in a letter of May 7, 1864, to the secretary of war. *O.R.*, series 1, vol. 36, part 1, pp. 107, 1078.
7. Gen. Horace Porter, *Campaigning with Grant* (New York: Century Co., 1897), p. 72.
8. Nichols, *A Soldier's Story*, p. 149.

Spotsylvania Court House. Lee had anticipated Grant's sideslip to the Confederate right toward Spotsylvania, and on May 7 the Rebel general had ordered the wounded Longstreet's command —already on the Confederate right—to march to Spotsylvania. Longstreet's First Corps, now under Gen. Richard H. Anderson, a South Carolinian, an experienced fighter, and senior major general of the army, was told to start for Spotsylvania before 3 a.m. on May 8. Anderson was off by 11 p.m. on the 7th. By 7 a.m. on May 8, his troops were near enough to Spotsylvania to support the Confederate cavalry holding off Grant's advance infantry units. Fierce encounters ensued, but by noon the Federal advances had been held off by Anderson's stubborn stand, and had provided more time for Confederates to arrive.[9] Ewell's Corps charged into the scene of battle about 5 p.m., just as Federals massed for attack in front of General Anderson's right wing. When Rodes' division of Ewell's corps swept forward, the Union attack, after some show of belligerence, was discontinued.

While all these marches and fights were being executed from May 6 to May 12, Lee was occupied with some necessary reorganization caused not only by the loss of the wounded General Longstreet, but also by the illness of the Third Corps commander, General Hill. On May 8, Lee wrote a confidential dispatch to General Ewell that affected Colonel Evans. Lee said that he had to put General Early in comand of the Third Corps because of Hill's illness. Lee continued: "In order to equalize your division, you will then transfer R. D. Johnston's brigade, or some other of Rodes' brigades, whose command is junior to General Gordon, to General Early's division, so that General Gordon may take command of the latter."[10]

This order was put into effect immediately, and Gordon took command on May 8. Simultaneously, Colonel Evans, the senior colonel, assumed command of the brigade. At various times both he and Gordon had temporarily filled these posts of higher command, but this time the promotions were permanent, even though confirmation did not take place until after the bloody days at Spotsylvania Court House. Evans' new commission was dated

9. *O.R.*, series 1, vol. 51, part 1, p. 902; and vol. 48, part 1, p. 1042.
10. *Ibid.*, series 1, vol. 48, part 1, p. 1078; and vol. 51, part 2, p. 926.

May 20, 1864, with the date of rank being May 19. Before this, on May 12, General Gordon had forwarded through channels to Adjutant General Cooper a new recommendation that Colonel Evans be promoted.

Gordon was very generous in his praise: "Col. Evans is a native of Georgia, is an intelligent and courageous gentleman well qualified in every respect for the position for which he is recommended and possesses in a high degree the confidence of both men and officers of the command. On the field he exhibits good judgment and tact in the management of his men." Therefore, by the time Ewell's corps came to the rescue of Anderson's men at 5 p.m. on May 8, John B. Gordon was in command of Early's division and Clement A. Evans was in charge of Gordon's former brigade.[11]

On the night of May 8 Gordon's division was held in reserve at Spotsylvania and began constructing "an awkward and irregular salient to the northward."[12] The terrain of the battlegrounds at Spotsylvania Court House lay about a mile in a northerly direction from that village, and had been studied by General Lee and his chief of engineers, Maj. Gen. M. L. Smith. Defense positions were established on a low ridge that was roughly crescent-shaped, except for the aforesaid "awkward and irregular salient" near the center, which Confederate soldiers first dubbed the "Mule Shoe." The apex pointed almost north, with the shanks on each side extending south in the direction of Richmond. This fortified area averaged about a half-mile in width and a mile in depth. Part of the interior was heavily timbered with hardwood trees and pines. Two houses stood within its confines: the McCoull (McCool) House and the Harrison House. Between the McCoull House and the arch at the northern tip of the "Mule Shoe" was a natural dividing line—a small stream running more or less east to west. On the north side of this stream, the land sloped up to the apex at a 45 degree angle. On the south side of the stream, the land sloped up at the same angle in the opposite direction, toward the McCoull House. Some ground between the McCoull House and the stream was clear, but on the north side toward the top of the salient, the woods were so thick no part of the front lines was visible. Thus, any Confederate units forced back from

11. A copy of Evans' commission and the recommendation are among Evans' papers.
12. Freeman, *Lieutenants*, vol. 3, p. 393.

the apex soon ran downhill, and any Confederates countercharging went first downhill from the McCoull House and, when over the stream, climbed uphill toward the apex at the ridge top.

As stated, Evans' brigade with Ewell's corps had been ordered into the salient on May 8, and participated in the construction of the fortification at its apex using earth and sharpened logs as abatis. The construction had gone on for two days. The original position of Evans' brigade was south of the stream, up the rising land, and behind the McCoull House, being between the McCoull House and the Harrison House.

On May 9, General Early's corps arrived at Spotsylvania and took its place on the extreme Confederate right, leaving Ewell's corps at the Confederate center to bear the brunt of the massive assaults upon the "Mule Shoe" three days later. No important actions on either side marked events of May 9, but on May 10, Early's corps became actively engaged in several skirmishes and Union feints on the Confederate right. However, it was not until late in the day that a major Federal foray was set in motion, and this was not against Early or the center, but against the left of Ewell's position on the west shank of the "Mule Shoe."[13]

About 6 p.m., Union Col. Emory Upton, hurled a furious and determined assault against George Doles' Georgia brigade of Rodes' division, which held this western edge. Assault after assault of Blue Coats—an array of twelve regiments—surged across a short, open space of two hundred yards in attacks referred to by one authority as "the best-known Federal column assault of the war."[14] Upton's strong attacks overwhelmed the Confederate entrenchments, and the Federals penetrated into the side of the "Mule Shoe" to a point more than one hundred yards to the rear of the line. Gordon's division was ordered to move rapidly to the left to support the beleagured defenders. Evans' brigade took part in charging the enemy, who were driven back with considerable loss.

May 11 dawned with lowering clouds, and during the day showers relieved the heat and dust as Evans' men, with their comrades, took advantage of inaction and dug on the fortifications at the "Mule Shoe" and worked on the reserve line at the Harrison House at the southern base of the salient.

13. Upton's report, *O.R.*, series 1, vol. 36, part 1, p. 667.
14. *O.R.*, series 1, vol. 36, part 1, p. 1078.

General Gordon gave the positions of the units in his official report. The forward echelons were General Rodes on the right, General Johnson on the left at the apex, and General Evans in the center at the rear, directly in front of the McCoull House.

Scarcely had midnight of May 11 passed into May 12 when the climactic battle of that memorable day commenced.

More details of the battle are given by Jed Hotchkiss, who said that:

> The shifting about of troops in the Federal lines, on the 11th, led Lee to the conclusion that Grant was about to draw back from the Spotsylvania Court House field of combat; so he made preparations to meet any new movement he might attempt by ordering all the artillery, placed in difficult positions, to be withdrawn to where it could be quickly assembled for marching. Obeying this order, General [Armistead] Long withdrew the guns from the northern portion of the great salient, so that Edward Johnson's division, at its apex, was left on guard with only muskets and two pieces of artillery. Near midnight, of the 11th-12th of May, Johnson discovered, through the dense foggy mist then prevailing, that the Federal troops were massing in his front, and asked General Ewell to have the supporting artillery returned. Not fully realizing the importance of time under the existing conditions, Ewell gave orders, not for the immediate return of the guns, but that they should be returned at daybreak of the 12th. Before that time arrived, Hancock's superb corps, in solid mass, rushed upon the apex of the salient, expecting to carry it by assault. Johnson's command . . . was on the alert and met this attack bravely; but musketry alone was not sufficient to drive back Hancock's many, massed battalions, which swarmed over the log breastworks and captured Johnson and 2,800 of his men.[15]

[Evans wrote his wife only one letter about the struggle at

15. Jedediah Hotchkiss, *Confederate Military History*, Clement A. Evans, ed., 13 vols. (Atlanta: Confederate Publishing Co., 1899), vol. 3, p. 451.

-EVANS- -GORDON- -LEE-

Spotsylvania. His letter picks up the sequence of events at the time Maj. Gen. Edward Johnson's command was overrun.]

> Battle Field
> near Spotsylvania C.H., Va.
> May 14, 1864

My dear Allie

The long continued series of battles are not ended yet. I have not had an opportunity to send you a letter for several days, nor have I any now, but will write the letter anyhow.

Since this fight commenced I have fought *five* hard battles. Think of that and my own wonderful preservation. Day before yesterday occurred the hardest fight of all. At daybreak the enemy broke our entrenchments where Jones' brigade [of Gen. Edward Johnson's division] was posted, and were rapidly pushing their columns through our lines. Our brigade was very close to the place where they broke through. So close that I did not have time to form the whole Brigade, but in order to check them I changed front of the Brigade and charged them immediately with such success that I checked their advance for the time & even recovered part of the works back. This part of the brigade I put in charge of Col. [J. H.] Lamar & moved the other three regiments by the flank under fire of the enemy until I got on their flank. Pegram's brigade was found on my left and I charged again. Drove them back across our entrenchments & pursued them 350 yards farther. The whole fight was most terrific. Grant has massed his army on one point. Our loss is heavy. Especially in officers. But the sacrifice had to be made to save the army from inevitable retreat.

I am not wounded (only in the clothes) thanks to the Great Preserver.

The 31st has lost very heavy. We are expecting another struggle every hour.

6 o'clock P.M.

The enemy have attacked our right & been repulsed.

They are moving farther to our right, You will hear of the fight in the papers.

Goodbye.

God bless you.   Your Husband

The stand organized by Evans, as mentioned in his letter, was a crucial moment in the Battle of Spotsylvania. It gave General Gordon the opportunity to gather his remaining units in the vicinity of the McCoull House and Harrison House for a counterattack.

While Gordon was forming his troops for this push, one of the most dramatic scenes of the war took place. General Evans told the story later when he gave an address as orator of the day on the capitol grounds in Atlanta when the equestrian statue of General Gordon was dedicated to the state:

> Gordon was on the field forming his division for the charge, and my own brigade was withdrawn into position with the general lines. It was at that moment the Virginia, the North Carolina and Georgia brigades of Gordon's general command were in line of battle ready, expectant, and eager to make the charge, when Lee rode through my brigade, having a sublime expression on his face, and in his *mien* which flashed the thrilling truth upon all the line of Confederate men that it was the heroic purpose of his great soul, for the third time in one week, to lead the charge of his Confederate comrades to victory or to death. Gordon read the purpose of Lee at a glance. In a moment he knew what should be done. With his characteristic intuitive discernment of the right action in that supreme crisis he rode to the side of the great commander, and in manner, voice, and by actual command remonstrated against the sacrifice, and spoke those historical words which were repeated and rolled up and down the lines of the army, "General Lee, you must go to the rear!" Men and officers were filled with the spirit of Lee, inspired by the enthusiasm of Gordon, and in a moment they moved, by his order, at double quick into the swirling vortex of battle.[16]

16. *Report of the Gordon Monument Commission*, p. 42. This is a paperback book with no publisher. It was printed just after May 25, 1907, when the ceremony took place on the capitol grounds. There is a copy in Evans' papers.

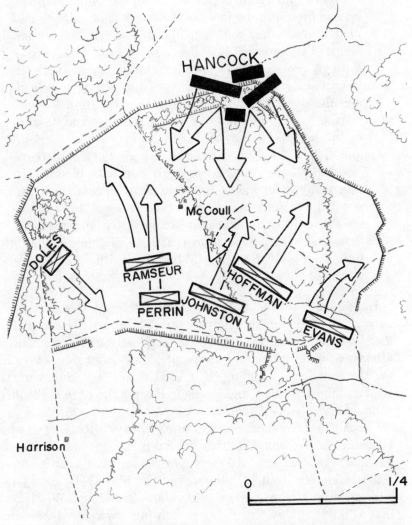

Battle of Spotsylvania Court House—May 12, 1864
General Gordon's counterattack in the Mule Shoe 5 a.m.-7 a.m.

395

Support of the counterattack by Gordon's division was given by units from the corps of Anderson, Ewell, and Early. The Federal attack was checked and driven back toward the apex of the salient. Wave after wave of Union soldiers were, during the remainder of the day, launched against the salient, and the struggle was further described:

> Infantrymen, from opposite sides of the works, climbed up and fired into the faces of their opponents; they grappled one another and attempted to drag each other across the breastworks; bayonet thrusts were made through crevices; the continuous musketry fire cut off large trees standing in the line of the works; the dead and the dying had to be flung to the rear to give room for the living, fighting ones, in the trenches and, to add to the horrors of the combat, a cold, heavy rain set in and partly filled the trenches, where the combatants stood, until they seemed to fairly run with blood. . . . The writer, who was on this field of awful combats, does not believe that human ear ever listened to a more steady and continuous roar of musketry and artillery than that which rose from that field of fierce contention, from the dawning to the day until late in the afternoon.[17]

In his conclusion of the 12th of May account Evans gives the reason for changing the name of the "Mule Shoe." He explained that "a bloody struggle continued from early morning until late afternoon, with unflinching desperation on either side, fairly filling the trenches and piling their borders, on each side, with the slain and the wounded, and giving to this portion of the salient the name of 'the Bloody Angle.' "[18]

Casualties were enormous in the eight days after May 4, when Clement had written Allie that he and his troops had "awakened this morning and found the extensive Yankee camps had all disappeared from our front." On the morning of May 11, General Grant informed the Union chief-of-staff, Maj. Gen. Henry W. Halleck, that as the sixth day of very heavy fighting ended he (Grant) had

17. Hotchkiss, *Military History*, vol. 3, pp. 453.
18. *Ibid.*, p. 452.

lost 11 general officers killed, wounded and missing, and probably 20,000 men.[19] General Ewell reported his Second Corps losses at the Wilderness as 1,250 killed and wounded. General Porter wrote that total casualties in the Wilderness were 17,666 for the Union army and then added a macabre note: "It will be found that on that bloody field every minute recorded the loss of twenty-five men."[20] At Spotsylvania, in Evans' old command alone (the Thirty-first Georgia regiment) there were 63 casualties.[21]

In the description of the battle at Spotsylvania in *Confederate Military History*, the following casualties were given: ". . . Lee's losses, from the 50,000 present, were only 8,000 men; but these were 18 per cent of his army. Grant had thrown twenty-two brigades against Lee's center, at the salient . . . from his 100,000 in hand, 16,000 were killed or wounded."[22]

[As an aftermath of these first two weeks of the 1864 spring campaign, one more of Clement's three surviving letters of this period tells Allie very little about his shattering battle experiences.]

Battlefield Spotsylvania C.H.
May 15, [18]64

Dear Darling

I wrote you a short battle field letter, just to keep you posted, provided my letters reach you at all.

Grant appears to be exhausted & the hope is that the fight is ended. but that is only a *hope*, for he is yet in our front & we may still fight another great Battle. I have written you many letters, sent you one dispatch but I fear no one has reached you. How terrible is my poor darling's suspense.

I cannot hear from Probe, but as bad news flies fast I take it for granted that he is all right.

I have been nearly exhausted several times & now feel scarcely able to travel. My face wound is well, but my wound in the knee still troubles me. Praise the good Lord for my safety.

Sam Everett has lost his arm. Tip Harrison safe.

---

19. *O.R.*, series 1, vol. 36, part 1, pp. 4, 1075.
20. Porter, *Campaigning*, p. 71.
21. Henderson, *Roster*, vol. 3, pp. 579-659.
22. Hotchkiss, *Military History*, vol. 3, p. 454.

I have such a violent headache that you will excuse my short epistle.

Goodbye. God bless you.

Your Husband

Evans' "hope" about Grant was far from fulfillment. In the midst of fighting and just before Evans' wishful thinking was expressed, Grant wrote what is probably his most oft-quoted dispatch to General Halleck: "We have now ended the sixth day of very heavy fighting. . . . I propose to fight it out on this line if it takes all summer."[23]

Between May 12 and 18, the armies maintained more or less static positions on the Spotsylvania battlefield. Ewell's corps was drawn back after midnight to a new line about nine hundred yards to the rear of the Bloody Angle, and all was quiet until May 18.[24]

It was at this juncture that General Lee took advantage of the brief lull in the fighting to issue, on May 14, General Orders No. 41. This timely message to the soldiers of the Army of Northern Virginia is a matchless example of the genius of General Lee in sustaining the morale and devotion of his men. An original copy distributed to General Gordon's division and signed with the personal autograph of General Lee was carefully saved by General Evans and is among his papers:

Hd. Qrs. Army of Northern Va.
14th May 1864

General Orders
No. 41

I.   The Commanding General takes great pleasure in announcing to the Army the series of successes that, by the favor of God, have been recently achieved by our arms.

II.   A part of the enemy's force threatening the Valley of Virginia has been routed by Genl. Imboden, and driven back to the Potomac, with the loss of their train and a number of prisoners.

III.   Another body of the enemy under Genl. Averell penetrated to the Virginia and Tennessee Rail Road at

23. *O.R.*, series 1, vol. 36, part 3, p. 627. This dispatch is dated May 11.
24. *Ibid.*, part 1, p. 1075.

Dublin Depot. A portion of this force has been dispersed by Genls. [John H.] Morgan and W. E. Jones, who are in pursuit of the remainder.

IV. The army of Genl. Banks sustained a severe defeat in Western Louisiana by the forces of Genl. Kirby Smith, and retreated to Alexandria, losing several thousand prisoners, thirty-five pieces of artillery, and a large number of wagons. Some of the most formidable gunboats that accompanied the expedition were destroyed to save them from being captured.

V. The expedition of Genl. Steele into Western Arkansas has ended in a complete disaster. Northern journals of the 10th inst. announce his surrender with an army of nine thousand men to General Price.

VI. The Cavalry force sent by General Grant to attack Richmond has been repulsed and retired towards the Peninsula. Every demonstration of the enemy south of the James River has up to this time been successfully repelled.

VII. The heroic valor of this army with the blessing of Almighty God has thus far checked the advance of the principal army of the enemy and inflicted upon it heavy loss.

The eyes and hearts of your countrymen are turned to you with confidence, and their prayers attend you in your gallant struggle. Encouraged by the success that has been vouchsafed to us, and stimulated by the great interests that depend upon the issue, let every man resolve to endure all and brave all until by the assistance of a just and merciful God, the enemy shall be driven back and peace secured to our country.

Continue to emulate the valor of your comrades who have fallen and remember that it depends upon you whether they shall have died in vain.

It is in your power, under God, to defeat the last great effort of the enemy, establish the independence of your native land and earn the everlasting love and gratitude of your countrymen and the admiration of mankind.

(signed) R. E. Lee
Genl.

Chapter 20

THE GEORGIA HOME FRONT IN 1864

And now, while the armies confronted each other, it is a good time to turn back to Georgia and read some letters[1] from Allie for the months of May and June 1864, and to realize again the contrast of her daily existence with the strenuous day-to-day life of Clement. Although she never intimates such a thought, Allie could not have helped but often wonder: "Is he dead even as I write this?"

Allie to Clement:

Lumpkin, Stewart Co., Ga.
May 8, 1864

My dear darling

You see I am still here. I expected to have been gone to Miller [County] long ago, but Sister hasn't sent yet. She will be sure to send this week I think. I will write to you as soon as the carriage gets here. I am all ready to start. I don't dread to go as much as I did, because I think you are writing to me there and when I get there I will find letters for me. I want to go now to get my letters. Ida and I both had a letter from you yesterday. I think Ida was very much relieved to find no geography questions in her letter. She wanted to know of me if when I went to her Aunt Annie's if I would ask her any questions in my letters. She carried paper with her to school this morning to write to you. She does her best in her geography but its all too hard for her. Mr. Graham is gone—left day before yesterday evening. I am so sorry —feel real bad about it. He did not get the appointment

1. Many family members are mentioned in this chapter. They will not be cited individually in footnotes to this chapter but will be in Appendix A on relatives.

I wrote you about. Jack Scott and John Richardson used their influence against him and they gave it to Mr. Seymour. Graham was so mad he was as white as cotton he was the maddest man I ever saw for awhile. Matt was furious. He says he has some wires working where they have no influence. I don't know what it is. He sent the trunk you sent up from Cuthbert. I am proud of my leather—everything in it will be useful to me. I am trying to make me another pair of shoes today. The jacket you sent is too good to cut up for shoes.

Georgia Richardson has just come over and stopped me in writing and I am afraid I will be too late for the mail. I wonder what you are doing this beautiful morning. I would give lots to know.

Matt says you must write to her and give her your advice about what to do with Jimmie—whether to let him go with his pa or to send him to you—tell her what you think would be best. She is getting ready to go to Eufaula. She says she will spend most of the time Mr. Graham is gone over there. The Columbus mail comes in this evening. I dread to see it, so afraid it will bring news of a fight. I do dread it so much darling but trust all will be well for me. Goodbye darling. Goodbye. God bless you.

Your Wife

Miller County, Georgia
May 16, 1864

My dear darling

I can't imagine what I shall fill this letter with to make it the least interesting to you. It has been raining all the week so we could go nowhere and we have seen nobody. It is dull dull times. Will this rain, if it continues, stop army operations for awhile? I hope so. Yesterday I received three letters from you the first I have had in ten days. I was getting really sick for a letter. I see from the papers there has been no fighting since the third. You think Grant wants to take our capital on the fourth of July. Can it be possible that this awful fighting will continue till then? Oh darling I am worn out with the suspense and anxiety. I wish it was December. I am tired of everything. I get so restless, dissatisfied, discontented sometimes I can scarcely live. I work all day as hard as I can. I don't know what I would do if I couldn't work to get ready to go to see you. I have just had to go out and part George and Lawton. They are the greatest fighting characters I know of. If they were old enough to join our army I think they would soon whip out the Yankees. Mama cut off his hair sometime ago, pa. Your letters were so long coming Ma thought she would cut it and risk the consequences. The curls are put away for you pa. He told me this morning he wanted to go home. I asked who did he want to go to see. He said Sister and Coon. How he will miss his little Negro when he goes home. I am trying to learn him to do without a nurse but he is lots of trouble. I can't afford to take a grown Negro to do nothing but nurse him.

You say I must stay down here a long time but I must go home. The first of August if not sooner. I have got so much to do before I can go to Virginia. I ought to be there now having clothes made for Hannah and Fillis. It makes me mad every time I look at them. They will be lots of expense on our hands. Will have to pay their board all this winter and I am troubled to know what I shall do for a Negro to carry with me. If it was Christmas I could get one from Sister, but all here are hired and then how would I get them to Lumpkin? I will try to make some arrangements to get one but at present I don't know what I shall do. I got a short letter from Clem yesterday. Mother has been sick but is better. Ida is well. Ma would give lots to see her. Sister had a letter from Probe too yesterday. He said Gen. Evans had filled his staff and left his brother in law minus. That he expected to stay with the second Ga. not get a transfer. We have nothing here but rain, rain, rain. I am so tired of it I don't know what to do. You must put up with my short and uninteresting letters, darling. There is nothing in the world to find to write here, only I want to see you worse and worse every day and if it was possible I would start to see you tomorrow. I wonder how long it will be before I see you. Goodbye. God bless you and take care of you my darling.

Your Wife.

Miller County, Georgia
May 18, 1864

My dear darling

Not a word from you yet. We got a Macon Telegraph this morning that had a list of some of the Georgia officers that were killed and wounded in it and more news from the fight than we have had before. I feel better than I did about you. I saw Major Pride was wounded in the abdomen. Lieutenant Hood was also among them. If there has been no fighting since the eighth I think you are unhurt. I got a letter from Clem yesterday and poor little Coon I reckon is dead. She said he was alive and that was all, had been having spasms all night. Battle had given him out. I do feel awfully sorry about it. He was a little sick the day before I left but I didn't think there was much the matter with him. He was a great deal better the morning I started and I thought of bringing him with me anyhow. I am glad that I didn't. I am so sorry. Clem wrote me to make up my mind to hear he was dead the next time she wrote for there was no hope for him. It is worms that ails him.

Ida was well and getting on finely but wanted to see me. She was still studying her geography. Sister has not heard from Probe yet. We are a right long face looking set. I am here by myself this morning. She has gone to see one of her neighbors on business. Lawton has got well I believe. What will he do without his little Negro to play with him, papa. I will miss him so much. I know that Mose will feel bad enough about him.

We are beginning to have real summer weather. It is very warm to-day—disagreeable. We are needing rain very much. It is right lonesome down here. We don't feel like visiting around until we know you and Probe are safe. I don't know what in the world to write you about. We haven't been anywhere and nobody has been here. We haven't seen a soul since I wrote to you last. I know my letters must be very uninteresting. I haven't had a letter from you in over a week. The last one was written on the second. I am so anxious for one written since the fight.

Goodbye darling. I want to see you and to hear from you so bad.

Goodbye. God bless you.

Your Wife

Miller County, Georgia
May 21, 1864

My dear darling

Yesterday I got a letter from Clem with a dispatch from you to Mr. Graham enclosed. I need not tell you my heart was made glad. You know that already. I have searched every paper anxiously since the fight commenced. I am so glad you are safe. I want a letter from you now telling all about everything. I feel like I hadn't had a letter in a year. It has been almost three weeks since my last was written. I do hope this is the last fighting to be done in Virginia. We have been spending the day at Mr. Trailer's, one of sister's neighbors. Sallie Campfield was there too. There was no church nearer than Bainbridge. We are going there before long. Sunday you know is always a dull day in town but it is awful down here in the piney woods. We have lots of everything good to eat but not much of the good company.

Poor little Coonie is dead. He died last Sunday evening. I feel so bad about it. What will he [Lawton] do for his little Negro, papa? Got nobody to play with him. Clem says brother will let me have one of his little Negroes—but it wont be Coon. I will miss him so much when I go home. I got good and bad news in the same letter. Mama is afraid she will have to cut his pretty hair, pa. He is so fat and it is so long and hot I don't think he can stand it all the summer. I am put up for something to write. Never had such little to put in a letter in my life. I have been persuading Sister to go to Lumpkin with me.

Miller County, Georgia
June 3, 1864

404

My dear darling

After a whole long week I have at last got another letter. I can't see why it takes my letters so much longer to come than it does Probe's. His written the same date came four or five days ago. I wonder if you are rested yet. I have been so uneasy all this long—long week for fear you were sick. I am miserable from one day's end to another about you. Are they done fighting. You say in your last letter that the hardest fighting is yet to come. I hope your prophecy will not come true. I of course am gratified to know you have received the appointment of Brigadier but had rather have you away from the Yankees' bullets than anything else.

How shall I back your letters. [in margin] How often I have wished that I didn't love you half as good as I do for then I wouldn't be so miserable about you. I got a letter from Ida too today. She wrote her Aunt Mat gets letters from you most every mail. That she had one from you telling her about your promotion. Sometimes she lets them read them and sometimes she won't. She is more lucky than I am in getting them. I will be so glad when the fighting is all over and you have time and can write me a good long letter. Such a one would do me good. Make me feel good a whole week. I want to see you so bad, darling. Sister and I went out to visit one of her neighbors this evening about three miles. A storm came up and caught us as we were coming home. We were the worst [scared] folks you ever saw. Got very wet. I didn't like the idea of being caught out in the woods and the trees falling all around me. I don't know how long I shall stay down here.

Sister won't hear to my going home before August. I like it very well but it is awfully lonesome. She can have plenty of company but it is such as I don't enjoy. Piney woods crackers—We are invited out to spend the day tomorrow with a very nice lady. Mrs. Swearengen [not identifiable]. Do you get all of my letters? I write three times a week. If you get sick darling do let me know it. I am miserable about you. Write as often as you can. I know you are tired and worn out and I am so sorry for you. If this is the last fighting of the war and we are to have peace sure enough then what a blessed time we will have. I am so thankful to the good being that he has spared you through so much and continue to ask his protection for you in all coming danger.   Your Wife.

Miller County, Georgia
June 10, 1864

My dear darling

I haven't written to you in several days because I haven't been at home. I have made that long expected trip to Bainbridge at last. Sister did not go. We would have had to stay all night away from the children and she preferred staying at home and taking care of them. I went to Mrs. Swearengen's Tuesday evening and from there Wednesday morning. I confess I was very much disappointed in the looks of the place. It looks old and dirty—so different from Lumpkin. I might take to it better if I were to stay longer perhaps and go all over the place. I saw only one pretty building, there are no sidewalks to the streets and all put together I have a very sorry opinion of the place although I had a very pleasant and agreeable time. Dined at the hotel. Made the acquaintance of some very nice agreeable ladies. I think it is what you might call a fast little place. The married ladies take on as much as the young ones and the same with the married gentlemen. You know that don't suit me. They think nothing of kissing another man's wife. They all do it. The married men take on with the girls more than the young ones and you very well know I never could stand that. I went out about a mile to the factory, bought me two bunches of thread. It cost forty dollars a bunch. It is very nice to make me and the children winter dresses. Would you like a nice homespun shirt or two? If you do I will have them ready for you by winter. Is there anything you need that I can get? If there is just say so. I am very much disappointed in not getting wool to make you a suit of clothes. I calculated on making you a nice suit. You must get you a fine uniform in Richmond.

I haven't had a letter in sometime but I am not complaining. I know you are so tired and worn out you don't feel like writing. Write whenever it is convenient but don't put yourself to any inconvenience about it. I shall be satisfied so long as you are safe. I see you are still fighting. When will it end? I wish I could sleep until it is all over and then wake and find my darling all safe. You have no idea how anxiously I look over every paper I can get my hands on. I do wish so much I could be with you just a little while.

I have so much to talk with you about. I can't write to you all I want to say. It will take me a long long time after this war ends to make up all lost time. I had another letter from Clem and Ida today. They report all well at home. That is of our folks but a lot of sickness in the country. I am getting right anxious to go home. I want to see Ida so much but Sister don't allow me to speak of it. She says she will send me home the first of August but not a day before. I get on finely down here. It is cheap living, don't cost anything and if it wasn't so lonesome I would be willing to stay until I got ready to go to Virginia. I travel it all over regularly every night before I can get to sleep. Last night I dreamed I was looking for you home expecting you every moment when I woke up I was so mad that you didn't come before I woke. Ida sent me another letter from Green Clifton and wanted to know if she must answer. I told her to do as she pleased about it. What do you think of the correspondence? Clem says she thinks Ida is the best child living, says she had no idea she was the child she is. That is very gratifying to me. Sister has gone this evening to see some of her neighbors. I dont like her piney woods folks and won't go with her. Mama has to whip your boy most every day—he called me old dog just now.

Goodbye. God bless and shield you, darling.

Your Wife

[The next letter is one of the rare ones from Ida. It is a remarkable one, too, from a nine-year-old.]

Lumpkin, Ga.
June 15, 1864

My dear Pa

I received your letter today and was so glad to hear from you it was the first time we had a letter from you in two weeks. Papa you say I don't write to you as often as I ought to but I am going to write once every week until vacation and I am going to write you two letters a week. Aunt Clem got a letter from Mama this evening and she says she won't be home until August. Oh that is so long for mama to stay away from home and I want to see her so bad. She says that little buddy has learned to talk right plain since she has been gone and that she has cut his hair off and he looks so sweet with his hair short. I go to school regular every day. Mrs. Hurley has put us upstairs. I stay up stairs all the time I am studying second arithmetic fourth reader and definer. Grandma has been sick a week with erysipelas in her face but she is getting better. Our school will be out two weeks from tomorrow. I will be sorry for I will not know what to do with myself in vacation while mama and little buddy is gone. It has been raining nearly every day for two weeks. Pa I wish you was at home to eat some plumbs apple and blackberrys they are getting ripe, and we have right smart. Aunt Clem wrote to you this evening and we will send our letters in the same envelope. Grandpa is down to uncle P D went down there today with Aunt Jane while he has gone up to Macon to report but they gave him a forty days' furlow but since he has come home he has got a detail and won't have to go at all.

How does Uncle Mose come on? Has he heard of Coonnie's death? Aunt Robie and Cousin Luella are spending the evening with us. Cousin Terita has got a mighty sweet little baby named Robert Lee but she says she is going to change his name for she is afraid the Yankees will come along here and kill him because he is named after General Lee. We all send you a heap of love and want to see you so bad. I will write to you next Saturday.

Goodbye dear papa.

Your affectionate daughter Ida

408

Allie to Clement:

My dear darling

I wrote to you day before yesterday but haven't had an opportunity of sending it to the office but I will write again any how and start both letters at once. I haven't had a letter in a week but I know from the papers you are safe if you are not sick. I noticed in the papers a few days ago that Gen. Evans had been severely injured by accident. It frightened me almost out of my wits for awhile until I had sense enough to read it over carefully when I saw it must be Gen. [Nathan G. "Shanks"] Evans of South Carolina. I am satisfied it is not you but was terribly frightened at first.

We have just got home from church. Ate a hearty dinner of vegetables and chicken. I had some nice ripe apples this morning which were highly appreciated. I think there will be a great deal more fruit than we all expected. Lawton is the greediest thing after fruit you ever saw, if he sees me with a plumb and I don't give it to him he jumps at me and almost tears me to pieces, pinches and scratches me, tries to pull my clothes off and when I slap him for it he runs off and says Old Dog dog dog, tells me to kiss his foot says all manner of saucy things. He is a torn down piece. He will get up in the chairs and let loose just to scare me. Sometimes he falls out and most breaks his head but he don't care for it. He has fattened up a good deal since he has been down here. He was fat enough before but he is a sight now. He is so well and full of life he don't know what to do with himself, has more monkey actions. He will run to me and point his fingers at me and then laugh like it was the funniest thing he ever saw. Everything that George or Walton does or says he tries to imitate it. He is learning to talk right fast. Can say almost anything he wants to. Asked for some sweetened water today the first thing when he got to the table I do wish you could see him. I know you will say these are some more of his smart doings that papa never saw. But mama sees them

409

and knows they are so. Everybody that sees him tells me I will never have another such a boy. We expected to go to the baptising this evening but it is thundering, lightning and raining and I am afraid we won't get off. I am sorry for anything with me to pass off the time. June is most half gone. I wish I could say it was gone. The two months since I saw you were like two years and that is only one third of the six months before I see you. I do everything I can to make time fly. Sleep until nine or ten o'clock every morning and then work hard until night. I want a letter so bad. I miss them. I can bear our separation so much better when I write. Do you get all my letters? I write three times a week. I hope you have had time to rest your poor tired self.

Goodbye. God bless you darling.

Your Wife

Chapter 21

SECOND COLD HARBOR

During the last span of Allie's letters, Clement was again at war, but no letters of his involvement for those days exist until June 18. The cessation of conflict for several days in May was in no way a diminution of General Grant's aggressive strategy. The cause of the delay was again rain.[1]

After a Union probe in front of Ewell's corps on May 18 had proved that the new Confederate line south of the Bloody Angle was impregnable, General Lee directed Ewell to demonstrate against the enemy in his front on May 19. Lee believed the Federals were moving to the left and wished to be sure. Ewell marched his command of about 6,000 men to the right of the enemy and met stout opposition when he attacked. His objective was attained: the Federal advances were designed to turn Lee's right. However, General Lee was disturbed that this intended "reconnaissance" had developed into a fight, and he felt that General Ewell's impaired physical and mental alertness were again demonstrated, as they had been on May 6 when Ewell held Gordon back from the attack in the Wilderness. There was no question that, since his lower right leg had been amputated, General Ewell's physical and mental condition had limited his field effectiveness.

In this latest engagement, Evans' command and Gordon's division were rather badly mauled. The corps casualties were about 900. Union losses were also sizeable. Grant reported 196 killed, 1,090 wounded, and 249 missing.[2]

As the Federals marched southeast, General Lee made quick countermoves and the Confederates again out-marched the enemy, guessing accurately what Grant would do. Lee ordered

---

1. *O.R.*, series, 1, vol. 36, part 1, p. 5.
2. *Ibid.*, p. 6, for Grant's report to Halleck and casualties.

Ewell to let him know "whether you discover any movement of the enemy in your front, and whether his rear is weak enough for you to strike."[3] This was early on May 20. By nightfall, it was clear to Lee the Federal units were moving from Ewell's front and at 8:30 p.m. Lee ordered Ewell to be ready to march at daybreak.

Lee had further reports confirming the enemy's intention to try to continue to turn Lee's right and drive toward Richmond. Lee hastened his forces southward toward Hanover Junction, forming them at a strong natural position on the banks of the North Anna River. This began about midday of May 21, instead of "at daybreak." Ewell's corps was instructed, as the first contingent, to start from Spotsylvania to the new position. By dark that same day, most of the Confederates were in motion toward the North Anna. By 2 a.m. on May 22, Evans' brigade had marched toward the new front, a distance of seventeen miles, to Dickson's Mill.[4] At 4 a.m. the men were roused and urged on, and about 9:30 a.m. had gone nine miles farther. General Lee accompanied Ewell's columns most of the way. This corps continued forward and was posted on the low ground on the south side of the North Anna River, on the Confederate right.

For four days, the armies confronted each other. Meanwhile, Grant had received reinforcements to replace his huge losses. The Confederates received some also, among whom were seven companies comprising the Twelfth Georgia battalion of 480, which was added to Evans' brigade,[5] General Lee had put his troops in such a strong position that he wanted Grant to attack. The latter maneuvered his forces across the river, made half-hearted thrusts, and then withdrew back over the river. One factor that deterred Grant was that he found Lee's defenses would force him to cross the North Anna River twice in order to get at the Confederates. This was the situation on May 26.

These few days were perplexing to Lee. On May 24 he became ill with intestinal trouble and was almost unable to command. His First Corps commander, General Longstreet (his Old War Horse), was recuperating from wounds suffered in the Wil-

3. *Ibid.*, part 3, p. 801.
4. *Ibid.*, pp. 814-15; *O.R.*, series 1, vol. 36, part 1, p. 1058.
5. Nichols, *Soldier's Story*, p. 161, cites 1,000 men. *O.R.*, series 1, vol. 36, part 2, p. 955, says the Twelfth Georgia Battalion had 480 men.

derness. A. P. Hill of the Third Corps had been *hors de combat* for about two weeks and was not well enough to resume command, even though he had done so. The Second Corps leader, peglegged Richard Ewell, whose alertness and physical stamina were in question, finally played out.

After an attack of diarrhea that lasted a week, Ewell was finally relieved, and General Early was named to temporary command of the corps on May 27. The change of commanders was made permanent on June 14. Ewell was placed in command of the defenses of Richmond,[6] where he would remain in charge of local forces until the retreat toward Appomattox.

Confronted with these circumstances, under which Lee could not delegate with confidence and could not personally supervise, Lee could not at the moment force an offensive. Grant, being outmaneuvered, could not assault, so he side-slipped once more to the Confederate right, sending his army down the north bank of the North Anna and Pamunkey on the night of May 26.

Evans' command moved toward Richmond with Ewell's corps (now under Early) on May 27. Lee rode with them, for the Second Corps had the reputation of outmarching any other large unit in the Army of Northern Virginia.[7]

From May 27 until June 1, the Confederates shifted to gainsay the Federals, as the latter continually sought to work around the right to capture the South's capital city. On June 2 and again on the 3d, the converging armies met for the second battle of Cold Harbor. Both were at maximum strength, for Lee had been reinforced from the Southside army of Gen. P. G. T. Beauregard and, as previously stated, Grant's losses of May had been more than amply replaced. Cold Harbor was where, two years before, General Evans, almost fresh from Georgia, had rushed with Stonewall Jackson's "foot cavalry" into the Chickahominy swamps, after Jackson's brilliant Valley Campaign of 1862.

Gordon's division was on the left of the Confederates and, contrary to its most recent experiences, was not at the brunt of Federal assaults. On June 2 the Second Corps (under Early) had attacked the enemy's right and gained some advantages. On June 3 the expected battle began about 4:30 a.m. Early renewed his

6. *O.R.*, series 1, vol. 36, part 1, p. 1074.
7. Freeman, *R. E. Lee*, vol. 3, p. 362.

attack on the enemy's right wing, but after two hours, had gained little. Meanwhile, the enemy massed in front of the Confederate center. Following his pattern, Grant sent assault after assault, and by 8 a.m. fourteen charges had been repulsed, with severe losses. By one o'clock the Federals were convinced that further frontal attacks were fruitless, although one final foray was made on Lee's center at dark.[8]

The Union casualties were again horrible. The loss in killed, wounded and missing was nearly 7,000. Grant acknowledged that Cold Harbor was a mistake.[9] Confederate losses were 1,200 to 1,500. The battle at Cold Harbor on June 3, 1864, was an "incredible success," but it was also the last great battle success of the Army of Northern Virginia.[10]

Matters were once more at a standstill. Ever mindful that his troops and supplies must be prudently nursed, Lee was reluctant to launch a direct offensive against Grant. Lee could not afford Grant's method of operation. Grant had to take stock of the prodigal sacrifice of men and material that had attended his efforts to date: "So far, Grant's campaign had been remarkable only for persistence—and some 55,000 casualties."[11]

General Grant now saw he could not accomplish by frontal attacks an entrance into Richmond. But Lee could not, for the moment, read his adversary's change of mind. The Union assault troops at Cold Harbor had been fought at close quarters, where they had been halted, and arm's-length observations of Grant's maneuvers were hampered. The Confederate cavalry, too, was not at top efficiency. Reports had come in late in the week, after the battle, that the enemy positions in front of Early and his new command had been abandoned after several days of hot skirmishes between snipers and small foraging parties. This had kept the Confederates on constant alert. But, with empty trenches there now, Early's corps was moved on June 11 from the left to the far right of the Southern army, behind the corps of Hill. This move was made because Grant's strategy had continually been to move in that direction. As President Davis expressed to Lee on June 9: "The indications are that Grant, despairing of direct at-

8. O.R., series 1, vol. 36, part 1, pp. 1032-33; and Porter, *Campaigning*, p. 177.
9. Porter, *Campaigning*, pp. 178-79.
10. Freeman, *R. E. Lee*, vol. 3, p. 391.
11. O.R., series 1, vol. 51, part 2, p. 1003.

tack, is now seeking to embarrass you by flank movements."[12]

But other pressures began to call General Lee's attention to a vital region of the Confederacy—the Shenandoah Valley—from whence the Army of Northern Virginia urgently needed the spring and summer harvests.

12. *O.R.*, series 1, vol. 51, part 2, p. 996.

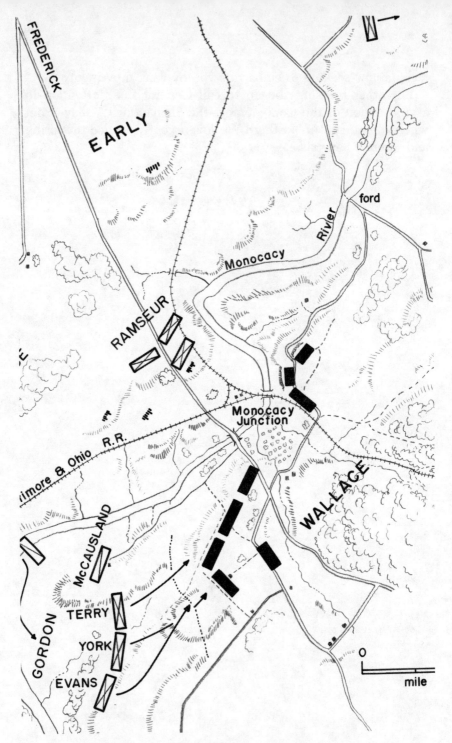

Battle of Monocacy, Maryland, July 9, 1864

416

Part IV

Chapter 22

MONOCACY AND THE ATTACK ON WASHINGTON

In May, 1864 Confederate Brig. Gen. John Imboden had delayed the Union advance under Maj. Gen. Franz Sigel in the Shenandoah Valley. Maj. Gen. John C. Breckinridge, former vice-president of the United States, was dispatched with additional Confederate troops to the lower Valley. They soundly defeated Sigel at New Market. In that battle, 264 V.M.I. cadets between the age of sixteen and eighteen participated and won the enduring admiration of the South, 10 of the cadets being killed and 48 wounded.

On May 21, nearly two weeks before Lee's victory at Cold Harbor, Sigel abandoned the Valley and was replaced by Gen. David Hunter, a Virginian who had chosen not to follow his state into secession. Hunter began an advance of devastation up the Shenandoah Valley on May 26, en route to becoming perhaps the most despised man in the South for a century to come. It was also reported that the Union cavalry's rising star, Maj. Gen. Philip Sheridan, was en route to join Hunter. Sheridan, during the earlier part of this spring when such desperate struggles in the Wilderness and at Spotsylvania were in progress, had led raids near Richmond, had cut rail connections behind Lee for a time, and had struck an enormous blow against the Confederacy when troops in his command mortally wounded the *beau sabreur* of the Southern cause, General Stuart, at Yellow Tavern.

When Grant attacked at Cold Harbor, Breckinridge had been called to join Lee. Even though reinforcements were sent to Imboden, his command mustered only five thousand, and now led by

Brig. Gen. William E. "Grumble" Jones, they were badly defeated on June 5 by Hunter's superior force at Piedmont. By this time, Brig. Gen. George Crook's columns joined Hunter and his eighteen thousand soldiers, and they started for Lynchburg.[1]

It was soon realized in Richmond that Hunter must be stopped if the Confederacy were to survive. Breckinridge, with twenty-one hundred men, had been directed to return to the Valley. His report from there was sent directly to President Davis. Based on that report, Gen. Braxton Bragg, now a presidential advisor, recommended that Hunter be expelled from the Valley. President Davis sent the report and recommendation to General Lee, who gave a hesitant reply on June 11: "If it is prudent to hazard the defense of Richmond, the interests involved by thus diminishing the forces here, I will do so. I think this is what the enemy would desire." And then he added a note that borders on sarcasm: "A victory over General Grant would also relieve our difficulties."[2]

Hunter's aggression, however, changed Lee's attitude. On June 12, Lee learned that Lexington had been taken the day before, and that Lynchburg was threatened. Since the Battle of Piedmont, Hunter had been free to cross the Blue Ridge Mountains. If the Valley were under his control, Hunter could plunder midland Virginia and then march to join Grant.

A Confederate success about this time (at the Battle of Trevilian Station on June 11 and 12) helped Lee to decide. Maj. Gen. Wade Hampton, who had succeeded Jeb Stuart, checkmated Sheridan in that engagement and Sheridan had to abandon his mission to join General Hunter in the Valley. So Lee ordered General Early to set out for the Shenandoah Valley on the morning of June 13. Early's mission was to clear the Valley of Yankees and, if possible, make a foray into enemy territory and threaten Washington. That would take pressure off Richmond, because, it was believed Grant would be compelled to weaken his army to protect the Union capital.[3]

The Shenandoah Valley had become familiar territory to Clement Evans as his command sallied forth a third time for this destination. It had been the scene of Evans' first combat experience

1. Joseph T. Derry, *The Confederate States of America* (Richmond, Virginia: Johnson Publishing Co., 1895), p. 324, *et seq.*
2. *O.R.*, series 1, vol. 51, part 2, p. 1003.
3. *Ibid.*, vol. 37, part 1, p. 346 is General Lee's statement of the mission.

with Lawton's brigade, when it was rushed from Georgia in 1862 to reinforce Stonewall Jackson. It was part of the same route he had traversed with Ewell's corps in 1863, in the Gettysburg Campaign, when Evans marched as far as York, Pennsylvania, and took the flag off the courthouse.

Two letters written to Allie on this third march reveal some of the details of Evans' movement from Cold Harbor to Lynchburg.

Bivouac near Charlottesville, Va.
June 18, 1864
Sunset

My dear darling

I have had no opportunity to write to you since the 12th inst. I sent you a letter then stating that we were near Cold Harbor about eight miles from Richmond. At daylight on the 13th we marched from that point, marching eighty five miles in four days. The weather is very dry, the roads exceedingly dusty, the sun hot, but we have kept up finely and are all here, except a few taken sick on the road. We are in excellent spirits and ready for the work before us. The telegram and newspapers will tell you the whole matter. I trust they will tell you only good news. We have heard not a word from Richmond since we left and do not know what has occurred down there. All we do know is that Grant changed his position during the night in which our portion of the army moved.

I received another letter from Ida. She expresses as being very lonely without you, congratulates me on being made a Brigadier General, and hopes to spend the winter with us in Virginia. To this end she says she is studying very hard, but does not mention *Geography*. I think we had better not encourage her to believe she will come to Virginia this winter although I shall be *miserable* about not seeing her.

The days pass off swiftly while marching through this lovely region. I saw Clark's mountain way off fifteen or twenty miles distant and thought of you. It almost looked like home was there. But never mind, it cannot be long before we will be with each other again. Four more months

419

will soon pass and I hope it is our last separation for this life. My soul is buoyant with anticipations concerning the early return of peace. Our enemies will soon give up their mad project of subjugation and we will be at peace. Then darling I contemplate with so much joy our future life of unmixed real happiness. Our duties, our occupations, all will make us happy.

Give my love to sister and her brats.

Take good care of your precious self. Your good report of yourself showing you could come to me, made me feel like a new man.

God bless you, preserve you, make you happy. Oh how grateful I am to Him for crowning my head with a wife so priceless.

Good bye.

Your Husband

Address me now as follows, so the letters will come safely.

Brig. Genl. C. A. Evans
Gordon's Division
Ewell's Corps
Richmond, Va.

Battlefield—
Lynchburg & Salem Turnpike
June 18, 1864

My dear Darling

I was just lying down to see if I could sleep a little, (for I was on horseback the whole night). But my conscience upbraided me for being so selfish as to go to sleep when I ought to write to you. I know you will say I ought to have slept & then write, but how do I know, but I shall be awakened with orders to move or fight or some other disagreeable thing and then I could not write.

We reached this place last evening at 6½ o'clock having come on the cars from Everett's crossing, which is about six miles beyond Charlottesville. As soon as I arrived I was ordered to march down the Salem Turnpike. I rode ahead to find my position and get orders, when I did get not only the orders, but a most disagreeable shelling. We found that the small force which was protecting this road had been driven in. But the night and ourselves checked them.

I went out after night on a reconnaisance, and spent two or three hours within six hundred yards of the Yankee Camp listening to the rascals. They were very careless and I wanted to pitch into them, but did not get permission.

I spent the remainder of the night entrenching, which work is still going on, accelerated by the Yankee batteries which give us an occasional benefit.

This is about all the present news which is proper for me to write. We shall certainly wind up all the long fighting with great success.

I had rather write to you about coming to see me. Does the next four months seem a long way off to you? As if they would never go by? But they will, darling, and we will be together again. Then how much we shall enjoy ourselves. I live in the future! Like a foolish school boy I build castles in the air—such glorious castles they are too—and not one fails to have you the center object of my fancy—Bless you my darling.

Just think of 44 days' fighting. Worse than the siege of Vicksburg. And likely to continue many more days. But it will also end some of these days, and we shall enjoy the end so much, shall we not?

Does Pa's boy talk any, Ma? What does he say? Pa thinks he must be a saucy boy—but Pa can't say whip yet, Mama.

Pa does want to see his baby so much—so much.

Give my love to sister and her picanninies. I take care of myself for your sake.

God bless you my darling.

Your Husband

Both General Evans' letters were dated June 18 from Lynchburg. The hasty departure of the Second Corps from Cold Harbor (the forced and dusty marches, and the cramming of men, artillery, ammunition, equipment, and supplies onto every available horse, mule, and passenger rail accommodation) paid off. The Second Corps beat Hunter to Lynchburg and when the Federals arrived, the Confederates were firmly dug in and made preparations during the night of the 18th to attack early next day. It had taken Hunter six days to get from Lexington to Lynchburg—a distance of 30 miles as the crow flies, but 60 miles by the route the Federals marched. Evans' command had covered 85 miles from Cold Harbor to Charlottesville and 60 miles from there to Lynchburg in five days—145 miles.[4]

Evans' brigade was settled on the left of the Confederate defense line, south of the Salem Pike leading to Lynchburg, in the rear of the division. On June 17, the Federals made an unsuccessful attack on the Confederate front about dark, and on June 18, a display of strength by Ramseur's and Gordon's divisions in a surprise counterattack broke Hunter's confidence. When Confederates stirred the morning of June 19, Hunter was gone.[5] He had gone so fast and was so far ahead that, even though they chased him for 60 miles, they could not come to grips with him. He had fled to West Virginia, leaving the Valley open for Early to advance deep into enemy territory.

After vainly chasing Hunter, the corps rested several hours, then took the Valley Turnpike for Staunton.

General Evans wrote several letters to Allie in the middle of these days. One of these letters was very short:

> North Bank James River
> opposite Buchanan, Va.
> June 24/[18]64
>
> My dear Allie
> I hope to be able to send this to you. We have just waded the James.

However, there was more to it than first appears. The corps had reached Buchanan on June 24. From Salem Pike near Lynchburg, where the brigade had helped thwart General Hunter on June 18, it had marched a distance of eighty miles. As the corps waded the upper reaches of the James River on June 24, the Confederates were two hundred miles from the next major river

4. *Ibid.*, p. 160.
5. Nichols, *Soldier's Story*, p. 166.

crossing, which was to be at the fords and bridges on the Potomac above Washington. Two days after passing Buchanan, the Confederates reached Staunton and spent two more days before stepping off down the Valley on June 28. The march to Staunton was comparatively pleasant. Many had a chance to see the great Natural Bridge, to inspect the ruins at Virginia Military Institute (which had been burned by General Hunter), to pay respects to Stonewall Jackson's grave at Lexington, and to draw supplies at Staunton.[6] General Early's strength can be assessed from reports at Staunton: about ten thousand infantrymen, two thousand cavalry troopers, and strength enough to man artillery that required three battalions. Increments of cavalry and others were added, and by the time the Potomac was reached, the Confederate concentration came to nearly twenty-five thousand.

General Early gave up-to-date information to General Lee from New Market on June 30. Early said his troops were in fine condition and spirits; there was no difficulty about supplies; and the crops in the Valley were fine and abundant. He assured Lee, "I shall lose no time."[7]

On July 1 General Evans once again began a diary, the Valley Campaign Diary, which contains almost daily details of his army service up to the close of 1864.[8] Entries for the first week bear out that Early was right in saying he would "lose no time." From the bivouac at Strasburg to the crossing of the Potomac at Shepherdstown, Evans' diary figures add up to eighty-one more miles of marches in five days.

STRASBURG BIVOUAC
July 1st 1864—Friday

Anniversary 1st day of Gettysburg—

Marched 3½ a.m. down valley pike to mill 1 mi. S.W. of Strasburg

Encamped near pike at 2½ p.m.

Pleasant until 11 a.m. Afterward very hot.

Rain 3½ p.m.

Hdqrs. on high hill overlooking the valley in which Strasburg lies, affording beautiful view.

Total distance marched 21 miles.

6. *Ibid.*, p. 168-69.
7. *O.R.*, series 1, vol. 51, part 1, p. 1028.
8. See Appendix B for full text of Valley Diary of 1864.

KERNSTOWN BIVOUAC
July 2nd—Saturday
Marched 3¼ a.m. Passed through Strasburg, Middletown,
Newton & Kernstown. Very hot.
Encamped ½ mile N.W. Kernstown near pike at 1 a.m.
Distance marched 18 miles.

July 3rd—Sunday
Marched 3½ a.m.
Passed through Winchester 4½ a.m. on valley pike toward
Martinsburg.
5¼ a.m. Artillery firing heard ahead.
Entered Martinsburg.
Place evacuated by Yankees.
Quantities of stores, etc.
—24 miles—

July 4
Encamped near Martinsburg.
2½ o'clock p.m.
Marched on Shepherdstown pike to Duffield Station.
Encamped—11 miles.

July 5th
Daybreak marched to Shepherdstown.
Crossed Potomac by wading. Marched on Sharpsburg
road 1 mi. turned to the right through fields leaving
Sharpsburg to the right, marching toward Harpers
Ferry, passing along a dull road running with the
canal. Halted about 6 mi. from Harpers Ferry & en-
camped near—iron works. Posted pickets—

July 6th
Marched on Harpers Ferry—
Skirmishing—cut a road with pocket knives & attacked
enemy in rear.

July 7th
Fought on Maryland Heights all day.
8th. March toward Frederick City.
9th. Battle of Monocacy.
Wounded severely—

This last succinct phrase refers to Evans' fourth wound of the war. His third wound had been a slight one in the Wilderness, "enough to draw blood." This next wound was serious. Some years after the battle, he wrote of this experience in notes among his papers:

The battle occurred on the banks of the Monocacy River near Frederick City in Maryland,[9] July 9, 1864:— and was brought on by the effort of Gen. Lew Wallace commanding United States forces to arrest the march of *Genl. Early on Washington City.*

The Federal army was thrown across our line of advance and entrenched across a *field* which had been reaped of the wheat & where the *shocks* were standing thickly all over it. Early ordered Gordon to attack with one of his brigades & follow up with others. Gordon selected my brigade to make the attack. We formed in the edge of a wood, and at the signal moved out into the open field in full view of the enemy (*posted* in *two* lines) who commenced firing at once. We advanced steadily without returning the fire immediately and in splendid line. The advantages were all on the side of the enemy as they had full sweep at us for 400 yards before we could reach them, and we advanced under the embarrassment of the interspersed *wheat shocks* which stood in our way. Just at the moment of the first shock of the two lines I was shot through my body from my horse and fell a hard stunning fall just immediately in front of my old regiment the 31st Ga. I was galloping along the front at the moment with Captain Gordon[10] my aide cheering the brigade forward & of course was a conspicuous mark for thousands of Federal rifles. I did that thing often before and after that day without being hit, but on that day I rode in the path of one bullet. Two soldiers took me up and bore me back across

9. The battlefield was on the farm of McCurdy family, ancestors of Senator Charles McCurdy Mathias of Maryland. General Wallace is more lastingly renowned for his famous book, *Ben Hur*, than he is for his defense of Washington.
10. Capt. Eugene Gordon, brother of Gen. John B. Gordon. Evans mentioned Captain Gordon in his diary of Winter Quarters, 1864.

the river on a blanket to a house. [Captain] Gordon knew what to do—He gave the Senior Colonel notice of my fall & the gallant line swept right on. The fire was exceedingly hot—The brigade suffered heavy loss in officers. At one point the charge hesitated and for a moment halted within a short distance of the enemy's breastworks. At this juncture [Captain] Gordon acted on my general instructions to do in my absence what he thought I would do if present and riding along the line inspired the brave fellows afresh so that they charged again and went so impetuously forward as to drive the Federal force before them—General Gordon meanwhile had advanced other brigades, and the victory was made complete. At dark the surgeons probed the wound and cut out the ball. I was shot in two places at this battle, one through my left arm, the other through my left side the ball lodging in my left side. The surgeons at my request worked fast and hurried me off because Early was moving to Washington. My wound was so threatening that my surgeons sought to dissuade me from my purpose to move with them on to Washington. But I had a horror of *Captivity*—so I refused to take an opiate during the surgical operation. I took the risk myself; the surgeons did the best they could, but as a consequence of that haste I suffered eleven years from the wound. Procuring a litter ambulance for myself and Capt. Eugene Gordon my aide who was also wounded I followed on that night at the rear of my brigade. I went down to Washington, was present at the demonstration made against it, then returned with the army, recrossing the Potomac & came to Richmond. My wound disabled me nearly three months from the field.

There is a family tradition that states that a complication made the wound more severe: doctors believed the ball had lodged on one side and probed for it there, only to find that it had penetrated to the other side of Evans' back so they had to operate there, also, to extract the ball.

What Evans meant by this wound causing him to suffer for eleven years relates to another circumstance. He carried a package of straight pins in the side pocket of his uniform jacket. When the ball that struck him tore through that pocket, it broke some of those pins into small pieces, and some bits were forced inside his body; these evidently were not extracted by his surgeons. For years after the war, he would have an infection appear some place and when he would open the spot, a part of one of those pins would be found to have worked to the surface.[11]

On July 10, after the victory at the Monocacy Bridge, General Early pushed on toward Washington in excessive heat and dust, marching thirty miles. On July 11, he advanced almost within sight of the White House, on the upper extension of what today is Sixteenth Street, and occupied the deserted home of Francis P. Blair, a presidential confident since Andrew Jackson's administration.

Early held a conference of war there that night. One of his staff, Capt. Henry Kyd Douglas, noted drolly that although the generals and their staffs were considerate of their enemies' real estate, he felt "compelled to say that the wine cellar of Mr. Blair was much depleted before they got away."[12]

Breckinridge, Gordon, and Ramseur met at that night conference, and an assault for the next day was agreed upon. However, the next morning, Early found the enemy had been strongly reinforced. After consulting his division commanders, Early became satisfied the assault would be attended with such great sacrifice that, even if successful, his army would be unable to win a victory. He reported to Lee that he "reluctantly determined to retire."[13]

The few days after Evans' wound at Monocacy are sketchily described in his diary:

[July] 10th & 11th—rode to Washing[ton]—in ambulance—
12 Crossed Potomac at Conrad's Ferry & went to Leesburg—
13th Stayed in Leesburg.
14th to 19th Trip to Richmond.
20—22—in Richmond.
23rd Started for home.

11. Myrta Lockett Avary, "Shot Full of Pins in Battle," *Atlanta* (Georgia) *Journal* (September 3, 1933), is a story on Clement Evans.
12. Douglas, *Stonewall*, p. 294.
13. *O.R.*, series 1, vol. 37, part 1, p. 348, for Early's report.

General Early had been almost too successful in drawing away enough Federal troops from around Richmond to relieve the pressure there on the main body of the Army of Northern Virginia.

Under duress from the powers of the Washington government, General Grant had sent Maj. Gen. James B. Ricketts' Sixth Corps infantry division to reinforce General Wallace. These were the veterans who shot General Evans off his horse at Monocacy. The Nineteenth Corps was ordered there from Fort Monroe, and the rest of the Sixth Corps at Petersburg was directed to proceed to relieve Washington.[14] However, Grant still had more than enough army to hold Lee and keep the pressure on Richmond and Petersburg.

Clement's route home was circuitous. He had ridden the most direct route through Tennessee with Lawton's brigade in June 1862. Allie had taken the same one when she joined her husband in Virginia in January 1863. By September 1864, this direct route had been cut between Atlanta and Knoxville by Sherman.[15]

The wounded Clement had to be transported on the alternate Confederate rail route south, which took him from Weldon to the seaport of Wilmington, North Carolina. From Wilmington he went to Branchville, South Carolina, on the main line from Charleston to Augusta. After he arrived in Augusta, his route dropped south to Millen, Georgia, in order to connect with the main line from Savannah to Macon.

When Clement made the statement in his diary for July 23, "Started for home," that home was in dire trouble, and not just from severed rail connections. Three days before the diary entry, Gen. William T. Sherman was knocking at the door of Atlanta, Georgia. On July 20 Federals had crossed Peachtree Creek and a battle had followed about two miles below Buckhead, and on July 22, they had launched the Battle of Atlanta.[16]

News of Clement's wound and its severity had preceded him, for he wrote to his daughter, Ida, from Richmond on July 19, on stationery "provided" by the U.S. Christian Mission. Printed on the letterhead was a message:

14. Porter, *Campaigning*, p. 237.
15. Coulter, *Confederate States*, vol. 7, p. 269.
16. William T. Sherman, *War is Hell! William T. Sherman's Personal Narrative of His March Through Georgia*, Mills Lane, ed. (Savannah, Georgia: Bee Hive Press, 1974), p. 974.

The U. S. Christian Commission sends this as the soldier's messenger to his home.

Let it hasten to those who wait for tidings.

"Fight the good fight of Faith."

July 19/[18]64
Richmond

My dear Daughter

I hope you all are not alarmed about my being wounded. I am doing very well, & shall soon go home. I will telegraph to you when I start. I want Ma to meet me in Macon.

My love to all.

Your Pa

[Clement was already on his way to Georgia before Allie heard of his wound. She was not in Lumpkin to see the letter to Ida because, as her letter of July 21 hereafter shows, she was in Albany. This is why he sent the letter to Ida.]

Albany, Georgia July 21, 1864

My dear darling,

I have not written to you in more than a week. I haven't had a letter from you in three. I thought if your letters couldn't come to me mine could not reach you and I concluded to wait until you were back on this side of the Potomac before I wrote again. I noticed the Yankee's account of Ewell's corps having recrossed this side and I do hope I will soon get letters from you my dear darling. I do want to hear from you so bad. I have read every paper that I could get my hands on carefully. I think you are safe if you are not sick. What if my poor darling is sick so far off and I know nothing about it. I shall prize a letter when I get it. I have been up here a few days and will stay a few days longer. I came up with Sallie Campfield. We are staying with Mrs. Catchings. Everything and everybody is all excitement about a Yankee raid [Lovell Rousseaus']. All the men have gone to Andersonville and they are looking for the Yankees there every day. When last heard from they were in ten miles of Columbus ten thousand strong. It would be awful if they should liberate all those prisoners and turn them loose here among us. They would ruin the whole country. Ma left the boy with his Auntie, pa. I want to see him real bad and haven't been from him but a little while. I expect to be home about the seventh or eighth of August. It will soon be here. I am almost crazy to see Ida but can't go any sooner. Sister begs me so hard to stay with her as long as I possibly can. I met Pike Hill in Albany the day we came up. He was apparently very glad to meet me, insisted on my spending some time with them. Mrs. Hill came over yesterday eve to see me and I am to go in the morning to see her and spend a day or so. Hill has gone to Anderson. Every man in the whole country has gone. There is nobody here but women and Negroes. It is distressing times. I hope they will not have to stay long though. I had a letter from Ida last week. She says she has written and written to papa and he dont get her letters. She seems very much distressed about it. Well darling another month is almost gone.

I shall be glad when the last day comes. I want to see you so bad. Got so much to tell you. When the war ends and we are together again I dont think I shall ever tire of talking with you. I don't think I should get through if I talked to you ten years. I am making all my arrangements to come to see you just as soon as the army gets quiet. How much happiness I have lain up and promised myself in the future. Ida is very anxious to come with me to see you but I will leave that all together with you. You will know how everything is situated and of course can judge what will be for the best. Must Ma bring he [Lawton], pa. I expect you will whip he lots when he gets there. He can talk real good, say anything. Mrs. Catchings sends her kindest regards to you and says she is not the same old sister Catchings she used to be. That she is the old woman now, got a grown daughter. She is fleshier than she used to be, a huge woman I tell you. I am having a good time up here, all but hearing from you. I know I will have a letter when I get back to Sister's. Fannie Catchings sends her compliments and says find her a gallant sweet heart. I will write again in a day or so. Good by darling. God bless you and grant that you are safe.

Your Wife

When Allie finally learned that Clement had been wounded, she began, without a moment's hesitation, to go and find him. She did not know when he might arrive, but she found out his route and started on her quest. Getting to Macon and anticipating going farther to intercept him, she was waiting at the railroad station to make connections when someone told her a wounded officer was there. Clement wrote about it after the war:

> She heard he was shot through the body in Maryland and the papers reported that he was killed. News came late sometimes but when this arrived she hastened away toward Virginia and by a special providence while she was trying to find some one "just from Virginia" in the Macon depot she was informed that Clement was aboard badly wounded. She soon found him of course and had him taken to the hotel. Next day [we] were on the way to Cuthbert & thence to Lumpkin.[17]

17. From a memorandum by Evans for his daughter, Lucy. See Kinfolk in Appendix A.

Portrait of General Evans which hangs in the
Georgia State Capitol Building, Atlanta, Georgia

432

Chapter 23

THE LAST VALLEY
CAMPAIGN BEGINS

Of course, there are no more letters or diary entries until September 1864, when Clement wrote to Allie from Macon on his way back to duty in Virginia. During this interim, Evans was at home, recovering from his wounds suffered at Monocacy.

Four occurrences of note transpired in Virginia while Evans was away on sick leave. Only three involved his command. The one that did not was a bizarre and unique incident of the war—the Battle of the "Crater"[1] at Petersburg, where a tunnel dug from the Federal trenches under Confederate defenses was exploded. Poorly led Federal forces, supported by Black troops, plunged forward after the mine exploded, and many became entrapped within the Crater. From above, Confederates shot the Yankees almost as in target practice.[2] Again, Grant came off with unequal losses of about four thousand, to fifteen hundred for the Confederates. Petersburg was saved.[3]

The next incident involved Evans' command indirectly. It was the burning of Chambersburg, Pennsylvania, by Brig. Gen. John McCausland and his cavalry. On the same morning the Crater blew up in Petersburg, the first incendiary torch was applied to Chambersburg. On specific orders from General Early, McCausland led his men to seek retribution and revenge for the wanton depredations against civilian property by Hunter in the Valley. McCausland was instructed by Early to exact a ransom of $100,000 in gold or $500,000 in cash as restitution for Hunter's damage, or, in lieu of payment, the Confederates would set fire to the town.

---

1. *O.R.*, series 1, vol. 40, part 1, pp. 556, 787.
2. *Ibid.*, p. 752. Lee's report.
3. Freeman, *R. E. Lee*, vol. 3, p. 467, *et seq.* Losses shown at p. 477.

No funds being forthcoming, Chambersburg was set aflame at 9 a.m. on July 30. The scrupulous execution of General Early's orders forever clouded the reputation of General McCausland, who was bitterly denounced by his companion on the raid, Brig. Gen. Bradley Johnson, for the unbridled and unrestrained behavior of McCausland's troopers.[4] The breech between Early's two cavalry commanders was exacerbated by an incident at Moorefield during the raiders' retreat from Chambersburg. Union Brig. Gen. William W. Averell attacked General Johnson in a surprise assault on August 7, and routed his Confederate brigade, while McCausland, three miles away, escaped the attack and did not come to his fellow general's aid. The future of General Evans' brigade was put in jeopardy by this quarrel, because General Early's inability to use the cavalry effectively was a problem for his valley army.[5]

Another event during Evans' sick leave was not foreseen as of such great importance, but developed into a major problem over the next few months in all the actions of Evans' brigade. The ineffective Federal general, David Hunter, was relieved of his command in the Shenandoah Valley, and Maj. Gen. Philip H. Sheridan, was appointed to succeed him. The latter was an energetic and forceful young West Pointer, a man of the same stamp as General Grant, who recommended Sheridan for the job.[6] The effective date of Sheridan's assumption of command was August 6.

The last episode that General Evans missed was the third battle at Winchester on September 19, followed by a Confederate retreat to Fisher's Hill, where another hard battle took place on September 22. Both engagements were defeats for General Early. However, the odds were not in his favor, for General Sheridan had been strengthened in men, equipment, and supplies, between August 6 and mid-September. As of September 10, Sheridan reported 45,509 officers and men present for duty, of whom 6,465 were the best-equipped cavalry heretofore in the war. Early's strength, in comparison, was about 12,150, of whom 2,900 were cavalry.[7]

4. *O.R.*, series 1, vol. 43, part 1, p. 7, dated August 10, 1864.
5. *Ibid.*, vol. 37, part 1, pp. 334, 354. Freeman, *Lieutenants*, vol. 4, p. 571, et seq.
6. *O.R.*, series 1, vol. 43, part 1, p. 709.
7. *Ibid.*, pp. 60-61, and note. Also Freeman, *Lieutenants*, vol. 4, p. 577.

For Abraham Lincoln, running for re-election, the battle at Winchester was especially good news because, up until this achievement, very little encouraging news for the North had come out of the Valley since Early's corps had gone there in June. On the day after Winchester, Lincoln dictated a message to Sheridan from the Executive Mansion: "Have just heard of your great victory. God bless you all, officers and men. Strongly inclined to come up and see you."[8]

In his report of Winchester, Early again blamed the cavalry for its comparative inefficiency, which he said turned the scales against him. About the fight at Fisher's Hill, Early said he had hoped to check Sheridan's progress but the enemy "drove back the cavalry . . . and got in the rear of my left flank, and when I tried to remedy this the infantry got into a panic and I found it impossible to rally it."

That night, Early began to retreat. He halted next day to drive back pursuing enemy cavalry and on the following day halted to stop Union infantry units. On the night of September 23, when Early arrived at Port Republic, most of his retreating command was fairly well reorganized and reunited.[9]

While the episodes at Winchester and Fisher's Hill were occurring, Clement was traveling. His diary was resumed on September 13: "Left home for the Army." What a dark day it was for Allie and Clement when he left to join his brigade in Virginia. By that time, the news in Georgia was black as night, for by September 15, General Sherman had consolidated his position in occupied Atlanta.[10]

Evans' rail trip deviated a little from Weldon Road along the coast, down which he had come to Georgia as a casualty, for one of his letters is posted from Greensboro, North Carolina. This was another alternate route that could be used instead of going over to coastal Wilmington.[11]

En route to Virginia, Clement wrote several letters home:

Macon, Ga. Thursday
Sept. 15, 1864

8. *O.R.*, series 1, vol. 43, part 1, p. 61.
9. *Ibid.*, vol. 43, pp. 555-57.
10. Sherman, *War is Hell*, p. 115.
11. *O.R.*, series 1, vol. 42, part 2, p. 1198.

My dear Darling

Parted again—I do so much long for the time to come when we can stay together—but we know how to submit to the separation and make the best of it. I felt so sorry for you when I looked back at the starting of the train, seeing you in the Carriage. I forgot my own grief, almost.

I obtained a seat in the ladies' car and slept to Smithville; then a fresh accession of Ladies brought me to my feet and for nearly all the way to Macon I had to stand up. At Smithville I offered my seat to a Lady who had just come in, which she very politely thanked me for, and commenced conversation with me. I found out that she was Mrs. Rose, living in Alabama, formerly Miss Kate Jones, related to the Jones of Cuthbert. Her father was Mr. Jones' brother. Between Anderson and Oglethorpe the train of the day before had run off the track killing and wounding a large number of Yankee prisoners and others, the precise number, however, I could not learn. The broken cars and torn up track prevented the trains from coming through and consequently, all had to get out and stay two or three hours in the woods, until the down train arrived and a change of baggage could be effected. I was assisting Mrs. Rose, and a young Lady who was with her, when I heard Mrs. Rose ask her if she had not been staying sometime with Mr. Hill at Albany. She replied that she had. This made me think she might have known you when I asked her, if it was at Pike Hill's she had been staying. She told me yes, there with her brother Ross Towns. When I told her that my wife had spent a day with Mrs. Hill, some few weeks ago she at once called your name and we drafted an acquaintance on the spot. Tony Hill was on the train, but I didn't know him until this incident occurred. I took care of them to Fort Valley when they got off the train to go to Columbus.

I had quite an interesting talk with old Mrs. Lewis, who was on a visit to her mother-in-law Elbert Lewis of Oglethorpe. She told me that [illegible] leaf was mighty good to smoke for cough, especially asthmatic afflictions. "Life

436

everlasting" was growing where we sat, and another old Lady sitting close by told me that it was heap better than hops or peach tree leaves to put in bread. I told her, that I had heard peach tree leaves were powerful good to make bread rise—It was a good old fashioned motherly talk about "ailments" etc., which you know I delight in.

I saw old Jimmy Clark at Fort Valley, but did not speak to him. He was telling a crowd around him about the Yankee doings at Atlanta. A Yankee General has made his house Head Quarters and promised to take care of his furniture etc. for him; I heard that Sidney Scott was here a day or two ago; but heard nothing of Ed. Ramsy.

In consequence of the delay yesterday I've failed to connect here, and I therefore had to remain, for twenty-four hours: How I wish I had not started—I came to the Lanier House where I have secured every attention. Being very tired I went to bed early, but had scarcely got off my clothes, before I was sent for to the bar room of the Hotel to see two Gentlemen, who had called to see me. I went down and who should be there but Clem Brown and Ben Watts.[12] They had been on the look out for me and seeing my name registered sent for me. Clem Brown is now staying at the Floyd Hospital. He still belongs to Benning's Brigade but has done hardly any service for eighteen months, in consequence of Chronic diarrhea. He now has also a very bad bone-felon on his middle finger left hand which has stiffened the two upper joints. Ben Watts is in the registration department, employed in getting up statistics of the Resources of the Confederacy. He is a very smart fellow and has accumulated a fund of valuable information; He says that there is no danger of our failing to feed our armies abundantly. That the present report will show a supply of bacon double the report of last year, with corn and wheat abundant. He says that the statistics gathered from the whole country show beyond doubt that we are growing steadily stronger every year in all the appliances

12. See Appendix A for relatives.

437

of war. Is it not strange that every year in all the appliances of war some people think the army will starve because the wheat crop of Stewart County has failed and the hogs dying with the Cholera? Clem Brown says his wife is very anxious to see me. He has not mentioned receiving my letter but spoke rather despondingly of his money matters. I was in hopes that in meeting him here I would replenish my purse. He drops many expressions of devotion to me which are doubtless entirely sincere. By the way, a page is due to Riddle. I met him this morning and he was delighted to see me. Showing me where his rooms were he made me promise to go over to have my photograph taken. I went, found him fixed up well and engaged in Government work. He is Chief of the Photograph bureau of this department and is lending very valuable service to the Government. My Photograph has more the appearance of a preacher than a fierce fighting Brigadier. I don't know how to look scary and belligerent. I am sorry I did not have my uniform in which "to secure my shadow."

Riddle lost all his furniture, his Negro woman, cow &c when Atlanta fell. He succeeded in getting off his family and has sent them to his father-in-law.

I find a great deal of despondency here on account of the military situation in Georgia—Everybody appears to look to reinforcements, from the Virginia army as being the only hope—They think that Genl [John Bell] Hood cannot successfully meet Sherman on any line which he may select for his advance and that he can take Augusta, Milledgeville and Macon. Sherman told a Lady a few days ago that he would take all these places. But the critical nature of affairs will arouse the Government and I believe that in a few weeks there will be quite a favorable turn. The Prisoners at Andersonville had become very restless and turbulent just before their removal, so much so that it was feared an outbreak would take place. I understand that the main body of them have been sent to Charleston.

Well, darling, I have given you all the news. If I had known that I should have to stay here twenty four hours

I certainly would have brought you along. Everything looks lonesome to me because you are not with me. I know too that you are feeling so badly. That is worse than if I suffered alone. I wish you could be perfectly contented about our separations, enjoying yourself just as if I was with you. Or at least that you would not grieve. Try to be cheerful. Put on a look of cheerfulness and the feeling itself will come after awhile.

I shall be anxious about the little man, and about Father until I hear from you. Go to see Father and read such parts of this letter to him as will be interesting. Tell him I will remember my promise to meet him in the Good World. Give my love to Ida. She must write to me every week.

Give my love to Mother, Clem, Mat and all the others—

And now good bye again. I will write on the route from Richmond.

Good bye, God bless you my precious Darling.

Your Husband

Branchville, So. Ca.
Friday, Noon, Sept. 16, 1864

My dear

I left Macon yesterday 4 o'clock p.m. [obliterated] took the train with me as far as his home which is sixty miles south of Macon on the Central railroad. He brags very much on his wife being so smart and energetic. Showed me a letter which he had recently received as a sample of her style, and handwriting. She is teaching school near her home. He incidentally mentioned "forty thousand dollars" as the value of his property. From his own account I expect he spent all of his own property before his second marriage. Well, I still have some hopes of our $350.00 though he did not refer to it. Ben May, [Col.] J. M. Clark, and Marshall Clark, were also on the train. I suppose you have heard the report that Ed. Rawson went Northward under Sherman's proclamations. Clark told me of it and said he always distrusted him. I understood Marshall Clark to say that Rawson would

439

go to Canada. But I doubt all that. Vermont will probably be able to hold him. Atlanta, in all probability, will share the fate of Fredericksburg in the event of its evacuation by Sherman. He will burn it to retaliate for Chambersburg or else will set it on fire under pretense of having Military stores in various buildings. Owners of real estate there can scarcely claim more than the land. At Griswoldville several hundred families are living in box cars along the railroad track. They have their beds, tables, chairs and &c in there arranged just like rooms in homes. I suppose they cook out doors. They are refugees from above Atlanta. This class of people are suffering very much.

There is a great deal of feeling against both Jeff Davis and [Georgia governor] Joe Brown. I heard men curse both together. Georgia is at this time more despondent than at any time during the war, but I believe that in a month the clouds will lift themselves and show us a bright sun and a clear sky beyond them.

I have had a good seat all the way, but especially since leaving Augusta. The crowd was very great from Macon to Millen, but since then the trains have not been packed. I have an entire seat to myself, which you know is something rare.

I will mail this somewhere. Have you received my photographs sent by Col. J. M. Clark. What do you think of them?

I suppose Sister is gone to Albany—I shall write to her from Richmond.

> Good bye, Darling.
> Your Husband

N. C. R. Road
Saturday Sept. 17/[18]64

[No salutation]

I can hardly realize that we are parted again, and that all the power of steam is rapidly hurrying me away from you. But a few days ago how I enjoyed being with you—now I close my eyes and see you so plainly— I embrace you in my arms, my lips rave to kiss you, but

440

it is my imagination procuring the deception. Four long, uneasy months! How can I bear it even as well as heretofore—I hated to leave you this time worse than ever before. What will I do if this wretched struggle continues another year? I do pray earnestly for peace—With that will come happiness to so many. So far I have missed no connection since leaving Macon and without further bad luck will reach Richmond tomorrow morning. I will stay there two days, (Sunday & Monday 18 & 19)—It will then take me four days to get to the army; unless Early has come up the valley. I will probably resume command on the 24th or 25th inst.

Rev. Mr. Hunter "Children's friend" still distributes tracts for donations on the train—I gave him $5.00.

My money holds out well—The "Old issue" is hardly current, but people will take it when one has no other sort. If you find any trouble with yours you had better send it up to Columbus to be exchanged, or send it to me.

Nothing of interest has occurred since I wrote yesterday. I cannot travel incognito successfully. Somewhere my rank becomes known in the car, and I am amused at the occasional looks of curiosity. The Soldiers as usual are as jolly as they can be. Many a poor citizen whose hat was uncouth has been seriously invited to [illegible]. All through South Carolina they begged everybody for "just one little chaw of [illegible] if you please, Mister."

I left my carpet-bag key in the Rockaway or at home. Did you find it?

Here we are at Greensboro—where I must mail this if possible. Love to all—Good bye. Kiss Ida & Pa's little rascal too. Good bye.

Your Husband

Richmond, Va.
Monday morning Sept. 19, [18]64
My dear darling,

Here I am in Richmond, again, separated so far from my dear little wife. Poor darling I am so sorry for you.

I know the last week has been an unhappy one to you.

I have not been on the Streets yet, nor even read the morning paper, consequently I have no news. Everybody appears to be expecting another great battle near Petersburg. I have not heard a word from old Jubal [Early] since I left home—I expect he is still in the valley.

The loss of my key to my carpet bag was the source of sore vexation this morning. I could devise no means to open it, and had to drag my clean clothes out of one corner. I will either get a key, or have to break the lock.

I am going to try for Probe's Commission to day or tomorrow, and a leave of absence for him at the same time—If I succeed Probe will start home about the 24th or 25th, and so will reach Albany about the 1st of October—

I feel worse about leaving you this time than ever before. I am afraid if I go home another time I shall be tempted to desert. It is so hard to be parted from you so long and at such a great distance. I will hear from you so seldom and the letters will be so long coming! How shall I make time fly? I wish I could sleep four months. Don't you think by making arrangements immediately about hiring the Negroes you could come in December, at least by Christmas? If you set your time to start to me on Christmas day, I think you could work up to it— Get Bob to see Fitzgerald, or write him a note proposing to hire him our Negroes taking half in provisions at Government price & the other half in money. I am so anxious to see you already that I am tempted to write to you to come the first of November.

This is my fourth letter since leaving home. The Photographs; have you rec'd them? I am very anxious to hear from the little man, and father. I do hope both are well. I know you have written to me, but it may be a week or two before I receive the letter.

I will write again—give Ida my love—Tell her to write me a long letter every week—My love to all—

Goodbye—God bless my darling.

Your Husband

My precious Darling

I have had the blues nearly all day. I think about you so far away from me, downhearted I know. Please try to be better satisfied and write so to me. I could bear our separation so much better if you were only contented.

I expected to leave Richmond tomorrow morning but the Yankees have made a raid on Orange C.H. and thereafter the Central Railroad so much that no train will leave tomorrow. For the same reason no train came from Staunton today—I am thus cut off from the valley for a day or two—

I took supper with McCrumby tonight. He insists on my staying with him while here and I shall put up there tomorrow. I went with him and Mrs. Saulsbury to hear Rev. Mr. Duncan preach tonight & have just returned.

The brigade is still in the valley near Winchester, but a part of Early's force (Kershaw's division) has come to Gordonsville. I think we are likely to remain in the valley for some weeks and then suddenly pounce on Grant. I hear of no probability of Hood being reinforced from here—Gen. Lee needs every man he has and has called for all the detailed men in Virginia.

I wish you would send Uncle Ira Potter word that I find I can do nothing about Capt. Potter's pay until I get to the Brigade & that then I will write him fully.

The prevailing opinion here seems to be that McClellan has no chance for election. His letter of acceptance has driven from him the support of the peace men and left him no support except the war democrats. Some hope however that Lincoln's re-election will cause another revolution and secession, but all admit that much depends on the bloody month of October. Gen. Lee, it is said, has the plan of deliverance in his head and that a few weeks more will unfold it all—

The Government is exchanging all the new issue [of money] for all the old which is preserved. If you find any difficulty in disposing of yours, send it in a letter by some one to Mr. E. Saulsbury, agt. Ga. Relief & C., No.

111 Main Street Richmond, Va. with a note requesting him to exchange it & keep it for me.

This is a poor letter, darling, but I could not make it better. God bless you my precious love. I hope before long to be again with your dear self. Give my love to all. Tell Ida to remember how smart I want her to be when I see her next—Kiss "The doodee" for papa.

Good bye—Good bye

Your Husband

Staunton [Va.] Sept. 22 [1864]

I am here safely & will have to stay here until the 24th, and will therefore reach the brigade on the 25th.

I can get no news from the casualties in Co. E, 31st [Georgia] during the fight of the 19th beyond Winchester.

Maj. [Rodolphus T.] Pride is wounded in the foot severely—Col. [John H.] Lowe very slightly wounded.

The command is perfectly safe so stated & holding a good position twenty miles from here. I write very hurriedly so as to give this letter in private hands. I will write you a long one tomorrow.

Good bye. Your Husband

Staunton, Va.
Friday Sept. 23, 1864

My precious Darling

I will first write to you—because I must write several letters to day, and yours must be written before I get at all tired. I did not get off this morning. Tomorrow the stage leaves very early and I have secured passage, but will not reach the brigade until the 25th.

Several of our wounded have reached this place, from the battle on the 19th and I have just returned from a visit to them at the hospital. There is not a single one here from Capt. Harrison's company, nor can I hear that any of his men were either killed or wounded. The accounts which I get from different quarters represent that we fought a largely superior force to ours, but had re-

444

peatedly repulsed them until the enemy forced a very heavy force of Cavalry against our left where our cavalry was posted, driving them in, and thus flanking us completely. This forced us to fall back. I have just talked with Genl. Breckinridge who says our entire loss in killed, wounded and prisoners, will not exceed twelve hundred. He captured a few over four hundred prisoners of the enemy, and I am certain from all the statements made that we inflicted a heavier loss in killed and wounded than we received—

Gen. Early marched back to Fisher's Hill which is about twenty two miles this side of Winchester, bringing off all his wagon trains. A few of our very severely wounded was left in Winchester. Early's present position is perfectly secure, and no fears of holding it are felt—Send word if you can up to Green Hill that Lieut. Green is slightly wounded; I. Graham severely in the face; and W. Ward very severely and left prisoner. They all belong to Capt. Cody's Company—So far as I can learn, but two were killed and some twenty five wounded. In my brigade about ten or twelve killed and fifty or sixty wounded—Three of [our] artillery [pieces] were taken from us by the enemy—Gen. Breckinridge has been ordered to command the department of Southwest Virginia and leaves here to day for Lynchburg. Possibly this may look to some movement against Knoxville, Nashville, Chattanooga &c to help out Hood—I understood yesterday that Pres. Davis & [Gen. P. G. T.] Beauregard had gone[13] to Georgia. If this is so, you know all about it by this time. I hope Beauregard will be placed in command there. I do not think it at all probable that any of Early's command will go to Georgia, but I still believe we will hold the valley awhile longer, and then re-inforce Gen. Lee at Richmond.

Prisoners taken from the enemy on the 19th report that Grant was in command, with reinforcements.

---

13. Jefferson Davis, *The Rise and Fall of the Confederate Government*, 2 vols. (New York: D. Appleton & Co., 1881), vol. 2, pp. 564-66. Davis tells of this visit with General Beauregard and discusses his controversy with Governor Joe Brown of Georgia.

Staunton is a busy depot now. Here all the wounded & sick are brought to be distributed elsewhere. Here the Advance Stores are collected & sent to the army, as well as Quartermaster & some commissary stores. And here they send all returning soldiers in bodies of one to two hundred to be armed and sent down the valley. Good rations of fine new flour and splendid beef are abundant. The apple crop is also good and of these the soldiers get a good share you know.

When I leave Staunton I shall feel like I am cut off from you sure enough; like I had severed the last remaining link, but I will try to endure it all patiently, very patiently; waiting in hope for the days to go by and [the] end of all this to come. No money could buy my hopes of the future. I find so much delight in building air-castles as they are sometimes called, but which will be glorious realities sometime. All day long my mind leaps beyond the present into the happy days to come, revels in the sweetest anticipation, & forgets its present sorrows in dwelling on future joys. I should go mad but for Hope. I would be utterly miserable did I not know that this could not last always. I am happy in thinking that a few months more is all that is before me of the present suffering and after that happiness with you. I will take as good care of myself as possible. I remember that your happiness is bound up in mine and that my life is so dear to you, so necessary to you, that I have no right to heedlessly put it in jeopardy. You know I will do my duty and in doing that can commit myself to the Good Lord. Bless your dear heart, my greatest suffering is mental, or from the heart, and on your account. My bodily hardships are pleasures compared to those. Write to me that you are resigned to the will of our Heavenly Father, that you patiently, contentedly, and even cheerfully endure our separation with the suspense of mind consequent upon the dangers surrounding me and I shall be so much happier than I am. My own contentment depends upon whether you are happy or not. Your feelings may always tell you precisely what mine are.

446

You are preparing now to come to see me are you not? Go ahead as briskly as possible and do not wait for January if you can arrange our business beforehand. Perhaps all the Negroes might be hired out in November, and you could come in December—I almost envy Col. [Rodolphus T.] Pride his wound. He has just returned from home, and now will go back again to stay two or three months; perhaps longer. I am afraid, though, to sigh for another wound, for fear that it might not be such as I could desire. But anyhow in less than four months you will be with me. All my dread is on account of your long fatiguing trip here. I will arrange to have you an escort and will try to meet you in Richmond—I suppose you can do with one trunk, but be sure to bring your nicest clothes and plenty of them, we may want to visit some. I will try to pick you up some valuables between now and then. Everett Harris mentioned my suit of Jeans. I told him about the visit of his Mother to us, & that you would bring the cloth when you came. If Mrs. Harris sends it in time I think it would be a good idea to send it to me by some one trusty and reliable, because you will not have room for it in your trunk. If you bring only one trunk I want that packed full of your own dressing. There are several ladies in the valley. Some of them left Winchester in such haste as to leave their trunks behind. Mrs. Gordon[14] was there, but I presume she is now at Woodstock, which is about 12 miles this side of the army— I have written 4 pages full & could write more, but I will write again tomorrow—Love to all—God bless you—

Your Husband

Staunton, Va.
Sept. 23, 1864

My dear Darling
I have written to you already to day and mailed the letter here, but I have an opportunity to send by safe hand to Richmond and will therefore write again. In my

14. Gordon, *Reminiscences*, p. 323.

today's letter I said that Early was safe at Fisher's Hill, and in a good position, from which the enemy were not likely to drive him, but the stage has just arrived bringing the news that the Cavalry again gave way, exposing our flank & compelling another retreat. The army was this morning at Woodstock, but I expect will fall back still farther this way. There was scarcely any fighting at Fisher's Hill, because as soon as Early was flanked his position was lost, and he ordered a retreat. The enemy are reported to be in heavy force, especially of Cavalry, while our Cavalry is not only weak but worthless. I cannot tell anything of the actual condition of affairs until I reach the army. If it is still unwhipped in spirit all will go as well because the valley affords many fine positions for defensive warfare, but if Sheridan or Grant (whichever is in command) more than doubles us in force, he may still flank us all the way to Staunton. I have not despaired from what I have heard of our ability to hold the valley because all these first accounts are usually exaggerations.

I will close my letter before going to bed, although I have obtained no new accounts of affairs which are at all encouraging. It is stated that we lost twelve more pieces of artillery at Fisher's Hill, but I cannot see how that is possible with the reported account of fighting. I am sorry that I have to rejoin my command under circumstances so discouraging, but as I have never yet participated in a defeat perhaps the tide will turn when I arrive. I think re-enforcements to Early are already on the way and that he may still be able to redeem all that he has lost.

As I go from here into almost immediate battle I place my trust in the Great One who so far has wonderfully preserved me, and will do with me as seemeth to Him best because I commit myself unreservedly to Him.

Give my love to my dear little daughter. Tell her to offer her little prayers to her Heavenly Father for her Pa—God bless her—Kiss Papa's "The doodee" for him. My love to all. I will write again tomorrow if I have any opportunity.

Goodbye. Goodbye my Darling. The good Lord keep you.

Your Husband

Chapter 24
EVANS RESUMES COMMAND

General Evans' Valley Diary entry for September 24, 1864, reads: "Reached the army at night retreating up the Valley. Camped about 15 mi. from Port Republic."[1] The letters, when he returned to his post of duty, are copious until the close of December 1864, and are more regular than ever before—almost daily. They contain a wealth of information on combat in the last campaign in the Shenandoah Valley.

> Brown's Gap. Sept. 26/[18]64
> Monday Morning

My dear Darling

Oh how mortified I was to find our splendid Corps in full retreat before the Yankee forces when I arrived at my command! My heart has bled with mortification; You have read the account of the Winchester battle of the 19th & the Fisher Hill affair; Both were defeats & both due to our weak & cowardly cavalry mixed with some bad Generalship. Our losses in *killed* & *wounded* are *very very* slight. We lost on the two occasions *18* pieces of artillery & many prisoners, but I cannot tell how many as they were scattered in the mountains & are still coming on to camp—I will give you a more detailed account in a letter which I will try to write to day. I was awake this morning to write this, and the mail carrier leaves at once.

Brown's Gap is in the Blue-ridge mountains, about 20 miles from Staunton and twelve or fifteen from the nearest main-valley-pike & Staunton. I suppose [it] is this morning in possession of the enemy!

I have seen Lucius, Archie, Cain, Rufe Thornton,

1. The Valley Diary is set out in full in Appendix B.

Henry Mansfield, Joe Clifton, Green Clifton, McKuthen—All were looking very well—The whole Brigade needs more clothing which I shall try to get.

I have not seen Lieut. Cox, but I suppose he is safe. The boys are all very glad to see me. It is a singular coincidence that just at this time two years ago I should return to the brigade from home and find it reduced in numbers just like it is now.[2]

I cannot tell what we are going to do. In fact it is useless for me to write prophecys to you because before the letter reaches you you will read in newspapers where we have been and what we have done.

It is getting very cold. It is nearly as cold now of nights as our winters usually are. These blankets hardly keep a body warm. I slept cold last night.

Of course there has not been enough time yet for me to have received a letter from you. How hard it is to wait in so much suspense, so long too, for your letters; You have already received five or six letters from me & know all about me, but I have not a word since I left.

Be content with a short letter this morning; If we stay here to day I will write you a long letter—Goodbye. God bless you.

Your Husband

Love to Ida—Bless her little heart—
How is "the Doodee?" [Lawton]

Brown's Gap, 3 m. from
Port Republic
Sept 26. 1864. Monday
10 o'clock A. M.

[No salutation]

I sent a letter off this morning—a short letter promising a longer one as soon as I had time. Perhaps I have time, now, but before I write another page orders to move may come.

I stayed one day in Staunton as I have already notified you. Saturday I took the stage to join my Command.

2. This was after sick leave, when he had typhoid fever and missed the Battle of Sharpsburg on September 17, 1862.

Rumors had already reached us of some great disaster at Fisher's Hill, which is a mile this side of Strasburg and is so strong sectionally and fortified so well, that all considered it impregnable to any direct attack, and that it could not be flanked except by a long detour. Therefore I stated publicly my disbelief of the report. But when we reached Harrisonburg the bad news was fully confirmed. Our army had been flanked and routed sure enough, about sunset on Thursday, at Fisher's Hill and were being re-organized near Mt. Jackson, but still retreating. Along the turn-pike to Harrisonburg the road was thronged with escaping citizens, hurrying along their cattle, sheep, with horses &c. Many soldiers without arms, and some wounded ones were also coming along the road with trains of wagons and ambulances. Our stage driver became alarmed and insisted that we should turn around and go back to Harrisonburg, but by persuasion & threats we forced him along. But horsemen coming along would say to him that he had better go no farther along the turnpike so excited his apprehension, that he finally turned around anyhow and would go no farther, leaving to us the alternative of going back to Harrisonburg, or being left afoot on the pike. We chose the latter alternative and shouldering our baggage set out to meet the retreating army which was about eight miles beyond us. Soon however our empty ambulance came along into which we got ourselves and proceeded on our journey. Here I met Green Clifton who had *dispersed* himself but bearing his brass horn gallantly on his shoulder, He told me that one half of my brigade was cut off in the mountains, under Col. Atkinson.[3] The balance being commanded by Col. Lowe.[4] From him I also learned that the brigade train of wagons had turned off on another road which I could get to, by leaving the

3. Henderson, *Roster*, vol. 3, p. 184. Col. Edward N. Atkinson, senior to Evans by three days in Lawton's brigade took command when Col. M. Douglass was mortally wounded at Sharpsburg. Atkinson was captured at Fredericksburg and Evans took command from December 1862 until General Gordon arrived, in April 1863. Atkinson was exchanged but was again captured at Fisher's Hill on September 22, 1864, as indicated in this letter.
4. *Ibid.*, p. 628. Col. John H. Lowe, succeeded Evans in command of the Thirty-first Georgia Regiment.

pike—orders to move at once. [Letter ends this way.]

Blue Ridge Mountains
Brown's Gap
Monday night.
Sept. 26, 1864

My dear Allie

This is my third letter written to you to day. I am sure you will not accuse me of neglecting you whenever I have the opportunity to write—Tired though I am still I remember how anxious you are to get the very latest intelligence from me.

In my last letter I was going on to tell you about leaving Staunton in the Coach Saturday morning, my difficulties on the way: how I heard rumors and then confirmations of the disaster at Fisher's Hill, how the Driver finally put myself & the other passengers out on the pike on account of his fear to go any farther, when I had to close my letter because orders came for me to move my brigade at once. I will not tell you the history of to day until I finish my narrative of Saturday and Sunday:—

After I got in the ambulance upon leaving the Stage Coach I continued to meet many citizens and soldiers on the road, all confirming the news that our army had been flanked out of Fisher's Hill in considerable disorder, and were still retreating before the enemy. When I met Green Clifton, he told me that the brigade train had turned off the pike on which the train was moving. Thinking I could certainly get my horse by this course I left the ambulance and walked in the direction pointed out but the train had passed before I reached the road. By this time our troops had reached & passed New Market, retreating in line of Battle by alternate divisions, followed by the enemy who posted artillery on the hills as they advanced, opening on our troops. I could see the firing, which was some six miles distant, but could not see the lines of troops. This was about five o'clock in the evening & having no horse I was obliged to be a spectator. About sunset an empty ambulance came along af-

453

fording me again an opportunity to ride, and I joined the general train which proceeded about six miles and then went into camp. The troops came on after night to the same place and also encamped until morning. Sunday we marched, not being pursued by the enemy, across the Shenandoah river, near Port Republic, not far from the celebrated Weyer's Cave, and came to this place.

I expect you have read full news-paper accounts of our defeat at Winchester on the 19th and at Fisher's Hill near Strasburg on Thursday the 22nd. The general blame is thrown on the cavalry who gave way on both occasions allowing the enemy to pour in on the left flank and rear of the infantry. Of course this happened, but the whole affair is due to that generalship which had the several divisions scattered so far apart on Sunday the 18th that they could not be on hand early Monday morning when the enemy advanced. Our forces had also been weakened by the addition of a new Corps [Wharton's division]—The troops were hurried into action confusedly, and the battle precipitated without sufficient reconnaissance. Our division had on Sunday been marched to Martinsburg, when considerable whiskey was obtained by certain officers, and marched back again ten miles, making nearly thirty miles in one day. Of course they were greatly fatigued, and Monday morning they were marched hurriedly about eight miles to the battle ground, thrown hastily into line and the fight commenced. Not withstanding all this we whipped their infantry force badly all the morning. The Signal Corps were reporting the fact that their wagon trains were moving to the rear, and their men running out of ranks back from the field when on our left the heavy firing gained ground down the Martinsburg road toward Winchester. Soon our Cavalry were seen dashing pell mell down the road, pursued hotly by the Yankees. It was an open rolling plain as far as the sight extended, bounded by the mountains, and the troops saw all, and when they saw heavy masses of Cavalry breaking through to their rear, and our own Cavalry flying in all directions, the timid first began to waver, and finally the lines gave way. The army was in

454

retreat. For the first time the whole Corps retreated from the battlefield during action and in daylight. The enemy however had been so severely handled that they were unwilling to pursue very closely, for we checked them from time to time close enough to save all our trains except a few wagons broken down and five pieces of artillery left on the field.

But Early wisely continued the retreat to Fisher's Hill where he reorganized his troops and placed the infantry in a strong position. They were burning to retrieve their reputation, and I have no doubt in the world that if the forces had been properly distributed along the line that [there would have been] no disaster, but on the contrary a real victory would have occurred had the enemy attacked. But strange to say the weak, wavering fearful Cavalry were placed where the position was naturally weak & without fortification, while the infantry were posted in the strongest natural positions well fortified. The enemy massed his force on our left against the Cavalry, notice was given but no movement was made to counteract this disposition of his troops. About five o'clock P.M. he attacked, the cavalry gave and in heavy force the enemy pierced his way to our rear and commenced firing down our lines. No brigade or division was in reserve; all were in the trenches, and the flanking force could not be met by any hasty change of front. The infantry [Ramseur's] on the left next to the cavalry retreated rapidly—my brigade was on the extreme right, but every division was gone before Gordon's men had notice of the extent of the break and the enemy had cut my brigade off before they were aware. Of course there was the most lamentable confusion. Part of the brigade retreated safely but about four hundred had to flee to the mountains for safety. Large numbers from other brigades did the same. However the main body had come in, and a heavy reinforcement of fresh troops [Kershaw's division] having arrived we will probably advance against the enemy on tomorrow.

Our losses in killed and wounded have not been heavy at all, nor do I think the enemy took very many prisoners, nevertheless the whole affair is of the most distressing and mortifying kind and I am truly glad I did not witness it. If I had left home on the 10th as I at first contemplated I should probably have been a participant—But the troops are revived now and everything looks much brighter. I trust a merciful Providence will yet crown our armies with victory—

This morning about ten o'clock I moved under orders first in one direction and then another, worried to death with marches and countermarches and coming into camp long after dark excessively fatigued. The enemy have appeared with three or four brigades of Cavalry and light skirmishing has been going on all day. So to morrow we will drive these fellows off and hunt up their infantry which is reported to be moving toward Staunton.

Probably it will be several days before I can write again but keep in good heart. The Good Being will take care of me.

Tell Mrs. Simmons that her brother is reported among the missing since the Fisher's Hill affair but I hope he will yet come up. Davy Adams still drives the ambulance and is a little feeble but nothing serious—The rest all well—

Goodbye now—I must sleep—Kiss my little Lady & "The Doodee" for papa. Love to all—Say that I'm so tired I cannot write to all yet. Goodbye. God bless you.

Your Husband

Bivouac near Weyer's
Cave on road to Port
Republic—Sept. 27, 1864

Dear Darling

To day records another fight, and the Good Being has graciously preserved me. Joe Clifton is wounded but not dangerously, by a minie ball. I have not seen him. We were advancing on the enemy [Brig. Gen. William Powell's cavalry division] & on being wounded he went back to the ambulance. John B. Woolridge[5] of Cody's Company [was] also wounded—No other casualties in the

---

5. *Ibid.*, p. 636. John B. Woolridge, Company C, Thirty-first Georgia Regiment.

31st. My whole loss was not a half dozen as I drove the Yankee Cavalry.

Oh how anxious I am to get a letter from you—I do so much want to hear from the "little man"—and Father too. I hope both are well. Surely no bad news from home is in store for me?

Give my love to all. Tell them I am writing by fire-light after a hard days work—so tired I can write only to you—

Kiss Pa's daughter—Bless her dear heart—

Goodbye—God bless & preserve my Darling.

Your Husband

Bivouac near Weyer's Cave—
about 2 m[iles] from Port Republic
Wednesday. Sept. 28, 1864

My dear Allie

I have written you many letters. Have they all reached you? I am well, except a cold which is getting better. It is now sunrise. I have slept well all night and although sore from fatigue I still feel quite in precise order. We have been in this neighborhood of Brown's Gap, in the Blue-ridge Mountains for the past three days, having *escaped*, as the Yankees say, from Sheridan. But yesterday we moved out against them and ran their cavalry away across the South [Branch of the Shenandoah] River & now we hold the country between [the] South and Middle rivers. I had only about a half dozen wounded yesterday, though I was engaged more than half the day, for my skirmish line drove the Yankees away. Joe Clifton is wounded, but not dangerously. Perhaps enough to give him a furlough home. J. B. Woolridge of Cody's Company is also wounded and in the mouth and hand: Lieut. Cox came in yesterday all safely and looking well. David Adams is improving. The rest of the home boys all well—

I think Early ought to be able to hold his own now, having received re-inforcements. A lot of new clothing & shoes also received & distributed this morning. So we will have very few barefooted or ragged men. I have given the boys several talks as I rode along among them, and I think their old spirit is with them again. I have never been in a retreat from the battle field during action and feel like I never shall be. I am very glad I did not witness the defeat at Winchester & Strasburg. Yesterday when I first formed my line I did it very coolly just like we were drilling, and then rode along the front rank & talked to the troops. You would have been amused to hear their assurances, "We won't leave you, General." "Don't be uneasy about us, General." "We'll go with you General." "We can whip them" &c &c—And when I gave the command forward, they moved off in beautiful order, not wavering though it was across an open field and the Yankees firing upon them from a battery—

—I felt glorious again. My old invincible brigade is itself again.

Kiss the little darlings. Love to all. I close hastily as the mailman is waiting.

God love you, My Darling.   Your Husband

Bivouac near Waynesburg, Va.
Thursday morning. Sept. 29 [1864]

My dear Allie

Yesterday the army moved from Weyer's Cave along the Waynesboro road up the valley and encamped at this point. A considerable skirmish occurred near Waynesboro late in the evening with the Yankee cavalry by a portion of our forces, resulting in driving the enemy away—Our missing men have been coming in rapidly renewing our strength. We have also been re-enforced as I stated in a former letter so as to be able to manage the Yankee infantry, but may yet suffer no little from their cavalry operations.

I expect our folks at home are very much disheartened on account of recent reverses, coupled with the apparent zeal and energy of the Yankees in filling up their armies with new recruits. This feeling of despondency is perfectly natural, but so long as it does not affect their resolve to be independent it will not materially affect our cause.

I anticipate an early and heavy assault on our lines at Petersburg. Grant will probably wait long enough to see if he cannot capture Lynchburg by Sheridan's operations, but whether failing or succeeding in that, he will doubtless attack Gen. Lee by or before the middle of October. Capt. J. Mitchell, will probably leave me, by transfer to the department commanded by Maj. Genl. [James] Kemper near Richmond—While I would be ever so anxious to retain Mitchell yet his Father's family have suffered so heavily in this war, I am really gratified at a transfer which exempts him from exposure of his life to a very great degree.

Don't You wish I could be so fortunate? I know you do. Poor agonizing darling. I am so distressed about you. Your suspense and anxiety I know are horrible. But bear it my love with all the fortitude you can summon, trusting His Divine Will, praying that He will give you His aid to it all.

Tell Mrs. Simmons that her brother has come in, and I delivered him her letter. He behaved very well at Fisher's Hill, and was cut off by the Yankees while himself and five others were trying to get off a piece of artillery. He held on to his rifle and accoutrements, bringing them safely back with him—Charley & Mr. Simpson both well—David Adams is on duty with his ambulance all well—Joe Clifton's wound very slight. He will not get a furlough. Green Clifton not come in yet.

I am well—No letter from you yet. Just think of that my dear, while you are receiving all of my many letters. My love to all. Goodbye—God bless you—

Your Husband

Bivouac near Waynesboro, Va.

Thursday Evening 29. Sept. [18]64

I have been engaged all day looking after my command in its various details, and also in riding over the country examining roads and posting pickets. The troops have been resting, washing &c.

—Your letter of the *22nd* Sept. was brought to me to day by Olenstein Farmer. How proud I was to get it for it was the first and brought me news from you not more than a week old—But I do sympathize with you so much in your trials & troubles. Poor Darling, how I wish I was with you to take much of the load off your Shoulders. I am very glad to hear that Father is well & "The Doo-die" all safe. I have been afraid to love the little fellow —God bless him I do hope he will be spared to us.

Why didn't you mention Ida at all in your letter? Did she have no word of love to send her Pa—?

It seems like we are to lose all our Negroes one by one from death—But the will of the Good One be done—If Fillis is dead do not grieve about it. We must be patient.

I have no further news for the evening, but believe that in a day or two we will be after them again with success.

Keep in good heart—All will be well—Good bye.

Your Husband

Valley Pike. below Staunton [Va.] 13 mi.
Oct. 2, 1864

My dear Allie

I am so glad to write October at the head of my letter. September with all its trouble is gone. October has come, I hope, with its triumphs, to be followed by the consumation of our Freedom in November.

You know how hopeful I am, but I will shortly write you a letter, to give you a history of my despondency, my heavy heartsickness, while trying to pry into our future, taking it for granted that the Yankees subjugated us and, of course, myself and you, exiles from our Country. But I am much too hurried to write about that now— You can see by our present position that we are advancing again. I believe the Yankees will retire before us as far as Winchester, and quite likely our fighting will be light here. But oh, at Richmond and Petersburg I fear already the greatest struggle of the war has begun. I shall begin to think that God's luck will attend me everywhere. We have not lost a skirmish since I came back.

I feel uneasy under Jubal's leadership on account of his utter disregard of the Sabbath and his great profan-

460

ity and habit of drinking.[6] I do believe that the good Lord sent us the defeats at Winchester and Fisher's Hill as punishment.

I received two more letters from you, both dated prior to the 22nd of Sept. I was so sorry for my poor darling— So much sickness—So much anxiety and trouble—So fatigued, and I could not be there to help and to console. Bear it all Darling—We are both being purified by fire— Like gold in a crucible. Our dross will all be consumed and we shall be made ready for the great and glorious work. Who knows how much is to be required of us, and what grand things we shall yet see before we die—

Of the future—the future—I live in it. I breathe its atmosphere—I draw my life from it—Hope—Glorious Hope —not for the world would I be without it.

Did I write to you that I had our box of medicines all safe? It was brought back by the Ambulance, which carried me to Rapidan Station. I have also another hat and will get another pair of pants. Have also another good pair of calfskin gaiter shoes—I am well fixed up in everything but a vest. That I will get.

I have no more news. Trammell—Adams—Simpson— Richardson—Clifton, Joe—Archie—Thornton and the others all well—my love to all—Today is Sunday—gloomy weather—Rained all day yesterday—We marched about sixteen miles.

Goodbye—God bless you

Your Husband

Camp near Burketown on
Valley Pike between Mt.
Sidney & Mt. Crawford—
Monday. Oct. 3rd, 1864

My dearest Wife
We are still here in camp, possibly to remain several

6. An old family story about the Spanish-American War relates that former Confederate general, Joseph Wheeler, was appointed a major general of United States Volunteers by President McKinley. One old Confederate soldier heard that and remarked: "When I die, I hope to go to hell because I sure would like to hear old Jubal Early cuss when he sees Joe Wheeler in that Yankee uniform."

days—but who knows? The infantry of the enemy reported to be fortified near Harrisonburg, with their front & flanks covered by their superior cavalry. How can we attack them successfully is the great question. Will they hazard an attack on us is the next great question. Perhaps after all October will not be so bloody here as at Petersburg, Richmond, and Georgia. But everyday has its little fight somewhere and by somebody— Yesterday I had my little time, today someone else has gone out, but all these little preludes may bring on a general fight—I do not know whether I ought to wish you were here. There would be so little comfort or company for you. Mrs. Gordon is at Staunton. I know you are so much more comfortable at home. Here you would be dragged around after the army. Yet my selfishness would say, "bring her here at once." But for your sake I will patiently wait for winter quarters. October has come—It will soon go by and drag November & December down with it, and then you will come. The clouds will lift—My sunshine will be here. How I crave to embrace my darling! To feel you once more in my arms, and know that I have you safely! Oh my love—I am a weak romantic love-sick boy again—I told you in a recent letter that I had tossed sleepless on my pallet a few nights since thinking of you and the little *bairns* in case of our subjugation. Have you thought about it, darling? I will be exiled—banished from the country as the least punishment, all our property taken from us, thrown homeless, pennyless on the world—If not sent to some prison-island for life, we will be allowed to take refuge in some foreign land. No country, no home, no money, no friends! Can you bear all this my poor darling—and go out into the wide world with me cheerfully? Think of your privations and sufferings. Would it not be best for me to accept of imprisonment for life, alone, leaving you at home with friends, relatives and protectors in comfort?

I have thought bitterly over all these things, and am fighting cheerfully to prevent the dire calamity befalling this country, of the wicked and despotic rule of the unprincipalled Yankee nation. But if our people become

462

faint-hearted and yield up our liberties I am prepared to trust our *Only Friend* in unwavering faith.

I am extremely anxious to hear from you. Your latest letter left you in great trouble. Fillis was extremely sick, and I fear that your next will tell me she is dead. We must sell all our Negroes. I would be glad now to exchange them for real estate somewhere.

I have no additional news—Application has gone up for the retirement of Sam Everett. Goodbye—Love to all —God bless you.

Your Husband

Camp on Valley Pike
between Mt. Sidney and
Mt. Crawford Va. Oct. 4, 1864

[No salutation]

I have a probable opportunity of sending you this letter by Col. [John H.] Baker 13 Ga., who is going home.

The horizon down the Pike toward Harrisonburg is lit up to night by the fires of burning barns. The Yankees are at their fiendish work and thousands of dollars worth of property has been consigned to the flames—I cannot say how many thousand bushels of wheat have been destroyed. The miserable Yankees will probably move farther down the valley to-night leaving us to contemplate the ruin they have wrought—[7]

My several letters have told you of my several successful skirmishes since I returned. Yesterday I had another using the 13th Ga. reg—one man wounded—none killed [at North River]. These little fights are of almost daily occurance and not attended with any great danger— I would not be surprised if we followed the enemy down the Valley tomorrow thus increasing the distance between us, and decreasing our chances of communication with each other by letter. I have received but three letters from you, the latest dated Sept. 22nd. I do hope my daily letters have all reached you. Tell me if you have them

7. See Sheridan's report to General Grant from Woodstock on October 7 about this destruction. *O.R.*, series 1, vol. 43, part 1, pp. 30-31.

all. Think how great my anxiety must be to hear from you since your letter of the 22nd. Then you were in so much trouble—Dear little "The doodee" was not entirely well—Fillis was in great danger—Hannah sick—My poor darling—how you suffer. If I was there to share your burdens it would be so much lighter for you—Instead of the enemy falling back they may advance upon us. In that event a battle may be imminent. But I command myself to the care of our Kind Heavenly Father—

Goodbye—excuse this short hasty letter—

Lumpkin boys all well—

Goodbye Love
Your Husband

New Market, Va.
Oct. 7, 1864

[No salutation]

Yesterday early in the morning the information was brought that the enemy had evacuated Harrisonburg, and we were immediately put in motion to *pursue* [obliterated] provided Sheridan continued to retreat but very wisely pursuing with so much deliberation that the enemy easily widened his distance from us every hour. We marched twelve miles & encamped a few miles north of Harrisonburg—This morning an hour past sun rise we rode in *pursuit*, again marching to New Market 17 miles, and encamped again. Such vigorous pursuit! With such *earnest anxiety* as we possess to overtake a *flying foe*, you may not wonder if we press them into the waters of the Potomac—*Sometime next year*. The role of both Sheridan and Early in the Valley is played. The smoking embers of five hundred barns tell how well Sheridan has performed his part. Perhaps now, the theatre of our operations will change. We will stay here a day or two, then in all probability *Culpeper* will see us again, and the mastery of Charlottesville, & Gordonsville will be tested. But these are only speculations which the telegrams will announce before this letter reaches you. By the defeats at Winchester & Fisher's Hill, Early has lost nearly all the fruits of the laborious

464

marching & fighting of June, July, and August—The harvested wheat and hay of the Valley has gone with these burning barns of which I have written. The fears of the North that Early might again cross the Potomac are all dissipated. The confidence of Grant that he can recruit his army, without endangering Washington has been increased, our people here have been deeply disappointed, at home greatly depressed, the Yankees jubilant, and Lincoln's election greatly assured—all by these reverses—And oh, they could have been so easily prevented! But the day brightens a little. We have hopeful news from Georgia—The newspapers are entertaining us with wonderful accounts of Forrest ['s raid into Middle Tennessee] & Hood['s crossing of the Chattahoochie and temporary lodgement on the Western and Atlantic Railroad, Sherman's lifeline].—The war will end soon—Do not fear.

I am well—I will send you, by the same one who carries this, a Yankee paper addressed to Ida.

How is she getting along with her music? & "The doodee," bless his heart. Pa wants to see both so bad. No letter from you since the 22nd. Don't you feel for me? Love to all.

Goodbye—God love you.   Your Husband

Oct. 8th in camp near New Market—same place—no orders to move—weather cool.

Camp near New Market
Oct. 8. 1864

My dear Darling

We are encamped here this morning with the prospect of remaining quiet a day or two longer. The cool winds blowing from the mountain sides indicate the near approach of winter. But still we have no frost, nor have I yet been forced to put on my flannels—I sent by private hands this morning a letter and a Yankee pictorial paper which I hope you will receive—It is possible that instead of going farther down the Valley, we may cross the Blue Ridge and go into Culpeper County, so as to cover Gordonsville & Charlottesville, for all appear-

465

ances indicate that Sheridan will be required to do something else now, than to hold the passes of the Potomac which we are not in condition to cross.

I have fears now only of affairs around Richmond—Grant does indeed appear to have gained some important advantages, but why make these speculations, when I know you will not read this letter within twenty days. Oh, how long is the time between the writing of a letter and its being read. Twenty days from now you will know that I *was here*, and *was well*, but that will be all—In that twenty days we may fight the enemy—What are you doing these days? Write to me all about your domestic life. How do you live? What about the cloth you were making? So much sickness has hindered you very much. Has it not? Are you coming by the first of January to see me. When this letter reaches you, you can say, "Only *two* months more."

My letters are very much alike, are they not? Remember that the language of love is always the same, and that my heart thinks only of our next meeting. I must meet you in Richmond. I think I can manage it in some way—All the Stewart boys are the same. I learned that Green Clifton is in Charlottesville. Is Jimmie Graham taking the steps to get his transfer to me? If his officers do not object it is quite a simple affair—Is Ida still as industrious and smart as ever—?

And "The Doodee," bad as ever? Must Pa love him?

My love to all. I write very hurriedly—Goodbye. God bless you.

Your Husband

Camp Shirley
Near New Market, Va.
4 o'clock p.m. Oct. 11, 1864

My dearest Allie

I wrote you a letter today to send by mail, but I will write another to send by private hands, thus taking all the chances which offer to communicate with you. We have been at this camp for four days, but we have just received orders to cook two days rations and to move at sunrise tomorrow. Does this mean down the valley, or across the Blue Ridge toward Richmond? It may mean either, but I incline to think we are going to cross the Blue Ridge. This is only a guess which I give you the benefit of—

I have received your letter of the 25th of Sept. bringing me the good news that "The Doodee" & Father have recovered and Fillis [is] better. I do hope these troubles of sickness have ceased and that you are now having nothing to do but prepare to come to see me. Come, Darling, just as soon as you can, even if it is the first of December. Anyhow get ready as fast as you can & then we will be governed by circumstances. It does not seem to me that I can do without seeing you three more long months. Only one month has gone since I left you and that seems an age—How long will the next four months be? I want to meet you in Richmond as you come on. We will stay there a few days to have my uniform made up. I wrote to you that I now have *three* coat patterns of nice cloth—Capt. Mitchell has been assigned to Maj. Genl. [James L.] Kemper at Richmond and will start to Richmond tomorrow. He will take one piece of cloth down for me. Send me an exact account of your finances. I know you have been put to very great expense in consequence of the sickness of our family. Shall I send you *five Hundred Dollars* by first opportunity? I can easily spare it.

I am glad you are pleased with my photograph. I did not like it, but if you do its all right. We have splendid news from Georgia about Hood & Forrest.[8] I hope it will turn out to be true.

The Lumpkin boys all the same. Joe Clifton is well of his wound. Green Clifton is here & well. David Adams

---

8. Gen. Joseph E. Johnston, who had contested Sherman every step of the way from Chattanooga, was replaced by Gen. John B. Hood, who attempted to draw the Federal general away from Atlanta by moving from west Georgia to get behind Sherman's railroad line to Chattanooga. Hood re-took Big Shanty and Acworth, but was rebuffed at Allatoona. About the same time, Maj. Gen. Nathan Bedford Forrest had led an operation that devastated Sherman's secondary railroad supply line, the Tennessee & Alabama Railroad linking Nashville, Tennessee, with Huntsville, Alabama.

does not look well but is still on duty—The balance all well—The weather, though becoming cooler, is still pleasant. We had our first frost last Sunday morning. Give my love to Ida & all the rest. It will soon be sunset when I will sit before my tent and wander in spirit far away from here to my dear little wife at home—God bless her—

Your Husband

Bivouac near Woodstock, Va.
Night—Oct. 12. 1864

Dear Allie

This morning at sunrise we moved from New Market down the Pike and after marching about nineteen miles have encamped at this place. We are under orders to move again at sunrise tomorrow and will probably go as far as Strasburg, which is about twelve miles below Woodstock in the direction of Winchester. The enemy are reported to be picketing with cavalry between us and Strasburg but it is supposed that their infantry are nearer Winchester. I do not anticipate an immediate engagement but one may take place and if so you will hear of it before this letter reaches you. I am getting now where the opportunities for sending letters to you are very scanty indeed. I will still write by the mail and by every other possible chance and thus I may get an occasional letter to you—But remember how few are the letters I receive from you. Only *four* yet and it is a *month* since we parted. Only *four* letter in a month when I have sent you *twenty four*. Have you received all of them?

It is now raining but is not very cold. However when the rain ceases I look for some bitter cold weather. I am very well prepared for it. Have good woolen shirts— 3pr. wool socks—good overcoat & cloth cape—good boots, &c &c—Don't be uneasy about my mere personal comfort. If that was all the war would be a small affair—It is the long separation from my darling which is distressing me so—Can't you come right away? I know how your dear heart jumps at the very idea of coming at once—I am impatient to get a letter telling me that you have

468

hired all the Negroes, made your arrangements & coming in December.

Give my love to all, at home—Lumpkin boys all still well—Lucius has two *full moons* [round holes] on the seat of his breeches, but that will be remedied by a new pair. I told him I was going to write to his sweetheart about it.

Give me a full description of Ida & her studies. I know she is the smartest little lady in Lumpkin.

Kiss "The Doodee."

Goodbye. God bless you.

Your Husband

Bivouac, Fisher's Hill.
Oct. 14. 1864
Friday morning

Dear Darling

Yesterday we left Woodstock and marched down the Valley Pike toward Strasburg, our Division marching first in order. About ten o'clock we reached Fisher's Creek which flows around Strasburg, and finding a few cavalry pickets just beyond the town, a small cavalry force was sent immediately forward, our Division was filed to the left and passed under cover of the hills around the town, and the other divisions were marched along the pike through Strasburg. The Yankee pickets gave way immediately and when we had marched some one and a half miles farther, we reached the highest points of the surrounding country, and looking across Cedar Creek, was the camps of the enemy, with his wagons in full view, the nearest camp being not farther than a mile and a half, and the Yankee troops lazily and unconcernedly lounging about. Evidently they were not apprised that we had our force so near them or they felt themselves so well prepared to receive us as to experience no uneasiness.

After a little while Early determined to shell their camp with some artillery which was accordingly brought up and placed in position [on Hupp's Hill]. The first fire was directed against a small Yankee brigade which was marching by the flank through a field. They literally *dispersed*, every man running for himself to the woods. Next the camps were shelled and we could see them dragging down their tents and hurrying off their wagons. About three o'clock p.m. notice was given that the enemy were passing a column of infantry [from Col. Joseph Thoburn's Army of West Virginia division] across Cedar Creek, and our line was disposed to intercept them. Conner's brigade of Kershaw's division on the right—Gordon's division Center & Wharton's Division left, the remaining troops in reserve. Pretty soon they came up sending their skirmishers forward and following with their line. As soon as they were near enough, we advanced to the attack. Conner's brigade moving first, then Gordon's Division, and next Wharton's Division. The Yankees made scarcely any stand at all, but fled with great precipitation—Our Division fired only with skirmish line—Wharton not at all—The main fight was on Conner like it was on me at Monocacy—We captured only about 60 prisoners—The prisoners stated that they supposed we only had cavalry here, and expected to drive us off easily. They also stated that they were taken by surprise when we shelled their camps. After nightfall we brought our troops back to Fisher's Hill and went into camp, where we are now—

You will join with me in thanks to the Great Preserver for my safety. We had our fifteen killed brought off the field, and when I saw the poor fellows laying in a road on the ground, in the moonlight, cold, stiff, bloody—dead—my heart was full of gratitude that I still lived for you—How many of those little minié balls which yesterday whistled around me were turned aside by the Hand of God! Be thankful my darling for death claims his victims in the small as well as in the great battles.

I received another letter from you yesterday, dated Sept. 27th. Fillis was still sick, and your troubles had not ended. I am very much put out about your failure to get wheat from Newsom. What do you suppose is the matter? Tell me all you think. Be sure to write to me fully all your troubles. Write everything to me about

470

yourself. Give me a little history of yourself—all you think—say—and do—

I am very sorry to hear of the death of Jno. Rockwell's little girl. We know indeed how to sympathize with the bitter distress of parents whose little ones are taken away. I do not know that such wounds ever heal. We feel ours deeply even until now—I dreamed last night that we were marching through a piece of woods when I observed a very handsome little tree, which had the foliage, bark & trunk of dogwood, and growing all over it very luxuriantly, as its proper fruit, was plump little grains of white corn. I said the tree itself looked like dogwood and taking out my knife I cut & tasted the inner bark which proved to have the exact bitter taste of that tree. Was this not a strange dream? A *bitter* tree bearing in such luxuriance the *staff of life*. A dogwood tree yielding grains of corn. What is its interpretation—? Tell Mrs. Richardson, Mr. Harrison & Mr. Bennard and ask them if they are prophets enough to interpret my dream— Real cold weather has not come yet although we had a touch of it yesterday & last night. But I am very well prepared for it, except in the item of gloves. Can you get somebody to knit me a pair of long woolen gauntlets.

Are you getting ready to come to see me. Suppose Grant gets the Danville road—what then?

My love to all—

All the home boys are well—

Goodbye—

Your Husband

Bivouac, Fisher's Hill
Saturday night. Oct. 15[18]64
Near Strasburg, Va.

My dearest Allie

I received your letter of Oct 3rd to day, announcing the death of Fillis. I sympathize deeply with you, my poor darling, in your many troubles. I know how cheerless is the life you now lead, and how heartsickening is the long suspense you endure in the continuance of our cruel separation. Surely out of all these bitter trials

471

we shall yet reap a rich harvest; and is not this the true interpretation of my wonderful dream? Did not Providence intend to say to me that the bitter tree shall bear such fruit as will sustain us happily in life? When I wrote to you to send me cheerful letters I did not intend to ask you to conceal your troubles from me. I wish you to open your heart with all its griefs and all its joys, and let me read them all. Who can sympathize with you as I do? Who can appreciate your efforts to endure all these trials like myself? To whom on earth can you go, with such confidence, in your hour of distress, as to your husband? Do not fear that you causelessly make me unhappy, for I should be more unhappy if I imagined you suffering secretly and concealing your troubles from me. Then tell me all, my darling—everything—So far as the mere property in our Negroes is concerned we should not regret its loss. Let Him who gave take away. Surely we can trust His assurances that "all things shall work for our good if we love Him."

I know you are so lonely at home. More so now than ever. Let your mind be diverted with preparation to come to see me. I will arrange to have you an escort from Lumpkin here, and you can stay as long as you wish—I am afraid "The doodee" will have to come. If you cannot come contentedly without him you will have to bring him and a nurse. But if you can leave him it will be much better—

We went out again to day in line of battle, but did not have a skirmish. At sunset we came again into camp leaving a skirmish line out for protection. I have no idea how long we are to stay here. Two weeks more will bring snow on us, with bad weather doubtless. This may cause a move of both armies across the Blue-ridge. In fact I do not expect to be in the Valley on the first of November.

I have no special news to write. Home folks all well— My love to my darling little daughter! Have Mother & Father received my letters?

Goodbye—God Bless you—

Your Husband

1864

Oct. 16th Sunday—noon—

[No salutation]

My letter of yesterday being still uncalled for by the mail-man I will add to it another sheet. I have just returned from preaching, for happily we have so far on this Sabbath been allowed to worship God in peace. We are abounding in good rumors from Georgia, from Forrest, Richmond, & Breckinridge. I suppose good news is now coming in from the Valley where we are. Our fight on the 13th [at Hupp's Hill] was a signal success, although but a small force was engaged. It gave our troops additional confidence in our ability to cope with Sheridan successfully so long as we have our present numbers—Probe must have been engaged in some of the recent battles around Richmond, as I see that his Division was in the fight. I am sorry that so far I am unsuccessful in getting him with me.

How is Bob getting on with his candidacy for Judge? What are his prospects? Ask him if he is going to send any *"election forms"* to me.

I suppose you have been in too much trouble to write me any Lumpkin gossip up to this time. But you must write me one gossiping letter about everybody and everything, so as to keep me posted about homefolks and home affairs—One half of October is gone—Before long I will be writing *"Nov."* at the head of my letters. I do long for the expiration of terrible 1864—Perhaps 1865 will be happier—You hardly know, Darling, how anxious I am to *hear* of Peace. How I dream over our *after life*— What visions of future joys are disclosed to me. We shall be so happy—So happy—My heart leaps in anticipation— It will be here after awhile—A little more of the bitter—& then the sweet.

My love to all home folks—To my little lady Daughter especially. You say *he* is bad boy Ma. Pa don't believe one word now—

Good bye—God bless you.

Your Husband

473

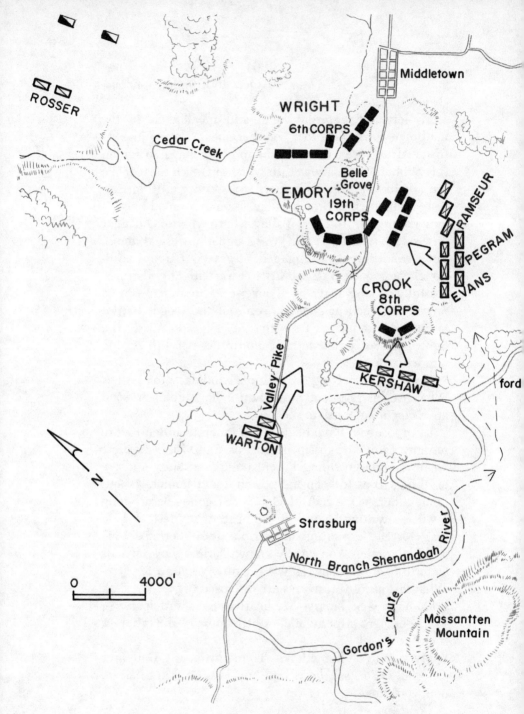

Battle of Cedar Creek, Virginia, October 19, 1864
5:30 a.m.-7:30 a.m.

474

Chapter 25

THE TRUTH ABOUT THE
BATTLE OF CEDAR CREEK

The high point in General Evans' next series of letters is his eyewitness testimony about the last "real" battle in the Shenandoah Valley. It was fought at Cedar Creek on October 19, and resulted in much controversy. These letters add agreeably to the story of what happened there. They contain what Evans knew from first-hand experiences, gained on *the very day* things happened.

The only published Confederate contemporary reports of events in the Valley are by General Early and Capt. Jed Hotchkiss.[1] Absent from the *Official Records* are any reports of the Battle of Cedar Creek by General Gordon and General Evans but they were made. A copy of Evans' official report sent to Early is included in this chapter. We can see that Gordon also conformed to military requirements and made an official report to Early. Evans says so in his letter of November 5, 1864.

Cedar Creek did more to enhance the fame and reputation of General Sheridan than any other action in which he commanded, including his postwar service in Indian Wars in the West. The epic poem by Thomas Buchanan Read has become familiar to many generations who thrilled to the cadence of the lines of "Sheridan's Ride."[2] Cedar Creek broke the lingering reputation and fame of General Early. First, he lost the battle. Second, he lost it by bad generalship. Third, he knew that and tried to hide it, glossing over it, even years later in his writings. What a contrast this was to his commanding general, Robert E. Lee, who after Gettysburg said: "It is all my fault."[3]

1. Hotchkiss, *Confederate Military History*, vol. 3, p. 476.
2. F. A. Matthiessen, ed., *Oxford Book of American Verse* (London: Oxford Press, 1934), p. 223; *O.R.*, series 1, volume 43, part 1, p. 32.
3. Freeman, *R. E. Lee*, vol. 3, p. 159.

We should examine General Early's account of Cedar Creek first. He started by blaming, in his initial report of October 20, "panic of the troops."[4]

His second report to Lee on October 21 (seven sentences) included the words "my men ran without sufficient cause."[5] Later that same day, Early gave a lengthier report. He outlined everything factually up to 10 a.m. of the day of the fight. He described the movement on the night of October 18: ". . . just after dark, Gordon's, Ramseur's, and Pegram's divisions [were] sent across the river and around the foot of the mountain, all under the command of General Gordon. . . ."[6] He reported that the concerted attack of all his units jumped off at 5 a.m., as ordered, and "swept everything before them, routing the Eighth and Nineteenth Corps. . . . They moved across the pike toward the camp of the Sixth Corps . . . which . . . was not surprised in camp . . . and this corps offered considerable resistance."[7]

At this point, Early's report became vague as to what transpired after 10 a.m. He did not state in his report that this was when he took active command of the field. He reported positions of units and small forays, and then wrote that the enemy cavalry was threatening the right flank and rear "and word was sent to General Gordon . . . and General Kershaw . . . to swing around and advance with their divisions, but they stated in reply that a heavy force of cavalry had got in their front, and that their ranks were so depleted by the number of men who had stopped in the camps to plunder that they could not advance them. . . ."[8] He elaborated upon this later in the report: "So many of our men had stopped in the camp to plunder (in which I am sorry to say that officers participated), the country was so open, and the enemy's cavalry so strong, that I did not deem it prudent to press farther. . . ."[9]

In conclusion, General Early came closer to admitting his culpability than at any other time:

4. *O.R.*, series 1, vol. 43, part 1, p. 560, for first and second reports.
5. *Ibid.*
6. *Ibid.*, p. 561.
7. *Ibid.*, pp. 561-64, gives all quotations from Early's lengthier report at this point and hereafter.
8. *Ibid.*, p. 562.
9. *Ibid.*

It is mortifying to me, general, to have to make these explanations of my reverses. They are due to no want of effort on my part, though it may be that I have not the capacity or judgment to prevent them. I have labored faithfully to gain success, and I have not failed to expose my person and to set an example to my men. . . . If you think, however, that the interests of the service would be promoted by a change of commanders, I beg you will have no hesitation in making the change.[10]

As previously noted, there are no other official reports by Confederates on record about the Battle of Cedar Creek, nothing contemporary to shed light on the truth, except for a few items in the journal of Captain Hotchkiss, a topographical engineer.[11]

First of all, Hotchkiss says the plan for a surprise attack on Sheridan's army was presented by General Gordon, not planned by Early:

> General Gordon, General Evans, [and] myself, by direction of General Early, went to the end of Three Top Mountain and examined the position of the enemy . . . with reference to an attack. . . . General Gordon and myself fixed upon a plan of attack to suggest to General Early. . . . There was a conference at headquarters at Round Hill. General Early decided to go by the route recommended by General Gordon and myself, and decided on a plan of attack to which all agreed.[12]

Hotchkiss' journal takes the movements in detail through the success of 10 a.m. on October 19. He did not mention when Early superseded Gordon on the field, but he gave a report on driving the Sixth Corps back beyond Middletown and the disposition of the Confederate forces at that time. Then he confirmed how little was done thereafter to consolidate the Confederate victory of the morning.

Hotchkiss concluded this journal notation of October 19 about

10. *Ibid.*, p. 563.
11. *Ibid.*, pp. 580, 582, for quotations from Hotchkiss Journal.
12. Jedediah Hotchkiss, *Make Me a Map of the Valley* (Dallas, Texas: Southern Methodist University Press, 1973), pp. 237-38.

the truth of what happened, but he did not say specifically who was to blame. He wrote on October 23: "Went to Richmond on the cars. . . . Saw General Lee and we had a long talk about matters in the Valley, commanding generals, etc. . . . General Early told me not to tell General Lee that we ought to have advanced in the morning at Middletown, for, said he, we ought to have done so."[13]

General Early's crowning affront came in a release to the press that was billed in the Richmond papers as "AN ADDRESS FROM GEN. EARLY TO HIS TROOPS." It was first published in the *Richmond Examiner* and was thereafter published on October 27 by the *Richmond Enquirer*. Early had dated his release October 23, and it began:

> *Soldiers of the Army of the Valley*:
> I had hoped to have congratulated you on the splendid victory won by you on the morning of the 19th at Belle Grove, on Cedar Creek, when you surprised and routed two corps of Sheridan's army and drove back several miles the remaining corps, capturing eighteen pieces of artillery, one thousand five hundred prisoners, a number of colors, a large quantity of small arms and many wagons and ambulances, with the entire camps of the routed corps; but I have the mortification of announcing to you that, by your subsequent misconduct, all the benefits of that victory were lost and a serious disaster occurred. Had you remained steadfast to your duty and your colors, the victory would have been one of the brilliant and most decisive of the war; you would have gloriously retrieved the reverses at Winchester and Fisher's Hill, and entitled yourselves to the admiration and gratitude of your country. But many of you, including some commissioned officers, yielding to a disgraceful propensity for plunder, deserted your colors to appropriate to yourselves the abandoned property of the enemy, and subsequently those who had remained at their posts, seeing their ranks thinned by the absence of the plunderers, when the enemy, late in the afternoon, with his shattered columns, made but a feeble effort to

13. *Ibid.*, p. 241.

retrieve the fortunes of the day, yielded to a needless panic and fled the field in confusion thereby converting a splendid victory into a disaster. Had any respectable number of you listened to the appeals made to you and made a stand even at the last moment, the disaster would have been averted, and the substantial fruits of victory secured; but, under the insane dread of being flanked and a panic-stricken terror of the enemy's cavalry, you would listen to no appeal, threat or order, and allowed a small body of cavalry to penetrate to our train and carry off a number of pieces of artillery and wagons, which your disorder left unprotected.

Now we can contrast Early's account with what General Evans wrote had occurred at Cedar Creek. Nowhere else is the answer more blunt and direct than in his letter to Allie of November 6: "It was General Early's miserable generalship which lost the battle. If history does not say so it will not speak the truth." General Evans' first-hand record on the battle of Cedar Creek speaks for itself. He began with the mountain reconnaissance, which he first described in his Valley Diary and then more completely in his letter. In the Valley Diary he wrote: "Oct. 17. Monday. Reconnaissance with my brigade toward Cedar Creek. Enemy found entrenched on the hills beyond Cedar Creek. 2 o'clock p.m. returned to camp. 2½ o'clock p.m. in company with Gen. Gordon & two or three staff officers went to the signal station on top of 'Three Top' mountain. From this position the entire camp of the enemy is visible. Also an extent of country twenty miles wide and thirty miles long."

Then, in the following letters, he enlarged on his diary entry:

Bivouac, Fisher's Hill.
Near Strasburg, Va. Oct. 18. 1864

My dearest Allie

Yesterday I made a reconnaissance with my brigade in the direction of Cedar Creek beyond which the enemy were found to be entrenched on the hills, and encamped behind their entrenchments. I returned to camp about two o'clock p.m. with the brigade, and hastily eating dinner set out to go to the top of the mountain on our

479

right where we have a signal station. I rode as far as possible, but found that I had to leave my horse and literally climb on foot about three fourths of a mile to reach the top and then to walk nearly a mile along the crest to get to the signal station. It was so steep that I had to travel on all fours, pulling along by the rocks and bushes. The face of the mountain is covered with occasional bushes of mountain growth, and small stunted trees. In many places for hundreds of yards it was all rocks, piled one against the other of various sizes, and over these I had to clamber like a coon. My strength was nearly exhausted when I reached the top, although I had rested frequently, but after another short rest I pushed on along the narrow ridge until I arrived at the Signal Station, or "look out" which was the extreme northern end of the mountain where a tremendous pile of overhanging rock makes a precipice down which you may jump half a mile with perfect ease but not with much safety. What a splendid sight was before me. You can form some idea of it, from the view you obtain by reaching the top of Clark's mountain. But it was far superior to that. Strasburg, Middletown, Newtown & Winchester were in sight visible to the naked eye. The vision was limited by the Blue ridge on the right, the Alleghenies on the left, and before you it melted far off into a hazy horizon—Like a narrow ditch filled with water the Shennandoah wound its way through the plain at the foot of the mountain toward the Blue ridge, while Cedar Creek like a placid rill showing here and there between the occasional patches of wood, finally buried itself below Strasburg in the bosom of the Shenandoah. So elevated is the position that the valley presented the appearance of a vast level, the highest hills scarcely undertaking its surface. The Valley pike like a white ribbon lay along the center, the country roads looked like foot-paths, the woods like little parks, and the fields like little gardens with nice little fences dividing. But the whole view presented a magnificent natural picture.

The interest of the scene was of course heightened by the full view presented of the enemy's camp. Nearly every tent was visible. We were able to locate precisely his cavalry, his artillery, his infantry and his wagon train. We could see precisely where he had run his line of entrenchments and where they stopped. Even the house where Sheridan made Hd. Qrs. was pointed out. There all was, with the roads leading to it, the place where he could be best attacked, and how the lines could move, how far to go, and what to do—just like a large map. I believe that we can utterly rout them, if we attack their left flank. I think we are going to attack but Gen. Early favors the attack on their right flank. To night we will probably move—Tomorrow in all probability we will have a great battle and I trust a brilliant victory.

How many poor fellows must die! How many be maimed for life! How many suffer from wounds! Poor men, poor widows, poor orphans, victims of this bloody work!

The weather is delightful during the day, but the nights are quite cool. I sleep with Capt. Cody and we join our covering, thus making enough for comfort. Do you still receive all my letters? I write nearly every day, because you reproached me when at home for not writing oftener. I suppose however it takes two full weeks or more for my letters to reach you. But it gives me a pleasure to think that when you get this letter October will be gone and only two months at the farthest will separate us. Time does pass so slowly does it not? The old saying *"Time flies"* fails now—*Time Creeps*—

I expect home folks are all mad because I do not write. You must beg for me and tell them to overlook the fault. After I have written to you I exhaust everything I can think of to write about.

I am glad to hear that Ida is getting on so well with her studies. Why does she not write to me? Give her my love—Tell Mat to write to me about Jimmie—Has he applied yet for his transfer? Where is he? I hope Graham has his detail. How about P. D. & Father?

Goodbye now—The Good Being keep & preserve you in his care.

Your Husband

"Camp Shirley"
Near New Market, Va.
Oct. 20. [18]64 night.

My dear Allie

Oh what a victory we had yesterday morning—What a defeat yesterday evening! I hardly know how to write about it to you. I am nearly dying for sleep. Just think I have slept but one hour in over sixty hours, besides undergoing the most constant & arduous labor. Will you therefore wait for a full account in my tomorrow's letter?

Then I will say briefly that at day break yesterday we attacked & routed the enemy completely, taking 11 pieces of artillery, several wagons & about 1500 prisoners. I commanded Gordon's division & led the attack with complete success.

But at 4 o'clock p.m. the enemy attacked our left flank, where Gordon's Div. was posted & by heavy force broke and drove us back to our camps, re-taking their artillery & capturing several of ours.

Oh how distressed I am.

Thank the Good Being for my safety. I have another bullet as a keepsake. It struck me & lodged in my clothes. David Adams is a prisoner—wounded seriously in the right lung and a prisoner. Trammell's sons both unhurt. Cliftons safe, Lucius and Archie safe—M. S. Thornton right foot amputated, wounded also in right arm—James Foreman in arm—J. N. Reeves in groin—Send word to their friends—

Gen. Gordon had command of three divisions and as long as his plans were followed by Early we were victorious, but about 12 o'clock Early took command, Gordon went back to his division, the place was changed & we were defeated. I was highly complimented on the field by many—Pardon my vanity—This is my first defeat on a battlefield. I did all I could. I hurled the brigade alone against the charging Yankee line, in the evening drove them back, but they came again, lapped me on all sides, when I retired with the balance—

Poor me—Poor me—What I did gain in the morning—and lost all in the evening.

But I must be thankful to the Good Being for my life—How grateful I am—We killed about 400 Yankees—wounded about 3000—captured about 1500—& utterly routed them.[14]

God bless you—Good bye.

Your Husband

October 21st 1864
"Camp Shirley" Near New Market, Va.

My dear Allie

I intended writing you to day a full account of the Battle of Cedar Creek, but I have been so much engaged that the mail man has come to tell me that the mail will go off at once. I must therefore put it off until tomorrow and give you a lengthy account. The newspapers will doubtless be full of it, and I expect many exaggerations will find their way into these accounts. But I can hardly see how anyone could describe a victory so glowingly as to exaggerate ours in the morning of the 19th, for on my word I never saw anything equal to it in all this war. The victory is due to the plan & management of Gen. Gordon, the defeat is due to Gen. Early. When shall we be relieved of this heavy incubus? Our army is not badly damaged in losses of men, as our loss in killed, wounded & known to be captured will not reach two thousand. We are already intact and can be fought to advantage even now under proper management. The infantry of the enemy have suffered terribly, but his cavalry is still all right. The immense amount of plunder on the battlefield caused a great deal of straggling and proper steps were not taken to prevent it. I have seldom seen a richer battlefield.

14. Sheridan gave the official count of casualties as 5,665. *O.R.*, series 1, vol. 43, part 1, p. 137. General Early reported in a second report of October 21: "The enemy's loss in killed and wounded was very heavy, and we took 1,300 prisoners, making with some taken by [Brig Gen. Thomas] Rosser, and others taken on the day of reconnaissance, over 1,500. My loss in killed and wounded was not more than 700 or 800, and I think very few prisoners were lost" (*Ibid.*, p. 560). Evans' letter of October 21, to be seen later, and his report of October 22, give some figures which would make Early's count seem low. Evans' letter, on the same day as Early's report, tells his wife that Confederate losses "will not reach two thousand."

I wish you would get hold of all the Georgia papers you can which give accounts of the fight cut out the statements and send them to me in your letter. We will have to fight these fellows again. We are not at all satisfied, on the contrary, if Pres. Davis will give us another Commander we can whip them completely.

Now if I could see you awhile I know I would feel better. It is no use for me to send you a dispatch, because it would stand a poor chance of reaching you from here. And you will know that I am safe. Why is it that I get hit in every battle without being much hurt? Is it not to remind me continually how dependent I am on the Good Being for my constant preservation?

I enclose you a Yankee Photograph to show you what profligates they are! But this one is truly decent compared to some of their vulgar monstrosities. I have also several letters which I will keep for you to read when you come, and some Yankee papers which I will send on any good opportunity.

I must stop writing. Pray for my continued safety. I begged the Good Lord on the night preceding the 19th to protect my life in the coming battle for your sake; Praise Him, therefore, my Darling for his goodness to us both.

Goodbye—God bless you, My love to all.

Your Husband

Camp Shirley, near New Market, Va.
Oct. 22, 1864

My dear Allie

I have never been so busy, scarcely during my life, or felt more indisposed ever to write a letter, much less do anything else. The promised description, therefore, of the Battle of Cedar Creek is not yet written, nor do I suppose it is now necessary because you will get full accounts from the newspapers.

The enemy did not follow us with their infantry at all. Their cavalry followed us next morning some twelve miles and went back. They were so badly crippled as to be incapable of pursuit. After all our defeat was not *ruin* by any means, and this army can still be made to win great victories. In fact we have heard that the Yankee army has moved back to Winchester.

I cannot foresee what is to be our future programme. I suppose Gen. Early will wait to hear from Richmond, before he makes any further move so that possibly we will still remain here a day or two longer. But you know how uncertain this is.

The *missing* men are coming into camp rapidly. I think very few were taken prisoners. My brigade is exceedingly small now, as may well be supposed after all its hard fighting through summer & fall, and the victories & defeats of the valley.[15] I believe however that those which remain are still in good condition for fighting and can yet be carried successfully with much more confidence than a small one because of the mere reliance on numbers. The weather begins to be wintry. From present appearances I would not be surprised to see snow falling in twenty four hours. We used to look to the approach of winter for a cessation of hostilities, but I think we are destined to undergo a winter campaign at least until the first of January next. Unless General Lee can give Grant a terrible thrashing and drive him away from Richmond, there is a strong probability that fighting will take place all through the winter. But do not let this divert you from preparing to come to see me. I can take care of you a few months anywhere.

I sent Ida, & Clem each a Yankee newspaper, this morning. I hope they will receive them. Besides I wrote you in a letter last night which was sent off this morning. I write so many letters, that you ought to receive one every mail.

I have no more news to write. There is a small prospect of having Gen. Early removed. I hope Gordon will

15. In the Evans papers there is a copy of his *Report of Casualties in Gordon's Division in engagement at Cedar Creek near Strasburg, Va., October 19, 1864.* (This report covers the largest part of Early's command that day. These are figures for Evans' Brigade, Terry's Brigade, and York's Brigade. The killed, wounded, and missing, both officers and enlisted men, in aggregate are 737. There were 52 killed and 230 wounded. The report is dated October 22, 1864, from New Market, Virginia.

take his place. Oh what a glorious corps we would make then!

Give my love to all—especially to my sweet little pets. Does Nellie complain, because her Pa don't mention her anytime? Well, she must not think her Pa has forgotten her. He thinks of her a great deal.

Did you receive the letter which enclosed one from Probe to me?

Good bye.   Your Husband

From Evans' letters up to October 22, we can put together, somewhat piece-meal, the Battle of Cedar Creek. Even if he had stopped there we would have had a *good* picture; posterity is fortunate that he continued, so as to complete a better picture. In Gordon's memoirs there is a lengthy account of the Battle of Cedar Creek, excoriating Early and agreeing with Evans' contemporary assessment. Early's memoirs, published after Gordon's, did not respond and scarcely touched the controversy. By then Early was too busy attacking the generalship of James Longstreet and others, perhaps to draw attention from Early's own failures as a leader. In Evans' last two letters on the subject of Cedar Creek, his summary, though repetitive, is brilliantly *definitive* of what happened at Cedar Creek.

Camp Shirley, near New Market, Va.
Oct. 23rd, 1864

My dear Allie

I have leisure this evening to write you a long letter, and ought to write you a full account of the battle of Cedar Creek according to promise, but I can give you only a general sketch.

On the 17th inst. Gen. Early made known to a few of his General Officers that he contemplated early next morning to attack the enemy on his right flank by moving his army during the night into position. There is a high mountain overlooking Strasburg, called Three Top Mountain, from which a full view of the enemy's camp was presented, and to that mountain Gen. Gordon, myself and a few Staff Officers, went for the purpose of understanding the ground on which the attack was to

486

be made. I gave you a full description of this visit in a previous letter written on the 18th inst. which I hope you have received, and I will only add that the view there presented convinced Gordon that Early should attack the left instead of the right of the enemy. Accordingly he arranged a plan of battle and presented it to Early on our return. On this account Early postponed the attack one day, and employed the decision to entrust the matter to Gordon's judgment. Three divisions were assigned to Gordon, his own, commanded by myself, with [John] Pegram's, and Ramseur's, to be conducted without artillery or any trains, as secretly as possible along a narrow winding trail along the mountain side, and to cross the Shenandoah at an obscure ford a few miles below Strasburg in time to march one and a half miles & be formed in line at 5 o'clock a.m. Kershaw was to cross higher up, and Wharton was to move down the Pike and cross with all the artillery as soon as the enemy were driven out of their works. [Tom] Rosser with the Cavalry was to attack their right at day break, while one brigade [Payne's] was to precede Gordon into their camps, trains &c creating as much confusion as possible. In continuation of the plan supposing the enemy to be driven from their camps.

The valley [pike] once gained was to be held by pouring troops and artillery upon it, constantly forcing back the left of the enemy into the rough country beyond Middletown, and if possible cut them off from Winchester which we hoped to capture with all its valuable stores.

Everything was to be ready and the attack to be made at 5 o'clock a.m.

[Col. William H. F.] Payne's cavalry, having driven in their pickets which were at the ford [McInturff's] when I was to cross, we hurried through the water and immediately double quicked along a road running nearly parallel with the pike, until we had gone about a mile, when we heard Kershaw's Musketry on our left. Forming immediately with sharpshooters in front we dashed in, in good style encountering the enemy after advancing a half mile, being received by a pretty heavy but badly directed fire. But the division without faltering pressed on, driving the enemy and gaining the pike, where it was joined by Kershaw on the left, and soon Ramseur & Pegram came up on the right. Without halting the consolidated lines still advanced upon the enemy who were flying in all directions. Wharton and the artillery soon came up, and Gordon ordered Kershaw on the left, Pegram, & Wharton, neither of which divisions had been scarcely engaged to move in three lines of battle down the pike with thirty pieces of artillery all to be launched against the 6th Corps which alone of the Yankee army had remained at all firm. This movement if it had been executed would have entirely ruined the Yankee army, but about this time Early had come up and Kershaw received an order from him to go to our left instead of the right. From this moment there was stagnation everywhere. Gen. Gordon resumed command of his division and I of my brigade. We were placed on Kershaw's left and halted. The enemy commenced threatening our left with cavalry and infantry. They eventually drove Rosser back behind us. Gen. Gordon sent me off with my brigade to watch the cavalry, and the enemy charged his division with their cavalry. I saw the danger and tried to avert it by charging into the Yankee lines with my brigade which I brought up for that purpose, but they broke the lines on my right, poured in on my left and forced me back, but I have the great honor of having brought off the best organized brigade from the field, fighting every foot of the way from hill to hill.

The Yankee ran some of their cavalry on ahead and captured some of our artillery & wagons but did not pursue with infantry beyond Cedar Creek. It unfortunately fell to the lot of Gordon's division to be on the left, when it received the attack and was forced back and there circumstances may be unfavorably commented on in the papers, but all who saw the situation give us credit for doing everything possible. I can say for myself that I offered to save the army, by charging along a Yankee advancing line several times as long as my own. I could do no more.

488

My own command and my Maj. Genl. [Gordon] are all satisfied—more than that, more than satisfied with our action, and this does me. I am not fighting for fame as you know—I enclose a map of the battle from which you will be able to understand the battle I think. There are a great many interesting incidents of the battle worth writing to you about, but I have scarcely ever felt so little disposed to write a letter in my life, as during the last three days. Some of the fighting of my brigade was done hand to hand, and many good anecdotes are afloat. I took part of the 12th G[eorgia] Batt[alion] & turned the enemy's guns on them before ours came up. This was in the morning. Oh if we had Gordons for Maj. Generals, and a Gordon for our leader we could thrash these Yankees back to Washington. I am earnestly hoping for a change of leadership and order to advance and attack.

We whipped them so badly in the morning that they have gone back down the valley—We are far superior to them in all else except cavalry & generalship.

The weather grows cold. I expect snow soon. Tell homefolks to knit cool socks and make clothes for their boys. I will continue to have them sent for. I have sent a list of casualties. I thought of writing to Mr. Kirksey & Jno. Richwell but I have been so busy until to day & so indisposed to write that it has been neglected. Send them this to read with the message that I will write soon. Good bye. I will write again tomorrow. Love to all.

Your Husband

I send by this mail to Mr. Kirksey a Yankee Lincoln paper for his edification.

Camp Shirley, near New Market, Va.
Sunday—Oct. 30—1864

My dear Darling

This is one of the loveliest Sabbaths I ever saw. It is so mild, so pleasant that I am writing in my shirt sleeves. For all the world like one of our mildest, most tranquil days in February which tempts us to go into the garden and begin planting our vegetables. I can hardly realize that this is the Valley of Virginia, hemmed in by tall mountains, now the last of October and yet such delightful weather. "Too bright to last." It is the time of Indian Summer which will soon give place to winds, rains, and snow of real winter. Our inactivity to this time is understood to be the result of orders, for it has not been considered necessary since the battle of Oct. 19th to again move upon the enemy. Grant will hardly withdraw troops from Sheridan until the weather reduces all danger of another invasion of Maryland impracticable, for the Northern people shiver with fear at the thought of just retribution which will overtake them for the destruction done in the Valley should their shores be accessible to us again. We have been re-enforced in Cavalry since the 19th by the arrival of two or three brigades, and now look for *Morgan's* old command under Brig. Genl. Basil W. Duke—These accessions to our strength may bring about activity on our part which will result in another engagement with Sheridan. Poor old Early has been so badly used up by this Yankee that he will always hate his very name. By the way a good joke, but a very practical one, was practiced on Early a few days since. Several pieces of artillery were on their way here from Richmond to supply the places of those lost at Cedar Creek, when some fellow marked on them very plainly—"To Maj. Gen. Philip *Sheridan, Care* of Lieut. Gen. Jubal Early."

My Brigade is now about the same in strength as before the battle of Cedar Creek. The brigade lost there twenty three killed and ninety wounded. Some fifty were captured by the enemy.[16]

The unhappy state of feeling between Gen. Gordon and Early has been increased by the recent "Address of Early to His Troops," in which some pointed allusions understood to refer to Gordon are made, and by some newspaper correspondent which eulogizes Gordon as the hero of the victory in the morning of the 19th. Early

16. On August 21, 1864, an inspection report made while Evans was absent because of his wound at Monocacy gave his brigade an aggregate present for duty as 1,344. *Ibid.,* p. 1002. Presumably, after the Battle of Cedar Creek the brigade strength was less than that.

is desperately jealous and will do everything in his power to work the downfall of Gen. Gordon, for he fears that Gordon's genius will obscure him as a department commander in the same way that it did last year as a division commander. The wholesale accusation of Cowardice against his command by Early in his late address, in order to shelter himself from the public disgrace which his want of Generalship has incurred upon him, is regarded very much out of taste, and has given much offense. There are certainly many untruths in it, and in all are exhibitions of gross ignorance of [what was] the actual state of affairs on the battle field. He pretends to say that no actual assault was made, when a dozen general officers know that he was repeatedly informed for two hours before the attack was made that the enemy were preparing for it. After our left was turned not a single disposition of troops was made by Early to arrest the retreat but all left to the unconnected efforts of Brigade & Division Commander[s]. He neither tried *to retreat*, nor stop the retreat by any maneuvers of troops, or any exercise of Generalship. He figured on the field only as a Company Commander, trying to huddle together a few men in a line, and this too after his broken army had recrossed Cedar Creek.

Before the attack a General officer was sent a message to "do the best he could" in answer to a message stating that the enemy were seriously threatening our left flank. In utter bewilderment he is said to have uttered a prayer, the first of his life, when he beheld his line, retreating; He said in general terms that "we will try to stop in the open field back here somewhere," but no line to halt upon was designated by any order. For him to talk about troops panic stricken, obeying no order, threat or entreaty is the sheerest stupidity and nonsense. Had he given sensible orders to Maj. Generals, they would have commanded these orders to Brigadiers, & they to Regiments. A retreat in order could have been conducted across Cedar Creek and all the fruits of the morning victory preserved. There will be no investigation. Early will be retained— The troops in sheer desperation may win a victory. 1

491

have announced that in the next fight we will win a victory or everyone of us be killed, wounded, or captured. I do not want a single member of my brigade to be left to tell how we came to be defeated. I expect therefore of course to be [the] victor when we fight again, and shall take every pain to get the advantage of whoever I fight. But oh, if we had Gordon at the head with a harmonious, co-operating set of Maj. Generals what a splendid army this would be.

The result of the quarrel between Gordon & Early will be their separation, but Gordon will be the one sent, as soon as operations in the valley are closed. I shall do everything to be sent with him, and hope we shall both land in Georgia. This is what I now hope for and am working for—But I will dismiss the disagreeable subject.

You will find a letter to Vones which I wish you to send to the Post-office. It is written in the most courteous & friendly manner, but I thought I ought not to submit to any imposition which is placed upon you. I leave the matter to your discretion. Perhaps before it reaches you, Vones may have full-filled his contract; if so of course you will burn the letter, but if not I want it sent to the office. Can you contrive in some way through Clem, to let Mansfield know about the letter. If Vones does not do right I shall write him a very different letter.

You say Papa must love "The doodee"—well Pa does love him Mama. But he is such a "Bad boy."

Both of Ida's letters have come & I have sent her another paper. I fear none will reach her.

Give my love to all—

Good bye—Your Husband

Be sure to seal the letter to Vones
I wish you would send me in your next letters, for three or four letters two or three sheets in each letter of that thin paper in the letter copying book, from which Clem wanted some paper to trace embroidery patterns. I think I can find a good use for it as Map Paper. If it will do I will want you to bring me a quire or two when you come. Only two months more—Oh joy—joy—

My dearest Darling

I take occasion to send you a letter by Sergeant Williard who goes to Georgia tomorrow but I have nothing of peculiar interest to write. The Richmond Newspapers are interesting themselves concerning the affairs in the Valley and the battle of Cedar Creek in particular. The question has resolved itself into a discussion whether the defeat is owing to a want of Generalship in Early, or to cowardice on the part of the troops. Consequently their has been produced in the army a new cause of bitter feeling between Early and the troops of his command. There was no love between them before, but Early has now published to the world an address, designed for the news-papers, but purporting to be to the troops, in which there is made by him a wholesale charge of *General misconduct and cowardice.* This too in terms so galling was to provoke the deepest resentment. We are most unhappily situated and I look for no further victories—no further glory to the old 2nd corps under its present leader—

—My former letters explain to you the battle of the 19th more truthfully than anything you will read in newspapers; of course in writing to you I have nothing to tempt me to omit, or to exaggerate; but news-paper writers have many temptations to do both—I care not whether anything I did is ventilated through the press or not. I am not fighting for *fame*—My heart I trust is dead to all worldly ambitions and looks only to preservation of honor untarnished so that I may enter untrammeled into the great and good work of the future—

Yours & Ida's letter of the 16th reached me to day. I have sent one letter & paper to Ida. I will send her another paper by Milliard. She writes a very nice letter indeed—spells some words wrong, but not many. Her language & ideas are very good. Tell her to improve her handwriting. She does not know how proud I am to say to my Staff Officers, "This is a letter from my little daughter only nine years old." I am keeping all her letters very carefully to show her again in a few years. I suppose Mat is now so much absorbed in her home distresses that she has entirely forgotten that such a being as myself exists—Tell her to remember me occasionally— As you did not mention P. D. in your last letter I take it for granted that he is doing well. Father also I hope has recovered his usual good health.

Can you send me any slips from any Columbus papers which you think would be interesting to me? I enclose the editorial of the *Richmond Enquirer*, which is the truth boldly spoken. Send it after you have read it to Graham, or Jno. Rockwell.

To all appearances our role is now quietude. Perhaps the present state of feeling in this army may cause Gen. Lee to pause before ordering Early to advance again. The weather is not very unpleasant—somewhat windy, but not very cold—No snow yet. Two years ago at this date, we were in the Valley nearer Winchester and had a pretty heavy snow, with quite cold weather.

I observed a movement to arm the slaves. That is to raise two hundred thousand Negro troops as a *Corps in reserve*, for the coming year. My position is *give up everything* even our Negroes for independence of Yankee rule. Therefore I am willing to muster our slaves as Soldiers in the last extremity, and believe that they will make better soldiers under their Southern Masters, than Negroes do, under Yankee Officers. But I hope we can still cope with the Yankees without drawing on this agricultural support to the war.[17]

Have you received my letters which beg you to make early arrangements to come to see me? Hire out your Negroes for Bread & Meat for yourself & family. You will of course keep Dan & Hannah, & I suppose *Nance* also,

17. The arming of slaves had been proposed earlier in the war, but not until 1864 was it taken seriously. One Federal unit was prominent at the Battle of the Crater. President Davis "in November, 1864, . . . threw out the hint that the Confederacy might ultimately be brought to a consideration of slaves as soldiers . . . and he threatened he would advocate such a measure if he could not secure a sufficient number of white soldiers" (Coulter, *Confederate States*, pp. 266-68).

to help you at home. Prepare for as comfortable living as possible next year, and then come, my Darling. Oh how I long to see you again! Your last letter is full of devoted love. You're happy to go anywhere—endure anything in company with me. The Merciful Father will reward the love of a wife so devoted as you.

Good bye. My love to all—
Good bye. God bless you.

Your Husband

There were several editorials about General Early in the *Richmond Enquirer* from October 25 to October 31, but the one Evans mailed home was probably the one of October 27, because it contained for the first time, the facts about the halt after Early took command, and it assessed him with the responsibility for the disaster, meanwhile praising General Gordon.

This scathing editorial was side-by-side with General Early's "ADDRESS TO HIS TROOPS," and covered almost as many columns:

Gen. Early's address to his army was apparently written more for the Richmond press than for his army. Nay, it seems to have been used to purchase the favor of a single newspaper rather than to inspire his soldiers. Its publication by favor in the "Examiner" one day before being read to his army is the first instance on record of a general officer descending to the pitiful expedient of forestalling public sentiment by muzzling with special favors the press of the capital. . . . General Early has failed, and feeling that his campaign is a failure, he is now bartering to cover up his blunders by buying the favors of the newspapers. Shameful as the subterfuge is, it is not worse policy than the effort of the address to throw upon his men and officers *all* the blame of his last disgrace. Plundering is, indeed, a heinous offense, but the General who cannot prevent it, who in General Orders maudlingly whimpers over it, stamps his unfitness for command upon the records of his country, and pleads for the pity, but deserves not the confidence of his countrymen. But is it a fact that plundering lost the victory? Notwithstanding that Gen. Early avows this,

we assert that the halt in Middletown from 1 o'clock
p.m. to 5 o'clock p.m. was the great and grievous error
of the day, and to which all others are directly refer-
able. At one o'clock p.m. General Early assumed the
immediate command. General Gordon having up to that
hour executed the orders and *won all the victory that*
was won. Up to that hour the victory was complete . . .
and then Gen. Early assumed the direction of the army.
Victory under Gordon. Defeat under Early: the first suppressed and the latter apologized for in a miserable excuse for a disgraceful disaster. It is not high time for a
a change of commanders?

Clement to Allie:

"Camp Shirley"
Near New Market, Va.
Sunday Nov. 5. 1864—Night

Dearest:

I have written and mailed a letter to Ida to day, but
as I have just been favored with one of your dear letters,
I will gratify myself by writing also to you. The dearest
enjoyment I have is reading the letters you send me, and
the next greatest enjoyment is writing to you. While I
read your writing I can almost fancy that it is you talking to me. I almost involuntarily stretch out my arms to
embrace you. How hard to bear is this separation! In my
eagerness to see you I have been begging you to come
in December, but I fear there was more love than judgment in the advice. It was selfishness in me to want you
to leave your preparations for another year unmade by
which you would be caused a great deal of inconvenience or even suffering. Come as soon as possible. I
know you will, for you are as eager to come as I can be,
but make your arrangements for another year first. A
party of us figured out a prophecy to day and pronounced that a cessation of hostilities will be proclaimed
on the *27 day of 1865,* but as we are not gifted with the
faculty of telling future events with much exactness you
need not rely *implicitly* on our declaration. At least it
will be best to prepare for another year of war.

At best our present separation will not be much over two months—I will make the time fly—I expect Probe and Sister are both surprised at my not fullfilling their expectations concerning the appointment of Probe on my Staff, but as I wrote to you before I could not get the appointment made until Congress meets and revises the Staff bill which was passed last session. The President would make no appointments under this bill. In due time I hope to elevate Probe from his *private* position and send him home for his outfit. The appointment of Sid Cheatham is in the same condition.

Tell John Richardson I am much obliged to him for his interpretation of my dream, but the laurels won on the morning of the 19th at Cedar Creek all withered in the afternoon.

Maj. General Gordon's official report pays me high compliments but what of those when the final report must go from Genl. Early who will do neither Gen. Gordon nor myself simple justice? The antipathy between Early and Gordon has grown into a mutual strong dislike. If the government will consult the interest of affairs here the two officers would be separated by the removal of Early from Command. I would expect our papers will publish Early's address and say the battle was lost because the men stopped to plunder—but this is not true. There was plundering done on this as on every other battle field, but it was Early's miserable Generalship which lost the battle. If history does not say so it will not speak the truth.

I am thinking of Lumpkin & Stewart County. The same griping, selfish, unfeeling spirit is still there. We ought not to feel many regrets in leaving there and yet how much happiness have we had there—and how much sorrow too—Fourteen years have we loved each other—loving on first acquaintance—loving through all these years, and loving still; how dearly still! Bless you my darling for these fourteen years which have borne me so much happiness. I do not know how to write to you all I feel when I think of our past life, or all I hope concerning the future.

Poor Ed Collier, I suppose, in dying, remembered his dislike to Sister, and accordingly bequeathed his property as you write. Probe is the only remaining one of the family is he not? How is Sister—Does she mention me in her letters? Do you intend sending Ida to see her this winter?

If Hurley has disappointed you as a teacher would it not be advisable to send Ida elsewhere next year? We cannot afford to waste her time now on any but the most efficient teachers. I know with the efforts you make at home for her improvement that Hurley must be very inefficient if she does not improve rapidly. Her handwriting does not suit me yet. There is not enough regularity in it—She writes rather too scattering—but do not discourage her by reading this part of the letter to her. I observe by some of her modes of expressing herself, that her poetic temperament is finding development— She will some day express herself beautifully. Just think of the wonderful difference between her letters of this date and those of twelve months ago—Her first letter was written to me two years ago. We cannot form her style yet. I do not want her to copy the style of anyone, but to be original in her mode of expressing her ideas, but at the same time she must be made acquainted in due time with the rules of taste taught in the books, and learned from specimens of the best writers—You know I want Ida developed to the highest style of an elegant and accomplished lady without destroying her naturally affectionate and loving disposition. First of all we would have her to be good, and next accomplished. "The doodee" must abide his time. Maybe Pa will begin to think of him in a few years, but Pa is afraid to love him.

Have I not written you several long letters?—This is four very closely written pages. The drums are beating tatoo—

Bedtime has come and I shall soon turn in on my pallet to dream of my sweet little wife.
                                                    Your Husband

To close the story of Cedar Creek, General Evans' unpublished "official report," dated October 31, 1864, must be studied. This report in Evans' papers is more restrained, naturally, than his candid remarks to his wife. But it is very significant that the account never mentioned any order, guidance, or directions from General Early in the conduct of the affairs of the battle, after the success of events up to 10 a.m., when Early came on the field. The first part of the report described the plan of attack and the "secret" way to get to the Federal left by a "dim and difficult path" over the mountain side, being almost verbatim what Evans had written in his letters to Allie. His report continued.

Five o'clock a.m., the time designated for attack having arrived, Gordon's Division was halted, faced to the front, placed in line of battle nearly parallel to the Valley Pike about one and one-quarter miles nearly east of the Pike, and immediately advanced. The ground over which the advance was made proved to be very rough, broken into ravines and hills and covered with woods, in consequence of which the unity of the line was not well preserved, but after an advance of something over three-quarters of a mile, the enemy being discovered in line about four hundred yards distance, posted nearly parallel with the Pike across a range of wooded hills, a temporary halt was ordered to reconstruct the line, which was very quickly done, the halt not lasting more than three or four minutes, when the division moved forward rapidly with spirit, encountered the enemy, who made a brief but somewhat stubborn resistance (part of the line actually engaging hand to hand), then fled.

Being joined by Kershaw's Division on the left and Ramseur's on the right the pursuit was continued across the Pike through the camps of the enemy beyond Bell Grove, the headquarters of Major-General Sheridan, U.S.A. and until about eight o'clock a.m., capturing in addition to artillery and colors a large amount of equipage, besides a number of small arms.

At this time I returned to the immediate command of my brigade, Major-General Gordon having re-assumed immediate command of his division.

In the last line of battle taken up by the army near Middletown my brigade was at first placed on the left of Gordon's Division, that division constituting the left of the line. About one o'clock p.m. it was observed that the enemy were moving cavalry to the left of our battle line about three-quarters of a mile from our front.

The central part of Evans' report gave the details of the Federal counterattack, which he said was begun about 3:30 to 4:00 p.m., when "the enemy advanced his infantry to the attack. It was a real attack as all who were present know, but one which might have been repelled if there had been troops enough in position on the left of the line occupied by Gordon's division to have covered the ground four hundred and fifty yards on the prolongation of that line." Step by step the Confederates were forced back, and Evans points out one of Early's shortcomings: "I conjecture now that the enemy did not continue immediately to advance forward that portion of his line which attacked Gordon's division, but employed his force in gradually turning the left of each brigade in succession."

Evans thus stated in his report the same fault that General Lee had already called to Early's attention as recently as September 27, after Winchester and Fisher's Hill. Lee told the latter that "As far as I can judge, at this distance, you have operated more with divisions than with your concentrated strength."[18]

Disorder came only after the field was lost:

The command retreated in line of battle to Belle Grove, Sheridan's Headquarters, where it again halted in support of two pieces of artillery which were here placed in position to fire upon the enemy. These pieces being withdrawn and the retreat still continuing on the right the brigade faced by the rear rank marched to the enemy's works near Cedar Creek on the west side of the Valley Pike, where another stand was made, the command by rapid fire checking the enemy until it was supposed that all artillery and trains were safely in the

18. *O.R.*, series 1, vol. 43, part 2, p. 880.

rear. This position was held so long that an organized retreat across Cedar Creek by its difficult crossing above the regular ford became impracticable. The enemy checked in our immediate front had moved cavalry around our left flank. Cedar Creek was only about two hundred yards distant with no crossing except a bridge of poles and fence railings and to attempt to cross these in order by the flank would have subjected half of the command to capture at the creek, or else the enemy reaching his works, which perfectly commanded the crossing in easy rifle range, could have killed and wounded large numbers of the troops. Orders were therefore given for a precipitate retreat and to reform as soon as the creek was passed. After the creek was passed I remained in rear to hurry up and organize the command which was reforming near the pike still moving on however, and it soon became so dark that various commands became mixed indiscriminately together.

In tacit reply to the public comments made by General Early, Evans concluded his statement by defending his soldiers.

I desire to remark that the Division behaved with commendable courage in the morning attack, there being remarkably few skulkers and plunderers, while the pursuit was vigorous. I desire also to remark in behalf of my immediate command that it would be the greatest injustice to characterize them as cowards.

I have caused charges to be preferred against men and officers in flagrant cases of cowardice during the recent battle. Officers so far as I could get information have caused plunderers to be punished and guns and accoutrement thrown away to be paid for—but have said in orders to the command that I do not join in any wholesale accusation of cowardice against brave men who have fought so often and so well where bullets fly the thickest.

After the letter of November 5 General Evans did not write anything more about the Battle of Cedar Creek. For the next three weeks his army duty was all marching.

In his Valley Campaign Diary, Evans mentioned the first snow on November 5 at Camp Moore (on the farm of Thomas Moore at New Market). Then he wrote that they "broke camp at sunrise and marched down pike, camped S of Woodstock" on November 10; "in the line of battle crossing the pike" near Newtown and "skirmish line at Chrisman house," then marching "to Fisher's Hill—9 miles—very cold" on November 12. By adding the miles he listed in the letters from November 5 to November 14, one finds that the Confederates covered 57½ miles in these maneuvers. Only one fight was recorded, and that was on November 22 at Rude's Hill, when "the enemy withdrew leaving about six killed."

Chapter 26

FROM CEDAR CREEK
TO PETERSBURG

A moment should be taken here to bring up-to-date what had been going on with General Lee's and General Grant's armies since Evans had departed on June 13 for the Valley Campaign. After the June 3 Cold Harbor attack, General Grant rested his army for nearly two weeks before beginning anew to press the Confederates at Richmond, but this time he made a more extensive movement to the right than in previous advances. He pulled farther down the peninsula and then, on June 14, commenced sending Federal troops across the James River well downstream from Richmand and advanced on Petersburg. Grant had ordered General Butler up from the lower peninsula and, with other additions, there were almost 113,000 Federals either south of the James or about to cross by June 15. General Beauregard's Confederate troops had rushed to Petersburg and, as Grant advanced, the Confederates fought a delaying action from first, the Dimmock, and then the Harrison's Bed line. Lee brought in units from around Richmond, reinforcing his strength to about 48,000 men. In a series of attacks, from June 15 to 18, Grant suffered approximately 10,000 casualties. After these efforts, the Federal commander settled back into a siege operation that lasted until late March 1865.

There were major affairs north and south of the James River, but no major battles during this time. This respite from major battles for the Army of Northern Virginia around Petersburg until the year's end was marred by alarming news from Georgia, already mentioned in the Evans' letters. By July 20, 1864, General Sherman had reached the environs of Atlanta and on the 20th, 22d, and 28th he was attacked by the Confederates now led by Gen. John B. Hood. The Confederates were repulsed and Sherman began siege operations. This bad news was somewhat offset by dispatches from Richmond stating that General Early was almost at the Washington White

House on July 11. However, the subsequent debacle in the Valley and the Battle of Cedar Creek dampened the hope of the Confederate army at Petersburg.[1]

And the news from Georgia got worse. General Sherman, instead of following Gen. John B. Hood's Confederates into Tennessee, as expected, detached only a part of his forces there to checkmate Hood. Sherman and his army, on November 15, set out from Atlanta for the march to the sea at Savannah. It was in late December that Sherman sent his telegram to President Lincoln, offering the city of Savannah and twenty-five thousand bales of cotton as a Christmas present.[2]

The stalemate and siege at Petersburg were the prevailing circumstances in Virginia when Lee re-called the Second Corps from the Valley—notably without General Early. General Gordon, age thirty-two, was the Second Corps commander, and acting Major General Evans, age thirty-one, was the division commander, positions they each held until the surrender at Appomattox Court House. Upon reaching Petersburg, Gordon's corps was assigned to hold the extreme right of Lee's infantry lines.[3]

Clement's last letters of the war, written in November and December, during that time of relative inactivity, dwell on army routine but with the underlying theme of his great desire to have Allie come to Virginia. In closing out these last war letters, the first is another delightful note to Ida:

> Camp Shirley
> Near New Market, Va.
> Nov. 6. 1864

My dear Daughter

I think I am due you another letter, and will write it now while I am at leisure. The little snow we had yesterday made me think of Ma and you and the fine times we had last winter. Do you remember the deep snows I had to ride through to come to see you and Ma at Mrs. Halloway's? I wish you were both here now I would enjoy myself so much better if I had Ma and my little

1. Freeman, *R. E. Lee*, vol. 3, pp. 444-46, 512.
2. Sherman, *War is Hell*, p. 181.
3. Gordon, *Reminiscences*, p. 376.

daughter to talk to every evening. I am very sorry that you cannot be taken from school now. You are improving so rapidly that I do not want you to miss a single month.

Traveling is also a great deal more annoying now than when you were here, and board much more difficult to obtain. I will not keep your Ma from you more than three months, and during that time we will write to you two or three times every week. "Uncle Mose" is so anxious to go home this winter that I think now I will send him next December to stay until Ma leaves home to come here. You must joke him about his "dark Virginia bride."

Ma says in her letters that "the little man" is so smart and sweet! Do you think so? I think he is a very bad little boy and gives Ma too much trouble.

For your amusement I send you, enclosed, a Yankee letter, written by a young lady to a Yankee officer. Also a photograph of a Yankee soldier for you to use as a "thrumble paper" in school. I am sorry you have failed to receive the Yankee pictorial papers which I sent you by mail.

Ask your Grandma [Lucy Walton] why she has forgotten me so soon. My letter to her written over a month ago is yet unanswered. You must continue to write regularly and take a great deal of pains in writing neatly, spelling correctly, and expressing your ideas carefully and grammatically. I will tell you some day why I am so anxious about this, as well as other accomplishments. You must believe that there is a great deal of importance in all my instructions and advice to you, although you cannot yet fully understand why it should be so.

In your last letter you tell me that you have overcome your extreme passion for dolls and have given them up. This is well. I encouraged your love for dolls until this year, but now I think you are old enough not to need these inanimate objects for the cultivation of an affectionate disposition.

Continue to write to me. Kiss Ma and "The doodee" for Pa. God bless you.

Your Pa.

Clement to Allie:

New Camp 3½ m. S.W. of
New Market. Va.
Nov. 9. 1864

My dear Darling

According to my statement in my letter of last Saturday we have changed camp to the place designated as above. We left camp "Shirley" (so named from the owner of the land on which we encamped), yesterday morning about ten o'clock marched up the Pike about three miles, and then turned off nearly due west, marched one and a half miles and encamped. This located our camp three and a half or four miles South West of New Market. Would it not be some satisfaction to you to have a map of Virginia, so you could see where we marched and encamped? Our camp, or rather my Hd. Qrs. are close to the dwelling of four maiden sisters, who have never enjoyed the sweets of matrimony. Do not be alarmed. They are old and ugly, not even tempting the imagination to go astray. Virginia is prolific of old maids who seem to be leading very useless and unprofitable lives. When you see a woman thirty years of age you naturally look around for a troop of romping boys and girls. Some of these Virginia maidens get to be too old to marry while waiting to get *old enough*, according to the Virginia theory. You and I will naturally take sides against long deferred matrimony, because our youthful leap proved to be one of happiness—

I have just received a present of a plate of cake and a *bottle of whiskey*. I enjoyed the cake but the whiskey is, and will be, untouched. Have I told you, that seeing the great evils being done in the army by the use of spirits, I have determined not to touch it in any shape during the war? I do this for the sake of example to officers and men—I have commenced a regular *crusade* against liquor drinking, and am determined to break it up in the brigade. My brigade is still large comparatively. I have a few over one thousand arms bearing men, this is exclusive of officers and those who do not carry guns.

506

Some entertain the opinion that Early will in a few days move down the Valley to give Sheridan another battle. If possible we ought to close the Valley campaign with a victory, and no one would go out with more cheerfulness than myself to aid in accomplishing an end so desirable, but writing to you in the fullness of confidence as I write to no one else—I must say that I shall be afraid of the results of any other battle under Early. We may win success even under him, but it will not be ensured by any confidence in his generalship.

The unsettled winter weather appears to have begun. It is not cold, but the clouds are dark, and rain is constantly looked for—then the sun comes out and we think it will be fair, but soon it is dark & cloudy again, and so it continues. But you remember that real winter does not begin here until after Christmas. There will be several weeks of such weather before this year closes as will admit of battles being fought—In fact I sometimes think that we may have no winter quarters at all, but through rain, sleet and snow continue to prosecute this bloody war to its end. Before this letter reaches you the result of the United States Presidential election will be known to both of us, but I think it does not require much wisdom to predict the success of Lincoln.[4] Do all my letters interest you?

This one for instance has no news, or anything else in it, which differs from a hundred letters which I have written to you heretofore. How can it interest you? I worry my brain sometimes to think up something which would amuse you, but nothing occurs worthy of mention now. If we could have another battle for me to describe to you—but I expect you would rather do without both battle and description. When I commence writing, the first idea uppermost is your coming to see me, and that keeps uppermost to the end so that I can

4. On November 8, 1864, the Republican ticket of Abraham Lincoln and Andrew Johnson beat the Democratic ticket of Maj. Gen. George McClellan and George H. Pendleton. Lincoln received 212 electoral votes to 21 for McClellan. The vote in the electoral college was overwhelming, but the popular vote was a different story. Lincoln received 2,209,938 votes and McClellan 1,803,787. Translated into percentages, Lincoln had 55% and McClellan 45%.

scarcely get any other idea to present itself. One third of November is gone—Two months of our separation have ended—only two more remain. I hope they will pass rapidly.

You mentioned in one of your letters that Bob was with Hood's army—What was the object of his visit there? What about his candidacy as to prospects of re-election? I expect our people in Georgia feel very much relieved since Hood has drawn Sherman after him on a Northern tour. It was Hood's best maneuver, but I am afraid he will accomplish very little toward destroying Sherman's army. I should think, however, that Atlanta will now be evacuated entirely and Sherman's army be collected nearer Chattanooga—Perhaps one valuable result will be that Sherman will have to commence his spring campaign from the same point at which he started this year. Then Hood can try his plans for defeating Sherman's advance into Georgia, where he differed from Gen. Johnston—When we look at the "Military Situation" closely it will be seen, that all the expenditure of men and means by the enemy this year have not secured them a single real advantage. I will close now—

Remember me to all Kinfolks and friends. Good bye— God bless you—

Your Husband

HEAD QUARTERS MIDDLE MILITARY DIVISION[5]

Night Nov. 9th, 1864
My dear Allie
Information has been received that Sheridan has moved from Middletown to Winchester, and therefore of course we will pursue with our accustomed vigor. The Richmond papers will have another opportunity of telling the public that Early is pressing Sheridan toward the Potomac. Our orders are to move at daylight tomorrow, which causes me to write this hasty letter to be

5. Evans' letter to Allie, as well as several subsequent letters and also his report of the Battle of Cedar Creek, were written on "captured" printed stationery from General Sheridan's headquarters at Belle Grove.

mailed at New Market in the morning so that there will not be such a long interval between my letters, for probably I may not write again in two or three days. This move will not necessarily bring on a battle, but instead thereof Sheridan may send his troops off to Sherman or Grant, and we may go to Lee. Who knows? From this point to Winchester & even to the Potomac the country has been stripped of army supplies. Therefore we cannot live down farther in the valley without getting our supplies from a distance. For that reason our campaign in the lower valley will be brief. I will write to you as usual on every opportunity and give you full details of the march, and everything of interest which occurs—Perhaps some of these days our letters will be read with interest by our grown up babies—

The Lumpkin boys are all well—Give my respects to all—

> Kiss the darling little ones.
> My love to Kinfolks—
> Good bye.
> God bless you.
> Your Husband

HEAD QUARTERS MIDDLE MILITARY DIVISION:
Camp—Near Woodstock, Va.
Nov. 11. 1864

We made a march yesterday of 23 miles down the pike and encamped at sunset, about 1 mile S. of Woodstock—I kept a topographic itinerary of the day's march, for my own amusement.

I write this hasty letter just at day break, on my knee, merely to keep you posted about myself—We march again this morning down the Valley & will probably come up with the Yankee cavalry, but their infantry is still beyond our reach.

Just received yours & Ida's letters of the 30th: You had heard of the battle of the 19th at last. And so our S-Camp turns out to be "Josephus" at last.

Ma must feed him on "thugar tane" [sugar cane]. Give him just as much as he can eat—Tell Ida I will write

509

to her soon. I have written two letters to her. I hope she has received them by this time.

Lumpkin boys all well—

Goodbye. Your Husband

HEAD QUARTERS MIDDLE MILITARY DIVISION,
Near Newtown—Va. 1864
Nov. 11. Night

I write again perhaps on the eve of another trial of skill & strength between Early & Sheridan—We marched to day 21 miles—through Woodstock—Strasburg & Middletown, and now are encamped in line of battle 2 miles S.W. of Newtown—The enemy are reported to be at Newtown with an additional Corps of infantry—Our orders indicate activity tomorrow.

With the same trust in the Good Being & the same faith that whatever he does is right, I shall enter the battle & do my duty—

This hasty note you know how to excuse. I write merely to keep you informed.

Kiss my little darlings for Pa. Love to all—Goodbye. God bless and preserve you. Your Husband

HEAD QUARTERS MIDDLE MILITARY DIVISION,
Line of battle
2 miles S.W. of Newtown,
Nov. 12, 1864

Dear Darling

We are still in line of battle at the same position from which I wrote to you last night. The enemy present a line of entrenchments two miles beyond Newtown on the N. bank of the Opequon (pronounced *Opekan*) Creek, which crosses the Valley Pike at that point. It is supposed that his infantry are there, consisting of the 6th, 8th, & 19th Corps—The report that an additional Corps had arrived is now doubted. We have had some cavalry skirmishing this morning taking a few prisoners.

I suppose we will move against the enemy.

I am in good health—

Goodbye—I am so glad you are now unconscious that

I am on the eve of another battle—God bless you—
Goodbye.

My love to Ida & "The doodee."

Your Husband

HEAD QUARTERS MIDDLE MILITARY DIVISION,
   Camp—Nov. 13, 1864

Instead of a fight yesterday we concluded the day's
operations by a march of nine miles commencing about
6 o'clock p.m.—arriving at the celebrated Fisher's Hill
about 10 o'clock at night. It was bitterly cold—The
sharp wind swept over the open fields along the line of
march, like it was trying to blow Early's little army off—
We were not defeated—did not run—but simply marched
back—The cavalry however fought with varying success
—but we lost *two* more pieces of Cavalry artillery—Early
appears really to be Sheridan's Chief of Ordnance. I
expect Sheridan will telegraph that he had another
fight & another victory—but it was the smallest kind of
an affair & the artillery was lost without being once fired
—We are now on our way back up the valley & will probably stop again near New Market for a few days—Some
of our Divisions will be sent off to Richmond—But I cannot yet tell which besides Kershaw's.

Send Mr. Trammel word that his son is dead. He died
& was buried at Mr. Stickley's house, near Cedar Creek,
about three miles from Strasburg. His grave is marked.
John Rockwell can send him the message for you.

I write hastily & by camp fire—I forgot to say we
marched in snow today—I have not become warm yet—
Oh it was so cold—I walked nearly all the way to keep
warm, but my rheumatism in the hip made walking
[not] nearly or quite as painful as freezing was—

But you will be here soon & cure all my troubles—
Goodbye—God bless you.

Your Husband

Camp Moore—Near New Market.
Monday—Nov. 14/[18]64
—night—

My dear Allie

We are back again to the same camp from which we

511

started five days ago to pursue Sheridan down the Valley—miles of marching—and one day of skirmishing—our loss about a dozen killed—Perhaps 50 wounded, and as many prisoners—with two pieces of artillery and three ordnance wagons captured by the enemy—Yankee killed & wounded unknown—Prisoners about sixty—The trip was very fatiguing and cold, with short rations to add to our troubles—But this seems to be the fate of the army of the Valley now—Kershaw's division has been ordered to Richmond—I hope we are to stay here; I have already written you several letters containing all this news, but I repeat it here in this, for fear that some of the former letters may not reach you. I will write you a good long letter tomorrow—as usual about nothing—for there is nothing here to write about—Are you *blue* about Lincoln's election and *four* more years of war? How do you think you can bear it? This letter will reach you about the last of November—and you can then be looking to the passing of only a month & a few days before you will be on your way to see me. Our meeting will be like our old friend in the cars said, sure enough.

I write again tomorrow—Goodbye—God bless you my darling—My love to Ida & The doodee.

Your Husband

Allie to Clement:

Lumpkin Ga.
Monday night Nov. 14, 1864

My dear darling,

One whole week has passed since I wrote to you and I have had no letter in that time. It has rained—rained, until the whole country has been flooded with water. All the bridges washed away and everything stopped for a while. The Cuthbert mail got in to day for the first time since last Monday. I was so anxious—so anxious for letters. The time seemed so long I expected at least a half dozen but got only one but that was thankfully received. It was a good long one written on the thirtieth of last month, two weeks since. You enclosed a letter to Mr. Jones. He did not let me have the flour but as I

have taken the money for Dan's work I have concluded
not to send it to him. I would like too for him to see it.
He did not treat me right but I would not contend nor
say anything to him. If I had not taken the money I
should send him the letter right away for I think it
would do him good to read it. He does not sell anything
from his mill now. Neither meal nor flour, because he
is compelled to take government prices. He says before
he will sell he will feed it to his hogs. He has been reported and I hope he will be sent to the army. It is the
place for all such as he is.

I am glad things are still quiet in the valley and hope
they will remain as long as you are there. You express a determination in your last letter to win a victory in the next
fight. When you are tempted to do anything rash or expose
yourself when it could be avoided darling, always think of
me and the two little darlings here at home before you go
too far. I have been thinking and wondering all day if
peace would ever come. I am prepared for it in any way. I
would almost welcome it even if we were subjugated. For
you to come home is peace to me and that is the only peace
for me. I am so worn out with this long separation from
you. Will it ever end. Three long—long—long years since
you first entered this dreadful war. What years of misery
for me. Have I three more just such to expend? If I have
then God help me. Matt heard to day that Mr. Graham
was not coming back any more, that they had sent him
on to camp from Macon. I am sorry if it is so, for he
would be so much assistance to me in hiring our Negroes. I am so frail I shall not be able to start to see you
before the middle of January. I did hope to get there by
Christmas.

It is now the middle of November and nothing close.
I saw Brother day before yesterday. He says he is afraid
he cannot hire the Negroes before Christmas as nobody
seems willing to make any engagements before that
time. I am afraid if I go off and leave it undone it will
not be for the best but I do want to come right away so
bad darling. I will try and bear it though as well as possible. The longer my visit is delayed, the more we will

enjoy the meeting. Hannah is at last in the bed for good. She has a nice little girl, born Friday night. It is a Negro. I am so glad it is not white. I think so much more of it. Ida is the proudest little thing of it you ever saw. Such nursing and taking on you never saw. She claims it as her own personal property. Hannah is in the house. I was afraid to trust her in the kitchen and put her in the dining room, so I can watch her and take care of her. She is doing first rate so far. I shall be glad enough when she gets well though. I get on pretty well cooking. I laugh heartily at my biscuits sometimes. I make them all sizes and shapes. I am learning how to work so if the Yankees should subjugate us and I should be obliged to do it. It is not so hard after all to get up in the morning and cook your breakfast. I am getting real smart. Necessity you know compels me to be so. My way of cooking amuses Hannah very much.

We had quite an excitement in town last night. A runaway match. Miss Frank Stokes and a Mr. Bussy. Mr. Frank Porter's brother. They went to William Mansfield's. He refused to marry them. They then went to William Thornton and he refused. They got uneasy and were afraid they would not get any body to perform the ceremony and about nine o'clock in the night went down to call [at] Thornton's house and told him he must marry them. He was about half drunk and cursing told them he would put them through faster than they were ever before. After they married they went out to Frank Porter's. Seven miles. Everybody is of course excited about it to day. You do not hear anything else but the runaway scrape. Every one knows something to tell.

Lawton has been saying all day, "My poor papa gone war," and begging me to go see papa. He is so fat that he is a sight to look at. He has said some bad things to day, papa. Too bad to write to you. I spanked him once this morning [and] he went right to Hannah. "Oh Hannah," he said, "Mama whipped poor me." He went out in the back yard to day and called Georgia Richardson and asked her how Al was. He asks everybody that comes in to take off their hats and when they leave he asks them to come to see us again. You do not know what a smart little mouth that is, papa. Ida has written you another letter. She was very much flattered by what you said about her letters. Will the next two months ever roll by? It seems an eternity to look to the end of them. Good bye darling. May God bless you and take care of you.

Your Wife.

Clement to Allie:

Camp Moore Nov. 15, 1864

My dear Allie

I am rested now, but you must not therefore say, why didnt he write me a longer letter? What shall I write about without repeating for the hundreth time what I have written before? It is no use for me to speculate on what is going to happen for I begin to believe now that I am not a prophet and cannot see any further into the future than other people. So far as the war is concerned we had better make our arrangements as if certainly another year must pass before we can have peace, for the whole Yankee nation appear to be determined on prosecuting the war to their own as well as to our destruction. Providence may arrest the strife in some mysterious way, unthought of by us, and for His interposition let us not forget constantly to pray.

I am dying to talk to you. Letter writing makes me impatient. I want to lay my head in your lap and look up into your face, and watch your lips and eyes—Will you not be repaid for your long and tiresome journey to Virginia, if you can have two or three months of my society. I would joyfully travel to California for the sake of yours.

Have I written to you that *D. A. Holloway*, whom you remember as the brother of Miss Virginia Holloway, is a surgeon in the brigade? I told him to send our love to his mother & sisters. He knows you, but did not meet with me during the winter you boarded with his mother.

I cannot say that we are going to stay here very long. There is much difference of opinion. Some think that

515

Gordon will be sent to Richmond & Early be left here. All agree that the two should be separated. I think however that we will be here at least a week longer.

I will write to Ida in a day or two—Give my love to all—By the way, tell me what that horrid dream was which you dreamed about me a month ago—Good bye. God bless you.

Your Husband

Night Nov. 15, 1864

I have concluded to re-open my letter to you and add another sheet merely to get in the last word. When I send off a letter I begin at once to think about writing you another and wonder what you will do or say when you receive and read them. Don't you think sometimes I am a romantic love sick boy who dotes on his sweetheart too much? How would you like for me to commence my letter somewhat in this style, viz: "My dear Mrs. Evans, I had the pleasure of receiving your last letter to day and in reply have to state that my health continues very good. I trust you are comfortably situated at home. Nothing of interest has transpired about which I could write to entertain you. Please give my respects to the children and our friends. I remain yours respectively. C. A. Evans."

How would you like to receive those kind of epistles? Or do you prefer a long warm love letter full of foolishness to the uninterested, but full of wisdom to the loved one written to? I know your answer before you write it. I know how you delight to read real love letters although nothing but nonsense is written.

Are you ready to ask me, why I have put in this extra sheet containing nothing? Well I will tell you. I have been wanting to day to tell you that I *do really love you so very much*, and I opened the letter just to gratify myself by writing it. That is very amusing is it not? So *new* too! Well, darling, I am going to sleep soon to dream about you. I intend to think about you until I fall asleep, and then I know I will employ myself about my dreams. How delightful it will be someday to be free from this war-bondage and be privileged to stay with my darling all the time.

Goodbye — One Kiss — another — another — and now Good night & sweet dreams to you—

Your Husband

HEAD QUARTERS 1st BRIGADE 2nd DIVISION[6]
2nd ARMY CORPS, Valley District
November 18th, 1864

My dear

I have just finished a good dinner. I expect you imagine I live very hard but if you could see my table you would change your opinion: For breakfast we have broiled chicken, beef steak, or fried ham, occasionally eggs—good biscuit & genuine coffee—For dinner baked turkey, roast beef, potatoes, sweet milk & apple pies. For supper warm biscuit, butter, syrup, coffee, and cake. Now what do you think of my hardships in the cause of liberty? I know now that you think I have given the accidental feasting of one day as my usual bill of fare. Of course we do not live quite this well every day, but yet we live well enough. I wish I knew that you always lived as well—Sheridan did not quite make the valley desolate, although his destruction of barns &c was very great indeed. Our general Court martial is still in session. I go there at 9 o'clock p.m. We have a good comfortable room, but the business is very tedious. It helps me however to pass off the time. When Christmas comes I am going to beg off if possible, so I can spend all my extra hours with you. I hope to get a camp somewhere near a good house where we can board together. The prospect of our remaining in the Valley brightens, but still we may receive an order any day to decamp.

It has rained all day along, and still rains, my tent is cozy and comfortable enough, but is not to be compared to our comfortable rooms at home. We used to delight in the raining days, because we claimed them as *dia*

6. This is Confederate stationery.

sacrae "sacred days" to be devoted to each other. Now the raining days only serve to call up those past joys and make us sigh for their return. It does seem to me that peace will bring more joy to us than to any other two people in the Confederacy—Would you believe that *Jubal* actually escorted a lady to church a few days ago—What do you think will happen next? It is reported that he lately refused to receive a barrel of whiskey as a present! A few more reverses will certainly humanize him. I was in hopes that we would bid him farewell, before you came, but present appearances indicate he will probably remain with us.

We are all a little uneasy at the rumors that Sherman has returned to Atlanta and is marching toward Augusta or Macon. It would be a heavy blow to us, should he succeed with such a daring enterprise.

Of course his march will be rapid and destructive. Communication between here and Georgia will be interrupted only for a little time. But he may succeed in destroying Augusta and capturing Savannah. I hope our fears on this subject are groundless.

Tell Mat that when she concludes to send John into service, if she wishes him to join me, not to let him enlist in any company, but write to me and I will send him orders. If she will buy him a horse I will keep him with me. It appears to be very difficult to get a transfer made. I suppose Jimmie is very well fixed—

Do you ever hear from Uncle Loverd these days? I wrote to him but he has not answered my letter.

I have no more to write—Love to Ida—Goodbye.

God bless you
Your Husband

Camp Moore
Near New Market, Va.
Saturday night. Nov. 26, 1864

[No salutation]

I'm writing another letter to be sent by hand into Georgia, with the hope that by some circuitous route it may possibly reach you. Sherman cannot hold our lines of communication very long, and I even now doubt whether he has any substantial foothold anywhere. What glorious news it will be to us to hear that this desperate struggle of the Yankee General has resulted in the total destruction of his army. Certainly we can gather enough men to meet his 30, or 40,000, before he can reach Augusta or Savannah—Affairs in Georgia constitute the topic of conversation here, and we all look with eagerness to the Richmond papers for the news.

The "Valley" is once more peaceful. Sheridan and Early appear to be willing to let each other alone for the present. Even Grant and Lee are looking [at] each other sullenly in the face like two mad bulls tired of fighting, while all eyes are turned to the Military comet, who has started on his eccentric course through Georgia. I suppose he has at least routed the Georgia legislature, thus dispersing the assembled wisdom of the Empire State of the Confederacy. Poor Joe Brown too has lost his house in Canton, including doubtless the whole of Mrs. Brown's winter supply of tallow for candles.[7] The good people of Georgia, begin now to feel the heel of the invader, and will awake to the folly which has kept back so many able bodied men from the field. We will probably leave our present camp in a few days for some locality nearer Staunton. I expect we will not be far from the Railroad. My first duty will be to secure a good *Head Quarters* for you and wait for you to come and take possession.

I wish I could now sleep six weeks—I would then wake up and find you here. I shall expect to meet you in Richmond about the 15th of next January.

Give my love to Ida, and Kiss both little darlings for Pa.

Good bye.
God bless you.
Your Husband

7. This reference goes back to the letter about Governor Joe Brown's reception at Milledgeville in 1859, when Evans was in the Georgia Senate.

Clement to Ida:

HEAD QUARTERS 1st BRIGADE, 1st DIVISION
2nd ARMY CORPS
Near New Market, Va.
Nov. 28th, 1864

My dear daughter,

I am afraid that wandering Yankee General Sherman, has destroyed so much railroad in Georgia, that all my letters will not reach home now.

Don't you think that our people ought to destroy his army before it can get to Savannah or Augusta?

I congratulate you, on the nice little waiting maid which you now have. You may take her for your own, and raise her to suit yourself. Her name is "Fannie Custer," after [the] Yankee Genl. Custer's wife. Her name is *Fannie*. You wrote to me that you had given up your dolls. It was a pretty hard trial was it not? But now little Fannie will engage your attention.

I am so proud to hear such good reports about your improvement in all your studies, I see that your letters improve. Each one is better than the preceding one.

You must excuse this short letter; Kiss "The Doodee" for Pa—"*Bad Boy*." Kiss Ma too—Good bye

Your Pa.

Allie to Clement:

Lumpkin, Stewart Co., Ga.
Dec. 2, 1864

My dear darling.

This evening I got two letters from you, the first I have had in two long—long weeks. I have missed my letters so much and been so anxious about you. I never rejoiced more to see your handwriting in my life than I did this evening—One of the letters was written on the ninth and the other on the eleventh three weeks ago, but they are later than anything I have had from you. I noticed in last night's paper that our mails would be sent around by Albany to Thomasville and on to Savannah, and had concluded to write to you anyhow for it has been two weeks since I wrote to you and I know

520

you are as anxious for letters as I have been. You have no doubt seen an account of Sherman's march through Georgia, in the Richmond papers. He is tearing up the railroad from Macon to Millen. When will it be rebuilt so I can go to see you? It almost kills me to think it may be that I cannot come in January. What will I do if I am disappointed? It is only about six weeks till I expected to leave. I am most ready to start now. I do hope there will be nothing to prevent my coming. I have done all my sewing. Christmas will soon be here. I hope to hire our Negroes for provisions. Get a plenty in that way to live on. I am so impatient for the time to come and so afraid the Yankees will not be out of the way so I can go.

They are tearing up the railroad from Cuthbert to Eufaula and Fort Gaines to get iron to rebuild the road to Atlanta. The Atlanta refugees are all returning to their homes. The Militia from here was in the fight at . . . [Griswoldville on November 21]. Stanley Bryan was shot through the head and killed instantly. Capt. Farwell was killed and a man by the name of Perkins. Jack Scott and John Rockwell have gone for their bodies and are expected back tomorrow. They will both be buried here in town. Tom Newsom was wounded through the arm, in the thigh and through the hip. He has eight holes in him, all made by one bullet. He is home. Charlie Humber was slightly wounded and come to bring him home. Ben Boynton lost his left arm. He is still in Macon and the last accounts from him he was not doing very well. His father started to see him today.

Wiley Pope was wounded in the thigh, is at home doing well. Henry Sherman was seriously wounded in the thigh too. The news came to town that he was killed last Saturday morning and they told his poor wife he was dead. Poor woman I was so sorry for her. It was just one week from her confinement. She thought all day he was dead but when the mail came in that night it brought her a letter from him, written by himself. As soon as I heard it I went down to congratulate her. She was the happiest looking woman I ever saw. She was

521

laughing, crying and talking. Now I rejoiced with her and was so sorry she could not go to nurse him. She has a nice little baby. [This letter ends here]

Here, Evans' Valley Campaign Diary fills a gap in the letters, and finally relieves his speculations on Early's fate:

Dec. 6 Broke camp at daylight & marched up the valley pike 25 miles; camped near Burkestown at same camp of Oct. 5th/[18]64.

Dec. 7 Marched to Waynesboro and took the cars to Richmond.

Dec. 8 At Richmond—marched to Petersburg Depot. Took cars to Dunlap about 10 o'clock p.m. Marched immediately to the line of works vacated by Heath's [Henry Heth's] Division.

Dec. 9th In quarters—very cold. Snow & Sleet.[8]

Clement to Allie:

Trenches, near Petersburg, Va.
Dec. 9. 1864

My dearest Allie

I know your heart failed you when you learned that I was again here in the trenches. I had hoped that we would remain and winter in the Valley, where there would be very little duty to perform, and where I could devote two or three months to you. But the pleasant dream is over, for I am one of the vast machine which is throbbing all around Richmond and Petersburg. Monday Morning 6th inst at dark near Burketown on the Pike. Tuesday we marched to Waynesboro, 22 miles and were immediately placed on the trains for Richmond, at which place we arrived by different trains during the day yesterday. As each regiment reached Richmond it was immediately marched to the Petersburg depot and sent by train to Petersburg. I waited for the last regiments, which left after dark and arrived at Petersburg about mid-night. From this point we marched miles to our position at the breast-works. Our trip was

8. *Confederate Military History*, vol. 3, p. 512, points out that Early's command "had marched, since the opening of the campaign on the 13th of June, 1,670 miles and had engaged in 75 battles and skirmishes."

so hurried that I came off with no comforts of any kind except a pr. of blankets. My horse was brought on the train to Richmond, but had to be ridden to Petersburg. Consequently I made the 7 miles march afoot—It has been bitter cold all night—all day the same, and to night colder than ever—windy and snowing—I have fortunately a hut to night and am comparatively comfortable—but I have left all my cooking utensils, rations and clothing in my wagon which I shall not see for a week yet—

Everybody says we are soon to have another great battle—You have of course seen the papers and will read all about it before this reaches you—I can only say that my trust is as ever [in] the Great Ruler who orders all things well. I have received no letter from you written since Nov 15th. I am uneasy—Continue your preparations to come to see me—I have not given up that hope yet—Good bye—my love to my darling little saints —God bless you.

Your Husband

Camp Gordon's Division
Near Petersburg, Va. Dec. 17, 1864

My dear Allie

Today your letter of the 2nd inst reached me. "Few and far between" of late days have come these delightful visitors. I have borne the deprivation with impatience and anxiety. When you wrote this letter I was in the Valley dreaming of winter quarters near Waynesboro, of your coming, and of a delightful winter. But, four days more and I was trudging to Richmond, and then to Petersburg. Now we are about eight miles from Petersburg close to the Southside railroad, building winter quarters. Gordon commands two Divisions. I command Gordon's Division, but this arrangement is only temporary. I sigh for the command of my brigade again. I have not given up your visit although Sherman has torn up and destroyed the Central Rail Road, and notwithstanding we are here right in the jaws of voracious Grant. I had my measure taken today for Uniform Coat, it will

523

cost me $550.00. I furnished the cloth. I shall be ready
for your coming. Moses will start home in two or three
days. I would have sent him sooner but no one has gone
home lately. He will stay and return with you. You will
not have to go to Richmond to get to me, but will come
to the Burkeville junction and take the Southside road
to Petersburg. In case of any difficulty I will ship you to
the relative of Mr. Harrison. I shall get a house close by,
[which] I will make Hd. Qtrs. There we will all stay—My
disappointment would be cruel if anything should prevent you from coming, but I do hope that nothing of the
sort will happen.

I am sorry to hear of the casualties you mention in
the Griswoldville fight. I saw a little account in the
papers of it and my impression was that our troops were
rather roughly handled there by the Yankees. Poor
Stanley—It is indeed hard that his hapless life should
terminate at last in such a sudden death. I expect Sherman's successes in Georgia have caused the people to be
more desponding than ever. But we must have the energy of despair, in this matter, when the sky looks
dark—You mentioned Johny Graham, but did not tell
me whether he was in service. If he is going tell Mat to
send him to me when you come, with a certificate of his
age. I want him—Tell her I can take care of him. If she
can furnish him a horse it will be better, but if not,
send him anyhow.

We are stationed on the extreme right of the infantry
line of defence. From here toward the left our lines beyond Richmond full 30 miles from this point is a connected line of works. Everything here reminds you of
war. All during the day & frequently during the night,
an occasional boom of cannon & musketry, near Petersburg. There is no firing near where we are. Petersburg
looks desolate, or rather looks ragged. One street has
business houses open, containing such things as soldiers
usually buy. The market price at that. Flour is from one
to one & a half doll[ar]s per pound. Pork five dollars per
pound, &c.

I am afraid the new staff bill will cause me a disap-

524

pointment about obtaining a position for Probe. But I still hope to do something for him.

I write you a short letter now, but I will follow it with daily letters from this time and long ones too. I am kept very busy and have to do a great deal of riding. I enclose a letter to Ida. I am so proud of her that I can hardly contain myself. I do think she is something extraordinary for her age. Pa loves "the boy" some too.

Goodbye—Give my love to Father, Mother, Mat, Clem, & all—Love also to Mr. Richardson & our other good neighbors. If possible Lucius & Archie shall come home soon.

Good bye.

Your Husband

Clement to Ida:

Hd. Qtrs. Gordon's Division
Dec. 19. 1864

My dear daughter.

We have left the Valley as you have perhaps already learned, and are now encamped near Petersburg. The Yankees are close by where we can see them every day if we wish, but they are very quiet and civil. I walked along within a hundred yards of their skirmish line for a half hour the other day, but they only gazed at me. We are now building our huts for the winter out of pine logs, and making ourselves comfortable. I wish you and Ma were both here close by me. Then I could enjoy my soldiers life so much better. Will you not be very lonely when Ma comes away to see me? I will not keep her long from you.

Ma writes to me that you are very fond of reading. I hope you will be able to get such books as will both entertain and instruct you. I desire you not to read any novels for another year. After that time I will select you some of the best, which I shall wish you to read. There are a number of novels which are very interesting and improving, but you must let me choose them for you. There are a large number which are not only worthless, but hurtful and such I do not wish your time wasted over. You will not find anything more useful for you to read now than books of travels, histories, biographies &c, written for persons of your age.—Do not neglect constant reading of the Bible. Your education will be very incomplete should you know everything else and be ignorant of the teachings of the Bible.

I am sorry to hear that your little Negro is not doing well. I hope however, that it will soon improve. How do you amuse your self now? You must not forget that much of your time should be spent in play. I do not want you to confine yourself too closely to study.

You must continue to write to me once each week. I will write to you as frequently as possible. Goodbye. God bless you—

Your Pa

Clement to Allie:

HEAD QUARTERS GORDON'S DIVISION
2nd Army Corps,
Camp Hunt. near Petersburg. Va.
Dec. 21st, 1864

My dear darling

To day it has rained nearly the entire day, and now the cold wind is blowing a young hurricane. I shall go to the bed shivering and think of you. My hand runs wild when I sit down to write to you now. I want to throw pen, ink and paper in the fire, and sit down by the road for the next three weeks and look for you to come. Ah me—will it not be joyful when I can see you again my darling—I do hope nothing will happen to prevent you from coming.

I have been mad all day—Mose let some one steal my winter's dried beef, about 40 lbs. last night! Was it not too bad? I thought of having him shot, but it would not have been too much trouble to have buried him. If it was not for returning with you I should recall my consent for him to go home. It is decidedly annoying these hard times to have forty days' rations stolen—Don't you think so?

It is rumored that Mrs. Genl. Gordon is expected to appear in this neighborhood soon. Gen. Gordon has an excellent house, conveniently situated. I must begin to find you a home soon. By the way, if the Yankees press us too hard here, you can easily run down into Halifax until the stir is over. I am afraid you have not kept up your correspondence, and cannot claim any indulgences in that quarter. I have been wondering whether I could get my wagon filled by sending it down into that section. What do you think of it?

Tell Mrs. Harrison, I will speak to Col. [John H.] Lowe tomorrow about a furlough for Archie, and perhaps it may be possible to get off some of the other Stewart [County] boys. You know I cannot interfere too much now with the arrangements of the 31st [Georgia]. And worse now than before as I am not even with the brigade. In the midst of all the excitement about the condition of Georgia I expect the Virginia troubles are forgotten. What will the people say if Savannah is taken? We all think here that it is better to have Atlanta than Savannah.

The heavy rains, and prospect of more, will perhaps make it comparatively inactive here, although there is some firing every day. But suppose we, our Corps, is ordered to Wilmington or Charleston! You see, the Yankees are collecting a force against Wilmington or some Southern port. Would you like the change?

Really I am almost prepared for anything provided it does not deprive me of the opportunity of seeing you, but I really fear that the "Wilmington Campaign" would "knock everything in the head"—But I will not dread the bridge until it is reached—

This is a hasty letter. I want to see you so much that I write with impatience. I know just how you feel. It takes ten days for your letters to reach me, and therefore you will cease to write ten days before you leave. But if you think it is necessary you can send me a telegram, on the day you commence your journey—a short one saying "I am coming."

527

Goodbye—God bless you—Love to Ida—and the boy—
Goodbye—

Your Husband

"Camp Hunt"
Near Petersburg, Va.
Dec. 23rd, 1864

My dear Allie

At last the time has come to commit Mose and my "dry goods" to the mercy of the rail-roads, and other unforeseen dangers of the route to Georgia. With fear & trembling I place the bundle in his hands and say to him "You old black rascal, if you do lose these things or let any other accident happen to them, the penalty is instant and merciless death." "Don't show your old wooley head here again, with any excuse for none will be received." I told him once to day that he "shouldn't go home to save his old life"—But I have repented and he goes tomorrow. Captain Kaigler, of 13th [Georgia], living in Randolph, has a 24 days leave of absence and will take Mose under his charge. I have also said to him, that you might desire to return under his escort. He will leave Randolph on the 12th of January. If you can get ready by that time, write him a note stating the day you will take the train at Cuthbert. But I am calculating on Johnny Graham coming with you. Tell Mat not to make any objections, and never mind about the horse. I will see to that, & keep John with me as a member of my staff. Say to her also, (but don't for the world let John know this) that I will keep him out of danger. Let him come as well provided with clothing as Mat pleases. I will have it carried for him in my wagon. He will mess with me & constitute one of my military family like the others. If she will do this John will return to her a man in every respect; I am not afraid of John's health in this climate like I was about Jim. I am bent on having him, and Mat must not object. In a few months more he will be subject to conscription, and then I cannot get him transferred. Remember how difficult it was to get Jim transferred; Lieut. Eugene Gordon will also

528

probably be coming about the same time, and I will write to him that you are coming. He will address you a note to know when you desire to come, provided he is able to come himself. Other opportunities will probably occur. I will try to meet you at Burkeville, or somewhere on the Rail Road, between Burkeville and Petersburg. I shall try to get a house close by the Rail Road and if I do, I will arrange for you to get off there. Bring but one trunk, if you can get along with one. Bring only your best dressing. Have you fixed up the "woolen felt hat & feathers" for yourself?

The grey cloth which Mose brings will make you a beautiful Talma. It is priced $125.00 per yard. They are very much in vogue now—Something on the cloak order. However the greater number are of black cloth—Pa wishes he had something to send his daughter. I know she will be very much disappointed, but tell her that her Pa could not spare money enough to buy anything for her worth sending—The shoes are for Hannah. The flannel shirts, dispose of according to your judgment.

I hope Hannah's little Negro is improving. I hoped that it would do well for Ida's sake, because she seemed to take such a fancy to it. Pa ought to put in a little switch for the boy. I expect he needs a present of that sort. What will he do when you leave? Poor Clem. I shall be sorry enough for her, if she has to manage that great boy. Well, I feel just like taking opium now and having a long sleep. I shall be so restless for the next 24 days, that I will ride myself almost to death. I shall commence tomorrow and ride day after day, until I know every path, creek, hill, and piece of woods for ten miles. My new uniform will be complete the first of January. But I shall wear very little until you come. Then I shall dress out in style daily. I intended to send you 500 dollars but the paymaster will have no fund, until next week. It will take about two hundred dollars to get you here. I suppose you have enough, but if not borrow and I will send it back at once. Tell Bob to come to Va. with you. If he is beaten for judge and goes into service I must try to do something for him if possible.

I hope you will make satisfactory provisional arrangements for another year in hiring the Negroes. I fear that we will have more trouble than usual in that quarter during the next twelve months.

I suppose you write to some of your young cousins in Va. or N.C. to visit the army with you. Tell them your stay will be so short that you will be unable to visit them on this trip. I could have obtained leave of absence to have spent the Christmas with you, and would have gladly done so if I had had any previous personal [illegible]. Well I am seeming wild. Have hardly any sense at all—Mose thinks doubtless that I am entirely crazy.

Goodbye, until we meet. I will continue to write until January 1st. So you may look for letters up to Jan. the 10th or 12th. Love to all. Tell my little curly head daughter that her Pa has not forgotten her.

Goodbye
Your Husband

Chapter 27
FORT STEDMAN

After this last ecstatic letter there are no more until after the war. Mose Evans *did* get to Georgia and Allie *did* get to Virginia. How she managed to do this is a marvel! This young twenty-six year-old girl left her two little children with her kinfolk in Georgia and stepped onto a train whose tracks were recently repaired just enough, behind Sherman's invasion, to afford passenger traffic. She threaded her way through places where the enemy had sought to interrupt rail transportation and met her husband in battlefield conditions seven hundred miles from where she had started.

Many years after this time, Clement wrote in the already quoted memorandum for his daughter, Lucy, telling of her mother's fortitude:

> Her husband recovered in 2 months after the Monocacy wound and returned to Virginia. In a short while she prepared to follow and joined him in the close siege of Petersburg sharing with a woman's heart all the sympathy and solicitude that was felt for the brave soldiers who were making their last stand. The small fightings along the line were almost incessant. The light from the curving mortar shells at night was in her full view; the sharp explosion of rifle cartridges all along the line was a familiar sound. Every day she knew that her husband was exposed but not once through all this did she in the least desire that the war should cease without Southern victory.

The desperate plight of the Army of Northern Virginia in the last few months of the Confederacy was dramatic, tragic, pathetic. Although matters remained in *status quo* in the vicinity of Richmond and Petersburg (except for an indecisive battle fought at Hatcher's Run below Petersburg the first week in February), developing events closed inexorably upon the Confederate army. After the affair at Hatcher's Run, Lee informed Secretary of War James Seddon on February 8:

> Yesterday, the most inclement day of the winter, they [the army] had to be retained in line of battle, having been in the same condition the two previous days and nights . . . heightened by assaults and fire of the enemy, some of the men had been without meat for three days, and all were suffering from reduced rations and scant clothing, exposed to battle, cold, hail, and sleet. . . . The physical strength of the men if their courage survives, must fail under this treatment. Our cavalry has to be dispersed for want of forage. . . . Taking these facts in connection with the paucity of our numbers, you must not be surprised if calamity befalls us.[1]

On February 19 General Lee sent a note to General Breckinridge, the new secretary of war: "I fear it may be necessary to abandon all our cities, and preparation should be made for this contingency."[2]

In a communication to General Longstreet on February 22, Lee pursued this further: "If Sherman marches his army to Richmond . . . and General [John M.] Schofield is able to unite with him, we shall have to abandon our position on the James River. . . . The want of supplies alone would force us to withdraw. . . ."[3]

Such were the harsh realities when General Lee called Gordon to his headquarters at 2 o'clock in the middle of a cold night, during the first week in March. Lee gave Gordon a summary of the Confederate straits, estimating that he could gather between 30,000 to 50,000 men from around Petersburg, while Grant could assemble more than 180,000 immediately and bring 20,000 more from the Valley. However, Lee could muster only 13,000 to 15,000 more Confederates from North Carolina, while Grant could

1. *O.R.*, series 1, vol. 46, part 2, p. 1209.
2. *Ibid.*, vol. 47, part 1, p. 1044.
3. *Ibid.*, vol. 46, part 2, p. 1250.

depend on General Sherman to come with 80,000 more Union soldiers. The final count would give Grant 280,000 men and Lee but 65,000.[4] It was a bleak but realistic assessment.

General Lee knew that General Grant could bring nearly 20,000 men from the Valley, because General Early's pitifully small army (after Gordon had departed) had been routed on March 2 by Sheridan at Waynesboro. Sixteen hundred of Early's command of scarcely 1,800 soldiers had been captured. In fact, General Early himself barely escaped capture.

After his conference with Gordon, General Lee consulted with all his senior commanders and came to the conclusion that the only chance to survive was to try to join, as soon as possible, the reinstated Gen. Joseph E. Johnston, now opposing Sherman's advance northward, after wreaking havoc in South Carolina.[5]

At the latter conference, the last big struggle of the Army of Northern Virginia was plotted. There would be an attack on Fort Stedman, a central part of the Federal entrenchments at Petersburg. The fighting units of the Confederates at this battle would be focused around Gordon's corps. One of the main reasons for the selection of the Second Corps was the fact that the plans for the assault were proposed to Lee by Gordon. The plan appealed to Lee because he knew he could not break away from Grant and move into North Carolina until Grant was severely crippled at Petersburg. Gordon's plan to attack Fort Stedman seemed to be the most likely way to succeed in doing that.[6]

Lee instructed Gordon to move his troops into the works around the city and make plans to attack.[7] General Evans explained the details of this movement in the first paragraph of his unpublished official report written several weeks later at Appomattox Court House:

> On the 14th of March 1865 Gordon's Division composed of Terry's Brigade on the right, commanded by Col. [Titus V.] Williams, Hay's and Stafford's brigades, commanded by Col. [Eugene] Waggaman, on the center, and Evans' brigade, commanded by Col. John H. Lowe on

4. Gordon, *Reminiscences*, pp. 385, 388.
5. Freeman, *Lieutenants*, vol. 4, pp. 635, 645.
6. Gordon, *Reminiscences*, pp. 389-94.
7. *Ibid.*, p. 397.

the left (the Division being commanded by myself) occupied the trenches before Petersburg, the right resting at the Otey Battery and the left on the right face of Colquitt's Salient, relieving portions of Major-General Johnson's Division.

After his men were moved into position, Gordon made an intensive study that lasted a week. He then came to Lee with a rather simple but daring recommendation. The study concluded that behind the first line of Federal entrenchments were three supporting troop concentrations in what were designated as "forts." Gordon's plan was to make a frontal attack in the middle of the entrenched line and push open a wide area, where advance units would stop as a holding force. He then suggested that three "bold colonels" be put in command of units of 100 picked men. As the major attack force held the line, these picked units were to thread their way behind the Federal lines and find and attack the forts separately. When they took the forts, they were to turn the guns on the rear of the Federal forces facing the line held by the first Confederate assault troops. A subterfuge was to be employed by the units of 100. The commanding colonels were to impersonate the Federal commanders in each fort, as ascertained through intelligence sources. By calling to the troops in those names, the officers were to give orders that would confuse the Federal defenders so they could be more easily overcome by the surprise attack. Lee was to supply guides who knew the area and could lead the three special units to the supposed forts.[8]

Just before daylight of March 25 (at 4:30 a.m.), the attack was launched. General Evans coordinated the first wave of Confederates. As commander of the major attack force, he was to establish and maintain the holding force. His official report, dated March 25 in his papers describes the part of the action for which he was responsible.

> Hdqtrs. Gordon's Division
> March 25, 1865

Captain V. [Virginius] Dabney, A.A.G.

I have the honor to submit the following general account of the action of this division in the affair of this morning on Hare's Hill. In accordance with instruction,

8. *Ibid.,* p. 405.

Fort Stedman (the enemy's work opposite Colquitt's Salient) was penetrated by this division, one by the division sharpshooters, one by the 31st and 13th Georgia regiments, Col. J. H. Lowe commanding, and one by the Louisiana troops Col. [Eugene] Waggaman [Tenth Louisiana] commanding. Immediately afterwards Terry's brigade was thrown across the enemy's works, formed and advanced along the breastworks in rear of them, driving the enemy from them for a space of about six or seven hundred yards, capturing a number of prisoners and several pieces of artillery. Evans' Brigade commanded by Col. [John H.] Baker [Thirteenth Georgia] co-operated with Brig. Gen. [William] Terry as soon as the Brigade was crossed from our breastworks to those of the enemy.

Day was breaking just as Terry's brigade was formed, and the enemy had been aroused. The division advanced as far as the orders which I received permitted and as far as prudence justified under the circumstances existing. Their orders were not to assault a line of breastworks and a fort directly in front, especially if protected by abatis or other obstructions. I communicated my situation to the Major-General commanding [General Gordon] with the statement that to advance further I must charge a strong line of the enemy aided by their artillery and was instructed to await further orders.

The orders to retire were afterwards received and the Division withdrawn under a galling fire of artillery and small arms to their original position.

The division is entitled to claim the capture of the south half of Fort Stedman and about six or seven hundred yards of the breastworks in which were very many mortars and other pieces of artillery—and at least four hundred of the prisoners captured. Among the prisoners was Brig. Gen. [Napoleon B.] McLaughlin, captured by Lieut. Gwin of Col. Lowe's regiment.

The Division lost 43 killed and 122 wounded.[9]

9. Also among Evans' papers is a Report of Casualties. It gives slightly different casualty figures. Evans' brigade had 24 killed, 88 wounded, and 157 missing. Terry's brigade had 15 killed, 97 wounded, and 118 missing. York's brigade had 3 killed, 26 wounded, and 25 missing. The aggregate of all the division casualties at Fort Stedman was 531.

I regret to state that Brig. Gen. Terry is severely wounded. To his skill and cool courage I was very greatly indebted during the morning. I could not but observe his own efficiency and of his admirable staff. Col. Baker commanding Evans brigade was slightly wounded also while in the brave discharge of his duty. We have to mourn over the loss of several gallant officers and good men among those killed and severely wounded.

To Brig. Gen. Terry, Col. Baker, Col. Waggaman, Col. Lowe I feel pecularily indebted for their conspicious zeal in executing the orders given.

Many of the troops behaved well, but in this as in former actions, I could but observe how sadly we need reorganization and discipline. It is almost impossible at times to maneuver the troops at all.

C. A. Evans,
Brig. Gen Commanding Division

Evans did not explain in this report that the plan failed because the special units of one hundred men, commanded by the three "bold colonels," were never able to accomplish their missions. General Gordon partially explained that it was because of the failure of the three guides. Neither Gordon nor Evans realized at that time what was perhaps the real reason why the Fort Stedman plan was a futile exercise from its inception: what Gordon had taken to be forts were actually remains of Confederate works lost during the fighting of June 15-17, 1864.[10]

General Lee's brief report to the secretary of war assessed no blame:

It was found that the inclosed works in rear, commanding enemy's main line, could only be taken at great sacrifice, and troops were withdrawn to original position. . . . All the troops engaged . . . behaved most handsomely. The conduct of the sharpshooters of Gordon's corps, who led the assault, deserve the highest commendation.[11]

Evans recalled the experience at Fort Stedman thus, when he

10. Freeman, *R. E. Lee*, vol. 4, p. 18 and footnote, p. 20.
11. *O.R.*, series 1, vol. 46, part 1, p. 382.

wrote the memorandum about Allie for his younger daughter: "Perhaps her height of devotion was reached at the midnight when her husband left her to go into the desperate assault on Fort Stedman and the height of her gratitude when he came safely through and was by her side at the next sunset."

The repulse at Fort Stedman on March 25 made it even clearer to Lee that the only chance of survival for the Army of Northern Virginia was to combine forces with General Johnston and evacuate the lines at Petersburg.[12] In effect, Lee realized the futility of continuing to try to protect the seat of the Confederate government at Richmond. Still, the drama or, more precisely, the tragedy, was not quite done. The last scene would have to be played before the curtain could be lowered on what would come to be called "The Lost Cause" in the South.

12. Freeman, *R. E. Lee*, vol. 4, p. 20.

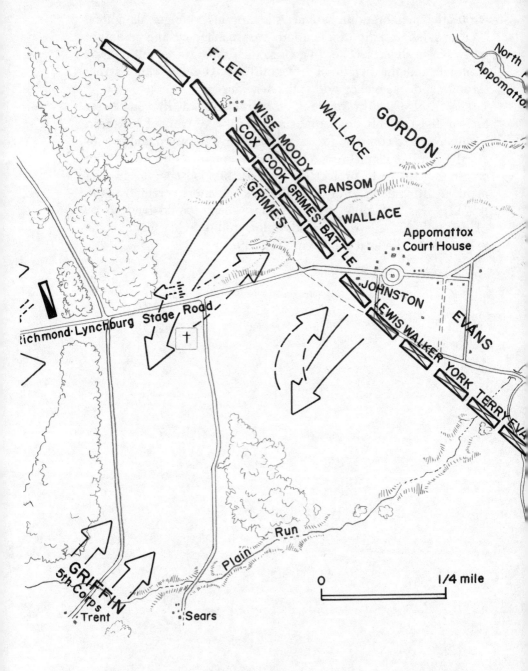

Battle of Appomattox Court House, Virginia, April 9, 1865
Gen. Gordon's last assault

Chapter 28

THE LAST TO SURRENDER

When the siege had commenced at Petersburg in mid-June 1864, the Confederate left was anchored on the Appomattox River, which flows north of Petersburg. The Confederate lines then faced east and ran vertically north and south for a distance of about two miles. At that time the Confederates numbered between 50,000 and 55,000, and the Federals had about twice that number.

This line and the strength of the opposing armies was more or less static until August 1864, when Grant began to move to the Confederate right as always. Every move the Federal commander made turned the Confederate defense lines south and west of Petersburg. Each turn extended the Confederate defenders. By November, there was only one man every four and a half feet."[1] By March, when the attack at Fort Stedman failed, the lines were spread even thinner. By April 2, when Petersburg was abandoned, the Confederates' original north-south line of two miles was curved and ran not only north and south but about twenty miles east and west, south of Petersburg as well. The same approximate number of Confederates that had defended two miles were now drawn out in a very thin array to defend ten times the same distance per man. While Lee's forces had remained the same, net reinforcements to Grant had about doubled his strength.

When Gordon's corps had been ordered on March 14 to occupy the trenches on the Confederate left to study the plan for the attack on Fort Stedman in the Federal center, this command not only filled the original, two-mile defense line set up in June, but also defended another two miles as the line curved south of the

1. Freeman, *R. E. Lee*, vol. 3, pp. 448, 497, 514; and vol. 4, p. 6.

city. The Second Corps still remained in place, chiefly on the north-south line, to recuperate after the March 25 attack on Fort Stedman.

On April 1 the Battle of Five Forks was fought on the far right of the Confederate lines. A. P. Hill's Third Corps (in the center) did not fight at Five Forks, nor did the Second Corps. Five Forks was a crushing defeat for Confederates under Maj. Gen. George Pickett of Gettysburg fame and resulted in the loss of more than four thousand men. Before daybreak on April 2, the Federals launched a heavy assault on the Confederate center near Fort Fisher, southwest of Petersburg, and on the far right end of Gordon's Second Corps. This sector was held by General Hill.

The right of Gordon's first line was driven in as Federals swept forward overwhelming troops of Hill's corps posted in the works. Hill's command was swamped, but stout resistance by a small detachment in Fort Gregg and delayed the advance sufficiently to allow Longstreet to establish a new defense position, west of Petersburg. Evans' division was heavily engaged but maintained its front. His official unpublished report describes this day of April 2:

Of the attack on Fort Stedman on the 25th of March an account has been given and no other movements occured until Saturday night, April first, about ten o'clock p.m. the enemy commenced a general fire of artillery and skirmishing which continued with short intervals until nearly day. About daylight I was informed that the enemy had carried a battery on the extreme left of the corps near the Appomattox River and hurrying in that direction I moved part of my division toward that point to be ready to aid in recovering the ground. But learning that Brig. General [William S.] Walker commanding division on extreme left had promptly regained the lost ground I was returning to my right when information was brought to me that Rives Salient occupied by [Bryan] Grimes' Division, on my right had been carried by the enemy.[2] I moved Col. Waggaman's command to the right at quick time along the trenches passing Terry's Brigade

2. Hill, after a conference with General Lee, rode toward the Boydton Plank Road and was shot off his horse and instantly killed—shot through the heart. Freeman, *Lieutenants*, vol. 4, pp. 677-79.

until I reached the position which I found to be carried. I found there a part of Cook's brigade of Grimes' Division, Col. [Edwin A.] Nash commanding. Directing him to follow in support immediately along the trenches I sent forward to attack the enemy [the] sharpshooters of Hays' and Stafford's brigades and directed Col. [Eugene] Waggaman to follow Cook's brigade.

On account of the nature of the ground and the constant threatening of several portions of my line I could not safely withdraw my entire Division to attack line, but in obedience to orders also received I pressed the attack along the trenches from traverse to traverse until I regained two hundred yards of the lost works, fighting often being hand to hand. I now found that I could go no further in this manner, the enemy having diligently fortified themselves and being constantly reinforced until their force far exceeded my small assaulting columns. I was enabled now to pass three hundred men of Terry's brigade along an entrenchment until I obtained a front against the enemy's left and determined to make an effort to carry another part of the line from that direction. Ordering Col. Nash and Col. Waggaman to attack heavily along the trenches I advanced the three hundred of Terry's brigade under the command of Col [Dorilas H. L.] Martz, a most gallant officer, to charge the enemy's line. The attack failed on account of the force of the enemy, the nature of the ground (an open field) over which the troops charged, and the fortifications which the enemy had rapidly made by changing our own breastworks. I found other efforts on my part to retake the works to be useless unless my whole division could be withdrawn for the purpose and even then the assault would have been attended with great loss of life. I omitted to mention that at the same time the enemy carried Rives Salient he also carried a part of my picket line in front of the Crater but was very promptly driven back by Col. Williams and during the evening they attacked and carried the picket line on my right, but were immediately driven out by Col. Waggaman.

About ten o'clock at night [April 2] I withdrew the

Division (under orders) from the trenches, having my skirmishers to be afterwards withdrawn, and marched across the Appomattox River at Pocohontas Bridge and from there toward Amelia C. H. . . .

The breakthrough dividing Lee's Confederate lines on April 1 and 2 at Petersburg had been achieved by 11 a.m. of April 2. About 7 p.m. on April 2, General Lee sent President Davis an urgent message that it was "absolutely necessary that we should abandon our position tonight."[3]

Lee's plans and conforming orders for the retreat from the defenses at Richmond and Petersburg had been made in the previous week. Even as early as February 22, he had revealed some of his design to General Longstreet: "The route for the troops north of the James River would have to be through Richmond, on the road to Amelia Courthouse at or near Burkeville. . . ."[4]

The concentration point at Amelia Court House was on the only rail connection from which the starving Confederate army could expect food supplies from three possible sources: from Richmond, from Danville, or from Lynchburg. It was also the site that offered the only hope of making a rail junction south via Danville in order to combine forces with Joseph E. Johnston, the last barrier against Sherman in North Carolina.

Gordon's corps, because of its position east of Petersburg on the Confederate left, was the logical choice to bring up the rear. All other units were nearer to the concentration point at Amelia Court House except, of course, the troops leaving Richmond. The soldiers around Petersburg needed only enough time to put the Appomattox River between them and the enemy. The Second Corps did not require much time to cross because they had simply to march slightly north through the eastern edges of the city and cross at the Pocahontas Bridge. This placed them automatically behind the other units on the Confederate right flank of the broken line and behind the troops that left Richmond with General Ewell.

Evans' report told nothing about the route or the retreat on April 3 to 5, when his command arrived at Amelia Court House,

3. *O.R.*, series 1, vol. 46, part 3, pp. 1378-79.
4. *Ibid.*, part 2, p. 1250.

thirty-six miles from where it started. There was not much to tell except for the exhaustion of underfed men and animals, spurred on by the expectation of rations at Amelia Court House. This phase of the retirement had gone as well as could be hoped. Lee's planning and clear orders of the routes gave the Confederates the advantage of one day's head start. By 11 p.m., April 4, all the major commands, with the exception of Ewell's troops from Richmond and Evans' rear guard, were at the appointed rendezvous. Confederates would not be engaged with the enemy until late in the afternoon of April 4, when Union cavalry were sighted but did not stand to fight as General Longstreet confronted them. Evans' troops did not come in until late, because his corps was stopped by General Lee about five miles from Amelia Court House in order to cover the arrival of General Ewell's columns. This made Evans join the other units early on the morning of April 5, which is the date Evans specified in his Appomattox report of April 10.[5]

The fate of the Army of Northern Virginia was sealed at Amelia Court House, if it had not been sealed before this. General Lee entered the town early on the morning of April 4, well ahead of most of the army. He found a host of hungry men in a country town where there were no rations. The supply trains from Danville, ordered from the commissary department, had not arrived. The marching men, who had already been on short rations at Petersburg, had not been supplied with food in three days. Food had to be found locally, and the army had to stand still while foragers were dispatched in every direction in all available army wagons. On April 4 an urgent appeal was broadcast by General Lee to the people in the vicinity: "I must therefore appeal to your generosity and charity to supply as far as each one is able the wants of the brave soldiers who have battled for your liberty for four years. We require meat, beef, cattle, sheep, hogs, flour, meal, corn, and provender in any quantity that can be spared."[6]

All day and all night the forage wagons roamed—all to no avail. As they creaked in on the morning of the 5th, the wagons were virtually empty. There was simply nothing in the countryside for the people to give. This night and day of seeking food for the army was a fatal blow for the Confederates. The one-day jump Lee had

5. *Ibid.*, part 3, p. 1385. Letter of Lee to Ewell.
6. Freeman, *R. E. Lee*, vol. 4, pp. 66, 67, 72.

on his antagonists was squandered, and Grant, with his well-fed, well-equipped and overwhelming numbers, caught up.

Later in the day of April 5, the despondent Confederates were urged on southwestward to try to reach Burkeville, where the South Side Railroad crossed with the Richmond-Danville line. Here it was hoped that some rations might be found. The movement began on April 5, and the report of Evans continues: "My division was ordered to march in rear and cover the retreat of the army aided by the cavalry of Major-General W. F. Lee."

It is interesting to note from Evans' report that he was in command of the rear guard of the Second Corps, covering the retreat from Amelia Court House. Already the corps had been rear guard out of Petersburg. It was a familiar assignment. Earlier in the war, Gordon's brigade, with Evans' Thirty-first Georgia Regiment in its rear, had been last to leave the battlefield at Gettysburg and had covered the retreat back to Virginia in July 1863. At the Battle of Cedar Creek, Evans held his troops until the final moment, being last to abandon that confused field.

Cavalry Maj. Gen. William Fitzhugh Lee, in his official report, added a little to the story of the retreat commencing April 5: "From Amelia Court-House, General Ewell's column, following that of [Lt. Gen. Richard] Anderson and followed by that of General Gordon, much impeded by the wagon trains, moved toward Jetersville and Amelia Springs, marching slowly all night."[7]

Scarcely five miles had been traversed on the wet and rainy morning of April 5, down the tracks of the Danville railroad toward Burkeville, when the Confederate advance led by Longstreet was halted. This was just before it reached Jetersville, where some of Sheridan's cavalry was found athwart the planned route. At first Longstreet thought it was a small detachment of horsemen, but by 2 p.m., when General Lee came up, reports arrived from Confederate skirmishers, proving that at least one Union corps blocked the road. Here General Lee changed the retreat path to a more westerly direction, north of the Danville rails to Farmville (twenty-three miles away), on the still-open South Side Railroad, where he had also ordered supplies and food to be sent from the stores at Lynchburg. From Farmville, Lee thought

7. *O.R.*, series 1, vol. 46, part 1, p. 1296. This is Ewell's report.

to circumvent the enemy, now holding the Burkeville junction, and to proceed south to Danville.

Beginning at 9:00 a.m. on April 6, the unremitting pressure from the Army of the Potomac's Second Corps of infantry under Maj. Gen. A. A. Humphreys is highly evident from Evans' report of April 10. This is what he reported of the continuous actions of the morning of April 6, after the all-night trek:

> The enemy came up about 9 o'clock a.m. soon after the last troops on trains had passed vigorously on my right and left flanks and the assaults of the enemy were resisted in a most determined manner by successive skirmish lines formed from the division withdrawn alternately, the division falling back in echelon by brigade, after notice of the moving on of the trains was received. The enemy came constantly on to the attack of my front and at the same time moved upon both flanks, so that it became necessary for me to keep my line crescent shaped pointing toward the enemy. His cavalry dismounted followed by mounted cavalry moved on my flanks while his infantry pressed the front.
>
> I received notice from Major-General Gordon that he would form successive lines by divisions and that I should pass through the line of Major-General Grimes. This I did and moving on was again placed in line where I threw up temporary breastworks for my line of battle and sent out a long line of skirmishers covering front and flanks. This was about one o'clock p.m. When the troops which had meanwhile taken up position to check the enemy were withdrawn through my lines and the enemy came on, formed line of battle in a piece of woods in my front. Two pieces of artillery were placed in position on my line and opened on their advancing line, but they were not checked until reaching easy rifle range. The infantry opened a destructive fire which caused them to break in great disorder to the rear. They were advanced again and again, broken in the same manner, the infantry and artillery both doing their duty in handsome manner. Finding his efforts useless to break my

line in front he moved a column to my right flank and was advancing again when [Brig. Gen. William G.] Lewis' brigade of [Brig. Gen. James A. Walker's] division was ordered forward and drove them back. But still moving to the right they were about to turn the flank of Gen. Lewis when orders came from the Major-General commanding to withdraw. This was done safely through other successive lines formed in rear.

Evans did not mention clearly in his report that these tactics were necessary for the protection of the Confederate wagon trains (as mentioned before by Fitzhugh Lee) and to cover the rear of Anderson and Ewell as their corps struggled to Sayler's Creek, a tributary of the Appomattox River. It had to be crossed before those units could get to Farmville. These running fights were the fiercest fighting of the retreat.

Evans' report showed how Gordon's corps had to fight. One Confederate unit would ward off an enemy assault while other units retreated to a new defensive position. When the new position was established, the first unit would pull back and, under the protection of the new lines, pass through the new defenses and through other units who were preparing the next defensive line to relieve the unit left holding the enemy. This game of leap-frog enabled slow-moving wagons to retreat safely in a steady fashion. In the middle of the morning of April 6, Gordon's troops became so sorely pressed that General Ewell halted and sent back help about 11 a.m.[8]

The decisive blow of the retreat was delivered by the Federals shortly after Ewell resumed the march (about 5 p.m.). The order of march had continued to be Longstreet in front, William's division, Mahone next, Anderson and Ewell in the middle, and Gordon's units bringing up the rear. Longstreet got to Rice's Station, followed by Mahone. However, owing to faulty staff communications Mahone did not know Anderson and Ewell had stopped to assist Gordon. Moving on, Mahone left a gap of unprotected wagon trains at Sayler's Creek. Federal cavalry struck the gap, destroyed the train, and Anderson had to halt his command because the road was a mass of confusion. He notified Ewell of his critical circumstance, and Ewell advised a joint attack to clear the way ahead of

8. *Ibid.*, p. 1294.

Anderson. But there was an even more serious mistake: Ewell failed to tell Gordon that he and Anderson had changed their route and had sent part of the wagons another way. Gordon had been escorting wagon trains from the start, and when the wagon trains continued on the route Gordon had been ordered to follow, he followed them.

Anderson, in Ewell's front, was overcome, as Ewell said, "in five minutes," and the enemy being in his own "front and rear" in great force, Ewell surrendered after a bitter fight, with a loss of 2,950 fighting men. Anderson's loss added 1,500 to the aggregate. This was, in effect, the final blow to Lee. The diminution by nearly 4,500 of his already depleted manpower at this time gave meaning to Lee's comment that "half of our army is destroyed."[9]

As Federals of Sheridan's Cavalry Corps and Wright's Sixth Corps were mopping up Ewell and Anderson, General Humphreys' Second Union Corps, on the route taken by Gordon's men, was viciously assaulting the latter in the final stages of this black Thursday, April 6.

Against this last and most determined attack, Evans reported he assigned the main job to his old brigade under the veteran Colonel Lowe, who had been Evans' second-in-command since they had left Savannah in June 1862:

> Again I deployed Evans' Brigade and about eight-hundred yards in rear of them Terry's Brigade supporting two pieces of artillery and sent Col. Waggaman farther to the rear. After all other troops had passed, the enemy again attacked Col. Lowe, the attack being resisted in front, but the right flank was again turned. Col. Lowe withdrew his brigade firing in retreat, slowly retiring through the line of Col. Williams [commanding Terry's brigade]. Col. Williams was in his turn attacked repulsing the enemy (with the aid of artillery) two or three times, but finding himself about to be overpowered, sent the artillery to the rear and withdrew his line re-forming the Division in rear of a new line taken up by Major-General Grimes.

The Confederate Second Corps was in desperate straits when

9. *Ibid.,* p. 1295; and Freeman, *R. E. Lee,* vol. 4, p. 91.

General Gordon sent a note by courier to General Lee about 5 p.m. on April 6: "I have been fighting heavily all day. My loss is considerable and I am still closely pressed. I fear that a portion of the train will be lost as my force is quite reduced & insufficient for its protection."[10]

This must have added to General Lee's frustration because he had no troops to send and was just getting in the full reports on the disastrous loss is at Sayler's Creek. Pausing only long enough to reorganize and to issue proper orders for units to proceed, Lee continued the retreat during the night of April 6. Gordon's corps moved along north of Longstreet's route to Farmville and crossed a loop to the Appomattox River at the High Bridge on the South Side Railroad.

On April 7, Gordon's corps, with Evans' division, was so worn from the fights of April 6 that General Lee ordered them to pass the relatively rested troops of General Longstreet at Farmville and to take the advance position of the army, covering the Confederate flank for part of the way to protect the wagons again. Evans continued in his report his command's activities for April 7: "Next day the Division marched on the railroad to Farmville and the march was continued toward Appomattox C. H. covering the passing trains of the army. During the day Col. Waggaman was ordered to report temporarily to Brig. General Walker and participated in a successful charge with that division gaining the applause of the officer with whom he temporarily served."

Evans did not comment on it, but his troops were among those fortunate enough to receive an issue of two days' rations that had come from Lynchburg—the first food received since Petersburg on April 2. Some of the rear echelon soldiers were not so lucky. High Bridge—the one remaining avenue for a rapid Federal crossing of the rain-swollen Appomattox—was supposed to have been burned, but the fires set to destroy it were extinguished by Federal infantry in time to save the span. General Humphreys' infantry crossed the bridge and forced the Confederates to cease issuing rations in order to repel the Federals.[11]

The Confederate progress, with weakened men and animals, and along terrible roads, was so slow that Union infantry closed

10. Freeman, *R. E. Lee*, vol. 4, p. 92.
11. Freeman, *Lieutenants*, vol. 4, pp. 715-16.

in on the rear guard of General Mahone, and the Confederate line had to be halted. Longstreet and Gordon detached elements that in a fierce fight at Cumberland Church drove the enemy back, and the attack was repulsed. This was the meaning of Evans' comment of April 7 that Colonel Waggaman had been sent temporarily to General Walker. With the success of that foray, the Confederate retreat was renewed.

After 9 p.m. on April 7, General Grant sent a message through to General Lee by flag of truce asking Lee to surrender: "The results of the last week must convince you of the hopelessness of further resistance on the part of the Army of Northern Virginia in this struggle." To this letter General Lee replied, asking "the terms you will offer on condition of its surrender."[12]

While this exchange was going on, Evans was still marching toward Lynchburg, the lines moving out about 11 p.m. The April 8 entry of his reports state: "During the night and the next day the division continued to march until it reached the vicinity of Appomattox C. H. and after resting about an hour I received orders to march my command to Appomattox C. H. in line of battle beyond the town. The order was executed, a skirmish line thrown forward and scouts sent out. The enemy was ascertained to be across the road toward Lynchburg. The division remained in line during the night."

Evans summed up the hopeless situation in that one simple clause: "The enemy was ascertained to be across the road toward Lynchburg." The end was in sight. The only thing pleasant about April 8 was that the sun finally came out to relieve the dismal rain.

The massively superior Federal armies had at last cut off the Confederate escape route to General Johnston in North Carolina. General Fitzhugh Lee wrote: "The enemy was enabled to take position across our line of march by moving up from Appomattox Station, which they reached earlier than our main advance, in consequence of our march being retarded by our wagon trains."[13]

Negotiations were continuing between Lee and Grant. Lee was aware by the evening of April 8 that Federal troops were across his advance line. Grant had replied to Lee's letter of April 7, and

12. Both letters are set out in *O.R.*, series 1, vol. 46, part 3, p. 619.
13. *Ibid.*, part 1, p. 1303.

on the night of April 8, General Lee agreed to meet with Grant at 10 a.m. on April 9.[14]

During the night of April 8, Lee consulted with his senior commanders and outlined the predicament. These officers knew the situation but were men who had gained their reputations as fighters and were reluctant to accede to surrender without one last effort to break the Federal lines—now almost encircling them —and escape to Lynchburg. Grant had not yet replied to Lee's last letter, and the commanders were fearful that the terms Grant might offer would be too humiliating to accept. To take one last chance at breaking through and go down fighting was preferable.

This one last chance was to begin at daybreak on April 9, with Fitzhugh Lee's cavalry leading the attack to clear the road and Gordon's Second Corps to take the left flank to keep the route secure for wagon trains to pass, while Longstreet protected the rear.[15]

After this 1 a.m. meeting, (when the troops were to move), Brig. Gen. William N. Pendleton reported to General Lee the most appalling news of enemy concentration in the path of the proposed escape route.[16]

At 5 a.m. on Sunday, April 9, Fitzhugh Lee and Gordon began to advance against the enemy with initial success, finding freshly thrown up breastworks manned by dismounted cavalry, who were driven off. This seemed a hopeful sign, because no infantry was met and the Confederate attack seemingly cleared the road to Lynchburg. Hope was of short duration, though, because, as Evans' report stated, after his division advanced in support of Gen. Bryan Grimes about 8 a.m. and "the enemy gave way in all points in front of the troops of the Corps" that was "eagerly pressing forward," orders to halt came "because the enemy were found to be advancing in force on the right and rear." Where Gordon and Fitzhugh Lee had expected dismounted cavalry only, they found infantry in the west, and cavalry to the southwest.

Confronted in every direction, Gordon sent his most famous message to Robert E. Lee: "Tell General Lee I have fought my corps to a frazzle, and I fear I can do nothing else unless I am

14. Freeman, *R. E. Lee,* vol. 4, p. 113.
15. *O.R.,* series 1, vol. 46, part 1, p. 1266. Lee's report to President Davis.
16. *Ibid.,* p. 1282. Pendleton's report.

heavily supported by Longstreet's Corps."[17] By this time, General Lee had decided the only action left to him was to seek the best possible terms of surrender, and this reality he reported to President Davis,[18] who was also in flight from the Federal army.

Although the tentative time Lee was to meet Grant was 10 o'clock, it was not until about 1:30 p.m. on April 9 that the two shook hands in the McLean residence on the road to Lynchburg. The conference continued until 3:45, when the terms were concluded. The generals shook hands again and General Lee departed to break the doleful news to his soldiers. During the meeting a cease-fire truce order had been sent to senior commanders, all except John B. Gordon.[19]

The prospects of immediate surrender were not generally expected by the lower echelon of command, who had remained in combat-ready positions on April 8 and had been fighting all the early part of the morning of April 9. This is clear from the actions Evans reported of the last day of the life of the Army of Northern Virginia in his report made on April 10 on the Appomattox battlefield:

> Sunday morning April 9th the division under orders from Major-General Gordon was formed on the Lynchburg road in front of Appomattox C. H. supporting the division of Major-General Grimes, and at about 8 o'clock A.M. was advanced with Grimes' Division on his left in echelon order by division, the division commanded by Brig.-General Walker following in echelon on my left. The enemy gave way in all points in front of troops of the Corps, and were eagerly pressing forward when an order came to halt was given because the enemy were found to be advancing in force on the right and rear. Suddenly in rear of my division the enemy came rapidly on driving back our cavalry force and pressing to the rear of the division. Two pieces of artillery happening to be near me I placed them quickly in position. At the same time ordered the division to counter march by brigades to face the new attack and threw forward the

17. Gordon, *Reminiscences*, p. 438.
18. *O.R.*, series 1, vol. 46, part 1, p. 1266.
19. Freeman, *Lieutenants*, vol. 4, p. 732.

division skirmishers at double quick. These movements, ordinarily so difficult under fire, were executed almost as promptly and with almost as little confusion as if done on the drill ground. The troops were perfectly cool, perfectly obedient, and awaited orders. The fire of the artillery and the charge of the skirmishers drove the enemy back temporarily, but the position was hazardous and orders to withdraw were given—from this and other causes the division was marched back again to Appomattox C. H.

What General Evans reported seems, historically, to describe the last charge ordered and led by a Confederate general officer of the Army of Northern Virginia. He never promoted the claim that his order at Appomattox launched the last charge. His only comment was that he wanted no part in any possible controversy on that subject, nor would he be drawn into any such contention.

In a memorandum in his papers Evans wrote for General Gordon after the war, Evans mentioned his indifference about the matter: "I do not want to make any special claim as to last fighting at Appomattox. All of us did the last fighting. But it does seem that my division had the good fortune to make this little battle after the moment of actual surrender. The firing you & Sheridan heard when you were together was clearly the few volleys of the charge of my Division."

Professor Joseph T. Derry in his book *The Confederate States of America*, which has been cited several times previously, contained an introduction by General Evans. Derry wrote about the surrender of April 9:

General C. A. Evans, whose division formed the left wing of Gordon's line of advance, was in front of his old brigade and had pushed out his skirmishers, under Captain Kaigler. The notice of the surrender had not reached him. Suddenly a Federal force appeared advancing on his flank and a small battery opened fire. Immediately forwarding his skirmishers under Kaigler, Evans led a desperate charge, capturing the battery with a number of prisoners, and driving his assailant from the field. At this moment General Custer came riding up to Evans on

552

a magnificent horse. After saluting, he asked where General Lee could be found, and stated that a surrender had been agreed upon. A few minutes later Evans received official notice of the surrender, and slowly drew back his command toward Appomattox. He and his gallant men, all unconscious of what was transpiring elsewhere, had gained one more victory for the falling Confederacy, and had shed a parting glory over the last hours of the Army of Northern Virginia.

General Evans' battlefield report of April 10 at Appomattox was prosaic until the closing paragraph. His conclusion, however, was in beautiful language:

> In this the last fight of the division before the surrender which has unavoidably taken place, every officer and man present was a hero. May we not think that if all the people of the south had been such as they that the struggle between the two sections would have accomplished different results. Never during my part of this war have troops behaved so cooly, so heroic, so determined. In the entire retreat these men endured the most terrible suffering from hunger, want of sleep, fatigue and fighting, but not one single man or officer of my division expressed the slightest wish to surrender. They at last bowed to it as a stern necessity, knowing that their beloved old Chief had done all—and was doing what was best.
>
> I will not particularize any of this small devoted band whose names however are preserved on the records of this brigade and this division.
>
> This report is hastily written under great difficulties and is not as full as I could wish.

Sentiments expressed by General Evans in his final report were matched only by his last poignant messages. One he wrote to his successor in command of the Lawton-Gordon-Evans Brigade, Colonel Lowe, in a small 3 inch x 5 inch memo book:

Hd. Qr. Evans, Divn, Appomattox C.H., Va.
Apr. 11, 1865

Col. Lowe

Please ask the officers of my Brigade to gratify me with their autograph signatures, and post office address in this book.

Res'ply
C. A. Evans
Brig. Genl.

The other message was on April 12 in his last general order:

Headquarters Evans Division, Appomattox Court House, April 12, 1865.

To Col. Eugene Waggaman Commanding Hays' and Stafford's Brigades:

The sad hour has arrived when we who have served in the Confederate Army so long together must part, at least for awhile. But the saddest circumstances connected with the separation is that it occurs under a heavy disaster to our cause. To you, Colonel and your brother officers and brother soldiers of Hays' and Stafford's brigades, I claim the right to say that you carry with you the proud consciousness you have done your duty. Tell Louisiana when you reach her shores, that her sons in the Army of Northern Virginia, have made her illustrious on every battlefield from First Manassas to the last desperate blow struck by your command on the hill of Appomattox Court House, and tell her too, that in the first so in the last, the enemy fled before the valor of your charging lines. To the sad decree of an inscrutable Providence let us bow in humble resignation awaiting His will for the pillar of cloud to be lifted. For you, your gallant officers and devoted men, I shall always cherish the most pleasant memories and when I say farewell, it will be with a full heart that beats an earnest prayer to Almighty God for your future happiness.

C. A. EVANS,
Brig. Gen'l Commanding Evans' Division.

EPILOGUE

Following the surrender, arms were stacked and the ragged flags furled for the last time in the Army of Northern Virginia. Each soldier was paroled, given a piece of paper to guarantee safe passage home with his horse and officers their sidearms, if he had either. General Lee made his final address to the tearful troops and then departed into quiet retirement. Federal soldiers in a generous display, shared their rations with their former enemies around common campfires at Appomattox. Thus, four years of war ended in surprising amity on the Virginia front, despite the fact that the war continued to the south and west.

Among Evans' carefully preserved papers and memorabilia is a one-inch-wide and five-inch-long strip of faded, red, white, and blue cloth showing two points of a white star, with this inscription on an accompanying sheet of paper:

> Fragment of a Confederate Battle Flag belonging to the Division commanded by Gen. Clement A. Evans. The flag was among those surrendered at Appomattox C. H. Virginia and had been used in most of the great and minor battles in which the Army of Northern Virginia was engaged. This fragment or scrap was cut from the flag and sent to Genl. Evans just before the flag itself was surrendered.

General Evans, who had written his wife of his concerns about recriminations, would not have to go into foreign exile as he had feared. There would be no charges against him, no imprisonment. A great burden was lifted from him and the others by the surprising generosity from General Grant.

Like the rest of the Southern soldiers, Evans signed his parole (in the last group to do so) and prepared to set out for the immediate purpose of finding his wife and what was left of his future.

Singly and in small groups, the Army of Northern Virginia dissolved into history and myth. Evans, still in his Confederate uniform, with wreath and stars upon his collars, rode off alone. At nightfall he came upon a camp of Federal soldiers and presented himself at the officers' tent. Although he was personally unknown to these recent enemies, he was greeted cordially and invited to join them for the night. Even his jaded horse was cared for and given forage. Years later General Evans would recall this nocturnal hospitality "as one of the pleasantest experiences of that eventful time."

But he would not tarry past the night, for he still had to find his beloved Allie, lost in the roar and smoke at Sayler's Creek.[1]

The last seven days of the Army of Northern Virginia, even in the telling, seem interminably long—so long that it seems ages since any mention of Allie has been made. Where was Allie during these traumatic death hours of the army?

Clement never forgot her part and, long after the war, lauded her devotion and brave conduct when the evacuation of Petersburg began. Allie left, too, with the army, and from the account Clement wrote for his daughter, his wife rode with the wagon trains in the midst of the meleé, incredible as it seems:

> Mrs. Evans moved with the retreating army of Lee and was amidst the battle when Ewell and Custis Lee's division were charged and captured & she was captured on her side at Sayler's Creek. When Mrs. Evans was captured a mounted Federal officer came to her to whom she gave her name. He at once directed some men to put two additional horses to her carriage and drive as rapidly as possible from the field. This order was executed so vigorously that she says she expected every moment to see the carriage hurled to pieces. But she was borne safely to the home of a citizen and next day went to the nearest railroad toward Petersburg. It was impossible for her to remain any more with the army of Lee. One incident occurring at this time is specially interesting. On

1. *Confederate Veteran* (1911): 252. Editor S. A. Cunningham heard this story from Evans in March 1911, less than four months before he died. Perhaps this hospitable display, on the way from Appomattox, partially accounted for the lack of rancor in Evans against his former foes.

the night before her capture, her husband found her carriage and told her that it was understood the Southern Army would break through Grant's army and assemble in the mountains, or that surrender was certain. Talking over the situation together it was agreed that she would return to Lumpkin, & that in case of disaster her husband would remain with his command & continue the war, even if it became necessary to go beyond the Mississippi. In any event, she was to be communicated with by him at Lumpkin. Upon this understanding they parted to meet again at Petersburg soon after the surrender.

She was kindly and cordially entertained at Petersburg when her husband joined her. As soon as the terms of the surrender were made, two Federal officers came into the Confederate camp and informed Evans of the safety of his wife at Petersburg.

From Petersburg, she and her husband reached home by going down the James River to Fortress Monroe, and from that place by ship *Ivanhoe* to Savannah, and from Savannah with a small party they made their way across South Georgia to the home of Mr. Needham Collier in Hawkinsville. While there, President Davis was captured in Irwin County, very near where she was stopping. An effort to see him and express her loyalty to him even in his captivity unfortunately failed.

At length, home in Lumpkin was reached. The two little children met her with rapturous embraces. The war—the cruel war was over.

Allie and Clement took the *Ivanhoe* sometime after April 19. His certificate as a "Paroled, prisoner of war of the Army of Northern Virginia" who had "permission to go to his home and remain undisturbed" was issued at Appomattox Court House on April 10. There is an official stamp in green ink imprinted on the face of the parole with the date of April 19, 1865, and the words "Ft. Monroe."[2] From this it can be presumed that they were there at that time for embarkment.

Clement does not leave any information on how he financed

2. The badly worn parole, creased and partly illegible is among Evans' papers.

the ship's fare home. As General Gordon facetiously remarked: "Confederate money . . . at that period of history was somewhat below par." Gordon had sold his war horse to a Federal general for United States dollars to pay for his and Mrs. Gordon's trip to Georgia.[3] Clement may have done the same thing.

The horse sale was made possible by an item which General Lee had asked Grant to include in the terms of surrender. He told Grant the practice in the Confederate army was different from the Union army. He pointed out that "the cavalry and artillerist own their horses in our army." Grant acceded to this by agreeing: "I will instruct the officers I shall appoint to receive the paroles to let all the men who claim to own a horse or mule take the animals home with them to work their little farms."[4]

In a memorandum of 1882 entitled "Items furnished a friend" Clement said: "Fortunately I made some money as a lawyer after getting home in '65."

This employment involved several months in a trip to Washington, D.C., on behalf of a number of Confederate soldiers, including Clement himself, who filed applications for pardons. He left Lumpkin on August 5, and due to disrupted railroad conditions, did not reach the capital until August 24. His route, he wrote Allie, took him to Nashville, Tennessee, through Kentucky, Indiana, Ohio, Pennsylvania, and Maryland. He did not get back to Lumpkin until the middle of September.

However, the first thing Clement had done when he got to Lumpkin was to follow up on his resolve to enter the Methodist ministry. He had not forgotten his *promise to God* made at Fredericksburg in 1862. In the same memorandum of 1882, he said: "When the war ended I returned home in May and applied for license, recommendation, etc. and applied to Annual Conference Dec. 1865 for admission." He said he had joined the church at the age of fourteen. He knew also, that his uncle, Loverd Bryan, had helped bring Methodism to Stewart County in its early days and had established there the first "Camping Meeting" ground.[5]

He initiated his application with a letter to his old pastor, Daniel C. Davies:

3. Gordon, *Reminiscences*, p. 104.
4. Freeman, *R. E. Lee*, vol. 4, pp. 138-39.
5. Terrill and Dixon, *Stewart County*, p. 152.

Lumpkin, Georgia
June 7, 1865

Dear Bro. Davies

You will perhaps be surprised to learn that the object of this letter is to make known to you a long settled purpose of mine and to get in full your counsel. This purpose is to offer myself to the Conference for the Itineracy. Many friends who have known me since my early connexion with the church will not be surprised that I am to preach, but on the contrary will express the opinion that I should have devoted myself to the Ministry in the beginning of life. That is a point about which I have always had a doubt and which has given me a little concern, but I think now that I have the clearest evidence, in my own mind of my duty in the future, and do really feel grateful that there is still a means of usefulness to my fellow man at my command.

I will not trouble you with my long experience of eighteen years connected with this very subject, my many examinations of the question "Does God will that I should preach"—all resulting in the resolve to abide his will in the matter and be guided by the evidence which He in His good way would furnish. These evidences came from time to time, and the preparation was made for the work, by the life of struggle, which had been mine. A thorough acquaintance with all classes of Society; with the motives which influence men to do evil; with their hopes, fears, joys and sorrows; with the mysterious avenues which lead to the inmost depths of human hearts—this knowledge my life has given me, by the will of God, and which I should not otherwise have gained. . . .

I prayed to God that if it was His will that I should *not* preach that he would in some way make it impossible for me to do so. I prayed earnestly for a loss of speech, or that some bullet might mutilate my tongue rather than I should deceive myself in regard to this solemn subject. I have in a singular manner felt that my life was safe during the entire war. Five times I have been struck

559

by bullets, enough to wound each time, and enough to keep me in humble trust in my Divine Protector. It is not affectation for me to say that God has graciously preserved me for a good purpose, and the deep sense of gratitude, of obligation and of Love I feel knows no bounds.

His application was accepted and in the fall of 1866 Clement began his career of service as a Methodist minister which covered a span of thirty years. Writing about this he said:

"I was appointed to Manassas Circuit in Bartow County. It was in Sherman's range and I found desolation and had a good time and stayed *three years*. Went to that people when they were broken-down, broken-hearted, poverty-stricken; took pot-luck with them also. I will never regret that appointment. It is in some respects the *best I* ever had."

In conclusion of the letters of Clement and Allie Evans, her last letter hereafter, and the final paragraph of Clement's memorandum for his daughter, Lucy, are appropriate:

Mrs. Evans subsequent life was passed as the wife of a minister in the North Ga. Methodist Conference. Her husband informed her in the beginning of 1863 amidst the war that he was persuaded in his own mind that when the war ended whatever that might be he would become a minister and spend the balance of his life in the Georgia Conference. He believed that his impressions coming upon him then for the first time in his life convinced him that such should be his future life. Without a word of dissent she declared to him that there could be no better life to live and she would gladly share it with him. This settled that matter and when the war ended she went with him through his ministerial life as a most faithful and efficient helper to the end. She was as devotedly loved during those years by all who knew her as she had been in her girlhood and young motherhood by the people of Lumpkin.

Just how descriptive this was of Allie becomes evident when her last letter in this collection is read. He was beginning his first charge and she was still at home in Lumpkin:

I am so anxious to get to house-keeping. I'm looking forward to so much happiness next year when we will have our family to theirselves. It is the greatest desire I have, to have you and our children all to myself. I know we will be happy. Just to think we have been married almost thirteen years and have never lived one year alone. Always somebody in the house with us. I haven't a word to say about where we shall go next year but like any obedient wife I leave it all to you. Shan't say a word. No matter where we are sent.

Clement Evans was an active Methodist minister from 1866 until 1896, holding charges in Cassville, Cedartown, Athens, Rome, Augusta, and in Atlanta at Trinity and the First Methodist churches.

On March 4, 1883, Alexander H. Stephens, the Confederate vice president died after serving for less than three months as governor of Georgia. Funeral services were on March 8, at the capitol (then on Forsyth Street in Atlanta), where his body lay in state. At 3 o'clock the casket was closed and carried into the hall of the house of representatives followed by the funeral party led by Senator Alfred Colquitt, General Evans, members of the family, the acting Governor Boynton and statehouse officers, members of the judiciary, and others. The choir sang "I waited for the Lord" followed by the opening prayer of Rev. Clement A. Evans:

We thank Thee for the life that Thou hast given to the State, to the country, the world; and now that Thou hast taken it back again, we thank Thee for all the good Thou hast accomplished through it in our behalf and in behalf of generations yet to come. We thank Thee for the kindliness, and sympathy, and gentleness which ever flowed from this departed life, which has taught those who still live how to deal justice and love and mercy, and to make themselves humble before Almighty God. . . . Grant that those of the young of our people rising up may emulate the virtues of this man, who loved God and loved his fellow-man, who was firm in his faith at last, and who, from first to last, was like the blessed

561

Master in this, that he sought only to do good. Grant that those who are being brought up in our midst may live and die like him.[6]

It is interesting to think that on this day General Evans had no way to foresee that twenty-four years later he would perform the marriage service of his daughter, Lucy Evans and Rob Stephens, the great-nephew of Governor Alexander Stephens. Those children in 1883 at the time of the funeral were only three and two years old, respectively.

On April 9, 1888, General Gordon, who had been elected governor, wrote Evans a letter offering to him the position of chancellor of the University of Georgia. Evans did not accept, but continued in the ministry until 1896 when he retired to run for governor of Georgia. Before the date of the Democratic primary, however, he withdrew from the race. William Y. Atkinson, who won, appointed him to Georgia's first prison commission. While serving in this position, Evans originated the idea that first offenders not be clothed in black-and-white convict stripes. He served for sixteen years in this office, while also managing the Methodist fund for superannuated ministers.

He edited the thirteen-volume series, *Confederate Military History* (Atlanta, 1899), and compiled a roster of Confederate soldiers of the state of Georgia.

Evans was never bitter about the war, but was actively interested in all things pertaining to the Confederacy. He was one of the founders of the United Confederate Veterans organization and acted as commander of the Georgia Division for many years. When Lt. Gen. Stephen D. Lee died, Evans succeeded him as commander-in-chief of the U.C.V. Ill health forced him to give up this post after two years, but he was made honorary commander-in-chief for life. He was in great demand all over the South as a speaker. His clear voice and beautiful diction held his audience. He offered dedication speeches for numerous Confederate monuments in the state and out. He gave the address at the unveiling of the monuments at Lumpkin, Athens, Augusta, and other places. He wrote the inscription for the Augusta monument. Evans was

6. R. M. Johnston and W. H. Browne, *Life of Alexander H. Stephens* (Philadelphia: J. P. Lippincott and Co., Revised ed., 1884), Memorial Volume, p. 664.

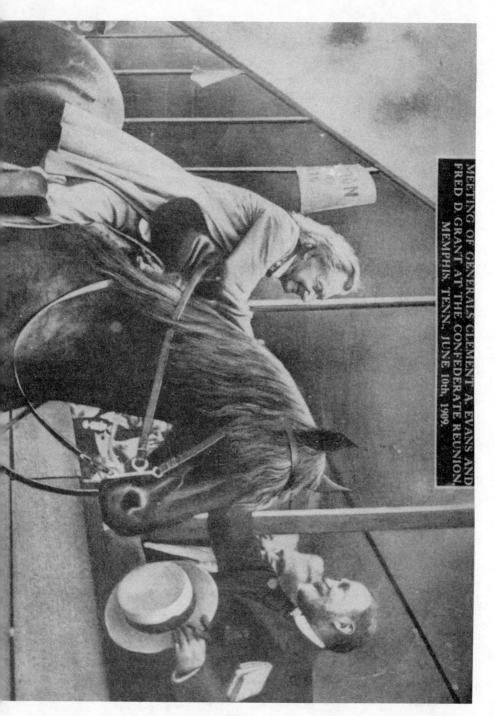

MEETING OF GENERALS CLEMENT A. EVANS AND FRED D. GRANT AT THE CONFEDERATE REUNION MEMPHIS, TENN., JUNE 10th, 1909.

563

the orator of the day when Battle Abbey was dedicated in Richmond. Evans fostered, at old Emory at Oxford, Georgia, the first student loan program and named the afflicted children's home in Richmond County, Georgia, "Gracewood."

At the Confederate Reunion in Memphis, Tennessee, in June 1909, he led the parade on horseback as commander-in-chief. Coming abreast of the reviewing stand, General Evans turned his mount aside to the stand and extended his hand to clasp the hand of a distinguished guest viewing the parade, Frederick D. Grant, son of wartime Union commander-in-chief, Gen. Ulysses S. Grant. This act was generally hailed as the first public, official gesture of reconciliation by the United Confederate Veterans.

In 1911 Governor Hoke Smith stated in the *Atlanta Journal* of June 9 that he had again tendered the position of adjutant general to General Evans and that "the general has agreed to accept it."[7] However, shortly after this announcement, General Evans had a stroke and was never sworn in. He died on July 2, 1911, at his home at 167 Capitol Avenue in Atlanta.

The next day, Governor Hoke Smith issued a proclamation:

It is with deep sorrow that I announce the death of General Clement A. Evans. . . . The state of Georgia has lost one of its most valuable and faithful public servants. He was a great Confederate general, a statesman of wide experience, a consecrated minister of the gospel, a faithful public official and a true citizen whose death will be mourned throughout the entire land.

Therefore, as an expression of the deep sorrow of the people of Georgia and as a mark of respect to his memory, it is ordered, that the flag on the state capitol be displayed at half staff for the period of ten days and that the offices in the capitol be closed during the hours set apart for the funeral services.

Hoke Smith. Governor.
Atlanta, July 3, 1911[8]

On Monday, July 3, the *Atlanta Georgian and News*, announced: "General Clement A. Evans' remains will lie in state in the central

7. *Atlanta* (Georgia) *Journal* (Jan. 9, 1911). On file at the University of Georgia Library in Athens, Georgia.
8. *Ibid.*, July 3, 1911. This was the new capitol still in use today.

rotunda under the dome of the state capitol Wednesday from 11:30 until 3:30 o'clock or until the funeral that afternoon."[9]

The same paper said both houses of the Georgia General Assembly passed laudatory resolutions and adjourned for the day of the funeral. The House resolution drawn by Dr. Hardeman of Jefferson stated: "We mourn with the people of this state in the sorrow of losing one of her citizens who in every walk of life, private and official, exemplified the type of Christian manhood and of moral elegance."

On July 6 Evans' funeral was reported thus in the *Atlanta Constitution*:

All that was mortal of General Clement A. Evans, soldier of the Confederacy and hero of peace as well as war, was followed to his last resting place by old comrades in arms, friends, admirers, surviving relatives and officials yesterday afternoon.

It was an impressive pageant which marked the passing of about the last of the foremost leaders of Georgia troops on the battlefields of Virginia. No such funeral will be seen again, for, so far as this locality is concerned, it may be said with truth that General Evans was the last of the great generals. And deserving tribute was paid him. . . .

From the time that the body, clad in a brigadier's uniform with the insignia of rank upon the collar of the coat, draped with the state flag, beside which he had sworn fealty to the southern cause a half century ago, and with old battle-scarred Confederate flags that defied bullets and swords on the blood-filled soils of Virginia, was taken to the state house at 11:30 a.m., until it was removed to the church at 3:30 p.m., a steady concourse of men, women and children, old broken veterans hobbling on canes, aged ladies whose memories took them back to the long ago, little children, flowers in hand to be laid on the bier of the fallen chieftain, poured through the rotunda of the building, each stopping to gaze once more upon the magnificent face of the aged hero.

9. *Atlanta* (Georgia) *Georgian and News* (July 3, 1911).

The veterans made the request that the casket be not used at the capitol, so those who passed through the rotunda during the day saw the body of General Evans lying, full view, upon a couch draped in Confederate gray as he appeared in life. He seemed as if sleeping rather than in death. There was a calmness upon his face which bespoke an eased soul, a grim resignation that he who had dared the cannon's roar had not hesitated in the slightest when death called. The long black hair, streaked with gray, which had never thinned, fell back from his forehead in stately profusion. The eyelids were closed as in slumber. The hands were folded upon the breast like a soldier at ease. In death there was that simplicity of bearing which characterized him in life.

About the bier were guards of honor, detailed from the local militia, and veterans from the Atlanta camps. Heaped around it were flowers in great profusion, the tributes of loving friends and admirers. . . .

The funeral march from the capitol to the First Methodist church was extended and impressive. A battalion of infantry, a troop of cavalry, a platoon of artillery formed the martial portion of the escort. Confederate veterans in uniform were out in full strength, under command of the camp commanders. . . .

State house officials, from governor to the clerks, were out in full numbers. The United States army was represented by General Albert L. Mills and staff from the department of the gulf. The board of trustees of Emory College, led by President Asa G. Candler, formed part of the escort, in honor of him who had long been one of them. The honorary escort, made up of friends of the general here, and from various parts of the south, consisted of more than fifty individuals. . . .

At the church Bishop Warran A. Candler officiated.[10]

Evans was buried near his friend and commander, Maj. Gen. John B. Gordon, in Oakland Cemetery in Atlanta. As the graveside

10. *Atlanta Constitution* (July 6, 1911). On file at the University of Georgia Library in Athens, Georgia.

services closed, cannon shots reverberated through the city from the cemetery and, in crowning tribute, the *Constitution* reporter concluded: "Before the blackest shadows had fallen on the scene, came the sweet, clear notes of a bugle sounding taps, the soldier's even-song, a call to sleep, and yet a promise that in God's good time another Trump shall sound above the *Bivouac of the Dead.*"

Appendix A

RELATIVES

Terrell & Dixon's, *History of Stewart County, Georgia*, has a section commencing at page 393 which is designated "Biographical sketches of some Pioneer Families of Stewart County." The Bryan Family is on page 418, the Evans Family on page 454, and the Walton Family on page 613. These sketches are very comprehensive, but for purposes of this appendix only the persons mentioned in the letters of Clement and Allie are given below:

1. *BRYAN FAMILY*

CLEMENT BRYAN and his wife, EDITH SMITH, grandparents of Clement Evans, had eleven children, seven of whom are mentioned in the letters. Those mentioned are aunts and uncles of Clement.

a. *Charity Bryan* (Cheatham) married Obadiah P. Cheatham and had Clement A., George, Sidney, Elizabeth, and Charles. George and Sidney left children. A son of Sidney Cheatham was Elliott Evans Cheatham, renowned professor of law at Columbia University in New York, onetime law teacher at Emory University, and assistant United States attorney in Atlanta. His middle name, of course, was from his father's first cousin, Clement Evans.

b. *Edith Bryan* (Brown) married Morton H. Brown and had one daughter and five sons. Georgia Brown married Robert Goss and lived in Hancock County, Georgia. Clement C. Brown, Loverd B. Brown, Morton J. Brown, and David Brown are the sons. Clement C. lived in Washington County, Georgia. Loverd resided in Texas. Morton J., killed in the war, married the daughter of Zadoc Sawyer and lived in Cuthbert.

c. *Emeline Bryan* (Watts) married Benjamin Franklin Watts. She was Clement Evans' aunt. Bryan Watts is her son, Thomas Bryan Watts. Ben Watts, mentioned in the same letter, may be another of her sons, William Benjamin Watts. However, it could have been her husband because Henderson, *Roster*, vol. 2, p. 592, lists "Watt, Benjamin Franklin—Private Apr. 9, 1861. Appointed 2d Corporal May 18, 1862. Transferred (from Co. B, Thirty-first Ga. Reg.) to Co. K, Mar. 2, 1863. Discharged. Furnished substitute, Mar. or Apr. 1863."

d. *Loverd Bryan* married Elizabeth Wyche of Thomas Co., Georgia. As identified in the early chapters, he was Clement's uncle, the brother of Clement's mother, Sarah Hinton Bryan Evans, and with whom Clement lived after his mother died.

In 1882 Loverd Bryan wrote an extensive genealogy of the Bryan family for Clement. It is among Evans' papers. In this letter, he said:

> Your kind letter came to hand a few days ago and I now sit down to the agreeable task of answering. . . . This is as I have said "an agreeable task," for the knowledge that I have now grown to be an old man, being now in my *seventy-eighth* year, admonishes me that whatsoever I know of interest to my family, I ought to communicate it now. And, let me say further, that it is with peculiar pleasure that I make this, perhaps my last communication on this, to *you* more than to anyone else, for my feelings are strongly drawn out towards you when I remember you as the only son of my oldest and favorite sister, and then as my dutiful ward—.

Cousin Texas (Kirksey) Watts told the family that Anselm Evans was "bad for drinking" and that Loverd and his brothers once sent him word that if he struck their sister one more time when drinking, they would not stand for it. See Clement's letter threatening to close the saloon in Lumpkin for a too-liberal supply to "Father."

2. EVANS FAMILY

ANSELM LYNCH EVANS ("Father" in the letters) and his wife, SARAH HINTON BRYAN, had three children. She was the granddaughter of Col. John Hinton of North Carolina.

a. *Jane Sarah Evans* (Hill), "Sis Jane," is Clement's sister, Jane Sarah A. Evans, who married Peyton D. Hill of Putnam Co., Georgia. In several letters he is mentioned as "P. D."

b. *Martha Ann Evans* (Graham), "Mat" (also referred to in Allie's letters as "Matt"), is Clement's sister, Martha Ann Evans. She was probably named for Clement's aunt who married a man named Gindratt, as shown in the Baldwin County, Georgia, marriage records. This aunt may have been married a second time to George T. Woods, who became governor of Texas. "Mat," Clement's sister, married James Graham first, and later, Charles J. Tucker. She had a daughter, Emma Graham.

c. *Clement Anselm Evans* married Allie Walton and had eight children.

(1) *"Miss Ida,"* the Evans' oldest child, was born on March 8, 1856, in Lumpkin. She was five when the war came and a month over nine when it concluded. She remembered much of the war, including her nurse holding her up high so she could see the train, draped in mourning, which bore to Richmond the body of Stonewall Jackson.

Clement was pastor of the First Methodist Church in Athens, Georgia, from 1869-1870. Walter B. Hill, who later became chancellor of the University of Georgia, was a student then at the university and met Ida. He wrote about her to his family:

> The young ladies of the Female Institute are going to give a May Entertainment, at night—a mixture of party, concert, tableaux, & supper. It is understood that invitations will not be very plentiful: so that those who receive them may deem themselves fortunate. A lady friend of mine has heard *Miss Ida Evans* (who is by the by, one of the prettiest & smartest girls I ever saw—she's the preacher's daughter) say that she was going to invite Harris & myself. I am a lucky "youth!"

Ida was graduated from the first college chartered by a state for education of women. This was the Methodist school, Wesleyan Female College at Macon, Georgia. She was a member of the founding chapter, Philomathians, that became the Phi Mu sorority. She married William F. Eve of Augusta, Georgia, longtime judge of the Court of Ordinary of Richmond County, Georgia. After Allie died in 1884, Ida took care of the youngest daughter of Allie and Clement, four-year-old Lucy Evans. After that, Lucy always called Ida, "Sister-Mama." Ida had four children: Ida, who died at thirteen; Allie Walton (Cabaniss), Sarah G., and William Frederick Eve, Jr.

(2) Clement and Allie had three boys between 1858 and 1861, all of whom died early. They were named Clement, Albert, and Charles Crawford. Charles Crawford is the child called "*Buddy*" in the early letters.

In March, 1884 the *Lumpkin* (Georgia) "*Independent*" newspaper was quoted:

> General Clement A. Evans of Augusta, Ga., was formerly a citizen of our town, and by 1862 lost three children who were buried here. One was a little boy of five years, one was an unnamed infant, and the other a small child. Mrs. Evans, who died in Augusta recently, requested that the bodies of these children be taken to Augusta to be reinterred with two others of their family. The coffins were exhumed last week, and the covering of the glass removed for inspection by a physician in order to obtain a certificate, which is required by railroads to protect them against infectious or contagious diseases. The bodies of the children were found to be in a remarkable state of preservation, and could be very easily identified. Their hair looked as if it had been just dressed and smoothed down, and their faces were almost lifelike, as if they had just dropped to sleep.

This article is among Evans' papers.

(3) *LAWTON BRYAN EVANS* was born on October 27, 1862,

571

and was named for Capt. Edward Lawton, killed at Fredericksburg. After the war, Lawton Evans was graduated when Emory University was at Oxford, Georgia, (now in Atlanta) and then attended the University of Georgia for his M.A. in 1881. At twenty he went to Augusta, and a month before his twenty-first birthday, he was elected as superintendent of the consolidated city and Richmond County public school system. For fifty-two years he held this job. When Nicholas Murray Butler, president of Columbia University in New York, came to Augusta in 1932 for Dr. Evans' fiftieth anniversary as school chief, he presented Lawton with an award known as the Distinguished Service Medal of Columbia. This was the first non-graduate ever to be given this honor by Columbia. In his time, Lawton was the foremost scholar of Georgia history. His grammar and high school *Student's History of Georgia* textbooks were used in the public schools for many years and his numerous books for young people included *America First, Heroes of Troy, Heroes of Israel, The Pathfinder*, and *With Whip And Spur*. He was made honorary Phi Beta Kappa by the University of Georgia, married Florence Campbell of Augusta; and died in 1933. They had three children: Sarah, Mrs. Edward Kent, who was a graduate of Smith College and longtime trustee of that institution; Lawton B. Evans, Jr., killed in a plane crash in Texas while training as a pilot in World War I; and Clement A. Evans, an Atlanta stockbroker for many years.

(4) *PAUL HINTON EVANS* was born in 1866. He became an electrical engineer and installed the first electrical utility system for Mexico City, where he died about 1916.

(5) *CLEMENT WALTON EVANS* never married. He went to Mexico with Paul Evans and died there, too, before his brother.

(6) *LUCY EVANS* (Stephens). Lucy was born on November 17, 1879. In 1967 her husband, Dr. Robert G. Stephens, wrote the following letter after her death:

In 1907 I married Miss Martha Lucy Evans, the youngest daughter of General C. A. Evans and his wife who was Miss Mary Allie Walton before she and Clement A. Evans in Lumpkin, Ga. were married. . . . He came out of the war a Major-General in 1865 and in 1866 he became a circuit rider minister in the Methodist church. His first assignment was at Cartersville. . . . He was sent to the First Church in Athens, Ga. The Grady family, the Nicholsons, the Kings were all members of that church and loyal, faithful workers in it. Dr. King, whose daughter married Henry Grady, was an officer. Ann Gartrell Grady and her sister, Martha Nicholson, took Allie Walton Evans, the General's wife into their hearts and homes and they became bosom friends. They called her "Sister Allie." The General after staying in Athens . . . was sent to serve the Methodist church in Rome, Ga. After being

572

in Rome sometime Allie Walton discovered she was going to have another baby. She decided she wanted to go to Augusta to have her baby where she could be with her daughter Ida, who was Mrs. W. F. Eve, wife of Judge W. F. Eve. . . . Ida Evans was born in Lumpkin, Stewart County, in 1855 and was ten years old when the war ended. . . . It was to her home that Mrs. Allie Walton Evans wanted to go, because Ida had a little girl and could not leave home to be with her mother when her baby was born. So the General took her to Atlanta and put her on the train for Athens where she was going to spend the night with the Nicholsons and then go to Augusta the next day. Mrs. Grady came over to her sisters to spend the night and see "Sister Allie." To the consternation and surprise of everybody during the night Mrs. Evans precipitated into labor and gave birth to a baby girl. It was all so sudden, there was no time to get the doctor and Mrs. Grady officiated at the birth of the baby. They named the little girl "Martha Lucy," the Martha being for Mrs. Nicholson and the Lucy for her grandmother Walton who was Lucy Harrison.

Lucy was graduated from Wesleyan College, in Macon, in 1899. She was a member of the Adelphian Club, now the Alpha Delta Pi Sorority. In 1899, at age seventeen, she traveled to Mexico City and lived with her brothers there for a year. It took her a week to make the trip. On October 22, 1907, she married Robert G. Stephens of Atlanta. They were married by her father, Clement Evans. They resided in Atlanta for thirty-one years. Dr. Stephens was the Atlanta public school physician for ten years, president of the Fulton County Medical Association and chairman of the Carnegie Library Board. In 1939 they moved to Washington, Georgia, where Dr. Stephens practiced for thirty-five years. In 1969 he was chosen "General Practioner of the Year" by the Georgia Medical Association. Lucy died in 1962 and Dr. Stephens died in 1974. They had four children: Allie Walton (Mrs. Dudley W. Reynolds), Emma Simpson (Mrs. Lucian C. Wilson), Robert G. Stephens, Jr. (the editor of these papers), and Ida Evans (Mrs. J. Mason Williams, Jr.).

* * * *

Clement Evans married a second time in 1886 after Allie died. His second wife was Mrs. Sarah Avary Howard of Decatur, Georgia, a widow. To them was born one daughter, Sarah Lee Avary Evans. Sarah Lee was only a young child when her mother died in 1902, and her half sister, Lucy, helped care for her while they both lived with General Evans in Atlanta. Sarah Lee married George E. Lippencott of Philadelphia, Pennsylvania, and had one daughter also named Sarah Lee. The latter is a well-known astronomer who taught at Swarthmore

573

College. In 1974 the governor of Pennsylvania named her as one of the twelve outstanding women of that state. She was married to a TV pioneer, Dave Garroway.

3. *WALTON FAMILY*

JAMES WALTON and his wife, LUCY HARRISON, (called "Mother" in the letters) the parents of Allie Walton, had four children. They came to Georgia from Person County, North Carolina, in 1850. James Walton's father and mother were Loftin Walton and Jane Boxley.

a. *Anne E. Walton* (Collier) married Probert Collier in Lumpkin, Georgia, in 1855. He is referred to in many letters as "Probe." "Annie" lived in Baker County and some of Allie's letters were mailed from there while she was on a visit. *Henderson Roster*, vol. 1, p. 431, gives Probert Collier's army record.

b. *Clementine E. Walton* (Thornton) married Dewitt C. Thornton in Lumpkin, Georgia, in 1856. They had one daughter, Nellie. When he died, she married J. M. Fulghum, a Baptist minister in Lumpkin. They moved to McKenzie, Tennessee. Their son was Guy Fulghum.

c. *Robert W. Walton* married Laura A. Davis in Lumpkin, Georgia, in 1859. After the war, he moved to Corsicana, Texas, and died there. He is generally referred to in the letters as "Bob."

d. *Walton relatives in North Carolina*

As letters show, Allie visited relatives in or near South Boston, Halifax County, Virginia, Black Walnut, Virginia, and across in Person County, North Carolina. Since she was thirteen or fourteen, when her parents came to Georgia from this section, Allie readily remembered these kinfolks, even though she had not seen them for some twelve years. She refers in these letters to Cousin William, Miss Sarah, Nancy, and Mrs. Phillips. At other places she mentions Cousin Lewis, Uncle Richard, Cousin Eliza, Thomas E. Owen, Cousin Mary, Mr. Fourquesan, Cornelia Williams, Joe Painter, Dr. Terrell, Uncle Sydney, and one or two others. At this late date, hardly any can be identified. "Uncle Sydney" was Sydney Walton. "Uncle Richard" may have been a Walton. Some were kin and some were probably not kin. "Nance" (also "Nancy") and Hannah were slaves mentioned in her letters.

Appendix B

PERSONAL DIARY OF GEN. CLEMENT A. EVANS, ARMY OF NORTHERN VIRGINIA, OF THE SHENANDOAH VALLEY CAMPAIGN FROM JULY 1, 1864, TO DECEMBER 15, 1864.

* * * *

"Strasburg Bivouac"

July 1st 1864 Friday

Anniversary 1st day of Gettysburg—Marched 3½ a.m. down valley pike to mill 1 mi. S.W. of Strasburg.

Encamped near pike at 2½ p.m.

Pleasant until 11 a.m. Afterward very hot.

Rain 3½ p.m.

Hdqrs on high hill overlooking the valley in which Strasburg lies, affording beautiful view.

Total distance marched 21 miles.

"Kernstown Bivouac"

July 2nd—Saturday.

Marched 3¼ a.m. Passed through Strasburg, Middletown, Newtown & Kernstown. Very hot. Encamped ½ mile N.W. Kernstown near pike at 1 a.m. Distance marched 18 miles.

July 3rd—1864 Sunday

Marched 3½ a.m.

Passed through Winchester 4½ a.m. on valley pike toward Martinsburg. 5¼ a.m. Artillery firing heard ahead. Entered Martinsburg. Place evacuated by Yankees. Quantities of stores, etc. 24 miles—

July 4th—

Encamped near Martinsburg 2½ o'clock p.m. Marched on Shepherdstown pike to Duffield's Station. Encamped—11 miles.

July 5th—

Daybreak marched to Shepherdstown. Crossed Potomac by wad-

575

ing. Marched on Sharpsburg road 1 mi. turned to the right through fields leaving Sharpsburg to the right, marching toward Harper's Ferry, passing along a dull road running with the canal. Halted about 6 mi. from Harper's Ferry & encamped near iron works—Posted pickets—

July 6th—
Marched on Harper's Ferry—Skirmishing—cut a road with pocket knives & attacked enemy in rear.

July 7th—
Fought on Maryland Heights all day.

*8th—*March toward Frederick City.

*9th—*Battle of Monocacy.

Wounded severely—

10th & 11th—rode to Washington in ambulance—

*12th—*Crossed Potomac at Conrad's Ferry & went to Leesburg—

*13th—*Stayed in Leesburg.

*14 & 19—*Trip to Richmond.

*23rd—*Started for home.

*29th—*July Arrived home.

[NO ENTRIES FOR A MONTH AND A HALF.]

*Sept 13th—*left home for the army—

*Sept 24th—*Reached the army at night retreating up the valley— Camped about 15 mi. from Port Republic.

*Sept 25th—*Marched to Brown's Gap in Blue Ridge mountains.

*Sept 26th—*Marched to & fro in the Gap. Enemy making demonstrations with cavalry.

*Sept 27th—*Weyer's Cave Skirmish—Marched from the gap around Weyer's Cave mountain. Drove the Yankee cavalry across the river. Casualties very few. 4 wounded. Camped on Port Republic road about 1½ mi. from Weyer's Cave.

*Sept 28th—*Marched from Weyer's Cave on Waynesboro road.

Camped about 1½ mi. N.E. of Waynesboro at Henger's Mill—

Sept 29th—Remained in camp at Henger's all day, 60th Ga. on picket 1¼ miles on main road from here to Port Republic road—Examined country and roads. Posted vedettes, etc.—12th Ga. bat. relieved 60th Ga. at 3½ p.m.

Sept 30th—Under orders to be ready to move. In camp all day.

Oct 1st—Marched from Henger's near Waynesboro to valley pike near Mt. Sidney—Marched through Mt. Sidney down the valley pike 4 mi. Encamped 1 mi. S.E. of Burketown on valley pike. Very cold & raining nearly all day. Marched 18 miles.

Oct 2nd—In camp all day. Light skirmishes with about 50 Yankee cavalry. Scouts on pike—Drove them across the river—1 man wounded 26 [th] Ga.

Oct 3rd—In camp—raining all day.

Oct 4th—Removed to new camp ½ mi. north of Burketown

Oct 6th—In camp. Enemy evacuated Harrisonburg early this morning & moved down the pike—Early in motion to follow about 10 o'clock a.m.—Marched through Mt. Crawford & Harrisonburg. Encamped two mi. north of Harrisonburg.

Oct 7th—7 o'clock a.m. marched down the pike through New Market. Encamped near New Market on land of Zach. Shirley.

Oct 8th—"Camp Shirley"—near New Market, Va—

Oct 9th—Sunday. Defeat of Lomax & Rosser [at Tom's Brook]. Loss of 11 pieces of artillery & missing wagons etc. Infantry moved out but not engaged.

Camp Shirley New Market

Oct 10th—Monday Weather cool—but not unpleasant. 1st heavy frost this morning.

Oct 11th—Tuesday. In camp.

Oct 12th—Wednesday marched from New Market to Woodstock 19 mi.

Oct 13th—Thursday. Marched from Woodstock to Strasburg—

Shelled enemy camp from hills w. of Strasburg, across Cedar Creek. Enemy advanced *Crook's* command of infantry—We attacked them & drove them back across the creek. Retd to camp at night on Fisher's Hill.

Oct 14th—Marched from bivouac across Fisher Creek to left of Strasburg. In line all day—Enemy displayed only cavalry. Light skirmishing. Retd to camp at sunset.

Oct 15th—In camp.

Oct 17th—Monday. Reconnaissance with my brigade toward Cedar Creek. Enemy found entrenched on the hills beyond Cedar Creek. 2 o'clock p.m. returned to camp. 2½ o'clock p.m. in company with Gen Gordon & two or three staff officers went to the signal station on top of "Three Top" mountain. From this position the entire camp of the enemy is visible—Also an extent of country twenty miles wide and thirty miles long.

Oct 18th—Further reconnaissance & preparation for battle.

Oct 19th—Battle at Cedar Creek—

Oct 20th—Retreat to New Market.

Oct 21th—Camp "Shirley" near New Market ¾ mile N.W. of New Market.

Nov 5th—Camp Shirley 8:30 o'clock a.m. Light snow—first of the season—

Nov 8th—Camp Moore. 4 miles S.W. of New Market—about ¾ mile west of valley pike on land belonging to Thomas Moore.

Nov 10th—Broke camp at sunrise & marched down pike, camped S of Woodstock 1 mi.

Nov 11th—Marched at sunrise down pike. Camped at Big Spring near Stickley's place, near pike between Middletown & Newtown—

Nov 12th—In line of battle crossing the pike on the ground encamped on last night. Skirmish line at Chrisman's house: Enemy skirmishers on north side of Newtown: Entrenched line of enemy on Opequon Creek two miles N.E. of Newtown. At night our lines withdrawn & march made to Fisher's Hill—9 miles—very cold—

Nov 13th—Sunrise, marched up pike and encamped about 3 mi. S.W. of Edenburg, on west side of pike.

Nov. 14th—Sunrise marched to Camp Moore, & placed in same quarters as before.

Nov 15th to 22nd—In camp at Camp Moore.

Nov 22nd—Advance of three cavalry divisions of the enemy to Meem's Farm, near Rude's Hill. Marched at sunrise to Rude's Hill: Found one Divn of Yankee cavalry on Meem's Farm, and two divisions in reserve near Mt. Jackson: Artillery was posted on Rude's Hill and opened on the enemy but with little effect; Infantry skirmishers were advanced & fight ensued. Enemy withdrew leaving about six killed—carried off their wounded;—Returned to Camp Moore at night.

Nov 23rd to Nov 27th to Dec 6th.

Dec 6th—Broke camp at daylight & marched up the valley pike 25 miles; camped near Burketown at same camp of Oct 5th/ [18]64.

Dec 7th—Marched to Waynesboro and took cars to Richmond.

Dec 8th At Richmond—Marched to Petersburg Depot. Took cars to Dunlap's about 10 o'clock p.m. Marched immediately to the line of works vacated by Heth's Division.

Dec 9th—In quarters—very cold. Snow & sleet.

Dec 10th—Took portions of 3 brigades on our right flank to drive back the enemy who had driven in our pickets the day before—successful. Ground covered with melting snow. Retd to quarters. *In command of Division*—

Dec 11th—In quarters.

Dec 12th—In quarters. Enemy moved troops from City Point by trains.

Dec 13th—Entire line aroused at four o'clock a.m.: Evening of 13th moved troops to temporary camp near Burgess Mill.

Dec 14th—Camped the Division in permanent quarters.

Dec 15th—Constructing winter quarters.

INDEX

581

582

586

592

U.S. Army Corps, Eleventh 223
U.S. Army Corps, First 223
U.S. Christian Mission 428
United Confederate Veterans 562, 564
United States of America xvii, 26, 31,
   417, 507
University of Georgia 562
Upton, Col. Emory 390
Ursula 309, 377
Valley Campaign Diary 423, 502, 522
Valley Campaign 413
Valley Diary 450, 479
Valley Pike 460-61, 463, 468-69, 480,
   487, 499-500, 506, 510
Valley Turnpike 422
Verdiersville, Virginia 191, 327, 385
Vermont 440
Vicksburg, Battle of 169
Vicksburg, Mississippi 131, 164, 180,
   183, 191, 207, 232, 244, 257, 368
Vigilance Committee 94
Virginia, State of xvii, xx, 30, 35, 48,
   54, 64, 67-68, 73, 100, 105, 111-12,
   114-16, 129, 132, 135, 143, 151,
   157, 184, 191-92, 216, 218-19, 232,
   238, 249, 252, 254, 265, 268, 286,
   296, 301-02, 304, 309, 316-17, 330-
   31, 338, 355, 361, 364, 366-68, 372,
   374, 376, 378, 383-84, 393-94, 402,
   404, 407, 418-19, 422, 428, 431,
   433, 435, 438, 443-45, 490, 504-06,
   515, 527, 530-31, 544, 555, 565
Virginia and Tennessee Railroad 398
Virginia Military Institute 417, 423
Vones 492
Waggaman, Eugene 533, 535-36, 541,
   547-49, 554
Walker, Col. 122
Walker, Freeman 115
Walker, Brig. Gen. James A. 546, 548-
   49, 551
Walker, Brig. Gen. William S. 540
Walker's division 546
Wallace, Gen. Lew 425, 428
Walt 53, 273
Walton 409
Walton, Anne E. 35

Walton, Clementine, M. 35
Walton, James 35
Walton, Lucy Harrison 35, 285, 505
Walton, Robert 35, 269, 409
Walton, Samuel B. 24-25
Ward, W. 291, 298, 308, 445
Ward's 52, 297
Warren, Charles 82, 104, 297-98, 314
Warren, Maj. Gen. Gouverneur K.
   385-86
Warrenton, Virginia 188, 191, 281
Washington County, Maryland 204
Washington, D.C. xix, 47, 68, 111,
   121, 178, 184, 222, 238, 248, 281,
   361, 363, 418, 423, 426-28, 465,
   489, 503, 558
Washington, George 342
Wats, Frank 69
Watts, Ben 112, 114, 437
Watts, Bryan 112-13
Way, Amos 56
Waynesboro, Pennsylvania 204, 210,
   212-13
Waynesboro, Virginia 233, 236, 459,
   522-23, 533
Waynesburg, Virginia 458
Webster County 102
Weldon, North Carolina 428
Weldon Road 435
Wellbron, Robert 31
West Virginia, State of 422
Western and Atlantic Railroad 465
Wethersby, Mr. 61
Weyer's Cave, Virginia 454, 456-58
Wharton, Gen. John Austin 487-88
Wharton's division 454, 470
White House 427, 503
White Oak Swamp, Battle of (Frayser's
   Farm, Glendale) 109
Wigfall, Brig. Gen. Louis T. 63-64
Wilderness 382, 385, 397, 411, 425
Wilderness Tavern 385
Wilderness, Battle of the xviii-xix, 382
   (map), 387
William, Cousin 144, 158, 161, 165-
   66, 169, 172, 175-76
William's division 546

597